Introduction to Counseling and Guidance

SIXTH EDITION

Robert L. Gibson
Indiana University

Marianne H. Mitchell
Indiana University

Upper Saddle River, New Jersey
Columbus, Ohio

Library of Congress Cataloging-in-Publication Data

Gibson, Robert L. (Robert Lewis)
    Introduction to counseling and guidance / Robert L. Gibson, Marianne H. Mitchell—
6th ed.
      p.   cm.
    Includes bibliographical references and indexes.
    ISBN 0-13-094201-4
    1. Counseling. I. Mitchell, Marianne. II. Title.
BF637.C6 G48 2003
158′.3—dc21

2002066215

Vice President and Publisher: Jeffery W. Johnston
Executive Editor: Kevin M. Davis
Editorial Assistant: Autumn Crisp
Production Editor: Mary Harlan
Production Coordination: Sharon Anderson, BookMasters, Inc.
Design Coordinator: Diane C. Lorenzo
Cover Design: Linda Sorrells-Smith
Cover Image: SuperStock
Text Design and Illustrations: BookMasters, Inc.
Production Manager: Laura Messerly
Director of Marketing: Ann Castel Davis
Marketing Manager: Amy June
Marketing Coordinator: Tyra Cooper

This book was set in Times by BookMasters, Inc. It was printed and bound by R. R. Donnelley & Sons Company. The cover was printed by Phoenix Color Corp.

Pearson Education Ltd.
Pearson Education Australia Pty. Limited
Pearson Education Singapore Pte. Ltd.
Pearson Education North Asia Ltd.
Pearson Education Canada, Ltd.
Pearson Educación de Mexico, S.A. de C.V.
Pearson Education—Japan
Pearson Education Malaysia Pte. Ltd.
Pearson Education, *Upper Saddle River, New Jersey*

Merrill
Prentice Hall

10 9 8 7 6 5 4 3 2
ISBN: 0-13-094201-4

To our parents—for a lifetime of guidance

Flora Lewis Gibson   *Helen Metzger Mitchell*
Alva Jason Gibson   *Frank Henry Mitchell*

About the Authors

Dr. Robert L. Gibson is Professor of Education, Department of Counseling and Educational Psychology at Indiana University, Bloomington, Indiana. In addition to his experiences as a counselor educator, he has been a high school teacher, counselor, and director of guidance, as well as a college counselor. His service activities include chairperson of the Guidance and Counseling Committee of the North Central Association of Schools and Colleges; member of the state guidance advisory committee in two states; president of two state counseling associations; treasurer of the Association for Counselor Education and Supervision (ACES); plus various state and national committee memberships.

His research activities include directing funded international research projects in the areas of pupil academic achievement, common educational problems of youth, and school dropouts. Recent studies include theoretical preferences of practicing counselors and studies of counselor functions in varied settings.

Dr. Gibson is co-director of Indiana University's programs in Bermuda and Scotland.

Dr. Marianne H. Mitchell is Professor of Education, Department of Counseling and Educational Psychology, Indiana University, Bloomington, Indiana. She has served as president of the American Counseling Association and as president of the Association of Counselor Education and Supervision.

Dr. Mitchell's research activities include international investigations of pupil personnel services and pupil achievement and common educational problems in the United States, the United Kingdom, and Europe. She has been the principal investigator in studies of career information delivery systems, career placement programs, and adolescent girls' attitudes toward vocational education. She serves as a consultant to the Ministries of Education and Health and Social Services in Bermuda, Moray House College of Education, Edinburgh, Scotland, and the Chinese University of Hong Kong.

Dr. Mitchell is co-director of Indiana University's programs in Bermuda and Scotland.

Preface

This book is designed for use in introductory counseling and guidance courses and in related fields for those who seek a comprehensive overview of the profession of counseling. In this text, readers will find a broad, general discussion rather than the in-depth treatment that students majoring in counseling can anticipate later in their specialized preparatory courses.

The objectives of this book are to provide the reader with an overview and general understanding of (1) historical perspectives and current activities of counselors, (2) the role and function of counselors in a variety of settings, (3) techniques utilized by counselors, (4) multicultural considerations in counseling, (5) the impact and role of technology on counselor functioning, (6) organization of counseling programs, and (7) legal and ethical guidelines.

Although counselors in all settings adhere to basically the same principles and practices, it is recognized through special attention in Chapter 3 that counselors function somewhat differently in these various settings. It is, therefore, our hope that counselors, regardless of their intended work setting, will find this book to be an appropriate introduction.

The initial chapter provides the reader with the historical development of the counseling profession. This chapter is followed by chapters discussing what counselors do and where they work. The chapters that follow provide an overview of the basic activities in which counselors are engaged. For example, Chapter 4 focuses on the primary and distinguishing activity of counselors—individual counseling—followed by chapters that discuss group counseling and multicultural counseling. Chapters 7 through 9 discuss other basic activities of counselors: assessment, career development, and consultation. Chapter 10 discusses the current trend of increased counselor attention to prevention. Chapter 11 presents a process and format for integrating the various counselor functions into a relevant and effective program designed to serve a specific target population. Chapter 12 recognizes the significant impact of technology on what we as counselors do and how we do it. The final chapter presents those ethical and legal considerations that confront all counselors.

As an introductory text, this book has been written and revised in a style that we hope is readable and enjoyable as well as informative. Your comments, suggestions, and reactions will be most welcome.

ACKNOWLEDGMENTS

We would like to acknowledge all those who have contributed directly and indirectly to the undertaking and completion of this book. These include, of course, the extremely helpful and responsive staff of Merrill/Prentice Hall, particularly our editor Kevin M. Davis.

Special thanks to Mary Harlan, Production Editor, whose good work kept us on schedule! Sharon Anderson at BookMasters, Inc., was efficient and helpful in assisting us to meet all our deadlines. Autumn Crisp, Editorial Assistant, has been especially prompt in meeting all our requests for assistance. It has been a pleasure to work with the entire staff at Merrill/Prentice Hall, all of whom have been supportive and responsive.

We would also like to acknowledge the valuable comments of our reviewers: Ronald D. Bingham, Brigham Young University; Jesse Brinson, University of Nevada–Las Vegas; Larry Golden, University of Texas–San Antonio; and Judy Lombana-Wren, University of North Florida.

We are extremely grateful to the many considerate authors and publishers who granted us permission to quote from their publications. It is appropriate to acknowledge the many useful suggestions from our departmental colleagues at Indiana University and our fellow counselor-educators who volunteered their time and comments for our guidance. In addition, we have appreciated the critical comments of our graduate students (who undoubtedly had in mind the well-being of their counterparts of the future). In conclusion, we would like to recognize our close friends and families, whose support and encouragement have been important to our work on this edition.

R. L. G.
M. H. M.

Discover the Companion Website Accompanying This Book

The Prentice Hall Companion Website: A Virtual Learning Environment

Technology is a constantly growing and changing aspect of our field that is creating a need for content and resources. To address this emerging need, Prentice Hall has developed an online learning environment for students and professors alike—Companion Websites—to support our textbooks.

In creating a Companion Website, our goal is to build on and enhance what the textbook already offers. For this reason, the content for each user-friendly website is organized by topic and provides the professor and student with a variety of meaningful resources. Common features of a Companion Website include:

For the Professor—

Every Companion Website integrates **Syllabus Manager™**, an online syllabus creation and management utility.

- **Syllabus Manager™** provides you, the instructor, with an easy, step-by-step process to create and revise syllabi, with direct links into Companion Website and other online content without having to learn HTML.
- Students may logon to your syllabus during any study session. All they need to know is the Web address for the Companion Website and the password you've assigned to your syllabus.
- After you have created a syllabus using **Syllabus Manager™,** students may enter the syllabus for their course section from any point in the Companion Website.
- Clicking on a date, the student is shown the list of activities for the assignment. The activities for each assignment are linked directly to actual content, saving time for students.
- Adding assignments consists of clicking on the desired due date, then filling in the details of the assignment—name of the assignment, instructions, and whether it is a one-time or repeating assignment.
- In addition, links to other activities can be created easily. If the activity is online, a URL can be entered in the space provided, and it will be linked automatically in the final syllabus.
- Your completed syllabus is hosted on our servers, allowing convenient updates from any computer on the Internet. Changes you make to your syllabus are immediately available to your students at their next logon.

For the Student—

- **Counseling Topics**—17 core counseling topics represent the diversity and scope of today's counseling field.
- **Annotated Bibliography**—includes seminal foundational works and key current works.
- **Web Destinations**—lists significant and up-to-date practitioner and client sites.
- **Professional Development**—provides helpful information regarding professional organizations and codes of ethics.
- **Electronic Bluebook**—send homework or essays directly to your instructor's email with this paperless form.
- **Message Board**—serves as a virtual bulletin board to post—or respond to—questions or comments to/from a national audience.
- **Chat**—real-time chat with anyone who is using the text anywhere in the country—ideal for discussion and study groups, class projects, etc.

To take advantage of these and other resources, please visit the *Introduction to Counseling and Guidance*, Sixth Edition, Companion Website at

www.prenhall.com/gibson

Brief Contents

Contents

CHAPTER 5   GROUP TECHNIQUES FOR COUNSELORS   181

CHAPTER 8   COUNSELING FOR CAREER PLANNING AND DECISION MAKING 304

CHAPTER 12   COUNSELING AND TECHNOLOGY 421

CHAPTER 13   ETHICAL AND LEGAL GUIDELINES 431

Historic Perspectives

COUNSELING: A RESPONSE TO HUMAN NEEDS

Many of you have recently decided to prepare for careers as counselors; some of you may be considering such a decision; still others may be interested in counseling because you are in or are preparing to enter various careers in which some introductory knowledge of this field may be helpful. In this process you probably asked yourself, Why have I selected this field? On occasion, you also may have even thought, Why do I have to work? Both are age-old questions that are vital to society and that have been discussed and researched extensively over the years.

Perhaps an equally important question but one not raised quite as frequently or researched as extensively is, Why do certain careers exist? What were the factors that led to their demand and creation? The answers to these questions are fairly obvious for such fields as medicine and law, for the need for physicians and lawyers in society has been clearly and universally recognized since the earliest recordings of civilizations. Less clear to many, however, is the role of occupations that are not so well known, such as ornithology, demography, and cytotechnology. Everyone in society does not have to understand and accept the need for all careers, but those studying the general areas encompassed by counseling will benefit from knowing the nature of the societal needs to which counseling and counselors are responding and, in turn, understanding the nature of those responsibilities and responses.

This first chapter, therefore, briefly reviews the historic antecedents leading to the development of counseling programs and the professional careers they represent. You may determine whether counseling and counselors are a response to human needs or just another fancy that will pass when the need is examined more closely and critically.

OUR HERITAGE FROM THE PAST

It is quite possible that the earliest (although unconfirmed) occasion in which humans sought a counselor was when Adam reaped the consequences of his eating the apple in the Garden of Eden. There is no proof of this early beginning to counseling, but an abundance of evidence suggests that persons throughout the ages have sought the advice and counsel of others believed to possess superior knowledge, insights, or experiences.

Perhaps the first counterparts of the present-day counselor were the chieftains and elders of the ancient tribal societies to whom youths turned or were often sent for advice and guidance. In these primitive societies, tribal members shared fundamental economic enterprises such as hunting, fishing, and farming. No elaborate career guidance programs were developed—or needed—because occupational limitations were usually determined by two criteria: age and sex. Later, as skills became more recognizable and important to societies, occupational trades began to be passed down, mostly within families. Thus, potters passed on the secrets and skills of their trade to their sons, as did the smiths and carpenters. Women passed on their skills to their daughters; however, their occupational opportunities were limited.

A study of early primitive life can lead one to conclude that most of the conflicts existing in present-day society regarding career decision making were absent. This lack of a career decision-making dilemma, however, should not be interpreted to mean that workers did not enjoy or take pride in a job well done. Even the earliest evidence of humankind's existence indicates that pride and pleasure resulted from developing and demonstrating one's skills—in developing one's human potential.

In the early civilizations, the philosophers, priests, or other representatives of the gods and religions assumed the function of advising and offering counsel. The historic origins of the concept of developing one's potential may be identified in the early Grecian societies, with their emphasis on developing and strengthening individuals through education so that all could fulfill roles reflecting their greatest potential for themselves and their society. Each person was believed to harbor forces that could be stimulated and guided toward goals beneficial to both the individual and the community. Of these early Greek counselors, Plato more than any other is generally recognized as one of the first to organize psychological insights into a systematic theory. Belkin (1975) notes that Plato's interests

> were varied, and he examined the psychology of the individual in all of its ramifications: in moral issues, in terms of education, in relation to society, in theological perspective, and so on. He dealt with such questions as "What makes a man virtuous—his inheritance, his upbringing, or his formal education? (Meno), "How can children be most effectively taught" (Republic), and "Why techniques have been successfully used in persuading and influencing people in their decisions and beliefs" (Gorgias). But it is not the specific questions themselves that prove important to counselors, but, rather, the method that Plato used to deal with these questions, a method which, more than any other in the history of human thought, sets the way for the counseling relationship. It is a dramatic method, in which profound questions are dealt with through the dynamics of very real human interactions, a method in which the characters are as important as the things they say. (p. 5)

The second great counselor of the early civilizations was Plato's student, Aristotle, who made many significant contributions to what was to become the field of psychology. One of these was his study of people interacting with their environment and others. Also, Hippocrates and other Greek physicians offered the opinion that mental disorders were diseases originating from natural causes.

Later, in ancient Hebrew society, individuality and the right of self-determination were assumed. The early Christian societies emphasized, at least in theory if not always in practice, many of the humanistic ideals that later became basic to democratic societies and, in the 20th century, the counseling movement.

Philosophers who were also educators, such as Luis Vives (1492–1540), recognized the need to guide persons according to their attitudes and aptitudes. Foreshadowing the more recent women's equity movement and the earlier women's liberation movement,

"Vives in his *De subventione pauperum* (Bruges, 1526) even demanded that girls should be prepared for useful occupations" (Mallart, 1955, p. 75).

In the Middle Ages attempts at counseling increasingly came under the control of the church. By the early Middle Ages, the duty of advising and directing youth had become centered in the parish priest. At that time education was largely under church jurisdiction. Sporadic efforts at placing youth in appropriate vocations occurred during the rise of European kingdoms and the subsequent expansion of the colonial empires. Books aimed at helping youths choose an occupation began to appear in the 17th century (Zytowski, 1972). A number of picture books also appeared depicting different occupations. One of the more popular publications was Powell's *Tom of All Trades: Or the Plain Path Way to Preferment*, published in 1631 in London. "Powell gives much information on the professions and how to gain access to them, even suggesting sources of financial aid and the preferred schools in which to prepare" (Zytowski, 1972, p. 447).

Also during this time, Rene Descartes (1596–1650) and others began to study the human body as an organism that reacted or behaved to various stimuli. These studies were to be forerunners for later, more accurate and scientific psychological studies.

In the 18th century Jean-Jacques Rousseau (1712–1778) suggested that the growing individual can best learn when free to develop according to his or her natural impulses; he advocated permissiveness in learning and learning through doing. At approximately the same time, the famous Swiss educator Johann Pestalozzi (1746–1827) expressed the belief that society could be reformed only to the extent that the individual in that society was helped to develop.

For centuries, however, many with mental illnesses, as well as those with physical illnesses, went underground and retreated. Whereas the wealthy could afford the attention of physicians, most mentally ill patients were almost always treated in the home. Those poor who received any treatment at all found help in hospitals run by religious orders. For the first 75 years of this new nation, the United States of America, few public facilities existed for the treatment of the mentally ill.

The newly independent United States did have leading citizens with a counseling viewpoint. One of its most versatile citizens, Thomas Jefferson, called for a plan to recognize and educate its male youth as a source of national leadership. The second president, John Adams, called for laws assuring the liberal education of youths, especially of the lower classes. He felt that no expense for this purpose could be thought extravagant.

The most famous U.S. educator of the 19th century, Horace Mann, included in his *Twelfth Annual Report* a notation of the advantages of the American common school system, advantages that were to be conducive to the development of counseling and guidance programs in U.S. education in the next century. Mann reported that "in teaching the blind and the deaf and dumb, in kindling the latent spark of intelligence that lurks in an idiot's mind, and in the more holy work of reforming abandoned and outcast children, education has proved what it can do by glorious experiments" (Johansen, Collins, & Johnson, 1975, p. 280). Mann also believed that education should have as one of its objectives the reform of society, and he continually stressed this view in his reports to the Massachusetts Board of Education.

In the wake of the political scandals of the Grant administration and other evidence of the decay of Christian morals, methods of moral instruction and moral education became significant in the later 1800s. In 1872, the noted educator A. D. Mayo stated that morality and good citizenship were indistinguishably intermingled and that moral education in the public schools should be based on concepts, principles, and models drawn from the Christian tradition of U.S. society.

During this period, the biologist Herbert Spencer (1820–1903) set forth his concept of adjustment. This biological concept held that forms of life that do not adapt to their environment eventually become extinct. From this, Spencer concluded that perfect life consisted of perfect adjustment. In other words, biological adjustment is a criterion of life. Adaptive behavior is that which maintains life.

Also important to the scientific study of behavior and of special significance to the eventual development of counseling as a psychologically based profession was the emergence of the field of psychology itself during the latter part of the 19th century. Preceded by physicists and physiologists who were conducting experimental investigations that led to reliable information on physical and physiological aspects of behavior, similar investigations launched psychology as a separate science in the late 1800s. Psychology's formal beginnings as a separate science occurred in 1879 when Wilhelm Wundt opened his Psychological Institute at the University of Leipzig. This was the beginning of the movement toward a systematic inquiry into human behavior rather than aimless and often biased observation. With William James (1892–1920) as its early American leader, psychology emerged over the next 100 years as a recognized discipline with its own distinct areas of specialization, inquiry, and training.

The rise of psychiatry as a specialty of medicine was another important and relevant development of this period. This field led to a decline in the support of moral treatment for mental disorders because psychiatry advocated organic treatment for organic causes. During this same time, the state mental hospital movement, led by Dorothea Dix, resulted in the development of these institutions and the removal of much of the care for at least the seriously mentally ill from local communities (Goshen, 1967).

A major contribution to the field of psychiatry and to all of mental health was the studies and writings of Sigmund Freud, an Austrian, in the early 1900s. His writings advanced the historical prominence of psychoanalytic theory and influenced later prominent theorists in the field such as Alfred Adler, Albert Ellis, and Fritz Perls. (Freud died in 1939 in London, England, where he had come as a refugee from the Nazi occupation of his country.)

As the United States entered the 20th century, its society was growing more complex, and finding one's appropriate place within it and adjusting to it were becoming increasingly complicated. Many adults were turning to such traditional sources of guidance as their family physician, minister, or employer. However, the 20th century seemed ripe for a considered and genuinely scientific approach to meeting many human needs. The time had come for the development of counseling and other psychologically oriented programs to meet these needs. We next examine how these programs emerged in schools and institutional and agency settings in the 20th century.

THE DEVELOPMENT OF COUNSELING AND GUIDANCE IN U.S. EDUCATION

History is often made when a person has an idea that meets a need and coincides with an opportunity. In 1908, Frank Parsons organized the Boston Vocational Bureau to provide needed vocational assistance to the many young people seeking employment and to train teachers to serve as vocational counselors. These teachers were to help select students for vocational schools and assist students in choosing a vocation wisely and making the transition from school to suitable work. Soon thereafter, Parsons (1909) published *Choosing a*

Vocation, a predecessor to this and other basic books in the field. In this publication he discussed the role of the counselor and techniques that might be employed in vocational counseling. This book is divided into three areas: personal investigation, industrial investigation, and the organization and the work.

Parsons's book is interesting reading even today, and few would find fault with what he considered to be three factors necessary for the wise choice of a vocation:

> (1) a clear understanding of yourself, your aptitudes, abilities, interests, ambitions, resources, limitations, and other causes; (2) a knowledge of the requirements and conditions of success, advantages and disadvantages, compensation, opportunities, and prospects in different lines of work; and (3) true reasoning on the relations of these two groups of facts. (p. 5)

Parsons suggested that in initiating the personal investigation, the client should first make an extensive self-study by answering questions on a "schedule of personal data." The counselor would then fill in the details by reading between the lines. Parsons stated that this approach would give clues to possible flaws such as defective verbal memory and slow auditory reactions. Such a client would make a poor stenographer, or as he put it, "would have difficulty in becoming an expert stenographer" (p. 7). The inventory suggested by Parsons includes such items as "How far can you walk? Habits as to smoking? Drinking? Use of drugs? Other forms of dissipation? How often do you bathe?"

An unusual feature of the intake interview was the observations Parsons suggested regarding the client's physical appearance:

> While I am questioning the applicant about his probable health, education, reading, experience, et cetera, I carefully observe the shape of his head, the relative development above, before, and behind the ears, his features and expression, color, vivacity, voice, manner, pose, general air of vitality, enthusiasm, et cetera.
>
> If the applicant's head is largely developed behind the ears, with big neck, low forehead, and small upper head, he is probably of an animal type, and if the other symptoms coincide, he should be dealt with on that basis. (p. 7)

Parsons advocated getting the client to see himself or herself exactly as others do and giving the client recommendations about methods that could be used for self-improvement—for example, reading suitable books to develop analytical power. Parsons also recommended using biographies of famous people, finding commonalities with the client in biographic details, and pointing these out to the client as a form of inspiration.

Parsons insisted that counselors be thoroughly familiar with all relevant details concerning job opportunities, the distribution of demand in industries, and courses of study related to these opportunities. Counselors were to make a detailed analysis of industrial job possibilities for men and women, including location and demand, work conditions, and pay. A similar detailed examination was to be made of offerings and openings in vocational schools.

Parsons also explained the need to train vocational counselors. This training was to be accomplished in one to three terms, and the applicants were to have some relevant occupational background and maturity. In addition to sound judgment, character, and maturity, Parsons (1909) believed the vocational counselor should have the following traits:

1. A practical working knowledge of the fundamental principles and methods of modern psychology.

2. An experience involving sufficient human contact to give him an intimate acquaintance with human nature in a considerable number of its different phases; he must understand the dominant motives, interests, and ambitions that control the lives of men, and be able to recognize the symptoms that indicate the presence or absence of important elements of character.

3. An ability to deal with young people in a sympathetic, earnest, searching, candid, helpful, and attractive way.

4. A knowledge of requirements and conditions of success, compensation, prospects, advantages, and disadvantages, etc., in the different lines of industry.

5. Information relating to courses of study and means of preparing for various callings and developing efficiency therein.

6. Scientific method analysis and principles of investigation by which laws and causes are ascertained, facts are classified, and correct conclusions drawn. The counselor must be able to recognize the essential facts and principles involved in each case, group them according to their true relations, and draw the conclusions they justify. (pp. 94–95)

Parsons's pioneer efforts and publications were popular and succeeded in identifying and launching a new helping profession: guidance counseling. Today, Parsons is generally referred to as the "father of the guidance movement in American education," but he probably did not envision the growth of the movement from the several dozen counselors he trained to approximately 115,000 school counselors by 1994 (Bureau of Labor Statistics, 1996). By 1913, the fledgling guidance movement (as it was initially called) had grown sufficiently in numbers and specialization to warrant the organization of the National Vocational Guidance Association and initiate, two years later, the publication of the first guidance journal, appropriately titled *Vocational Guidance*. The term *guidance* was the popular designation for the counseling movement in schools for well over 50 years. However, in recent generations *guidance* has been sometimes viewed as an outdated label. Additionally, the early years of the movement had a vocational orientation that was primarily concerned with those aspects of youth guidance dealing with vocational choice, preparation, and placement. (Sixty years later, many of the same characteristics would once again be reasserted in the career education and guidance movements.) Hence, in these early years, the movement was often referred to as one of vocational guidance.

According to Rockwell and Rothney (1961), other early leaders in the guidance movement in the United States were Jessie B. Davis, Anna Y. Reed, Eli W. Weaver, and David S. Hill. Their contributions should also be noted. Davis's approach was based on self-study and the study of occupations. His descriptions of counseling (Rockwell & Rothney, 1961) seem to suggest that students should be preached to about the moral value of hard work, ambition, honesty, and the development of good character as assets to any person who planned to enter the business world. In their discussion of early pioneers of the guidance movement, Rockwell and Rothney (1961) wrote:

Davis's position within the social gospel philosophy was enhanced by his use of the "call" concept of the ministry in relation to the way one should choose a vocation. When an individual was "called," he would approach it with the noblest and highest ideals which would serve society best by uplifting humanity. (p. 351)

In the same era, Anna Reed was an admirer of the then-prevailing concepts and ethics of the business world and the free enterprise system. She believed that guidance services could be important to the Seattle school system as a means of developing the best possible educational product. Contrary to today's philosophy, she placed the system's (business world's) needs above those of the individual. As a result, the guidance programs she developed were designed to judge a person's worth by his or her employability.

Another early leader, Eli Weaver, succeeded in establishing teacher guidance committees in every high school in New York City. These committees worked actively to help youths discover their capabilities and learn how to use those talents to secure the most appropriate employment (Rockwell & Rothney, 1961).

The fourth of these early pioneers, David S. Hill, was a researcher in the New Orleans school system who used scientific methods to study people. Because his research studies pointed out the wide diversity in student populations, he advocated and worked for a diversified curriculum complemented by vocational guidance. He viewed this model as most appropriate if the individual student were to develop fully.

In the first quarter of the 20th century, two other significant developments in psychology profoundly influenced the school guidance movement: (a) the introduction and development of standardized, group-administered psychological tests and (b) the mental health movements.

The French psychologist Alfred Binet and his associate Theodore Simon introduced the first general intelligence test in 1905. In 1916, a translated and revised version was introduced in the United States by Lewis M. Terman and his colleagues at Stanford University, and it enjoyed widespread popularity in the schools. However, when the United States entered World War I and the armed services sought a measure that would enable them to screen and classify inductees, the first so-called group intelligence measure, the Army Alpha Test, was subsequently administered to thousands of draftees. The possibilities of applying these and other psychometric techniques to pupil assessment resulted in the rapid development and expansion of standardized testing in education in the decade immediately following World War I.

The 1920s was a lively decade in many ways. That noble experiment, Prohibition, was launched; in turn, such names as Al Capone and Baby Face Nelson appeared in the nation's newspaper headlines. Socially, jazz, flappers, and bathtub gin were in vogue. For the professional educator, the Progressive movement ensured a lively educational era as well. This movement, thought to influence the further development of a people-oriented philosophy, stressed the uniqueness and dignity of the individual pupil, emphasized the importance of a facilitating classroom environment, and suggested that learning occurred in many ways. Many of today's counselors would have embraced the Progressive education suggestions that pupils and teachers should plan together, that the child's social environment should be improved, that the developmental needs and purposes of the student should be considered, and that the psychological environment of the classroom should be a positive, encouraging one.

Organized guidance programs began to emerge with increasing frequency in secondary schools in the 1920s and more often than not modeled themselves after college student personnel programs, with titles of deans (separately for boys and girls, of course) and similar accompanying functions of discipline, school attendance, and related administrative responsibilities. As a result, many programs of this decade began to have a remedial emphasis, as pupils who experienced academic or personal difficulties were sent to their deans for help modifying their behavior or correcting their deficiencies. Nevertheless, a counselor of the mid-1920s, if projected by a time capsule into a school counselor's meeting 80 years later, could converse easily with his present-day counterparts—at least about their common concerns and involvement in vocational or career counseling, the use of the standardized testing instruments, assistance to students with their educational planning, the need for a more caring school environment, and their role as disciplinarians and quasi-administrators.

It is probable that the elementary school counseling movement also had its beginnings in the mid-1920s and early 1930s, stimulated by the writings and efforts of William Burnham who emphasized the role of the teacher in promoting children's mental health in the elementary school. Efforts to develop guidance in elementary schools during this period were scarcely noticeable, but a few notable programs were undertaken. One of these, in Winnetka, Illinois, established a department of elementary counseling with resource personnel for guidance. These personnel included (although not all on a full-time basis) psychiatrists, psychometrists, psychologists, an educational counselor, a psychiatric social worker, and supporting clerical services. Their basic responsibilities were counseling, child study, psychotherapy, pupil analysis, parental assistance, and referrals.

College campuses also began to reflect the influences affecting the guidance movement in the 1920s as student personnel workers began utilizing standardized tests for admission and placement purposes. A few institutions even began to offer vocational guidance. By the end of the 1920s, it was evident that the early guidance pioneers believed that there was a need for guidance services and the school was the proper institution for the delivery of these services. Some even thought that pupil guidance should encompass all grades.

It is also important to note that the word *counseling* was rarely used during these early years as the label *guidance* was broadly applied to those activities utilized to guide students and other clients into appropriate educational choices and career decisions. The reversal in popularity of these labels is noted by Hoyt (1993) in his article "Guidance Is Not a Dirty Word." Perhaps the first delineation of counseling as a psychological process was expressed with the publication of *Workbook in Vocations* by Proctor, Benefield, and Wrenn in 1931 (cited in Lewis, Hayes, & Lewis, 1986).

While the American public debated the policies of FDR and the threat of Hitler to world peace, the guidance movement of the 1930s continued to develop, becoming increasingly popular as a topic for discussions and debate in educational circles. Questions and criticisms concerning guidance activities were increasingly noted in the professional literature of the era. Educational associations appointed committees to study the movement, and many issued reports with descriptions and definitions of guidance and guidance services. The New York State Teachers Association published a report in 1935 in which guidance was defined as "the process of assisting individuals in making life adjustment. It is needed in the home, school, community, and in all other phases of the individual's environment" (p. 10).

As in the 1960s, when concern was often expressed about the interchangeability of the words *guidance* and *counseling,* in the 1930s a similar concern was expressed over the interchangeability of the terms *student personnel* and *guidance.* Adding to the confusion, leading spokespeople for the movement during that period, such as John Brewer (1932), used the terms *education* and *guidance* synonymously.

Sarah M. Sturtevant (1937) sought to deal with some of these growing concerns by addressing questions regarding the developing secondary school guidance movement: What do we mean by the guidance movement? What are the essentials of a functioning guidance program? What personnel and what qualifications should guidance workers have for a good guidance program? And the inevitable question, What are the costs of individualizing education? These questions would not be outdated more than 60 years later.

During the late 1930s and early 1940s, the trait-factor approach to counseling became increasingly popular. This often-labeled directive theory received stimulus from the writings of E. G. Williamson (*How to Counsel Students: A Manual of Techniques for Clinical Counselors*, 1939) and others. Whereas critics of this measurement-oriented approach claimed it was rigid and dehumanizing, Williamson stresses its worth: "You are trying to improve your understanding by using data with a smaller probable error of estimate, such as test data—instead of judgments, which have a much larger probable error of estimate: variability" (Ewing, 1975, p. 84).

Also during the 1930s, possible directions for guidance in the elementary school were put forth by the child study movement, which took the position that it was the teacher's role to provide guidance for each pupil in the self-contained classroom. Publications by Zirbes (1949) and others described the ways in which the learning experiences of children could be guided. The intensive study of each child was recommended, with the objective of understanding how children achieved or failed to achieve certain developmental tasks. This popular approach found some following at the secondary school level and ultimately led to the suggestion of "every teacher a guidance worker."

As the United States emerged from World War II, the counseling and guidance movement appeared to be taking on new vitality and focus. A significant contributor to this new direction, with an impact on counseling in both school and nonschool settings, was Carl R. Rogers (1902–1987). Rogers set forth a new counseling theory in two significant books, *Counseling and Psychotherapy* (1942) and a refinement of his early position, *Client-Centered Therapy* (1951). In *Counseling and Psychotherapy*, Rogers offers nondirective counseling as an alternative to the older, more traditional methods. He also stresses the client's responsibility in perceiving his or her problem and enhancing the self. This self theory soon was labeled nondirective because it appeared to be the opposite of the traditional counselor-centered approach for dealing with client problems.

Rogers's suggestion that the client rather than the therapist assume the major responsibility for solving the client's problem provoked the first serious theoretical controversies in the school guidance and counseling movement. Rogers's follow-up publication, *Client-Centered Therapy*, was the result of this continued research and application effort. The book promotes the semantic change from nondirective to client-centered counseling but, more important, places increased emphasis on the growth-producing possibilities of the client.

Perhaps more than any other person, Rogers influenced the way American counselors interact with clients. Furthermore, his view of the client as an equal and his positive view of a person's potential seem more consistent with the American way of life and democratic traditions than do the European-based theories. The tremendous influence of Rogers resulted in an emphasis on counseling as the primary and most significant activity in which counselors would engage. He further provided a theory that was easy to understand and optimistic in its orientation.

Over the years Rogers continued to research, test, revise, and challenge others to test his theory. In summary, Carl Rogers's impact and contributions to the counseling movement in this century might be considered analogous to Henry Ford's contribution to the development of the automotive industry.

Another dimension to the techniques of counselors of the late 1940s and one to which Rogers, again, was a significant contributor was group counseling. Others, utilizing research data gathered by the armed services and their investigations into small-group dynamics, developed a theoretical framework within which school counselors could integrate the skills and processes of individual counseling with the dynamic roles and interactions of the individual in a group setting.

Other opportunities also appeared on the horizon for the counseling and guidance movement. Feingold (1947), writing in *School Review*, called for a new approach to guidance. He indicated that guidance counselors cannot stop with mere educational direction—they must go beyond that goal, must provide guidance, "not only for the anointed, but for those pupils who really need it—the pupils who run afoul of rules and regulations" (p. 550). Feingold and others also called for "guidance of the whole child," an outgrowth of the child study movement of the 1930s. Three years later, Traxler (1950), writing in the same publication, identified emerging trends in guidance.

- More adequate training of guidance personnel.
- Guidance as an all-faculty function.
- Closer cooperation with home and community agencies.
- Orderly accumulation and recording of individual information.
- Use of objective measures.
- Differential prediction of success on the basis of test batteries that yield comparable scores in broad areas.
- Increased interest in improved techniques in the appraisal of personal qualities of pupils and the treatment of maladjustment.
- Trend toward "eclectic" guidance (rather than directive/nondirective).
- Recognition of the relationship between remedial work and guidance.
- Improved case study techniques.
- Availability and better use of occupational-educational information. (pp. 14–23)

In 1957, the Soviet Union made headlines around the world by successfully launching the first earth satellite, *Sputnik I.* An indirect but nevertheless significant result of this accomplishment was the lift-off of the counseling and guidance movement in the United States. This boost came about through legislation resulting from the public's criticism of education and its failure to supply trained personnel for careers deemed vital for national well-being. This legislation, labeled the National Defense Education Act and passed in September 1958, became a most important landmark in American education as well as the guidance movement for its acknowledgment of the vital link among our national well-being, personnel needs, and education.

This act provided special benefits for youth guidance in 5 of its 10 titles or sections. Of these, perhaps Title V was the key to the upsurge in counseling and guidance program development. This act provided for (a) grants to states for stimulating the establishment and maintenance of local guidance programs, and (b) grants to institutions of higher education for the training of guidance personnel to staff local programs.

Six years later (September 1964), the impact of the act could be detected in announcements from the U.S. Department of Health, Education, and Welfare, which pointed out that the act had, in that short period of time, achieved the following:

- Made grants to states of approximately $30 million, thereby helping bring the number of full-time high school counselors from 12,000 (one for every 960 students) in 1958 to 30,000 (one for every 510 students) in 1964

- Through the end of the 1964–1965 academic year, supported 480 institutes designed to improve counseling capabilities, which were attended by more than 15,700 secondary school counselors and teachers preparing to become counselors
- From 1959 to 1964, made it possible for 109 million scholastic aptitude and achievement tests to be given to public secondary school students and over 3 million to private secondary school students
- Helped 600,000 students obtain or continue their college education with federal loans
- Trained 42,000 skilled technicians to meet critical manpower needs
- Granted 8,500 graduate fellowships, a first step toward meeting the need for many more college teachers

Stimulated by this rapid growth in counseling and guidance, standards for the certification and performance of school counselors were developed and upgraded; the criteria used by accrediting associations for school guidance program evaluation were strengthened; and noticeable progress was made in counselor training. Many writers in the field noted that guidance had come of age, that there was a new era.

For example, Donovan (1959) wrote about a new era for guidance in which he pointed out that "the test expert and professional counselor enter the picture to give scientific aid in getting each child in touch with those teachers and courses best calculated to free his abilities" (p. 241). He and others further discussed the movement from an era of mass education to one in which each child was treated as an individual with "counseling personnel becoming indispensable auxiliaries to administrators and teachers" (p. 241).

The following year, Klopf (1960) called for an expanding role for the high school counselor. He pointed out that "as populations increase, schools will become larger and taxes become greater in most communities. Instructional services will increase in communities, but guidance programs may not increase accordingly" (p. 418). He suggested that new uses and approaches to homeroom group guidance, small discussion groups, and group counseling needed to be explored. He also suggested that guidance workers should view themselves not only as counselors but as individuals concerned with total learning, including the personal and social relations of the student: "If he has a knowledge of individual behavior, the social structure of the school and the community and awareness of the world of today and the future, this in all the ongoing activities of the school he should share" (p. 418).

In the 1960s one of the most important developments for the school counseling and guidance movement was the *Statement of Policy for Secondary School Counselors* (American School Counselor Association, 1964), which was developed and approved as an official policy statement by the American School Counselor Association (ASCA). This effort to specify the role and function of the school counselor involved more than 6,000 school counselors plus teachers, school administrators, and other educators.

C. Gilbert Wrenn's classic contribution of the 1960s, *The Counselor in a Changing World*, also examined the counselor's role in a society with changing ideas about human behavior and changing schools. Wrenn (1962) noted the growing complexity of the counselor's task:

> It is not enough for the counselor to understand youth in isolation, as it were. More than ever before, the counselor must understand not only the student, but himself and his adult contemporaries as they attempt to adjust to a rapidly changing technology and the world order. (p. 8)

C. Harold McCully (1965) implied that if school counselors were to move toward bona fide professionalization, "they cannot afford to define their function on the basis of a retrospective analysis of what counselors have done in the past as technicians" (p. 405). He forecast needed new directions in which the counselor functioned as a consultant and agent for change, directions that would require substantive study of the dynamics of cultural and social change.

By the 1970s the school guidance counselor had inherited a series of stereotypes, the value and validity of which had to be determined. What historians recorded about guidance in the 1970s attested to their concern for these generalizations and their behavior in dealing with them. These stereotypes were as follows:

The Stereotype of Responsibility. The belief by parents and others that counselors have certain responsibilities such as ensuring that the student takes the "right" courses, selects the appropriate college, takes necessary standardized examinations, meets application deadlines, and so forth.

The Stereotype of Failure. The belief that the counselor is responsible for keeping individuals from failing—that the counselor is a buffer between success and failure. As a predictor of outcomes that determine decisions, the counselor can assess risks and chances for success or failure.

The Stereotype of Occupational Choice. Perhaps more consistent and widespread than any other is the view of the counselor as the person who can tell a student what occupation to enter—who can make this "once-in-a-lifetime" decision for individuals. After all, the counselor is the one with the various interest and aptitude tests and occupational fields—and one is constantly referred to as the person to see about industrial, armed services and educational recruitment materials. (Munson, 1971, pp. 16–17)

In 1973, the National Commission on the Reform of Secondary Education published its report, with 32 recommendations for the improvement of secondary education. Although the majority of these held implications for the functioning of the secondary school counselor, the following were of particular importance:

- Recommendation 6, dealing with bias in counseling
- Recommendation 9, focusing on career education
- Recommendation 10, emphasizing suitable job placement as a part of career education
- Recommendation 12, recommending alternative routes to high school completion

During the mid-1970s and early 1980s, a number of developments influenced counselors in schools and frequently in other settings as well. As noted in more detail in chapter 11, the accountability movement of this period influenced many school counseling programs to develop more relevant data-based programs usually based on objective needs assessments. A major publication of this period, *Guidance and Counseling in the Schools* (Herr, 1979), was the outgrowth of a national survey directed by Dr. Edwin L. Herr and jointly sponsored by the American Personnel and Guidance Association and the Counseling and Guidance Office of the U.S. Department of Education. (Note: The American Personnel and Guidance Association officially changed its name to the American Association for Counseling and Development—AACD—in 1983. In 1992, the AACD changed its name to the American Counseling Association—ACA.)

Although state certification laws have in recent generations governed the credentialing of counselors in schools in all states, school counselors also became increasingly interested in the movement to license counselors for practice outside school settings. By 2001, 46 states plus the District of Columbia had passed legislation to license counselors (Alabama, Alaska, Arizona, Arkansas, California, Colorado, Connecticut, Delaware, Florida, Georgia, Idaho, Illinois, Indiana, Iowa, Kansas, Kentucky, Louisiana, Maine, Maryland, Massachusetts, Michigan, Mississippi, Missouri, Montana, Nebraska, New Hampshire, New Jersey, New Mexico, North Carolina, North Dakota, Ohio, Oklahoma, Oregon, Pennsylvania, Rhode Island, South Carolina, South Dakota, Tennessee, Texas, Utah, Vermont, Virginia, Washington, West Virginia, Wisconsin, and Wyoming), and others are preparing to follow suit.

CACREP (the Council for Accreditation of Counseling and Related Educational Programs), the accrediting arm of the American Counseling Association (ACA), was incorporated in 1981. This independent council was created by ACA and its divisions to develop, implement, and maintain standards of preparation for the counseling profession's graduate-level degree programs. Its purpose is to work with institutions that offer graduate-level programs in counseling and related educational fields so that they might achieve accreditation status. Eight common core curricular areas are required for accreditation:

- Professional Identity
- Social and Cultural Diversity
- Human Growth and Development
- Career Development
- Helping Relationships
- Group Work
- Assessment
- Research and Program Evaluation

The National Board for Certified Counselors, Inc. (NBCC) was established in 1982 to establish and monitor a national certification system, to identify for professionals and the public those counselors who have voluntarily sought and obtained certification and to maintain a register of such counselors. This process grants recognition to counselors who have met predetermined NBCC standards in their training, experience, and performance on the National Counselor Examination for Licensure and Certification (NCE).

Thirty-seven states and the District of Columbia have adopted the NCE as part of their statutory credentialing process. Initially created by the American Counseling Association (ACA), NBCC is now an independent credentialing body with close ties to ACA. While ACA concentrates on professional development, including publications, workshops, and government relations in the counseling field, NBCC focuses on promoting quality counseling through certification.

Since October 1985, NBCC has been accredited by the National Commission for Certifying Agencies (NCCA). NCCA is an independent national regulatory organization that monitors the credentialing processes of its member agencies. Accreditation by the commission represents the foremost organizational recognition in national certification (Hollis, with Dodson. 2000, p. 32). By the year 2000, there were 31,342 nationally certified counselors. (*The National Certified Counselor,* 2000)

In 1983, the presidentially appointed National Commission on Excellence in Education issued its report, entitled *A Nation at Risk* (Bell, 1983). This report cited as its primary evidence the decline in standardized achievement test results and recommended longer school days, more effective school discipline, a return to basics, and more. Although there are no specific references to school counseling programs, many inferences for such programs could be drawn.

During the 1980s and 1990s a number of social concerns affecting children stimulated an accelerated growth of elementary school counseling. Issues such as substance abuse, child abuse, sexual abuse, and latch-key children plus increased interest in and attention to prevention led to mandated elementary school counseling in 24 states by 2000 (Lum, 2001).

During the 1990s dramatic changes in the world of work significantly affected school counseling programs and their career guidance services. Among the significant changes were the shift from a goods and services economy to an information-based economy; the movement toward international marketing and a global, rather than a national, workforce; multiple careers for the individual across the working life span, rather than a single, life-long occupation; and dual-career couples being the norm rather than the exception. These are just a few of the changes totally reshaping the world of work and workers.

In 1986 a significant report, *Keeping the Options Open*, was published by the College Entrance Examination Board. This report focused entirely on school counseling and guidance programs with an important emphasis on their role in providing career assistance. In the late 1980s and early 1990s, counseling, especially career counseling, was extended in various new directions. This included outreach services for the poor and homeless, out-placement services for middle-aged workers and senior executives, prevention and early intervention programs for alcohol and other substance abusers, and emerging concerns with retirees, stress management, and sports and leisure counseling. The 1990s also brought a dramatic increase in interest in multicultural counseling.

Another direct influence on school counseling programs was the School-to-Work Opportunities Act of 1994, which provides the framework for creating school-to-work opportunity systems in all states with career counseling and guidance being a high priority activity.

The computer and its accompanying technology have had a tremendous impact on educational institutions at all levels beginning in the 1990s. Individuals could suddenly access information and communicate instantly via electronic mail, the Internet, or cellular phones with people almost anywhere in the world. For example, school counseling programs utilize computers and Web sites especially for career guidance purposes, to access information about job sites and opportunities as well as educational opportunities and requirements.

THE DEVELOPMENT OF INSTITUTIONAL AND AGENCY COUNSELING PROGRAMS

The mental health movement, like the vocational guidance movement, owed much of its impetus in the early 1900s to the efforts of one person. This was Clifford Beers, who was neither a physician nor a psychologist, but for several years a patient in a mental institution suffering from schizophrenia. During his confinement Beers (1908/1953) wrote:

> I soon observed that the only patients who were not likely to be subjected to abuse were the ones least in need of care and treatment. The violent, noisy, and troublesome patient was abused because he was violent, noisy, and troublesome. The patient too weak, physically or

mentally, to attend to his own wants was frequently abused because of that very helplessness which made it necessary for the attendants to wait upon him. Usually a restless or troublesome patient placed in the violent ward was assaulted the very first day. This procedure seemed to be a part of the established code of dishonor. The attendants imagined that the best way to gain control of a patient was to cow him from the first. In fact, these fellows—nearly all of them ignorant and untrained—seemed to believe that violent cases could not be handled in any other way. (pp. 164–165)

In another statement, Beers (1908/1953) wrote:

Most sane people think that no insane person can reason logically. But that is not so. Upon unreasonable premises I made most reasonable deductions, and at that time when my mind was in its most disturbed condition. Had the newspapers which I read on that day which I supposed to be February 1st borne a January date, I might not then, for so long a time, have believed in special editions. Probably I should have inferred that the regular editions had been held back. But the newspapers I had were dated about two weeks ahead. Now if a sane person on February 1st receives a newspaper dated February 14, he will be fully justified in thinking something wrong, either with the publication or with himself. But the shifted calendar which had planted itself in my mind meant as much to me as the true calendar does to any sane businessman. During the seven hundred and ninety-eight days of depression I drew countless incorrect deductions, and essentially the mental process was not other than that which takes place in a well-ordered mind. (pp. 57–58)

These and similar descriptions aroused the public to initiate humanitarian reforms and scientific inquiry into the problems of mental illnesses and their treatment. With the help of a few psychologists of the time, such as William James and Adolph Meyer, the mental hygiene movement was launched to educate the general public to a better appreciation of the plight and treatment of disturbed persons.

At the same time the viewpoint that persons are products of both their environment and their heredity was reemerging. As a result, a new type of institution for dealing locally with mental illness was gaining support. This institution was to become the forerunner of our present-day community mental health center. It was called a psychopathic hospital. These hospitals were located in communities and were designed to provide outpatient treatment, rather than custodial care. Although many believed these hospitals were based on controversial ideas, they did result in community efforts to raise standards of treatment and prevention of mental disorders and to establish local clinics for disturbed children. As the public became increasingly aware of the extent and impact of mental illness, the possibility of prevention, or early treatment, was increasingly examined.

World War I not only stimulated the development and postwar usage of standardized group psychological tests, it also resulted in two acts significant to the development of one of the early specializations in counseling: rehabilitation counseling. The first of these, the Civilian Vocational Rehabilitation Act (Public Law 236, 1920), was followed in 1921 by Public Law 47. The latter created the Veteran's Bureau and provided, among other benefits, a continuation of vocational rehabilitation services for veterans, including counseling and guidance.

The term *rehabilitation counselor*, however, did not appear in professional literature until the late 1930s. Since then, rehabilitation counseling has generally come to be recognized as basically psychological counseling that specializes in the rehabilitation of persons with physical as well as social and emotional problems. In the history of its development, the practice of rehabilitation counseling seems to have gone through several models, as described by Jacques (1969):

1. Vocational agent, trainer, or worker model
2. Vocational counselor or coordinator of services model
3. Psychotherapeutic model
4. Community-centered team counselor model (p. 17)

The quarter century from 1904 to 1929 was a period of rapid growth in solid scientific research in many different areas. This included the development of a scientific basis for many areas of standardized testing, human development and learning, and psychology as a science.

One of the prominent theorists of this period was another Austrian, Alfred Adler, a one-time disciple of Freud, who migrated to the United States in 1932 to avoid the Nazi rise to power in his country. His lectures and writings formed the basis for Adlerian counseling. Adler was one of the pioneers of family counseling and his theories have, in recent years, also influenced the counseling of children.

During the first half of the 20th century, the community mental health movement reflected a good deal of diversity and encompassed both ideological and practical features. Jeger and Slotnick (1982) note:

> As a philosophy, it has its roots in the fields of social psychiatry and public health, which recognized the iatrogenic effects of institutionalization, redefined "mental illness" as a social problem, advocated alternatives to hospitalization and called for community change for purposes of preventing mental health problems. As a methodology, community mental health refers to specific programs that sought to translate this ideology into practice. (p. 15)

After World War II a series of federal legislative acts defined the mandates of agencies and in so doing provided operational definitions of community mental health practices. The federal government's first major entrance into the public mental health arena began with the passage of the National Mental Health Act of 1946, which established the National Institute of Mental Health, thus announcing the federal government's interest and involvement in public mental health. The National Mental Health Act also encouraged each state to designate a single agency as the state mental health authority and initiated a state grant-in-aid program to assist these authorities in the improvement of community mental health services.

In 1944 the Veterans Administration (VA) established centers to provide counseling for those receiving benefits under the GI Bill, which provided training and education for veterans. Many counselors were trained in VA-supported counseling services on college campuses. The VA did much to broaden and professionalize the role of the vocational counselor. In 1951, the VA established the position of counseling psychologist, in line with new concepts from psychology and related disciplines (Borow, cited in Humes, 1987, p. 16).

During and immediately after World War II, counselors also found increasing opportunities in the VA vocational rehabilitation and educational services as these were rapidly expanded to accommodate the needs of U.S. armed services personnel and ex-service personnel.

Counseling, as a recognized specialty in the field of psychology, also emerged during this time. In 1946 Division 17 (Counseling Psychology) was created with Dr. E. G. Williamson as the first president. The specialty gained further recognition and acceptance in 1951 following a conference at Northwestern University called by Dr. C. Gilbert Wrenn. Another prominent contributor to the movement was Dr. Carl R. Rogers whose writings (noted earlier in this chapter) promoted psychological and public interest in psychotherapy.

Also in the 1950s, another specialty began to emerge: marriage and family counseling. Although historically this movement appeared to have been initiated in the early 1930s, the dramatic post–World War II increase in the separation and divorce rate of young couples led to rapid developments in marital therapy. In the 1960s, dramatic increases in new styles of coupling, marriage, and living together further stimulated interest in providing professional counseling assistance to couples and families. During this period marital therapy moved increasingly from individual analysis to conjoint marital therapy (Brown & Christensen, 1986).

This period after World War II also saw a rapid expansion of community mental health services. In 1955 Congress passed a Mental Health Study Act, which established a joint commission on mental illness and health. This study resulted in a report entitled *Action for Mental Health* in 1961, which led in 1963 to the Community Mental Health Centers Act (Public Law 88-164). Two thousand centers were expected to provide five essential services:

1. Inpatient (for short-term stays)
2. Outpatient
3. Partial hospitalization (e.g., day and/or night hospitals)
4. Emergency care (e.g., 24-hour crisis services)
5. Consultation (e.g., indirect service) and community education (i.e., prevention)

For a center to be considered "comprehensive," five additional services were required: (a) diagnostic, (b) rehabilitation, (c) precare and aftercare, (d) training, and (e) research and evaluation (Jeger & Slotnick, 1982).

The first decline in the number of patients in state mental institutions was recorded in 1955. This decline was to continue steadily over the next 20 years despite increases in the number of admissions. This trend had obvious implications for the growth of local mental health services.

The trauma of the Vietnam War and the postwar era for many veterans and their families created another population in need of mental health counseling. Also during the 1960s and 1970s, increased substance abuse and public awareness of the extent and seriousness of the problem at all age levels led to research, the development of training programs, and the growth of another area of specialization for counselors. Additionally, attention to preparing specialists for correctional counseling and counseling for the elderly reflected a concern for the needs of these populations as well.

The Community Mental Health Centers Amendments of 1975 (Public Law 94-63) redefined the notion of a comprehensive community mental health center from the five minimum and five optional services to a mandated set of 12 services. They include the five originally established services plus these seven:

1. Special services for children
2. Special services for the elderly
3. Preinstitutional screening and alternative treatment (as pertains to the courts and other public agencies)
4. Follow-up for persons discharged from state mental hospitals

5. Transitional living for persons discharged from state mental hospitals
6. Alcoholism services (prevention, treatment, and rehabilitation)
7. Drug abuse services

In addition, the 1975 amendments also obligated centers to allocate 2% of their operating budgets for program evaluation.

The mandated delivery of these 12 services was further modified in the Community Mental Health Extension Act of 1978 (Public Law 95-622). Specifically, new centers were required immediately to provide six services (inpatient, outpatient, emergency, screening, follow-up of discharged inpatients, and consultation/education) and were allowed to phase in gradually the remaining six over their initial 3 years of operation (i.e., partial hospitalization, children's services, elderly services, transitional halfway houses, alcohol abuse services, and drug abuse services).

In considering all the services mandated by legislation since the 1970s, we can chart the progress and intent of the community mental health movement. The 10 characteristics delineated by Bloom (1984) as differentiating community mental health from "traditional" clinical practice help to identify both the ideological and operational aspects of the movement:

- First, as opposed to institutional (e.g., mental hospital) practice, the *community* provides the practice setting.
- Second, rather than an individual patient, a *total population* or community is the target; hence the term *catchment area* to define a given center's area of responsibility.
- A third feature concerns the type of service delivered, that is, offering *preventive services* rather than just treatment.
- *Continuity of care* among the components of a comprehensive system of services constitutes the fourth dimension.
- The emphasis on *indirect services,* that is, consultation is the fifth characteristic.
- A sixth characteristic lies in the area of *clinical innovations*—brief psychotherapy and crisis intervention.
- The emphasis on *systematic planning* for services by considering the demographics of a population, specifying unmet needs, and identifying "high-risk" groups represents a seventh characteristic.
- Utilizing new *person-power resources,* especially nonprofessional mental health workers, constitutes the eighth dimension.
- The ninth dimension is defined in terms of the *community control* concept, which holds that consumers should play central roles in establishing service priorities and evaluating programs.
- Finally, the tenth characteristic identifies community mental health as seeking *environmental causes* of human distress, in contrast to the traditional intrapsychic emphasis. (Jeger & Slotnick, 1982, p. 17)

"Although a majority of community mental health workers might agree that these characteristics reflect the orientation of community mental health, there is much less agreement on the emphasis of these concepts in practice" (Bloom, 1984, p. 38).

In the 1970s, significant federal legislation in the form of the Mental Health Systems Act passed Congress and was signed into law by President Carter. In addition to continuing many of the provisions of the original act, other provisions broadened the scope of care for disturbed children and adolescents. President Reagan's election in 1980, however, led to new economic policies at the federal level, which included repealing the budgetary authorizations of this act. As a result, in the 1980s, states and local communities were increasingly called on to assume the financing of mental health care facilities and programs.

In spite of such setbacks, the counseling profession can mark several important milestones. As previously noted, the counselor licensure movement was initiated in Virginia in 1976. The formation of CACREP as an accrediting body for counselor training programs and the establishment of the NBCC with its process for voluntary national counselor certification have been major accomplishments in the professionalization of counseling. To date, 46 states, plus the District of Columbia have passed licensure laws protecting the practice of professional mental health counselors.

In the late 1980s and early 1990s, counseling, especially career counseling, was extended in various new directions. This included outreach services for the poor and homeless, outplacement services for middle-aged workers and senior executives, prevention and early intervention programs for alcohol and drug abusers, and emerging concerns with retirees, stress management, and sports and leisure counseling. The 1990s also showed a dramatic increase in interest in multicultural counseling.

In 1986, the College Entrance Examination Board's *Keeping the Options Open* placed important emphasis on the role of counseling and guidance programs in providing career assistance. In 1994, Congress continued to recognize the role of counselors in providing career assistance with the passage of the School-to-Work Opportunities Act, which provided a framework for creating school-to-work opportunity systems in all states, with career counseling being a high priority.

In 1996 the U. S. Congress passed the Mental Health Insurance Parity Act (effective January 1, 1998), which is very significant to mental health professionals. This act prevented health plans from placing unequal caps on dollar amounts covering mental health services if these same caps are not placed on the coverage for other medical services. This legislation was a major step toward parity of insurance coverage for the provision of mental health services by mental health counselors. In 1998, another significant congressional act was the Health Professions Education Partnership Act, which recognizes professional counselors who are trained in various mental health professional training programs, including counseling students in counselor education programs. More specifically, these education programs may be eligible for the various programs operated by the federal Health Resources and Services Administration and the federal Center for Mental Health Services.

At the end of the 20th century, the counseling profession was being impacted by both globalization and technology. The impact of these movements will be discussed at greater length in chapters 8 and 12. Counselors in agencies and private practice were also being increasingly confronted with the restrictions imposed by HMOs (health maintenance organizations) and managed care as we entered the new millennium.

The United States can look back on many accomplishments of the last century and anticipate further triumphs in the new century. However, the nation still faces significant societal problems that affect millions of its citizens. These problems include the ever-increasing AIDS epidemic; the continuing addictions of millions to drugs and alcohol; the alarming numbers of abused children and spouses; pregnancies, suicides, and criminal activities among the teenage population; the persistent school dropout problem; the disgraceful numbers of homeless; the resurfacing of various forms of prejudice; a bankruptcy of values in all areas ranging from the political to the private sector; and a myriad of career needs affecting all age groups and socioeconomic levels. The United States could still be labeled a nation on the verge of being psychologically and sociologically at risk.

Further, in examining these problems we would note that many of these issues require not only remedial treatment but also preventive efforts if they are to be ameliorated to any degree. Treatment or punitive actions alone cannot solve societal problems. Only prevention has the prospect for diminishing the numbers of potential victims of nearly all these social ills. In this context, then, we can conclude that most of these problems are in our realm. Counselors, with their access to and work with many different populations, are uniquely positioned to emphasize prevention as well as early intervention and treatment.

Thus, as we begin a new century, we see the opportunity for counseling to become *the* helping profession and respond to society's needs in the coming years. The chapters that follow will acquaint you with the skills and knowledge counselors must acquire to serve society's mental health needs and the settings in which counselors will function to provide their services in meeting these great challenges in the years ahead.

SUMMARY

We have examined the need of humankind, from the time of Adam and Eve down through the ages, for advice and counsel, to understand themselves and their relationships to their fellow human beings, and to recognize and develop their own potential. In responding to these needs, the chieftains and elders of ancient tribal societies were perhaps the first forerunners, the ancient counterparts, of the present-day counselor. Later, in the early civilizations, the philosophers, priests, or other representatives of the gods were seen in roles offering advice and counseling. Often treatment for the mentally ill was cruel, even when administered by physicians. The role of religion in the counsel and advice of the young in particular, but not exclusively, continued through the Middle Ages, supplemented by sporadic efforts of talent identification and development and even planned career placement. From the Middle Ages onward, teachers also were increasingly expected to provide guidance for their pupils, often of the most directive kind. To supplement these efforts, books began to appear with increasing frequency from the 18th century onward that focused on providing advice and counsel to youth in meeting many of the problems of the times, especially those concerning occupational choice. Meanwhile, many leading statesmen, philosophers, scientists, and educators were laying a philosophical groundwork that would eventually support and nurture

an embryonic movement to establish psychology as a science and academic discipline in its own right, with an impact on school and community settings.

The school counseling and guidance movement, which for many years was unique to U.S. education, in its beginning had a vocational guidance emphasis but was shortly to be influenced by a multitude of other movements, especially psychological testing, mental health, and progressive education. Later in the 20th century, the interdisciplinary character of the movement was further emphasized through influences from such movements as group dynamics, counseling psychology, education of the gifted, career education, and placement.

The public or community aspects of the mental health movement initially focused on home confinement and little treatment. An early significant development was state support for the establishment of state mental hospitals in the United States in the 19th century. However, at the turn of the century (1908), the mental health movement was stirred by the writings of Clifford Beers, and local mental health treatment centers began to emerge. These community aftercare services were the forerunners of the present-day community mental health centers.

Three significant legislative acts that further stimulated the counseling movement were the Civilian Vocational Rehabilitation Act (1920), the Mental Health Study Act (1955), and the Community Mental Health Center Act (1963). Later in this century, public need led to the development of specializations in marriage and family, substance abuse, corrections, and gerontological counseling.

Over the years the movement has not been without its pioneers and heroes. Of course, the great humanistic teachers of history—Christ, Mohammed, Buddha—and farsighted leaders such as Plato, Aristotle, Pestalozzi, Rousseau, and Charlemagne would have been charter members and undoubtedly elected officers of any counseling association of their time in history. In the United States, one can easily envision Franklin, Jefferson, Lincoln, and the Roosevelts receiving honorary life memberships in the American Counseling Association for their contributions to the eventual growth of the movement. But the real heroes have been persons such as Parsons, Beers, Davis, Reed, Weaver, and Hill—those early, persistent, and farsighted pioneers of the movement whose efforts were later recognized and advanced and then further enriched by the giants of the last half of the 20th century: Carl R. Rogers, E. G. Williamson, C. Gilbert Wrenn, Albert Ellis, and Donald Super.

It is said that a movement must have a cause and leadership to survive. This brief review of some historic highlights of the development of counseling and guidance in the United States should indicate that neither has been lacking. As the past illuminates the future, it is possible to predict that regardless of the wonderful scientific and technological advances that await humankind, many persons will search out the counsel and advice of the trained, while others will still seek self- and other understandings for the development of their potential or the solution of their problems. Also, as we look at the current major social concerns in society, we see unprecedented opportunities for the counseling profession to serve society. In the next chapter, we examine some of the activities of the trained professional counselor.

DISCUSSION QUESTIONS

1. Discuss factors and events that influenced your decision to enter or consider entering the counseling profession.
2. Have you had your fortune told? If so, who and when, how accurate, and what results? Which do you believe is most likely to be accurate in pre-dicting futures: palmists, astrologists, graphologists, or others? Defend your selection.
3. National and state legislative acts have had significant impact on the counseling profession. In view of current national social problems, what current legislation might you suggest that would affect the field of counseling and enable it to make a more significant contribution to our national well-being?
4. Discuss differences and similarities in the historic development of counseling in schools versus counseling in agency and institutional settings.
5. Discuss Parsons's three necessary factors that aid in the wise choice of a vocation, as stated in chapter 1. Why did he deem these factors necessary? Would you adjust these three factors in any way? Please explain.
6. Discuss how technology has changed your life in recent years.

CLASS ACTIVITIES

1. Have students create an intake interview (i.e., updated version of Parsons's interview).
2. Go to the library and find the earliest article you can on the subject of counseling or guidance. Report your article, its date, author, publication, and content to the class.
3. Divide the class into small groups and give this assignment: Identify significant characteristics of today's society and examine these to see whether they have implications for the development of any new careers or occupations. What are the implications of these developments for the counseling profession?
4. Have the class members each select and write down any historic leader's name; then allow 15 minutes for a one-page description of how the leader would have benefited from counseling at some particular point of his or her career. Permit a few students to read their description in class.
5. Review current newspapers and popular publications for reports or articles that would imply a useful role that the counseling profession can play in responding to human needs in today's society.

6. Go to the library and examine the major journals in the field of guidance and counseling today. Select three journals and examine current issues; then compare them with the issues discussed 20 and 30 years ago. What changes do you see in the contents?

7. Read an "advice" column in a newspaper (e.g., Ann Landers) or magazine. Review your horoscope in a newspaper or magazine column. Share and discuss your reactions in small groups.

SELECTED HISTORICAL READINGS

Adler, A. (1959). *Understanding human nature.* New York: Premier Books.

Anastasi, A. (1954). The measurements of abilities. *Journal of Counseling Psychology, 1*(3), 164–168.

Borow, Henry. (1996). Vocational guidance and social activism: A fifty year perspective. In Rich Feller & Garry Walz (Eds.), *Career transitions in turbulent times: Exploring work, learning and careers* (pp. 3–10). Greensboro: School of Education, University of North Carolina at Greensboro. (ERIC Counseling and Student Services Clearinghouse; ERIC/CASS Publications.)

Conant, J. (1959). *The American high school today.* New York: McGraw-Hill.

Dugan, W. (1962). An inward look: Assumptions and expectations. *Counselor Education and Supervision, 1*(4), 174–180.

Ellis, A. (1957). Outcome of employing three techniques of psychotherapy. *Journal of Clinical Psychology, 13*(4), 334–350.

Gummere, R. (1988). The counselor as prophet: Frank Parsons. *Journal of Counseling and Development, 66*(9), 402–405.

History of psychology. (1997). [Special section]. *American Psychologist, 52*(7).

History of psychology circa 1900. (2000). [Special section]. *American Psychologist, 55*(9), 1014–1024.

Hooper, D. (1996). Counselling psychology: Into the new millennium. In R. Woolfe & W. Dryden (Eds.), *Handbook of counselling psychology* (pp. 630–648). London: Sage.

Howard, G. S. (1992). Behold our creation! What counseling psychology has become and might yet become. *Journal of Counseling Psychology, 39*(4), 419–442.

Professional counseling: Spotlight on specialties. (1995). [Special issue]. *Journal of Counseling and Development, 74*(2).

Murphy, G. (1955). The cultural context of guidance. *Personnel and Guidance Journal, 34*(1), 4–9.

Odegaard, C. (1987). A historical perspective on the dilemmas confronting psychologists. *American Psychologist, 42*(12), 1048–1051.

Strawbridge, S., & Woolfe, R. (1996). Counselling psychology: A sociological perspective. In R. Woolfe & W. Dryden (Eds.), *Handbook of counselling psychology* (pp. 605–629). London: Sage.

Watkins, C. E. (1994). On hope, promise, and possibility in counseling psychology or some simple, but meaningful observations about our specialty. *Counseling Psychologist, 22*(2), 315–334.

Whitely, J. (Ed.). (1984). Counseling psychology: A historical perspective. *The Counseling Psychologist, 12*(1), 1–126.

Williamson, E. G. (1964). An historical perspective of the vocational guidance movement. *Personnel and Guidance Journal, 42*(9), 854–859.

Woolfe, R. (1996). The nature of counselling psychology. In R. Woolfe & W. Dryden (Eds.), *Handbook of counselling psychology* (pp. 3–20). London: Sage.

Wynkoop, T. F., & Dixon, D. N. (1994). Organizational and political issues in counseling psychology: An accounting of the Georgia Conference recommendations. *Counseling Psychologist, 22*(2), 342–356.

RESEARCH OF INTEREST

Beale, A. V. (1986). Trivial pursuit: The history of guidance. *School Counselor, 34*(1), 14–17.

Abstract   This article quizzes the reader with 15 trivia questions and provides the answers regarding the history of guidance. Additional resources, as well as references to the article, are provided for readers who are interested in learning more about the history of the school guidance movement.

Danzinger, P. R., & Welfel, E. R. (2001). The impact of managed care on mental health counselors: A survey of perceptions, practices, and compliance with ethical standards. *Journal of Mental Health Counseling, 23*(2), 137–150.

Abstract   A sample of 108 mental health counselors in four states was surveyed about their experiences and perceptions of the impact of managed care on their work with clients and the effects of managed care on their compliance with professional ethics. The majority reported that managed care has negatively affected their work with clients and that the protection of the confidentiality of client disclosures has been the most troublesome ethical issue. The study revealed gaps in accuracy of diagnosis, appropriateness of treatment, management of termination, and informed consent procedures with managed care clients. It also showed limited use of ethics codes and other resources developed to help professionals resolve ethical questions responsibly.

Pope, M. (2000). A brief history of career counseling in the United States. *The Career Development Quarterly*, *48*(3), 194–211.

Abstract   The author presents the six stages in the development of career counseling in the United States. In the first stage (1890–1919), placement services were offered for an increasingly urban and industrial society. In the second stage (1920–1939), educational guidance through the elementary and secondary schools became the focal point. The third stage (1940–1959), saw the focus shift to colleges and universities and the training of counselors. The fourth stage (1960–1979) was the boom for counseling and the idea of work having meaning in a person's life came to the forefront; organizational career development began during this period. The fifth stage (1980–1989) saw the beginning of the transition from the industrial age to the information age and the growth of both the independent practice of career counseling and outplacement counseling. The sixth stage (1990–present), with its emphasis on technology and changing demographics, has seen an increased sophistication in the uses of technology, the internationalization of career counseling, the beginnings of multicultural career counseling, and the focus on the school-to-job transition.

Ray, C. G., & Finley, J. K. (1994). Did CMHC's fail or succeed? Analysis of the expectations and outcomes of the community mental health movement. *Administration and Policy in Mental Health*, *21*(4), 283–293.

Abstract   This article establishes a historical context for assessing the impact of the Community Mental Health Center (CMHC) program. The program was based on the social engineering themes of comprehensiveness, centralized service delivery to meet all needs within a catchment area, and self-sustainment that would be integrated over time with mainstream health care. However, competition for valuable economic resources and the rise of social ills (including family disintegration, drug abuse, and urban violence) required that CMHCs target their services to specialized areas. Deinstitutionalization caused CMHCs to face large numbers of nonpaying patients who, in the past, would have been hospitalized. Although CMHCs today contribute substantially to meeting mental health service needs, their services are severely limited.

Resnick, R. J. (1997). A brief history of practice—expanded. *American Psychologist*, *52*(4), 463–468.

Abstract   Psychology can trace its origins from philosophy, through experiential introspection and behaviorism, to a major branch in the evolution of the discipline called practice. This article presents a history of practice, with emphasis on major events that altered the direction and focus of practice. The history begins with the "first" patient of Lightner Witmer and traces the movement into assessment, psychotherapy, and primary health care. It examines the impact of the federal government, the Veterans Administration system, and World Wars I and II on the evolution of practice. The expansion of the availability of services along with the movement to credential-qualified professionals is delineated within the context of licensure laws, freedom of choice acts, and third-party reimbursement. Finally, the impact of health reform on psychological practice is described. These events are viewed as an integral part of the history of psychology as well as the evolution of practice.

Truax, C. B. (1966). Reinforcement and nonreinforcement in Rogerian psychotherapy. *Journal of Abnormal Psychology*, *71*(1), 1–9.

Abstract   Explores the possibility of important reinforcement effects from therapy encounters with a client-centered therapist. Four eclectic and one analytic clinical psychologist rate three therapist behaviors identified as potential reinforcers and nine patient behaviors identified as theoretically significant, from an unbiased sample of 40 typewritten (TAT, Therapist, Patient, Therapist) interaction units. Findings support the Skinnerian view that reinforcement occurs and influences behaviors in Rogerian therapeutic encounters.

2 ◆ What Do Counselors Do?

In studying any profession, you may ask, What is the profession of ... (e.g., counseling)? What do they (e.g., counselors) do? The objective of this chapter is to respond to those questions. We begin by examining counseling as a helping profession and then identify the activities professional counselors do to meet their responsibilities.

COUNSELING AS A HELPING PROFESSION

Counseling as a helping profession is the concept that underlies the role and function of the counselor in today's society. A helping profession is one in which the members are specially trained and licensed or certified to perform a unique and needed service for fellow human beings. Helping professionals serve; they are recognized by the society as the sole professional providers of the unique and needed services they offer.

The helping professions include medicine, law, dentistry, education, psychology, and social work. The roots of each lie in the nature of humankind and society, past and present. It is on these bases that services are determined and programs for providing these services are developed. We will briefly review some of the basic concepts of humankind and society as a basis for the helping profession in general and the profession of counseling in particular.

In the instance of the helping professions, including counseling, it is appropriate to begin with the very foundation of their existence—namely, the human client. This client has certain distinguishing characteristics that provide a basis for the counseling profession and the institutions and agencies through which this profession contributes its special knowledge and skills. Although any attempt to characterize such a versatile and ever-changing species as human beings is perilous, we have certain stable yet unique traits that set us apart from other living species. In the main these are what we might term the privileges of the human race. They provide not only the basis or focus of our being, but the basis for our doing as well. They also suggest roles that human beings can play in helping their fellow human beings. These distinguishing characteristics include the following:

- *Humans are among the weakest species at birth.*

We are born without the genetically imprinted behaviors possessed by many forms of life. Whereas many young animals in the forests and jungles of the world can survive without adult help, young human life cannot. Our early survival is dependent solely on the attention, care, and affection of others. The human need for love and care and the degree to which it is provided becomes a critical basis for the lifelong adjustment or lack of it for the individual.

- *Humankind has the greatest potential for growth and development of all the species.*

The brain itself triples in physical size, and grows even more in capacity as a child develops. This brainpower, coupled with a surplus of energy (more than other species), gives us almost limitless possibilities. The realization of human potential does not, however, rest with the individual alone; we are all dependent on many environmental variables and assistance to develop our potential.

- *Humans have the highest level of communication skills, skills that enable us to express our thoughts in detail to many others; to teach our language to others (even other animal species at certain levels); to record, send, and receive information.*

These dual capacities, sending and receiving, in both word and gesture, form the bases for human relationship skills and for love and affection, which in turn form the primary stimulus for the human race. This ability to relate to others thus becomes the core of a happy, well-adjusted life.

- *The human species exhibits a wider range of differences than any other.*

These differences not only clearly distinguish each human from every other human, but also multiply the potential of the society and stimulate the advancement of civilizations. The concept of individual differences provides the rationale for client analysis in the helping professions.

- *Human beings manipulate and are manipulated by their environment.*

The behavior of a human being cannot be adequately understood apart from the environmental context within which it occurs. Thus, environmental analysis is becoming increasingly important to the professional counselor.

- *Humans are the only living organisms that understand past and future time.*

We can recall the past, act in the present, and plan for the future. This gives us the capability for building on our experiences, avoiding past mistakes, anticipating the future, and planning for the development of our potential.

- *Humans have the ability to reason and to gain insight.*

We are able to make reasoned choices among alternatives and to change. This aptitude for planned individual change is significant in the important arenas of individual development and social adjustment (relationships with one's peers). Our ability to understand ourselves and act rationally also contributes to the maturing process.

From images of the human species, McCully (1969) drew inferences for counseling and other helping relationships as follows:

1. All people at birth possess the potential for the distinguishing characteristics of the human species; and
2. The environmental conditions the individual experiences from birth on may either nourish or suppress their realization. (pp. 134, 135)

In light of these premises, we can suggest, at even this early point in our discussion, that a fundamental basis for counseling program development must be rooted in our understanding of the characteristics and needs of all our clientele, plus an understanding of the environment that shapes them. For counselors, this implies learning in human growth and development and our sociocultural foundations.

Societal needs and expectancies also play an important role in a profession's development and functioning. The brief historic review in chapter 1 indicated some of the social influences on the development of the counseling profession.

THE PROFESSIONAL COUNSELOR

As a beginning student in a counselor preparation program, you have made a commitment to prepare yourself for entry into the counseling profession. Membership in a profession mandates that the member assumes the expectancies and characteristics of a professional. The term *professional counselor* distinguishes the professional from those who may use the title counselor in conjunction with another primary occupation (e.g., loan counselor, sales counselor, investment counselor). Professionals are full-time active representatives of their profession. They accept the responsibilities of professionalism. For professional counselors, these responsibilities include the following.

1. Professional counselors must become fully trained and qualified to meet the needs of the client population they elect or are designated to serve. Training requires an appropriate graduate level (master's degree at least) program that leads to an understanding and awareness of the systematic theories guiding professional practice.
2. Professional counselors actively seek and obtain the certification or licensure appropriate to their training, background, and practice setting.
3. Professional counselors need to be professionally and personally committed to constantly updating and upgrading their skills and knowledge to reflect the latest and ongoing progress in their professional field.
4. Professional counselors are aware of and contribute to the advancement of the profession by conducting and participating in research studies designed to increase knowledge for the profession. In addition, they assure the dissemination of such studies to the profession through professional writings and program presentations at professional meetings.
5. Professional counselors are active participating members of appropriate professional organizations at all levels (national, regional, state, local).
6. Professional counselors are aware of and adhere to all legal and ethical guidelines pertaining to the profession and the practice of counseling. Note that in the majority of states the use of the title counselor is protected by law.

COUNSELING AS A DISCIPLINE

As we examine our roots and the emergence of counseling as a helping profession, we should also note the foundations for counseling as a discipline. Much of this foundation has been derived from the field of psychology. The contributions from psychology have included counseling theory and process, standardized assessment, individual and group counseling techniques, and career development and decision-making theories.

Specialty areas within the field of psychology have further contributed to a knowledge base for counselors to draw on. These include *educational psychology* and its studies of learning theories and human growth and development and their implications for educational settings. *Social psychology* helps us understand the impact of social situations on individuals, including the environment's influence on behavior. *Ecological psychology* is also concerned with the study of environments and how individuals perceive and are shaped by, as well as influence in turn, their environments. *Developmental psychology* helps us understand why and how individuals grow and change over their life span.

We acknowledge that our strongest disciplinary ties are to the field of psychology, but we must also recognize the important contributions of other sciences to the counseling profession. For example, sociology has contributed to our understanding of human groups and their influence on social order and social change. Anthropology has provided counselors with insights into the cultures of peoples, cultures that in turn provide guidelines for the behaviors and viewpoints of their members. Biology has helped us understand the human organism and its uniqueness. The health professions have made us aware of the importance of wellness and prevention.

TRADITIONAL ACTIVITIES

The historic review of the counseling movement in chapter 1 noted the contributions of the many disciplines and influences that have consistently been adding to and expanding their areas of emphasis. Among these were vocational or career guidance, mental health, standardized testing for client analysis, education as guidance, group activities, and the identification and college placement of the gifted. Other influences were the community mental health agency movement; the counseling psychology movement; the development of specialized counseling programs for rehabilitation, substance abuse, correctional, marriage and family, and gerontological counseling; reemphasis of the impact of environment on the individual's growth and development; a currently renewed stress on prevention and early intervention; and the impact of technology on how services are delivered. However, despite the relatively short time that counseling has existed as a profession, certain traditional activities, basic principles, and identifiable patterns of program organization have emerged. An understanding of these can provide some insights into the not infrequently asked question, "Why do counselors do what they do the way they do it?"

Because the early training programs often emphasized school counselor preparation, many of the influential texts had this orientation as well. Early authors tended to discuss counselor functions in terms of services. For example, more than 40 years ago, Froehlich (1958), in discussing counseling and guidance services to pupils in schools, identified basic services to pupils in groups and individually, services to the instructional staff, services to the administration, and research services. After passage of the National Defense Education Act (NDEA) of 1958, the 1960s were a period of rapid growth for counseling programs, especially in schools. Writers of that period, such as Hatch and Costar (1961), also noted that

> it seems more desirable to think of the guidance program as a program of services—services which can be defined, recognized, administered, and evaluated. It is then possible to define a guidance program as a program of services specially designed to improve the adjustment of the individual for whom it was organized. (p. 14)

Hatch and Costar made the following suggestions:

- Guidance services are for all concerned.
- Guidance services are for all school levels.
- Guidance services are primarily preventive in nature.
- The teacher plays a major role in the guidance program.
- The program of guidance services needs trained personnel.
- The program of guidance services requires coordination.
- The guidance program uses and improves on present practices.
- Guidance services are not an added activity.
- Guidance services are a group of facilitating services.
- The training background of guidance workers presupposes certain elements.

Hatch and Costar identified the following services as desirable for a school counseling program:

- Pupil inventory service
- Information service
- Counseling service
- Placement service
- Follow-up and evaluation service

Zeran and Riccio (1962) listed the basic services or activities of counselors as analysis of the individual, counseling, placement and follow-up, and informational services. Gibson and Higgins (1966) noted that although semantics and labels varied, the basic services of counselors were usually identified as pupil analysis, individual counseling, informational activities, group guidance, placement and follow up, and evaluation and research.

In the 1980s, Shertzer and Stone (1981) saw the necessary elements of guidance programs in schools as (a) an appraisal component; (b) an information component; (c) a counseling component; (d) a consulting component; (e) a planning, placement, and follow-up component; and (f) an evaluation component. Blocher and Biggs (1983), in discussing counseling in community settings, noted that counseling psychologists engage in individual and small group counseling centered around concerns involving educational and vocational planning, personal problem solving and decision making, family problems, and other activities related to personal growth, prevention, consultation; at times, the helper acts as a psychological educator. Blocher and Biggs believed that assessment strategies must be developed and mastered to permit an understanding of individuals as they interact in natural environments. Counselors must understand processes of human development as they apply to both individuals and social organizations.

Additional insight comes from the Council for Accreditation of Counseling and Related Educational Programs (CACREP). This organization specifies that all counselors should study eight core areas: human growth and development, social-cultural foundations, helping relations, group work, career and lifestyle development, appraisal, research and program evaluation, and professional orientation.

In summary, certain traditional or basic activities have evolved for counselors across all settings. These include individual assessment, environmental assessment, individual counseling, group counseling and guidance, career assistance, placement, and follow-up. Currently, these traditional activities have expanded to include referral, consultation, research, evaluation, accountability, and prevention. Preventive intervention has also received renewed attention. These are discussed briefly in the sections that follow and will be considered in greater detail in later chapters.

Individual Assessment

Individual assessment seeks, systematically, to identify the characteristics and potential of every client. This activity is often considered a primary skill of the professional counselor because it provides a database for more readily understanding the person in the counseling setting, the effective planning of group counseling activities that reflect client interests and needs, the development of responsive career and human potential development programs, and the organization of systematic placement and follow-up programs. Often referred to as *individual inventory, assessment,* or *appraisal,* this activity promotes the client's self-understanding as well as assisting counselors and other helping professionals to understand the client better.

Individual assessment emerged as a result of the standardized testing movement. Even today, standardized test results are the most frequently used objective data in individual analysis. Other popular and traditional techniques are observation and observation reports, and self-reporting techniques such as the autobiography. Note that other helping professional specialists also have diagnostic skills and responsibilities. For example, a school counselor will often consult with school psychologists and psychometrists for their expertise in psychological assessment, including individual testing, and with school social workers as specialists in environmental and case study analysis. These and other techniques for human resource assessment will be discussed in greater detail in later chapters.

Individual Counseling

Individual counseling, since the early days of the counseling movement, has been identified as the core activity through which all the other activities become meaningful. *Counseling* is a one-to-one helping relationship that focuses on a person's growth and adjustment and problem-solving and decision-making needs. It is a client-centered process that demands confidentiality. This process is initiated when a state of psychological contact or relationship is established between the counselor and the client; it progresses as certain conditions essential to the success of the counseling process prevail. Many practitioners believe that these include counselor genuineness or congruence, respect for the client, and an empathic understanding of the client's internal frame of reference.

Although each counselor will, in time, develop his or her own personal theory to guide personal practice, established theories provide a basis for examination and learning. Effective counseling not only requires counselors to have the highest levels of training and professional skills, but to have certain personality traits as well. Counseling programs will suffer in effectiveness and credibility unless counselors exhibit understanding, warmth, humaneness, and positive attitudes toward humankind. Chapter 4 discusses individual counseling in greater detail.

Group Counseling and Guidance

Groups have become increasingly popular as a means of providing organized and planned assistance to individuals for a wide range of needs. Counselors provide such assistance through *group counseling* or *group guidance,* including task groups and psychoeducational groups. In schools, students have been organized into groups for what might be called guidance purposes since long before any counseling or guidance label was attached to the activity. The organization of courses and group meetings to dispense primarily occupational information can be traced back to before the evolution of the counseling movement. Homeroom grouping served a guidance as well as an administrative function long before being labeled as such. However, in 1934, H. C. McKown wrote a textbook titled *Home Room Guidance*, recognizing the guidance function. With the increasing importance and attention given to extracurricular activities in schools in the 1920s and 1930s, some suggested these activities also were a type of group guidance experience.

Although various activities from time to time have been given the label group guidance, the most consistent definition of this service is an activity designed to provide individuals with information or experiences that promote their career or educational understanding and personal social growth and adjustment. Some traditional group guidance activities that have become familiar to most high school students are career days, college days, and orientation days.

Group Guidance

In recent generations, group counseling has also been viewed as a basic but different activity from group guidance.

Group guidance refers to group activities that focus on providing information or experiences through a planned and organized group activity. Examples of group guidance activities are orientation groups, career exploration groups, college visitation days, and classroom guidance. Group guidance is also organized to prevent the development of problems. The content could include educational, vocational, personal, or social information, with a goal of providing students with accurate information that will help them make more appropriate plans and life decisions.

Group Counseling

Group counseling is the routine adjustment or developmental experiences provided in a group setting. Group counseling focuses on assisting counselees to cope with their day-to-day adjustment and development concerns. Examples might focus on behavior modification, developing personal relationship skills, concerns of human sexuality, values or attitudes, or career decision making.

We might conclude that group guidance activities are most likely to be found in schools. Group counseling will be popular in agency and institutional settings and utilized somewhat, though not as frequently as group guidance, in school settings; group psychotherapy will most frequently occur in clinics and agency or institutional settings. Group counseling and other group responsibilities of the counselor are discussed in greater detail in chapter 5.

Career Assistance

Since their earliest inception, both the school guidance movement and the counseling psychology movement have had a strong vocational influence. Traditionally, this activity has been viewed as one in which standardized tests were used for career assessment and planning. Descriptive materials and media were accumulated, organized, and then disseminated through planned group activities, as well as used in individual advising and counseling.

For many years in school settings this activity was referred to as the *information service* (providing occupational and educational information). In the 1970s the concept of this basic service was broadened and a new (now more appropriate) label assigned: *career guidance*. This term seemed more compatible with the rapidly developing career education movement and also represented in the minds of many (but not all) a broadening of the school counseling program's responsibility in the career development of school-aged youths. This approach, a developmental one, suggests that a person should have certain experiences and understandings at each stage of growth that will provide appropriate foundations for later career planning and decision making.

The attention to and preparation for providing career assistance to client populations is one of the distinguishing and unique characteristics of the counseling profession. Dramatic changes taking place in the world of work have greatly altered the workplace and affected the traditional planning and careers of millions of workers. As a result, the counseling profession is being called upon once again to renew and update its efforts in one of its most traditional areas of service and to provide career guidance and counseling, not at selected stages in life's development, but across the entire life span.

Technology is also keeping pace with the rapid change affecting work, workers, and preparation for work. Computer-based programs, the Internet, distance learning, and interactive learning systems are but a few of the technological developments impacting the ways counselors provide career assistance and information to their clients.

Counselors in a wide range of settings are called on to provide career planning and adjustment assistance to clients. In some agencies, such as community career centers and career centers for special populations, the focus is almost exclusively on the career needs of individuals. Counselors in government employment offices and rehabilitation services have an obvious responsibility to provide career counseling and guidance. Even those counselors in more broadly based programs such as community agencies, secondary schools, and institutions of higher education are expected to address the career-oriented needs of the populations they serve.

Placement and Follow-Up

Placement and *follow-up* have more traditionally been a service of school counseling programs with an emphasis on educational placement in courses and programs. In actual practice, this has meant that many school counselors have had responsibility for student scheduling, a very time-consuming task that has been viewed with considerable controversy as an administrative rather than a counseling function. Another aspect of educational placement is activities associated with college admissions.

The other obvious component of the placement service—employment placement—has had much less emphasis and planning in schools. However, concerns for youth unemployment in the 1990s resulted in increasing attention to this aspect of placement in schools. Job placement in school counseling programs strives to match students seeking part-time or regular employment with available jobs. It also frequently involves a form of referral in which the individual is directed to a particular job setting.

Follow-up activities are a way to assess the effectiveness of a program's placement activities. Placement and follow-up activities have taken on increasing significance in schools in which career education and planning are emphasized. Of course, employment counselors and rehabilitation counselors are very active in the referral, placement, and follow-up of their clients. Also, as counselors are increasingly employed in business and industrial settings, these procedures are an important aspect of their services. Counselors in all settings should use follow-up procedures for assessing counseling outcomes. Placement and follow-up activities are discussed further in chapter 8.

Referral

Referral is the practice of helping clients find needed expert assistance that the referring counselor cannot provide. It directs the client to another counselor with a higher level of training or special expertise related to the client's needs. Counselors in all settings will find it an advantage to their clients to establish a network of qualified helping professionals for referral purposes. Of course, counselors themselves will be the recipients of referrals from their various work settings and the populations they are expected to serve.

Consultation

Consultation is a process for helping a client through a third party or helping a system improve its services to its clientele. The former, usually labeled *triadic consultation,* is popular in working with parents of troubled children or teachers with problem pupils. The latter, appropriately labeled *process consultation,* focuses primarily on the processes that an agency or institution may be using to carry out its mission. Thus, consultation is a form of outreach in which counselors function as team members to assist individual clients or systems that serve clients.

In community and other agency settings, consultation is receiving increased attention as a way of preventing severe mental illnesses. In fact, the Community Mental Health Centers Act requires centers to provide consultation as one of five essential services. In school settings, especially elementary schools, the counselor is being increasingly used as a consultant to teachers and parents. Consultation is discussed in greater detail in chapter 9.

Research

Research is necessary to the advancement of the profession of counseling. It can provide empirically based data relevant to the ultimate goal of implementing effective counseling. It is a means for producing additional knowledge in our field, providing factual data to reinforce or guide the counselors' professional judgments, and seeking answers to questions and issues of professional concern. Research results and the research process are important to program managers and other counselors who find it advantageous to have factual data to reinforce or guide their professional judgment.

Whether one is an active researcher or not, a counseling professional cannot afford to ignore or gloss over important research in the field. Different client populations, more diverse and usually more intense client problems, plus greater variation in staff backgrounds and, hence, treatment approaches offer counselor-researchers the opportunity for unique and significant research investigations.

Interest has also grown in *outcome research*—research that measures the outcomes of various counseling practices and activities. The American Counseling Association Foundation has sponsored studies of counseling outcome research. For example, Whiston and Sexton (1998) summarized school counseling outcome research published between 1988 and 1995. Also, the professional publications of the American Counseling Association and the American Psychological Association regularly report the findings of counseling research studies. A brief sampling of counseling research studies is provided at the end of each chapter, and research is discussed in general in chapter 11.

Evaluation and Accountability

Although *evaluation* and *accountability* are not synonymous terms, they are interrelated, and counselors and counseling programs are expected to engage in both. *Evaluation* is a means or process for assessing the effectiveness of the counselor's activities. It is fundamental to the verification and improvement of professional and program performance.

The use of the term *accountability* is an outgrowth of demands that schools and other tax-supported institutions and agencies be held accountable for their actions. In other words, some evidence of accomplishment must be provided in return for tax investments. Accountability also implies that these accomplishments must be relevant to the purpose for which the agencies or organizations were established.

Accountability establishes a basis for relevance, effectiveness, and efficiency. In this context, evaluation can be viewed as a component of the accountability model. More attention is given to accountability and evaluation in chapter 11.

Prevention

The past 20 years have seen a substantial number of reports of important studies that examined the promotion of mental health through primary prevention using a social-psychological perspective. These and other studies suggest that a most attractive alternative to traditional remedial mental health practices is primary prevention, which seeks to prevent the occurrence of the disorder in the first place. Such an alternative suggests a shift in focus to the settings and life conditions that shape early adaptation. In this regard, the school and the family are the social institutions that most profoundly affect early human development. Increasingly, this focus is on the school as a vital ongoing shaping force with organizational advantages for the initiation and development of mental health programs for primary prevention.

Thus, potential benefits for society may be derived from devising programs in schools that facilitate positive mental health interacting with a mastery of cognitive development. Basic human needs, both sociological and psychological, are to a large measure met either successfully or unsuccessfully in major social institutions. For youth, the schools become not only a resource for intellectual achievement but also institutions that, in a larger and more important sense, shape the entire social group, subject to its experiences. As such, the schools have a major role in the promotion of positive mental health. In this effort, a significant contribution can be made through effective primary intervention strategies.

Community and other mental health–oriented agencies are becoming active in working with families to head off anticipated stresses as well as in working with other stress-prone groups, such as divorced individuals, widows and widowers, and so forth. We can anticipate that counselors in a wide range of settings will be increasingly called on to develop and implement prevention strategies for their clientele. Chapter 10 gives further attention to prevention and wellness.

Closely allied with prevention is the concept of *wellness,* which recognizes both the mental and physical well-being of the individual. Although the professional counselor may assist clients more directly in becoming mentally healthy, the possible interrelationships between mental and physical health cannot be overlooked. Counselors will, therefore, work to establish linkages with health care professionals. Too, as we are concerned with the total well-being of the individual, we may consider the *holistic approach* to counseling, which embodies the dimensions of body, mind, spirit, and emotions.

BASIC PRINCIPLES

Principles tend to form a philosophical framework within which programs are organized and activities developed. They are guidelines that are derived from the experiences and values of the profession, and they represent the views of the majority of the profession's membership. As such, they become fundamental assumptions or a system of beliefs regarding a profession and its role, function, and activities.

For Schools

Indicated here are some principles suggesting how school counseling programs can make their contributions more effective:

1. School counseling and guidance programs are designed to serve the developmental and adjustment needs of all youth.
2. The school counseling program should be concerned with the total development of the students it serves. This program also recognizes that individual development is a continuous, ongoing process; therefore, school counseling programs must themselves be developmental.
3. Pupil guidance is viewed as a process that is continuous throughout the child's formal education.
4. Trained professional counseling personnel are essential for ensuring that helpers have professional competencies, leadership, and direction. (This does not imply that paraprofessionals cannot make worthwhile contributions.)
5. Certain basic activities are essential to program effectiveness, and these must be specifically planned and developed if they are to be effective.
6. The school counseling program must reflect the uniqueness of the population it serves and the environment in which it seeks to render this service; thus, like individuals, each school guidance program will be different from other programs.
7. Relevant to the preceding point, the school counseling program should base its uniqueness on a regular, systematic assessment of the needs of the student clientele and the characteristics of the program's environmental setting.
8. An effective instructional program in the school requires an effective program of pupil counseling and guidance. Good education and good guidance are interrelated. They support and complement each other to the student's advantage.

9. Teacher understanding and support of the school counseling program is significant to the success of such programs.
10. The school counseling program is accountable. School counselors recognize the need to provide objective evidence of accomplishments and the value of those accomplishments.
11. The school counselor is a team member. The counselor shares a concern and programs for youths with psychologists, social workers, teachers, administrators, and other educational professionals and staff.
12. The school counseling program must be designed to recognize the right and capability of the individual to make decisions and plans.
13. The school counseling program must be designed with respect for the worth and dignity of the individual—every individual.
14. The school counseling program must be designed to recognize the uniqueness of the individual and the individual's right to that uniqueness.
15. The school counselor should be a role model of positive human relations—of unbiased, equal treatment.

Although counseling is a relatively young profession, counselors are developing traditions and establishing their role and worth; they will cope resourcefully and imaginatively with the demands of the future. The following discussion considers some traditions, activities, and effective counseling program organization and functioning.

For Community Agencies

Counseling programs in community and other institutional or agency settings represent a wide range of approaches for delivering services. The development and implementation of these services is based on certain underlying assumptions and basic principles. The basic assumption that community involvement is necessary for relevant and accountable community mental health agencies has implications for the essential principles of those agencies that are community based. It is important for community mental health agencies and the counselors they employ to be aware of the following.

- It is important to understand the characteristics of both the population and environment of the catchment area the agency is designated to serve.
- These data must be factual, not theoretical. Therefore, an objective, fact-finding needs assessment, such as suggested in chapter 11, should be conducted on a regular, ongoing basis.
- It is important to communicate to the community, as well as to the agency staff, what is learned about the community and its population.
- Organizational goals should be specified, priorities established, and procedures for achieving the goals identified.
- A comprehensive communications and public relations program must be developed to ensure that the community is aware at all times of the activities and accomplishments of the organization.
- A planned, ongoing program of evaluation is essential to both program improvement and public support.

FUTURE DIRECTIONS FOR THE PROFESSION

As we enter a new century, we are mindful that the future and change are inseparable. Progress for the counseling profession itself depends on the generation of new knowledge and the changes new knowledge stimulates. Certainly a number of these changes affecting our profession are already under way so we cannot lay claim to any crystal ball magic in noting the following future directions for the counseling profession.

1. *Increasing standards for counselor preparation.* Counselor preparation programs, which have moved from 32–36 credit hour programs to 45–48 master's credit-hour programs in the last decades of the 20th century, are anticipated to move to 65 hours and beyond in the early years of the 21st century. Increases in new knowledge and the broadening of counselor responsibilities will be the major contributors reflected in new and additional course work requirements. Additionally, as in other professions, counselors must increasingly in the years ahead anticipate a lifetime of learning—of constantly updating their skills and knowledge if they are to optimally serve their clients and the public in general.

2. *Increasing attention to specialty fields.* As professions develop and gain public confidence, specialty fields tend to emerge within these professions. For example, specialties have proliferated in the traditional helping professions of medicine and law. Specialties are also emerging in the profession of counseling. We note such specialties as marriage and family counseling, multicultural counseling, crisis counseling, substance abuse counseling, career counseling, elementary school counseling, secondary school counseling, community/agency counseling, gerontological counseling, rehabilitation counseling, mental health counseling, and so forth. As we look to the future we can anticipate that increased attention will be given to the specialty fields that have already evolved in our profession and can project that new and perhaps at this point unidentified specialty fields will emerge.

3. *Increased use of technology.* The technology explosion projected for the 21st century will undoubtedly impact and influence all of the helping professions, including counseling. We are already aware of the influence that computers, automated testing programs, fax machines, electronic mail, and distance learning have made on the workplace and within counseling organizations. Those involved in the worlds of developing technology indicate that "we ain't seen nuthin' yet!"—that we are really just experiencing the tip of the iceberg. Currently, we are witnessing clients receiving personal counseling through utilization of the Internet. An article in *USA Today*, May 22, 2001, noted that currently more than 500 counselors are practicing online (p. 19).

Many in the counseling profession question the use of technology to the exclusion of the personal interaction that occurs between client and counselor. Many also question the ability to maintain confidentiality with the various electronic means of communication. In any event, we can anticipate an exciting era in which counselors and the counseling profession will be called upon to adjust to, utilize, and cope with rapid technological advancements.

4. *Increasing focus on empirical results.* Although not necessarily justified, counseling has long been considered suspect by many of its critics due to a presumed lack of empirical evidence supporting counselor activities and results. In recent years the profession has devoted more attention to informing the public of factual evidence documented by empirical research supporting counselor activities and ensuing results. This trend must continue and, in fact, be accelerated with particular attention to counselor effectiveness in

prevention programs, human relationships, and other areas of critical national need. Not only prospective clients but the general public must be made aware of what our profession can do to improve our national well-being.

5. *Updating the profession's traditional theories.* The counseling profession's traditional theories of counseling and career development have been under scrutiny in recent years as many have challenged their relevancy in view of the changing characteristics and dynamics of society and the world of work. It has been suggested that the original data and bases on which the theories were founded are no longer appropriate. Without involving ourselves in this debate, we would simply note that most of the leading theorists today are engaged actively in researching and updating the traditional theories of our profession. We can assume that others are researching and testing new theories that may well emerge in the 21st century. (Attention to these traditional theories and possible new and emerging ones as well will be provided in chapters 4 and 8.)

6. *Renewing attention as well as expanding career counseling parameters.* The world of work has undergone dramatic and in many instances unanticipated changes in the last generation of the 20th century. Influencing these changes are the closing out of certain traditional careers and the emerging of completely new careers. Here are just a few examples of the sweeping changes that have occurred in recent years in the world of work: the U.S. economy's expansion into the world marketplace and the necessity of competing in a global economy, resulting in many industries and careers being shifted out of the country; downsizing that has affected the stability of heretofore lifetime career paths; the concept of career counseling across the life span as retirement barriers fall; and legislative activities stimulating school-to-work transition planning. These shifts have produced an upheaval in the career planning of countless adults and have confused young people planning their entries into a career and the world of work. This has focused new attention on the counseling profession as *the* profession with specialized training in the area of career counseling. It is also resulting in increased opportunities for counselors to function in specialized career settings. This renewed attention to a traditional area of concern and expertise in the counseling profession offers many exciting possibilities for our profession to provide special expertise and service to the general public in the years ahead.

7. *Increased attention to public communication and political activity.* Many leaders in the counseling profession have called on counselors to become more politically active (not in a partisan sense but in a public information sense)—to publicly communicate what counselors do, what they are accomplishing, and so forth. All too frequently, the general public appears to be misinformed, partially informed, or uninformed regarding the significant contributions that the counseling profession can make to individuals and to society's wellness. Although there is no challenge to our recognized expertise in communicating in a "counseling booth," we very frequently appear to have let our communication skills stop at that point. It is now apparent that if we are to compete and be recognized for what we do in the public service area, we must make the public aware of our skills and contributions. This has been a major deficit standing in the way of our profession's advancement and it is only now beginning to be recognized and remedied. This action must continue.

8. *Increased attention to program relevancy.* The accountability movement in the last generation of the 20th century has brought about a recognition that to adequately serve our

client populations, we must be relevant. Programs must address the real needs of their client populations, not theoretical or assumed needs. The basis for developing relevant programs is objective needs assessments which then lead to the development of relevant and accountable counseling programs.

9. *Increased multicultural sensitivity and activity.* Although as a profession we justifiably claim to be experts in human relationships, we have failed to transform our skills in individual counseling and small group relationships to the broader community and even national relationship issues. Certainly progress has been made in recent decades in the area of racial relationships; however, the overall picture of relationships among our population indicates many elements of our citizenry are at odds with each other. These differences are expressed in everything from subtle prejudices to extreme violence that constantly threatens our national stability and well-being. There appears to be little concerted effort to mitigate or improve these situations. As a profession espousing positive human relationships, we must step forward and assume a national leadership role in dealing with this human crisis.

10. *Increased globalization of the profession.* The increased globalization of the workforce and the attending significant changes affecting both employers and employees will undoubtedly create stress and uncertainty among the millions affected. As the majority of those affected will be well beyond school age, assistance in decision making and adjustment must come from counseling agencies, EAPs (employee assistance programs), or private practitioners in the community.

SUMMARY

Most of the basic principles and traditional activities enumerated here have, as chapter 1 suggested, a historic relationship with the development of the counseling movement. Although the organization of these activities into program formats differs across the various settings, the mention of the importance of individual assessment, one-to-one counseling, group activities, career information, and placement and follow-up would evoke a ringing round of applause from our professional forebears. Additionally, in recent generations we have come to view consultation as an expected professional service, and the current emphasis on prevention indicates it will be a major role for counselors in the future.

Traditions are the hallmarks of a profession. They are often seen as indices of the professional maturity of a discipline and synonymous with the guiding principles for a profession. They represent guidelines for newcomers (and reminiscences for the old-timers) to the profession. They become powerful determinants of the profession's goals and actions and, in time, extremely resistant to elimination or alteration. Thus, although we

sometimes hear a call for drastic change (even elimination of counseling programs in some settings), it is not the fundamental beliefs or traditional activities of the counselor that must change, but rather, how the activity is interpreted or viewed and carried out that will determine the merits of a counseling program in any setting.

Relevancy is a key to the success or failure of a program's activities and services. For example, it is doubtful that the counseling skills and understandings that we possessed when we first entered the profession would be relevant to the demands of today's youths, and it is certain that both the concept of careers and the career information at our disposal then would not be in any way relevant today. As C. Gilbert Wrenn stressed in his classic book *The World of the Contemporary Counselor* (1973), "the need of the counselor is to attempt to understand contemporary youth and the world in which they live" (p. 3). That is relevancy—seeing and understanding the environment that surrounds our clients, as well as our clients themselves.

We move from this broad overview of counselor activities to more specifically examining where counselors work in chapter 3.

DISCUSSION QUESTIONS

1. When you hear the term *professional,* what does this imply to you? What does the label "profession" mean to you?
2. Discuss characteristics attributable to those in the helping professions (medicine, law, dentistry, education, psychology, and social work) and how these characteristics help or hinder professional performance.
3. Do some current societal needs have implications for new directions in educational or societal services? Identify and discuss.
4. List five environmental variables that positively influenced the development of your human potential as well as five environmental variables that detracted from your human potential growth. Next, examine present environmental variables.
5. Are there traditions you associate with other professions such as medicine and law? Discuss these and how you believe they may have evolved.
6. Are there any special responsibilities that a profession has to the public? Identify and discuss.
7. In view of current societal needs, what changes in the traditional counselor role and function might be envisioned, if any?
8. Discuss any relevant experience you have had with (a) individual assessment, (b) individual counseling, (c) group counseling, (d) career assistance, (e) placement and follow-up, (f) referral, (g) research.

CLASS ACTIVITIES

1. Pursue one of the following categories to find out more information:

   - **Individual Assessment:** What questions are asked? What does an intake look like?
   - **Individual Counseling:** What is the client-centered process? What are some activities to help clients engage in personal growth, adjustment, problem solving, and decision making? How do counselors develop good rapport with clients?
   - **Group Counseling and Guidance:** What are some activities for group guidance? What are some activities for group counseling?
   - **Career Assistance:** What are some career development activities for individuals across the entire life span (e.g., leaving high school, leaving college, changing careers, nearing retirement)?
   - **Placement and Follow-up:** Give examples of how counselors follow-up to assess counseling outcomes.
   - **Referral:** Make a list of people in your community that you could refer people to (e.g., drug and alcohol counselors, marriage and family counselors, career counselors, psychiatrist, psychologist, physician).
   - **Consultation:** Explain systems theory and present to the class.
   - **Research:** Research a counseling theory you are interested in and find empirical evidence to support it.
   - **Evaluation and Accountability:** How does one evaluate the effectiveness of the counselor's activities? What are ways to evaluate a counseling program's performance? How can we evaluate the accountability of schools and tax-supported programs in terms of relevance, effectiveness, and efficiency?
   - **Prevention:** Describe some intervention strategies for a clientele you are interested in working with. How do counselors incorporate the holistic approach, which embodies the dimensions of body, mind, spirit, and consciousness? (What are some specific activities counselors use with clients?).
   - **Basic Principles:** What are some specific activities for meeting the developmental and adjustment needs of all youth? How can a school systematically assess the student clientele's needs and the characteristics of the program's environmental setting?

2. Organize the class into small groups to interview professionals in medicine, dentistry, law, nursing, and teaching. Interviews should seek information regarding (a) training, (b) regulation of the

profession by the profession, and (c) traditions of the profession. Report findings orally to the class.

3. Have class members interview counselors in various settings to ascertain the major activities they typically engage in as professional counselors. Report these findings to the class.

4. Organize the class into small groups and have each group member discuss his or her contact with counseling programs and the perceptions of those programs for each of the educational levels: elementary, secondary, and higher education. Have each group develop a list of recommendations based on its experiences for improving school counseling programs.

SELECTED READINGS

Etringer, B. D., Hillerbrand, E., & Claiborn, C. D. (1995). The transition from novice to expert counselor. *Counselor Education & Supervision, 35*(1), 4–17.

Herr, E. L. (1982). *Why counseling?* [Monograph]. Washington, DC: American Personnel and Guidance Association.

Hollis, J. W., with Dodson, T. A. (2000). *Counselor preparation, 1999–2001: Programs, faculty, trends* (10th ed.). Philadelphia: Accelerated Development/NBCC (National Board for Certified Counselors).

McCully, C. H. (1962). The school counselor: Strategy for professionalization. *Personnel and Guidance Journal, 40*(8), 681–689.

Meier, S. T., & Davis, S. R. (1997). *The elements of counseling* (3rd ed.). Pacific Grove, CA: Brooks/Cole.

Pedersen, P., & Leong, F. (1997). Counseling in an international context. *Counseling Psychologist, 25*(1), 117–121.

Whiteley, J. M. (1980). Counseling psychology in the year 2000 A.D. *The Counseling Psychologist, 8*(4), 2–62.

RESEARCH OF INTEREST

Brehms, C., & Johnson, M. C. (1997). Comparison of recent graduates of clinical versus counseling psychology programs. *Journal of Psychology, 131*(1), 91–99.

Abstract   This study assessed similarities and differences of aspects of programs and job-related activity in 129 recent graduates (aged 28 to 56 years) from clinical or counseling graduate psychology programs. Subjects were given a graduate activities questionnaire, which was developed specifically for this study, and the short version of a theoretical orientation survey. Results revealed only minor differences. Counseling psychologists were more likely to (a) provide group therapy, career counseling and assessment, public lectures and workshops; (b) have more knowledge of the Strong-Campbell Interest Inventory; (c) be more likely to work in university counseling centers; and (d) endorse humanistic theoretical orientations. Clinical psychologists were more likely to (a) work in medical school settings; (b) ascribe human behavior to internal states rather than to social causes; and (c) have greater knowledge of the Rorschach. However, the similarities between the two specialties relative to work setting, theoretical orientation, service, research, and teaching activities far outweigh these minor differences. Implications of these findings are placed in the context of previous research that has suggested the possible merger of the two specialties.

Brehms, C., Johnson, M. E., & Gallucci, P. (1996). Publication productivity of clinical and counseling psychologists. *Journal of Clinical Psychology, 52*(6), 723–725.

Abstract   This study compared the research productivity of 500 clinical versus 500 counseling psychologists and found surprisingly few differences. A serendipitous finding was low productivity across the board, and a question was raised about the success of the scientist-practitioner model in both clinical and counseling psychology doctoral programs in instilling a research-publication ethic among professional (as opposed to experimental, social, etc.) psychologists.

Forsyth, D. R., & Leary, M. R. (1997). Achieving the goals of the scientist-practitioner model: The seven interfaces of social and counseling psychology. *Counseling Psychologist, 25*(2), 180–200.

Abstract   Counseling and social psychology have commingled theoretically and empirically for many years, but both fields have much to gain from a more complete integration across seven domains: educational (learning, teaching, and training), professional (relationships between researchers and practitioners), practical (integrated attempts to solve individual and societal problems), methodological (shared empirical procedures and standards), theoretical (attempts to construct conceptual models that span disciplines), metatheoretical (shared assumptions about the phenomena under study), and epistemological (fundamental assumptions held in common about how knowledge is expanded). After estimating the strength of the union between social and counseling psychology on each of these seven planes, suggestions for fortifying the weaker links and enhancing the vitality of the stronger links are offered.

Romano, J. L., & Hage, S. M. (2000). Prevention and counseling psychology: Revitalizing commitments for the 21st century. *The Counseling Psychologist, 28*(6), 733–763.

Abstract   This article advocates the need for a much stronger emphasis on and commitment to the science and practice of prevention in counseling psychology. Historical and recent developments in the profession are highlighted, as are the changing U.S. demographics and societal needs that mandate an enhanced prevention focus for the field. A prevention-based agenda of four fundamental goals for counseling psychology is articulated. The goals include eight training domains and objectives as well as skills needed to support a prevention agenda for counseling psychology. Barriers and adjustments needed to give renewed vitality toward prevention are discussed. Prevention resources and funding opportunities are presented.

Sawatzky, D. D., Jevne, R. F., & Clark, G. T. (1994). Becoming empowered: A study of counsellor development. *Canadian Journal of Counselling, 28*(3), 177–192.

Abstract   This study examined the experiences of nine doctoral students in counseling that contributed to the development of their effectiveness as counselors. Data were collected from interviews with subjects in the final stages of their internship in a variety of professional settings. Based on a thematic analysis of the interviews, a cyclical model of counselor development, Becoming Empowered, was proposed. This model included four recurring themes: experiencing dissonance, responding to dissonance, relating to supervision, and feeling empowered. The model developed from recognizing gaps in skills and knowledge, and experiencing emotional turmoil about acquiring new skills and experiences and changing attitudes. Feelings of empowerment were enhanced by changing perspectives and experiencing increased competence.

3

Where Counselors Work

Currently, counselors are employed in a variety of work settings. In some they may function as generalists; in others, they may provide specialized services to specific populations (e.g., marriage and family counselors). Both the settings and the number of emerging counseling specialties have increased in recent years and we can anticipate, especially as we move into the global village, additional specialties reflecting international perspectives and technological advances. The objective of this chapter is to briefly describe the various settings in which professional counselors may work.

Currently, counselors are most frequently employed in educational settings and mental health facilities (see Table 3-1). According to Hollis (with Dodson, 2000 p. 56),

> Approximately three out of five (58%) students in community counseling programs accept positions in public agencies the first year after graduating. The next largest group (graduating from community counseling programs, 13%) take work in private practice or private agencies. Ten percent of graduates from community counseling programs continue their advanced graduate education. (p. 56)

More than one half of the graduates (52%) take jobs in public agencies after graduating from the entry level mental health counselor programs (see Table 3-2). Another one fifth (21%) accept employment in private practice or private agencies. Nine percent continue their education in advanced graduate programs (Hollis with Dodson, 2000, p. 71).

Hollis (with Dodson, 2000) indicates that 90% of graduates from school counseling programs accept positions in schools (see Table 3-3). Of these job placements, 38% were in secondary schools, 30% in elementary schools, and 22% in middle schools. Four percent of graduates from school counseling programs continue in their graduate education (Hollis with Dodson, 2000, p. 83).

COUNSELORS IN EDUCATION SETTINGS:
ROLE AND FUNCTION

Counselors in any work setting need to be aware of what services school counselors and school counseling programs provide. Therefore, a purpose of this chapter is to orient potential counselors, including those interested in school settings, to the following:

- Training of counselors for educational settings
- Credentialing of school counselors
- Role and function of counselors in various educational settings

Table 3-1   Job settings first year after completing entry level community counselor preparation program.

Job Placement After Graduation	1996 Study		1999 Study	
	NPR	Percent of All Graduates	NPR	Percent of All Graduates
Advanced graduate programs	122	11	109	10
Managed care	89	8	78	9
Private practice/agency	125	22	98	13
Public agency	141	48	129	58
Other	53	7	35	4
School—Elementary	8	0	17	1
Middle	6	0	12	1
Secondary	9	0	14	1
Higher education student affairs	30	2	43	3
Total		100		100

NPR = Number of programs responding
Number of programs surveyed for 1996 study was 193.
Number of programs surveyed for 1999 study was 204.

Source: Copyright © 2000. From *Counselor Preparation 1999–2001: Programs, Faculty, Trends* (10th ed., p. 57), by J. W. Hollis, with T. A. Dodson. Reproduced by permission of Taylor & Francis, Inc., http://www.routledge-ny.com

TRAINING PROGRAMS FOR COUNSELORS IN EDUCATIONAL SETTINGS

Counseling and guidance programs in schools are an educational development of the 20th century and they have, until recent years, been unique to the United States and Canadian educational systems. The same has been true of training programs for counselors. Similarly, since the initial years of the National Defense Education Act (1958–1960), both the number and size of counselor training programs have grown rapidly. In 1964 there were 327 institutions of higher education supporting counselor preparation programs with 706 faculty. Hollis (with Dodson, 2000), in the 10th edition of *Counselor Preparation*, identified 542 academic departments that offered counselor training with 2,510 faculty (pp. 17, 30). Also, if you had entered a counselor training program in 1964, you could have anticipated a training staff of slightly more than two full-time faculty members; however, if you delayed your entry until 2000, you could have expected, on the average, a staff of eight full-time faculty members.

Because many of you may already be enrolled in programs of counselor education, this chapter's initial discussion may serve only to remind you to see your adviser about the course work that lies ahead or show you how your own program may differ from others. We are certain, however, that you recognize the significant relationship between what you are trained to do and your role and function once you are on the job.

Table 3-2   Job settings first year after completing entry level mental health counseling program.

Job Placement After Graduation	1996 Study		1999 Study	
	NPR	Percent of All Graduates	NPR	Percent of All Graduates
Advanced graduate programs	61	14	37	9
Managed care	46	11	32	12
Private practice/agency	60	21	36	21
Public agency	68	46	48	52
Other	24	6	12	3
School—Elementary	3	0	8	1
Middle	1	0	3	0
Secondary	0	0	5	1
Higher education student affairs	6	2	6	1
Total		100		100

NPR = Number of programs responding
Number of programs surveyed for 1996 study was 104.
Number of programs surveyed for 1999 study was 100.
Source: Copyright © 2000. From *Counselor Preparation 1999–2001: Programs, Faculty, Trends* (10th ed., p. 7), by J. W. Hollis, with T. A. Dodson. Reproduced by permission of Taylor & Francis, Inc., http://www.routledge-ny.com

As a means of putting into perspective who functions at what level and with what training or expertise, Table 3-4 indicates that persons with appropriate experience or training and the skills to communicate can function at the advice-giving level. In the school setting, for example, all teachers and most staff would qualify as advisers for many occasions and should serve in this important role in the school's program of pupil guidance. At the second level, special training to at least the master's degree level is required, which provides the school counselor with special expertise as a counselor. This expertise sets the counselor apart from other professionals in the school setting and establishes the unique qualifications needed to interact with or on behalf of students in meeting their routine development, adjustment, planning, and decision-making needs. The third level represents the highest degree of professional training available, usually an earned doctorate. As practicing counselors, these professionals are most frequently used as resource personnel for referrals and consultation. Their clients usually have serious personality disorders requiring intensive and long-term counseling. In addition to counseling, these more highly trained counselors may also seek careers in research or university teaching or in supervisory positions (see Table 3-4).

If you examine the content of training programs available, you will notice course content consistency among master's degree programs across the United States. Much of this conformity is undoubtedly the result of state certification patterns for school counselors that

Table 3-3 Job placement during first year after completing entry level school counselor program.

Job Placement After Graduation	1996 Study		1999 Study	
	NPR	Percent of All Graduates	NPR	Percent of All Graduates
Advanced graduate programs	116	5	84	4
Managed care	1	0	4	0
Private practice/agency	17	0	11	0
Public agency	17	1	34	2
Other	50	5	21	2
School—Elementary	229	30	184	30
Middle	220	21	180	22
Secondary	238	37	195	38
Higher education student affairs	29	2	26	2
Total	N = 248	101	N = 200	100

NPR = Number of programs responding
Number of programs surveyed for 1996 study was 332.
Number of programs surveyed for 1999 study was 314.

Source: Copyright © 2000. From *Counselor Preparation 1999–2001: Programs, Faculty, Trends* (10th ed., p. 83), by J. W. Hollis, with T. A. Dodson. Reproduced by permission of Taylor & Francis, Inc., http://www.routledge-ny.com

Table 3-4 Levels of training and responsibility.

Level	Training	Responsibility
First	Appropriate educational and/or experience background	Advising; information giving
Second	Master's degree in counseling and guidance	Developmental and normal adjustment counseling
Third	Doctorate in counseling and guidance, clinical mental health, or counseling psychology, or M.D. with specialty in psychiatry	Serious personality disorders

reflect, with little deviation, an expectancy of training to perform the traditional basic services noted in chapter 2. Many counselor education programs are guided by the eight core areas specified by the Council for the Accreditation of Counseling and Related Educational Programs (CACREP). These core areas are

- Professional identity
- Social and cultural diversity
- Human growth and development
- Career development
- Helping relationships
- Group work
- Assessment
- Research and program evaluation

A number of counselor training institutions also offer a specialist or sixth-year degree for counselors planning to work in educational settings, as many school systems recognize, for pay purposes, the specialist degree. Also, in many states this degree qualifies an individual with appropriate experience for certification as director or supervisor of guidance or director of pupil personnel services.

Approximately 180 counselor training institutions in the United States and Canada offer programs leading to an earned doctorate. These programs tend, according to the nature of the program, to prepare their candidates for a variety of positions in addition to educational settings. These include positions in community counseling centers, business and industry, health facilities, and correctional institutions, and in such specialties as mental health, marriage and family, substance abuse, and rehabilitation counseling. Some individuals may also elect to enter private practice. Variations in program emphasis and preparation patterns are more commonplace at the doctoral than at the master's level. Also, in many institutions, several counselor education or related programs may exist because of specialized training (e.g., departments of counselor education, rehabilitation counseling, counseling psychology, marriage and family).

THE CREDENTIALING OF SCHOOL COUNSELORS

Today, the title counselor seems to be used with ever-increasing frequency in a variety of settings. There are home buyer counselors, financial counselors, landscape counselors, used car counselors, and diet counselors. There are also counselors who may be distinguished from the first group on the basis of certification or legal licensure. These include legal counselors, investment counselors, psychological counselors, mental health counselors, marriage and family counselors and school guidance counselors. Differences between licensure and certification will be discussed later in this chapter. Licensure or certification indicates that the holder has successfully completed training and has been examined on learning and experience criteria recommended by the representative professional organizations and the appropriate licensing boards or agencies. The late C. Harold McCully, in his classic discussion "The School Counselor: Strategy for Professionalization" (1962), suggested, "A profession is an occupation in which the members of a corporate group assure minimum competence for entry into the occupation by setting and enforcing standards for selection, training, and licensure or certification" (p. 682).

Certification is a process that verifies the qualifications of individuals to engage in professional practice, usually in specific settings such as schools, utilizing a title authorized by the certification agency. Education and its subspecialties is an example of a profession that certifies qualifications usually through state departments of education guided in many instances by state laws. In addition, certification may be awarded by agencies and volunteer organizations. School counselors are required to be certified under such guidelines in all states.

The process requires that the candidate for certification produce evidence of meeting the criteria for such certification. Minimally, for those seeking certification as counselors, this process requires evidence of appropriate academic course work at a recognized and in some states regionally accredited institution of higher education. In addition, at this writing, 21 states and the District of Columbia require teaching experience or related experience. An additional five states require applicants for an entry-level credential as a counselor to have previous teaching or related experience but permit these requirements to be satisfied by completion of a one-year supervised, school-based internship (Lum, 2001, p. 3). A few states also require specific course work in areas such as state history, special education, computers, and so on. Twenty-three states use one or more standardized examinations as part of the credentialing process. An additional eight states use only state-administered tests. (Lum, 2001, p. 4).

Because credentialing for school counselors is usually through certification, the other major process of credentialing, licensure, will be addressed later in the discussion of counselors in noneducational settings.

Another activity that has significance for the credentialing process, whether it be certification or licensure, is *accreditation.* Most programs preparing school counselors are accredited by their regional accrediting associations. Counselor training programs in schools or colleges of education may also have accreditation by the National Council for Accreditation of Teacher Education (NCATE), and programs both within and outside education may qualify for approval by the Council for Accreditation of Counseling and Counseling Related Programs (CACREP). As of April 2001, 124 school counseling programs had CACREP accreditation (Ginter, 2001). Doctoral programs preparing counseling psychologists may seek accreditation by the American Psychological Association. As of December 2000, 71 counseling psychology programs had been accredited by the American Psychological Association. In addition, many state departments of public instruction accredit higher education training programs within their jurisdictions.

All states require certification for those who will be school counselors. Generally very similar across states, these requirements account for the considerable degree of reciprocity by which candidates certified in one state may be eligible for certification in other states. For example, the vast majority of certification programs require a counselor's minimal completion of a master's degree. Also, most certification patterns require course work appropriate to the basic counseling services. That includes courses in assessment or sometimes standardized testing, career and educational information, career counseling or career development, individual counseling, group counseling, and principles of counseling. Courses in consultation and research and program evaluation are also frequent requirements. In addition, some sort of supervised practicum experience is required. As noted previously, 21 states and the District of Columbia require applicants for a school counselor credential to have previous teaching or related experience (1–3 years) (Lum, 2000, p. 3). An increasing number of states, however, have recently amended their certification requirements to provide for an alternative experience to teaching, such as in internship.

It is probably a chicken or egg situation to attempt to determine whether training influences practice or vice versa, and it is not the intent of this chapter to enter that argument. We have, by choice, discussed training and resulting certification first. In the paragraphs that follow, counseling practices in various educational settings are described. Note the relationship between these practices and training patterns previously presented. Remember, though, that this discussion is a brief overview only, and greater detail and specificity will be provided later.

Advantages

The following advantages accrue from some sort of a credentialing process:

1. *Credentialing protects the public against those who would masquerade as possessing certain skills and training.* A number of years ago, an article in the old *Look* magazine entitled "Beware of the Psycho-Quacks" gave examples of the various guises for preying on the public under counseling and psychological titles. Many have read the book or seen the movie *The Great Imposter*, in which one individual successfully assumed a variety of professional careers. Although such reports sometimes amuse and often attract admirers for those who have beat the system, very few people would knowingly ask for help from a physician who is not a physician, a lawyer who is not a lawyer, or a counselor who is not a counselor. These examples remind us of the need for some sort of a procedure that protects the public against professional misrepresentation and fraud.

2. *It provides, at the very least, minimally accepted training and experience requirements.* Credentialing and training requirements (and experiences) are closely interrelated. This interrelationship provides for a common core of learning experiences and achievement expectancies. These are related to the profession's concept of preparatory standards for entry into the profession. These standards are not only helpful to candidates considering entry into training programs and protect them from misleading training schemes, but they also reassure employers as well as the general public who use the services.

3. *Credentialing can provide a legal base for protecting the membership of the profession.* Because credentialing suggests standards that benefit the public, lawmaking bodies are prone to provide the profession and its membership with certain legal forms of protection. For example, individuals cannot legally practice medicine without a license, and lawyers legally have the right of privileged communication with their clients. In many states, the right to enter private practice in such fields as psychology and professional counseling is limited by law.

4. *It may provide a basis for special benefits.* In addition to legal benefits, credentialed professionals may also qualify for certain financial benefits. Physicians' and lawyers' fees may qualify for reimbursement by insurance payments. Physicians, including psychiatrists, also qualify for national health insurance payments such as Medicaid for their eligible patients. Psychologists and appropriately credentialed counselors may also qualify as mental health providers for insurance payments in some states. Credentialed school counselors

have, on occasion, been qualified to receive special training grants to increase their qualifications. Because credentialing qualifies individuals for membership in professional organizations, they become eligible for the benefits such memberships provide (e.g., special training, publications, group insurance).

THE ROLE AND FUNCTION OF COUNSELORS IN SCHOOL SETTINGS

An Overview

All states require counselors to be certified to be employed in a public elementary, middle, or secondary school setting, but not all states mandate schools to have counseling programs. As of 2000, 24 states and the District of Columbia mandated the provision of guidance and counseling services in public elementary and/or secondary schools (Lum, 2000 p. 40). However, the major regional accrediting bodies *do* require secondary schools to have functioning and effective counseling programs. These bodies specify certain activities that are expected of programs in elementary, middle, and secondary schools. These activities may vary from accrediting agency to accrediting agency, although they have a considerable degree of similarity basically reflecting the traditional role and functions of counselors in school settings. Recent descriptions of the school counselor's role and function are noted in the American School Counselor Association's statements as presented in Appendix A (Sharing the Vision: The National Standards for School Counseling Programs–1997) and Appendix B (The Role of the Professional School Counselor–1999).

The variety in school settings, of course, will account for some differences in the ways counselors may carry out their roles. However, some common influences determine the role and function of counselors, regardless of the setting. The first of these is what might be called *professional constants* or determinants that indicate what is appropriate and not appropriate to the counselor's role. These include guidelines and policy statements of professional organizations, licensing or certification limitations, accreditation guidelines and requirements, and the expectancies of professional training programs. In addition to these professional constants, personal factors inevitably influence role and function. These include the interest of the counselor, such as what he or she likes to do; what the counselor gets encouraged to do and is rewarded for doing by the school, community, or his or her peers; what the counselor has resources to do; what the counselor perceives as the appropriate role and function for a given setting; and finally, how life in general is going for the counselor. The counselor's attitudes, values, and experiences both on and off the job can influence how he or she views the job.

Counselors and other professional helpers are recognizing more and more that traditional roles and delivery systems in human services may have imposed real limitations on their ability to deal directly and effectively with clients' critical needs. We would also note the current call for counselors and counseling programs to become increasingly active in preventive interventions and developmental guidance. Thus, as we further view the role and function of counselors, we are seeking to integrate for you, our reader, not only those concepts that have proven themselves over the years but also current and promising directions that seem necessary for the counselor to remain a viable entity in the school setting.

How Counselors in Educational Settings Spend Their Time

During the 1996–1997 school year, the authors of this text conducted a role and function study of practicing counselors in school and nonschool settings. Participants in the study were randomly selected from the membership directory of the American Counseling Association and asked to complete a survey form indicating the comparative amount of time (good amount, fair or average amount, little, or none) spent on 14 possible activities. Space was also provided to indicate additional activities. School respondents were summarized according to educational levels (i.e., elementary, middle or junior high, and secondary education). A numerical value was given to each of the time spent categories (i.e., good amount = 3; fair or average amount = 2; little = 1; none = 0). Total scores were then tabulated for each activity, producing an unscientific but reasonably accurate indication of the rank order of time spent on various common activities that practicing counselors engage in for each of the specified settings. Table 3-5 presents results from counselors in elementary, middle/junior high school, and senior high school settings. Individual counseling, guidance activities, consultation, and group counseling are major activities as measured by time commitments. Administrative and clerical responsibilities increase from elementary to senior high school.

Hardesty and Dillard (1994) in an earlier study examined the tasks and functions counselors at different grade levels view as important. Three hundred sixty-nine elementary, middle, and high school counselors were surveyed regarding their activities in schools. The authors found three major differences in the ranking of counselor activities by elementary counselors compared with their middle and secondary school counterparts: (a) elementary counselors perform more consultative and coordination activities; (b) elementary counselors may perform less administrative-type activities (scheduling and paperwork); and (c) whereas secondary and middle school counselors seem to work with student concerns on an individual basis, elementary school counselors tend to work systematically with families, teachers, and community agencies.

A study reported by Burnham and Jackson (2000) indicated that school counselors, in addition to the traditional activities of their role, spent on average 20 percent of their time in nonguidance duties in rank order as indicated in Tables 3-6 and 3-7.

The Elementary School Counselor

Elementary schools are a powerful socializing force in human development. For better or worse, virtually all members of modern society carry important imprints of their elementary school experiences throughout their lives. In this setting the young pupil is expected to acquire basic mastery of increasingly difficult bodies of knowledge as well as learn to meet the school's behavior and social expectancies. Failure to learn generates behavioral problems just as inappropriate behaviors and social skills handicap learning.

In the 1970s it became increasingly evident that the developmental requirements of elementary-age youth were often neglected and even unrecognized. As a result, a number of states—22 by 2000—(Lum, 2001) have mandated elementary school counseling. We believe this trend will continue as the public becomes increasingly aware of the vital role of the elementary school in primary prevention. The characteristics of the elementary pupil and the elementary school dictate certain features in program organization that distinguish elementary school counseling programs from those in secondary schools and at other educational levels. Thus, the elementary school counselor's role and function will also reflect

Table 3-5 How practicing school counselors spend their time.

Activity	Elementary	Middle/ Junior High	Senior High
Individual counseling	2.5	2	2
Organizing & conducting counseling groups	10	10.5	10.5
Classroom & other group guidance activities	4	6	10.5
Standardized test administration and interpretation	7	6	
Nonstandardized assessment (e.g., case studies, observation, information gathering interviews, questionnaires)	5	4	
Needs assessment (to determine priority needs of the target population)	9		
Consultation activities	1		8
Providing career guidance and information		3	5
Providing educational guidance & information (including scholarships, college placement, student scheduling)		9	1
Prevention planning & implementation activities	2.5	8	4
Developmental activities	7	10.5	9
Administrative activities	6	1	3
Information dissemination, public communications, and public relations	8	5	7
Other			

Source: Based on a survey by Robert L. Gibson and Marianne H. Mitchell, 1997.

these differences. The differences, however, are not so much in what the elementary school counselors do, but in *how* they do it.

For example, counselors and other elementary school specialists must work closely and effectively with classroom teachers. Guidance activities, usually classroom oriented, are a major time-consumer (see Table 3-8 for a rank ordering of elementary school counselor activities as indicated by counselors). This context naturally leads to an emphasis on consultation and coordination. In addition to counseling, consulting, and coordination functions, the elementary school counselor has responsibilities for pupils' orientation, assessment, career and other development needs as well as significant attention to the prevention of undesirable habits and behaviors.

Counselor

Although one-to-one counseling in the elementary school may take correspondingly less of the counselor's time than counseling at other levels, the counselor should be available to meet individually or in groups with children referred by teachers or parents or identified by the

Table 3-6 Nonguidance duties (in rank order).

1. Requesting and receiving records
2. Scheduling
3. Permanent records
4. Enrolling students
5. Special education referrals and placement
6. Record keeping
7. Filing paperwork
8. Withdrawing students
9. Computer time, word processing or typing
10. Checking immunization records
11. Grades and report cards
12. Duplicating material
13. Working with testing materials or test results
14. Scholarship recommendations
15. Telephone reception
16. Office reception
17. Nurse/medical coordinator

Source: From "School Counselor Roles: Discrepancies Between Actual Practice and Existing Models," by Burnham, J. J., & Jackson, C. M. (2000). *Professional School Counseling, 4*(1), p. 45.

Table 3-7 Nonguidance duties.

Duty	Number of Counselors with Duty	Percentage with Duty
Student Records	52 of 80	65
Scheduling	46 of 80	56
Transcripts	39 of 80	49
Office Sitting	35 of 80	44
Clubs and Organizations	32 of 80	40
Bus Duty	30 of 80	38
Attendance	22 of 80	28
Hall, Restroom, and Lunch Duty	21 of 80	26
Averaging Grades	16 of 80	20
Homeroom	10 of 80	13

Source: From "School Counselor Roles: Discrepancies Between Actual Practice and Existing Models," by Burnham, J. J., & Jackson, C. M. (2000). *Professional School Counseling, 4*(1), p. 46.

Table 3-8   Major functions of elementary school counselors.

Order	Function	Percentage Engaged In
1	Individual counseling	98.8
2	Group guidance and counseling	81.0
3	Working with parents	79.2
4	Consultation with teachers and administrators	78.9
5	Classroom guidance instruction	65.5
6	Assessment activity	39.3
7	Coordination with community agencies	39.1

counselor or other helping professionals in need of counseling. Too, counselors in elementary schools can anticipate that individual pupils will come to the counseling offices for assistance, advice, or support. Such current social issues as substance abuse, child abuse, divorce, and discrimination are a frequent basis for individual counseling in the elementary school.

Consultant

As a consultant, the counselor may confer directly with teachers, parents, administrators, and other helping professionals to help an identified third party, such as a student, in the school setting. In this role, the counselor helps others to assist the student-client in dealing more effectively with developmental or adjustment needs.

Coordinator

Elementary school counselors have a responsibility for coordinating the various guidance activities in the schools. Coordinating these with ongoing classroom and school activities is also desirable. As the only building-based helping professional, the elementary school counselor may be called on to coordinate the contributions of school psychologists, social workers, and others. Other similar activities could include intraschool and interagency referrals.

Agent for Orientation

As a human development facilitator, the elementary school counselor recognizes the importance of the child's orientation to the goals and environment of the elementary school. It is important that the child's initial education experiences be positive ones. In this regard, the counselor may plan group activities and consult with teachers to help children learn and practice the relationship skills necessary in the school setting.

Agent of Assessment

The counselor in the elementary school can anticipate being called on to interpret and often gather both test and nontest data. To the counselor will also fall the task of putting these data into focus not only to see but to be able to interpret the child as a total being.

Beyond the traditional data used for pupil understanding, the counselor should also understand the impact of culture, the sociology of the school, and other environmental influences on pupil behavior.

Career Developer

The importance of the elementary school years as a foundation for later significant decisions underscores the desirability of planned attention being given to the elementary pupil's career development. Although the responsibility for career education planning rests with the classroom teachers, the elementary school counselor can make a major contribution as a coordinator and consultant in developing a continuous, sequential, and integrated program.

Agent of Prevention

In the elementary school, there are early warning signs of future problems for young children: learning difficulties, general moodiness (unhappiness, depression), and acting-out behaviors (fights, quarrels, disruptions, restlessness, impulsiveness, and obstinacy). There is an accumulation of evidence to demonstrate that children who cannot adjust during their elementary school years are at high risk for a variety of later problems. Further, substance abuse, violence among peers, vandalism, problems associated with latchkey children, and so forth have increased among elementary school pupils raising additional concerns and public calls for preventive efforts.

A study (Gibson, 1989) of 96 elementary school programs recommended as "outstanding" by their state departments of public instruction indicated that prevention was a major program emphasis in 85% of these programs. Elementary school counselors are increasingly called on and challenged to develop programs that seek to anticipate, intervene in, and prevent the development of these problems. Table 3-9 ranks the emphasis of the programs in this 1989 study. (See Table 3-8 for a rank ordering of elementary school counselor activities as indicated by counselors.)

In our 1996–1997 role and function study, a survey of 224 elementary school counselors indicated that they spend their professional time engaged in the following activities, in order from most to smallest amount of time:

- Consultation with teachers, parents, and other educational personnel
- Prevention planning and implementation; individual counseling
- Classroom and other group guidance activities
- Nonstandardized assessment of pupils such as case studies, observation, individual interview, and so forth
- Administrative duties, such as record keeping, reporting, and preparation of materials
- Developmental activities
- Information sharing, dissemination, and public communications and relations
- Needs assessment
- Organizing and conducting counseling groups

Other activities frequently noted were administration and/or interpretation of standardized tests; providing for educational guidance, such as study skills, assistance, and peer tutoring; and participation in orientation programs and various parental assistance groups.

Table 3-9 Prevention objectives of elementary school counseling and guidance programs.

Rank	Objective	Percentage
1	To prevent child and/or sexual abuse	69.7
2	To prevent substance abuse	64.9
3	To promote self-concept development	35.8
4	To promote personal safety	17.6
5	To promote social-skills development	15.0
6	To prevent teenage pregnancy	6.3
7	To prevent premature school leaving	4.4
8	To prevent school vandalism	2.1

Source: From "Prevention and the Elementary School Counselor," by R. L. Gibson, 1989, *Elementary School Guidance and Counseling, 24*(1), p. 34. © 1989 American Counseling Association. Reprinted by permission. No further reproduction authorized without written permission of the American Counseling Association.

A few elementary school counselors reported their involvement in such nonprofessional activities as lunchroom monitoring, recess and playground duties, monitoring crossing guards, and school bus duties. The benefits of counseling programs in elementary schools are outlined in Table 3-10.

The Middle/Junior High School Counselor

Among the educational changes in the last quarter of the 20th century was a change in concept from junior high toward middle school. These changes have not been without their attending controversies, but the middle school in concept and function may not really be all that different from the more traditional junior high school. For example, many contend that the junior high school was originally conceived as an institution to meet the developmental and transitional needs of youth from puberty to adolescence, from elementary to secondary school. Early in the middle school movement, it was suggested that a rationale for the middle school concept was based on data indicating that modern youth reach physical, social, and intellectual maturity at a younger age than did previous generations and that the junior high school may no longer meet the developmental needs of these students.

Regardless of whether a school system adopts a middle school type of intermediate school or stays with the more traditional junior high school, it would appear that either institution will reflect such characteristics as providing for (a) the orientation and transitional needs and (b) the educational and social-developmental needs of their populations. In such a setting, middle or junior high school counselors will be actively involved in the following roles.

Student Orientation

This would include the initial orientation of students and their parents to the programs, policies, facilities, and counseling activities of their new school and later, their pre-entry orientation to the high school they will attend.

AN OVERVIEW OF THE ELEMENTARY SCHOOL COUNSELOR'S ROLE*

Children are scattered on the sidewalks, laughing, playing, crying, some hugging poles. It is early morning and as I walk through the safety of the gate, I am welcomed with a deluge of hugs from what seems like a thousand arms. In the distance there are faces with eyes eagerly waiting their turn for mine to acknowledge theirs.

The elementary school is a gloriously fulfilling environment for a school counselor. In my opinion the elementary school counselor is the ultimate human resource for hundreds of children. We are perceived by them as an adult who never judges or belittles them. We are their friend. Children depend on us to be loving, understanding, happy, always willing to help, incredibly flexible and genuine. In essence we are our positions.

Truly, our jobs are energizing and rewarding. In the lives of many children, we are possibly the only positive force. Our presence in schools allows all children to experience feeling warm and fuzzy and accepted.

The multifarious position of an elementary school counselor begins as I enter the gate of the school yard. Following my regal entrance into the building, most often I am greeted by teachers who need consultation on discipline problems or to refer a child. They follow me inside. Once in my office, I can find paper and pencil to take necessary notes.

With all their needs met, I get ready for the parent conference that is scheduled next. Many parents work and are unable to come in after school, so they prefer early morning appointments. Teachers may or may not be included depending on the issue.

This type of conference is intervention. When a problem or concern exists, the counselor intervenes, for example, by suggesting ways of modifying behavior or some other form of problem solving.

In addition to intervention, another major thrust is toward prevention. The purpose and underlying hope is to help children, early in their lives, to become problem solvers, to develop self-confidence, to become more responsible and thoroughly practice being the best they can be.

We incorporate prevention strategies primarily through classroom guidance activities. In my school, teachers are allowed to choose either the first period of the day or their period before lunch for classroom guidance.

It is now time to gather audiovisual equipment and scurry off to a classroom. Sometimes I pack a cassette player, puppets, posters, handout sheets, books, stickers, but always high energy and a smile. Also, the rule at my school is that, as the counselor walks by, it is not acceptable to get out of line to give hugs. They all raise their hand for a high-five as I walk by their line. This saves the teacher frustration from lining up again, and I am not late for my scheduled activity.

As I open the door and enter the classroom, there's clapping and happy glowing faces. The children are thrilled that I have come to be with them. The teachers sit in the back of the room or at their desks. I invite the children to enter the world of affective education—feelings, thoughts, decision making, understanding who they are and how to be the best they can be. Through clever and outwardly un-academic techniques of teaching, whether it is musical or magical, the children gain understanding of themselves and life skills that will forever be useful to them. In addition, they are uplifted, excited, and eager to learn.

On my way back to the office, I am inevitably stopped by a teacher or two for a quick suggestion or a follow-up comment on a child they referred. Since I am often stopped on my way to or from a classroom, it is necessary to invite them to come to my office at their activity period or after school.

With a few minutes before my next scheduled activity, I stop in the attendance office to welcome any new students who have registered.

Next is a small-group counseling session consisting of children who have been referred for similar reasons. My group size is limited to six children. Guidelines for conducting group counseling are followed.

After group, there are phone calls to return to parents, district office person-nel, the school psychologist, doctors, or other counselors.

Now it's time to administer a series of screening tests and counsel with individuals before leaving for the next classroom guidance presentation. If time permits I will join a class for lunch. It's always a treat for children when the counselor shares extra time.

After lunch, again there are phone calls to return and messages that need at-tention. It may be necessary to visit a classroom to do an observation or go to the rescue in an emergency situation. This time is also used for paperwork. On days when I make an abuse or neglect report to the Department of Social Services, three copies of the report must be made and sent to appropriate agencies. Afternoons are scheduled for individual and small-group counseling also.

After children leave for the day, typically there is a constant flow of teachers in the guidance office. This time is also used for parent-teacher conferences and staffings of children into programs for students with disabilities.

On days when the school psychologist is working in my school, I work closely with her as a liaison for teachers who have referred children for psychological test-ing. Teachers depend on the counselor to make accurate reports to the school psy-chologist related to the special needs of their children. It is often advisable to set up times for her to observe in these classrooms.

After testing and proper discussion of test results, we set up staffing dates and parent conferences to explain test scores and recommendations. I send letters of invitation to parents and teachers a week in advance of the meetings. Administra-tors are also included in these staffings.

By now, the school day has come to an end. I pack my school bag, exchange hugs, and say my good-byes. It could be an evening when I'm conducting a par-enting class at school. If so, things at home are put into fast-forward so I can leave again for school. There are parents who are a little nervous yet eager to learn how to better care for their children and relieved that other parents share their woes. Parenting groups are very supportive and encouraging ways to reach the children. Our jobs are made easier because of them.

Elementary school counselors are special, caring people who are dedicated to educating children in the affective domain. We help them become more self-confident, productive, and successful adults. Our day is ended with a feeling of accomplishment because of the constant feedback we get from children, parents, and teachers about the difference we make in the lives of people they care about. Elementary school counselors: every child deserves one!

*This description of a day in the life of an elementary school counselor was written by Sherry K. Basile, Ph.D., at that time an elementary school counselor at Berkeley Elementary School, Monck's Corner, South Carolina. Dr. Basile is currently employed by Hendricks County Community Hospital (Indiana).

Table 3-10   Benefits of counseling programs in elementary schools.

The Elementary School Exists to Provide	The Counseling Program in the Elementary School Can Contribute By	This Implies the Following:
1. Foundations for learning and living	1. Providing classroom guidance to enhance learning and relate learning to preparation	1.1 Classroom guidance 1.2 Consultation with teachers and administrators
2. Transmission of our culture and historical heritage	2. Developing multicultural awareness; pride in our cultural diversity and respect for the uniqueness of all cultural/ethnic groups	2.1 Classroom guidance activities 2.2 Consultation with teachers and administrators 2.3 Group guidance and counseling
3. Development as a social-psychological being	3. Providing for the socialization (social development) of all children, including respect for self and others	3.1 Group guidance and counseling focusing on prevention, development, and remediation 3.2 Individual counseling 3.3 Consultation with parent
4. Preparation for citizenship	4. Providing for the development of each individual's human potential	4.1 Career development 4.2 Individual assessment 4.3 Talent and skill enhancement

Source: From Gibson, R. L., Mitchell, M. H. and Basile, S. K., *Counseling in the Elementary School: A Comprehensive Approach.* Copyright © 1993 by Allyn & Bacon. Reprinted with permission.

Appraisal or Assessment Activities

In addition to typical school record and standardized test data, counselors may increasingly encourage the use of observation and other techniques to identify emerging traits of individual students during this critical development period.

Counseling

Both individual and group counseling should be used by school counselors at this level. In practice, it appears that middle and junior high school counselors tend to use group counseling more frequently than individual counseling.

Consultation

Counselors will provide consultation to faculty, parents, and, on occasion, school administrators regarding the developmental and adjustment needs of individual students. Counselors will also consult with other helping professionals in the school system.

Placement

Counselors are usually involved in course and curricular placement of pupils, not only within their own schools, but also cooperatively with their counterparts in the feeder secondary schools.

Student Development

As one notes the role of the middle school, it is obviously important that student development be given specific attention by the school counselors, faculty, and the other helping professionals (e.g., social workers, psychologists). This means understanding the developmental characteristics of this age group and the developmental tasks and planning programs that are appropriately responsive to their needs.

Seventy-one middle and junior high school counselors reported (in our 1996–1997 survey) that they spent their professional time involved in the following activities, in order from highest to lowest:

1. Administrative activities
2. Individual counseling
3. Providing career guidance assistance and materials
4. Student assessment using nonstandardized procedures
5. Dissemination of information regarding program; public relations activities
6. Group guidance activities
7. Standardized test administration and/or interpretation
8. Planning and implementation of prevention activities
9. Providing educational guidance and information
10. Group counseling; developmental activities

A number of the responding counselors mentioned significant amounts of time spent in meetings, serving on committees, meetings with parents, and sponsoring student organizations.

AN OVERVIEW OF THE MIDDLE SCHOOL
COUNSELOR'S ROLE*

Part of my joy as a middle school counselor is the endless variety that exists; part of my challenge is being not only prepared but flexible for that variety. There is rarely a "typical" day, but if there were, it would begin early with smiles for staff arriving early to prepare for a day with young adolescents. Leftover business from yesterday receives attention; a discussion with a teacher about the student who needs encouragement to keep working hard even though that test score was discouragingly low; a discussion about the student who needs extra support during difficult family changes; support for a teacher who seeks suggestions for motivating and connecting with a hard-to-reach young student; acknowledging the information from an administrator about a parent concern; and thank you's to the secretaries for yesterday's assistance and wishing them an outstanding day.

At 7:45 A.M. the early bell announces the opening of the day. Students stream into the Guidance Office for appointment passes, to set a time to discuss a concern, to look for or turn in lost items, to make a phone call home to ask a parent to retrieve and deliver forgotten items. At this time of day, there are multiple reminders that these young adolescents can be quite forgetful and quite needy. A bit of extra attention brings open smiles and can set the student off to a positive day.

Shortly after the day begins, a new student and parent arrive to enroll. Following a meeting with the Dean to register and go over all required documents, it is my turn to welcome the student and parent, find out about their likes, dislikes, and preferences, introduce them to the academic program they will experience; discuss elective options, devise a schedule, provide a tour (using a student assistant as ambassador, if available) and introduce them to one or more of their teachers. A typical orientation for a new student takes up about one hour. A very important role for me is to make the student feel welcome and important and to present an open and warm atmosphere for them.

Upon returning to the office, a quick check of phone calls and the daily schedule occurs. On tap for today are: a meeting with one of the academic teams to discuss student needs and teacher concerns; a parent/team conference to consider the special needs for a particular student; a classroom presentation on career skills, appointments with students to follow up on academic progress reports. An important part of my focus is to assist in ensuring the success of all students. This occurs through individual sessions with students that touch on accountability, motivation and skill building, small group counseling, classroom guidance, consultation with parents, teachers, teaching teams, outside counselors, and administrators.

As the day moves forward, students frequently present themselves with a desire for assistance with a peer conflict, to talk about a family or personal concern, to question how to achieve in a given teacher's class, especially when the student believes the teacher does not like him or her. Phone calls and personal consultation with the Dean of Students, the School Nurse, and caseworkers from Child Protection fill the time between scheduled meetings, classroom visits, and student conferences. Informal visits with students occur during "lunch duty" supervision and chance meetings in the hallways during passing periods. Students respond well to "hellos" and being called by name when seen in the hallway. A school of 700+ can seem overwhelming for a young adolescent. Being known by adults helps make it seem less scary!

As students leave for the day, time is spent returning phone calls to parents and making phone calls to community members for assistance with career activities. Upcoming activities include our program, "Catch Your Dream," giving students and parents feedback from the Career Interest Inventory. Another is "Reality Store," a collaborative effort with the local Business and Professional Women's Association in which students experience a day in adult life. Career Day is when students hear a variety of career speakers. Organization of each of these activities requires many phone calls and follow-up calls as well as meetings to finalize these important events.

Some days require other meetings: a community-wide committee "Care Teams," a district-wide K-12 Guidance Steering Committee, a district Pupil Services Network, middle school Parent Advisory Committee, Team Representative Committee, Remediation Committee, as well as faculty meetings. These meetings are all important to the functions of a middle school as well as the effectiveness of the developmental counseling program.

In addition, my own professional development provides support for the energy required to be effective in my work. Attending professional conferences and meetings enhances my effectiveness as a middle school counselor. All that I do is underscored by an effort to positively support success by all students. It is a privilege to be involved in this work.

*This description of a middle school counselor's responsibilities was written by Rochelle House, a middle school counselor at Central Middle School in Columbus, Indiana.

The Secondary School Counselor

Although the role and function of the secondary school counselor has expanded over the years, it is clearly the most traditional and most readily identified, even though it has been more frequently and seriously challenged than that of elementary or collegiate counselors. However, despite these challenges, any drastic changes are unlikely. Although the emphasis and techniques will undoubtedly change, the role and function of the secondary school counselor will continue to be built around the traditional expectancies discussed in chapter 2. These expectations are, for the most part, confirmed in a study by your authors as illustrated in Table 3-5.

The 109 secondary school counselors who responded to our function and role survey (1996–1997) reported their involvement in the following activities in order from most to least involvement:

1. Providing educational guidance and information, including student scheduling, and college placement and scholarship information
2. Individual counseling

3. Administrative activities and record keeping
4. Prevention activities
5. Providing career guidance and assistance
6. Standardized test administration and/or interpretation.
7. Information dissemination, public communication, and human relations
8. Consultation activities
9. Student development activities
10. Group guidance; group counseling

As with their elementary and middle/junior high school counterparts, secondary school counselors were engaged in noncounseling activities. Prominent among these were hall duty and monitoring student lunchrooms. Some also indicated duties as substitute teachers. In a study of teacher opinions of secondary school counseling programs, Gibson (1989) reports that teachers view the most important functions of counselors as (a) providing individual counseling, (b) offering career planning assistance and information, (c) administering and interpreting standardized test results, and (d) assisting in college guidance and placement.

The roles and functions of the secondary school counselor are not dissimilar to those of counselors in the elementary and middle/junior high schools. The differences occur in how counselors in the secondary school discharge their role and function and in the various emphases appropriate to the secondary school setting. For example, the emphasis at the secondary school level shifts slightly from the preventive to the remedial in dealing with many common counseling concerns. Many of these issues are potentially serious life problems, such as addiction to drugs and alcohol, sexual concerns, and interpersonal relationship adjustments. Furthermore, there is less client emphasis on preparing for decisions and more emphasis on making decisions. These include immediate or impending career decisions or further education decisions, decisions relevant to relationships with the opposite sex and perhaps marriage, and decisions involved in developing personal values systems.

In addition to these different emphases in contrast to counseling needs at other educational levels, counselors anticipate more emphasis on consultation and on a broader understanding of the impact of environment on students' behavior; a shifting emphasis toward a closer relationship with the classroom teacher in the school environment, as opposed to the traditional "medical" model (in which the client in need comes to the office for a "prescription"); and finally, a shift in emphasis from being reactive to becoming a proactive change agent in both the school and the community.

Counselors in Vocational Schools

The image and the significance of vocational education changed markedly in the 1970s. Once regarded as a dumping ground for the unwilling or unable student (with facilities usually appropriate to this image), vocational education programs have made a dramatic turnaround. Today they are some of the finest educational facilities in the country, attracting students at all ability levels and preparing them for jobs in demand. School counselors need to become aware of both the nature of vocational education programs and the opportunities available to those who complete them. Additionally, counselors in preparation need to recognize some differences in the role and function of the counselor in the vocational school.

AN OVERVIEW OF THE SECONDARY SCHOOL COUNSELOR'S ROLE*

Typical Day's Activities of a High School Counselor

- Typically arrive at 7:00 A.M. and leave at 5:00 P.M.
- Host parent calls to explain her foreign student's broken elbow and premature return to Brazil
- Coordinator of Career Academy calls to see whether student who was recommended for the special program and put on a waiting list last semester is still interested in participating
- Student from Czech Republic discusses schedule change
- Student from Germany adds two classes to his schedule for second semester; checked with teachers for approval
- Senior brings in college application and wants school recommendation completed by tomorrow
- Local employer calls for recommendation for a 1993 graduate who is seeking employment
- Interpretation of PSAT/NMSQT test results to 200+ juniors and sophomores
- Conference with former student's parent (her daughter graduated in 1979; currently her granddaughter is a freshman at NSHS) who is concerned with her granddaughter's well-being
- Conference with a sophomore who is interested in participating in an international exchange program for his junior year
- Conference with senior who needs help with college application
- Phone call from senior parent re FAFSA form and Financial Aids Workshop
- Conference with senior (returning from a semester of study in Japan at our sister city school) who will be returning for his eighth semester at North Side; also needed help with college applications
- Conference with senior and Student Assistance Counselor re possible abuse by parent
- Conference with parent (whose daughter graduated in 1993) and daughter's fiancé who wants to get GED certificate
- Phone conversation with soccer coach who had borrowed a videotape of soccer game from one of our Spanish exchange students and had not returned it
- Conference with female junior who is interested in hosting a Japanese girl
- Phone conversation with former student (who was a peer facilitator and now a teacher at South Side High School) who is interested in starting such a program at his school and wanted some help in writing his proposal
- Conference with Japanese businessman who brought me a present from parents of one of our exchange students

- Conference with a journalism student who was writing an article on the FAFSA and financial aid
- Chat with senior football player whom I had moved, at his request, from an Essentials of English class to an Academic English class, checking on his grades; currently earning a B+
- Conference with sophomore soccer player to see whether his family would consider taking the Rotary Exchange student from Turkey for the second semester
- Phone conversation with counselor from Educational Opportunity Center regarding one of our students
- Phone conversation with probation officer downtown to discuss the student's being transported to North Side to take the SAT test
- Appointment downtown with Media Services person in Fort Wayne Community School Channel 20 regarding production of a videotape about PURSUITS career development program (which I coordinate)
- Phone conversation with Educational Testing Service regarding providing test center for the PLUS Academic Abilities Assessment Program (for sixth graders)
- Conference with parent of junior dropout regarding plans to reenter school next semester
- Area coordinator for Center for Cultural Interchange needs signature for student from Argentina who will enter North Side High School second semester
- Phone conversation with Indiana University Admissions Office regarding appeal process for senior who was not admitted; followed up with letter confirming the telephone conversation
- Phone conversation with mother of senior transfer student who is experiencing adjustment problems
- Parent request for progress reports for student; advised secretary to prepare reports
- Conference with teacher regarding need to find shadowing sites for Advanced Biology students
- Phone conversation with tutor at Benet Learning Center regarding a student he is tutoring
- Conversation with North Side graduate who is currently a professor at Earlham College
- Conference with parent of sophomore regarding college opportunities for minority students
- Discussion with athletic director regarding NCAA Clearinghouse for student-athletes
- Prepared memo for science and math teachers regarding National Engineers Week and the need to recommend seniors who are serious about pursuing a career in engineering
- Senior Interview (all counselors assist in interviewing each senior individually)

- Phone conversation with Purdue nutritionist who will teach the "Have a Healthy Baby" class
- Case conference with student-athlete, his mother, and a teacher to discuss inappropriate behavior and attitude
- Conference with student regarding possibility of sexually transmitted disease; referral to Board of Health; appointment scheduled
- Letter to mayor regarding nomination of student for Mayor's Youth Achievement Award
- Letter and applications completed for Hoosier Girls state delegates and alternates
- Meeting with two community consultants and Student Assistance Counselor regarding plans for conflict management training sessions
- Conference with *Journal-Gazette* reporter regarding teens and "Sexuality in the 1990s"
- Phone conversation with two counselors in our feeder middle schools arranging for home stays for eleven Japanese middle school students and one teacher
- Financial Aid workshop, 7–9 P.M. with 96 parents participating

This is a typical day!

Additional Responsibilities on a Regular Basis

Monthly Meetings:

Faculty Advisory Committee (first Tuesday 2:45–4:00)

Faculty meetings (first Thursday, during teachers' plan periods)

Family and Children's Service board meeting (third Thursday, 11:30–1:00); PR Committee meets second Tuesday for lunch

Sister Cities Committee (first Wednesday, 5:00–6:15)

Integrated Guidance Program staff (first Thursday, 8–10 A.M.)

Curriculum and Instruction division (second Tuesday, 8–10 A.M.)

Other Meetings:

North Side High School administrative staff and guidance staff meet weekly for about 2 hours each

Performance Based Accreditation Steering Committee meets weekly at 7 A.M.; School Climate Committee (which I chair) meets weekly at either 7 A.M. or 2:45 P.M.

Peer facilitator training, 7 A.M. on Tuesday, Thursday, Friday

PURSUITS (career development program) board meets quarterly; I serve as coordinator of this program, which is funded by a private foundation, currently serves all high schools in Allen County and 11 Fort Wayne

Community Schools middle schools, and pilots a career development program for elementary schools

Dave Hefner International Exchange Fund Board meets twice a year; I serve as president

Indiana Counseling Association Foundation meets yearly; I serve as treasurer.

North Side Area Guidance Leadership Project (3-year project funded by the Lilly Endowment) core team meets quarterly; North Side High School CAIT (Child Advocacy/Inquiry Team) meets regularly

· Regularly attend professional conferences and workshops as well as serve on various ad hoc committees (e.g., the State of Indiana GED study group)

· Supervise test center for the American College Testing, Scholastic Aptitude Testing, ASE Technician Test, PLUS, and U.S. Postal Service exams

· Prepare college applications/scholarship recommendations on an ongoing basis (usually after school and on weekends)

· Attend/supervise various fine arts programs, athletic events, dances, and other programs

*Ms. De Klocke, at the time a counselor at North Side High School in Fort Wayne, Indiana, lists her activities in a typical day as a high school counselor.

Counselors in Higher Education

A wide variety of counseling services are available to students in programs of higher education across the United States and Canada. Some of the counselors providing these services function in specialized facilities such as career centers and college admissions and placement offices. The majority of counselors, however, are employed in university counseling, mental health, or psychological service centers. These centers typically offer personal, academic, and vocational counseling, although group counseling has increased in popularity in recent years. Many of these centers are interdisciplinary in terms of staffing.

Some insight into anticipated responsibilities of counselors on college campuses may be provided by noting the CACREP standards for the training of college counselors. These standards suggest that college counselors will need preparation in (a) career counseling, (b) group work, (c) additional studies (e.g., academic assistance, promoting interpersonal relationships, leadership training, consultation, assessment, referral).

A noticeable trend in the activities of college counseling center programs is their move to assist larger numbers of students on their campuses through such activities as outreach programs, special workshops, residence hall groups, and peer counseling. On some campuses, counselors are also becoming more active in consultation with their faculty peers, campus administrators, and leaders of student organizations.

Counseling Services in Community and Junior Colleges

The community and junior college has increased significantly in popularity in recent decades. Increasing numbers of students have been attracted to community and junior colleges as a way of easing the financial cost of a 4-year degree and the transition from high school to college. Counselors in these settings have assumed important roles in the educational, social, and emotional development of students attending these institutions. They are also called on to provide counseling services for student populations from diverse socioeconomic and cultural backgrounds and from varying levels of academic backgrounds and abilities. The challenges facing the counselor in these settings are immense and include the following:

- academic motivation
- the development of adequate study skills
- the development of appropriate communications and human relationship skills
- the management of time and personal responsibilities
- the development of appropriate academic and personal goals and plans for implementing these
- maintaining adequate mental and physical health

Counselors in junior and community colleges are often called on to provide services for stimulating the educational opportunities of individuals with learning disabilities. Such responsibilities would include not only the traditional personal counseling and individual guidance activities but also inclusion of special orientation programs, support groups, study skills courses, and career development activities. As we enter the 21st century, labor market predictions imply significantly increasing importance in the role of the junior and community college. Many, perhaps the majority of individuals entering the workforce in the early generations of this century, will experience three to seven distinctly different careers. The training and retraining for these different careers are predicted to be the responsibility of local community colleges. Further, as the nation becomes more dependent on new and developing technology, appropriate technical training programs as well as cooperative programs between area businesses and industries and relevant training programs will further enhance the role of the community college. These developments will also emphasize the important role of counseling services in bringing students and appropriate training programs together. Vocational guidance and career counseling are anticipated to become significant to both the individual and the institution in the achievement of personal and program goals.

TEACHER AND ADMINISTRATOR ROLES IN THE SCHOOL COUNSELING PROGRAM

The Classroom Teacher

Although it seems heresy to the counseling profession, it has been and could continue to be possible for schools to exist without the benefit of counselors. Many students possibly would not achieve their potential, solve their problems, or make appropriate decisions and plans, but nonetheless most of them would learn, progress, and be viewed as educated. It is also possible for schools to exist without the presence of an even more prominent member—the school principal. Although teachers would be even more overburdened with administrative responsibilities, and their teaching effectiveness would undoubtedly suffer, students would still be taught, learn (perhaps at a slower rate), graduate (even without the principal's handshake), and be viewed as educated.

Schools without teachers, however, cease to be schools. They become, instead, detention centers, social clubs, or temporary shelters, but they are not schools, and any learning that takes place would be both incidental and accidental. It therefore becomes obvious, and has been since the beginning of schooling, that the teacher is the most important professional in the school setting. Teacher support and participation are crucial to any program that involves students. The school counseling program is no exception. Further, today's teachers feel that they should have responsibilities in the school counseling program beyond those performed in the classroom (Gibson, 1990). Gibson also notes that

> notwithstanding changing roles and calls for new directions, it can be concluded that secondary school teachers continue to believe that counseling and guidance programs make a positive contribution to the total program of their schools. Interviews further confirmed that teachers have high respect for the skills and dedication of the counselors in their schools. This was especially noted in those schools in which counselors interacted with every teacher on a one-to-one basis at least once per semester (1990, p. 254)

It is therefore important to examine the role and function of the classroom teacher in the counseling program, recognizing, of course, that differences may be anticipated at differing educational levels and in different educational settings.

Listener-Adviser

Most classroom teachers see their pupils every day, 5 days a week, for at least 45 minutes per day on the average of 180 school days per year, often for several years, all of which represents a staggering amount of contact time exceeded by no other adults except parents, and that exception does not always hold true. Inevitably, the teacher more than any other professional in the school setting is in the position to know the students best, to communicate with them on an almost daily basis, and to establish a relationship based on mutual trust and respect. The teacher thus becomes the first line of contact between the student and the school counseling program, a contact in which the teacher will frequently be called on to serve in a listening/advising capacity.

Referral and Receiving Agent

The classroom teacher is the major source of student referrals to the school counselor. Because the counselor's daily personal contacts with students are necessarily limited, the counselor's personal awareness of students needing counseling is similarly limited. The counseling program must, therefore, depend on an alert faculty to ensure that students with counseling needs will not go unnoticed and uncounseled. School counselors need to encourage their teacher colleagues to actively search for these students, because much evidence exists to suggest that only the tip of the proverbial iceberg has been touched in efforts to identify all students with serious counseling needs.

Of course, simply identifying these students to a counselor may not be enough. In many instances, the teacher must orient and encourage the student to seek counselor assistance.

Nor does the teacher's responsibility necessarily end when the student has entered a counseling relationship. The teacher may still be involved, if only in the role of supporting the student's continuation with the counseling process. Teachers may also anticipate a role as a receiving agent, not only for those students they have referred but for others in their classes as well. In such situations, the teacher in a sense receives the counseled student back into the classroom environment and, it is hoped, supports and reinforces the outcome of the counseling. The importance of this reinforcer role cannot be overemphasized. Teachers can also play a valuable role as a member of study teams for pupils they refer.

Discoverer of Human Potential

Each year teachers witness a talent parade through their respective classes. Most teachers have the expertise to identify those who may have some special talents for their own particular career specialty. That expertise, multiplied across the many career specialties, represents a near army of talent scouts that should ensure that each student will have his or her talents and potentials identified and his or her development encouraged and assisted. This teacher role as a discoverer of human potential is significant in fulfilling not only a mission of the school counseling program but also in meeting the responsibility of education to the individual and to society.

Career Educator

Closely related to the foregoing is the teacher's central role in the school's career education program. Because career education is recognized as a part of students' total education, it is important also to recognize the classroom teacher's responsibility to integrate career education into teaching subject matter. Career education cannot succeed without career guidance and vice versa. The success of the career guidance program is tied to the success of the career education program, a success that rests largely with the classroom teacher.

The career education responsibilities of the teacher include developing positive attitudes and respect for all honest work, a challenging responsibility in view of the many adult-imposed biases with which the student is constantly confronted. Additionally, the teacher must promote the parallel development of positive student attitudes toward education and its relationship to career preparation and decision making. Students must also have the opportunity to examine and test concepts, skills, and roles and develop values appropriate to their future career planning. The security of the classroom group provides an ideal setting for these experiences.

Human Relations Facilitator

The potential for success of any school counseling program depends to a considerable degree upon the climate of the school, an environment that is conducive to the development and practice of positive human relations. The influence of the classroom teacher on that environment is dominant, as ably expressed by Haim Ginott:

> I have come to the frightening conclusion
> I am the decisive element in the classroom
> It is my personal approach that creates the climate
> It is my daily mood that makes the weather
> As a teacher I possess tremendous power to make a child's life miserable or joyous

I can humiliate or humor, hurt or heal

In all situations it is my response that decides whether a crisis will be escalated or de-escalated, and a child humanized or dehumanized.

(cited in Gross & Gross, 1974, p. 39)

Among the research emphasizing the importance of a favorable classroom and school environment for learning is that reported in Benjamin Bloom's book *Human Characteristics and School Learning* (1976). Bloom suggests that it is possible for 95% of the students to learn all that the school has to teach at or near the same achievement level. His research indicates that most students will be very similar in both learning and their motivation to learn when they are provided the favorable conditions or environment for learning. His research also demonstrates that when the environment in the classroom is unfavorable, differences occur that widen the gap between high and low achievers. In this role as a human relations facilitator, the classroom teacher has the opportunity to be a model to demonstrate positive human relations. The teaching and practicing of these skills should occur as a regular procedure in the classroom as the teacher plans and directs group interactions that promise positive human relationship experiences for each individual participant.

Counseling Program Supporter

Someone once said, "Counselors are the most human of all humans." Be that as it may, counselors, like all humans, need and respond to the encouragement and support of their fellow beings. Therefore, a significant contribution that the classroom teacher can make to the school counseling program is one of counselor encouragement and support and the creation of a motivating environment. Support can be especially influential in determining how pupils view and use the services of the school's counseling program. Teachers' reactions also do not go unnoticed by school administrators and supervisors. Of course, evidence of teacher support for counseling ideally should extend to parents and others in the community as well.

Despite the importance of the classroom teacher in any school counseling program at any educational level, evidence indicates that, in far too many settings, the classroom teacher is still only incidentally involved in the program. Many classroom teachers may feel uncertain about the goals of their school programs and may lack communication and involvement in the counseling programs. In such situations, the student is the real loser, and both the counselor and the teacher must share the blame.

Because the school counseling program is the responsibility of counselors, they must initiate communications and interaction with their teaching faculties; they must actively pursue teachers' involvement and assistance, and they must exemplify their claim to human relations expertise. Blum (1986) suggests the importance of counselors having visibility—being seen—and sociability—being known by the teachers in their school. They must also recognize that although most teachers are willing to accept their role in the school counseling program, as many studies have indicated, teachers may lack some understanding of what that role and function are.

Of course, not all teachers will or can be "all things," as suggested in this section. Most can and will accept many of the roles, however. These role opportunities also can be enhanced by preparing teachers to recognize, accept, and enjoy their roles in the school counseling program. Unfortunately, most teachers do not seek and are not required to take coursework in counseling and guidance and, therefore, are limited in realizing their full potential as team members.

The Chief School Administrator

Whether a building principal or a university president, the chief on-site administrator is potentially (and usually) the most important person in the development of any educational program in his or her respective setting. Most staff members of schools (including principals and college presidents) think of chief administrators in terms of power—what the chief administrators permit them to do and not to do. Previous studies (Gibson, Mitchell, & Higgins, 1983) have noted that administrative support was ranked in the highest priority category in the establishment and development of school counseling programs. These studies emphasize the significant role the school principal and other educational leadership can and should play in any program of counseling within their jurisdiction. This role may be appropriately expressed through leadership, consultation, advice, and resource support. Some of the characteristics of these activities are described next.

Program Leader and Supporter

The leadership behavior of the school principal on behalf of the school counseling program is a major determinant of the program's prospects for success. Because school administrators represent the educational leadership in both the school and the community, they have the responsibility of giving clear, open, and recognized support for the school program. This will include responsibilities for communicating program characteristics, achievements, and needs to school boards and others within the educational system and to the tax-supporting public.

Program Consultant and Adviser

The chief school administrator has the best overview of all activities and planning within the institution. This position enables the chief administrator to make a valuable contribution to the school counseling program as adviser and consultant on school needs that can be served by the school program, school policies that affect counseling program functioning, resolution of problems encountered by the program, and procedures or directions for program development and improvement.

Resource Provider

Chief school administrators are usually responsible for the institution's budget—its makeup and utilization. In this role, they provide advice and direction to all school programs regarding budget expectations, staffing possibilities, facilities, and equipment. They may also be aware of possible external resources such as state or federal funding, which the school counseling program may wish to explore.

THE COUNSELOR AND RELATIONSHIPS WITH OTHER HELPING PROFESSIONS

One of the school counselor's important roles is as a team member. Unlike the gifted athlete who may have to limit membership to one team, the counselor may play on several teams. One of the most important and logical of these is the helping professions team. This team typically includes the school psychologist, social worker, speech and hearing specialists, and health personnel. To work effectively with each other, members must understand the expertise and responsibilities of their fellow team members and how they support each other. This is not always easy because their roles often seem to overlap, especially at the elementary school level. The All Handicapped Children's Act of 1975 has had the most consistent influence over the past 25 years in role determination for elementary school personnel. Unfortunately, most training programs do little in the way of interdisciplinary planning or training. Therefore, it becomes the responsibility of the school counselor and other helping professionals to initiate and develop positive, cooperative working relationships consistent with the team concept.

The School Psychologist

By some estimates, more than 23,000 school psychologists are currently practicing in the school systems of the United States. In these settings they assist classroom teachers, parents, and other school personnel, including counselors, in developing classroom management strategies, assisting students who are disabled or gifted, and in general, improving overall teaching and learning strategies. School psychologists give special attention to learning and behavioral problems. They also administer and interpret the results of standardized assessment instruments to teachers, parents, and others. The training programs that prepare these psychologists emphasize psychological and educational foundations with special attention to measurement and evaluation. Students in programs preparing school psychologists are further instructed in the application of these foundations to the behavioral, social, and academic problems that students experience in schools.

In recent generations state and federal laws that mandated educational services for students with disabilities contributed to a significant increase in the number of school psychologists. These laws also resulted in a dramatic growth in special education and also emphasized the role of the school psychologist in evaluating students to determine their eligibility for special education services. Federal laws, including the Individuals with Disabilities Education Act (IDEA), indicate that the role of the school psychologist would include assessment, consultation, and provision of services to students with disabilities and also their families.

School psychologists have been traditionally trained in the medical model for conceptualizing and providing their professional services. In practice, this means assessing, diagnosing, and treating the internal pathologies of their clients. However, in recent years many in the field of school psychology have felt that although relevant, this model is too restrictive in scope, as many problems must be looked at in the context of a multilayered, proximal-distal, and interactive system. This means considering individual differences, educational contexts, environments, family, and community variables. (Information in the paragraphs that follow were contributed by Nancy Waldron, Ph.D., Associate Professor of Education, Florida State University.)

As the focus in special education and other remedial education programs switched during the 1980s from eligibility and identification to intervention and prevention for students with mild disabilities and others at risk for school failure, school psychologists became increasingly involved in intervention and remediation programs for all students. The school psychologists' skill with individual assessment tools—including measures of cognitive ability; academic achievement; and behavioral, personality, or adaptive behavior—are often used to meet specific student needs and deliver possible intervention alternatives. Increasingly, these assessment skills are expanding beyond individual test administration to include interviewing, observation, and alternative techniques such as curriculum-based assessment.

Because the school psychologist is heavily trained in the use of clinical tools such as those that measure the mental and personality characteristics of the individual, counselors may often find it desirable to refer students to the school psychologist for clinical diagnosis. And the school psychologist will often identify, through his or her diagnostic evaluations, pupils in need of counseling.

School counselors will often work directly with school psychologists in providing psychological and support services to students with disabilities, families, and classroom teachers working with these students. Thus, school counselors and school psychologists will frequently collaborate on building-based and student support teams that consult with teachers and parents and provide direct services to students with academic and/or behavioral problems in school.

The School Social Worker

Social workers are trained to assist people, including all youth of school age, to deal effectively with their problems and concerns. These may include environmental adjustments, personal relationships, and personal and family problems.

The school social worker provides helping services for those children who are unable to make proper use of their educational opportunities and who find it difficult to function effectively in the school environment. In this role, the social worker is a referral source for children who appear to have emotional or social problems that are handicapping their learning and social adjustment to school. The school social worker has special interviewing and casework skills that are used within a school-child-parent context. The school social worker works closely with community agencies and nonschool professional helpers, such as physicians, lawyers, and ministers.

The school social worker is an important member of the school services team. Counselors and other helping professionals may depend on the social worker to provide better understanding of the child, especially in regard to the home environment and the nature of the pupil's behavioral problems.

Special Educator

In 1975 The Education for All Handicapped Children Act (Public Law 94-142) was signed into law. This law's intent was to provide normal and integrated educational opportunities for children with disabilities. A major impact of the act, stemming from the desire to educate the student in the least restrictive environment, was the mainstreaming of most students with disabilities into regular classrooms. The regular classroom teacher was also made responsible for the progress of such students in his or her classroom, and the law forbade any categorical labels (e.g., emotionally disturbed, retarded). Other aspects of the law provided for due process or the equal protection of the rights of people with disabilities and individualized programs designed to maximize the potential of each student.

One outcome of these provisions has been the addition of the special educator to the school's helping services team. Obviously, the school counselor has special skills in terms of assessment and placement, individual counseling, group guidance, and career assistance that can help this population. Consulting with parents can also be helpful. In all of these aspects the school counselor will work closely with the special educator and others concerned with maximizing the educational opportunities for these students.

School Health Personnel

Most school systems employ professional health services personnel, at least on a part-time basis. Most common are the school nurse and the dental hygienist; a number of school systems also employ school physicians. Your personal recall of these helping professionals may consist of memories of immunization shots, opening your mouth to say "Ahh," the taste of the tongue-depressor, and the admonition of the dental hygienist when she discovered you weren't brushing regularly. Such recalls are fairly characteristic of the role of these providers of basic, preventive health services for all school children. These professionals also identify children who need special medical treatment or referrals for the correction or alleviation of defects. Counselors will find these medical specialists a resource for making referrals and determining whether or to what extent physical ailments or defects are an obstacle to a student's anticipated development or adjustment. These personnel are usually responsible for covering a number of schools rather than a single institution. As they visit different schools, they tend to treat a wide variety of health problems. Most common among these are medication problems in schools where students are not allowed to carry any medications to school with them; emergency and first-aid assistance; digestive problems and relatively simple discomforts such as headaches, stomachaches, and skin rashes. Most school systems also have vision screening, hearing tests, and dental examinations and vaccination screening. Medical personnel will usually follow up on teacher reports of child abuse, substance abuse, suicidal students, and teen pregnancies.

Psychiatrists

Psychiatrists are physicians with specialized training in the treatment of behavioral abnormalities. As physicians, psychiatrists are permitted by law to use drugs and other physical means of treatment for mental problems. Counselors often suggest to parents that they refer their son or daughter to a psychiatrist if it is suspected that the child may have an emotional disturbance requiring the use of medication. Many psychiatrists perform an important consultative role to other mental health professionals as well.

It is clear that there are many overlapping functions especially among school counselors, school psychologists, and school social workers and particularly in the elementary school. There remains a uniqueness to each specialty, however. The question to be answered, then, is, Who does what? It can be argued that there is enough work to spread around if the dollars and jobs exist. Student nonadjustment and incidence of social ills suggest that there are not enough mental health professionals. Then what is the issue? The problem seems to be territoriality. The three specialties (elementary school counselors, school psychologists, school social workers) remain eager to protect professional boundaries even though similarities are acknowledged when actual situations require broad services to pupils. Perhaps the main solution to the teamwork dilemma is a multidisciplinary examination of organizational patterns and line-staff relationships (Kameen, Robinson, & Rotter, cited in Humes & Hohenshil, 1987, p. 43). Working together as a team is clearly desirable, with each helping professional enhancing the contributions of the others.

PATTERNS OF COUNSELING PROGRAM ORGANIZATION IN EDUCATIONAL SETTINGS

We noted earlier in this chapter that school counseling programs must reflect the differences in their populations and settings; therefore, it is appropriate to assume that these differences will also result in differing organizational structures for programs. Consequently, it must be recognized that there are many successful yet differing patterns of program organization for all educational levels. Furthermore, these structures differ according to the educational levels (elementary, middle, secondary, or higher education) they serve. This section attempts to briefly illustrate a few of the most traditional and popular program formats.

Counseling in Elementary Schools

As we noted in the discussion of the historical development of guidance in American education, counseling programs are continuing to develop rapidly in the elementary schools of this country. A wide variety of organizational formats has emerged in the development of elementary school counseling programs; so rather than attempting to present the most desirable organizational form, we examine some of the possible considerations.

In determining appropriate approaches to program organization and development in the elementary school, elementary educators have considered the characteristics and goals of the elementary school, especially those that highlight the special role of the elementary school as an educational institution. These include orienting elementary schoolchildren to the educational environment and providing them with the basic educational-developmental experiences essential for their future development. Other special characteristics of the elementary school are also important as considerations in the organization and development of their counseling programs, including the following:

- Most elementary schools are homeroom-teacher centered. The elementary pupil is in a self-contained classroom with one teacher for most of the day, and the pupil is with this teacher for at least one academic year. As a result, pupil and teacher get to know each other better in the elementary school than in schools at higher levels.
- There is an emphasis on learning through activity. Physical activity and exercises related to learning are characteristic of the elementary school.
- The elementary school pupil is a member of a reasonably stable group. Although some school populations are relatively transient, it is not uncommon for a child to be with the same group of fellow pupils for most of each school year, and in many elementary school situations, with many of the same children throughout all the elementary school years.
- Elementary schools are usually smaller and less complex than secondary schools.
- Parental interest and involvement are generally greater at the elementary school level.

Further reflected in the educational approach and structure of the elementary school are the characteristics of the elementary schoolchildren. Anyone who has ever set foot in an elementary school knows that there is no such thing as the typical elementary school pupil. And parents and teachers who interact with these children on a daily basis can further testify to the difficulties of characterizing this age group. It is therefore appropriate to suggest that the common characteristic all elementary youths share is that no two are alike. Despite this, it is not inappropriate to briefly note some broadly recognized needs and characteristics of this youthful population, even though there have been and will continue to be innumerable studies made and volumes written about the needs of children.

As a basis for guidance in the elementary school, we will view these needs from two standpoints: (a) basic needs that continuously demand satisfaction, and (b) developmental needs that must be met during different life stages.

People's basic needs have been presented by Maslow (1970) in a hierarchy or priority ordering of needs in which the higher order needs will emerge only when the lower order needs have been fairly well satisfied. Maslow points out that the best way to repress the higher motivation of humankind is to keep individuals chronically hungry, insecure, or unloved. According to Maslow's theory, as the teacher and counselor view the elementary pupil and his or her ability to become self-actualized and develop potential, the teacher or counselor must be concerned with the degree to which the pupil's lower order needs are being met.

The developmental needs of humankind, according to his life stage, have been well presented by Havighurst (1953) in his popular "developmental tasks." Counselors and teachers in the elementary school should still take note of the following developmental tasks for middle childhood:

1. Learning physical skills necessary for ordinary games.
2. Building wholesome attitudes toward oneself as a growing organism.
3. Learning to get along with age-mates.
4. Learning an appropriate masculine or feminine social role.
5. Developing fundamental skills in reading, writing, and calculating.
6. Developing concepts necessary for everyday living.
7. Developing conscience, morality, and a scale of values.
8. Achieving personal independence.
9. Developing attitudes toward social groups and institutions.

The presentations of Maslow and Havighurst stress both the personal and the cultural nature of the needs of children as they grow and develop. There is also an implied developmental task for educational programs: the task of providing learning experiences appropriate to the needs, both basic and developmental, of the elementary school child.

In addition to the needs of children, plans for counseling in the elementary school should take into consideration the following characteristics of the student:

- The elementary school student is experiencing continuous growth, development, and change.
- The elementary school student is constantly integrating experiences.
- The elementary school student is relatively limited in the ability to verbalize.
- The reasoning powers of the elementary school pupil are not fully developed.
- The ability of the elementary school pupil to concentrate over long periods of time is limited.
- The enthusiasm and interest of the elementary school pupil can be easily aroused.

- The decisions and goals of the elementary school pupil serve immediate purposes; he or she does not yet make long-range plans.
- The elementary school pupil displays feelings more or less openly.

The implications of these characteristics and needs for programs of counseling in the elementary school must be reflected in both counseling program structure and counselor role and function.

On the basis of these identifiable features of the elementary school and the characteristics and needs of elementary school students, any successful program in the elementary school that focuses on the student must have not only the approval but also the significant involvement of the faculty. It must be teacher centered. Furthermore, close and frequent contact with parents must be anticipated, especially in the primary years. Any program that relies too heavily on "talking at" the elementary school student, even when supplemented with films and other media or material aids, is doomed to failure. The elementary school is activity oriented, and the counseling program in this setting must "do as the Romans do." Finally, the elementary school years are developmental years. The elementary school guidance program must, therefore, respond with a developmental rather than a remedial emphasis— an emphasis that suggests, for example, less individual adjustment counseling and more developmental group guidance activities.

Counseling in Secondary Schools

Since their early, sometimes timorous, and sometimes tenuous beginnings in the 20 years after Parsons through their experimental growth years of the 1930s and 1940s into the boom years of the 1950s and 1960s, school counseling and guidance programs have been almost the exclusive property of high schools in the United States. Although different influences and emphases in both the secondary school and the counseling and guidance movement have often altered concepts of program structure and function, the movement maintained a steady growth in both numbers and professionalization through the last half of the 20th century and developed recognizable images of program structure, role, and function. These, however, may also be more readily understood with a renewed acquaintance with the characteristics of the secondary school (so well eulogized in the classic publication *Is There Life After High School*, Keyes, 1976) and with the high school student as well.

Although adolescence is identified as that period between puberty and adulthood, nothing defies standard definition or description more than adolescents. They are as varied, unpredictable, and uncontrollable as their peer group permits. They give meaning to the expression "generation gap," of which many adolescents are proud and, before it's over, for which many adults are thankful. Most persons view their adolescent years as different from those of today. They probably were, for adolescents today not only exhibit a wide variation in individual characteristics, but the group characteristics also seem to change rapidly from generation to generation. As an extreme example, many may recall that some of their grandparents seemed to go directly from childhood to work and adulthood. They completed their 8 to 10 years of schooling and went to work. Today, some youths stretch their adolescence into their 20s, resisting growing up or accepting responsibility, and rejecting independence.

For all who are concerned with youth during these magical years, for those who may hope to ease their passage, it is important to recognize some of the characteristics of adolescence:

- It is a period of continuous physical growth, not the least of which is the awakening of sexual impulses. Girls discover boys, and boys discover girls who discover boys. Puppy love becomes a serious crush that becomes undying love (at least for the moment).
- It is a period of movement toward maturity with all its implications for independence, responsibility, and self-discipline; a period often very trying to parents who want to keep little Sasha tied to her mother's apron strings or Johnnie still passing the football to old "butterfingers" Dad.
- Reveling in their newly acquired independence and the discovery of their rapidly developing abilities to reason and hypothesize, many adolescents exaggerate their ability to solve the problems of the world and those that are personal for them. At the same time, many become critical of adult solutions to social problems, lifestyles, and values but deny that adults are in a position to evaluate life among the adolescents.
- Furthermore, with the acquisition of the privileges of adulthood—independence, responsibility, and self-direction—there is a movement from childish to adult forms of expression, reaction, and behavior. For better or worse, adult behavior is mimicked and often exaggerated.
- Self-selected (not adult-imposed) peer group memberships are important to the adolescent. The peer group becomes the center of most of their significant social-recreational activities and, in the eyes of many parents (and many authorities as well), their initial sex education "program." Also, while demanding their independence from parents and other adult controls, adolescents in turn may surrender much of their independence and individuality to peer group conformity.
- It is a period when teenagers seek direction, a set of values, and their own personal identity. The last demands treatment as an individual—a demand that the home and the school often appear to overlook. In the quest for this new identity, the adolescent encounters, with peers, many of the common problems of this journey. Although a multitude of studies have investigated the priority concerns of youths, most of these tend to be outdated immediately after their publication. Recognizing this limitation, we would use three categories to classify a consensus of common adolescent problems from current studies.
  a. *Developing as a social being.* This includes problems of one-to-one personal relationships, particularly dating, love, sex, and marriage. It also involves group living and acceptance and, in general, the development of human relationship skills.
  b. *Developing as a unique being.* Adolescents are concerned with the development and recognition of the uniqueness of individuals. It is a time when they are seeking to develop their own value system and often find they face value conflicts. Anxieties are often created as a result of constant demands to measure up made by evaluative testing and other appraisal techniques that appear to standardize them. They are also concerned when they fail to gain parental or other support for their new self.

c. *Developing as a productive being*. In this regard, youths are concerned with their educational adjustments and achievements, their career decisions, future educational directions, impending financial needs, and employment prospects. Many become concerned because school is not providing them with a marketable skill. Others feel that staying in school is delaying their earning a living.

We can also note some of the significant characteristics of the secondary school. Although there are, of course, exceptions to any attempt to characterize schools at any level, the following are generally appropriate for many secondary schools in the United States and Canada.

- Secondary schools are generally large, complex institutions populated by a heterogeneous student body. The size and complexity of the secondary school have implications for both counseling program development and program activities. Because the larger student bodies tend to be more heterogeneous, often representing many cultural minority groups, the identification of these groups and the response to their needs can represent a major challenge to the program.
- Secondary school faculties represent a variety of academic specialties. The secondary school faculty member tends to concentrate on a particular subject area. As a result, the secondary school faculty represents a variety of specializations, which provides a reservoir of resources that the school counseling program may use in the career, educational, and personal-social development of students.
- Secondary school years are important decision-making years for the individual student. During students' secondary schooling, they are usually confronted with at least two lifetime-influencing decisions. The first is whether to complete secondary schooling. Various dropout studies indicate that approximately one fourth of high school youth make the decision to leave school before finishing their secondary school program. Second, many students make important decisions regarding careers or choice of college. The wide variety of course offerings and activities available in most secondary schools prompts a nearly continuous series of minor decisions for the students as well. They may also be confronted with significant personal decisions regarding sex and marriage; use of tobacco, alcohol, and drugs; and friends and friendship.
- Secondary schools are subject-matter oriented. Schedules and classes tend to be formal and rigidly organized in many secondary schools, with considerable emphasis on academic standards, homework, and grades (rather than personal growth). Emphasis on standardized test achievements and school discipline can be expected. The homeroom that many students have experienced in the elementary school years ceases to exist in most high schools, except as an administrative checkpoint. As a result, at a time when students are accelerating their development as social beings, the secondary school structure often tends to inhibit this growth and development by placing them in a series of formal, academically oriented subject-matter class experiences. At the same time, many schools fail to provide students with an organized scheduled group (such as homeroom) where they might develop social skills and attitudes. This suggests a challenge to the

subject-matter teacher and the counselor to work cooperatively to incorporate social development experiences into the academic program.

- School spirit, or esprit de corps, is usually more evident in secondary schools than in any other educational institution. This school spirit is usually reflected in the quest for winning athletic teams, championship bands, and other public indications of excellence. Often the competition among students for participation in significant school events is keen. Social divisions may often arise between those who have made it and those who have not in terms of these activities. On the positive side, however, school spirit in competitive activities can often be a potential factor in motivating students to remain in school, making them seek higher academic achievements, and promoting pride in the school. Recently, frequent suggestions and efforts have been made to increase the visibility of academic competition as well.

- The school principal is the single most influential person in the secondary school setting. Decisions, policy development, and practices all emanate or are subject to the approval of the school principal. Unlike the elementary school principal, the secondary principal is frequently assisted by several assistant principals, supervisors, department heads, and specialty chairs. In addition, probably no other person is so significant in establishing the tone or atmosphere of the school and its inhabitants.

Although the adolescent and the adolescent's school share many characteristics, wide variations also prevail between them. Counseling programs in secondary schools seem to reflect these ambivalences as counselors engage in many of the same basic activities but within a variety of organizational structures. Figures 3-1 through 3-3 present three of the more traditional organizational models of school counseling programs. Bigger schools in larger school systems may have resource specialists and specialized services (computer and data processing, test scoring) available in the administrative offices of the school system. These resources are available to supplement the efforts of the local building counselors. Small schools may often have to share counseling and other specialized personnel. These personnel may operate out of the central administrative offices of the school system and be available on certain days to each school that shares their assignment.

Counselors in school settings at elementary, middle, and secondary school levels should be aware of the National Standards for School Counseling Programs, adopted by the American School Counselor Association and published in 1998 (Dahir, Sheldon, & Valiga, 1998). These standards facilitate student development in three broad content areas:

- academic development
- career development
- personal/social development

The Standards are outlined here:

I. Academic Development

Standard A: Students will acquire the attitudes, knowledge, and skills that contribute to effective learning in school and across the life span.

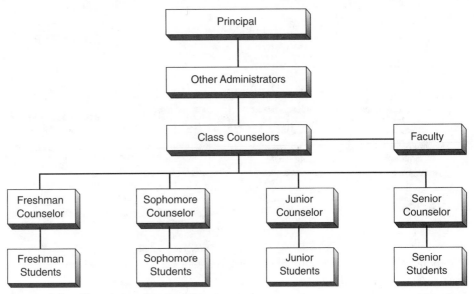

Figure 3-1 Class counselor model.

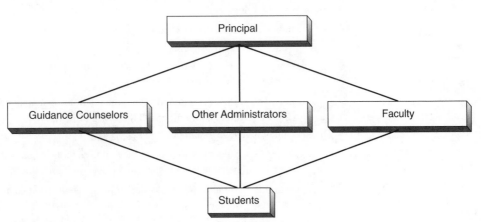

Figure 3-2 Guidance counselor (generalist) model.

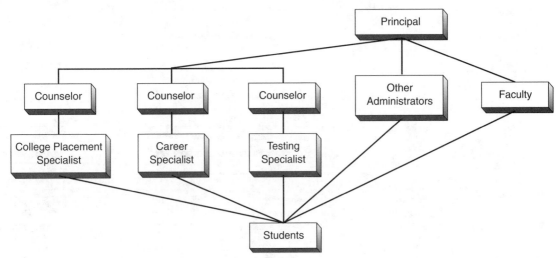

Figure 3-3 Guidance counselor (specialist) model.

Standard B: Students will complete school with the academic preparation essential to choose from a wide range of substantial postsecondary options, including college.

Standard C: Students will understand the relationship of academics to the world of work, and to life at home and in the community.

II. Career Development

Standard A: Students will acquire the skills to investigate the world of work in relation to knowledge of self and to make informed career decisions.

Standard B: Students will employ strategies to achieve future career success and satisfaction.

Standard C: Students will understand the relationship among personal qualities, education and training, and the world of work.

III. Personal/Social Development

Standard A: Students will acquire the attitudes, knowledge, and interpersonal skills to help them understand and respect self and others.

Standard B: Students will make decisions, set goals, and take necessary action to achieve goals.

Standard C: Students will understand safety and survival skills.

(Dahir, Sheldon, & Valiga, 1998, p. 6)

Counseling in Institutions of Higher Education

Although the popular view from the ivory tower seems to most frequently focus on the football stadium, the attractive students, and sometimes (but rarely) the distinguished professor, a serious look at most college and university campuses confirms the existence of counselors and programs of counseling and other student services—or student development

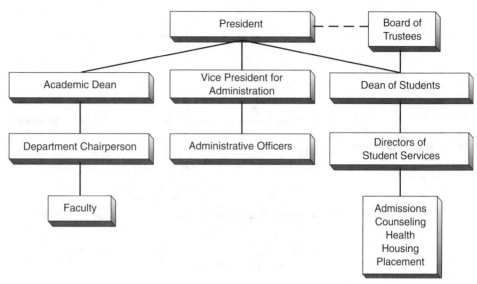

Figure 3-4 Organization chart for a four-year college.

as it is now called. These programs are as unusual or as traditional as the institutions they represent. The burgeoning junior and community college movement appears to be developing programs that often suggest an open marriage between elements of secondary school counseling programs and traditional university student personnel services programs. Four-year colleges and universities maintain, although often with interesting innovations, programs based on traditional student personnel services models—programs in which counseling services are frequently provided through campus counseling centers or clinics, residential counselors, and career counseling offices. Today, the field continues to grow.

Figure 3-4 illustrates an organizational chart for a four-year college with counseling services provided as a part of the student services of the college or university. Figure 3-5 displays counseling services as a unit of a large university program.

THE ECOLOGY OF THE SCHOOL

Environment or ecology is important in our lives. We select vacation spots because of their beauty and/or climate; we decide where we want to build our home based on its reputation as a nice, quiet neighborhood; flowers are planted and landscaping is done at our place of employment; all are examples of our recognizing the importance and impact of environments on our life.

In discussing the ecology of the school, we are, in fact, examining the climate of the school, its environment. Ecological psychology has, since the early pronouncements of Kurt Lewin (1936), stressed the importance of the environment on individual behavior. The growing field of specialists in ecological psychology are concerned with how individuals perceive, are shaped by, value, influence, and are influenced by their environments.

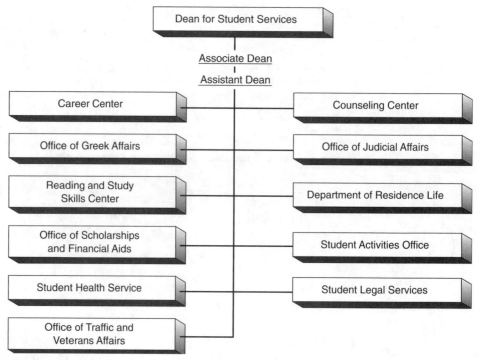

Figure 3-5   Organization chart for student service division in a large university.

Certainly, the school is a significant environment and one that will influence the behavior, values, and plans of its student inhabitants. However, Conyne (1987) notes that only recently has increased interest in the application of this viewpoint to the practice of counseling been noted. Within this context, school counselors can improve their understanding of their student-client population by recognizing the following concepts:

1. Environment is a significant influence on behavior. Therefore, school counselors must understand this influence if they are to predict, modify, or prevent undesirable behaviors in their student clientele.
2. Because stable, long-term settings such as the school pass on expectations and norms for behaviors, values, and attitudes, school counselors, with their teaching colleagues, must plan accordingly.
3. Environmental understandings provide a basis for the development of meaningful prevention programs.
4. Students, like all others, strive for optimal environments in which to develop adequate self-concepts, fulfill their needs, and maximize their potential. Such settings provide supportive relationships and a climate that is motivational and enjoyable.

Influential environmental factors include weather, population density, cleanliness, accessibility, housing, natural resources, attractiveness, and such other aspects as educational, health, economic, spiritual, cultural, and leisure facilities.

Schools and students cannot be understood on the basis of records and data (test scores, grades, attendance, etc.) alone. They are performers on the stage of life. To understand the roles they are playing, we must understand the setting. Ecological psychology thus helps us better understand students by understanding their psychological interplay with their environment.

From an ecological perspective, then, we view students and their environments as being in a reciprocal relationship, with each mutually influencing the other, sometimes in subtle and sometimes in very obvious ways. Thus, in understanding clients, counselors seek to recognize the relevant ecological transactions between an individual and his or her life space.

FUTURE DIRECTIONS FOR SCHOOL
PROGRAMS OF COUNSELING

All of us engage in predicting the future. Much of our speculation on what lies ahead is, of course, short range—we predict that the weather will be better tomorrow, the price of gasoline will go up again next month, or the football team will be a winner next fall. Predicting the future is fun, but it is also risky, especially if one is bold enough to put these speculations into print. However, despite the many uncertainties attending even the most scientific efforts (and highly reputable scientific institutes are engaged in such studies today), we still read our horoscopes and annual New Year's predictions, have our palms read or handwriting analyzed, and note that books projecting the future often become bestsellers. Science fiction, books, movies, and television programs set in the distant future are especially popular with children and adolescents.

Although the high level of interest in knowing what the future holds for us and our societies does not appear to have diminished over the centuries, both the nature and need for future insights have undergone significant change. We have noted the emergence since World War II of a futuristic science, with an emphasis on scientific, data-based, and computer-assisted forecasting, and the development of organizations such as the Institute for the Future (Middletown, Connecticut), the World Future Society (formed in Washington, DC), and the Hudson Institute (Indianapolis, Indiana). The need for some form of reasonably accurate future forecasting has become increasingly evident.

One indicator that change will probably take place in a product, activity, or organization is strong and significant criticism of its present state. For example, public criticism of airline service has resulted in modest improvements in their services. Criticism of certain automotive products has resulted in correctional changes, and political criticism of public education has led to change initiatives.

We are already aware of the change that computers and technology have made on the way people are educated, and they will increasingly impact the schools of the future. (There is no suggestion, however, that the schools will not continue to have their important social education function—a function that cannot be learned via the computer but must be based on face-to-face interactions between and among individuals.)

Some indication of the extent of the technological invasion and its impact on today's student can be gleaned from a study by the National Center for Education Statistics (2000). This study indicated that 78% of students in grades 1 through 12 used the Internet at school, and 58% had computers in their homes. Nineteen percent of students use the Internet at home on a regular basis to take education courses or do research for school. Fifteen percent of the students use the Internet at home on a regular basis for e-mail (electronic mail).

Certainly in the midst of the rapid technological development predicted for the new millennium, it is quite probable that many individuals will become frustrated and discouraged at their inability to master both the technology and their future. Counselors must help their client populations recognize that technology is designed to improve lives rather than complicate them!

This new generation of counselors must also be computer competent and alert to the technological advancements of the information age that have implications for their practice. Distance education and multimedia approaches, among others, will dramatically influence new approaches to learning. Counselors will increasingly network via the Internet with counselors locally, nationally, and internationally to exchange ideas, solutions, and information.

Counselors must recognize and take advantage of the reality that the growth of the information industries means we will have a more informed society. Better information dissemination offers the opportunity to the counseling profession to inform all segments of society of their services and the means of accessing those services.

New curricular emphases will include increased attention to technological and vocational curricula, plus renewed attention to the arts. The schools may also stress the importance of environmental conservation. Increased international orientation may also be anticipated. A longer school day and school year may be part of future school systems in the United States. Finally, the schools are being envisioned as centers for lifelong learning.

As in the past, counselors will continue to counsel and consult and give attention to the career development needs of all populations. These needs, however, will be dramatically different from the one person—one career approach of the past as we view a century when individuals entering the workforce (with the exception of the professions) can anticipate three to seven distinctly different careers over their working lifetime. Many of these will require a return to educational settings, adapting to new technologies, and movement to new geographic locations. Counselors in all settings must assist their clients in becoming both adaptable and flexible if they are to maintain employment in the global workplace. Workers must be prepared for tomorrow's career world rather than yesterday's. It is also important to realize that counselors will be providing career assistance in nearly all settings in which they are employed, as many adults will be experiencing constant changes and turbulence in the world of work.

There will be increasing emphasis not only in schools but with adult populations as well on the prevention of such societal concerns as child and spouse abuse, substance abuse, AIDS and other human sexuality concerns. The increasing recognition that prevention programs are needed and are more promising than after-the-incident treatment of these social issues will present counselors with unprecedented opportunities to establish their uniqueness and value to society. Mental health counselors will have increased opportunities for consultation with businesses and industries as well as community organizations and groups. This consultation may focus on topics such as stress management, substance abuse, people abuse, decision making, and career planning.

As the United States becomes a more diverse and multicultural society in the generations ahead, counselors, as human relations experts, will again have unprecedented opportunities in every setting to take an active role in preventing prejudice by promoting multicultural understandings and teaching positive human relationship skills. We are, after all, experts in communication and human relations. As a result, we should be active in promoting positive and productive relationships among all racial, cultural, ethnic, and religious populations at all age levels.

Our workplaces will also be more diverse from an age standpoint, as the percentage of older workers will continue to increase. With increased longevity and improved health, people are working longer and retiring later. This trend is predicted to continue and retirement counseling as a specialty is beginning to emerge.

The urgent need for counselor involvement is further suggested by the recognition that although considerable progress has been made in legislative enactments and judicial decisions, much more remains to be accomplished at the levels of personal awareness, understanding, respect, and acceptance. The urgency for this progress is further highlighted when we note that an estimated 25% of our population are minorities. This proportion is projected to increase to 32% by 2010 and 47% by the year 2050. Here again, we note that the elimination of prejudice and the substitution of respect and understanding in human relations must begin in the school setting. To achieve this goal, counselors must be models of awareness, understanding, and acceptance.

Counseling for educational options will be greatly altered in the years immediately ahead because of the proliferation of new educational opportunities via the Internet. Distance learning is also promising to drastically alter educational traditions as individuals can now earn degrees with the click of a mouse or the use of a fax machine without ever setting foot in a classroom. Counselors of the 2000s will also be expected to be more professionally competent in assessing differing environments (e.g., community and school) and their impact on their clients.

Accountability mandates will demand increased counselor knowledge in the areas of measurement and standardized testing. The rapidly developing field of family therapy and specialty areas such as substance abuse counseling can also have a "spillover" influence on school counseling in the immediate decades ahead.

Additionally, the vast majority of homes with children in the United States will be either dual-career or single-parent homes. The implications of these new models of family life are many, not the least of which will be, What happens to the children? So far, there has been little planning to provide for these "latchkey" youth. Obviously, the failure to make adequate provisions guarantees disastrous consequences to both the individual and society. Counselors in all community settings should work together to develop comprehensive and effective programs for latchkey children. Whether dual-career or single-career, the family is, and always has been, critically important to the academic success of students. The family is the basic institution of our society and the one that has the longest period of impact on the individual. Parental conferences are significant, not only to the family/school relationship, but also to student behavior and achievement. All research data indicates that the significance of the home, plus major societal changes affecting the home, will stimulate the need for increased school/family relationships in the decades ahead.

We believe that school counselors of the future increasingly will be called on to engage in research in their settings to hasten the solutions to many constant youth problems such as those previously noted. Only through an all-out professional effort involving those on the scene can we hope to make real headway in dealing with these problems.

Another responsibility of schools in the future will be preparing students to enter a rapidly changing job market. If the United States is to continue to compete in the worldwide marketplace, American workers will need to be more highly trained than at present.

Schools will be responsible for preparing individuals who are adaptable and able to respond quickly to the changing requirements of new technologies as many workers' jobs will change dramatically and often in the span of just a few years. This means schools will train and retrain both youth and adults. Future workers will be displaced frequently, and they will be moving constantly from one occupation to another, thus needing periodic retraining because each new job will be different from the previous one.

One significant and factually recognized change in the counseling profession itself will be the new wave of counselors entering our profession as a majority of the NDEA (National Defense Education Act) trained counselors of the 1960s move into retirement. This, coupled with the increased nationwide demand for elementary school counselors, could result in an acceleration in employment opportunities for counselors in schools. Many states and counselor preparation programs are also revising their training requirements for counselors in schools, community agencies, and mental health facilities.

AN INTERNATIONAL PERSPECTIVE: COUNSELORS IN OTHER COUNTRIES

As counseling is a rapidly growing profession in the United States, it is also experiencing rapid growth in other countries. Canada, the United Kingdom, and the English-speaking islands close to the United States are all experiencing the growth of counseling services in schools. In the pages that follow, descriptions of a day in the life of school counselors from some of these places are presented. Note the similarities as well as the interesting contrasts with the daily routine of counselors in the United States.

COUNSELORS IN COMMUNITY AND AGENCY SETTINGS

Many of you may eventually consider employment as counselors in community, agency, or other nonschool professional situations. The purpose of this section is to acquaint you with the counselor's role and function in a variety of these settings. They include community and mental health agencies (as noted earlier in Tables 3-1 and 3-2), employment and rehabilitation agencies, correctional settings, and marriage and family practice. Pastoral counseling, gerontology counseling, and private practice are also discussed.

Insights into possible employment opportunities for counselors interested in marriage and family, and rehabilitation positions may be gained by examining Tables 3-11 and 3-12, which identify first-year job placements of graduates of such programs.

TRAINING PROGRAMS FOR COUNSELORS IN COMMUNITY AND AGENCY SETTINGS

The training of counselors for the various community and agency settings is very similar to the training of school counselors, and in the past there was little distinction in many master's degree programs with the possible exceptions of practicum and internship settings and a few specialized courses. However, new standards for the preparation of counselors in specialty

A DAY IN THE LIFE OF A GUIDANCE OFFICER IN AUSTRALIA*

As I reflect on my role as a guidance officer in Outback Queensland, Australia, I am struck by the uniqueness of my situation. Firstly, a school counsellor in Queensland, Australia, is not referred to as a school counsellor but a "Guidance Officer". Even more specifically, I perform the duties of a Senior Guidance Officer in the Longreach District which means in addition to providing guidance in schools, I coordinate a team of guidance officers and plan for services across the district.

There are four guidance officers or school counsellors in the Longreach District. We service a vast area with Longreach as our base. Longreach is approximately 800 miles from Brisbane, the capital city of Queensland, and has a population of about three thousand people. There are 23 schools in the district and each one of us has a number of schools which we service. We service three schools in Longreach and the remainder are in small rural towns across the district. Some visits are day trips and others are so far away that we are away for two or three days. We typically drive to most schools in department vehicles. Most of the vehicles are four-wheel drives as the roads are often narrow and when it rains become quite hazardous. It is not unusual to get bogged in the wet times or have to change a tyre on the very rough roads. There are some schools like Birdsville and Bedourie which are so remote that we are flown there in a twin-engine aeroplane. We typically go to those schools once or twice a term.

The schools which we service also vary in nature and size. Of the 23 schools in the district, at least half of them are what we call Teaching Principal Schools. As the name suggests the Principal is the teacher and is assisted by teacher aides. The school may have anywhere from five or six students to twenty students. The schools range from primary schools (preschool to year seven) to schools which have grades from preschool through to year twelve. The larger schools vary in size with the larger ones having about 250–300 students. There are only about 2,000 students in the district but spread over a vast area.

One of the schools in the Longreach District which is very unique in its delivery of education is the Longreach School of Distance Education, located in Longreach. I have had the privilege of working with students and their families from LSODE for three years. The school caters for students (preschool to year ten) who are unable to access the local school due to distance. The children typically live on cattle and sheep properties or "stations" and receive their education from a distance. Teachers work from the central location and provide instruction over the telephone or via a radio hence its former name "School of the Air". The students are taught at home by home tutors [usually their mothers]. The students come into Longreach for mini-school for a week, twice a year, and also meet for what is called a "cluster" which occurs in a central town closer to home once a term. Teachers go to the clusters and provide an action-packed day for the students. It is an opportunity for the children to have social interaction with their peers rather than just their voices over the air every day.

At first I wondered how I would provide a guidance service to students in a non-traditional setting. The motto of the school is "Effort Conquers Distance" so I have tried to stretch the limit in terms of providing guidance. I typically write in the "Bush Telegraph", the school newsletter which reaches over 200 families. I try to provide information on issues such as communication, self-esteem, protective behaviours, mental health, and other topical issues. I have worked with groups of students when they come in for minischool on social skills, communication, career planning, et cetera. Counselling is more difficult but once the relationship is established, I rely on telephone contact between visits. One of the highlights of working at LSODE has been "home visits." I often spend the day driving two or three hours to visit the family on a property. The child may be experiencing some difficulty with his/her learning and given the learning environment is at home on the property, I appreciate the opportunity to observe the child in his/her own setting. . . . I am often shown the family pets, the new "four wheeler" used for mustering, and am treated to the hospitality so often seen in Outback Queensland. It is a wonderful opportunity for me to chat to the parents in a non-threatening environment and give support to the home tutor who is typically the mother and has many roles in the management of the family and property. I am always tired at the end of the day, but it's a very satisfying feeling.

A large part of our work as guidance officers in Queensland is the assessment of children who are having difficulties in learning. There is a formal process called "Ascertainment" which aims to provide varying levels of learning support for children. Guidance officers provide much of the data for the ascertainment process by way of assessment, case conferences and observations. Unlike the process in the USA, where psychologists test children, guidance officers are responsible for giving cognitive assessment to children [in Australia]. Assessments and report writing take up a large percentage of our time. Working with the family and preparing parents for the ascertainment process is also quite time consuming but necessary for a successful outcome.

Retention of students to year twelve is a major thrust in Queensland. We are aiming to raise the rate to 88%. We are having a Career Fair this term with exhibitors coming from universities, rural colleges, government departments, employment agencies, et cetera. It is an opportunity for students to get a broader view of career prospects. I have been very busy planning for this activity in collaboration with the Marketing Manager at the Longreach Pastoral College where the career fair will be held. As guidance officers we are aiming to work with every year eleven and twelve student towards the development of individual career plans.

Counselling is another key part of the guidance officer's role. The issues we work with are similar to those in other areas. A limitation to our work is the infrequency of our visits. Children who require more intensive work are referred to a visiting team of specialists. A group of specialists—Paediatrician, Child Psychologist, and Child Psychiatrist—visit Longreach every term. We work very closely with the team and enjoy a collaborative approach. We provide detailed reports for them and provide follow-up between visits.

Guidance Officers in Outback Queensland have a varied role. We work from preschool through to year twelve so require a range of skills and expertise. Not everyone wants to live in western Queensland so we have difficulty recruiting guidance officers. This makes the load heavier for the other guidance officers.

Given the type of schools we service, we develop close links with principals and parents. I have found the experience very rewarding as the context is unique—vast spaces, rural culture and wonderfully warm and generous country people.

*Contributed by Denise Patton-King, Ph.D., Outback Queensland, Australia

GUIDELINES FOR A GUIDANCE COUNSELLOR IN MT. ISA, AUSTRALIA NORTHERN TERRITORY BORDER*

Seven program goals guide the activities of guidance counsellors for this district. They are:

1. Quality curriculum programmes for all students
2. Effective teaching
3. Improving learning outcomes for all students
4. A skilled, confident and responsible work force
5. Confidence in public education
6. Adoption of technology to enhancing learning, teaching, and management
7. A safe, supportive and productive environment

In the pursuit of these program goals, data will be collected and analyzed in conjunction with other data to identify trends, areas of need, areas of professional development required, and the setting of future directions. In general, there are two types of data to be collected: client service data and outcome data. The role of a guidance officer can be divided into five areas: (a) proactivity; (b) reactivity; (c) crisis intervention; (d) school development; and (e) administration. When developing the school's guidance programme, consideration will be given to the following:

· core duties (i.e., essential activities)
· supplementary activities (i.e., to meet the specific needs of the school)
· appropriate means of evaluating the guidance program
· reporting relationships and procedures
· changing priorities throughout the year
· responding to unforeseen demands (e.g., critical incidents, systemic demands)

In conclusion, we would note that the guidance officers complete an annual operation plan that is submitted to their line manager at the base school. This plan covers their general duties, timelines, and budgeting information.

*This information has been abstracted from *The Guidance Program Information Handbook*, ISIS, Burnett District (Queensland, Australia), adapted from the Handbook originally written by Ms. Carol Beechey.

COUNSELING AND GUIDANCE IN SCOTTISH SCHOOLS: BACKGROUND INFORMATION*

Formal 'guidance' structures were introduced within Scottish secondary schools in 1970 with the appointment of 'guidance teachers.' Each guidance teacher has responsibility, on average, for the pastoral welfare of approximately 150 students, aged between 12 and 18 years. Guidance teachers tend not to be specialist counsellors, but are, in fact, subject teachers who take on additional responsibilities for guidance. A typical guidance teacher will spend approximately half the week teaching her specialist subject and, in the time remaining, will contribute to the work of the subject department as well as involving herself in guidance. Guidance responsibilities fall into three main areas: curricular guidance, vocational guidance and personal guidance.

The guidance teacher will monitor students' progress and provide counselling support at times of transition, such as the end of Year 2, when important course choice decisions have to be made. She will help her students to prepare for the major transition from school to tertiary education or the world of work. Her students will learn to trust her and will discover that she is someone they can talk to, who will listen without offering criticism or judgment and who will support them when they face major and difficult decisions. She will know each students' parents and siblings at the school and will encourage a free flow of communication between school and home. She will be involved in the delivery of the school's personal and social education programme (PSE), incorporating health education, careers education and lifeskills. In addition, she will be the first point of contact for outside agencies seeking reports and references and she will liaise very closely with the visiting educational psychologist, social workers, health specialists, police, employers and various community groups.

The fact that a guidance teacher is both teacher and counsellor is at once an advantage and a disadvantage. It is a disadvantage insofar as the demands on her time and energy are considerable and she has to work extra hard to play a full part within her subject department and retain her credibility as a teacher. Her teaching commitment limits the time available for pastoral activities. However, being a teacher with guidance responsibilities enhances her credibility with students, parents, and, not least, colleagues. She is in every sense involved in the life of the school: its academic life, its social life, its pressures and its frustrations. She is seen as someone who understands and who often mediates on the students' behalf, with other students, with teachers or even with the students' parents.

*Contributed by Bob Cook, Head of Resource Development, Department of Education and Cultural Services, West Dunbartonshire Council, Scotland

'TAKE TIME'*
SCHOOL STUDENTS COUNSELLING SERVICE
ABERDEEN, SCOTLAND
AN OPEN DOOR

NEW ROLE

My role is a new one within our Education Authority: a full-time, School Students Counsellor, on-site, dedicated to working with students who choose to refer themselves. I have been seconded for a period of twenty three months from my Guidance post in another school to set up this service. My background is in teaching; alongside this, I am in advanced integrative psychotherapy training, preparing for examination.

'TAKE TIME' is a two-year project supported by funding from the Scottish Executive Excellence Fund: a fund to support the raising of standards and the promotion of social inclusion in Scottish schools. The progress of the project is monitored through regular Steering Group meetings; the evaluation of the project is managed by the Educational Psychology Department, Aberdeen City Education Department.

I work with students aged 8–17 years, in one large secondary school and a number of primary schools in an area of social deprivation in the city. I am also available in the community centres, out-of-school-hours—dependent on the student's individual choice. The aims of the service are as follows:

· To create a safe environment where young people can explore their thoughts, feelings and behaviours.
· To create a self-referral system which gives young people options of where and when to meet.
· To foster self-confidence in young people.
· To encourage self-awareness, problem-solving skills and a growth towards autonomy in the young people.
· To encourage open communication between the counsellor and staff and/or parents, while respecting the confidences of each young person.

Students refer themselves, sometimes with the help of a friend, a family member, a teacher, their Guidance teacher. Parental permission is sought for working with primary students, a requirement I explain to the young people who come to me. Family members or carers can also make arrangements to see me to help to clarify what I do before giving permission. We may agree to set up a further meeting to discuss *their* thoughts and feelings once I have been working with the young person for a time—if this would be helpful to the young person concerned. These agreements are open to discussion with the young person and respectful of the confidentiality working with me carries with it. Some students actively want my intervention with another student or an adult. We spend time clarifying what they want to happen with that intervention and what our roles are to be.

THE COUNSELLING SESSION

We discuss what counselling is, including confidentiality and Child Protection issues, what their expectations are, and what brought them to see me. In the course of our first session together, we make an agreement about how we will work together, when and where we will meet. This contract provides the structure for our time together, encourages mutuality and review, and models a possible way to approach problems. My experience shows that young people respond to this structure given that it is balanced by my recognition of their concerns.

Building a relationship can be hard for many of the young people I work with. They may have experienced a significant absence of appropriate care and have developed strong defences. In these cases, we work slowly together, respecting those defences, which have been so essential to survival. The use of play materials like puppets, Play Doh, coloured pens or sand tray can provide valuable options for communicating without the apparent pressure of face-to-face contact. Others students may come with a specific issue, which can be resolved in a few sessions. Depending on the nature of the issue brought, and the needs of the young person, I may show him/her a model to illustrate what we are discussing—e.g., the Transactional Analysis diagram 'the drama triangle' which represents what can happen in friendships or families. This can provide a 'short-hand' way into further discussions.

Current national research pointing to worrying levels of depression in young people may be supported by our findings so far, that anxiety about their families has the highest incidence in presenting problems across the age-range of our project. Amongst the students I have seen so far, this seems to be connected to a number of issues: complicated relationships within the family, inconsistent care arrangements, conflict within the family or between divorced or separated parents, addiction of one or more family members, loss of a significant, secure career. Bleak as many of these issues are, many young people have developed powerful survival strategies which have allowed them to get on with life. Sometimes they come to me when these strategies are no longer working or are now holding them back.

GETTING KNOWN

Taking part in Circle Time or Personal and Social Education classes, early in the term gives me an opportunity to introduce myself to students and encounter them in a group setting. I am careful to describe my role within the community and to encourage students to clarify how my role differs from that of other people who will support them. This is especially true of the role of Guidance teacher who has a multitude of functions within the secondary school: to teach; deliver social education programmes; provide career guidance; negotiate timetables; liase with parents and outside agencies; write reports, et cetera. Added to these is the responsibility to provide pastoral care for a specific group of young people.

Going around the school, open to contact, sitting with an open door before and after school, break-times and lunch-times also has encouraged students to make contact with me. Some young people come regularly at these times, individually or in a group, seeking support. They bring their lunch, their friends—we may even go for a walk. They tell stories about what they've done, share jokes in a light and safe time before afternoon classes begin. They have an investment in this service and like to check-out from time to time that I will be around for another year. My room has been set-up to be a safe and welcoming environment, distinct from the bustle of the rest of the school. Students bring pictures to put on the wall and quickly notice anything new. One quiet student brought a wind-chime to claim her place there. Others, often senior students, acknowledge me with the barest of facial gestures in public places and come to see me discreetly.

A TYPICAL DAY

Each day is different in its balance; however, the main thread running through each is the one-to-one contact with students—a rich and varied experience. A day usually involves eight to ten scheduled sessions with any number of other, informal contacts as I move around the schools. In secondary school, sessions usually last for 40 minutes—a neat time slot for the school timetable; in primary school, sessions are more usually thirty minutes. In each context, there is some flexibility to respond to emergency situations.

Contact with staff usually takes place before school begins as this seems to suit staff best. When other agencies are involved, we will organise meetings during class time, and cover is organised for the teacher concerned. Getting to know staff has been important to my being accepted as part of each school's team, albeit a specialist who is independent of other school structures. Due to current demands on teacher time, we have not been able to participate in more than a few, short, in-service sessions. However, in day to day contact, informal chats as we go about our work, we continue to build the trusting relationships which are so essential to the well-being and progress of all within the school.

Class teacher, Guidance staff, school nurse or doctor, educational psychologist, school manager, social worker, parent or carer—any of these might wish to raise a concern about a young person with me. Sometimes, this leads to me working with the willing student; at other times, the student is not ready to look at the issues identified by others. Consultation may lead to contact with another agency or, an equally important outcome, a confirmation that what is currently happening for that student is appropriate and needs to continue.

In my turn, I take my concerns to a meeting with my supervisor. We review my cases and the progress of aspects of the service for one hour, every two or three weeks. Alongside this, steering group meetings are scheduled every four to six weeks.

Other regular commitments include parents evenings when parents/carers can meet me; evening sessions at youth clubs when young people can request individual or small group time with me; network meetings to update other interested staff on how we are progressing; meetings with other mental health services to monitor changes in referral patterns, et cetera.

THE FUTURE

· In the coming session, I begin to run groups:

The primary begins first with a group of primary 6 and primary 7 boys. 'How we get on with others' will look at what our responses are when we're in a group, what we do with the feelings and options for change.

In the secondary school, we hope to run a personal development group for seniors to improve their interpersonal skills, prior to launching a new 'buddy' scheme for junior pupils.

· The interim report on the project will be produced and distributed to interested parties. The final report will follow in 2002.
· The evaluation process will continue with a satisfaction questionnaire and a series of focus groups involving students and staff. These will add to the data already gathered through questionnaires to staff and students *before* the project started and will be further supplemented by the responses to the same questionnaire *after* the allotted time is completed.

I anticipate that, in the drive to grow and develop, students will continue to come through that open door, close it behind them, sit down and 'take time' to explore the thoughts, feelings or behaviours which are keeping them 'stuck'.

"It helps me to talk and not to compress my feelings."
Secondary student, March 2001.

"I can't tell you how much appreciation Mrs. M has given me and I am sure much other people like her appreciation."
Primary student, June 2001.

* 'Take Time' was contributed by Ms. Sandra Mojsiewicz, a School Students Counsellor for the Aberdeen City Council Education Department in Aberdeen, Scotland.

A TYPICAL DAY: GUIDANCE TEACHER*

The skill in being a guidance teacher in a Scottish secondary school consists of the ability to sustain an often precarious juggling act between the demands of a fairly full teaching commitment and the pastoral care of approximately 160 students.

I teach English to students from S1 (age 12 years) to S6 (age 17/18 years) and my subject carries a particularly heavy load of preparation and marking. Workload is particularly challenging when, for example, reports are due for any year group and I must first establish grades and write reports for my English students and then collate all the reports for my guidance group and write a comment on each. Another difficult period is in the autumn term (fall) when I give considerable time to helping students complete applications for university while also having to prepare my English students for their prelim exams. This can be a very stressful experience.

A typical day recently included the following:

8:15 A.M. Check memos from year heads and teachers regarding concerns about any of my students, and from office staff regarding parental phone calls explaining absence.

9:00 A.M. Registration, make the rounds of all my guidance groups (five in number), checking on attendance and being available to speak to anyone who needs to see me.

9:10–10:00 A.M. "Higher" English class.

10:05–10:25 A.M. Counselling S5 student experiencing difficulty with chemistry and wishing to drop the subject.

10:25–10:50 A.M. Attendance at Joint Assessment Team for discussion with educational psychologist, social worker, head teacher and year head of students giving cause for concern.

10:50–11:05 A.M. Break for coffee; colleagues take chance to update me on various issues involving my students.

11:05–12:00 noon S1 English class

12:00–12:10 P.M. Discussion with chemistry teacher regarding S5 student who spoke to me earlier.

12:15 P.M. Telephone call from parent concerned that his daughter is being bullied.

12:25–12:55 P.M. Investigation of bullying issue with this student and others involved. Write up this incident for student's file and copy to year head.

1:00–1:20 P.M. Lunchtime supervision of students in social areas.

1:20–1:45 P.M. Lunch

1:45–2:40 P.M. S3 English class

2:45–3:35 P.M. Writing report on student who has been referred to the Reporter to the Children's Panel (a statutory body serving as an informal 'court' for children who have offended or are at risk). This is a time-consuming and exacting, but extremely important exercise, which will often have to be finished at home.

3:35–3:45 P.M. End of school day. Signing 'record of work' and 'behaviour' cards and briefly discussing the day's progress with individual students;

3:45–5:00 P.M. Catching up on phone calls and paperwork; writing up phone calls, incidents and records of discussions; filing materials in students' records (clerical support has been erratic because of staff shortages).

An average of two hours spent in the evening marking students' work, preparing for the next day and catching up on paperwork.

* Contributed by Ms. Rosemary Cook, Assistant Principal Teacher of Guidance, Gourock High School, Inverclyde Council, Scotland

A DAY IN THE LIFE OF A SCHOOL COUNSELOR IN HONG KONG*

I have been a counselor for adolescents and their families for more than 10 years. During this period, I have made every effort to reach out to parents, teachers, and social workers as well as many other professionals who are concerned with the well-being of young people. I have found that support systems, especially the family, have great impact upon the development of adolescents.

Early in the morning, while I was walking toward the school, a cluster of students passed by. They hesitated to greet me. It is no surprise that being a counselor, I present an objective figure to the students and maintain a certain distance with them in the school's daily life. Therefore, if they need to see me when they are in need, they are able to present a true self and do not need to react to my expectations. However, I would break this principle if students actively come close to me.

I started the day by checking my schedule to find out the time of appointments. At that moment, a student squeezed into my room and immediately closed the door. She asked if I could offer her an alternate time-slot for an interview as she wanted to cancel the appointment she had previously made. She had been my client for a year and was accustomed to making appointments with me. By the way, she still kept our interviews a secret and feared that her friends might tease her.

It was almost time for the morning assembly. I hurried to the playground where the students line up every morning. From the far end of the corridor, I saw a young guy waving his hand passionately. I guessed there was another teacher behind me and the guy was greeting him. I turned back and found nobody there. Then I recognized that he was the one I met the day before. He was referred to me because he had been found to steal the wallet of his schoolmate. In that session, he looked confused and anxious. I gave him an empathic response. While he felt that he was being understood, he told me of the frustration he felt concerning his academic failure. His dreams were gone. I did encourage him to keep his dreams. Just having connected with him once, I wondered about his treating me like an old friend.

Before the first appointment of the day, I had some time to prepare materials for the parent workshop scheduled for the next evening. At this time, a teacher came to me urgently and asked me to give a hand.

Ann, who had a wrist-slashing problem, came for counseling last year. From this school term, she did not happen to have an act of self-injuring anymore. As I opened the door of the interview room, Ann, like a child of three, was sitting on the floor, yelling and striking herself with her fists. The teacher told me that a conflict between Ann and a teacher had triggered Ann's hysterical behavior. In fact, her hysterical behavior intensified the tension of the relationship with her teachers. She was labeled a difficult student. In my experience, lots of the hostility and the anger of a teenager like Ann often indicates family problems. It may be partially true that underneath the "bad" or "mad" teenager is a "sad" person.

When I came toward Ann, I tried to hold her shoulder and grasped her hands, stopping her self-hurting gesture. She claimed that she was faint and she would like to lie down on the floor. I understood that if I could not insist that she get to her feet at once, it would be harder for me to get control of the situation. Ann and I had built up a trusting relationship previously. I spoke to her in a firm and steady, but caring voice. She finally followed my instructions and sat in a chair. Thus, through the process of listening and responding, I tried to reconstruct her behavior, so that she could act like an adult again. Ann was able to gain insight. She expressed that she did not know how to relate to the teacher. After the session, she decided to try to talk to the teacher again.

I feel tremendous relief and am full of hope when I am able to get parents to join the sessions with their children. In the afternoon, the mother of a student made a call to me. She told me that her husband agreed to join the session, but the interview had to be arranged in late evening. Of course, I would not reject her request because it was a great chance to get the absent-father involved, although I would have another long day.

Ted and his parents arrived right on time. They took their seats in the interview room with some awkwardness. Each of them seemed to make an effort not to sit too close to one another. In the session, Ted's mother complained all the time and expressed her disappointment about her son. Ted was not submissive to her and grasped his chance to show his disagreement and argue with her. Ted's father listened quietly and he sometimes spoke a few words to show that he allied with his wife. However, Ted's mother did not appreciate him and started to blame him. She accused that he was a silent man and she could not know him much. She seemed to face the ups and downs of life by herself only. Her husband only concentrated on his work. This was typically a triangular relationship. The underlying problem of parenting was the problem of the marriage and the relationship between the husband and wife.

It was important for me to know their family organization, then I could plan the intervention in a more successful way. Finally, after lots of tears and complaints, I came up with a contract with Ted's family. They were willing to come again. It came to the end of the day. Even though I felt exhausted, I had to prepare myself for another new day.

* This description in the life of a school counselor was written by Agnes Yuk-yin Ho, who has been working in the counseling center of a youth organization as well as in secondary schools. She is presently the school counselor of China Holiness Church Living Spirit College.

THE DAILY WORK OF A SECONDARY SCHOOL COUNSELING TEACHER IN HONG KONG*
DAILY ROUTINE

Counseling Role

- Usually arrive at 7:40 A.M. and leave at 6:30 P.M.
- Walk around the playground during the morning assembly to welcome students and identify any drastic changes in them so as to show care and concern for them
- Share with students in some sessions of the morning assembly to create a loving, encouraging, appreciative, and helpful learning environment in school
- Pay attention to those usually late for school and show concern for them, then cooperate with disciplinary teachers to explore their reasons for being tardy and assist them to overcome their difficulties
- Work with disciplinary teachers to help students in overcoming their difficulties with behavioral problems
- Answer phone calls from parents who are in need of help
- Discuss preventive programs with the social workers of different organization directly or by telephone
- Cooperate as a partner of the disciplinary team leader to plan preventive and proactive programs for strengthening students' self-control and self-esteem
- Attend meetings with core members of the administrative committee to discuss issues of the school as a whole
- Talk to parents who would like to improve parenting skills in helping their children
- Discuss with teachers concerned to identify students' problems at an early stage and to decide if some students need counseling service and to make referral

- Refer students who are having severe learning, emotional, social, and behavioral problems to relevant professionals for counseling and therapeutic service
- Follow-up counseling cases with school social worker, teachers, or parents
- Meet with educational psychologists, inspectors of the education department, parents, and subject or form teachers to follow up on the individual educational plan of the inclusive hearing-impaired students
- Discuss preventive programs and group work with the school social worker and the school counselor or team members to help students develop a better understanding of themselves and raise their awareness of feelings and develop skills in handling emotions
- Supervise and evaluate the work of the school social worker and the school counselor
- Nominate students for different types of awards to help them build up self-confidence
- Plan and implement developmental activities with students for some primary school students to enhance their self-esteem and confidence
- Prepare preventive drug abuse program for a session of the student assembly to promote desirable learning and social behavior
- Chair the counseling meeting discussing programs and cases throughout the school year to enhance the whole-person development of students
- Conduct periodic evaluation on guidance work delivered to ensure students' and teachers' current needs are catered for
- Organize an "Appreciation Day" to create an encouraging, loving, and supporting atmosphere for the whole school
- Coordinate the "Orientation Day" and program for newcomers
- Draft proposals on the program of volunteer work for students, helping them to develop empathy and concern for the community
- Attend or conduct parent training groups in the evening
- Attend or conduct class or form meetings to discuss issues of students in a class or the form as a whole to understand their needs or difficulties and give guidance advice
- Work with the career team leader to provide individual/group guidance and counseling to assist students to understand their interests, abilities, needs, and priorities in relation to further education, vocational training, and job opportunities
- Share the needs of students with all school personnel through formal and informal paths
- Incorporate the needs of students into both formal and informal curriculum
- Make use of community resources and integrate them into counseling programs or groups
- Develop the guidance teachers' awareness of and common belief in the principles and practices of guidance and counseling

- Keep systematic records of cases handled and compile statistical information to provide insights of the trends of students' problems and their contributing factors
- Attend various counseling seminars or training courses after school or on weekends

Teaching Role

- Teach the lessons in different classes (this is the major part of my work)
- Prepare exercises, tests, and examination papers and mark them
- Organize activities of volunteer work for students
- Supervise students who need help in doing homework or projects
- Deal with students who have complaints among peers
- Attend regular meetings of the academic committee
- Chair the regular meetings of life education in planning the curriculum and monitoring the instruction work among form teachers
- Integrate guidance elements into formal and informal curriculum
- Encourage the organization of class activities to promote and enhance class spirit so as to develop a sense of belonging for students in school
- Design the teaching schedule and the plans for subject teachers of life education and social and civic education
- Prepare teaching schedule and plans for geography class
- Improve my teaching by attending seminars of new teaching strategies or thinking skills
- Keep up with the current changes in educational policy or reform
- Attend various training courses after school or on weekends.

* Ms. Lydia To is the counseling mistress in China Holiness Church Living Spirit College. She is the head of the counseling team and is responsible for planning and implementing the developmental and preventive programs and remedial activities for her students. She is also the panel chairperson of life education responsible for planning the curriculum and coordinating the teaching progress of 26 form teachers. Other than these duties, she also has to teach geography for the upper grades (forms) and social and civic education for the lower grades (forms). Having a glance at her positions in the school, it may be anticipated that, in addition to her role of a guidance teacher, her teaching and administrative duties are both very heavy. This narrative indicates some of her varied activities.

Table 3-11 Job setting first year after completing entry-level marriage and family counseling/therapy preparation program.

Job Placement After Graduation	1996 Study		1999 Study	
	NPR	Placement for All Graduates (Percent)	NPR	Placement for All Graduates (Percent)
Advanced graduate programs	59	13	41	12
Managed care	40	9	28	11
Private practice/agency	60	26	37	19
Public agency	67	41	47	52
Other	4	0	12	4
School				
Elementary	3	0	5	2
Middle	4	0	5	1
Secondary	4	0	3	0
Higher education student affairs	25	9	2	1
Total		98		102

NPR = Number of programs responding

1996 Study—N = 112 programs surveyed.

1999 Study—N = 110 programs surveyed.

Source: Copyright © 2000. From *Counselor Preparation 1999–2001: Programs, Faculty, Trends* (10th ed., p. 63), by J. W. Hollis, with T. A. Dodson. Reproduced by permission of Taylor & Francis, Inc., http://www.routledge-ny.com

Table 3-12 Job settings first year after completing entry level rehabilitation counseling program.

Job Placement After Graduation	1996 Study		1999 Study	
	NPRP	Percent of All Graduates	NPRP	Percent of All Graduates
Advanced graduate programs	47	7	29	5
Managed care	30	5	22	7
Private practice/agency	56	28	37	20
Public agency	64	51	41	60
Other	1	0	13	6
School—Elementary	0		2	0
Middle	3	0	3	0
Secondary	4	0	3	0
Higher education student affairs	25	8	8	1
		99		99
	N = 12		N = 42	

NPRP = Number of programs reporting placement

Source: Copyright © 2000. From *Counselor Preparation 1999–2001: Programs, Faculty, Trends* (10th ed., p. 77), by J. W. Hollis, with T. A. Dodson. Reproduced by permission of Taylor & Francis, Inc., http://www.routledge-ny.com

areas as officially indicated by appropriate professional organizations have resulted in an increase in specialized courses. In some training programs counselors may be trained in separate departments or in programs with distinctly different emphases. Even greater distinctions will be noted at the doctoral degree level, where preparation tends to focus on the anticipated professional work setting.

The Council for Accreditation of Counseling and Related Educational Programs (CACREP, 2001) specifies that community agency counselor preparation programs will require a minimum of 48 semester or 72 quarter hours of graduate course work. This course work will include studies in each of eight common core areas: professional identity, social and cultural diversity, human growth and development, career development, helping relationships, group work, assessment, and research and program evaluation. In addition to the common core courses, curricular experiences and demonstrated knowledge and skills are required in (a) foundations of community counseling, (b) contextual dimensions of community counseling, and (c) knowledge and skill requirements for the practice of community counseling. A 600-hour internship in a community setting is also required.

Programs in mental health counseling are at the graduate level, with a minimum of 60 semester-hour or 90 quarter-hour credits. In addition to the core courses indicated above, additional course work is required in three specialty areas: (a) foundations of mental health counseling; (b) contextual dimensions of mental health counseling; and (c) knowledge and skill requirements for mental health counselors. A mental health counseling internship requires a minimum of 900-clock hours.

Programs in marital, couple, and family counseling/therapy require courses in the eight core areas plus course work in three additional areas: (a) foundations of marital, couple, and family counseling/therapy; (b) contextual dimensions of marital, couple, and family counseling/therapy; and (c) knowledge and skill requirements for marital, couple, and family counselor/therapists. A 600-clock hour internship is required.

Both training and on-the-job functioning are influenced by the provisions of the Community Mental Health Centers Act of 1963, which provided for the establishment of a network of mental health centers throughout the nation. Each center was to provide at least the five basic services of (a) in-patient care; (b) out-patient care; (c) partial hospitalization; (d) emergency care; and (e) consultation, education, and information.

Many counselors and managers in community mental health centers are Ph.D. graduates of counseling psychology programs. In addition to their preparation in individual and group counseling, their training programs typically include coursework in psychological measurement, research design, biological and cognitive and other bases of human behavior, intervention strategies and service delivery systems, plus course work leading to competence in an area of specialization.

Thus, as we proceed to examine the role of the counselor in a variety of community, agency, and institutional settings, we emphasize that these counselors deal with the developmental and growth needs of clients as well as the more traditional remedial and adjustment concerns.

THE IMPORTANCE OF LICENSURE

The movement toward licensure is one that, in the long run, will protect both the public and the profession. Licensure is particularly important to many professional counselors practicing in community agencies or private practices, in which client reimbursement is significant to the agency's or individual's fiscal wellness. This reimbursement, usually referred to as third-party payment, is made by insurance companies and Medicare for services rendered to clients by eligible (licensed) providers. The process of licensure in each state is established by legislative action. State licensure boards administer the legislated licensing program.

Currently, counseling psychologists may be credentialed in any of the 50 states. Minimally, to be eligible for such licensure, candidates must hold an earned doctorate in psychology, have completed a predoctoral internship, and have passed the national licensure examination and whatever special examination an individual state may require.

Professional counselors trained in programs of counselor education may currently secure licensure in 46 states and the District of Columbia. Although this process differs from state to state, it typically requires candidates to have an earned master's degree and often to have passed the National Board for Certified Counselors' National Counselor Examination. Graduates of programs accredited by CACREP may, in some instances, be eligible to take this examination upon completing their graduate training program, rather than having to acquire experience to become eligible.

COMMUNITY AND MENTAL HEALTH AGENCIES

Community mental health agencies provide counseling services for the general population within a specified geographic locale. Many community mental health agencies have been initiated under the provisions of the Community Mental Health Act of 1963, which provides initial funding for such centers that must be developed following the guidelines of the National Institute of Mental Health. These agencies were designed to provide preventive community mental health services. Typically, they offer inpatient and outpatient, emergency, and educational and consultation services. Many centers also provide partial hospitalization services, diagnostic services, and precare and aftercare in the community through programs of home visitations, foster home placement, and halfway houses.

Senator Edward M. Kennedy (1990) noted,

Experience has demonstrated that a number of key features must be included in any effective community-based program of care for the seriously mentally ill. These include the following:

1. Quantitative analysis of the population to be served, so that the number of people to be helped and their specific needs can be determined.
2. Case management, so that someone is responsible for coordinating and monitoring necessary services.
3. A program of support and rehabilitation to provide services appropriate for each client's age, functional level, and individual needs. Psychotherapy, regular social contact to assist reintegration into the community, vocational training, supervised work, and assistance in obtaining and keeping competitive employment should be available to adults, and an appropriate range of services should also be available to children. The goal is to enable individuals to function at the maximum feasible level.
4. Medical treatment and mental health care, available on a continuum from day hospitalization to periodic appointments, to regulate medication and monitor mental status.

5. Assistance to families who often provide the frontline care for the mentally ill in the community and who are often left to cope with the severe strains of mental illness without assistance from the society at large.
6. Housing services, ranging from half-way houses with staff in residence who provide continuous supervision to largely independent living. Outreach to the homeless mentally ill should be seen as an essential part of these services. (pp. 1238–1239)

Data in Table 3-13 show how agency counselors reported spending their professional time, with activities ranked from highest amount of time to lowest.

The Agency Team

In most community mental health agencies, counselors are employed as team members with other helping professionals. These typically include psychiatrists, clinical and counseling psychologists, and psychiatric social workers. Psychiatrists are usually considered to be the leaders of the team, inasmuch as they have a medical background and may perform physical examinations, prescribe drugs, and admit people to hospitals for the treatment of behavior abnormalities. In addition to basic medical training, certification as a psychiatrist typically requires 3 years of residency in a psychiatric institution plus 2 years of further practice.

Table 3-13   How practicing agency counselors spend their time.*

Activity	Agency
Individual counseling	1
Group counseling	8
Couples/family counseling	4.5
Crisis intervention	
Standardized test administration and/or interpretation	
Nonstandardized assessment (e.g., case studies, information gathering interviews, questionnaires)	6.5
Needs assessment (to determine priority needs of your target population)	6.5
Consultation activities	3
Case management	4.5
Dealing with managed care organizations (MCOs) as a provider (e.g., making application, precertification, concurrent review of cases, appealing decisions)	
Prevention activities	10
Clinical supervision activities	9
Administrative activities	2
Information dissemination: public communication and public relations	
Other	

* Based on a survey by Robert L. Gibson and Marianne H. Mitchell, 1997.

Counseling or clinical psychologists are prepared in programs that require a minimum of 3 academic years of full-time resident graduate study, plus a full year's internship in an appropriate setting. Although emphases in programs will vary somewhat from institution to institution and depend on whether the person is trained in a clinical or counseling psychology program, the psychologist receives general training in basic psychology, counseling and psychotherapy, psychological assessment, and psychological research.

Some contend that the difference between clinical and counseling psychology has never been entirely clear, but distinctions do exist. One distinction might be that clinical psychologists appear to work more frequently with behavioral abnormalities and personality reorganization, whereas counseling psychologists emphasize increased understanding of the adjustment problems of normal persons.

Psychiatric social workers are trained minimally to the master's degree level in 2-year programs. One year of this program is devoted to supervised internship in a clinical or hospital setting. Social workers are trained to help people experiencing economic or other problems. Often these people are being assisted through welfare and other programs. Psychiatric social workers, however, are more frequently found in hospital or community mental health settings. In such settings, they may gather data regarding patients and their families and often will work with the patient's family in assisting the client's adjustment. In many community mental health centers, psychiatric social workers may also conduct treatment of a nonmedical nature.

Counseling in the Agency Setting

What is it like to counsel in an agency setting? The following represents a day in the life of a licensed mental health counselor in Rangely, Colorado, working for Colorado West Regional Mental Health.

Counselors in community settings deal with extremely diverse populations and a wide variety in both the type and nature of human concerns. These range from continuous developmental needs of people to crises requiring immediate emergency attention.

In addition to community mental health agencies, a variety of what might be labeled alternative and nontraditional yet related community counseling services have developed over the past several generations. These nontraditional service centers have had different titles, but most of them can be categorized under the labels of hot lines or crisis centers, drop in or open-door centers, and specialized counseling centers such as those catering to drug and alcohol abusers or dealing with special populations such as women, minorities, or the aged.

Hot lines or crisis phones have been one of the most popular and older alternative services offered. They are frequently staffed by nonprofessionals or paraprofessionals with, in some settings, professional volunteers available or a professional supervisor on call. Usually hot lines or crisis phones are designed to provide sympathetic and helpful listeners and reliable information for dealing with common concerns such as drug overdoses, suicide, spouse abuse, alcoholism, and mental breakdown.

Open-door or drop-in centers provide havens for people who need a place to come to and, in larger cities, to get off the streets—a place where they can feel secure and receive sympathetic attention and counseling assistance. Some of these centers actually provide minimal accommodations where a person can "sleep it off." For the most part, however,

I'm* a licensed professional counselor working for Colorado West Regional Mental Health, which serves ten counties in Northwest Colorado, an area roughly the size of the state of Vermont. Rangely, where I live and work is a one-person satellite office on the westernmost edge of that empire. The most daunting aspect of my life here is the isolation, however, that's easily compensated by my enjoyment of earth's wild beauty. The greatest benefit living on the frontier is that I get to take my dog to work.

Agatha and I go to the office early every morning. I make tea in the microwave, clear messages from the answering machine and prepare for the day's sessions which, unless I've made an exception, begin at nine o'clock. Between 8:00 and 9:00 A.M. I return and take phone calls. Keeping this routine is crucial because the community has learned that's when I'm directly available. Once I go into session, when the phone rings, the answering machine picks up. I seldom check messages between sessions. However, if the phone rings more than four times, I know it's an emergency and interrupt the session to answer. This rarely happens. I schedule three sessions in the morning, three or four in the afternoon. Lunchtime commonly is spent attending meetings. Because of our extreme isolation, interagency cooperation and camaraderie is one of the pleasures of my work environment. We value each other so highly because there's no one else, literally for hundreds of miles, to count on.

One day a week I drive an hour through spectacular wilderness along the White River to Meeker for a staff meeting with our program director and two colleagues who work out of that office. I share the road from time to time with herds of sheep, range cattle, elk, and deer and once or twice in the distance, wild horses. My client population in Meeker is primarily abused children referred by Department of Social Services. In Rangely I serve whoever walks through the door. In both settings and with all populations, Agatha is my most versatile therapeutic tool.

Always the first to greet people when they arrive, she trots into the waiting area aglow with her dachshund/Chihuahua charm. I begin assessment watching both her reactions and the reactions of people to her. First time in a therapist's office is stressful for anyone. Commonly, the most nervous and agitated people visibly relax and often laugh when they see this sassy little dog. She normalizes and disarms the environment into a homelike setting and acts as an immediate container into which huge energy can be safely transferred while [the client is] learning to trust me.

Traumatized children, especially, bond with Agatha long before they can allow vulnerability with an adult. From the very start when a child sees this tiny animal trusts me, they know I'm safe and can grow into that truth at their own pace. I've spent many hours listening to children who curl up in my bean bag chair and pour their hearts out to Agatha as if I weren't there. She snuggles with them, puts her little paws on an arm or leg and mirrors the child with her soft brown eyes. Sometimes children with tactile defensiveness cannot tolerate even Agatha's touch and have acted out towards her with aggressive behavior. I'm able to use her fearful reactions to help the child acknowledge their own fear and how hard it is to be touched after someone physically hurts us. I also tell Agatha's history of abuse before I rescued her from a shelter and how she's had to learn that not every human will treat her that way. Then kids say, "She's just like me," and the two of them go through a parallel process of learning to trust each other as the child replaces internalized violent behavior with gentleness.

Rangely doesn't have a nursing care facility for the elderly so the hospital operates a swing bed unit to serve this need and I am required to perform mental status exams on the residents at admission and quarterly thereafter. Agatha loves this duty most of all and the old folks love her back. Even the cranky guy at the end of the corridor that hates everybody and everything and refuses to cooperate whenever possible, beams when Agatha comes. He holds her in his lap and repeats, "She's a dandy!" while the nurses scurry around taking advantage of his improved disposition to get things accomplished in his room. Once, when he was being unusually difficult, the nurses called the office and asked me to bring Agatha up to help them. She saved the day.

One of our greatest adventures together involved an emergency call requiring a three hour drive high into the mountains in the northeast corner of our county to Pyramid, Colorado. The sheriff's department had been searching all night for a man missing since the day before. They found his body at dawn and were left with a distraught widow and several others in that weekend party exhausted from the vigil and in shock. That time of year, I could only drive so far up the mountain before I had to pull over and be taken by snowmobile the rest of the way. I did a six-hour intervention with that grieving group ending with me standing by the widow at the site of her husband's death. Agatha and I were truly a team, the two of us in a world at the top of the world, containing crisis. She did her best work that endless day, sustaining and comforting me.

* Written and contributed by Ms. Katharine Unthank, who is currently in private practice in Lafayette, Indiana.

they simply provide an opportunity for the person to face emergency counseling assistance. In many of these centers, record-keeping is at a minimum and clients may not even be required to give their name or other personal data unless they wish.

In a number of more populous communities, various specialized counseling service centers are on the increase. These centers tend to serve special populations, defined by the nature of the problem—such as alcohol or drug addiction, spouse abuse, marital relations, or sexual problems—or by age classifications or racial or religious groups. These specialty centers tend to be staffed by a mixture of professionals, paraprofessionals, and volunteers. Facilities are equally diverse. For example, the Norfolk, Virginia, Redevelopment and Housing Authority has established a system of community-based counselors who function with aides to assist individuals and families living in 11 public housing parks in that city. These counselors and their aides give support to residents in crisis situations and provide the information they need to cope with their problems, including the rules and regulations of the housing authority. Counseling activities tend to focus particularly on strengthening families. An organizational chart depicting an agency organization is shown in Figure 3-6.

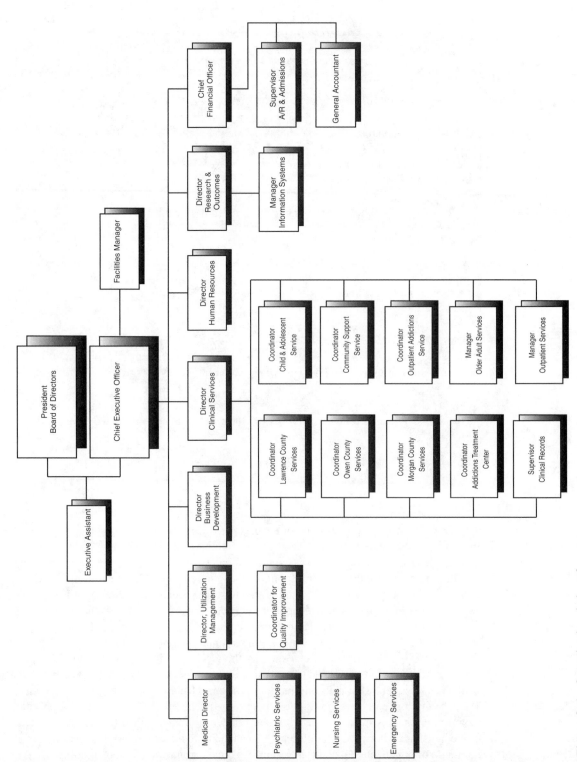

Figure 3-6 Organizational chart for an agency.
Source: Center for Behavioral Health, Bloomington, IN.

Employment Counseling

In 1933, the U.S. Department of Labor established employment security offices, which were to provide job placement and advising or counseling functions for the unemployed. Counseling was more specifically provided for in the G.I. Bill of 1944, which provided job counseling for veterans returning from World War II. By the 1960s, the Department of Labor was encouraging states to upgrade their counselors to the professional or master's degree level of training.

In the fall of 1970, the Manpower Administration of the Department of Labor initiated a massive inservice training program for selected employment service personnel. Originally, 88 colleges and universities in 33 states participated in the training program. Approximately 2,500 employment service personnel were initially involved in the training. The training was intended to increase the overall skill level of the trainees in dispensing employability assistance to those persons comprising the client population of the U.S. Public Employment Service.

Within the Department of Labor, an employment counselor is defined as one who performs counseling duties and who meets the minimum standards for employment counselor classification. The employment service system is designed to bring together workers seeking employment with employers seeking workers in order to improve the functioning of the nation's labor markets. Each state is expected to administer a labor exchange system to facilitate this service and to participate in a system for sharing information among the states, including the use of standardized classification systems issued by the secretary of labor. Employment counselors may also administer the work test requirements of the state unemployment compensation system.

Although the focus of employment counselors, as with other employees of the U.S. Employment Service (now called Job Service), is appropriate job placement of its clientele, the counselors are expected in the process to counsel clients on personal problems and assist them in developing attitudes, skills, and abilities that will facilitate their employment. Counselors are also involved in data gathering from their clients and in the administration and interpretation of standardized tests. Employment counselors tend to consider the National Employment Counseling Association (a division of the American Counseling Association) as their professional organization. Some insight into both the qualifications and role and function of employment counselors may be gained from looking at the National Employment Counseling Competencies adopted by their association in March 2000 for use in workforce development, welfare reform, and such direct service as school-to-work, one-stop, job service, and other employment counseling programs.

National Employment Counseling Competencies

- **Counseling Skills:** The ability to establish a trusting, open and useful relationship with each counselee, accurately interpreting feelings as well as verbal and nonverbal expressions, and conveying to the customer this understanding and whatever pertinent information and assistance is needed. Knowledge and awareness of career development theory and the ability to support the customer through transitions and facilitate decision-making and goal setting. The ability to recognize the need to refer the customer to appropriate resources to remove barriers to employment. The ability to conduct effective intake to insure that the applicant is suitable and able to benefit in the agency's programs.

- **Individual and Group Assessment Skills:** The ability to provide ongoing assessment utilizing individual and group assessment skills and to use formal and informal assessment methods that comply with Equal Employment Opportunities Commission (EEOC) regulations. The ability to provide ongoing assessment in individual and group settings involving the appraisal and measurement of the customer's needs, characteristics, potentials, individual differences and self-appraisal. The ability to recognize special needs and characteristics of all types, e.g., minorities, women seeking nontraditional occupations, culturally different immigrants, disabled, older workers and persons with AIDS.

- **Group Counseling:** The ability to apply basic principles of group dynamics and leadership roles in a continuous and meaningful manner to assist group members in understanding their problems and taking positive steps towards resolving them.

- **Development and Use of Employment-Related Information:** The ability to access, understand and interpret labor market information and job trends. The ability to develop and use educational, occupational and labor market information to assist customers in making decisions and formulating employment and career goals that lead to self-sufficiency. The ability to develop and use skill standards.

- **Computer Related Skills:** The ability to apply employment counseling principles to the use of the internet and other online services, including, but not limited to, employment testing, job banks, job search, job matching, resume writing and sharing, case management reports, counseling and maintaining the confidentiality of customer data.

- **Employment Plan Development, Implementation and Case Management:** The ability to assist the customer in developing and implementing a suitable employment plan that helps move the jobseeker from current status through any needed employability improvement services, including training and supportive services, into a suitable job. Knowledge of educational and training resources, sources of financial support, community resources and local labor market requirements is needed. The ability to manage cases through placement and retention.

- **Placement Skills:** The ability to ascertain and to communicate an understanding of employer's personnel needs, to make effective job development contacts and to assist the customer in the presentation of their qualifications in relation to the employer's needs. The ability to teach job seeking skills and to develop jobs. The ability to assist the customer in making decisions related to the work environment in which he/she might be most successful. The ability to advocate for employment and career development of special groups.

- **Community Relationship Skills:** The ability to assist customers in obtaining the services needed to address barriers to employment which might interfere with successful employment and career directives. The ability to make presentations to community groups and participate on community task force groups. The ability to develop information packets. The ability to partner and link resources with other agency staff in a One Stop setting.

- **Workload Management and Intra-Office Relationship Skills:** The ability to coordinate all aspects of the whole employment counseling program as part of a team effort, resulting in a continuous and meaningful sequence of services to customers, agency staff, employers and the community. The ability to operate a comprehensive employment resource center.

- **Professional Development Skills:** The ability to develop skills individually and within the profession and to demonstrate by example the standards and performance expected of a professional employment counselor.
- **Ethical and Legal Issues:** The ability to comply with the ethical standards developed by the American Counseling Association. The knowledge of regulations and legislation effecting employment and training, job service and social reform, such as EEOC, American with Disabilities Act, professional testing standards, Multicultural Issues, Personal Responsibility and Work Opportunity Reconciliation Act, School-to-Work and One Stop Centers.

Source: National Employment Counseling Association, Fall, 2000, p. 10. (A division of the American Counseling Association).

Employee Assistance Counselors

More and more counselors are practicing in business and industrial work settings. The impact of substance abuse on the workforce plus a heightened recognition that employees' general mental health affects productivity stimulated the initial development of many of these programs. Economic opportunity and labor legislation also created opportunities. However, as counselors proved their worth in the industrial sectors, many programs expanded their activities to include career assistance, retirement planning, educational guidance, and family counseling. Additionally, the rapidly changing nature of the employment picture in the decades ahead continues to create challenges for employers and employees alike and their programs for assisting employees. Recent trends toward downsizing, merging, the hiring of temporary workers, and the movement of whole industrial complexes to new geographic locales are just a few of these new and emerging challenges.

Counselors in business and industrial settings are frequently organized into Employee Assistance Programs (EAPs). Most counseling in EAP programs would be labeled brief or short-term therapy. Too, the diversity of worker needs in most settings requires that EAP counselors have an extensive knowledge of referral sources and client options. An example of a day in the life of an EAP counselor is included at the end of this chapter under the heading "Counselors in International Settings," submitted by Ms. Martha Pitman, executive director of the EAP program in Bermuda.

Correctional Counseling

Practitioners of correctional counseling are employed in various law enforcement settings, ranging from those involved with first-time juvenile probationary offenders to persons incarcerated in penal institutions. Counselors in these settings usually have training backgrounds in counseling, psychology, sociology, criminal justice, or forensic studies. Their duties include counseling and interviewing; the use of various analytical techniques, including standardized testing; referrals; parole recommendations; and placement. In some juvenile institutional settings, counselors may be employed as live-in advisers. Counselors of youthful juvenile offenders work closely with police officers and other authorities.

Examples of counselors in juvenile correctional institutions are those in the Kennedy Youth Center of Morgantown, West Virginia, and the Indiana Boys' School, Plainfield, Indiana. These and similar institutions utilize the differential treatment approach, which takes into account individual differences in matching inmates with counseling staff on the basis of personality or behavioral categories. In other correctional settings, counselors function as key agents in converting closed, traditional, punitive systems into those that are more positive, helping, and rehabilitative. In these settings, the emphasis is on the formation of positive interpersonal climates and open lines of communication among the various members of the prison community, including inmates and correctional officers, or guards. An example of such an activity in recent decades has been the training by correctional counselors of prison guards and other security personnel in racial relations and/or multicultural awareness.

Counselors in the field of correctional counseling may join the International Association of Addictions and Offender Counselors, a division of the American Counseling Association.

Rehabilitation Counseling

Society has always admired people who have overcome physical handicaps to achieve notable success: Franklin D. Roosevelt, who was paralyzed by polio in both legs at 39 but later became president of the United States of America and a wartime world leader; Helen Keller, who was deaf and blind from the age of 2 but became a successful author and lecturer; Ludwig van Beethoven, who wrote his majestic Symphony No. 9 after he lost his hearing; and Sarah Bernhardt, who continued to act after losing her leg in an accident. Clifford Beers, who was mentioned in chapter 1, is an example of an individual who triumphed over mental illness. These are just a few of the many who have overcome real adversity.

Their achievements were notable, but history has failed to record the tragic losses in human potential that were allowed to occur because of lack of attention, other than medical, for people with disabilities. Since World War II, however, rehabilitation counseling has expanded into public agencies so that these individuals may receive special counseling assistance in overcoming their disabilities.

Although the central role of rehabilitation counselors has remained quite consistent over the years, their functions and required knowledge and skill competencies have expanded. Regardless of their employment setting and client population, most rehabilitation counselors (a) assess client needs, (b) develop goals and individualized plans to meet identified needs, and (c) provide or arrange for the therapeutic services and interventions (psychological, medical, social, or behavioral) needed by clients that may include job placement and follow-up services. Counseling skills are considered an essential component of all of these activities (Jenkins, Patterson, & Szymanski, 1992).

Research by Leahy, Szymanski, and Linkowski (1993) indicated that the following 10 knowledge domains represent the core competency requirements of rehabilitation counselors: (a) vocational counseling and consultation services; (b) medical and psychological aspects; (c) individual and group counseling; (d) program evaluation and research; (e) case management and service coordination; (f) family, gender, and multicultural issues; (g) foundations of rehabilitation; (h) workers' compensation; (i) environmental and attitudinal barriers; and (j) assessment. The specialized knowledge of disabilities and of environmental factors that interact with disabilities, as well as the range of knowledge and skills required in addition to counseling, differentiates the rehabilitation counselor from other types of counselors in today's service delivery environments (Leahy & Szymanski, 1995, p. 163)

Rehabilitation counselors help clients overcome deficits in their skills. They may work with a special type of client such as those with vision or hearing loss, people with mental illness, or those who are physically disabled. In some settings, they see all of these plus people with other kinds of disabilities as well.

Vocational rehabilitation counselors help clients with disabilities prepare for gainful employment, frequently assisting them in appropriate job placement. In recent decades, much effort has been expended on the rehabilitation of substance abusers, with counselors prominent in both inpatient and outpatient facilities. We have also noted increased efforts to rehabilitate those with mental disabilities. Rehabilitation counselors also work with ex-offenders in preparing for adjustment to life in society's mainstream.

The role of rehabilitation counselors is a complex one; they provide a broad range of psychological and career-oriented services and work with and often coordinate the efforts of community agencies in their client's behalf. They also function as resource persons who seek to encourage the optimum adjustment and development of their clients. Their preparation has been described by Capuzzi and Gross (1997):

> Academic training of counselors whose interest lies in working with clients with disabilities is accomplished almost invariably through Rehabilitation Counselor Education (RCE) programs. These training programs are typically graduate (master's level) programs and are offered by Counselor Education or Counseling Psychology departments. Completing the programs normally requires two years of academic and clinical training when pursued full time.
>
> The curriculum content pursued in most of these training programs has been developed and verified by the Council on Rehabilitation Education (CORE). CORE was established in 1971 as an accreditation body to oversee the academic and clinical training of rehabilitation counselors and to promote effective delivery of rehabilitation services to people with disabilities. Of the approximately 100 RCE programs in the United States, 84 are currently CORE-accredited. These programs must show evidence of a graduate-level curriculum that provides its trainee with a course of study that includes, but is not limited to, the following knowledge and/or skill areas: (1) history and philosophy of rehabilitation; (2) rehabilitation legislation; (3) organizational structure of the rehabilitation system (public and private, nonprofit and for-profit service delivery); (4) counseling theories, approaches, and techniques; (5) case management; (6) career development and vocational counseling theories and practices; (7) vocational evaluation, occupational information, job analysis, and work adjustment techniques; (8) job development and placement; (9) medical aspects of disability; (10) psychosocial aspects of disability; (11) knowledge of community resources and services; (12) rehabilitation research; (13) measurement and testing; (14) legal and ethical issues in rehabilitation counseling; (15) independent living; and (16) special topics in rehabilitation (such as transition from school to work, supported employment, rehabilitation engineering).
>
> In addition, rehabilitation counseling trainees are required to participate in supervised practicum and internship experiences totaling a minimum of 600 clock hours in approved rehabilitation sites and under the supervision of a certified rehabilitation counselor. (pp. 487–488)

Marriage and Family Counseling

Although the marriage vows read "until death do us part," the high divorce rate in this country in recent decades indicates that thousands of couples have decided they cannot wait until their entry into eternity to part. In addition, thousands of other couples suffer through phases of their marriages or seek adjustment to marriage difficulties by means other than separation or divorce.

Certainly, an abundance of statistical empirical evidence indicates that family discord and divorce is continuing to increase. The stresses of the actual divorce process for spouses and children and the later adjustment requirements for all involved are well documented and include such problems as the feelings of failure that often accompany divorce as well as other emotions such as anger, regret, and depression. Adjustment problems may also arise in terms of separation, child rearing, and single parent roles. In addition to these emotional and psychological stresses, there are practical concerns that center on the legal issues and financial responsibilities for persons in divorce or separation. Also, the adjustment problems of children whose parents divorce cannot be overlooked. Concerns about loyalty, parental dating, and custody can have severe psychological consequences, especially when coupled with the feelings of guilt and devalued self-concept commonplace in children of divorce.

We can conclude that the traditional image of the home and family as a cozy nest of love, security, togetherness, and never-ending happiness has been severely battered (as have many of the nest's inhabitants) in recent generations. The need for counselors who can effectively counsel outside the one-to-one relationship, who can work in this new dimension—the family or family system—has evolved. Yet, providing effective counseling assistance to families and couples in today's complex and stressful society is a challenging and often difficult task, frequently complicated by advice from nonprofessionals, cultural traditions, and environmental pressures.

The first marriage and family help centers were established in the 1930s, but only within the past several decades has marriage and family therapy emerged as a counseling specialty. With over 40,000 counselors engaged in the practice, the American Association of Marriage and Family Therapy represent this specialty area as does Division 43 of the American Psychological Association and the division of the American Counseling Association entitled the International Association of Marriage and Family Counseling.

Whereas individual counseling addresses the individual person and his or her concerns, family therapy focuses on the family system. Even if only one member of the family is being counseled, if the counseling is concerned primarily with the family system, it can be viewed as family counseling. In other words, regardless of the number of family members involved, the family counselor tends to conceptualize problems in terms of the systems perspective or the context in which clients exist. Interventions, therefore, focus on relationships and communication.

An objective of family therapy may be to bring about change in the family structure and the behavior of family members. Communication among the family will probably be examined as well as how the members resolve their conflicts.

We must continue to recognize the rising numbers of dual-career couples, single-parent families, and latchkey children as issues in family living that are more characteristic of recent generations. These stresses, plus those accompanying the necessitated major career changes predicted for most adult workers in the immediate decades ahead, would indicate complex factors challenging marriage and family counselors.

An outgrowth of the stress on marriage and families has been the development of specialty areas represented by the International Association of Marriage and Family Counselors (IAMFC), a division of the American Counseling Association, and the American Association of Marriage and Family Therapy (AAMFT). These associations may include members from diverse professional preparation backgrounds, including psychiatrists, psychologists, attorneys, counselors, as well as priests, rabbis, and ministers.

Many counselor education programs offer courses in the marriage and family area. Popular courses include marriage counseling, family counseling, human sexuality, and marriage/family counseling. For those who wish to specialize in the field of family therapy, credentials can be earned in one of two ways. An individual can complete an advanced degree in one of the traditional disciplines, such as clinical psychology, counseling, pastoral counseling, expressive therapies, social work, or psychiatry. Either within the course of study for that degree or after completing the degree, the student must complete specific course work that meets the educational requirements for a degree in marriage and family counseling.

Pastoral Counseling

From the standpoint of sheer numbers and geographic coverage, pastoral counseling provides a significant mental health resource. Not only are clergy members generally available to listen to the concerns and personal problems of their parishioners, but they also are frequently the first source to which people in trouble turn. In fact, many churches offer counseling on family issues including marriage problems, bereavement counseling and youth counseling and guidance. The American Association of Pastoral Counselors certifies individuals and also accredits training programs.

Churches are also increasingly utilizing professional counselors in their youth programs. In recognition of the mental health function of the clergy, many theological training programs include courses in pastoral counseling, related psychology, and general counseling subjects. Special programs have also been developed in clinical pastoral education for theology students and clergy who want further training. Although many of these specialized programs are comparatively short term, others provide intensive training in clinical settings.

GERONTOLOGY COUNSELING

The "graying of America" is the phrase frequently used to note the dramatic increase in the older population. The *U. S. Bureau of the Census Current Population Reports* (1995) noted that the group 65 years of age and older constitutes approximately 11% of our total population, contrasted to 4.1% in 1900, with predictions of continued increases well into the 2000s.

With increased representation has also come an increased sensitivity to the needs, including counseling, of this special population. Also, as this group becomes more politically potent and active, the aged themselves are demanding the same range of social services and attention to their needs that are provided for other age groups. Certainly the presidential election of 2000 highlighted both the increased political importance of this group and their concerns for appropriate health care and financial security.

A dramatic change that occurs in the lives of most of the working elderly is retirement. No longer is the engraved watch or the upholstered rocking chair sufficient to ease the transition of the worker from employment to retirement. For many workers, including the elderly, their job is an important source of their identity—"I'm a teacher, I'm a salesperson, I'm a secretary." The loss of this identity, through retirement, can be difficult for the elderly who, in addition, may have depended on their coworkers at the job for social contacts. Loneliness is a not uncommon problem among aging retirees. Further, retirees as well as many older individuals have not developed avocational interests or leisure time pursuits, resulting in boredom and frustration for many. The loss of spouses and other loved ones is particularly noticeable among the elderly. Bereavement counseling should be available during these difficult periods. Depression, stress, and alcoholism are also common among the elderly.

The increased recognition of the needs of this population is further reflected in the growth of course offerings in counselor preparation programs and substantive increases in professional publications addressing the counseling of older individuals.

Private Practice

The possibility of establishing a full-time private practice has appealed to an increasing number of counselors and many, employed by other institutions or agencies, have done so on a part-time basis. Those interested in private practice may consider whether they wish to practice alone or in a partnership or group practice. They must also determine whether to enter general practice or specialize in such areas as addictions, career, children, or others.

A basic consideration in entering private practice is whether one's professional interest and expertise are relevant to a sufficient client population in the geographic area of practice to adequately support the private practitioner. As in any situation, knowledge of and adherence to legal and ethical guidelines are critical in private practice. The importance of licensure and eligibility for third-party payment must also be considered. Other concerns that the individual private practitioner must address are fiscal (fees, billing policies, insurance, office overhead), logistical (office location, hours, furnishings, record keeping, secretarial help), and public relations or communications, including advertising of services.

Future Directions

In 1980, *The Counseling Psychologist* had a special theme issue (Volume 8, Number 4) entitled "Counseling Psychology in the Year 2000." In this issue, Whiteley concluded:

> In order to have an increased impact in the changed world of 2000 A.D., counseling psychology will have to enlarge its substantive bases to include environmental psychology and environmental planning; life-span developmental psychology including aging, developmental tasks, and transitions between phases of life; the psychology of men and women, the growth of men and women within relationships, sex roles, parenting, sexuality, and child rearing; more refined approaches to building a psychological sense of community; assertion training and social organization self-renewal; psychobiology; information and computer science; and, finally, systematic study of the expected future and its alternatives. (p. 7)

In 1987, Division 17, the Counseling Psychology division of the American Psychological Association, held its third national conference focusing on the theme "Planning the Future." Reporting on this conference, Rude, Weissberg, and Gazda (1988) noted:

> Across the five work groups that comprised the Third National Conference for Counseling Psychology a number of common themes emerged. Discussions of identity affirmed the value of the scientist-practitioner model and of traditional strengths such as prevention, life-span development, and skill-building as well as innovative and nontraditional functions. Among the ideas that were endorsed multiple by work groups were strategies to enhance counseling psy-

chology's visibility and political strength and to build mechanisms for proactive planning into governance. Ways to improve the training of counseling psychologists by enhancing rigor, scientific thinking, professional identity, and ability to work in diverse and emerging settings also received substantial attention. Overall, deliberations of the groups resulted in substantial convergence and a set of specific goals and plans for the future. (p. 423)

Details of the conference were reported when another special issue of *The Counseling Psychologist* (Fretz, 1988) featured the theme and reports from this conference, "Planning the Future."

More than 20 years ago, Leona Tyler (1980) made predictions for counseling in the year 2000:

Counseling psychology (and counseling psychologists) will be dealing with the significant reality problems of that day, just as they have been oriented toward the reality problems of the 40s, 50s, 60s, and 70s.

What are these reality problems of 2000 likely to be? (Fortunately, I can treat this as an academic exercise.) No one really knows, of course, but it is useful to speculate. Here are my speculations concerning those trends that are likely to involve counseling psychologists:

The single-cycle sequence of family life, education, work and labor-force retirement will break down. Education will be a life-long process, interspersed and interacting with work and family.

There will be more explicit attention to a broader scope of life skills. Just as we now have organized training in educational skills and job skills, so there will be organized training in family skills, community skills, recreational skills, and so on.

Mental health will be a recognized aspect of our total health system. Just as we go to the dentist twice a year and have an annual medical exam, so we will periodically go to the psychologist for a "psychological check-up."

In all of the above, counseling psychologists, with their history of dealing with the normal, everyday reality problems of the entire spectrum of age and level of adjustment will have an increasingly important role to play. They will be located in a variety of settings—educational institutions, government, community and social agencies, and private business and industry. And if psychology ever develops a "general practitioner" (as I think it will), professional training in counseling psychology will be the best preparation for this role. (p. 22)

Many of these predictions have now emerged as reality. We would note also that advancements in "futuristic science," as in other fields, are making it possible to be increasingly accurate in seeing the future.

For community, agency, and other counselor settings, it is appropriate to note that the increased attention to prevention, multicultural, family, and career issues will apply to non-school counselor settings as well. For example, the growing European and Asian economic competition as well as the trend among U.S. companies to move their production to locations where workforces are more efficient and/or cheaper have mandated the development in the United States of a world-class workforce. This has necessitated training and retraining, plus worker transitions to new careers and locations. For orderly and meaningful career planning and development, career counseling has been increasingly in demand in the public sector. Because of the potential for at least temporary unemployment or underemployment and the accompanying frustrations, people abuse, substance abuse, and crime will continue to be national social concerns unless the major nonschool institutions of society (government, business, and industry) demonstrate more caring through counselor/directed human assistance programs.

Counselors in nonschool settings must be prepared for the fallout from an older workforce; a drastic scaling down of traditional promotional opportunities in many fields; more women in management positions; the downsizing of government, military, and related industries leaving the former workers of these organizations seeking new options; and the creation of a large pool of workers in temporary or transitional jobs. We also must be aware of the rapid scientific and technological advances that have moved us well beyond the computer revolution into a new age of communications, home-based economic ventures, and human services via the Internet. Thus, although the future will present many opportunities for counselors, whether we as a profession serve the population will depend to a large degree on how vigorous and successful we are in communicating to the political and general publics our capabilities and readiness for rendering our much-needed services in the decades ahead.

INTERNATIONAL SETTINGS: COMMUNITY/AGENCY COUNSELORS

School counseling programs and counseling services in a variety of nonschool settings are developing rapidly in a number of other countries. Descriptions of counselors functioning in several of these settings are presented in the pages that follow.

A DAY IN THE LIFE OF MARGARET JARVIE (EDINBURGH, SCOTLAND)*

It began with the telephone ringing about 7:30 A.M. In the Scottish scene, that is early. Nine A.M. is the usual time for beginning the working day. However, I run a company, called Interface, which offers a 24-hour, seven days a week, counselling service. Fortunately, it runs from my home and, therefore, provided I am sufficiently wide awake to attend to the caller, it does not matter greatly whether I am in a state of dress or undress. I dread the introduction of video telephoning!

On this occasion, it was a request for a counselling appointment from a client who was clearly trying to hold back the tears. Having assured her that it was all right to cry, it was fully ten minutes before she was sufficiently composed to give me some information about what was troubling her. It was a relationship problem. As she was telephoning from approximately 250 miles away, I would need to arrange for her to see a counsellor much nearer to her than I was. Nonetheless, I encouraged her to continue to talk to me until she was calmer. I also needed her to continue to talk so that I could make some assessment of whether or not she was potentially suicidal. Fortunately, she was not.

Our conversation finished with my promising to get one of our counsellors to contact her within 24 hours to make an appointment and assuring her that she would be seen by the counsellor within a few days. I also informed her that she should not hesitate to telephone my number if she felt the need to talk to someone. I explained that the service was a 24-hour one and that, if I was not here, the calls would be diverted to another counsellor.

Interface began in 1986 when I was first appointed to be Hewlett-Packard's counsellor and expanded in 1988 when I was asked by one of our national banks to help their staff after a raid situation. Having agreed to try, I had to ask some other counsellors to help me as I already had a full-time job teaching in one of the local universities. After I retired from working at the university, both companies asked me to continue to be their counsellor. When I agreed to do so, the bank immediately changed my contract into one which offered a general counselling service to all employees anywhere in Britain. At that point, Interface became an Employee Assistance Provider (EAP).

One of the tasks facing the reconstituted Interface was to set down the principles on which our work would be based. One of these was that clients would be seen within a few days of asking for help. In Scotland, for historical and cultural reasons, there is still a hesitancy about going for counselling and, on occasions, it takes considerable courage for a client to ask for help. I, and my associates in Interface, therefore decided that, whenever possible, we would respond quickly. In this instance, the counsellor whom I contacted was able to arrange to meet the client later on the day that the request was received.

After breakfast, I tackled my mail. It was the usual mixed bag. It contained invoices from several of our counsellors whose monthly ones are due to reach me by the beginning of next week when I shall collate the information contained in them and dispatch the invoices to the companies who employ us. As well as the invoices there were some 'Completion Forms.' These are forms completed by our counsellors at the end of each case which gives us very little information but does enable us to give statistical feedback to the company without disclosing anything personal about our clients and, at the same time, enabling the company to identify any trends.

The kind of information the form contains is—what were the main reasons for seeking counselling; were they mainly work or non-work related; did the counsellor think that all, most, some or none of the client's issues had been resolved; how many sessions the client has had; and whether or not the case is continuing on a private basis? As one of our principles is that we shall not abandon a client until they are able to function independently, we have had to face up to the implications of what that means when we are employed on the basis of a limited number of sessions. Right at the beginning of working with any company, we negotiate a contract which stipulates that if both the client and the counsellor think that a few more sessions, in addition to those stipulated, will conclude the case, we may contact the company and ask for an extension without breaking confidentiality. If that is not enough, the counsellor and the client are allowed to convert the contract into a private one.

Among the other items in my mail was a request from the professional body to carry out an assessment of a course which a Highland College wants to offer and for which the College is seeking validation. As education is a top priority with me, I gladly accepted this invitation. Also, included in the mail, was a request from a company for our literature. Fortunately, we now do have literature. For years, we resisted having some printed on the basis that we did not need it because we have never had to look for work. Companies, as well as private individuals, have tended to seek us out, so we have not had to market ourselves.

The same applies to recruiting new counsellors. We get a considerable number of applications to join us. We demand high standards both in respect of qualification and reputation from our counsellors and our vetting system is a rigorous one. However, what pleases us enormously is our reputation for being a good company to work for is spreading. This has surprised us because we pay the minimal going rate while some of the bigger EAPs pay considerably more. What our counsellors tell us is that what appeals to them is that, in spite of the fact that there are now over 200 counsellors throughout Britain working for us on a part-time basis, they feel that they are personally known to us and that they feel that they are part of a team working with a counselling company whose principles they approve of. That pleases us. We have reserve lists of counsellors waiting to join us.

The mail also includes letters from counsellors. Some of these are in response to an invitation I have extended to our counsellors in Cheshire to join me for lunch next Tuesday. I have a morning appointment with the staff of the Human Resources Division of one of our companies and thought that, as I am rarely in that part of the country, I would take the opportunity to catch up with our counsellors before flying back to Edinburgh.

Attending to the mail and to the e-mails takes me about two hours but doing so extends considerably beyond that time because the telephone rings frequently for a variety of reasons. Sometimes it is clients looking for appointments, sometimes it is counsellors wanting to discuss something or other, sometimes it is requests for information. Today it includes a request to talk at the local meeting of the Association of Counsellors at Work, a sub-section of our professional body. They want me to lead a discussion on the pros and cons of an integrative versus an eclectic model of counselling. That's a tall order and will take a considerable amount of preparation!

Another one was to ask if we could supply a counsellor to be on the premises while a non-routine interview was taking place. A non-routine interview is where a member of staff is disciplined. After a suicide, we helped this company to review their disciplinary procedures. Part of the new procedure is that the employee will be offered counselling immediately *after* the disciplinary hearing. This means a counsellor has to be present in the building but, I hasten to add, definitely not involved in the disciplining.

A pleasant interruption to my responding to the mail occurred today when a very beautiful bouquet of flowers was delivered. Two days ago I met with a man who wanted information about how to train in counselling. I spent a pleasant hour trying to inform him. The flowers were his way of thanking me. Getting them was a lovely surprise.

In the afternoon, I had two supervision sessions. The first was a trainee who is on his practicum. The other was a counsellor who has been successful in her bid to establish a counselling service in the maternity section of our local hospital. The service is for parents who lose their babies. In between these two sessions I had time to do a bit more of my preparation for the diploma course that I am running for members of the Lorn Counselling Service. Lorn is in Argyll, which is a sparsely populated area in the west and includes some of the inner isles of the Western Hebrides. I am committed to taking courses to outlying districts so, I am very pleased at having been asked to do this. It does, however, mean a three-and-a-half hour's drive each time I go up.

My day closed with a three hour teaching stint on a Certificate in Counselling Skills in a Further Education College located about 20 miles from Edinburgh. Having got home about 10:00 P.M., I was tired but well satisfied. Although I had not done any one-to-one counselling, I had done some teaching which I thoroughly enjoy doing. So, my day had finished on a high.

*Counselor in Private Practice, EAP Director, and Counselor Educator

A DAY IN THE LIFE OF A SCOTTISH COUNSELLOR IN PRIVATE PRACTICE*

Without being awkward, fanciful or inaccurate, I can safely state that my life as a counsellor holds no two weeks the same. Each day is varied, interesting and different—a definite attraction of my chosen career path. Naturally some routine may creep in, perhaps taking the form of a weekly commitment, for example a regular college class input at a set time on a specific day each week or a monthly supervision session, arranged a few months in advance. Most of my training demands are on a short term or modular basis which is advantageous for committing to future pieces of work.

On thinking about a "day in my life", it has been useful to check back in my diary to give me an indication of the distribution of my time. Perhaps the most obvious trend is the inconsistencies from day to day. Some days I can see up to eight clients whilst on others, I may see one or two or none! In my defence, this is not all poor time management on my part, but rather, attempting to accommodate the clients' days off, shift patterns, lunch hours, baby sitting arrangements and so on.

On days I have fewer contact hours, there is no excuse but to catch up on case notes, phone calls, filing or some current reading material. You will have gathered that I am not purely a counsellor as I also supervise both trainee and qualified counsellors either on a private basis or for organisations. In addition, as an accredited trainer, I run various courses, including the recognised COSCA (formerly

The Confederation of Scottish Counselling Agencies) counselling skills modules and am a Visiting Lecturer in counselling skills at a local university for a few hours a week.

A typical day? I try not to make appointments before my two school-age children leave mum to get on with 'seeing the worried people'. It is usually a surprise to check my diary, on which I am totally reliant, to confirm the day's proceedings. Ideally, I like to begin the day with some exercise which varies and includes running, squash, tennis, swimming, or if entirely unavoidable, the dreaded gym. This somewhat energetic start helps me focus on the hours ahead and is in direct contrast to the potential sedentary nature of the rest of my day. If this is not possible due to other commitments, I try to schedule it in later in the day. I do make a conscious effort to leave spaces between sessions and although I do have a waiting room, there is usually no-one there to answer the door. A space between sessions therefore makes sense. Sessions adhere to a 'fifty minute hour', leaving time to make another arrangement if required. Somewhere I do try to fit in a light meal or snacks along the way. I make every effort to keep noise and possible disruption to a minimum. However, there is always the client who arrives early, at the wrong time, on the wrong day, et cetera, and I have to make the difficult decision whether to interrupt the session to answer the door. This is also the case for any caller. I have no way of telling who is on the other side of the door! Our ever-changing persistent postmen often have to be educated. Most friends and neighbours know and respect the nature of my work and check before calling. The telephone is simply in another room with the answer machine to take messages. Many interested parties when acquainted with the fact that I work at home often ask if I'm not tempted to become involved in housework and other domestic chores. Well, I can categorically state that mainly due to my anathema to household duties, this is not the case! Occasionally it has been known for me to load the dishwasher in a spare ten minutes or to throw a few dishes in the sink at the news of a cancellation, but I am never prone to getting too carried away. I do, however, have a little treasure in the form of Hazel, 'my lady who does' who comes in once a week to wash, clean, polish and iron. She, too, is respectful of the need for a noise-free zone and vacuums between sessions.

The fact that I mainly work at home also raises the question from the curious as to whether I'm not tempted to while away my spare moments in front of the television or other idle pursuits. Again, I think it is fair to state that this will only happen on the rare occasion and due to the inevitability of working quite a few evenings, I am justified in having some 'chill out time' now and again. On the other hand, I do think working for yourself in your home environment demands a certain self-discipline and conscientiousness.

In relation to being home-based, I do try to keep the room comfortable but not too cosy with the distinction made between displaying pictures as opposed to personal photographs. My framed qualifications are also visible for all to see. I have the usual set-up of chairs facing, which are re-arranged to accommodate couple or family work. A small occasional table offers a glass of water each and a box of tissues. Interestingly, I do offer supervisees coffee or tea, perhaps highlighting a perceived difference in our relationship. There is a CD and tape machine facility in order to play relaxation or guided fantasy tapes if appropriate. I also have on display a variety of drawing materials, clay, buttons, plastic animals, stones, et cetera for more creative forms of expression.

Back to my time-management, I do try to keep evening work to a minimum, but due to issues around babysitting, confidentiality, not wishing to come in work time, reliant on husband/wife's car, et cetera, this is sometimes unavoidable. Weekends I keep faithfully clear of client work—a time for friends and family. However, this seems to be a prime time for courses and workshops—both facilitating and participating so I endeavour to spread these out as much as possible throughout the year. This is an essential and recognised part of my role. As an accredited counsellor I am required to complete a number of hours each year as a contribution to my Professional and Personal Development. Possibly as importantly, the life of a home-based counsellor is potentially an isolated one. I feel I have a need to meet, mingle and network for my sanity and socialisation!

The question of safety is often raised when I disclose my chosen career and situation. This, to date, has not been a problem, but I am aware that I tend to see first time and particularly male clients when my partner is about. I also have access to a room in the town centre if for reasons of accessibility or safety this is deemed more appropriate. Occasionally, I do make home visits, but as this setting can raise many issues, including lack of control over environment, safety, and the time factor it only tends to happen for good reason.

I have been known to take a telephone referral, mainly for geographical or health reasons. I am also about to enter the world of on-line counselling with not a little apprehension and as yet, need to be convinced of its effectiveness. Ideally, I work face-to-face with a wide and varied caseload. This would include a cornucopia of presenting issues from an inclusive age range of individuals and couples with the occasional family. I do some private work for which I operate a sliding scale. I am, however, reliant on Employee Assistance Programmes for the majority of my referrals.

As EAPs work with many different companies and organisations, I must make a considerable effort to keep on top of the numerous systems which exist. Each EAP provider has a unique set of paperwork, case management style, number of sessions and follow-up procedures. The varied demands of each provider does influence my record keeping and note-taking. This said, I do keep at least brief notes for all clients.

Before a session, I refer to the previous meeting if only to remind myself of names of partners, children, dogs and significant others. I have to state that over the years, I have been challenged by some clients' companions. These have included a baby who just might require to be breast-fed mid-session; an energetic Dalmatian puppy who could not possibly be abandoned in the car on such a hot day; a robust toddler who was too much for the childminder; a neighbour who thought she may like to try it and wants to see what we do; and many partners who feel duty-bound to attend. Not conducive conditions for counselling, and often a decision has to be made as to whether to re-arrange our time together. To me, it illustrates some clients and sometimes their dependents' difficulty with the concept that this time is exclusively for them.

In conclusion, I am aware I have barely referred to my approach which is eclectic with a person-centered bias. From this position, I believe wholeheartedly that the effectiveness of my work is based on our relationship. If I can offer the core conditions of empathy, unconditional positive regard and congruence, hopefully, the client will feel safe and trusting enough to make for meaningful and worthwhile time together. As long as I believe this to be happening, I will continue to pursue a career in the counselling world!

*Contributed by Maggie Murray Harris, Edinburgh, Scotland

EMPLOYEE ASSISTANCE PROGRAMME OF BERMUDA*

An Employee Assistance Program offers a wonderful opportunity for counsellors who are looking for a lot of variety and stimulation in a team work environment. The Program of which I am Executive Director, is a non-profit consortium of 200 member companies, and we provide services to over 17,000 employees and their immediate families. A member company pays, in advance, a fee to cover all their employees for a year, so that employees and family can see us at no cost to themselves. The EAP therefore opens up the doors to counselling for a huge number of people who may otherwise not have the means or motivation to seek help privately.

We service many types of organizations, including Government, banks, insurance companies, law firms, retail, schools, hotels, to name a few, and we see all tiers of the organization, from the CEO down to junior staff members. And we deal with all types of problems: relationship, family, psychological/emotional, substance abuse, grieving, etc. Our focus is on assessment, referral when appropriate, and short-term counselling, but we also provide critical incident debriefing, case management, supervisor consultation and workshops on EAP and mental health issues.

A counsellor's typical day may include four sessions with individual clients, an EAP orientation with a member company, a meeting with staff, and an hour to do phone calls and client notes.

As the Executive Director, my tasks are many and varied. I must respond to the demands of my Board of Directors, the staff, and member companies. As I enjoy counselling and continue to develop my skills, I also maintain a client load of six to twelve clients.

A typical (is there such a thing?) day would start at 8:30 A.M. with chatting casually with my colleagues for a few minutes and checking the schedule for the day as well as telephone and e-mail messages. If this is a staffing day, we would then have a two hour meeting when all the counsellors present all their new cases and any other cases that they need help with. As we have four full-time counsellors, as well as any clients I may have, it can be quite a challenge getting everything accomplished in two hours. For new cases, typically three to five each counsellor, the counsellor provides brief demographics for the client, as well as presenting problem, assessment and plan. Other cases may be more time-consuming as the counsellor seeks input from colleagues on how to move forward with a case. Due to the nature of our community and some limitations on available resources, we do a lot of short-term counselling at our EAP, and thus input from others is valued so that we can effectively, albeit quickly, help the many people we see within the six to eight session model we attempt to follow.

After staffing, I may have an hour or two to do some administrative work as well as respond to phone calls and any case management I may have. After a lunch break, which I often take in the staff room so I can "catch up" with my colleagues, I may then have a meeting with a new company to implement a contract. Back at the office I may then have one or two clients, or administrative tasks to complete.

Every week the staff meets for an administrative meeting, at which time any issues may be discussed relating to projects we are working on, policies and procedures we are constantly working on, or any issues of concern to staff. I also meet with my Chairman every few weeks to get feedback and support on issues as they arise, and I meet with the Executive Committee monthly and the entire Board quarterly.

In an EAP such as ours, there is a lot of scope for development. EAPs are constantly looking at better ways to provide a quality service to member companies and their employees. It is always important to focus on the core services that people have traditionally expected of an EAP, but there are many areas that can be developed, such as wellness, mediation, organizational development, work/life programs, risk management, elder care and conflict resolution.

EAP work is always interesting and varied in terms of activities performed, type of problems presenting, and the cross section of people seen. It provides great opportunities for personal and professional growth, and a true sense of helping a lot of people in the community.

* Written by Ms. Martha Pitman, Executive Director—December 2001

SUMMARY

An article in *Better Homes and Gardens* noted that "if you graduated from high school before 1960, chances are the only school counselors you have known are your child's" (Daly, 1979, p. 15). This chapter assumes that most of those who graduated from high school before 1960 also knew little about how counselors were trained or licensed and had little familiarity with their role and function. Perhaps this very lack of understanding has led the counseling professionals in the past decade to move more energetically into the public communications arena to "tell what they're about," upgrade their training, and seek protection of their profession from unqualified intruders through certification and licensure. Much has been accomplished in a short period if one considers that at the turn of the 20th century, there were no counselors in schools. More than 100 years and approximately 125,000 school counselors later, we can identify tremendous progress in training, certification, and practice.

Counselor training today is available at the master's specialists and doctoral levels and postdoctoral courses as well. All states specify some type of counselor preparation or certification for employment in school settings, with the exception of postsecondary institutions. These requirements in general reflect role and function expectancies. Differing characteristics of various school levels, settings, and clientele, by necessity, result in variations in that role and function. However, school counselors cannot go it alone. They must view themselves as member players on the school team and work for the cooperation and contributions of teachers, administrators, and other helping professionals who are vital to the success of any school counseling program.

School counselors and school counseling programs must be able to adapt to the demands of the future if they are to become or remain relevant and valuable to the populations they are intended to serve. This is, of course, no less true for counselors functioning in various community and agency settings.

This chapter has also discussed the role, function, and training of counselors for community and various agency settings. Community mental health agencies are perhaps the most versatile in terms of their readiness to deal with a wide range of developmental as well as remedial needs. Also, the staffing of these agencies is usually more diverse, often including professionals trained in medicine and social work as well as psychology. If one is seeking less conventional settings, many communities have crisis centers, hot line counseling, open-door agencies, centers for human growth, and other nontraditional approaches to providing mental health services.

Assume you have a problem, and you need to see a counselor, but you are no longer in school and besides, your old school counselor is too busy with the current student body. So what are your options? This chapter has suggested a number of these opportunities for both employment as counselors and assistance for clients in nonschool settings.

If your problem is one of career decision making or job placement, you might want to seek the assistance of a government employment office counselor (unlike private employment agencies, government employment offices charge no fees and are more likely to employ trained counselors). Additionally, career counseling centers, both government and nongovernment sponsored, are available in a number of communities. These specialized centers are also popular on college campuses.

Of course, if you are confined to a correctional institution, your only option may be your institutional counselor. Unfortunately, in many such institutions counseling personnel may not be employed.

For assistance in overcoming a physical or mental disability, rehabilitation counselors can be a valuable resource because they have received special training to work with the developmental needs of the handicapped. Veterans can seek such assistance through the Veterans Administration, of course, and other "rehab" counselors may be found in community and other governmental agencies and hospitals. A small number are in private practice.

If your problem is marriage- or family-related, there can be help for you too, since marriage and family counseling is a growing area of specialization. Like many of your friends and neighbors, you may turn to your family clergy. The likelihood is increasing that your minister, priest, or rabbi will have received some counseling preparation in his or her ministerial studies, or will have some assistant specially trained to provide counseling services. Another source of counseling assistance, if you are by chance a member of the armed services, would be your service counselor. If you are among our older readers, specialized counseling assistance may also be available to you to help you plan for your retirement or other needs.

A final option, one that would probably cost you more dollars, is to seek out a counselor in private practice. Large population centers, university-oriented communities, and upper socioeconomic suburbs are the more likely habitats of the private practitioners. Obviously, evidence of appropriate training, such as licensure, is important for private practitioners.

Having examined the historical development of our profession, the activities of counselors and their role and function in various school and nonschool settings, we now move to a more detailed examination of specific counselor services and activities. We shall begin in the next chapter with our most important skill and service: individual counseling.

DISCUSSION QUESTIONS

1. Discuss contacts that you can recall during your schooling with differing helping professionals (e.g., school psychologist, school social worker, school counselor, school nurse, and other health personnel). Compare the role of each of these in the school program.
2. As a potential counselor, are there some special preparations or subject matters that you would like to see as a part of your training program? Identify and present a rationale.
3. Discuss differences in lifestyle one might anticipate as a
   a. school counselor
   b. correctional counselor
   c. counselor in private practice
4. Should all counselors for school and nonschool settings come under one broad general counseling license? Discuss.
5. Should counselors in community agencies be involved in such community problems as substance abuse, crime and delinquency, the homeless, unemployment, and so on? If so, in what way?

6. How should school counseling and guidance programs respond to major societal programs such as substance abuse, child abuse, AIDS, school dropouts, underemployment, the homeless? Are there other major societal problems that school counseling programs should address? If so, what are these problems and how should school counseling programs respond to them?
7. Discuss the growth of specialty areas in the counseling profession (e.g., marriage and family, sports, gerontology). Are there other areas of counseling specialization that you see emerging in the next 25 years?
8. How can the counseling profession increase the public's awareness and appreciation of counseling services and their potential contribution to our society?

CLASS ACTIVITIES

1. Shadow a marriage and family counselor, an employment counselor, a counselor in private practice, or a counselor in an agency or school setting and report your experiences to the class.
2. Interview a minister, rabbi, or priest regarding the counseling aspects of his or her ministry.
3. Assume you (the class) are a group of experts called together to formulate a model school counselor preparation program for the first years of the 21st century. Outline such a model.
4. Survey a small sample of your community population to ascertain their perceptions of the profession of counseling and their awareness of local school and agency counseling services. Discuss the implications of your findings.
5. Identify some activities that elementary, middle, and high school counselors might use to facilitate students' learning and practice of human relationship skills necessary in the school setting, with special attention to the elimination of racial, religious, or economic prejudice. Share with your classmates.
6. Explore a counseling specialty area you are interested in (e.g., schools, rehabilitation, marriage and family). Provide up-to-date information from

professionals and current literature in the field. Report findings to your classmates.

SELECTED READINGS

Bell, T. (1983). *A nation at risk: The imperative for educational reform.* Washington, DC: The National Commission on Excellence in Education.

Burnham, J. J., & Jackson, C. M. (2000). School counselor roles: Discrepancies between actual practice and existing models. *Professional School Counseling, 4*(1), 41–49.

Casey, J. A. (1995). Developmental issues for school counselors using technology. *Elementary School Guidance and Counseling, 30*(1), 26–34.

College Entrance Examination Board. (1986). *Keeping the options open.* New York: Author, Commission on Precollege Guidance and Counseling.

Davis, K. M., & Garrett, M. T. (1998). Bridging the gap between school counselors and teachers: A proactive approach. *Professional School Counseling, 1*(5), 54–55.

Dahir, C. A., Sheldon, C. B., & Valiga, M. J. (1998). *Vision into action: Implementing the national standards for school counseling programs.* Alexandria, VA: American School Counselor Association.

Dean, L., & Meadows, M. (1995). College counseling. Union and intersection. *Journal of Counseling and Development, 74*(2), 139–142.

Dennis, D. L., Buckner, J. C., Lipton, F. R., & Levine, I. S. (1991). A decade of research and services for homeless mentally ill persons. *American Psychologist, 46*(11), 1129–1138.

Gibson, R. L. (1990). Teacher opinions of high school guidance programs: Then and now. *The School Counselor, 37*, 248–255.

Herr, E. L., & Fabian, E. S. (Eds.). 1995. [Special issue]. Professional counseling: Spotlight on specialties. *Journal of Counseling and Development, 74*(2), 113–224.

Howard, G. S. (1993). Sports psychology: An emerging domain for counseling psychologists. *The Counseling Psychologist, 21*(3), 349–351.

Kelly, J. A., Murphy, D. A., Sikkema, K. J., & Kalichman, S. C. (1993). Psychological interventions to prevent HIV infection are urgently needed: New priorities for behavioral research in the second decade of AIDS. *American Psychologist, 48*(10), 1023–1034.

Kelly, K. R., & Hall, A. S. (Eds.). (1992). Mental health counseling for men. [Special issue]. *Journal of Mental Health Counseling, 14*(3).

Kunkel, M. A., & Newsom, S. (1996). Presenting problems for mental health services: A concept map. *Journal of Mental Health Counseling, 18*(1), 53–63.

Lawless, L. L., Ginter, E. J., & Kelly, K. R. (1999). Managed care: What mental health counselors need to know. *The Journal of Mental Health Counseling, 21*(1), 50–65.

Leahy, M. J., & Holt, E. (1993). Certification in rehabilitation counseling: History and process. *Rehabilitation Counseling Bulletin, 37*(2), 71–80.

Lenhardt, M. C., & Young, P. A. (2001). Proactive strategies for advancing elementary school counseling programs: A blueprint for the new millennium. *Professional School Counseling, 4*(3), 187–194.

McAuliffe, G. J. (1992). A case presentation approach to group supervision for community college counselors. *Counselor Education and Supervision, 31*(3), 163–174.

McCarthy, C. J., & Lambert, R. G. (1999). Structural model of coping and emotions produced by taking a new job. *Journal of Employment Counseling, 36*(2), 50–66.

Milburn, N., & D'Ercole, A. (1991). Homeless women. *American Psychologist, 46*(11), 1161–1169.

Neukrug, E. S. (1991). Computer-assisted live supervision in counselor skills training. *Counselor Education and Supervision, 31*(2), 132–138.

Pace, D., Stamler, V. L., Yarris, E., & June, L. (1996). Rounding out the cube: Evolution to a global model for counseling centers. *Journal of Counseling and Development, 74*(4), 321–325.

Paisley, P., & Borders, D. (1995). School counseling: An evolving specialty. *Journal of Counseling and Development, 74*(2), 150–153.

Psychotherapy with lesbian, gay, and bisexual clients. (2000). Guidelines for psychotherapists with lesbian, gay, and bisexual clients. Division 44/Committee on lesbian, gay, and bisexual concerns, joint task force on guidelines for psychotherapy with lesbian, gay, and bisexual clients. *American Psychologist, 55*(12), 1440–1451.

Rafferty, Y., & Shinn, M. (1991). The impact of homelessness on children. *American Psychologist, 46*(11), 1170–1179.

Reschly, D. J. (2000). The present and future status of school psychology in the United States. *School Psychology Review, 29*(4), 507–522.

Robbins, S. B., Lese, K. P., & Herrick, S. M. (1993). Interactions between goal instability and social support on college freshman adjustment. *Journal of Counseling and Development, 71*(3), 343–348.

Shapiro, E. S. (2000). School psychology from an instructional perspective: Solving big, not little problems. *School Psychology Review, 29*(4), 507–522.

Short, R. J., & Talley, R. C. (1997). Rethinking psychology and the schools: Implications of recent national policy. *American Psychologist, 52*(3), 234–240.

Sports psychology. (1993). [Special issue]. *The Counseling Psychologist, 21*(3).

Srebalus, D. J., Schwartz, J. L., Vaughan, R. V., & Tunick, R. H. (1996). Youth violence in rural schools: Counselor perceptions and treatment resources. *School Counselor, 44*(1), 48–54.

Towner-Larsen, R., Granello, D. H., & Sears, S. J. (2000). Supply and demand for school counselors: Perceptions of public school administrators. *Professional School Counseling, 3*(4), 270–276.

Worthington, R. L., & Juntunen, C. L. (1997). The vocational development of non-college-bound youth: Counseling psychology and the school-to-work transition movement. *Counseling Psychologist, 25*(3), 323–363.

RESEARCH OF INTEREST

Benjamin, B. A. (1992). Career counseling with couples. *Journal of Counseling and Development, 70*(4), 544–549.

Abstract This article examines a career counseling model that takes into account the couple dynamics active in the career choice process of the adult individual. It describes facilitative elements of career counseling with couples, the role of couple assessment, precautions in counseling couples, and future directions.

Casey, J., & Ramsammy, R. (1992, February). *MacMentoring: Using technology and counseling with at-risk youth.* Paper presented at the Annual Conference of the California Association for Counseling and Development, San Francisco.

Abstract The MacMentoring Project was designed to reconnect disenfranchised youth back into school through activities focused on enhancing self-esteem while also teaching them transferable computer skills. Among the subjects (N = 45), improvements of on-task behaviors, expression of creativity, benefits from a nondirective counseling strategy, and success at meeting expectations were demonstrated.

Danzinger, P. R., & Welfel, E. R. (2001). The impact of managed care on mental health counselors: A survey of perceptions, practices, and compliance with ethical standards. *Journal of Mental Health Counseling, 23*(2), 137–150.

Abstract A sample of 108 mental health counselors in four states was surveyed about their experiences and perceptions of the impact of managed care on their work with clients and the effects of managed care on their compliance with professional ethics. The majority reported that managed care has negatively affected their work with clients and that the protection of the confidentiality of client disclosures has been the most troublesome ethical issue. The study revealed gaps in accuracy of diagnosis, appropriateness of treatment, management of termination, and informed consent procedures with managed care clients. It also showed limited use of ethics codes and other resources developed to help professionals resolve ethical questions responsibly.

Fagan, T. K., & Jenkins, W. M. (1989). People with disabilities: An update. *Journal of Counseling and Development, 68*(2), 140–143.

Abstract This article provides information regarding disabling conditions in school-age and adult populations. It presents changes in federal legislation and interpretations of this legislation. The focus is on adult disabling conditions and rehabilitation services.

Fairchild, T. N., & Seeley, T. J. (1996). Evaluation of school psychological services: A case illustration. *Psychology in the Schools, 33*(1), 46–55.

Abstract This article describes how school psychological services were evaluated in two elementary schools serviced by the same school psychologist. Twenty-one students who had received individual counseling services and 183 students who had participated in classroom guidance activities were asked to complete questionnaires evaluating their experience. Forty-four teachers completed the one-page School Psychological Services Evaluation Scale, and 37 partners of students who had participated in psychoeducational assessment were asked to complete the Assessment Service Evaluation: Parent Rating Scale. The school psychologist also provided an accountability report. Results from the available sample show that school psychological services were positively viewed by students, teachers, and parents. Based on suggestions obtained during the evaluation, the school psychologist was also able to make improvements to the service.

Fisher, P. J., & Breakey, W. R. (1991). The epidemiology of alcohol, drug, and mental disorders among homeless persons. *American Psychologist, 46*(11), 1115–1128.

Abstract This article discusses recent research regarding the prevalence of alcohol, drugs, and mental (ADM) disorders and the personal characteristics of homeless substance abusers and individuals with mental disorders. It emphasizes that these individuals are impacted by extreme poverty; underutilization of public entitlements; isolation from family, friends, and other networks of support; frequent contacts with correctional agencies; and poor overall health. The conclusion is that awareness of those issues must take place in advocating more suitable services for persons experiencing homelessness.

Hardesty, P. H., & Dillard, J. M. (1994). The role of elementary school counselors compared with their middle and secondary school counterparts. *Elementary School Guidance and Counseling, 29*(2), 83–91.

Abstract This study examined the tasks and functions counselors at different grade levels view as important. Three hundred sixty-nine elementary, middle, and high school counselors were surveyed regarding activities in schools. Three major differences in the ranking of counselor activities by elementary counselors were found compared with their middle and secondary school counterparts: (a) elementary subjects perform more consultative and coordination activities; (b) elementary subjects may perform less administrative-type activities (scheduling and paperwork); and (c) whereas secondary subjects and middle school subjects seem to work with student concerns on an individual basis, elementary subjects tend to work systematically with families, teachers, and community agencies. Elementary school counselors need to actively demonstrate how their work contributes to the overall school environment and the development of students.

Hosie, T. W., West, J. D., & Mackey, J. A. (1993). Employment and roles of counselors in employee assistance programs. *Journal of Counseling and Development, 71*(3), 355–359.

Abstract Employment and roles of master's level counselors in employee assistance programs (EAPs) as well as the services offered by the diverse EAP organizations are examined. It was found that master's level counselors were similar to individuals with master's degrees in social work in employment rate and percentages among EAP staff. Differences in the roles of counselors among the EAP types are presented.

Lapan, R. T., Gysbers, N. C., & Petroski, G. F. (2001). Helping seventh graders be safe and successful: A statewide study of the impact of comprehensive guidance and counseling programs. *Journal of Counseling and Development, 79*(3), 320–330.

Abstract The researchers examined the relationships between statewide implementation of comprehensive guidance and counseling programs and indicators of safety and success for seventh graders. Hierarchical linear modeling was used to analyze data from 22,601 seventh graders attending 184 Mis-souri schools and 4,868 middle school teachers. After researchers controlled for differences between schools due to socioeconomic status and enrollment size, students attending middle schools with more fully implemented comprehensive programs reported (a) feeling safer attending their schools, (b) having better relationships with their teachers, (c) believing that their education was more relevant and important to their futures, (d) being more satisfied with the quality of education available to them in their schools, (e) having fewer problems related to the physical and interpersonal milieu in their schools, and (f) earning higher grades.

Leigh, B. C., & Stall, R. (1993). Substance use and risky sexual behavior for exposure to HIV. *American Psychologist, 48*(10), 1035–1045.

Abstract This article reviews research literature on the relationship between substance use and high-risk sexual behavior through global association studies, situational association studies, and event analysis procedures. It concludes that both sex and substance abuse are complicated behaviors and wonders whether related comprehension of the dynamics of the relationship is necessary.

Lombana, J. H. (1989). Counseling persons with disabilities: Summary and projections. *Journal of Counseling and Development, 68*(2), 177–179.

Abstract The findings of various articles pertaining to counseling individuals with disabilities and the progress recently made regarding provision of services to these individuals is presented here. Issues of concern in counseling persons with disabilities are discussed and guidelines for counselors in their future work with persons with disabilities are provided.

McCarthy, C. J., & Lambert, R. G. (1999). Structural model of coping and emotions produced by taking a new job. *Journal of Employment Counseling, 36*(2), 50–66.

Abstract The relationship of preventive and combative coping resources to appraisals and emotions produced by taking a new job was investigated at two separate times. Participants consisted of 231 graduate students who completed inventories measuring these variables regarding their last employment experience. The results of the structural model suggested that preventive coping resources may affect the appraised desirability of taking a new job as well as initial emotions related to this event, and that combative coping resources may affect subsequent emotional responses. The implications of these results for timing interventions by employment counselors using stress counseling techniques are discussed.

Mooney, S. P., Sherman, M. F., & Lo Presto, C. T. (1991). Academic locus of control, self-esteem, and perceived distance from home as predictors of college adjustment. *Journal of Counseling and Development, 69*(5), 445–448.

Abstract This article examines the academic locus of control, self-esteem, and geographic distance from home (actual and perceived) as predictors of college adjustment for female college freshmen (N = 88). Results indicate that internal academic locus of control, high levels of self-esteem, and a belief that the distance from home was "just right" for the individual related to personal, academic, social, and attachment adjustment.

Paulson, B. L., & Edwards, M. H. (1997). Parent expectations of an elementary school counselor: A concept-mapping approach. *Canadian Journal of Counselling, 31*(1), 67–81.

Abstract A concept-mapping process was used to understand parental expectations of an Edmonton elementary school counselor's role. The 25 parents who participated generated 91 statements that were subsequently sorted by each parent and analyzed to develop a seven-theme conceptualization of parental expectations. Parents requested that the counselor become highly involved in providing services that involve support, referral, education, and information. In addition to perceiving the counselor as a provider of direct counseling services, parents expected that the school counselor would collaborate extensively with them. Additional expectations include developmental programming for all children in the school and services involving teacher consultation, special needs programming, and community liaison.

Ritchie, M., Partin, R., & Trivette, P. (1998). Mental health agency directors' acceptance and perceptions of licensed professional counselors. *Journal of Mental Health Counseling, 20*(3), 227–237.

Abstract Two hundred three directors of mental health agencies responded to a survey designed to examine their level of acceptance and satisfaction with licensed professional counselors (LPCs) in Ohio. The directors reported hiring and salary rates for LPCs compared with other therapists. They rated the qualifications of LPCs and rated them on their ability to perform their duties. Most directors were licensed as social workers. Results revealed that there were three times as many social workers as counselors employed in the agencies. The directors' responses to the questionnaire suggest a preference for hiring social workers over counselors. Starting salaries for counselors were similar to those of social workers with similar educational levels. LPCs were rated as most competent in counseling skills but less competent in diagnosis. The directors reported a need for LPCs to have more training and experience in diagnosing using the *Diagnostic and Statistical Manual of Mental Disorders (DSM)* of the American Psychiatric Association and in making insurance reimbursement claims. Implications for training mental health counselors are discussed.

Roberts, A. H., & Rust, J. O. (1994). Role and function of school psychologists, 1992–1993: A comparative study. *Psychology in the Schools, 31*(2), 113–199.

Abstract This study examined the roles and functions of 52 school psychologists from Iowa and Tennessee. Three multivariate analyses of variance (MANOVAs) were used to test differences between (a) reported time spent on prereferral, assessment, intervention, consultation, and curriculum-based assessment; (b) reported actual time spent and desired time spent; and (c) desired time spent on the five variables. Significant differences were found for the time spent in all areas, in actual time spent versus desired time spent in consultation, and in desired time spent in curriculum-based assessment. Results suggest that school psychologists in Tennessee and Iowa occupy different roles. School psychologists in Tennessee reported spending the majority of their time on assessment activities, whereas the Iowa sample balances their time among the five functions.

Schmidt, J. J. (1995). Assessing school counseling programs through external reviews. *School Counselor, 43*(2), 114–123.

Abstract External reviews were performed in two southeastern school systems to respond to questions each school system had about the services being provided by counselors; the perceptions of students, parents, and teachers about those services; and the extent to which the current staff was meeting the needs of these audiences. Results indicated that accountability continues to be an important issue for the school counseling profession. Neither school system had a clearly defined school counseling program. The lack of evidence to support a comprehensive program with stated goals and objectives, a job description for school counselors, and guidelines for professional practice prevented either review team from recommending an increase in counseling positions. Findings reveal perceptions of school counselors as being overwhelmed with case loads, administrative duties, clerical tasks, and crises that occur in schools.

Shelby, J. S., & Tredinick, M. G. (1995). Crisis intervention with survivors of natural disaster: Lessons from

Hurricane Andrew. *Journal of Counseling and Development*, *73*(5), 491–497.

Abstract   This article presents anecdotal evidence from mental health work with Hurricane Andrew survivors in south Florida and discusses implications for general disaster counseling. The mental health workers served a predominantly lower socioeconomic group with diverse ethnic identities, all of whom had been left homeless by the 1992 hurricane. Interventions were based on the belief that enhancing clients' perceived power would restore or improve predisaster functioning. Issues presented by adults included helplessness and a sense of loss, both of which were dealt with through individual counseling, stress reduction techniques, and helping the adults increase their sense of mastery. Children experienced regression and anxiety and were treated through play therapy, drawing, and positive reframing. The effects of multicultural issues are noted.

Stinnett, T. A., Havey, J. M., & Oheler-Stinnett, J. (1994). Current test usage by practicing school psychologists: A national survey. *Journal of Psychoeducational Assessment*, *12*(4), 331–350.

Abstract   This study surveyed 123 members of the National Association of School Psychologists to examine the assessment activity of practicing school psychologists. Results indicate that assessment activities still account for about 50% of the practice hours of school psychologists, followed by consultation (20%) and treatment (19%). Subjects reported frequent use of intellectual, behavioral-social-emotional, achievement, and perceptual assessment methods but were less likely to be involved in vocational or preschool assessment. Familiar instruments, such as the Wechsler scales, the Woodcock-Johnson Psychoeducational Battery–Revised, the Wide Range Achievement Test–Revised, and the Vineland Adaptive Behavior Scales were the most used tests. In the social-emotional domain, direct assessment methods (e.g., interview and observation) were more frequently used and were rated as more important than standardized measures.

Szymanski, E. M., Leahy, M. J., & Linkowski, D. C. (1993). Reported preparedness of certified counselors in rehabilitation counseling knowledge areas. *Rehabilitation Counseling Bulletin*, *37*(2), 146–162.

Abstract   This study investigated the perceived preparedness of certified rehabilitation counselors and assessed differences in perceived preparedness across respondent characteristics. A sample of 1,535 rehabilitation counselors who renewed their certification between March 1991 and October 1992 reported that they were at least moderately prepared in the following areas that constituted the majority of rehabilitation counseling knowledge: vocational services; foundations of rehabilitation; case management and services; group and family counseling; medical and psychosocial aspects; workers' compensation, employer services, and technology; individual counseling and development; social, cultural, and environmental issues; research; and assessment. Significant differences in perceived preparedness on at least one subscale were found for preservice education level, gender, job setting, job title, and years of experience.

Watts, R. E., Trusty, J., Erdman, P., & Canada, R. (1996). Texas LPCs' perceptions of their counselor training: A brief report. *TCA Journal*, *24*(1), 9–14.

Abstract   This study examined counseling professionals' perceptions of how well their counselor training program prepared them for their work as professional counselors. A survey was made of 212 master's level counselors licensed by the Texas State Board of Examiners of Professional Counselors. Results show the subjects to be somewhat neutral regarding the effectiveness of their preparation. Subjects perceived their training in normal human development and theories of counseling to be adequate, whereas their training in substance abuse counseling, treatment planning, private practice, and the *DSM* system was perceived as inadequate.

Whiston, S. C., & Sexton, T. L. (1998). A review of school counseling outcome research: Implications for practice. *Journal of Counseling and Development*, *76*(4), 412–426.

Abstract   In this review, the authors summarize school counseling outcome research published between 1988 and 1995. Gysbers and Henderson's (1994) comprehensive developmental guidance model served as the organizing model through which the status of empirical literature regarding school counseling is examined. Results indicated that research focused more on remediation activities than preventive interventions. This review found tentative support for career planning, group counseling, social skill training activities, and peer counseling. Practical implications and future research direction are drawn from these conclusions.

Individual Counseling

Counseling is, of course, the single most important activity in which counselors engage. They are called counselors not because they give tests, offer career planning information, or provide consultation, but because they counsel. Counseling is a skill and a process distinguished from advising, directing, perhaps listening sympathetically, and appearing to be interested in many of the same concerns as professional counselors. To introduce this topic, the objectives of this chapter are to (a) orient the reader to traditional and popular theories of counseling, (b) introduce and briefly discuss the counseling process, and (c) examine some basic counseling skills.

Individual counseling has, since the early days of the movement into both school and nonschool settings, been identified as the heart of any program of counseling services. All other professional activities of the counselor lead to this most important function. Test results, career information, and autobiographies are all relatively meaningless if they do not provide information that enhances the effectiveness of the counseling process.

Many definitions of counseling are available to students of counseling. There are semantic differences, of course, but most definitions begin by suggesting that individual counseling is a one-to-one relationship involving a trained counselor and focuses on some aspects of a client's adjustment, developmental, or decision-making needs. This process provides a relationship and communications base from which the client can develop understanding, explore possibilities, and initiate change. In this setting, it is the counselor's competence that makes positive outcomes possible. The counselor's skills and knowledge provide the appropriate framework and direction that maximize the client's potential for positive results. Untrained and unskilled helpers, regardless of their best intentions, cannot duplicate the functions of the professional counselor.

Though counseling is viewed as a helping relationship, with the counselor as the helper, it is also a relationship in which the client must assume some responsibility to participate fully, cooperatively, and willingly. Only then can the potential benefits of the counseling relationship and process be realized.

THEORIES OF COUNSELING

Because the various definitions of counseling differ little in actual meaning, one might assume that all counselors function similarly in like situations; that, like so many robots, we would all respond similarly, interpret client information in the same manner, and agree on desired outcomes in specific counseling situations. Thus, a chapter on counseling techniques might read like a cookbook in which recipes were specified for the kinds of situations and the kinds of outcomes desired for these situations. Of course, nothing could be further from the truth. As definitions vary in counseling, the approaches that professional counselors use vary even more. Although the variety of these approaches may, at times, confuse the beginning student and the general public as well, it is fair to say that unlike recipes, they have proven useful in the provision of counseling services to various populations. These approaches are usually distinguished and described under their theoretical labels.

Theoretical models for counseling have their origins in the values and beliefs of persons who, in turn, have converted these into a philosophy and a theoretical model for counseling. These values and beliefs form a rationale for what one does, how one does it, and under what circumstance. It predicts probable outcomes for different sets of conditions. Theory summarizes the information base of the philosophy and draws conclusions.

For the beginner, as well as the experienced counselor, theories provide guidelines that have been tested by experienced counselors. They explain behaviors. They may predict desirable or undesirable outcomes in given circumstances. Theories can also assist counselors in organizing client data into a coherent and meaningful framework and the development of counseling strategies appropriate to the situation.

Of course, for the established theories, research has played an important part in bridging the gap between theory and practice through verifying or proving theoretical premises. This progress from theory to practice is depicted in Figure 4-1.

In the next section, we present brief descriptions of some of the popular counseling theories. Counselors in training, and certainly the proactive professional counselor, should be knowledgeable about the popularly recognized theories of counseling—their premises, characteristics, differences or similarities, and implications for practice. Note, however, that these and other recognized theories in the field of counseling provide only a base that the practicing counselor will modify to suit the unique situation in which he or she functions and his or her unique personality.

The roots of these traditional theories of counseling are in European and North American cultures. The pioneering theorists did not consider multicultural perspectives in their work. Thus, all these theories can be enhanced by multicultural awareness and considerations. In fact, counselors who fail to recognize the unique cultural background of clients from diverse backgrounds will handicap their client interaction. This suggests that counselors consider the extended background—family, support networks, coping styles, and so forth—plus the cultural context of the client for integration into their theoretical orientation.

Finally, we believe that eventually every counselor will adopt the theory or combination of theories, plus a multicultural perspective, that is most appropriate for him or her;

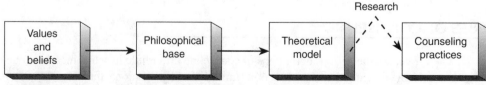

Figure 4-1   Bridging the gap from theory to practice.

with which he or she is most comfortable and effective; and that reflects what he or she is as a person *and* a professional.

Psychoanalytic Theory

For beginning counselors, the study of psychoanalytic theory is more important from a historic perspective than as a model for adoption. Sigmund Freud and Freudian therapy were prominently associated with the practice of psychoanalysis and psychotherapy throughout the 20th century and influenced the development of numerous other theories as well. Freud developed and popularized worldwide the first accepted comprehensive theory of personality development, which included not only a theory of personality but a method of therapy as well. Freud broadened the field of psychology and gave it a new and exciting look, though not without controversy, and assured himself of a prominent place in the history of the fields of counseling, psychology, and psychotherapy.

Psychoanalytic theory views the personality as divided into three major systems; the id, the ego, and the superego. The id is inherited and thus is present from birth. The id is believed by many to work on the pleasure principle and provides the drive for the pursuit of personal wants.

The ego is viewed as the only rational element of the personality. The ego also has contact with the world of reality. Because of this contact with reality, it controls consciousness and provides realistic and logical thinking and planning and will moderate the desires of the id.

The superego represents the conscience of the mind and operates on a principle of moral realism. It represents a person's moral code, usually based on one's perceptions of the moralities and values of society. As a result of its role, the superego in a sense is responsible for providing rewards, such as pride and self-love, and punishments, such as feelings of guilt or inferiority to its owner.

In this triangle, the superego, because it resides largely in the subconscious, is most aware of the impulses of the id and seeks to direct the ego to control the id. As a result, psychoanalytic theory views tension, conflict, and anxiety as inevitable in humans and believes that human behavior is therefore directed toward reduction of this tension. In this context (reduction of tension) Freud's daughter Anna further advanced psychoanalytic theory when she expanded on the concept of defense mechanisms. These may be characterized as mechanisms that help individuals reduce tensions, adapting or adjusting to situations through distortion or denial that would otherwise create high levels of stress or anxiety. It is fair to say that all of us use these techniques on occasion—perhaps to assuage our guilt feelings regarding something we failed to do or to tell ourselves (and maybe others) that we were not supposed to do it in the first place. For the most part, these are normal and operate at an unconscious level. Of course, excuses can become troublesome—for example, in the individual who rationalizes his or her consistently inappropriate and destructive behavior.

Indicated below are several commonly employed defense mechanisms.

- *Repression* represents memories, feelings, and thoughts that are stored in the unconscious because their recall may be painful or fearful. Much of what is repressed occurs in childhood and therefore, may not be readily verbalized. Because repression is usually limited to specific areas or topics, only behavior related to the area will be affected. Repression is viewed as the basic defense mechanism and psychoanalysis seeks to bring the repressed into the conscious.

- *Rationalization* is a commonly practiced defense mechanism that seeks to justify or provide a seemingly reasonable explanation to make undesirable or questionable behaviors appear logical, rational, or acceptable. It is frequently used to modify guilt feelings because the valid or true explanation for the behavior would produce feelings of guilt or anxiety.
- The return to an earlier form of behavior or stage of development is called *regression.* This usually occurs when the more mature or appropriate behavior is blocked by feelings of uncertainty, anxiety, fear, conflict, or lack of reward. In some instances, it will also represent a retreat to earlier more automatic responses.
- *Identification* gives one satisfaction or compensation by identifying with others and their achievements. In identification with others an individual may actually acquire new and useful behaviors.
- *Displacement* represents movement away from one object to another that is less threatening or anxiety producing. A common form of displacement is sublimation, wherein unacceptable urges may be channeled into more acceptable behaviors as, for example, the conversion of sexual interests and energy into nonsexual activities such as sports, religion, or work.
- *Overcompensation* (reaction formation) is the display of behaviors as attitudes that represent the opposite of one's repressed feelings. Anxiety and guilt feelings are repressed and their opposites expressed instead.

In summary, these and other defense mechanisms represent behavioral responses designed to protect the individual's current self-concept against threat.

In the psychoanalytical context, then, reducing tension becomes a major goal of counseling. Because personality conflict is present in all people, nearly everyone can benefit from professional counseling. Inasmuch as the psychoanalytic approach requires insights that in turn rely on openness and self-disclosure, multiculturally oriented counselors would be aware that some Asian, African, and Native Americans would see these traits as signs of immaturity.

Psychoanalytic theory usually views the client as weak and uncertain and in need of assistance in reconstructing a normal personality. The counselor is in the role of the expert who will facilitate or direct this restructuring. The client will be encouraged to talk freely, to disclose unpleasant, difficult, or embarrassing thoughts. The counselor will provide interpretation as appropriate, attempting to increase client insights. This in turn may lead the client to working through the unconscious and eventually to achieving the ability to cope realistically with the demands of the client's world and society as a whole. In this process, among the techniques the psychoanalytic counselor may employ are projective tests, play therapy, dream analysis, and free association, all of which require special training for the counselor, usually available only at the doctoral level.

Individual Psychology

Individual psychology is often called Adlerian therapy because its initial developer was Alfred Adler, a colleague of Freud who disagreed with him on some basic issues. This disagreement led Adler to break away entirely from Freud's circle. The works of Adler have had, in turn, a profound impact on many therapists who followed, such as Albert Ellis, Victor Frankl, Rudolf Dreikurs, Rollo May, and William Glasser.

Individual psychology sees the person holistically and focuses on the uniqueness of individuals. Adler's view of humans offered a positive and refreshing alternative focus to Freudian psychoanalytic theory. At the core of his theory was the belief that within the human being is an innate drive to overcome perceived inferiorities and to develop his or her own potential for self-actualization, and that given a positive environment, this growth will take place.

What is it that keeps a person from moving in a fast and easy manner toward this full realization of self? For Adler it was feelings of inferiority. A person permits himself or herself to experience these feelings through three sources: (a) our biological dependency and dependency in general as infants, (b) our image of ourselves in relationship to the grandeur of the universe, and (c) organ inferiority. The drive within ourselves, however, enables us to compensate for these feelings and strive for superiority and perfection.

Adlerian theory has been, on occasion, referred to as socioteleogical for its viewpoint of individuals constantly striving to achieve their goals. He also stressed the importance of developing the client's social interests and reeducating clients so that they can live in society as individuals who give to the society as well as receive from it.

When a person comes for therapy, he or she is assumed to be experiencing incongruence and discomfort in (a) work, (b) friendship, or (c) love. The counseling process then is seen as a means by which the therapist and counselee work together to help the counselee develop awareness as well as healthier attitudes and behaviors so as to function more fully in society on the more useful side of life. Developing social interest is seen as the salient variable of one's mental health.

The Adlerian counseling process involves four stages: (a) establishing a relationship, (b) diagnosis, (c) insight/interpretation, and (d) reorientation. In the first session the counselor establishes a relationship with the client through a subjective/objective interview in which the client is helped to feel comfortable, accepted, respected, and cared about. Through an "objective component of the interview, the client is encouraged to explain what specifically has helped him or her determine the need for counseling. The client is asked to discuss how things are going in each of the life task areas. Also during this first session the counseling process is explained and discussed with the client. The diagnostic stage involves the "lifestyle interview," a formal assessment procedure that looks at things such as family constellation, perceptions of self in relationship to siblings, perceptions of parents, early recollections, and recurrent dreams.

The interpretation phase is the time during which the counselor and the client develop insight from the lifestyle interview into the client's "basic mistakes" by analyzing and discussing the convictions, goals, and movement that the client developed early in life and the ensuing thought, emotional, and behavioral patterns and attitudes.

The reorientation stage is perhaps the most critical, for it is in this stage that the therapist helps the counselee to move from "intellectual" insight to actual development and expression of healthier attitudes and behaviors. Here the client—with the counselor's support, encouragement, and direction—actively pursues changing unhealthy ways of thinking, feeling, and behaving to ways that are more satisfying and healthy for himself or herself and society.

Adler was one of the pioneers in family therapy who made "spin off" contributions to the field of elementary school counseling. Today, concepts of Adlerian counseling are also being utilized in working with children of divorce and/or remarriage.

Person-Centered Theory

Person-centered (formerly referred to as client-centered) counseling is another historically significant and influential theory. This theory was originally developed and described by Carl R. Rogers as a reaction against what he considered the basic limitations of psychoanalysis. As a result of his influence, this particular approach is often referred to as Rogerian counseling. The Rogerian approach stresses the client's capability and responsibility to identify ways to more accurately identify and cope with reality. The better clients know themselves, the more likely they are to identify the most appropriate behaviors for themselves. Rogers emphasized the importance for the counselor to be a warm, genuine, empathic, and caring individual.

In understanding the client- or person-centered approach to counseling, be aware of the personality basis for this theory, as presented by Rogers (1959a) in the form of 19 propositions. The lead statements for each of these propositions are as follows:

1. Every individual exists in a continually changing world of experience of which he is the center.
2. The organism reacts to the field as it is experienced and perceived. This perceptual field is, for the individual, "reality."
3. The organism reacts as an organized whole to this phenomenal field.
4. The organism has one basic tendency and striving—to actualize, maintain, and enhance the experiencing organism.
5. Behavior is basically the goal-directed attempt of the organism to satisfy its needs as experienced, in the field as perceived.
6. Emotion accompanies and in general facilitates goal-directed behavior, the kind of emotion being related to the seeking versus the consummatory aspects of the behavior, and the intensity of the emotion being related to the perceived significance of the behavior for the maintenance and enhancement of the organism.
7. The best vantage point for understanding behavior is from the internal frame of reference of the individual himself.
8. A portion of the total perceptual field gradually becomes differentiated as the self.
9. As a result of interaction with the environment, and particularly as a result of evaluational interaction with others, the structure of self is formed—an organized, fluid, but consistent conceptual pattern of perceptions of characteristics and relationships of the "I" or the "me," together with values attached to these concepts.
10. The values attached to experiences and the values which are a part of the self-structure, in some instances, are values experienced directly by the organism, and in some instances are values introjected or taken over from others, but perceived in distorted fashion, *as if* they had been experienced directly.
11. As experiences occur in the life of the individual, they are either (a) symbolized, perceived, and organized into some relationship to the self; (b) ignored because there is no perceived relationship to the self-structure; (c) denied symbolization

or given a distorted symbolization because the experience is inconsistent with the structure of the self.

12. Most of the ways of behaving which are adopted by the organism are those which are consistent with the concept of self.

13. Behavior may, in some instances, be brought about by organic experiences and needs which have not been symbolized. Such behavior may be inconsistent with the structure of the self, but in such instances the behavior is not "owned" by the individual.

14. Psychological maladjustment exists when the organism denies to awareness significant sensory and visceral experiences, which consequently are not symbolized and organized into the gestalt of the self-structure. When this situation exists, there is a basic or potential psychological tension.

15. Psychological adjustment exists when the concept of the self is such that all the sensory and visceral experiences of the organism are, or may be assimilated on a symbolic level into a consistent relationship with the concept of self.

16. Any experience which is inconsistent with the organization or structure of self may be perceived as a threat, and the more of these perceptions there are, the more rigidly the self-structure is organized to maintain itself.

17. Under certain conditions, involving primarily complete absence of any threat to the self-structure, experiences which are inconsistent with it may be perceived, and examined, and the structure of self revised to assimilate and include such experiences.

18. When the individual perceives and accepts into one consistent and integrated system all his sensory and visceral experiences, then he is necessarily more understanding of others and is more accepting of others as separate individuals.

19. As the individual perceives and accepts into his self-structure more of his organic experiences, he finds that he is replacing his present value system—based so largely upon introjections which have been distortedly symbolized—with a continuing organismic valuing process. (pp. 483–524)

In the counseling relationship, six conditions account for personality change in the client. These were presented by Rogers (1959a, 1967).

1. Two people (a therapist and a client) are in psychological contact. (Rogers, 1967, p. 73)
2. The client is experiencing a state of anxiety, distress, or incongruence.
3. The therapist is genuine (truly himself or herself) in relating to the client.
4. The therapist feels or exhibits unconditional positive regard for the client.
5. The therapist exhibits empathetic understanding of the client's frame of reference and conveys this understanding to the client.
6. The therapist succeeds to a minimum degree in communicating empathetic understanding and unconditional positive regard to the client. (Rogers, 1959a, p. 213)

Some of the changes expected from a successful utilization of this approach are these:

- The person comes to see himself differently.
- He accepts himself and his feelings more fully.
- He becomes more self-confident and self-directing.

- He becomes more the person he would like to be.
- He becomes more flexible, less rigid, in his perceptions.
- He adopts more realistic goals for himself.
- He behaves in a more mature fashion.
- He changes his maladjustive behaviors, even such a long-established one as chronic alcoholism.
- He becomes more acceptant of others.
- He becomes more open to the evidence, both to what is going on outside of himself, and to what is going on inside of himself.
- He changes in his basic personality characteristics in constructive ways. (Rogers, 1959b, p. 232)

Thus, Rogerian theory is optimistic in its view of humankind. Clients are seen as being basically good and possessing the capabilities for self-understanding, insight, problem solving, decision making, change, and growth.

The counselor's role is that of a facilitator and reflector. The counselor facilitates a counselee's self-understanding and clarifies and reflects back to the client the expressed feelings and attitudes of the client. Giving information for problem solving in a client-centered context is not usually considered a counselor responsibility. The client-centered counselor also would not seek to direct the mediation of the counselee's "inner world"; instead, he or she would provide a climate in which the counselee could bring about change in himself or herself.

Another label, *self-theory,* has also been used instead of the traditional labels. This has probably resulted from the emphasis on enhancement of the self, the capacity of one's self, self-actualization, and self-perceptions. Regardless of one's choice of label, this theory, originated by Rogers, continues to exert its influence on the field of counseling.

Regardless of label changes, Rogers's popular writings have, for over 40 years, advanced the public image of the counselor and counseling. His tremendous contributions to the profession itself in the areas of both individual and group counseling created a whole new wave of person-centered counselors and left a positive and lasting impact on the whole field of mental health and the helping professions.

Behavioral Theory

Each of us has our own unique patterns of behavior and most of us believe we understand at least why we behave the way we do and perhaps even the behavior of identifiable others as well. We may have only anecdotal rather than scientific evidence; nonetheless, as countless others have done, we may develop our own personal theory of behavior. The scientific development of behavioral theory and conditioning can be traced directly from Pavlov's 19th-century discoveries in classical conditioning. Important foundations for the behavioral approach later were discovered from the system of psychology called behaviorism, founded by American psychologist John B. Watson (1913) and expressed initially in his article "Psychology as the Behaviorist Views It."

Significant research and publication on the subject were conducted by Watson, Thorndike, and others, but it was not until B. F. Skinner systematically refined and developed his principles of behaviorism that the behavioral theory moved toward its current popularity. The behaviorist views behavior as a set of learned responses to events, experiences, or stimuli in a person's life history. The behaviorist believes that behavior can be modified by providing appropriate learning conditions and experiences. The experimental origins of the behaviorist's approach explain their indifference to concepts that cannot be empirically observed or measured. Thus, rather than being concerned with the emotional dynamics of behavior characteristic of the insight approaches of either Freudians or Rogerians, the behaviorist focuses on specific behavioral goals, emphasizing precise and repeatable methods. The behavioral theoretical approach to counseling has grown steadily since the 1950s and today is utilized by therapists in a wide variety of settings. This approach has been successful in the treatment of smoking, weight control and other eating disorders, substance abuse, speech difficulties, behavior problems, and others.

For the behaviorist, counseling involves the systematic use of a variety of procedures that are intended specifically to change behavior in terms of mutually established goals between a client and a counselor. The procedures employed encompass a wide variety of techniques drawn from knowledge of learning processes. A current leader in behavioral psychology, John D. Krumboltz (1966), historically placed these procedures into four categories:

1. *Operant Learning.* This approach is based on the usefulness of reinforcers and the timing of their presentation in producing change. Reinforcers may be concrete rewards or expressed as approval or attention.
2. *Imitative Learning.* This approach facilitates acquisition of new responses by exposure to models performing the desired behaviors.
3. *Cognitive Learning.* This technique fosters learning of appropriate responses by simply instructing the client how he may better adapt.
4. *Emotional Learning.* Involves substitution of acceptable emotional responses for unpleasant emotional reactions, using techniques derived from classical condition. (pp. 13–20)

John Krumboltz popularized behavioral approaches to counseling by identifying counseling as a way to help people learn to solve their problems. Learning and relearning are viewed as ways to help people make changes. Krumboltz also applied behavioral theory in terms of quantifying and measuring baselines and successes in counseling.

Arnold Lazarus developed a systematic multimodal approach to counseling and psychotherapy based on a behavioral model. In his model, he uses the acronym BASIC-ID to account for all of the facets of a client's life. Multimodal therapy is not considered behavioral purely because it is based on reconditioning but because it is action oriented and focuses on what is observable.

The cognitive-behaviorists helped popularize behavioral methods of skill practice and homework assignments. Meichenbaum, for example, has created a cognitive-behavioral approach to skill improvement using self-monitoring and self-verbalization.

Behaviorists believe that stating the goals of counseling in terms of behavior that is observable is more useful than stating goals that are more broadly defined, such as self-understanding or self-acceptance. This means that counseling outcomes should be identifiable in terms of overt behavior changes. Three examples of behavioral change appropriate to counseling are the altering of behavior that is not satisfactory, the learning of the decision-making process, and problem prevention.

In many ways, practicing behavioral counselors follow an approach similar to that of other counselors in clarifying and understanding the needs of their clients. They use reflection, summarization, and open-ended inquiries. But rather than probing for deeper feelings, they are seeking to better understand dimensions of the client's situation and environment. Feelings are secondary to behaviors. Behavioral counselors attempt to uncover the specific antecedents, circumstances, and consequences of client situations so they will be able to develop specific goals, objectives, and treatment plans.

Behavioral counselors also take a more directive role than many counselors in initiating and directing therapeutic activities. Sessions tend to be structured and action oriented. Behavioral counselors often take on roles of teacher or coach.

Counselors utilizing behavioral theory assume that the client's behavior is the result of conditioning. The counselor further assumes that each individual reacts in a predictable way to any given situation or stimulus, depending on what the person has learned.

Current behavior therapy often involves the client in all aspects of the procedure. According to Gilliland and James (1998),

> Most modern behavioral counselors approach the helping process from a much broader perspective than was the case a few years ago. Rather than viewing the counselor as the expert who scientifically develops and imposes behavior-modifying processes on the client, the modern approach strives to involve the client in the analysis, planning, process, and evaluation of his or her behavior-management program. Modern behavioral counselors seek to help the client extinguish a wide range of maladaptive behaviors and learn adaptive behaviors needed to establish and maintain targeted goals and consequences. The counselor collaborates with the client. The counselor is expected to have training and experience in human behavior modification and also to serve as consultant, teacher, adviser, reinforcer, and facilitator. (p. 206)

Success with behavioral interventions will generally come to clients with particular characteristics:

- People with a strong goal orientation—motivated by achieving goals or getting results.
- People who are action-oriented—need to be active, goal-focused, participating in the helping process (this includes several cultural groups, including Asians and African Americans).
- People who are interested in changing a discrete and limited (two to three) number of behaviors. (Hackney & Cormier, 1996, p. 213)

Rational Emotive Behavior Therapy

Often, one person—for instance, Carl R. Rogers—is associated with the formulation and development of a theory. In the case of Rogers, it is client-centered therapy. Similarly, rational emotive behavior therapy (REBT), formerly known as RET, was formulated by Albert Ellis. This theory is based on the assumption that people have the capacity to act in either a rational or irrational manner. Rational behavior is viewed as effective and potentially productive, whereas irrational behavior results in unhappiness and nonproductivity. Ellis assumes that many types of emotional problems result from irrational patterns of thinking. This irrational pattern may begin early and be reinforced by significant others in the individual's life as well as by the general culture and environment. According to Ellis, people with emotional problems develop belief systems that lead to implicit verbalizations or self-talk resting on faulty logic and assumptions. And what a person tells himself or herself is intimately related to the way that person feels and acts. The main propositions of REBT can be described as follows:

- People are born with a potential to be rational (self-constructive) as well as irrational (self-defeating).
- People's tendency to irrational thinking, self-damaging habituations, wishful thinking, and intolerance is frequently exacerbated by their culture and their family group.
- Humans perceive, think, emote, and behave simultaneously.
- Although all the major psychotherapies employ a variety of cognitive, emotive, and behavioral techniques, and although all (including unscientific methods such as witch doctoring) may help individuals who have faith in them, they are probably not equally effective or efficient.
- Rational emotive behavior therapists do not believe a warm relationship between client and counselor is a necessary or a sufficient condition for effective personality change, though it is quite desirable.
- Rational emotive behavior therapies use role-playing, assertion training, desensitization, humor, operant conditioning, suggestion, support, and a whole bag of other "tricks."
- REBT holds that most neurotic problems involve unrealistic, illogical, self-defeating thinking and that if disturbance-creating ideas are vigorously disputed by logico-empirical and pragmatic thinking, they can be minimized.
- REBT shows how activating events or adversities (A) in people's lives contribute to but do not directly "cause" emotional consequences (C); these consequences stem from people's interpretations of these events—their unrealistic and over-generalized beliefs (B) about them. (Corsini & Wedding, 2000, pp. 169–170).

Ellis has identified a series of 11 values or ideas that are universal in Western societies and inevitably lead to neurotic behaviors.

1. I believe I must be loved or approved of by virtually everyone with whom I come in contact.
2. I believe I should be perfectly competent, adequate, and achieving to be considered worthwhile.
3. Some people are bad, wicked, or villainous, and therefore should be blamed and punished.
4. It is a terrible catastrophe when things are not as I would want them to be.
5. Unhappiness is caused by circumstances that are out of my control.
6. Dangerous or fearsome things are sources of great concern and their possibility for harm should be a constant concern for me.
7. It is easier to avoid certain difficulties and responsibilities than it is to face them.
8. I should be dependent to some extent on other persons and should have some person on whom I can rely to take care of me.
9. Past experiences and events are what determine my present behavior; the influence of the past cannot ever be erased.

10. I should be quite upset over other people's problems and disturbances.
11. There is always a right or perfect solution to every problem, and it must be found or the results will be catastrophic. (Hackney & Cormier, 1996, p. 182)

The goal of REBT is to reduce or eliminate irrational behavior. In order to change this undesired behavior clients have to learn how their thinking, emotions, and behavior are interrelated. Negative and self-defeating thoughts and emotions must be reorganized so that the client's thinking becomes logical and rational.

The REBT therapist may frequently challenge, provoke, and probe the irrational beliefs of the client. In the relationship the counselor is viewed more as a teacher and the client as a student. As a result, procedures may include not only teaching and related activities such as reading or other assignments, but also questioning and challenging, even confrontation tactics, contracts, suggestions, and persuasion. REBT can be applied not only to individual therapy but also to group therapy, marathon encounter groups, marriage counseling, and family therapy.

REBT is frequently relatively short term and is not helpful with the seriously disturbed. Clients usually have little difficulty in learning the underlying principles and terminology of REBT. Although REBT therapists may challenge clients, such confrontations with minority clients should not bring into question the client's cultural values and background.

Reality Therapy

Another theory of counseling that has gained popularity in recent decades is that of reality therapy, largely developed by William Glasser. Glasser's approach is a fairly straightforward one that places confidence in the counselee's ability to deal with his or her needs through a realistic or rational process. From a reality therapy standpoint, counseling is simply a special kind of training that attempts to teach an individual what he should have learned during normal growth in a rather short period of time. Glasser (1984) suggested that reality therapy is

> applicable to individuals with any sort of psychological problem, from mild emotional upset to complete psychotic withdrawal. It works well with behavior disorders of the aged and the young, and with drug- and alcohol-related problems. It has been applied widely in schools, corrections institutions, mental hospitals, general hospitals, and business management. It focuses on the present and on getting people to understand that they choose essentially all their actions in an attempt to fulfill basic needs. When they are unable to do this they suffer, or cause others to suffer. The therapist's task is to lead them toward better or more responsible choices that are almost always available. (p. 320)

Glasser originally (1981) conceptualized reality therapy in eight steps:

- Make friends or get involved, or get along; create a relationship or gain rapport.
- De-emphasize the patient's history and find out what you are doing *now*.
- Help the patient learn to make an evaluation of his or her behavior. Help the patient find out if what he or she is saying is really *helpful*.
- Once you have evaluated the behavior, then you can begin to explore alternative behaviors—behaviors that may prove more helpful.
- Get a commitment to a plan of change.

- Maintain an attitude of "No excuses if you don't do it." By now the patient is committed to the change and must learn to be responsible in carrying it out.
- Be tough without punishment. Teach people to do things without being punished if they do not; it creates a more positive motivation.
- Refuse to give up. Once clients realize the counselor will not give up, they feel more support and work proceeds with more efficiency and promise.

In 1989, Glasser's *Control Theory* was published, elaborating on his reality theory. In his control theory, Glasser identified his concept of the components of total behavior as (a) active behavior, (b) thinking, (c) feeling, and (d) physiology as the capacity to produce voluntary and involuntary body mechanisms. Glasser believes that control theory could help individuals take more effective control of their lives; that human beings are control systems and this is how they function to fulfill their needs. Reality therapy (and control theory) suggest that humans have four needs, which are encoded in their genes:

- the need to belong, to love, cooperate, and share
- the need for power
- the need for freedom
- the need for fun and recreation

Reality therapy focuses on present behavior and consequently does not emphasize the client's past. When using this approach, the counselor functions as a teacher and a model. Reality therapy is based on the premise that there is a single psychological need that is present throughout life: the need for identity, which includes a need to feel a sense of uniqueness, separateness, and distinctiveness. This need, which accounts for the dynamics of behavior, is seen as universal among all cultures.

Reality therapy is based on the anticipation that the client will assume personal responsibility for his or her well-being. The acceptance of this responsibility, in a sense, helps people achieve autonomy or a state of maturity whereby they rely on their own internal support. Whereas many of the counseling theories suggest that the counselor should function in a noncommital way, reality therapists praise clients when they act responsibly and indicate disapproval when they do not.

Glasser has, throughout his writings, expressed an intense interest in education. In his book, *Reality Therapy* (1965), he described his concepts for helping children in problem solving. Glasser believed that the public schools were failure prone; he promoted a success model for schools rather than what he saw as the traditional model of failure. As a result, reality therapy has been successfully implemented not only in agencies and mental health institutions but also in many schools and school systems. He later published his ideas regarding education in his bestseller book, *Schools Without Failure* (1969), in which he suggested a program to eliminate failure and to replace the traditional model of memory work, irrelevant instruction, and discipline with a model stressing relevance, prevention, and success. He sought to create an environment that would motivate and involve students in the development of responsible behavior. He also sought to establish ways of involving parents and the community in the schools and in their children's education.

Both in and out of school, reality therapy stresses the importance of making a plan through which the client can improve his or her behavior. This plan should lead to behavior that enables the client to gain satisfaction and often favorable recognition as well.

Transactional Analysis

Transactional analysis is a cognitive-behavioral approach that assumes a person has the potential for choosing and redirecting or reshaping his or her own destiny. Eric Berne did much to develop and popularize this theory in the 1960s. It is designed to help a client review and evaluate early decisions and to make new, more appropriate choices.

Transactional analysis views normal personality as a product of healthy parenting (I'm OK, you're OK). Abnormal personality results when the child "must play games" to gain approval. Transactional analysis then seeks to understand the transactions between individuals in order to understand the different personalities that are a part of each of us. Each of these personalities behaves in its own distinct pattern and is, at different times, in control of the individual. When one of the three ego states is unwilling to relinquish its control and asserts it rigidly, especially at inappropriate times, the client is in difficulty and in need of psychological assistance. Transactional analysis will seek to restore a damaged ego and develop the client's capacity to use all ego states appropriately, especially the adult, which is needed to govern one's life.

Thus, transactional analysis (TA) places a great deal of emphasis on the ego, which, from this viewpoint, consists of three states: parent, adult, and child.

CHILD: A set of behaviors, feelings and/or attitudes that are the relics of the individual's childhood and are important in building a person's adult self-concept.

PARENT: A product of "recordings" from an individual's parents that are passed on and/or acted on. This is sometimes referred to as parental conditioning.

ADULT: This ego state develops from the assimilation of the individual's unique experiences from childhood on. These are translated into facts which then become regulatory in the individual's life and thus, the "adult" is the most changeable of the three ego states.

Each of these states can take charge of the individual to the point that his or her observable behavior indicates "who's in charge" (adult, parent, or child). The client is assisted in gaining social control of his or her life by learning to use all ego states where appropriate. The ultimate goal is to help the client change from inappropriate life positions and behaviors (life scripts) to new more productive behaviors while coming from an "I'm O.K." position." (Gibson, Mitchell, & Basile, 1993, p. 74)

An essential technique in TA counseling is the contract that precedes each counseling step. This contract between counselor and counselee is a way of training or preparing people to make their own important decisions. In addition to the contract technique, transactional analysis also utilizes questionnaires, life scripts, structural analysis, role playing, analysis of games and rituals, and "stroking" (reinforcement). Although recording is not a counseling technique, transactional analysis sessions are tape recorded in their entirety.

At each stage of counseling the decision to go ahead is squarely up to the counselee. (This is the way the counselor protects himself or herself from implications that the counseling is being forced on the counselee.) The counselor may specify conditions for client participation in contracts, such as requiring the counselee to define, in advance, what advantage might ensue from their joint effort.

Although transactional analysis, like all theories, focuses on the individual, it is basically a procedure for counseling people within a group setting. TA counselors feel that the group setting facilitates the process of providing feedback to persons about the kind of transactions in which they engage. The counseling group, then, represents a microcosm of the real world. In this setting, the individual group members are there to work on their own objectives and the counselor acts as the group leader.

Gestalt Counseling

"Gestalt therapy, developed by Frederick Perls, is a therapeutic approach in which the therapist assists the client toward self-integration and toward learning to utilize his energy in appropriate ways to grow, develop, and actualize" (George & Cristiani, 1995, p. 66). The primary focus of this approach is the present—the here and now. This approach implies that the past is gone and the future has yet to arrive; therefore, only the present is important.

Gestalt counseling also has as its major objective the integration of the person. In popular terminology, this might be called getting it all together. Perls (1948) wrote,

> The treatment is finished when the patient has achieved the basic requirements: a change in outlook, a technique of adequate self-expression and assimilation, and the ability to extend awareness to the verbal level. He has then reached that state of integration which facilitates its own development, and he can now be safely left to himself. (p. 58)

In order to achieve this togetherness, the counselor seeks to increase the client's awareness. As a result, the counselor functions in a way that provides the client with an atmosphere conducive to the discovery of client needs, or what the client has lost because of environmental demands, and in which the client can experience the necessary discovery and growth.

In this process the counselor will engage the client in what Perls labels a here and now discussion. The counselor attempts to provide the client assistance in identifying what she needs to become independent—to not be dependent on others. In order to accomplish this, the client must work on getting her act together in order to function as a systematic whole encompassing behaviors, feelings, thoughts, and attitudes. In this process, clients must also learn to take responsibility for themselves.

Cited by George and Cristiani (1995), Passons lists eight assumptions about the nature of humans that act as the framework for Gestalt counseling:

1. Individuals are composite wholes made up of interrelated parts. None of these parts—body, emotions, thoughts, sensations, and perceptions—can be understood outside the context of the whole person.
2. Individuals are also part of their own environment and cannot be understood apart from it.
3. People choose how they respond to external and internal stimuli; they are actors, not reactors.
4. People have the potential to be fully aware of all their sensations, thoughts, emotions, and perceptions.

5. Individuals are capable of making choices because they are aware.
6. Individuals have the capacity to govern their own lives effectively.
7. People cannot experience the past and the future; they can experience only themselves in the present.
8. People are neither basically good nor bad. (p. 66)

From these assumptions we can conclude that the Gestalt therapist has a positive view of the individual's capacity for self-direction. Furthermore, clients must be encouraged to utilize this capacity and take responsibility for their own lives—and do that *now,* in the present; they must experience the here and now! Counseling techniques may include "how" and "what" questions, confrontations, "I" statements, and sharing awareness with clients emphasizing "this moment."

Other Theories

In addition to the traditional theories of counseling previously described, there are several other popular theoretical approaches of which beginning counselors should be aware and which they can explore further if they choose. Then, there is the traditional eclectic approach that enables a counselor to employ the strengths of the various approaches without being wedded to any one specific theory.

Existential

Individuals define who they are by their choices even though there may be factors beyond their control that restrict their choices. It is important for all of us to find meaning in our lives through awareness. This awareness is underlined through the experience of being, or the "I am" experience, known in existential therapy as an ontological experience that translates into the science "of being." A basic concept of existential therapy is called "being in the world." This implies that the counselor must understand the phenomenological world in which the client exists and participates. This world is not limited to the environment, which is viewed as only one model of the client's world, but must also include the human world that is the structure of meaningful relationships in which the client exists and in the design of which the client participates.

> From the point of view of existential psychotherapy, there are three modes of world. The first is *Umwelt,* meaning "world around," the biological world, the environment. The second is *Mitwelt,* literally the "with-world," the world of one's fellow human beings. The third is *Eigenwelt,* the "own-world," the relationship to one's self (May & Yalom, 2000, p. 276).

Within the existential framework, counselors may help clients recognize outmoded ways of life and become willing to take the responsibility to change, to expand, and to find meaning in their life that is unique to them. Counselors can also help clients improve their human relationships with others and recognize their own importance in society.

Family Systems Therapy

Family systems theory is based on the assumption that the client cannot be completely understood apart from his or her family. For example, when dramatic changes take place in the family unit, all members of the unit will be affected. Interactions between the individual and her or his family members are usually significant. Mentally healthy people have good family relations and satisfactory relationships outside the family. Counselors help individuals who need better relationships with important people in their lives in or out of the family unit. The basis for improving these relationships often comes from the need to promote better communications among family members. It is also important that counselors assist families in learning a process for successful problem solving.

Multimodal Therapy

Multimodal therapy is a systematic and comprehensive approach developed originally by Arnold Lazarus. This approach is characterized by unique assessment procedures and by significant emphasis and detail with sensory, imagery, cognitive, and interpersonal factors and their interactive effects on the client. Multimodal therapy presumes that clients are more frequently troubled by a multitude of problems that can be more effectively dealt with by using a broad range of special methods. The emphasis of this therapy on assessment leads to an examination of each area of a client's BASIC ID:

B = Behavior

A = Affect

S = Sensation

I = Imagery

C = Cognition

I = Interpersonal relationships

D = Drugs/Biology

(Lazarus, 2000, p. 340)

This theory is personalized and individualistic. The assessment of the client seeks to identify his or her exceptions to general rules and principles and identify the appropriate intervention for the client. In a manner of speaking the counselor functions somewhat like an eclectic theorist, using techniques and procedures drawn from a variety of sources without necessarily subscribing to them. This, according to Lazarus, "is a consistent, systematic, and testable set of beliefs and assumptions about human beings and their problems, and an armamentarium of effective therapeutic strategies for remedying their afflictions" (Lazarus, 2000, p. 341).

Integrated Theories

In recent years we have seen continued efforts not only to reinforce and expand on the many traditional theories of counseling but also to develop new multidimensional and integrated models. One of these, Actualization Counseling and Psychotherapy, presented by Brammer, Shostrom, and Abrego (1989), represents a creative synthesis approach to counseling theory and human growth. Actualization Counseling is based, in part, upon assumptions drawn from major theoretical approaches.

> Actualization counseling represents a developmental therapy derived from *historical and psychodynamic approaches* to counseling. The person is viewed from a perspective of development over time: past, present, and future.

1. Development is cumulative in the sense that early experiences influence the kinds of later experiences a person will have. The meaning and impact of events is influenced by past history, which shapes our expectations and desires.

2. Unresolved conflicts and grief from previous generations can become transmitted in an intergenerational process, which may constrict current personal growth and contribute toward symptom development.

3. Personal development becomes actualized as individuals develop clear internal boundaries. Clear boundaries within oneself involves an awareness of one's own moment-to-moment thoughts and feelings, inner polarities and conflicts, and defensive style.

4. Personality development is dynamic, changing its focus and pattern over time.

5. Development is enhanced by a consistent core identity, which can orchestrate changing life structures or "season," and a broad repertoire of skills to anticipate and manage situational and developmental stress.

6. Insight into one's development over time can be an invaluable assistance in self-actualization. However, insight is of limited usefulness unless it is accompanied by the experience of changed behavior patterns.

Actualization therapy derives important assumptions from *phenomenological approaches* to counseling.

7. We affirm the uniqueness of each individual. We believe that personal development involves learning to become aware of one's own unique strengths, limitations, and purpose.

8. One's representation of events determines behavior more than events themselves. These internal beliefs guide one's behavior with others. Concurrently, circular recursive interactional patterns with others shape one's expectations and interpretations of events. This ongoing feedback from others intentionally or unintentionally confirms or disconfirms existing internal psychological beliefs and structures.

9. One has freedom to choose much of one's future. While much of human behavior is shaped by personal history and systemic forces, the actualizing process assumes that one's future is largely undetermined and a person has wide ranges of freedom to choose.

10. The assumption of freedom places corresponding responsibility on the person for his or her own actualizing. Even though growth takes place in a social context, each person is responsible for initiating and maintaining changes for his or her own life, based on an examined and considered choice of values and principles. The therapist maintains an active neutrality, emphasizing accurate empathic understanding while valuing the person's responsibility to choose his or her own goals.

Behavior therapy contributes an action focus to actualizing therapy as well as an understanding of how change occurs.

11. While some primitive behaviors are reflexive, hence largely genetically determined, and some are the result of chemical or neurological changes, a fundamental assumption of actualization counseling is that social behavior is learned and changes in

behavior follow an active learning process. Important life skill deficits, such as competencies in social and work roles, may be mastered through new learning.

12. Most human learning is not automatic but is mediated by cognitive processes. A reciprocal interaction takes place between thoughts, emotions, actions, and feedback from others. Change can begin at any of these processes.

Systems approaches remind us that each individual is embedded within a larger relational context.

13. Actualization is achieved primarily in social interaction with a counselor, teacher, minister, group, friend, or family, but it can also be achieved through self-help methods, such as meditation and imagery. Social interaction becomes the main vehicle for conditions of actualization such as honesty with feelings, awareness of self, freedom of expression, and trust in oneself and others. Therapist support is an important component in helping others to achieve their potential.

14. Transactional patterns play an important role in shaping behavior. Therapeutic change is facilitated by disrupting dysfunctional interactional patterns and providing new feedback. This usually involves altering either the client's interpretation of other people's behavior or the behavior itself.

15. Actualization involves learning to set clear external boundaries with others. These boundaries are evidenced by the ability to maintain a clear sense of self in the midst of an anxious emotional field. Additionally, an actualized person has a capacity for intimacy and a readiness for closeness based on a firm sense of identity to risk the self with others.

16. Actualization is reflected in an attitude of interdependency. An actualizing person has a systemic ethic of responsibility. Personal decisions are made in terms of their impact on the total web of relationships that the person is involved in, both in the present and in the future. An interdependent person attempts to balance his or her own rights against the claims of others and learns to deal with the inevitable tensions that this will involve.

17. Actualization is in part a byproduct of an interdependent attitude in which one transcends self-interest to cooperate with others working for the common good of justice and love. Actualization involves widening the inclusiveness of the circle of those we consider as our "neighbor" from the narrowness of our familiar beginnings toward real solidarity with a commonwealth of people. Pursuit of self-actualization apart from an attitude of interdependency produces alienation from others. (Brammer, Shostrom, & Abrego, 1989, pp. 54–55)

Ivey, Ivey, and Simek-Morgan (1997) indicate that

integrative theories are currently becoming more numerous and influential. Meichenbaum's construction of cognitive-behavioral theory brings diverse theories together in a coherent fashion and thus offers a broader scope than traditional behavioral frames of reference. Developmental counseling and therapy integrates theory and practice in a different format and provides an overall rationale for moving from sensory to behavioral to cognitive to systemic approaches. Developmental counseling and therapy, perhaps more than other theories, emphasizes sensorimotor and systemic/cultural foundations of experience, arguing that a network approach is essential if change is to be maintained over time. (p. 407)

Eclectic Counseling

The eclectic approach to counseling is one of long-standing tradition and equally long-standing controversy. It originally provided a safe, middle-of-the-road theory for those counselors in the early years of the profession who neither desired nor felt capable of functioning as purely directive or nondirective. The directive approach championed by E. G. Williamson and others at the University of Minnesota took control and in effect, influenced directly the client's decision making and exerted major influence on the outcomes of the counseling process. The nondirective approach, with Carl R. Rogers as its chief spokesperson, believes that the counselor's role is more that of facilitator than decision maker and that clients must achieve the necessary insights and self-confidence to make their own decisions.

Defenders of the theory suggested eclecticism as an approach that allowed each individual counselor to construct his or her own theory by drawing on established theories. It has often been suggested that the eclectic counselor can choose the best of all counseling worlds. Others contend that eclecticism encourages counselors to become theoretical "jacks of all trades." Certainly, the many theoretical models currently available can be confusing in the absence of a model or definitive guidelines for theory and technique selection.

Eclecticism is not intended to compound the confusion. Rather, it enables the counselor to build a personalized yet professional system that allows components of various established theories to blur into an integrated whole. Eclecticism assumes that the diversity among individuals and the diversity in human needs and concerns and the environments in which they occur can be best responded to when the counselor has theoretical options and the flexibility to use these within a conceptual and organized framework.

We would conclude this discussion by noting that eclecticism does not mean the absence of theory, nor can it be an excuse for "doing whatever grabs you at the moment" in your counseling. Current literature indicates a decline in the use of the label and practice of eclecticism. This approach has never been intended to be a short-cut to a counselor's personal theory formulation, but if properly pursued, it can be a difficult and challenging path to follow.

THEORETICAL PREFERENCES OF PRACTICING COUNSELORS IN EDUCATIONAL SETTINGS

Students in counselor preparation programs, beginning counselors, and even experienced practicing counselors may very appropriately ask, "Which theories are the most popular in practice?" To provide some current indications, your textbook authors conducted a brief, simplistic survey in 1996–1997 of 420 practicing counselors (randomly selected from the American Counseling Association membership directory. An initial pilot study involved Indiana counselors only). The results of this survey are displayed in Table 4-1; a total of 286 responses were received (representing a return rate of 68%). The number of theoretical orientations that practicing counselors reported drawing on frequently in their practice ranged from 2 to 7 with a mean of 4.1, indicating a desire for flexibility in meeting the needs of different clients and situations.

Table 4-1 represents responses from 170 counselors in educational settings and 116 counselors in nonschool settings. Somewhat surprisingly, only insignificant differences were noted for the differing educational levels, so the responses are summarized in Table 4-1.

Table 4-1   Survey of theoretical preferences of practicing counselors.

Theory	Schools		Agencies and Nonschool Settings	
	Percentage Preferring	Rank	Percentage Preferring	Rank
Psychoanalytic (Freudian)	0	13.5	5	10.5
Individual psychology (Adlerian)	14	2	10	5.5
Person-centered (Rogerian)	22	1	14	2.5
Rational emotive	12	4	12	4
Reality	10	5	5	10.5
Existential	2	10	2	12
Directive	13	3	10	5.5
Behavior	3	9	6	8
Family systems	1	11.5	14	2.5
Solution-based	4	7.5	2	12
Gestalt	1	11.5	2	12
Transactional analysis	0	13.5	6	8
Eclectic	7	6	16	1
Other	4	7.5	6	8
	N = 170	N = 116		

*Source: From a survey conducted by Robert L. Gibson and Marianne H. Mitchell, 1996–1997.

BUILDING A PERSONAL THEORY

As Table 4-1 demonstrates, most counselors can identify a traditional theory that has greatly influenced their own personal theory and practice of counseling. Although beginning counseling students should become familiar with the traditional and proven theories, eventually, in practice, they will develop their own variation or eclectic approach. Your own personal theory will be modified to fit you as a unique individual and perhaps adjusted to more effectively serve special client populations. As George and Cristiani (1995, p. 119) point out, "All counselors interact with clients on the basis of a set of beliefs they have about people and how people change; therefore, the importance of counselors clarifying those beliefs and developing them into a theoretical foundation is emphasized." Counselors must develop a theoretical framework that fits them personally—a framework in which they can work comfortably, be themselves, and be maximally effective.

Theories are like a road map, they indicate to you, the counselor, differing but established routes for reaching a final destination—in this instance, the goal of providing maximum assistance to the client in an efficient and enhancing way. When your experience and professionalism grow, you may develop your own personal eclectic theory. In so doing, you will seek to identify a framework or system of parts that will be in harmony with who you are as a person and as a professional—what you believe in, value, and stand for. In all endeavors we are most comfortable when we are engaged in something we are sure about and competent in doing. If you know yourself—your strengths and limitations—and have a valid theoretical framework that you understand and feel comfortable with, you may proceed with ever-increasing confidence to providing counseling assistance to your clients.

THE CASE OF GEORGE

The application in practice of the differing counseling theories can, of course, lead to differing approaches and interactions with clients experiencing similar needs. Though approached from different perspectives, each has a high probability of success in the hands of the skilled theoretician-counselor.

In this section we present the case of George to illustrate how he might be counseled from seven different theoretical orientations. (We also recognize that not all therapists of a given theoretical orientation will approach the same client concern in the same manner.)

Client	George, 28-year-old male
	2-year technical college degree in air-conditioning & refrigeration
	Twice divorced; no children; three different jobs in 8 years
Problem:	Interpersonal relationships
	(can't interact positively with people)
	(easily irritated by others, especially supervisors)

Suffering theoretical orientations:

Psychoanalytic Counselor is in charge. Initial focus is on client's recall of earliest childhood experiences. Were his parents aggressive personalities? What angered him then? Are there particular events in the past that especially angered him? Discuss his "history" of personal relationships. Be alert to resistance or transference. Free association, dream analysis, hypnosis may be used. Resistance is confronted. Role of sexuality may be explored. Analysis and interpretation precedes treatment, which will be long term.

Adlerian (Individual Psychology) Process is a joint responsibility of client and counselor. Client's inappropriate social beliefs will be challenged in a humanistic way. Client is encouraged and assisted in developing social skills. Basic assumptions about self (weaknesses) are restructured.

Person-Centered (Rogerian) Counselor is helper; major responsibility is the client's. Relationship building with George is the first task; trust must be developed. At the same time, George is encouraged to believe in himself;

that he has the capacity to get along with others—to make friends. Case histories, analysis in a traditional sense, probing and questioning is out; focus is on building a relationship that is facilitative.

Behaviorism   A relatively short-term approach in which the counselor becomes a teacher to the client. First step would probably be developing a case study of George. George's inappropriate behaviors will be examined and he will be taught new more appropriate behaviors (hence, the term *behavior modification*).

Rational Emotive Behavior Therapy (REBT)   Counselor-client connection is almost a business or teacher/student relationship. Client will be shown that anger, hostility, and suspicion are nonproductive emotions. George may be asked to examine how another person would normally or rationally react in his circumstances. George may be taught more appropriate behaviors.

Reality   Time will initially be spent building a relationship with George, but here again, the counselor assumes a teaching role. George will be helped to realistically view his problem and to become more responsible in solving it. Contracts would probably be used.

Gestalt   A warm, caring relationship is established with George. George will be encouraged to become more aware of his inappropriate behaviors and to take responsibility for changing them now. (Action now—not talk.) Confrontation, role playing, questioning (how? why?) may be used, but always in a caring sense.

GOALS OF COUNSELING

Obviously, counseling goals may be simply classified in terms of counselor goals and client goals or the immediate, intermediate, or long-range goals of therapy. Regardless of how one chooses to classify the goals, counseling, like all other meaningful activities, must be goal driven, have a purpose, or seek an objective. Broadly speaking, counseling goals may also be separated into the following categories:

Developmental Goals: Developmental goals are those wherein the client is assisted in meeting or advancing her or his anticipated human growth and development (that is, socially, personally, emotionally, cognitively, physical wellness and so on).

Preventive Goals: Prevention is a goal in which the counselor helps the client avoid some undesired outcome.

Enhancement Goals: If the client possesses special skills and abilities, enhancement means they can be identified and/or further developed through the assistance of a counselor.

Remedial Goals: Remediation involves assisting a client to overcome and/or treat an undesirable development.

Exploratory Goals: Exploration represents goals appropriate to the examining of options, testing of skills, and trying new and different activities, environments, relationships, and so on.

Reinforcement Goals: Reinforcement is used in those instances where clients need help in recognizing that what they are doing, thinking, and/or feeling is okay.

Cognitive Goals: Cognition involves acquiring the basic foundations of learning and cognitive skills.

Physiological Goals: Physiology involves acquiring the basic understandings and habits for good health.

Psychological Goals: Psychology aids in developing good social interaction skills, learning emotional control, developing a positive self-concept, and so on. (Gibson, Mitchell, & Basile, 1993, pp. 87–89)

Goals serve three important functions in the counseling process. First, goals can have a motivational function in counseling. Secondly, goals can also have an educational function in counseling in that they can help clients acquire new responses and three, goals can also meet an evaluative function in counseling whereby the client's goals help the counselor to select and evaluate various counseling strategies appropriate to the client's goals. (Hackney & Cormier, 1996, pp. 104–105)

THE COUNSELING PROCESS

Having briefly introduced some of the popular counseling theories, let us now move on to examine the translation of these theories into action. This action is frequently referred to as the counseling process, a process usually specified by a sequence of interactions or steps. Although various authors will conceptualize these stages or phases differently because of different theoretical models, there is considerable agreement that initially the process is concerned with relationship establishment, followed by some method of problem identification and patterns of exploration, leading to planning for problem solution and remediation and concluding with action and termination. Hackney and Cormier (1996) identified the stages as follows:

1. relationship establishment
2. problem identification and exploration
3. planning for problem solving
4. solution application and termination

A brief description of each of these stages will be helpful.

RELATIONSHIP ESTABLISHMENT

As often stated in definitions, counseling is a relationship. Furthermore, it is defined as a helping relationship. If it is to be a relationship that is helpful, the counselor must take the initiative in the initial interview to establish a climate conducive to mutual respect, trust, free and open communication, and understanding in general of what the counseling process involves.

Although responsibility will later shift increasingly to the client, at this stage the responsibility for the counseling process rests primarily with the counselor. Among the techniques the counselor may use are those designed to relieve tensions and open communication. Both the counselor's attitude and verbal communications are significant to the development of a satisfactory relationship. In the latter instance, all of the counselor's communication skills are brought into play. These include attentive listening, understanding, and feeling with the client. Certainly, the quality of the counselor/client relationship will influence counseling outcomes.

Among the factors that are important in the establishment of this counselor-client relationship are positive regard and respect, accurate empathy, and genuineness. These conditions imply counselor openness, an ability to understand and feel with the client, and valuing the client. This counselor-client relationship serves not only to increase the opportunity for clients to attain their goals but also to be a potential model of a good interpersonal relationship, one that clients can use to improve the quality of their other relationships outside the therapy setting.

Counselors must keep in mind that the purpose of a counseling relationship is to meet, insofar as possible, client needs (not counselor needs). The counseling process within this relationship seeks to assist the client in assuming the responsibilities for his or her problem and its solution. This will be facilitated by the counselor's communications skills, the ability to identify and reflect clients' feelings, and the ability to identify and gain insights into the clients concerns and needs.

A relationship must be established with the client early in the counseling process, as this will often determine whether the client will continue in therapy. Suggested goals for the initial counseling interviews might include the following.

Counselor's Goals

- Establish a comfortable and positive relationship.
- Explain the counseling process and mutual responsibilities to the client.
- Facilitate communications.
- Identify and verify the client's concerns that brought her or him to seek counseling assistance.
- Plan, with the client, to obtain assessment data needed to proceed with the counseling process.

Client's Goals

- Understand the counseling process and his or her responsibilities in this process.
- Share and amplify reasons for seeking counseling.
- Cooperate in the assessment of both the problem and self.

PROBLEM IDENTIFICATION AND EXPLORATION

Once an adequate relationship has been established, clients will be more receptive to the in-depth discussion and exploration of their concerns. At this stage, clients assume more responsibility because it is their problem and it is their willingness to communicate as much of the nature of the problem to the counselor as possible that will determine to a large extent the assistance the counselor can give.

During this phase, the counselor continues to exhibit attending behavior and may place particular emphasis on such communication skills as paraphrasing, clarification, perception checking, or feedback. The counselor may question the client, but the questions are stated in such a way as to facilitate the continued exploration of the client's concern. Questions that would embarrass, challenge, or threaten the client are avoided. Throughout this phase, the counselor will recognize cultural differences and their implications in terms of how techniques should be modified to be culturally appropriate.

Now the counselor is seeking to distinguish between what might be called surface problems and those that are more complex. The counselor also strives to determine whether the stated problem is, in fact, the concern that has brought the client to the counselor. This may be a time for information gathering. The more usable information the counselor has, the greater will be the prospects of accurate assessment of the client's needs. It is therefore helpful for counselors to recognize the various areas of information that must be tapped.

We have, rather arbitrarily, grouped the information desired under three headings: the time dimension, the feeling dimension, and the cognitive dimension. Subsets of information under each of these headings are indicated as follows.

1. The *time dimension* includes the client's experiences, especially those he or she may view as influencing experiences. The present dimension would cover how well the person is functioning presently, especially those current experiences that may have influenced the client to seek counseling. The future time dimension would include future hopes, plans, and goals, and also how the client plans to achieve these.
2. The *feeling dimension* includes the emotions and feelings of the client toward himself or herself as well as toward significant others. Included are feelings about groups, attitudes, values, and self-concept. All are a part of the feeling dimension.
3. The *cognitive dimension* includes how the client solves problems, the coping styles she or he employs, rationality in making daily decisions, and capacity and readiness for learning.

At this point, some counselors may use appraisal techniques such as standardized tests for problem diagnosis. Subproblems of the problem may also be identified. During this stage, the client not only explores experiences and behaviors but also may reveal feelings and the relationship of concern to the way he or she is living life in general. The counselor is seeking to secure as much relevant data as possible and to integrate it into an overall picture of the client and his or her concern. The counselor also shares these perceptions with the client. A goal of this stage is for both the counselor and the client to perceive the problem and its ramifications similarly. One of the counselor's goals during this stage is to help the client develop a self-understanding that recognizes the need for dealing with a concern—the need for change and action.

Obviously, this is a busy stage of the counseling process. This is when much of the real work occurs, especially when extensive exploration is needed. Facilitative conditions must continue in order to promote the client's understandings of action plans for resolving problems. Although problem-solving activities are likely to be initiated during this stage, the major steps in implementing the activities take place in the third stage.

The steps or stages in problem identification and exploration are these:

1. *Define the problem.* The counselor, with the cooperation of the client, is seeking to describe or identify the problem as specifically and objectively as possible. It is important that the counselor and client have the same understanding of the problem. In addition to the accuracy desired in defining the problem, it is important for the client to identify the components or contributing factors and the severity of the problem as to its recency and longevity.

2. *Explore the problem.* The kinds of information needed to fully understand the problem and its background are gathered at this point. Once the kinds of needed information have been identified, counselor and client must determine how this information can be obtained, who will have responsibility for gathering it, and what the timelines for gathering the data will be. Within this context, decisions may be made regarding the administering, for example, of standardized psychological measures. To test or not to test is a decision in which the client must have a major voice. Regardless of how desirable it may be to obtain data through standardized psychological measures, the effect on the client and his or her willingness to participate fully in the counseling process may be threatened by this data-gathering technique. In some situations, the counselor may wish to complete a detailed case study. Obviously, this is a decision that will depend on the seriousness of the situation, the amount of data needed, and the amount of time available to both counselor and client for this purpose. In many agency settings, intake interviews will gather basic information that is deemed useful in most counseling situations. In this process, it is obviously important that the counselor continue to employ facilitative behavior.

3. *Integrate the information.* In this step all the information collected is systematically organized and integrated into a meaningful profile of the client and the client's problem. At this point it would be appropriate to begin the exploration of changes that may be needed and barriers that may exist to these changes. The actual identification of possible solutions will be discussed in the next section. Note that in brief therapy, also discussed later in this chapter, this stage, as well as all stages in the counseling process, are condensed or collapsed in such a way as to expedite the process.

Planning for Problem Solving

Once the counselor has determined that all relevant information regarding the client's concern is available and understood and once the client has accepted the need for doing something about a specific problem, it is time to develop a plan to solve or remediate the concern of the client.

At this point, effective goal setting becomes the focus of the counseling activity. Mistakes in goal setting can lead to nonproductive procedures and the client's loss of confidence in the counseling process. In this stage we again suggest certain steps in sequence to guide the process.

1. *Define the problem.* It is important that both the counselor and the client view the problem from a similar perspective and have the same understanding of its ramifications.

2. *Identify and list all possible solutions.* At this point, it is appropriate to brainstorm all possibilities. Both the client and counselor participate, but the client should be given the opportunity to list as many possibilities as may come to her or his mind. If there are some

obvious solutions that are overlooked, the counselor may suggest to the client, "Have you also thought of —?" When listing solutions, none should be eliminated simply because at first glance they appear to be impossible to implement. Those that will be eliminated for various reasons will be taken care of in the next step.

3. *Explore the consequences of the suggested solutions.* Here the client, with encouragement and even an occasional suggestion from the counselor, will identify the procedures needed to implement each of the suggested solutions. As he or she does so, some procedures will appear too complex or for other reasons impossible to apply. Other solutions may produce more problems or more serious consequences than the problem that is the focus in this counseling sequence. In any event, the projected outcomes for each solution must be explored thoroughly.

4. *Prioritize the solutions.* Following exploratory stage 3, the client, again with the counselor's encouragement, will prioritize the solutions from best possibility down to least likely to produce the desired results. Once the decision has been made and the best solution selected, the client is now ready to move on to the application and implementation.

In the further development of this plan, the counselor recognizes that the client will frequently not arrive at basic insights, implications, or probabilities as fast as the counselor will. However, most counselors will agree that it is better to guide the client toward realizing these understandings himself or herself, rather than just telling the client outright. To facilitate the client's understanding, the counselor may use techniques of repetition, mild confrontation, interpretation, information, and, obviously, encouragement.

Solution, Application, and Termination

In this final stage, the responsibilities are clear-cut. The client has the responsibility for applying the determined solution, and the counselor, for determining the point of termination. In the first instance, the counselor has a responsibility to encourage the client's acting on his or her determined problem solution. During the time the client is actively engaged in applying the problem solution, the counselor will often maintain contact as a source of follow-up, support, and encouragement. The client may also need the counselor's assistance in the event things do not go according to plan. Once it has been determined, however, that the counselor and the client have dealt with the client's concern to the extent possible and practical, the process should be terminated. As noted before, this responsibility is primarily the counselor's, although the client has the right to terminate at any time. The counselor usually gives some indication that the next interview should just about wrap it up and may conclude by summarizing the main points of the counseling process. Usually, the counselor will leave the door open for the client's possible return in the event additional assistance is needed. Because counseling is a learning process, the counselor hopes that the client has not only learned to deal with this particular problem but has also learned problem-solving skills that will decrease the probability of the client's need for further counseling in the future.

In concluding this section on the counseling process, we are aware of our frequent reference to the client's "problem" and we would like to remind our readers that problems are not always based on perceived inadequacies or failures requiring remediation and restorative therapy. Clients can have equally pressing needs resulting from concerns for developing their human potential—for capitalizing on their strengths. In these instances the emphasis is on development, growth, or enhancement rather than remediation.

COUNSELING SKILLS

Thus far in this chapter we have discussed the importance of the counselor's having a theoretical framework within which to function and a knowledge of the process or stages through which client counseling moves. Equally important are the skills that the counselor must possess to apply a given theory and implement the process. The skills of counseling have their roots in both theory and process and have been reinforced through both practice and research. The counselor acquires these skills through learning and practice.

Communications Skills

Nonverbal Communications Skills

All of us communicate nonverbally. Through the use of facial expressions, body posture, and physical movements we send messages, usually intentional but sometimes not intentional. We also usually "read" messages that others communicate to us in a similar manner. In our society, nonverbal language is a popular means of communication and in counseling, it is a social interaction process important to both the counselor and the counselee. For example, from the onset and throughout the counseling process, visual clues will influence the client's perception of the counselor. As noted earlier in this chapter, one of the nonverbal ways in which the counselor deals with this factor is by exhibiting attending behavior, by communicating nonverbally, "I am interested in you and your concerns; I respect you, and I'm going to give you my undivided attention," and so forth. Attending behavior accomplishes several purposes.

1. It indicates to the client that she or he is the object of your undivided attention. It further indicates the respect that you have for him or her as an individual.
2. It indicates your acceptance of the client and your readiness to assist with his or her concerns to the full limit of your professional abilities.
3. It facilitates the flow of communication by demonstrating your undivided attention. This conveys to the client your interest and will encourage further verbalization on the client's part.
4. It tells the client that not everything that he or she needs to communicate has to be put into words.
5. It keeps you, the counselor, aware and alert at all times. It enables you to follow the client's communication.
6. It enables you to identify clues that the client may subconsciously or even consciously reveal during the course of the counseling interview.

Verbal Communications Skills

Strange as it may seem, we will initiate our discussion of verbal communications skills by discussing listening. Listening, however, is a prerequisite to effective verbal communicating. Listening also is implied in attending behavior, but because of its importance, we emphasize the point again because listening is the basis of counselor competence.

Effective listening enables counselors to adroitly manipulate their verbal counseling skills. These skills include using attending responses that indicate to the client that you are listening ("I understand," "I see") and what we might label as "stimulus responses," those that encourage the client to continue to comment ("Can you tell me more about that?" "Could you clarify that for me? "Please continue if you wish").

Effective listening is mandatory for feedback, another important verbal (as well as non-verbal) communication skill. Feedback is the verbalization of the counselor's perceptions and reactions to the client's behaviors, feelings, concerns, actions, expressions, and so forth. It offers the client the opportunity in turn to feed back—react, perhaps validate or expand on the counselor's feedback. It offers the counselor the opportunity to periodically summarize and validate what has transpired and ensure that both counselor and counselee are accurately "receiving" each other's messages before moving further in the counseling process.

Also important in verbal communication is the art of questioning. Skill in questioning involves timing, wording, and types of questions. The skillful counselor does not inject questions that will stop, alter, or slow down a client's open discussion of a concern. Questions are injected to keep the discussion moving ("Why do you think they reacted that way to your behavior?"), to clarify ("What do you mean? Am I right in understanding you?"), and to validate ("How do you know? Give me an example").

The type of question used should be appropriate to the desired outcome from asking it. Open questions ("How did you feel about that?") provide opportunities for the client to express feelings, provide greater detail, and gain new insights whereas closed questions ("Will you go back next week?") get an answer rather than an evasive or rambling reply. The counselor may also decide when to use direct questions ("Tell me, are you an alcoholic?") or nondirect questions ("What do you think about alcoholism today?"), which do not directly identify the client with a problem or issue.

Effective communication is also facilitated by knowing what not to do. George and Cristiani (1995) list these barriers to communications:

1. Giving advice
2. Offering solutions
3. Moralizing and preaching
4. Analyzing and diagnosing
5. Judging or criticizing
6. Praising and agreeing; giving positive evaluations
7. Reassuring (pp. 126–128)

Obviously, the effectiveness of counseling is determined by the effectiveness of counselor/client communication. From the counselor's standpoint, communication is primarily designed to influence and motivate the client. Table 4-2 presents descriptions of some of these influencing skills and their motivation function in the counseling interview.

SHORT-TERM COUNSELING OR BRIEF THERAPY

Recent years have witnessed increased interest in and practice of short-term or brief therapy. In practice, brief therapy is probably as old as therapy itself; however, it has only recently been recognized and written about as a viable approach for the delivery of counseling assistance. This increase in popularity can be attributed to a number of factors, including the escalating costs of treatment; the managed care movement; limitations on payments

Table 4-2 Influencing skills.

Skill	Description	Function in Interview
Interpretation/ reframing	Provides an alternative frame of reference from which the client may view a situation. May be drawn from a theory or from one's own personal observations. *Interpretation may be viewed as the core influencing skill.*	Attempts to provide the client with a new way to view the situation. The interpretation provides the client with a clear-cut alternative perception of "reality." This perception may enable a change of view that in tum may result in changes in thoughts, constructs, or behaviors.
Directive	Tells the client what action to take. May be a simple suggestion stated in command form or may be a sophisticated technique from a specific theory.	Clearly indicates to clients what action counselors or therapists wish them to take. The prediction with a directive is that the client will do what is suggested.
Advice/information	Provides suggestions, instructional ideas, homework, advice on how to act, think, or behave.	Used sparingly, may provide client with new and useful information. Specific vocational information is an example of necessary use of this skill.
Self-disclosure	The interviewer shares personal experience from the past or may share present reactions to the client.	Emphasizes counselor "I" statements. This skill is closely allied to feedback and may build trust and openness, leading to a more mutual relationship with the client.
Feedback	Provides clients with specific data on how they are seen by the counselor or by others.	Provides concrete data that may help clients realize how others perceive behavior and thinking patterns, thus enabling an alternative self-perception.
Logical consequences	Interviewer explains to the client the logical outcome of thinking and behavior— if/then.	Provides an alternative frame of reference for the client. This skills helps clients anticipate the consequences or results of their actions.
Influencing summary	Often used at or near the end of a session to summarize counselor comments; most often used in combination with the attending summarization.	Clarifies what has happened in the interview and summarizes what the therapist has said. This skill is designed to help generalization from the interview to daily life.

Source: From A. E. Ivey, M. B. Ivey, and L. Simek-Morgan, *Counselling and Psychotherapy: A Multicultural Perspective* (4th ed., p. 66). Copyright © 1997 by Allyn and Bacon. Reprinted by permission.

imposed by insurance companies; a "busy public" that wants as much time as possible to devote to career and family; and the results of studies, some highly publicized in the popular media, indicating that for most situations, short-term therapy is at least as effective as long term, if not more so; produces lasting or durable results; and more frequently responds to the client's anticipation of treatment time.

Descriptions of "short term" seem to vary somewhat, but it seems to be in the range of one to five sessions with the average length of one hour. The process itself is characterized by (a) promptness of treatment (no lengthy intake interviews), (b) openness and cooperation, (c) rapid assessment and focus on the problem, (d) an emphasis on the client's positive traits in solution identification, and, of course, (e) some attention to time limitations. In addition to the goals of responding to the needs that brought the client to counseling, short-term therapy also seeks the development and enhancement of the individual's potential for fruitful behaviors, including learning to solve his or her own problems.

Good (although not the only) candidates for short-term or brief therapy are clients who are (a) motivated to change, (b) can establish positive personal relationships readily and easily, (c) expect and want only a brief treatment, and (d) are not psychologically impaired.

Basile (1996) summarized strategies that contribute to the effective application of a solution-based brief therapy model as follows:

1. Foster the development of a therapeutic or working alliance.
2. Assess the client's motivation for change (as a visitor, a complainant, or a customer).
3. Establish a goal for treatment.
4. Use presuppositional and solution-focused language.
5. Search for strengths, solutions, and exceptions.
6. Connect and stay connected with your client's sense of humor.
7. Be pragmatic.
8. Brief therapy moves slowly; stay on track. (pp. 8–9)

SPECIAL COUNSELING POPULATIONS

Counselors in nearly all settings deal with a variety of individual problems and concerns. Because increasing attention is being given to certain populations, it seems appropriate to note several of these special client populations.

People Who Abuse Drugs

Information about the use of alcohol and drugs and the ill effects of abusing these substances are well publicized. The four most commonly used are nicotine, caffeine, alcohol, and marijuana. At any given time in the United States, substance abuse is either directly or indirectly related to up to 50% of emergency room admissions, over 50% of domestic violence cases, and half of all homicides (Stevens & Smith, 2001, p. 1).

An excellent source of demographic information concerning drug abuse, and perhaps the largest collection of data, is the National Household Survey on Drug Abuse conducted by the Substance Abuse and Mental Health Services Administration. The preliminary results of the 1997 study describe the following patterns of use:

- An estimated 13.9 million Americans are current illicit drug users (in all categories "current" is defined as having used within the previous 30 days). This does not indicate a significant change from 1995.
- Of youth ages 12 to 17, 11.4% reported current illicit drug use. Although this figure was stable from 1995 to 1996, the current illicit drug use for youth ages 12 to 13 increased significantly from 2.2% to 3.8%.
- One in 10 youth are current marijuana users, with the prevalence of use doubling between 1992 and 1997 and significantly increasing from 1996 to 1997.
- An estimated 1.5 million Americans are current cocaine users.
- Approximately 111 million Americans ages 12 and above are current alcohol drinkers. Thirty-two million are binge drinkers (five or more drinks on one occasion in the past month), and 11 million are heavy drinkers (five or more drinks on 5 or more days in the past month). This demographic has remained stable since 1988.
- Eleven million current drinkers are between the ages of 12 and 20. (Stevens & Smith, 2001, pp. 8–9)

Further, the 1995 National Household Survey of Drug Abuse indicated an estimated 1.5 million had used cocaine within the past month; 60% of the cocaine users are between the ages of 18 and 34 (Stevens & Smith, 2001, p. 4).

People Who Use Tobacco

Until recent generations, tobacco has generally been overlooked as an abused substance; on occasion, it was and still is glamorized. Now, however, we are much more aware of the deadly effects of its addiction. Further, even though the U.S. Surgeon General in 1964 pointed out the highly addictive nature of nicotine and its health hazards, the alarm bells raised by this report were severely muted by the tobacco industry's media responses. Although medical reports, lawsuits, and legislative actions have made the public much more conscious of the deadly effects of habitual use of tobacco, it is currently estimated that over 60 million people in the United States over 12 years of age continue to smoke regularly. An alarming 4.5 million of our children ages 12–17 smoke regularly (Stevens & Smith, 2001, p. 6). Further, recent reports indicate an increase in the percentage of teenage girls smoking.

People Who Abuse Alcohol

In recent generations the concept of alcoholism as a disease has gained popularity; in some respects this has placed less emphasis on drinking as a weakness of willpower and more attention on treatment. Alcoholics Anonymous, the most popular self-help movement, has emphasized this approach in its 12-step treatment program. Within this concept, researchers are continuing to explore various treatment possibilities.

Beginning in the mid-1970s, alcohol has been the single most abused drug in adolescent culture. It is estimated that currently 11 million drinkers are between the ages of 12 and 20 (Stevens & Smith, 2001, pp. 8–9) and that more than 3 million of these teenagers are alcoholics, most of them enrolled in schools. No one knows exactly why this is, but it may represent a characteristic of adolescent rebellion against the adult—what the teenagers view as a restricting and nonunderstanding adult society.

The manifest symptoms of alcohol abuse among teenagers are as evident or more evident than the symptoms of drug abuse, which at times may be obscure. Adolescent problem drinkers are likely to have a high absentee rate, be poor achievers academically, appear resentful of adult interest in their personal lives, have little interest in school activities, and often have an alcoholic aroma about them.

Counselors may be involved in prevention, intervention, and crisis treatment or remediation. However, specialized training is important for counselors who are working with substance abusers. Because the traditional counseling approaches frequently have limited effectiveness, counselors who work extensively with substance abusers usually acquire specialized training. Clients who are substance abusers are very resistant to change, and the conditions facilitating their abuse are often beyond the therapist's control. Counselors working with these clients need dramatically different techniques proven to have some chance of success with substance abuse clients. Also, counselors must be aware of client conditions that merit referral to more highly trained specialists for long-term treatment and monitoring.

Counselors in all settings need to be aware of the resources available for the treatment of substance abuse clients. These may include emergency clinics, specialized centers, hospital care (both inpatient and outpatient), halfway houses, crisis centers, and special assistance groups such as Alcoholics Anonymous and Narcotics Anonymous. Counselors working with such populations generally have a specialized knowledge of the pharmacological, physiological, psychological, and sociocultural aspects of the use of alcohol and drugs.

In addition, counselors should also be engaged in a continual interaction with teachers, ministers, juvenile authorities, industrial personnel managers, and others who can help in implementing prevention, early intervention, and addictive treatment programs.

In many programs, both individual and group counseling are used. In some settings, counseling teams are effective for group counseling with this special client population. Obviously, counselors who work with drug and alcohol abuse should have more than a superficial knowledge of the causes, symptoms, and potential outcomes of the problem. In many individual situations, medical treatment may be needed, and referral to or "teaming" with a psychiatrist may be necessary.

Following the client's diagnosis, the appropriately qualified counselor will usually develop a treatment plan. This plan is designed to provide structure and direction for both the client and the counselor in achieving the desired and clearly specified goals of the treatment. Factors that influence the characteristics of this plan include the seriousness of the client's condition, the client's motivation, projected length of treatment, external factors influencing the treatment, and the counselor's prognosis for success of the treatment.

Women

Even though federal and state legislation has sought to promote opportunities for women to achieve their potential by stimulating legal equality of the sexes, abundant evidence indicates a lack of consistency at both the national and state levels in the application and enforcement of such legislation. In fact, in many ways, discrimination has become much more subtle since passage of the Civil Rights Act of 1964.

The changing role of women in the world of work has produced changes in both the lives of women and family life. Working women are experiencing greater financial freedom and less need to get married or to stay married. This has resulted in later marriages, more living together, and higher divorce rates. Even so, the majority of women still work because of economic necessity, and they continue to work for less money than men. In most organizations, men still control the fiscal management and decision making, thus reinforcing the "glass ceiling" that limits women's advancements, salaries and opportunities. Further, of the single-parent families living in poverty, approximately 58% are headed by women. Teen-age girls in poverty environments are especially at risk.

Another growing and increasingly recognized outcome of women's continuing to work after marriage is the dramatic increase in the number of dual-career couples. This has created issues regarding whose career takes priority, how household responsibilities will be divided, and who will care for the children. The bothersome issue of latchkey children, often left on their own without supervision for long periods of time, has become especially troubling.

The counselor's role in counseling women is often further complicated by not only the woman's perception of what is appropriate for her but also by society's expectations. Counselors must be careful when counseling female clients not to reflect societal sex-role stereotypes.

Another complicating factor in counseling women is the multiple role expectations held for a woman as wife, mother, and employee. With increasingly greater numbers of women seeking counseling, especially for career planning and decision making, counselors must be alert that sexism does not limit their perception of career opportunities. The counselor has the responsibility to help women understand their own values, abilities, aptitudes, and interests and to utilize these to develop their potential to the fullest. In so doing, the counselor must, as always, function as a nonbiased, nonstereotyping helper.

Finally, it is important for counselors to remind themselves of the importance of practicing the basic skills of empathy and respect in establishing productive professional relationships with their female clients. It is also important for counselors to treat women as individuals who are, like all clients, unique in their own right.

Older Adults

In the 1980s we became increasingly aware that our population was growing older, living longer and more actively, and becoming another special population for counseling services. Although in the past the elderly were in a sense often "out of sight, out of mind," it is clear that in the 1990s they increasingly came into the mainstream of public thought and activity. Popular books like *Old Friends* by Tracy Kielder (1993) and *The Fountain of Age* by Betty Friedan (1993) told us of the increasing age of our population and made as aware of this aging, and the American Association of Retired People became an increasingly influential organization representing the interests of the elderly. (Betty Friedan [1993, p. 40] noted that life expectancy in the United States has increased 30 years in the 20th century and that in 1970–1985, the number of people over 65 increased by 30%!) As we enter this new century, we can anticipate an elderly population (65 and older) of over 31 million. Further, this population will not only live longer but may work longer if they choose, since the Employment Act of 1967, as amended in 1986, made it possible for workers to work beyond age 65.

An interesting observation is that even though older individuals are now living longer and healthier with the option of continuing to work, they are, as a group, declining to take advantage of their employment opportunities, as the age at which people retire continues to gradually move downward. Of course, some of these people will return to work when they experience restlessness in retirement, but for many, the option of early retirement may offer an escape from boring and unsatisfying jobs. Too, retirees seeking reentry into the workforce, rarely find opportunities equal to the positions they left or commensurate with their abilities and previous experiences.

Regardless of when an elderly worker chooses to retire, the experience can be both significant and traumatic. For many retirees, adjusting to life without work is difficult because they feel a loss of status; workers are more valued in our society than nonworkers: For many it means a loss of planned involvement with other people, and some have developed so few supplemental leisure time/recreational activities that life suddenly becomes meaningless because they have excess time on their hands. But there is promise of a better transition for these older adults, and this promise appears to rely heavily on counseling.

As employee assistance programs (EAPs) are increasingly helping older workers plan for their retirements and make psychological adjustments, such assistance is becoming an increasingly significant employee benefit and opportunity for counseling.

Counseling assistance to this population stresses

- orientation to retirement with attending personal adjustment counseling
- financial planning
- career assessment and assistance for those desirous of some form (part time or full time) of continued employment
- leisure planning

Additionally, most older adults will face other major changes in their twilight years that may be eased by counseling. These may include

- the loss of a spouse
- the decline of physical and often mental capacity and well-being
- a decline in financial security
- a decline in mobility—not just their own physical ability but also a time when they can no longer drive, which in itself may increase their isolation
- a decline in social contacts and increased loneliness
- an increase in mental health problems

Counselors will thus have opportunities, primarily through community services and outreach programs, to meet the needs of another distinct and worthy segment of our population. The aged, like most special populations, must confront societal expectations and prejudices. Although some individuals *do* become more absent-minded, senile, or physically disabled, these are not appropriate characteristics to assign all aged individuals. Counselors working with older clients must again exhibit acceptance, openness, and respect for clients and their values. Even the oldest client must be permitted to look ahead and plan for a different future if this is the client's desire. If the older clients are willing, counselors can help them find new meanings and roles in life.

Business and Industry

Recent generations have witnessed a steady broadening of the opportunities for counselors to function in a variety of settings. This is partly because organizations, agencies, and special populations have recognized that they share needs and concerns with other populations and settings where these needs and concerns are known and dealt with. Increasingly, business and industrial organizations and their workforces have realized that they may benefit, from both a corporate and individual viewpoint, from programs of counseling assistance. Counseling in EAPs tends to emphasize short-term or "brief therapy" treatment. Clients with more serious problems that may require long-term treatment are usually referred. Counselors in EAP settings also frequently work with groups, particularly in dealing with such issues as stress management and retirement planning.

Counselors can also provide worthwhile programs to facilitate the career development and placement or replacement of workers and management personnel. In recent years, the downsizing of many corporations and the merging of others have led to lay-offs, reassignments, and relocations that have also increased the emphasis on career counseling. Personnel training, especially in human relationship and communications skills, is another area of promise. Increased emphasis is also noted on prevention and wellness programs for employees. In some business settings counselors are being hired on a contractual basis rather than as full-time employees of the organization.

Many government agencies have also developed EAP programs. For example, the U.S. Postal Service EAP suggests that their professional counselors are prepared to assist their employees with such common concerns as marital and family issues, alcohol and other drug abuses, job-related problems, and emotional disturbances.

Counselors may also work with executives and management personnel to assist them in improving their communication skills and ability to recognize and facilitate the solution of personality conflicts and interdepartmental disputes. In another area, EAPs can provide support and assistance in helping home life and work life fit together and complement each other.

People with AIDS

Acquired immunodeficiency syndrome (AIDS) was recognized and labeled more than 2 decades ago. Since that time it has become one of the most feared of diseases and health epidemics. The rapid spread of AIDS, its incurability, and its fatality rate have caused worldwide alarm. The scope of the disease is indicated by the data published in 1995 in the *Morbidity and Mortality Weekly Report* of the Centers for Disease Control and Prevention. According to this report,

> During 1994 state, local and territorial health departments reported to the Centers for Disease Control and Prevention 80,691 cases of acquired immunodeficiency syndrome (AIDS) among persons in the United States, which followed the 106,618 cases reported in 1993.
>
> Of the total 80,691 reported cases, 79,674 (99%) occurred among adolescents and adults (i.e., persons aged ≥13 years) and 1017 among children <13 years. The number of cases reported in children during 1994 (1017) increased 8% over those reported during 1993 (942). Of the 1017 children, 50% were female, most were black (62%) or Hispanic (23%) and 92% were infected through perinatal transmission (Centers for Disease Control and Prevention, 1995, p. 1).
>
> Newer data appeared in the *Morbidity and Mortality Weekly Report* in February 28, 1997. This information indicates that from 1981 through 1996, a total of 573,800 persons aged ≥13 years with AIDS were reported to the Centers for Disease Control by state and local health departments. . . . The expansion of the AIDS surveillance case definition in 1993 resulted in a large increase in reported cases during 1993 followed by declines in numbers of AIDS cases

reported each year from 1994 through 1996. The 68,473 AIDS cases reported during 1996 was substantially higher (47%) than the number reported during 1992.

From 1992 through 1996, non-Hispanic blacks, Hispanics, and women accounted for increasing proportions of persons reported with AIDS. In 1996, non-Hispanic blacks accounted for 41% of adults reported with AIDS, exceeding for the first time the proportion who were non-Hispanic white, and women accounted for an all-time high of 20% of adults reported with AIDS. (Centers for Disease Control and Prevention, 1997, pp. 166–167)

AIDS is also a disease of the young. More than 13,000 of the victims are younger then 24 years of age, and 124,000 are between 25 and 35 (Brunner, 2000, p. 556).

Treatments to extend the life of AIDS victims are continuing to be developed. Many AIDS patients are also eager to improve their quality of life, including their psychological well-being. As patients and their close friends and relatives increasingly seek counseling to help them cope with the emotional stresses resulting from AIDS, counselors must become more knowledgeable about the disease and the psychological reactions to it that are most likely to occur. Initial shock and panic are typical reactions of those learning they have contracted AIDS. Additionally, they frequently feel isolated and punished (Why me?!). Low self-esteem is often reinforced by discrimination, including difficulty in securing and holding a job and developing and maintaining social relationships.

Counselors providing assistance to clients with AIDS must recognize that they (the clients) have frequently lost social support from both friends and family, which can adversely affect their ability to cope. Serious depression is not uncommon among this group. Many will also demonstrate anger and frustration. Counselors can be helpful in assisting and educating the support systems of patients—families, friends, employers—and in helping the patients themselves focus on life and living. This may include helping them develop adequate coping styles, identifying and entering careers they can achieve in, and encouraging them to join AIDS support groups. Counseling AIDS clients requires great sensitivity and understanding of the complexities of the disease. Counselors must also guard against their own possible prejudices and fears.

Victims of Abuse

Domestic violence characterized by spouse abuse or child abuse is rampant in the United States and the personal, social, and economic costs are staggering. The number of children abused annually is estimated to be over one million, and reports indicate that one third of all married people engage in spouse abuse. As public awareness of the extent of the problem has increased, so have efforts to provide assistance and refuge for adult victims and frequent relocation for the children.

Spouse abuse is often associated with poverty, substance abuse, and career disappointments. For abused spouses, the most popular response has been providing shelters and crisis lines. Most of the personnel for these settings are drawn from the ranks of paraprofessional and volunteer workers, although helping professionals such as counselors, social workers, and psychologists are increasingly being utilized.

In recent years the public has also become more aware of the nature and extent of child abuse in the United States. Even so, we suspect the real extent of this national tragedy is largely unreported. Not only does child abuse destroy the joys and memories of youth, but its damaging aftereffects can cause psychological problems throughout the victims' adult life. The federal government and all states have passed legislation to stop child abuse. School counselors are legally required to report suspected child abuse in most states and can be penalized for failing to do so.

Baker (1996) suggests several steps to follow in reporting child abuse as a school system employee:

1. Report suspected cases of child abuse to the building principal immediately; that is, children under age eighteen who exhibit evidence of serious physical or mental injury not explained by the available medical history as being accidental; sexual abuse or serious physical neglect, if injury, abuse, or neglect has been caused by the acts or omissions of the child's parents or by a person responsible for the child's welfare.
2. Each building principal will designate a person to act in his or her stead when unavailable.
3. The principal may wish to form a team of consultants with whom to confer (e.g., school nurse, home and school visitor, counselor) before making an oral report to public welfare service representatives. This should be done within twenty-four hours of the first report.
4. It is not the responsibility of the reporter to prove abuse or neglect. Reports must be made in good faith, however.
5. Any person willfully failing to report suspected abuse may be subject to school board disciplinary action. (p. 287)

Because children spend so much time at school, a special responsibility for reporting abuse rests with school personnel.

School counselors are the central helpers in any school system's child abuse prevention efforts. They must recognize the symptoms of possible abuse and their legal reporting responsibilities. They must also recognize their responsibility to take a leadership role in developing and implementing an effective program of child abuse prevention. Allsopp and Prosen (1988) emphasize the increasing need for counselors to provide appropriate training and information for school personnel who might be involved in cases of suspected child abuse. They discuss a model program which has been successfully implemented in the training of over 2,000 teachers and administrators to deal with sexual abuse cases. The program consisted of (a) information related to offenders, victims, and non-offending family members; (b) present laws and proposed legislation; (c) requirements and procedures for school systems in reporting suspected child sexual abuse; and (d) available community resources for victim's use. Ninety-eight percent of teachers reported that the program increased their awareness of victims and offenders; 92 percent stated that the program provided them with a clearer understanding of the school system's procedures for reporting child sexual abuse; 93 percent expressed they had increased their knowledge of county services currently available to victims; and 98 percent reported that as a result of participation in the program, they felt more adequately prepared to deal with a situation in which a child was sexually abused. (Gibson et al., 1993, p. 109)

The American School Counselor Association (1999) indicates that

it is the responsibility of the school counselor to report suspected cases of child abuse/neglect to the proper authorities. Recognizing that the abuse of children is not limited to the home and that corporal punishment by school authorities might well be considered child abuse, the

ASCA supports any legislation which specifically bans the use of corporal punishment as a disciplinary tool within the schools. (p. 1)

Please refer to Appendix C for the full text of the American School Counselor Association (ASCA) statement concerning child abuse (1999).

In recent years, we have also been made much more aware of the incidence of sexual abuse as victims come forward and discuss the harmful effects of their experiences.

- Incidence research shows that between 8% to 38% of women and 5% to 9% of men in the United States have been victimized.
- Sexual abuse is an international concern, although specific statistics are not available.
- Sexual abuse essentially, by definition, is harmful.
- The most common ages of victims are 8 through 12, with many cases outside of that span.
- Stepfathers may be five times as likely to victimize a daughter sexually than fathers are, although other family members (brothers, uncles, grandfathers) could be offenders.
- Most female victimization occurs within the family.
- Boys are more likely to be abused outside the family than are girls. (Rencken, 1989, p. 3)

Further, the American School Counselor Association (ASCA 1988) encourages its members to participate in the implementation of the following guidance and counseling activities:

- Coordinate team efforts involving the principal, teacher, counselor, school nurse, protective services workers, and the child.
- Serve as a support to teachers, and other school personnel, especially if the child was abused as a result of a report sent home about the child from school.
- Emphasize the non-punitive role of protective services and allay fears that the child will be removed immediately from the home.
- Facilitate the contact between the child and the social worker. The issue of confidentiality and re-establishing the trust of the child after the report is made is critical to the child-counselor relationship.
- Provide ongoing counseling services to the child and/or family after the crisis is over, or refer to an appropriate community agency.
- Provide programs designed to help prevent child abuse. Counselors can help children with coping skills and ways to prevent their own abuse by improving their self-concepts, being able to recognize stress in their parents, and being sensitive to cues that abuse may occur if their own behavior is not changed.
- Help teachers and administrators in understanding the dynamics of abuse and abusive parents, and in developing a nonjudgmental attitude so they can react more appropriately in crisis situations.
- Provide developmental workshops and/or support groups for parents focusing upon alternative methods of discipline, handling anger and frustration, and enhancing parenting skills. (p. 263)

We can only assume that the extent of reported sexual abuse is minimal and that because of guilt, stigma, and fear, many, many incidents continue to go unreported. Regardless, the effect of abuse can be traumatic. The emotional effects can be a sense of being guilty or responsible for the abuse, low self-esteem, depression, anger, fear and the inability to trust others, helplessness, and negative attitudes toward sexuality.

Again, it is important to note the role of prevention programs. Such programs require careful planning and a coordinated effort involving school and community agency counselors, social workers, school teachers, administrators, nurses, and significant community groups. Parents obviously should be involved and educated regarding their responsibilities. Children themselves need to be educated and informed regarding sources of help if needed. The local media should also be requested to fully publicize the efforts to prevent child sexual abuse.

Sexual abuse is, of course, not limited to children. Adolescents are also frequently victimized, and rape, including date rape, is being increasingly reported. Prevention is the desired antidote, but we must still be prepared to assist the victims through crisis lines, crisis centers, and specialized rape assistance programs.

The victims of child abuse may be placed in temporary shelters or, in extreme cases, foster homes. The current trend, however, is to hold the family together if at all possible. An effort is made to give the parents the training and support they need to become adequate parents. Groups are commonly used for this purpose. The goal is to help them break the cycle of abuse. Remember that effective parenting does not always come naturally but for some people must be learned in a step-by-step fashion.

Counselors functioning in settings serving abused spouses or children need special skills in individual and group counseling as well as crisis and short-time interventions, plus a knowledge of marriage and family dynamics.

Gay Men and Lesbian Women

In recent generations the counseling profession has become more aware of issues relating to the counseling of lesbian women and gay men. As many of this population are now readily acknowledging their sexual orientations and moving more openly into the public mainstream, more members of this group can be expected to seek assistance from counseling professionals, as they are frequently the victims of harassment, violence, discrimination, and isolation.

Given that the research on the lesbian and gay populations to date is complex, often contradictory, and in some cases biased as well, counselors may find it confusing to find agreed-upon guidelines for providing effective counseling. However, many of the profession's proven approaches would appear to provide a basis for assistance inasmuch as many of the common problems faced by gays and lesbians are not unique to this population. These include problems of (a) societal prejudice, (b) family conflict, (c) peer ridicule and rejection, and (d) health fears (especially AIDS).

In counseling, then, we would assume that awareness, acceptance, and understanding would provide a basic foundation. Going beyond these basics, counselors must also be aware of the impact of societal prejudices, including the social stereotypes that exist regarding sexual minorities. The attitudes of some religious people toward gays and lesbians are frequently troublesome to these clients, especially those with their own strong religious ties. Family awareness and interactions, and support or nonsupport for the gay or lesbian client is frequently an issue. Confidentiality is a hallmark of the client/counselor relationship, but counselors must often emphasize to gay and lesbian clients that the highest level of confidentiality will be maintained within the limits permitted by the law and ethical guidelines. Counselors must also recognize that in some circumstances management, such as school administrators, may demand to be made aware of employees or students who are gays or lesbians. Parents can also be demanding about this issue. Regardless of the circumstances, confidentiality (within legal and ethical guidelines) *must* be maintained.

In working with gay and lesbian clients, counselors may utilize a variety of techniques and draw on a range of theoretical approaches. At times, person-centered approaches may assist the client in self-examination and expression of repressed feelings. Gestalt techniques may be effective in helping the client to develop his or her awareness of the ambivalence and confusion centering around homosexual affiliation. Family systems approaches are obviously important in assisting clients and their families in adjusting to their gay and lesbian members.

Counselors should anticipate gays and lesbians among their clientele at all ages and be comfortable as well as knowledgeable in working with this population. They should learn about the lifestyle- and gender-specific issues common at different stages across the life span of gays and lesbians. In some settings and situations, counselors may find it useful to identify therapists who are themselves gays or lesbians for referral or consultative purposes.

People with Disabilities

It is estimated that there are over 6 million Americans of working age with varying degrees of physical or mental disabilities in the United States. Nearly two thirds of this group are unemployed. Many who are employed face significant environmental and attitudinal barriers, often subtle. Because of the special needs of this population, rehabilitation counseling emerged as a specialty after World War I and accelerated in the period following World War II. Today, within the profession, it is recognized as an area requiring specialized training. However, in many locales, rehabilitation counselors are not available. Data indicate that in business and industrial settings, employment and retention are enhanced for the disabled with counseling and even more so when training and support groups are available. Counselors should be aware that the career development issues of individuals with disabilities will be very similar to those experienced by all populations, but this group will usually require a recognition of the particular disability in strategies for facilitating career development, including the education of employers. Counselors, as well as employers of people with disabilities, must be aware that the goal of the Americans with Disabilities Act is to remove all barriers that have restricted people with disabilities from achieving their potential in employment and in the community.

People in Poverty

The concept of people living in poverty may seem inconsistent with the "American Dream," but over 34 million people were living below the poverty level in the United States in 1998. Dispelling the theory that the majority of these people are minorities, statistics indicate that 23,400,000 are white, 9 million are black, and 8 million are Hispanic. The most commonly recognized geographic settings of these populations are the large metropolitan industrial areas and rural settings with few natural resources. In these locales, many individuals are born into the cycle of poverty: their parents lived in poverty, they will live in poverty, and their children will live in poverty. To many in these settings, there appears to be no way out.

The public schools in these environments are usually the poorest; there is little educational stimulation or motivation to prepare children to move out of this cycle. In addition, there is generally public apathy and little political action (although a great deal of shouting at election time). This population of the poor has little political influence; they are certainly, not big contributors to the campaigns of politicians. Unfortunately, career counseling and career training programs are rare in these settings; where they *do* exist, they are often viewed with suspicion or simply ignored because the people they might help know little about them and trust them even less. To be effective in these settings, counselors must first understand the "culture of the poor." This is essential if a meaningful public information program is to be undertaken. Of course, informing the potential client population is not an end in itself. Counselors in these settings must be able to relate to these clients on a one-to-one basis. Group work can also be very helpful when counselors recognize the special characteristics of the poverty populations and the problems of poverty.

SUMMARY

Counseling is the heart of the counselor's activity. Although there is general agreement in broadly defining counseling, a variety of theoretical concepts have emerged over the years. Traditional approaches such as psychoanalytic and client-centered theories are still popular, but in recent generations, the behavioral theory, the rational-emotive therapy theory, the reality therapy theory, and the integrative theory have attracted followers. However, counselors may still opt for the eclectic approach, one that gives the option of selecting from any and all the existing theories.

The counseling process initially focuses on relationship establishment, then seeks to identify and explore the client's problem with the objective of establishing client goals. The process then proceeds to the planning and problem-solving stage and, finally, to the applying of the solution and termination of the counseling relationship. Although these stages tend to blend into each other, they serve as a guide to a logical sequence of events for the counseling process. The effective application of the process is dependent upon the basic counseling skills required of the counselor.

More and more attention has been given to the counselor's responsibility and need for special preparation in dealing with our population's diversity and a range of special problems. Recent generations have also noted increased usage of group counseling and other group techniques by counselors. These will be discussed in chapter 5.

DISCUSSION QUESTIONS

1. What theoretical orientation would you prefer for your own counselor?
2. What theoretical orientation do you believe you would feel most comfortable with as a counselor?
3. How can counseling help improve the quality of life for (a) children of elementary school age? (b) the elderly of postretirement age?
4. When, or under what circumstances, would you encourage a friend to see a counselor?
5. How do you interact in establishing a relationship when you meet someone for the first time? What impresses you most about an individual when you meet for the first time?
6. What are the differences and similarities among advising, providing guidance, and counseling an individual?
7. Discuss counseling as a growth enhancement and development activity.

CLASS ACTIVITIES

1. Interview a practicing counselor regarding his or her theoretical orientation and ask how the counselor determined that this theory was the most appropriate for her or him.
2. Identify the counseling theory that at this early point in your training you feel would be most appropriate for you. Share your rationale (in a

group) with others in the class who have selected the same theory.

3. Conscientiously practice the basic counseling skills of attending behavior in your interactions with others for a week. Report your reactions or results.

4. Keep a log noting the effectiveness of your communication skills with others over a 3-day period. What are the implications of your findings?

5. Organize the class into groups of three. Each individual in the triad is to alternate role-playing the role of counselor, client, and observer. The client is to role-play a client with a problem; each of the three role-playing counselors is to practice, in the first round, the skill of attending behavior; in the second round, attending behavior plus reflection of feelings; in the third round, attending behavior, reflection of feelings, and facilitative communications. The observer, in addition to observing the process, is to evaluate the effectiveness of the counselor in practicing the basic skill or skills, in addition to being the time keeper for each session (approximately 5–7 minutes for the first round, 10 minutes for the second and third rounds). After the conclusion of each counseling "session," counselor and client should also assess the process (allow about 15–20 minutes after each session for this activity).

SELECTED READINGS

American Psychological Association. (2000). Guidelines for psychotherapy with lesbian, gay, and bisexual clients. *American Psychologist, 55*(12), 1440–1451.

Atkinson, D. R. (1985). A meta-review of research on cross-cultural counseling and psychotherapy. *Journal of Multicultural Counseling and Development, 13*(4), 138–153.

Brammer, L. (1988). *The helping relationship* (4th ed.). Upper Saddle River, NJ: Prentice Hall.

Claiborn, C., & Ibrahim, F. (Eds.). (1987). Counseling and violence [Special issue]. *Journal of Counseling and Development, 65*(7), 338–390.

Cooney, J. (1988). Child abuse: A developmental perspective. *Counseling and Human Development, 20*(5), 1–10.

Davenport, D. S., & Woolley, K. K. (1997). Innovative brief pithy psychotherapy: A contribution from corporate managed mental health care. *Professional Psychology: Research and Practice, 28*(2), 197–200.

Gerber, S. (2001). Where has our theory gone? Learning theory and intentional intervention. *Journal of Counseling and Development, 79*(3), 282–291.

Glauser, A. S., & Bozarth, J. D. (2001). Person-centered counseling: The culture within. *Journal of Counseling and Development, 79*(2), 142–147.

Gold, J. R. (1996). *Key concepts in psychotherapy integration.* New York: Plenum Press.

Hill, C., Helmer, J., Tichenor, V., Spiegel, S., O'Grady, K., & Perry, E. (1988). Effects of therapist response made in brief psychotherapy. *Journal of Counseling Psychology, 35*(3), 222–233.

Ivey, A., & Goncalves, O. (1986). Developmental therapy: Integrating developmental processes into the clinical practice. *Journal of Counseling and Development, 66*(9), 406–413.

Kelly, K. R., & Hall, A. S. Mental health counseling for men. [Special issue.] *Journal of Mental Health Counseling, 14*(3).

LaFromboise, T. (1988). American Indian mental health policy. *American Psychologist, 33*(5), 388–397.

Lesbian, gay, and bisexual concerns. (2000). Report of Division 44/Committee on Lesbian, Gay, and Bisexual Concerns Joint Task Force on Guidelines for Psychotherapy with Lesbian, Gay, and Bisexual Clients. *American Psychologist, 55*(12), 1440–1451.

McFarland, W. P., & Dupuis, M. (2001). The legal duty to protect gay and lesbian students from violence in school. *Professional School Counseling, 4*(3), 171–179.

Maki, R. H., & Syman, E. M. (1997). Teaching of controversial and empirically validated treatments in APA-accredited clinical and counseling psychology programs. *Psychotherapy, 34*(1), 44–57.

Okun, B. (1987). *Effective helping: Interviewing and counseling techniques* (3rd ed.). Monterey, CA: Brooks/Cole.

Shaikur, B. (1988). The measurement and treatment of client anger in counseling. *Journal of Counseling and Development, 66*(8), 361–365.

Smith, E., & Vasquez, M. (Eds.). Cross cultural counseling [Special issue]. *The Counseling Psychologist, 13*(4), 531–720.

Stalikas, A., & Fitzpatrick, M. (1996). Relationships between counsellor interventions, client experiencing, and emotional expressiveness: An exploratory study. *Canadian Journal of Counselling, 30*(4), 262–271.

Switzky, H. N. (1997). Individual differences in personality and motivational systems in persons with mental retardation. In W. E. MacLean, Jr. (Ed.), *Ellis' handbook of mental* deficiency, psychological theory and research, (3rd ed., pp. 343–377). Mahwah, NJ: Lawrence Erlbaum Associates.

Tracey, T., & Dundon, M. (1988). Role anticipation and preparations over the course of counseling. *Journal of Counseling Psychology, 35*(1), 3–14.

Weinrach, S. G., Ellis, A., MacLaren, C., DiGiuseppe, R., Vernon, A., Wolfe, J., et al. (2001). Rational emotive behavior therapy successes and failures: Eight personal perspectives. *Journal of Counseling and Development, 79*(3), 259–268.

RESEARCH OF INTEREST

Atkinson, D. R. (1985). A meta-review of research on cross-cultural counseling and psychotherapy. *Journal of Multicultural Counseling and Development, 13*(4), 138–153.

Abstract   Analyzes four major reviews of the research on the effects of race on counseling and psychotherapy in terms of client use of mental health services, client preferences for counselor race or ethnicity, counselor prejudice and stereotyping, differential diagnosis of client problems, differential counseling process, differential treatment strategies, and differential outcomes. An attempt was made to examine research outcomes across ethnic groups, research designs, and research settings. Several observations regarding methodology are discussed, and several conclusions derived from analog, survey, and archival studies are reached. Recommendations for future research on cross-cultural counseling and psychotherapy are presented.

Bloch, S., Szmukler, G. I., Herrman, H., & Benson., A. (1995). Counseling caregivers of relatives with schizophrenia: Themes, interventions, and caveats. *Family Process, 34*(4), 413–425.

Abstract   This study evaluated an intervention designed to reduce the burden and increase the physical and emotional well-being in 60 caregivers of patients with schizophrenia. Subjects were randomly assigned to experimental or control groups. Experimental subjects underwent 6 one-hour weekly individual counseling sessions. Coping, family, and social themes arose among subjects. Cases associated with those themes are described. Principal interventions applied by the counselors included active listening, recognition of the caregiver's experience, clarification of problems arising in counseling, and use of educational approaches. Counselors were given caveats to treatment as the program evolved. Caveats addressed issues including therapists' blurring of professional boundaries and subjects' addressing concerns other than those unique to caregiving. Thirteen themes emerged.

Holloway, E. L., & Wampold, B. E. (1986). Relation between conceptual level and counseling-related tasks: A meta-analysis. *Journal of Counseling Psychology, 33*(3), 310–319.

Abstract   Meta-analysis was used to review 24 studies that applied conceptual systems theory (CST) (a) to investigate the effect of counselor's conceptual level (CL) on the counselor's performance and (b) to investigate the matching of CL and environmental structure. Results corroborate the predictive power of CST in the context of the counseling situation. The prediction was corroborated that counselors who were matched with a compatible environment (i.e., low-CL Ss with high structure and high-CL Ss with low structure) would perform better than those who were mismatched. It was also found that low-CL Ss generally performed significantly better in more highly structured environments, whereas high-CL Ss showed only a slight improvement in their matched low-CL environment. Due to the lack of standardization in the task stimulus, it was unclear whether higher CL Ss generally performed better than low CL Ss. Methodological, conceptual, and training issues were discussed.

Howard, K. I., Orlinsky, D. E., & Lueger, R. J. (1994). Clinically relevant outcome research in individual psychotherapy: New models guide the researcher and clinician. *British Journal of Psychiatry, 165*(1), 4–8.

Abstract   This article recommends a more systematic exploratory methodology for clinical research, emphasizing the generalizability and constructive replication of findings. This quasi-experimental, case-study approach entails the use of objective data, continuous assessment, a model of problem stability, diverse and heterogeneous samples, and clear evidence of an effect that can be ensured for magnitude and treatment applicability.

Lambert, M. J., & Okiishi, J. C. (1997). The effects of the individual psychotherapist and implications for future research. *Clinical Psychology Science and Practice, 4*(1), 66–75.

Abstract   A body of research concerning psychotherapy outcome is reviewed with the intent of establishing the importance of the individual psychotherapist to treatment process and outcome. Although particular therapy techniques have not been shown to be especially important in therapy process and outcome, they have been the focus of most research and training for the last two decades. In the past, extensive study of the individual therapist was difficult, but the rising trend of managed health care organizations has created opportunities to conduct research on this topic. Hypothetical outcome data for individual clinicians are presented in graphical form. An attempt is made to show how patient typing can be used to adjust outcome by case-mix methods. Suggestions for future research are made.

Racism and Psychological Health. (1999). [Special issue]. *The Counseling Psychologist, 27*(2).
Thompson, C. E., & Neville, H. A. (1999). Racism, mental health and mental health practice. (1999). *The Counseling Psychologist, 27*(2), 155–223.

Abstract   In this article, the authors present an interdisciplinary discussion of the multiple dimensions of racism and formulate conceptions of its impact on the formation of healthy personalities. They describe both the ideological and structural components of racism and discuss how it perpetuates itself recursively at the macro- (e.g., group, institution) and microlevels (e.g., interpersonal). As one consequence of the embedded, cyclical nature of racism, efforts to treat client problems that involve issues of race and racism will necessarily entail piercing distortions in reality, encouraging self-moral development, and eliciting risk-taking behaviors. To take part in transforming current structures of racism, counseling psychologists are urged to extend these strategies beyond the therapeutic milieu. Implications for practice, training, and research are presented.

Waller, G. (1997). Drop-out and failure to engage in individual outpatient cognitive behavior therapy for bulimic disorders. *International Journal of Eating Disorders, 22*(1), 35–41.

Abstract   This study explored the characteristics of bulimics who fail to complete therapy. Noncompleters were divided into those who failed to engage and those who dropped out, so that these groups could be directly compared. Subjects were 50 women (bulimia nervosa or anorexia nervosa of the bulimic subtype) recruited from a case series of referrals to an eating disorders clinic who were offered individual cognitive-behavior therapy. The women (28 completers—mean age 22.3 years) were compared on standardized measures of eating, psychological, and family characteristics. The noncompleting groups both had high levels of borderline psychopathology and more severe perceived bulimic characteristics than the completers. However, the dropouts and failure to engage subjects had very different patterns of perceived family emotional involvement, with the failure to engage subjects reporting relatively healthy functioning.

Weisz, J. R., et al. (1987). Effectiveness of psychotherapy with children and adolescents: A meta-analysis for clinicians. *Journal of Consulting and Clinical Psychology, 55*(4), 542–549.

Abstract   Conducted meta-analysis of 108 well-designed outcome studies using 4- through 18-year-old subjects to examine effectiveness of psychotherapy with children and adolescents. Overall, findings revealed significant, durable effects of treatment that differed somewhat with client age and treatment method but which were reliably greater than zero for most groups, most problems, and most methods.

5 ◆ Group Techniques for Counselors

The rugged individualist has been extolled over the years in U.S. history. The sagas and accomplishments of Daniel Boone, Davey Crockett, "Wild Bill" Hickok, Wyatt Earp, Buffalo Bill, Susan B. Anthony, Charles Lindbergh, and others have been told and retold. We still pay certain homage today to the "lone wolf" who can make it alone, ignore the system, or shun the spotlight. Perhaps one of the reasons we so admire this rugged individualist is that we recognize it is almost impossible to go it alone in today's group-oriented, group-dominated, and group-processed society. In fact, today, to be well adjusted in a given society usually means that the individual has mastered the society's norms of social interaction—of functioning appropriately in groups.

The objectives of this chapter are therefore to (a) identify the various types of group settings used by counselors to assist their clients, and (b) introduce the process and values of group counseling, group guidance, and values clarification techniques.

We can see the influence and dependence on groups from examining the individual's functioning in today's society. Such an examination leads to the following conclusions:

1. Humans are group oriented. People are meant to complement, assist, and enjoy each other. Groups are natural venues for the emergence of these processes.
2. Humans seek to meet most of their basic and personal-social needs through groups, including the need to know and grow mentally; thus, groups are a most natural and expeditious way to learn.
3. Consequently, groups are most influential in how a person grows, learns, and develops behavioral patterns, coping styles, values, career potentials, and adjustment techniques.

For counselors, teachers, and others who work with groups in leadership, facilitative, and teaching capacities, the following additional assumptions can be made:

1. An understanding of the influences and dynamics of groups can improve your assessment and understanding of individuals.
2. An understanding of the organization and utilization of groups can help you in teaching and guiding others.
3. Group counseling may be more effective for some people and some situations than individual counseling.
4. Special populations can benefit from groups specially designed to recognize their uniqueness or their needs.

DEFINITIONS AND EXPLANATIONS

In any study of groups, particularly one that is introductory, it is important at the onset to clarify the various labels in group counseling and guidance, including a definition of *group*. Webster's *Third New World International Dictionary* (unabridged) defines a group as "a number of individuals bound together by a community of interest, purpose, or function." However, within and across the professional disciplines engaged in the study and practice of groups, there are wide variations in defining a group. To narrow the definition of *group* for discussion here, note that counseling groups are characterized by interaction. They are functional or goal-oriented groups. Aggregate groups without interaction of the members are not functioning groups.

Counselors may view various group activities as occurring at three levels. These are the guidance level, the counseling level, and the therapy level. Definitions of these and other group configurations are given in the next sections.

Group Guidance

Group guidance refers to group activities that focus on providing information or experiences through a planned and organized group activity. Examples of group guidance activities are orientation groups, career exploration groups, college visitation days, and classroom guidance (discussed later in this chapter). Group guidance is also organized to prevent the development of problems. The content could include educational, vocational, personal, or social information, with a goal of providing students with accurate information that will help them make more appropriate plans and life decisions.

Group Counseling

Group counseling refers to the routine adjustment or developmental experiences provided in a group setting. Group counseling focuses on assisting counselees to cope with their day-to-day adjustment and development concerns. Examples might focus on behavior modification, developing personal relationship skills, concerns of human sexuality, values or attitudes, or career decision making.

Group Therapy

Group therapy provides intense experiences for people with serious adjustment, emotional, or developmental needs. Therapy groups are usually distinguished from counseling groups by both the length of time and the depth of the experience for those involved. Therapy group participants often are individuals with chronic mental or emotional disorders requiring major personality reconstruction. Group therapists obviously require a higher level of training.

T-Groups

T-groups are derivatives of training groups. They represent the application of laboratory training methods to group work. T-groups represent an effort to create a society in miniature with an environment designed especially for learning.

T-groups are relatively unstructured groups in which the participants become responsible for what they learn and how they learn it. This learning experience also usually includes learning about how people function in groups and about one's own behavior in groups. A basic assumption appropriate to T-groups is that learning is more effective when the individual establishes authentic relationships with others.

Sensitivity Groups

In actual practice, the label *sensitivity groups* appears to be applied so frequently and broadly as to be almost meaningless. In a more technical sense, however, a sensitivity group is a form of T-group that focuses on personal and interpersonal issues and on the personal growth of the individual. There is an emphasis in sensitivity groups on self-insight, which means that the central focus is not the group and its progress but rather the individual member.

Encounter Groups

Encounter groups are also in the T-group family, although they are more therapy oriented. Rogers (1967) defines an encounter group as a group that stresses personal growth through the development and improvement of interpersonal relationships via an experiential group process. Such groups seek to release the potential of the participant:

> In an intensive group, with much freedom and little structure, the individual will gradually feel safe enough to drop some of his defenses and facades; he will relate more directly on the feeling basis (come into a basic encounter) with other members of the group; he will come to understand himself and his relationship to others more accurately; he will change in his personal attitudes and behavior; and he will subsequently relate more effectively to others in his everyday life situation. (p. 262)

Extended encounter groups are often referred to as *marathon groups*. The marathon encounter group uses an extended block of time in which massed experience and accompanying fatigue are used to break through the participants' defenses.

Although encounter groups offer great potential for the group members' increased self-awareness and sensitivity to others, such groups can also create high levels of anxiety and frustration. Obviously, if encounter groups are to have maximum potential and minimal risk, they must be conducted by highly skilled and experienced counselor leaders.

Task Groups

Task groups are organized to meet organizational needs through task forces or other organizational groups or to serve individual needs of clients through such activities as social action groups. These groups are frequently useful to organizations seeking ways to improve their functioning. In agency counseling centers, task groups may be organized to assist clients in dealing with a wide spectrum of needs ranging from spiritual to educational.

Psychoeducation Groups

Psychoeducation groups emphasize cognitive and behavioral skill development in groups structured to teach these skills and knowledge. Psychoeducational groups are oriented more toward guidance than toward counseling or therapy. These groups tend to be short term in duration and focused on specifically delineated goals. Attention is directed at current life situations and interactions within the group related to the group theme.

Minigroups

Although technically two or more people can constitute a group, the use of the term *minigroup* has become increasingly popular in recent years to denote a counseling group that is smaller than usual. A minigroup usually consists of one counselor and a maximum of four clients. Because of the smaller number of participants, there can be certain advantages resulting from the more frequent and direct interaction of the group members. Withdrawal by individuals and the development of factions or "cliques" are less likely in minigroups.

Group Process and Group Dynamics

Two terms commonly used in describing group activities are *process* and *dynamics*. Although often used interchangeably, they do have different meanings when used to describe group counseling activities. The beginning counseling student should note that *group process* is the continuous, ongoing movement of the group toward achievement of its goals. It represents the flow of the group from its starting point to its termination. It is a means of identifying or describing the stages through which the group passes.

Group dynamics, on the other hand, refers to the social forces and interplay operative within the group at any given time. It describes the interaction of a group, and can indicate the impact of leadership, group roles, and membership participation in groups. It is a means of analyzing the interaction between and among the individuals within a group. Group dynamics is also used on occasion to refer to certain group techniques such as role playing, decision making, "rap" sessions, and observation.

In-Groups and Out-Groups

Although *in-groups* and *out-groups* are not formal groups organized or overseen by counselors, they are often important influences on client behaviors. These groups can be based on almost any criteria—socioeconomic status, athletic or artistic accomplishments (in schools especially), a particular ability, racial-cultural origins, and so forth. In-groups are characterized by association mostly with peers who share the defining characteristic, and out-groups consist of those who are excluded from in-groups. For example, there are nonparticipants in athletics or drama who have not been invited to participate in such things as social clubs. In many counseling situations, it is important for counselors to understand how clients see themselves and others in terms of "in" or "out."

Social Networks

Although not a group in a formal sense, a *social network* results from the choices that individuals make in becoming members of various groups. As counselors we may be concerned with how these choices are made and what their impact is on individuals. Sociologists engage in social network analyses to determine how the interconnectedness of certain individuals in a society can produce interaction patterns influencing others both within and outside the network.

PROFESSIONAL STANDARDS FOR THE
TRAINING OF GROUP WORKERS

The Association for Specialists in Group Work (ASGW) advocates the incorporation of core group competencies into master's degree–level training required in all counselor education programs. It also supports preparation of group work specialists at the master's degree level and the continued preparation of group work specialists at the post-master's level—through the Education Specialist (Ed.S.) degree, certification, doctoral degree, continuing education, etc.—recognizing that the recommended levels of group work specialty training in many programs will have to be preceded by completion of the master's degree.

The year 2000 revision of the *Professional Standards for Training of Group Workers* contains two levels of competencies and related training that have been identified by the ASGW Standards Committee:

1. *Core Training Standards:*

    Coursework Requirements: Core training shall include at least one graduate course in group work that addresses ... but [is] not limited to scope of practice, types of group work, group development, group process and dynamics, group leadership, and standards of training and practice for group workers.

    Experiential Requirements: Core training shall include a minimum of 10 clock hours (20 clock hours recommended), observation of and participation in a group experience as a group member and/or as a group leader.

2. *Group Work Specialists:* Advanced competencies that build on the generalist core in the four identified group work specialties of

    • Task/work groups, including knowledge, skills, and supervised practice beyond core group training (additional minimum: 30 clock hours; recommended: 45 clock hours);

    • Guidance/psychoeducation groups, including knowledge, skills, and supervised practice beyond core group training (additional minimum: 30 clock hours; recommended: 45 clock hours);

    • Counseling/interpersonal problem-solving groups, including knowledge, skills and supervised practice beyond core group training (additional minimum: 45 clock hours; recommended: 60 clock hours);

    • Psychotherapy/personality reconstruction groups, including knowledge, skills, and supervised practice beyond core group training (additional minimum: 45 clock hours; recommended: 60 clock hours). (Association for Specialists in Group Work, 2000, pp. 4–10).

For the training of those who engage in group psychotherapy, the distinguished scholar in the field, Irvin D. Yalom, suggests four major components essential to a comprehensive training program beyond the didactic and theoretical: (a) observing experienced group therapists at work, (b) close clinical supervision of one's maiden groups, (c) a personal group experience, and (d) personal psychotherapeutic work (1995, p. 512).

GROUP COUNSELING

More than 100 years ago, the psychologist William James (1890) wrote:

> We are not only gregarious animals liking to be in sight of our fellows, but we have an innate propensity to get ourselves noticed and noticed favorably, by our kind. No more fiendish punishment could be devised, were such a thing physically possible, than that one should be turned loose in society and remain absolutely unnoticed by all the members thereof. (p. 293)

James, as well as others, noted over the years the importance of human relationships in meeting people's basic needs and influencing their individual development and adjustment. For most, the vast majority of these relationships are established and maintained in a group setting, and for many, daily routine adjustment problems and developmental needs also have their origins in groups. Interest has increased in encouraging social skills development among groups in the elementary school grades and in fostering positive group relationships and communications skills across all ages of the adult population.

Counseling, as a facilitative science, is based in helping relationships, which must also be human relationships. Because the most frequent and common human relationship experiences occur in groups, groups also can provide positive developmental and adjustment experiences for many people. The next sections examine some of the potential values of group counseling and the ways these values are realized. Also discussed are the importance to the counselor of selecting participants and forming groups carefully, and of mastering the skillful use of group techniques.

Theoretical Considerations

In the previous chapter, we discussed popular theoretical orientations as well as the important rational base that theory provides for good counseling practice. As in individual counseling, effective group counseling emanates from a sound theoretical base. Therefore, let us briefly reexamine the popular counseling theories in the context of their application to group rather than individual counseling settings.

In groups led by counselors with a *psychoanalytic* theoretical orientation, the counselor interprets transference and resistances in order to free the clients' unconscious. The analysis may focus on the behavior of individual members of the group and/or the behavior of the group as a whole.

Individual or *Adlerian* group leaders are somewhat direct and active in the group process while recognizing that the group members can decide what to do for themselves. The group setting is viewed as a safe opportunity for members to examine themselves, develop self-respect, and improve their social interactions as they strive to develop their potential.

Client-centered counselors have always had an active interest in group counseling. Carl Rogers coupled his beliefs about human behavior with his observations of therapeutic groups to formulate his ideas of group counseling and therapy, labeled a *basic encounter group*. The client-centered approach assumes that people have a natural tendency to grow and improve themselves. Group counseling can provide an atmosphere within which members feel safe to reveal their needs and ultimately to improve their lives. The group leader also models behavior that contributes to a positive group environment and the overall group process.

The *behavioral* counselor in the group setting proceeds to systematically identify the members' problems in behavioral terms. Behavioral objectives are established for members and the counselor reinforces the behaviors that clients wish to acquire.

In group counseling the *rational-emotive* therapist, not the environment, is prominent in promoting client change. He or she does this through reason, persuasion, role playing, and so forth. The counselor seeks to bring about cognitive and rational behavior change. Within the group, members help each other identify illogical, emotionally driven behaviors.

Reality-oriented groups provide a caring environment in which clients can feel worthwhile and secure enough to explore more satisfying behavior. The counselor may function as a teacher in leading the group members to adapt more appropriate behaviors and make more realistic choices.

As noted in chapter 4, *transactional analysis* (TA) is essentially a process for counseling individuals within the group setting. TA counselors usually feel that the first step in establishing a TA group is teaching group members to recognize ego stages.

Gestalt therapists focus on the integration of the person—"getting it all together"—with counselor-client interaction considered a key to this process. This focus does not change in the group setting, as is evident in the goals of such groups, shown in Table 5-1.

Eclectic counselors, in group counseling situations as in individual counseling, will utilize a number of different theoretical perspectives to respond to a variety of clients, interactions, and problems. Table 5-1 offers a comparison of the group goals of the different theoretical viewpoints.

Values of Group Counseling

Group counseling is not a team sport. The goal is not to have a winning group. The goal of group counseling is to achieve the goals of, meet the needs of, and provide an experience of value to the individual members who constitute the group. Following are some of the opportunities that group counseling can offer:

1. *Individuals can explore, with the reinforcement of a support group, their developmental and adjustment needs, concerns, and problems.* Groups can provide a realistic social setting in which the client can interact with peers who not only are likely to have some understanding of the problem or concern that the client brings to the group, but who will, in many instances, also be sharing the same or a similar concern. The counseling group can provide the sense of security group members need to interact spontaneously and freely and take risks, thus promoting the likelihood that the needs of each member will be touched on and that the resources of peers will be utilized. The old saying that "misery loves company" may in fact provide a rationale for group counseling. People are more comfortable sharing a problem with others who have similar experiences, and they may also be more motivated to change under these conditions.
2. *Group counseling may give the client an opportunity to gain insights into his or her own feelings and behavior.* Yalom (1995), in discussing the group as a social microcosm, stated that "a freely interactive group, with few structural restrictions, will, in time, develop into a social microcosm of the participant members" (p. 25). He also points out that given enough time in the group setting, clients

Table 5-1   Comparative overview of group goals.

Model	Goals
Psychoanalytic therapy	To provide a climate that helps clients reexperience early family relationships. To uncover buried feelings associated with past events that carry over into current behavior. To facilitate insight into the origins of faulty psychological development and stimulate a corrective emotional experience.
Adlerian therapy	To create a therapeutic relationship that encourages participants to explore their basic life assumptions and to achieve a broader understanding of lifestyles. To help clients recognize their strengths and their power to change. To encourage them to accept full responsibility for their chosen lifestyle and for any changes they want to make.
Psychodrama therapy	To facilitate the release of pent-up feelings, to provide insight, and to help clients develop new and more effective behaviors. To open up unexplored possibilities for solving conflicts.
Existential therapy	To provide conditions that maximize self-awareness and reduce blocks to growth. To help clients discover and use freedom of choice and assume responsibility for their own choices.
Person-centered therapy	To provide a safe climate wherein group members can explore the full range of their feelings. To help members become increasingly open to new experiences and develop confidence in themselves and their own judgments. To encourage clients to live in the present. To develop openness, honesty, and spontaneity. To make it possible for clients to encounter others in the here and now and to use the group as a place to overcome feelings of alienation.
Gestalt therapy	To enable members to pay close attention to their moment-to-moment experiencing, so they can recognize and integrate disowned aspects of themselves.
Transactional analysis therapy	To assist clients in becoming free of scripts and games in their interactions. To challenge members to reexamine early decisions and make new ones based on awareness.
Behavior therapy	To help group members eliminate maladaptive behaviors and learn new and more effective behavioral patterns. (Broad goals are broken down into precise subgoals.)
Rational emotive behavior therapy	To teach group members that they are responsible for their own disturbances and to help them identify and abandon the process of self-indoctrination by which they keep their disturbances alive. To eliminate the clients' irrational and self-defeating outlook on life and replace it with a more tolerant and rational one.
Reality therapy	To guide members toward learning realistic and responsible behavior. To assist group members in evaluating their behavior and in deciding on a plan of action for change.

Source: From *Theory and Practice of Group Counseling,* 1st edition by G. Corey, © 2000. Reprinted with permission of Brooks/Cole, an imprint of the Wadsworth Group, a division of Thomson Learning. Fax 800-730-2215.

will begin to be themselves, interact with others, and create the same interpersonal universe they have experienced, including the display of maladaptive, interpersonal behavior to the group. Yalom also states that corrective emotional experiences in groups may have several components, including these:

- A strong expression of emotion which is interpersonally directed and which represents a risk taking on the part of the patient

  - A group supportive enough to permit this risk taking

- Reality testing which allows the patient to examine the incident with the aid of consensual validation from the other members

  - A recognition of the inappropriateness of certain interpersonal feelings and behavior or of the inappropriateness of certain avoided interpersonal behaviors

- The ultimate facilitation of the individual's ability to interact with others more deeply and honestly. (p. 6)

As clients gain new insights into their behaviors and feelings from interactions with members of the counseling group, their self-concept formation may also be affected. Because of the significant influence self-concept has on an individual's personal-social adjustment and his or her perception of school and career decision making, the opportunity to bring about positive change in self-concept through new insights provided by the group counseling experience can be a very valuable benefit.

3. *Group counseling provides clients with an opportunity to develop positive, natural relationships with others.* The personal interactions that take place within the group counseling structure provide an excellent and continuous opportunity for the group member to experiment with and learn to manage interpersonal relations. This includes developing sensitivities to others—their needs and feelings. It also provides opportunities for members to learn of the impact their behavior has on others. Thus, through the group process and its interactions and sharing of experiences, clients may learn to modify earlier behavior patterns and seek new, more appropriate behaviors in situations that require interpersonal skills.

4. *Group counseling offers opportunities for clients to learn responsibility to themselves and others.* Becoming a member of a counseling group implies the assumption of responsibilities. Even when clients show initial tendencies to avoid assuming responsibility for their own behavior, contributing to the group's interactions, or accepting their "assignment" within the group, these avoidance techniques will usually fade as group relationships develop and group goals are established.

Selection of Group Members

All of us have had experience in organizing groups. When deciding on group members for a social occasion we select good old Charlie because he is a laugh a minute; Diane, because she gets along with everybody; Harry, in case we need some serious conversation; and Olga, because she is a good listener. On the other hand, if the purpose of the group is a more serious one, such as planning a neighborhood park, we might choose Rosalie, because of her knowledge of flowers and shrubbery; Jim, because he is a landscaping expert; Jane, because of her architectural skills; and Jerry, because of his proven fund-raising abilities. In each instance, people are usually selected because they can contribute something to the group and its interaction.

Forming counseling groups is obviously not approached as casually as creating social groups. Professionally we must have some criteria beyond "guesstimates" of what is needed. One way to gather objective data that can help in the formation of counseling groups dealing with specific and identifiable needs is the needs assessment.

A needs assessment is important to stay fully informed about the current needs of your constituents. Without tapping in to them on a regular basis, you may be providing services that are not relevant or that do not accurately meet their requirements. Not only does a needs assessment tell you what topics are important, it provides you with data useful in persuading reluctant administrators and teachers to permit children to leave the classroom for the group experience.

There are formal and informal ways to conduct a needs assessment. In a school setting, you could informally poll parents, teachers, children, and administrators by directly asking them for their opinions on what group topics/issues need to be addressed. A more formal way to gather these important data is to develop a simple survey instrument that can more accurately assess the current state of needs, thus providing more in-depth information for both planning and evaluating future groups (Smead, 1995, p. 23).

Although group counseling focuses on the needs of the individual, the importance of group membership to the achievement and adjustments of individuals in the group cannot be overestimated. Group member selection is one key to a successful counseling group. The following are possible criteria for the selection of group members: (a) common interest, (b) volunteer or self-referred, (c) willingness to participate in the group process, and (d) ability to participate in the group process. A popular criterion for group selection also may be a common interest of the potential members in a similar problem, concern, or issue.

Many group specialists believe that the best group member is self-referred. Group counseling should be an option chosen by the group participants. Choice guarantees the protection of each client's rights. It also further enhances the motivation for counseling should the client decide to be in a counseling group.

Corey (2000) notes that

> screening should be a two-way process. Therefore, the potential members should have an opportunity at the private screening interview to ask questions to determine whether the group is right for them. Group leaders should encourage prospective members to be involved in the decision concerning the appropriateness of their participation in the group. (p. 87)

In the selection of potential group members, both the counselor and the potential participant are involved. It is important that *both* determine the readiness of the individual to participate positively with prospects for desirable outcomes in the counseling group.

In some instances, potential group members may lack the ability or desire to communicate with others or to relate to and assist others. From the standpoint of temperament, not everyone will be a suitable group member. In short, a person must possess certain abilities or aptitudes if he or she is to profit from and contribute to the group experience. Thus, although any number of procedures may be used by counselors to form a group, inviting clients to participate once the counselor has become familiar with each of them and his or her concerns is a procedure that is the most realistic and professionally sound. We cannot emphasize enough the importance of clients' being comfortable and satisfied with their decision to participate.

The following should be considered during the process of screening interviews for possible group membership.

- Identify the ground rules that group members are expected to follow. These would include (a) the right of all group members to express their views, (b) the suggestion that no personal viewpoint is unimportant, (c) the absolute necessity for confidentiality.
- Describe how a counseling group develops and functions. Special attention should be given to how the group members individually can benefit the most from the group experience.
- Emphasize honesty and openness as critical components throughout the duration of the group.
- Point out that although an objective of the group is to help members enhance interpersonal relationship skills, frustrations and disappointments are likely; however, these should be considered opportunities for personal growth.
- Discuss guidelines pertaining to the duration of group therapy.

Another consideration in the formation of the counseling group is size; what should the size of the group be to get the best results? Yalom (1995) notes that his own experience and a consensus in the clinical literature implies that the

> ideal size of an interactional therapy group is approximately seven or eight with an acceptable range of five to ten members. The lower limit of the group is determined by the fact that a critical mass is required for an aggregation of individuals to become an interacting group. When a group is reduced to a size of four or three, it often ceases to operate as a group; member interaction diminishes, and therapists often find themselves engaged in individual therapy within the group. Many of the advantages of a group—the opportunity for broad consensual validation, the opportunity to interact and to analyze one's interaction with a large variety of individuals—are compromised as the group size diminishes. (p. 276)

. . .

> The upper limit is determined by sheer economic principles; as the group increases in size, less and less time is available for the working through of any individual's problems (p. 277).

It is certainly appropriate to note that as group sizes increase, the intimacy and comfort that exist in small or modest-size groups may begin to diminish. The number of group members can also influence the difficulty of scheduling meetings and hence, the number of and time between meetings. Larger groups often have a tendency to become less personal and more mechanical in their process. Larger groups also increase the risks that some members may be inadvertently overlooked to the extent that their needs are not satisfied.

At the other end of the size continuum, the very small group of only two or three members, despite the advantages of closeness and feelings of security, often suffers from a deficit in the human experiences, viewpoints, and value resources found in groups of five to eight.

Meeting time for groups in nonschool settings should be based on predetermined or mutually convenient times. In schools, however, Stockton and Toth (1993) note:

> It is important to involve teachers in the group planning process (i.e., how many times, and when, will students be called out of class?). Some counselors have found it effective, at the middle or high school level, to schedule the group during different class periods each meeting time so as not to have a student miss the same class time over and over again. (p. 74)

GROUP LEADERSHIP

Few would dispute the oft-noted suggestion that leadership, while constantly sought after, is a very elusive and misunderstood phenomenon. The nature and quest for leadership at all levels and across all settings has been a continuing challenge to humankind. Historically, it would appear that leaders frequently emerge because of the wants and needs of the population they are seeking to serve.

Whereas different characteristics of leadership have asserted themselves in different settings and situations, the following seem to apply generally to effective group leadership.

- The leader conducts himself or herself honestly, openly, and ethically at all times.
- The leader is open to and accepts the input of all group members, even those with whom the leader may disagree.
- The primary interest of the leader at all times is in the personal growth and well-being of all the group members.
- The leader models values and behaviors that can enhance the lives of the group members.

Helen Driver (1958), an early leader in the group counseling movement, identified leadership techniques for the group counselor:

1. Support: giving commendation; showing appreciation.
2. Reflection: mirroring feelings.
3. Clarification: making meanings clear, showing implications of an idea.
4. Questioning: bringing out deeper feelings, inviting further response.
5. Information: providing data for examination, serving as a resource person, teaching.
6. Interpretation: explaining the significance of data, using analogy.
7. Summary: asking for client summary first, pointing out progress, alternatives. (pp. 100–102)

Stockton (1980) reviewed the importance of training in four areas as preparation for group leadership responsibility:

> (1) didactic knowledge (e.g., potential group leaders should understand theories of group counseling, ethical principles, research); (2) individual clinical skills such as those involving assessment, interpreting nonverbal behaviors, ability to use self-disclosure, confrontation and other standard therapeutic tools; (3) knowledge of group dynamics, most particularly developing a keen sense of the importance of timing and knowing how to pace a variety of specific group leader techniques and interventions; and (4) achieving a healthy personality oneself. (p. 57)

Stockton and Morran (1982) surveyed the group leadership research and reported that the results are inconclusive: "There is very little research that provides clear evidence for a particular style of leadership as being most effective" (p. 48). A significant result from their survey is that leadership is multidimensional, which thus creates difficulty in controlling for unidimensional examination. Stockton and Morran also concluded that the Lieberman, Yalom, and Miles (1973) study of encounter groups comes closest to supporting a specific style of leadership. This study's results are summarized as follows:

> The most effective encounter group leaders (a) were moderate in amount of emotional stimulation (emphasizing disclosure of feelings, challenging, confronting, etc.), (b) were high in caring (offering support, encouragement, protection, etc.), (c) had meaning-attribution utilization (providing concepts for how to understand, clarifying, interpreting, etc.), and (d) were moderate in expression of executive functions (setting rules, limits, norms, time management, etc.). (Stockton & Morran, 1982, pp. 70–71)

Corey and Corey (2002) identified personal characteristics of effective group leaders as including the following:

- courage
- willingness to model
- presence
- goodwill and caring
- belief in group process
- openness
- becoming aware of your own culture
- nondefensiveness in coping with attacks
- personal power
- stamina
- willingness to seek new experiences
- self-awareness
- sense of humor
- inventiveness
- personal dedication and commitment

An examination of these suggestions for group leadership indicates the group counselor's responsibility for the structure, conduct, and general overseeing of the group sessions. Note that conscientious group leaders do not become involved in group activities beyond their depth of professional preparation. Group counseling emphasizes factors of association rather than deep emotional disturbances. The counselor's depth of psychological understanding and skill in group dynamics are individual considerations in the level of group counseling that he or she undertakes. For counseling groups that focus on specific and narrow concerns, such as family relations, human sexuality, or substance abuse, it is obviously desirable that the counselor-leader have some special understanding of the topic.

GROUP PROCESS

The elements of the group counseling process share much in common with those of individual counseling. These may be separated into their logical sequence of occurrence.

The Establishment of the Group

The initial group time is used to acquaint the new group membership with the format and processes of the group, to orient them to such practical considerations as frequency of meetings, duration of group, and length of group meeting time. Additionally, the beginning session is used to initiate relationships and open communications among the participants. The counselor also may use beginning sessions to answer questions that clarify the purpose and processes of the group. The establishment of the group is a time to further prepare members for meaningful group participation and set a positive and promising group climate.

The group counselor must remember that in the initial group sessions the general climate of the group may be a mixture of uncertainty, anxiety, and awkwardness. It is not uncommon for group members to be unfamiliar with one another and uncertain regarding the process and expectancies of the group regardless of previous explanations or the establishing of "ground rules."

It is important in this initial stage of group establishment for the leader to take sufficient time to ensure that all the groups' members have their questions and concerns addressed; that they understand the process and begin to feel comfortable in the group. Of course, the impression that the group counselor makes in this initial stage is of utmost importance to the smooth and successful process of the group.

Identification: Group Role and Goal

Once an appropriate climate has been established that at least facilitates a level of discussion, the group may then move toward a second, distinct stage: identification. In this stage, a group identity should unfold, the identification of individual roles should emerge, and group and individual goals should be established. These may all develop simultaneously or at different paces, however, they are significant at this stage of the group counseling process. It is also important to make the group counseling goals operational.

Most of us have few undirected, non-goal-oriented activities in our typical everyday plan of action. Those who work with groups frequently, whether in teaching or other capacities, can well predict the outcome if you were to appear before such a group with the question, "How would you like to spend your time today?" At worst, chaos would result, and at best, considerable time would be lost before a determination could be made of how the group could best utilize the time available.

Goal setting is no less important in group counseling than in any other activity that seeks to be meaningful. The early identification of goals in group counseling will facilitate the group's movement toward a meaningful process and outcomes. Establishing these goals is the joint responsibility of the counselor and group members. Goals are most readily identified and implemented when they are specified in behavioral terms. It is important to make the group counseling goals operational from the outset. They should be stated in objectives that are not only measurable but are also attainable and observable and likely will be realized in view of the group strategies planned. It is also important in this process that the subgoals of each individual group member be recognized and responded to.

Counselors need to be aware of the probable, or at least possible, conflict and confrontation that may emerge during this stage of the group's development. Yalom (1995) labels this second phase "the conflict, dominance/rebellion stage." He considers it a time when the group shifts from preoccupation with acceptance, approval, commitment to the group, definitions of accepted behavior, and the search for orientation, structure, and meaning, to a preoccupation with dominance, control, and power. The conflict characteristic of this phase is between members or between members and the leader. Each member attempts to establish for himself his preferred amount of initiative and power, and gradually a control hierarchy, a social pecking order, emerges. (p. 297)

In this second stage, often referred to as the confrontation stage, conflict and even open hostility will often occur. As members attempt new patterns of behavior and new approaches to group goals, differing perceptions as well as differences in solutions generated by the individual members can lead to a range of behaviors from normal discussions to active and open confrontation. In this stage, the counselor must function to keep the discussions "in bounds" and prevent them from becoming personal attacks on individuals' values and integrity.

The counselor should not misjudge silence as a sign of group compliance in this stage; rather, the counselor must be alert to the possibility that silence may signal resistance on the part of the group members. Not all groups will experience this stage with the same degree of intensity or conflict. In groups with younger clients, such as high school students, the perception of the counselor as an authority figure may inhibit expressions of conflict, doubt, or anger.

This second stage in the group process is frequently one in which group members express their dissatisfaction with the group process or leadership. Sometimes this results from differences between the way a group member sees himself or herself and the way the group has stereotyped that individual, which leads to the member's challenging the reactions or impressions of the rest of the groups. Differences may also emerge when controversial issues are discussed or the issues are more complex than anticipated. Demands that group members change can also result in frustration and dissatisfaction. Finally, premature termination from the group can have negative effects on the group from which the member has withdrawn.

When conflicts and confrontations do occur, a more cohesive group usually emerges, with resulting increased openness in communication, consensual group action and cooperation, and mutual support among the members. Premature termination can result in negative effects on the group from which the member has dropped. Initial work stages of the group require membership stability in order to develop therapeutic potential from group treatment, and loss of members makes this task more difficult (Stockton, Barr, & Klein, 1981).

Productivity

In the third stage of the group's development, a clear progression toward productivity is noted. As the group has achieved some degree of stability in its pattern of behaving, the productivity process can begin. Also, because the members are now more deeply committed to the group, they may be ready to reveal more of themselves and their problems.

This is the period of problem clarification and exploration, usually followed by an examination of possible solutions.

The emphasis of this stage is on recognizable progress toward the group's and individual members' goals. In this process, however, each group member is exploring and seeking an understanding of self, situation, and problem or concern, and each member develops a personal plan integrating these understandings. The three subphases of this stage may be (a) assessment, (b) understanding, and (c) planning. The group structure tends to be functional.

In group counseling productivity can be frequently equated with successful problem solving. Group counseling thus often becomes a process seeking to promote change.

In this regard, the group counselor must (a) determine where the group is; (b) identify where the group wants to go, what it desires to accomplish; (c) identify the most promising process to help the group move from where it is to where it desires to go, and then (d) employ the selected processes to achieve the desired outcomes. Here again, it is important to have the agreement and hence the participation of all involved in assessing where the group is, where it wants to go, and how it can best get there; then do it!

Although group strategies may be selected by the group for any or all of these phases, it is important that they make sense to each member in terms of that person's individual needs. The counselor may note that progress is being made when progress can be seen. Of course, progress is not always constant during this time, and occasionally regression, stagnation, or even confusion may occur. It is appropriate that when the group does not understand what it is doing, it should stop until understanding is achieved. Sometimes uncertainty occurs when members don't understand how they are to participate. Sometimes they may feel they have nothing to contribute.

On these occasions the counselor is alert to prevent process problems from handicapping progress and group achievement. Often, a simple reminder by the counselor of the stated goals or objectives of the group can prevent activities or discussions that tend to sidetrack members or the group as a whole from maintaining progress. However, because of the relationships and the group climate previously established, groups should overcome these difficulties and regain their productivity.

During this phase, the problem or concern should be clarified to everyone's satisfaction and ownership should be verified. This clarification includes a thorough understanding of the nature of the problem and its causes. Only when this has been achieved can resources for problem solutions be realistically examined. This phase may be successfully concluded when all possible solutions have been considered in terms of their consequences. These solutions should be practical or capable of being realized (obtainable), and the final choice of a solution should be made only after appropriate consideration and discussion. This is not the time for snap judgments and hurried commitments. At this point, the group members have examined themselves and the problem as it applies to them and have explored these considerations in considerable depth; have looked at possible solutions and their consequences; have determined the course of action that appears most appropriate; and are ready to move into the next stage, one in which they will try out or experiment with their chosen solution. In this process, by making their own decisions they have established their ownership of the problem and the chosen solution.

Realization

When members of the group recognize the inappropriateness of their past behaviors and begin to try out their selected solutions or new behaviors to implement their decisions in practice, they are making progress toward realizing their individual goals. At this time, the individual members have taken the responsibility of acting on their own decisions. The counselor encourages the sharing of individual experiences and goal achievement both within and outside the group. Although general success with the new behaviors may provide sufficient reinforcement for many members to continue, for others a support base of "significant others" outside the group should now be developed to help them of maintain the change once the counseling group is terminated. In school settings, for example, counselors might consult with parents and teachers to implement this strategy.

Termination

Most of us have experienced occasions of regret and even sorrow when temporary groups to which we have belonged reach the breakup point. Regardless of the purpose for which the group is organized, we may try to prolong its eventual dissolution by promising get-togethers, planning social activities, and in general agreeing that "this has been too much fun to let it end." On many such occasions, casual strangers have become the best of friends in relatively short periods of time, and they resist—at least psychologically—the threatened termination of the relationship.

For these same reasons, members may resist the termination of a counseling group. The very nature of counseling groups, with their emphasis on interpersonal relationships, open communication, trust, and support, promises the development of a group that the membership may want to continue indefinitely. It is therefore important from the very beginning that the group counselor emphasize the temporary nature of the group and establish, if appropriate, specific time limitations. The counselor also reminds the group, as the time approaches, of the impending termination. This does not mean that the counselor alone is responsible for determining the termination point of a group. Although the counselor may, of course, assume this responsibility, termination may also be determined by the group members or by the group members and the counselor together.

Termination, like all other phases or stages of the group counseling experience, also requires skill and planning by the counselor. Termination is obviously most appropriate when the group goals and the goals of the individual members have been achieved and new behaviors or learnings have been put into practice in everyday life outside the group. The group will also be ready to terminate when, in a positive sense, it has ceased to serve a meaningful purpose for the members. Under less favorable circumstances, groups may be terminated when their continuation promises to be nonproductive or harmful, or when group progress is slow and long-term continuation might create over-dependency on the group by its members.

Members may be terminated from a group at any time during the group's existence. Members who are disruptive, seriously handicap the other members, may be more effectively assisted through individual counseling, or personally desire to terminate are often subjects for individual terminations. Group counselors should be aware that this is a common happening, especially in the beginning stages of a group, when several members may voluntarily terminate. The counselor should accept these departures as a matter of course and refrain from exerting pressure on such persons to remain in the group. At the same time, however, the counselor may indicate a willingness to see the leavers on an individual basis.

The point of termination is a time for review and summary by both counselor and clients. Some groups will need time to allow members to work through their feelings about termination. Even though strong ties may have developed and there are pressures from the group to extend the termination time, those pressures must be resisted, and the group must be firmly, though gently, moved toward the inevitable termination.

GROUP GUIDANCE ACTIVITIES

In a broad, general context, group guidance is probably as old as formal schooling. Good teachers through the years have used groups for what today would be called pupil guidance purposes. In schools, group guidance activities have been designed to provide information to students in groups or experiences beyond those associated with the day-to-day learning activities in the classroom. In nonschool settings, group activities have been planned to provide information, help in skill building, opportunities for personal growth and development, orientation, and assistance in decision making.

Values

Over the years certain values have been attributed to group activities of a guidance nature. Some of these are discussed in the following sections.

Facilitating Personal Development

Certain experiences that lead to personal development can take place only in the group setting. These include the opportunity to learn and play certain roles, such as group leader, group follower, or member; the development of patterns of cooperation with others; and the learning of group communication skills.

Stimulation of Learning and Understanding

In group settings people can be given opportunities to learn more about themselves and their relations with others and to understand these better. They can also acquire information about the external world. In this context, group guidance activities are important in providing learning and understanding—relevant to career and educational decision making and personal-social adjustments. Care must be taken in how the information is presented and perceived. Clients must feel that the information is important to them if they are to assimilate it.

Advantages of Group Interaction

By actively participating in groups organized for guidance purposes, members have the opportunity to broaden their scope of understanding regarding the subject or purpose for which the group is organized. Additionally, participants should grow in their understanding of group interactions and dynamics as well as understanding their own behavior in groups.

Economy

Groups should not be organized for guidance purposes solely on the basis of economy. However, when effectiveness of outcome is not lessened, the saving of both counselor's and clients' time through the use of groups can be of considerable value.

Organizing Group Guidance Activities

All of us have been participants in some type of group activity, social or otherwise, that has been organized on the spur of the moment. Occasionally these unanticipated activities have been enjoyable or worthwhile, but probably more often, they have resulted in confusion, uncertainty, perhaps even frustration, and have been considered a waste of time. The popularity of group activities has, in some instances, led to their being scheduled without appropriate preparation, but that is not and should not be the pattern. If group guidance activities are to achieve their potential, a great deal of consideration and organization must go into their planning, conducting, and evaluation. Although the organization process is very similar to group counseling, discussed earlier in this chapter, the differences, though often subtle, should be noted and the similarities should be reemphasized. The following guidelines may be helpful.

Determining That There Is a Need for Group Guidance

All too often group guidance activities are simply scheduled. On occasion, the scheduled activities may be a response to an actual need. If we are to ensure the group's success, however, we must determine beforehand that there is a need a group shares in common and for which a group guidance response is appropriate. Questionnaires, problem surveys, or checklists administered to specific populations often will provide a factual basis for determining possible group guidance activities.

Determining That Group Guidance Is the Most Appropriate or Effective Response

Once needs have been determined, the counseling staff must identify those for which a group guidance activity would be appropriate, in contrast to group counseling or individual counseling, or perhaps even some form of instruction. Group guidance activities are those that may be useful to nearly every one in a specific population or setting; hence, the total group would experience the activity. Examples might be a stress management program for employees in an industrial setting; a behavior workshop for public relations workers; or a career day for high school students.

Small group guidance activities, in broad general terms, are designed for specific outcomes and cater to the needs of smaller subgroups within the total population served by the school or agency counseling and guidance program. These activities may focus on providing information for decision making and planning purposes, activities for personal development purposes, and assistance for educational adjustments. Small group guidance activities can emphasize smaller components or follow-up activities for the larger college, career, or orientation programs. Other specific examples are guidance groups organized to develop job-seeking and interviewing skills, how-to-study techniques, assertiveness training, career education, values clarification activities, discussion groups, and experiences in nonverbal communications.

Determining the Characteristics of the Group

Once the nature of the group guidance activity has been established, certain group characteristics must be determined. Obviously, size of the group must be one consideration. Here, the counselor must determine what size group will be most appropriate for the activities planned and outcomes anticipated. Size will also have an influence on the operational format of the group. Format planning includes determining the types of activities of the group, the length of time allotted for each group session, the number of sessions, and the setting.

A final consideration affecting the group characteristics will be the role of the counselor. Will the counselor be an active participant or an inactive observer who remains in the background once the group's activities are under way? Will the counselor direct the group? Will the counselor be a group arbitrator? What information will the leader provide the group? Will roles be assigned or will roles evolve as the group progresses?

Establishing the Group

Once the characteristics of the group have been determined, members may be selected. They may volunteer or they may be invited to participate. Invitation implies that the person may refuse to participate. In establishing the membership of the group, the leader must verify that the planned activity will respond to the needs of the individual member and that the structure or operational format will be comfortable for the group member. In large groups, such as those organized for orientation purposes, career needs, or other special information purposes, this is not necessarily essential, but for smaller, intimate groups, it is an important consideration.

Monitoring the Ongoing Activities

Once the group has been established and the members oriented to its purpose and processes, the counselor or facilitator assumes the responsibility for keeping the group "on track." It is relatively easy, especially considering the participants' lack of experience and understanding of the group process, to deviate from the purposes of the group, become bogged down in irrelevant discussions and activities, or encounter personal factors that inhibit or impede the functioning of the group. The counselor must, therefore, be constantly on the alert to detect such symptoms and to use his or her skills to minimize these effects. The ongoing activities of the group are meaningful only as long as they promote the progress of the group and its members toward their goals.

Evaluating Outcomes

The importance of evaluation in assessing the outcomes of groups cannot be overemphasized, and evaluation and the accountability process are discussed in greater detail in chapter 14. The goals or projected outcomes of the group must be stated in clear, objective, and measurable terms. The criteria for measuring goal achievement must be identified and stated, and data then collected that, when analyzed, will present an objective evaluation of outcomes. Such evaluations can assist counselors and others involved to determine which group guidance activities are most effective and which techniques within groups are most and least effective. Implications for group membership, roles, and leadership may also result.

Classroom Guidance Activities

Classroom guidance is a planned process for helping school populations acquire useful and needed information, skills, or experiences. The classroom has been found the most effective setting for carrying out such programs, and the guidance program generally does not detract from and, in fact, may even enhance the regular curricular offerings.

Classroom guidance activities are characterized by (a) being developmental, (b) being ongoing, and (c) having counselors as instructors (but they may be planned with faculty assistance). The substance of the instruction is based on specific needs of the population for whom the program is designed. Their needs provide the rationale for the program and in turn are translated into program goals. Program procedures (including timetables), feedback, and evaluation planning are developed in the next step. School counselors will have responsibility for developing a communications plan for orienting all interested parties to their role and function. They will also be responsible for identifying the topics that need attention, gathering resource materials, and preparing handouts.

School counselors will have responsibility for developing a communications plan to inform interested parties of the counseling program's goals and the activities related to the achievement of those goals. For example, obviously students should be aware of the services provided for them and the activities related to these services. Likewise, parents should be informed and additionally, encouraged to participate in and support program activities where appropriate. Faculty and school administrators need information regarding all major activities within the school, including those of the counseling program. The counseling program will be enhanced by teacher and administrator participation and support. School counselors will also be responsible for identifying the topics that need attention, gathering resource materials, and preparing handouts.

Programs of classroom guidance help ally school counselors with the teaching faculty by bringing the counselor into the individual teacher's classroom on a regular basis. This activity not only enriches the instruction of the classroom teacher, but enhances the counseling program of the school. Classroom guidance provides additional opportunities for student/counselor interactions and natural settings for counselors to identify and react to student needs.

Values Development Activities for Groups

When we say that we believe in free speech, freedom of the press, equal rights for women, and access to education for all, we are, in effect, expressing values. Those values might appropriately reflect the consensual values of our society. Each society is characterized by well-defined, articulated values that are passed on to and practiced by the members of the society. On the other hand, when we extol the pleasures of travel abroad, the virtues of exercise and careful diets, and the inspiration of a specific religious faith, we may, in effect, be expressing our personal values. Thus, values also represent what a person considers important in life, and these ideas of what is good or worthwhile are acquired through the modeling of the society and the personal experiences of the individual.

A discussion of values is basically a discussion of what people believe in, what they stand for, and what is important in life. In recent years we have seen a dramatic increase in public and political attention to "values" in relationship to violence and other crimes, political and corporate scandals, the decline in morality, and disrespect for laws and rights. There has also been much discussion regarding who is responsible for imparting desirable values.

We do know that values are the reasons people behave and even think the way they do. They motivate us to plan and act and serve as a standard for judging the worth of activities, achievements, things, and places. In short, values give direction to life and, hence, behavior. On the other hand, people who do not know what they value often engage in meaningless, nonproductive, and usually frustrating behavior. In both individual and group counseling, understanding the client's values can help the counselor understand the client's behavior, goals, or lack of goals, and what is or has been of significance in the client's life.

Values Defined

Values have become increasingly a topic of discussion and concern in recent years. Government leaders, magazine and newspaper editors, leading educators as well as countless concerned citizens have suggested that as a nation we are on the verge of moral bankruptcy. They cite financial scandals, political abuses, Medicare fraud, misleading advertising, child molestation, drug peddling, and more, evidencing a loss of values. One result has been a call to re-instill our traditional national values, with school populations being especially targeted. The resulting proliferation of values clarification techniques and the increasing examination of values education in the school curriculum, as with any popular movement, have clouded traditional definitions and brought forth complex explanations of what is meant by values. We do not propose to add to this confusion but rather to present several of the more prominent definitions appropriate to those engaged in counseling.

First, the dictionary defines *values* as ideals, customs, and institutions that arouse an emotional response, for or against them in a given society or a given person—a simple straightforward, and, we think, acceptable definition. Another equally clear definition is that values represent the comparative worth we attach to anything (behaviors, people, material goods, experiences, environments). Values may be generated and reflected in individuals, organizations, institutions, and societies.

In developing their own value system, children are constantly examining, testing, and acquiring values based on their experiences and learning. In these early and formative years the developing child and adolescent are also influenced by the impact of significant others; the impact of socializing institutions, such as schools; the perceived values of the cultures in which they are immersed; and the influence of groups they may associate with or hold membership in.

It is in the last instance, groups, that counselors, as group experts, have a role to play in both school and nonschool settings. Values and counseling have always been intertwined, have always complemented each other.

VALUES AND COUNSELING

Historic Concerns

Rockwell and Rothney (1961) indicate that from the very beginning of the counseling and guidance movement in the United States, leaders have expressed concern with values. The "father" of this movement, Frank Parsons, has been described as a "utopian social reformer," believing in the perfectibility of humanity. He viewed guidance as a means to a mutualistic society and the counselor's role as one that would lead to social goals by offering prescriptive advice. Jessie Davis preached the moral values of hard work, ambition, honesty, and the development of good character as assets in the business world.

Later, Carl Rogers stated his beliefs in the goodness and worthwhileness of people and their abilities to chart their own destiny. C. Gilbert Wrenn, in *The Counselor in a Changing World* (1962) and *The World of the Contemporary Counselor* (1973), discussed the values of the counselor and his or her clients. In *The Counselor in a Changing World* he wrote:

> It has become increasingly clear that the counselor cannot and does not remain neutral in the face of the student's value conflicts. Even the counselors who believe most strongly in letting the student work out his own solutions have firm values of their own and cannot help commu-

nicating them. They communicate their values in what they do and don't do even if they never mention their beliefs verbally. Furthermore, we expect more and more of the counselor with reference to the needs of society. Just to accept the need for the full development of abilities in the interest of a stronger nation as well as the interest of the individual is a manifest expression of a social value. Because the counselor cannot escape dealing with values and expressing values in his own behavior, he must be clear about the nature of his own values and how they influence his relationships with other people.

A second developing conviction about values is that they are now seen by some psychologists as the central difficulty for many troubled people. Fifty years ago values were clearly defined, and acute maladjustment seemed to result from a willful violation of them. Psychological treatment consisted primarily of freeing the individual from an overwhelming sense of guilt over his transgression against his parents and other representatives of society. But today the picture seems almost the reverse of what it was. The maladjusted person feels himself more lost than guilty. Social expectations have become more diverse, less well defined, less insistent. The social processes of inculcating strong values are less effective today, in part because family and community are less cohesive.

As a consequence the individual feels a lack of purpose and direction. He feels estranged from others and even from himself; he feels worthless and unsure of his identity. He must discover character in himself for himself. Values strongly felt are the foundation upon which he can build an increasingly satisfying personal existence. Thus, clarifying values and perhaps acquiring new values becomes a major task for the individual in counseling, as in education generally. (pp. 62–63)

In the later publication, *The World of the Contemporary Counselor*, Wrenn discusses the counselor's and client's values:

The Counselor's Values

A first concern is that the counselor examine his own hierarchy of values and check it against the contemporary scene. I do not suggest that the counselor must change his values to meet changing assumptions, but rather that he attempt to increase his openness to the intrusions of change. A feeling of great certainty that what he now thinks is right and is right for all time can become a simple rigidity. It is too easy to retreat into a secure castle of one's own construction and close the gates to all that might disturb. It is healthy to be disturbed, for this means that one is required to think, to test assumptions, to question thoughtfully the bases for conduct. It is more realistic to confess confusion than to parade conviction.

On the other hand, admitting confusion could be interpreted as justifying having no convictions, no assurances of vital values. I must anticipate at this point what I want to discuss more carefully later, that one can be committed to values and goals even though they are tentative. In fact, one must be committed to be real, but the commitment may be to values which are seen as subject to modification, as changing with experience. "Tentativeness and commitment" paralleling each other are powerful principles.

The Client's Values

The second area of concern is the acceptance of the client's right to be different in his values. This difference between the values of the client and those of the counselor is often a difference between generations or between cultures. Always, of course, the values of the client are the product of his life experience, unique to him and often markedly different from the experience of the counselor. The 30-year-old, middle-class, socially accepted, college-educated counselor cannot be expected to understand in all cases the values of a 16-year-old, ghetto-reared, socially rejected boy or girl or those of an affluent, socially amoral, parentally rejected youth. In fact, experiential understanding of another is rare. What is most important, however, is that the counselor accept the client's values as being as real and as "right" for him as the counselor's values are for the counselor. There is too frequently a tendency to protest inwardly, "He can't really meant that," when the value expressed by the client is in sharp contrast to a related value held by the counselor. The point is that the client does mean that; his value assumption is as justifiable to him as yours is to you.

So far I have said nothing about the counselor's responsibility for helping the client to examine a given value assumption, particularly if the value is likely to result in behavior harmful to another or to society. He has such a responsibility, I am sure, differing widely from client to client and varying often with the client's psychological readiness to examine values. Basic to the success of any such confrontation, however, is the counselor's acceptance of the "right" of the client to have different values. If a counselor enters into a discussion of another's point of view with the implicit assumption that he is "right" and the other is "wrong," failure is assured. (pp. 34–35)

Counselors using values clarification techniques must be aware of the criticism that this frequently arouses, especially from religious groups. Critics of values clarification techniques suggest that they encourage the permissiveness associated with secular humanism and, further, that they detract from the role of the home and church in teaching values.

Values Theory and Process

In the development of values theory, no individual has made a greater contribution than Lawrence Kohlberg. His research was significant in formulating a theoretical viewpoint on moral (or values) development. Kohlberg's early conclusions were that children go through six stages of moral development as follows:

1. Heteronomous morality—Obeying the rules to avoid punishment.
2. Individualism, instrumental—purpose and change—Following rules when it is in one's best interest. Serving one's own interests.
3. Mutual interpersonal expectations, relationships and interpersonal conformity—Living up to what is expected of you by others. Being a good person in your own eyes.
4. Social system and conscience—Fulfilling duties, contributing to the group and society. Satisfying your conscience.
5. Social contract or utility and individual rights—Obligation to the law—commitment to family, friends, work.
6. Universal ethical principles—Follows universal principles of morality. (McCandless & Coop, 1979, pp. 163–164)

Kohlberg believed that the individual's development could become fixed at any one of the six stages. He

proposed a moral education program centered around discussions of real and hypothetical dilemmas. The ultimate goal of the program was the moral maturity of the student with moral maturity being defined as "the principled sense of justice." Realizing there might be a disparity between the values the schools said they wished to foster and those they exemplified in their hidden curriculum, he insisted that the hidden curriculum be made "explicit in intellectual and verbal discussions of justice and morality." (Pyszkowski, 1986, p. 22)

A major hypothesis of group values activities that has significant implications for counselors utilizing these techniques suggests that the skillful and consistent use of the valuing process by an individual increases the likelihood that the individual will make appropriate decisions that will be satisfying both to him or her and to society.

Having broadly viewed values and their impact on behavior, noted a basis for values theory, and described similarities between the valuing and counseling processes, let us examine further some of the relationships between values and counseling.

Values development techniques appear to emphasize group participation—and although this is true, it does not necessarily limit their utilization or inclusion in individual counseling. Many of the techniques can be completed by an individual client and then shared and examined within the framework of the counseling process. Such exercises (some of which are included at the end of this chapter) as drawing a hobby plaque, listing 20 things you like to do, selecting from alternatives, and discussing situational anecdotes are examples of activities that can be satisfactorily completed by the client, then discussed and examined with the counselor. They may in turn help the client confirm and practice more appropriate and satisfying behavior.

Because values education or clarification techniques are popularly practiced in groups, their potential for group counseling and guidance is considerable. For example, numerous values clarification techniques designed to promote getting acquainted and developing interpersonal relationship and communication skills would have their appropriate moments in group counseling and guidance. Group values exercises designed to facilitate self-assessment, self-concept clarification, and reinforcement for change would have their usefulness for the group counselor. Exercises that give a person the opportunity to compare, examine, and defend his or her behavior, values, and interests against the norms of others can also be useful in group counseling.

MULTICULTURAL ISSUES AND GROUPS

Counseling or guidance groups can provide counselors with both challenges and opportunities for promoting multicultural awareness and sensitivity to their group clients. This assumption is based on recognizing (a) the opportunities groups provide for promoting positive multicultural relationships and (b) the opportunities for counselors themselves to model and be perceived as individuals who are aware, sensitive, and attentive to a diversity of populations, approaching them in an appropriate manner. Coleaders of groups in which one leader is from a cultural minority can be helpful. Here again, as in individual counseling with multicultural clients, counselors must be aware of their own cultural background and how it influences their perceptions and behaviors. Counselors, whatever their background, must conscientiously prepare themselves to work with the wide range of culturally diverse groups that populate our country. Whatever their professional position, counselors must be prepared and ready, even assertive, to step forward to assist their communities in overcoming the misunderstandings, biases, and insensitivity that threaten the fabric of community life and our national well-being.

SUMMARY

Today's society is group oriented and each person belongs to many groups. These groups serve a variety of purposes and in them one plays a variety of roles. Because of this group orientation, group counseling and guidance have become increasingly recognized as a means of assisting individuals in meeting their adjustment and developmental needs in both school and nonschool settings. These group activities are distinguished by the nature of their concern and the type of group experience provided. Group guidance activities are confined primarily to school settings with an emphasis on providing information or experiences helpful in decision making. Group counseling tends to focus on routine adjustments and developmental needs or problems of individuals, whereas group therapy provides an intense experience that may last for a considerable length of time for individuals with serious adjustment, emotional, or developmental needs. The counselor's role and leadership are important to the success and accomplishment of both guidance and counseling groups. The group counselor must also be skillful and aware of the steps through which the group process moves. This process begins with the selection of members and the initial establishment of the group as a group, the identification of group goals, the clarification and exploration of the group's and its individual members' problems and/or concerns, the exploration of solutions and consequences, decision making regarding solutions, implementation of the decision, and finally, termination and evaluation.

In recent years much media attention has been given to the values of youths, the shifting values of the adult world, and the significance of personal values for satisfaction in the world of work. Values have also become increasingly important to professional counselors. Group values activities can provide a helpful and nonthreatening approach for assisting clients in groups and appraising individuals. In a planned program of values development, the individual initially engages in exercises designed to identify his or her values, then shares them; next, he or she examines, confirms, and finally, practices values. Varied group exercises are available for counselors to use.

Of course, for counseling—whether group or individual—to be maximally effective, the counselor should know the client as well as possible. Assessment techniques that counselors may use to learn about clients are discussed in the next two chapters.

DISCUSSION QUESTIONS

1. In how many different groups do you actively participate during a typical day? How does your role and function differ across groups?
2. What are the differences among group counseling, group guidance, and group therapy?
3. What are some typical guidance needs of school-age youth that can be dealt with effectively in groups?
4. Identify counseling situations in which you believe group counseling might be more effective than individual counseling.
5. How do you account for the great popularity of sensitivity groups, T-groups, and encounter groups in recent years? Do you see any potential dangers in the popularity of these groups?
6. Can individuals with differing personality traits be equally effective as group leaders?
7. Discuss differences in the values generally held by three different client populations: adolescents; working, middle-age adults; and older Americans approaching retirement.
8. Are there any general societal values that ought to be taught to all youth through a deliberate program of values education?

CLASS ACTIVITIES

1. Divide students into small groups with the goal of each group member to be the identification of a new behavior that he or she would like to develop. Have the group work together to write a contract to be used by all group members. In one week, the group will reconvene to discuss progress/setbacks as well as possible changes in the contract.
2. In small groups, discuss situations in which you would like to improve your communication skills with others. Include both in-school and career settings.

3. Organize the class into small groups. Each group will identify a growth or learning activity agreed on by the group members and proceed to accomplish the goal of their group (insofar as time will permit). Each group will then analyze the dynamics and varying roles of members in the group.

4. Organize the class into small groups. Groups are to assume they are being exiled to an island for one week. Transportation to the island will be furnished by a rowboat. In addition to normal clothing for mild, but rainy, fall weather, each member of the group may bring six items (not to exceed 20 pounds) for the group's survival. These items should include the necessary foodstuffs and liquids for the group's nourishment during their period of internment. After the exercise ends and is reported to the class, each group should reconvene to analyze the dynamics of the group experience, noting the various roles played by members of the group.

5. Organize the class into small groups. Each group will design a meaningful group activity and demonstrate this activity. (You may use another classroom group for the demonstration if this would be more meaningful.)

6. Observe the dynamics of a group outside this class and report your observations.

SELECTED READINGS

The following special issues of the *Journal for Specialists in Group Work:* Critical issues in group work: Now and 2001, *10*(1), 115 pages; and Support groups, *11*(2), 122 pages.

Brantley, L. S., Brantley, P. S., & Baer-Barkley, K. (1996). Transforming acting-out behavior: A group counseling program for inner-city elementary school pupils. *Elementary School Guidance and Counseling, 31*(2), 96–105.

Gilbert, M., & Shmukler, D. (1996). Counselling psychology in groups. In R. Woolfe & W. Dryden (Eds.), *Handbook of counselling psychology* (pp. 442–459). London: Sage.

Karniauski, C. (1988). Using group development theory in business and industry. *Journal for Specialists in Group Work, 13*(1), 30–43.

Kivlighan, D. M., Multon, K. D., & Brossart, D. F. (1996). Helpful impacts in group counseling: Development of a multidimensional rating system. *Journal of Counseling Psychology, 43,* 347–355.

Mallinckrodt, B. (1997). Interpersonal relationship processes in individual and group psychotherapy. In S. Duck (Ed.), *Handbook of personal relationships: Theory, research and interventions* (2nd ed., pp. 671–693). Chichester, England: John Wiley.

Riordan, R. J., Beggs, M. S., & Karniauski, C. (1988). Some critical differences between self-help and therapy groups. *Journal for Specialists in Group Work, 13*(1), 24–29.

Stockton, R., & Morran, K. (1985). Perceptions on group research programs. *Journal for Specialists in Group Work, 10*(4), 186–191.

RESEARCH OF INTEREST

Hines, P. L., Stockton, R., & Morran, D. K. (1995). Self-talk of group therapists. *Journal of Counseling Psychology, 42*(2), 242–248.

Abstract To identify group leader cognitions and the role experience may play in leader cognitive schemas, 60 participants were placed in one of three groups on the basis of group-leading experience and were exposed to a 20-minute videotape of the group session, during which they completed a thought-listing instrument. Two judges free sorted the 1,299 collected thoughts and identified and defined 17 distinct thought categories. Three trained judges then placed 1,271 (97.8%) of the thoughts into these categories. Differences among experience levels were also explored through correlation and stepwise multiple regression analysis. Two thoughts, interpretation of group process and internal question regarding member, were found to account for 56% of the variance in experience level. Findings are discussed in terms of group leader cognitive processing, and suggestions for future research are provided.

MacKenzie, D. R. (1994). Where is here and when is now? The adaptational challenge of mental health reform for group psychotherapy. *International Journal of Group Psychotherapy, 44*(4), 407–428.

Abstract This article outlines the present state of group psychotherapy from the perspectives of the health care and psychotherapy service delivery systems and emphasizes the importance of designing a comprehensive group program, adapting group psychotherapy to a managed care environment, and adapting to professional changes. An examination of psychotherapy service-use patterns shows the importance of time categories and the relevance of group techniques and clinical investigations. The author suggests that traditional interpersonal and psychodynamic group techniques may be modified for time-limited use without sacrificing basic values and with demonstrated effectiveness. Clinicians must also undertake a process of transition in adapting to a more fiscally stringent practice environment. Psychotherapists must let the health care system know that proper practice guidelines are necessary to achieve effective treatment for patients.

MacNair, R. R., & Corazzini, J. G. (1994). Client factors influencing group therapy dropout. *Psychotherapy, 31*(2), 352–362.

Abstract   This study investigated client factors influencing group therapy dropout and continuation in 155 groups clients (aged 17–48 years) assigned to open-ended interpersonal therapy groups and classified as either dropouts or continuers as defined by the therapist, pattern of attendance, and method of leaving the group. Predictor and criterion variables were coded, and interpersonal variables were condensed using principal component analysis. A discriminant analysis found six significant variables predicting dropout: alcohol/drug problem, somatic complaints, roommate difficulties, general fighting, fighting with partner, and introversion. The strongest variable in the discriminant function was alcohol/drug problem. Previous individual counseling was found to predict continuation in group. The discriminant analysis correctly classified over 76% of cases as dropouts or continuers.

Marcus, D. K., & Holahan, W. (1994). Interpersonal perception in group therapy: A social relations analysis. *Journal of Consulting and Clinical Psychology, 42*(4), 776–782.

Abstract   Although group therapists have emphasized the importance of interpersonal perception and feedback during therapy, there has been little systematic research on how group members form impressions of one another. D. J. Kiesler's interpersonal circle provided a framework for studying interpersonal perception and relations. Twenty-seven women and 18 men from nine time-limited therapy groups reported their impressions of their fellow group members using the Impact Message Inventory, and they also completed two self-report scales. A social relations analysis of these data indicated that subjects' perceptions included both assimilation and consensus. There was also a relationship between how subjects saw themselves before therapy and how they were seen by other group members. The results demonstrated the utility of the social relations model for group therapy research and provided modest support for Kiesler's interpersonal circle.

Merta, R. J., Johnson, P., & McNeil, K. (1995). Updated research on group work: Educators, course work theory, and teaching methods. *Journal for Specialists in Group Work, 20*(3), 132–142.

Abstract   This article updates research on various aspects of training group counselors, using the results of a national survey of counselor educators. Two hundred thirty-six responses were analyzed. Group counselor educators are described, required course work in group work and theoretical or philosophical bases for group work are examined, and training components and teaching methods used to educate group counselors are presented. Training practices of counselor educators who are members of both the American Counseling Association and the Association for Specialists in Group Work are compared with those who are not. Implications for training specialists in group work are discussed.

Merta, R. J., Wolfgang, L., & McNeil, K. (1993). Five models for using the experiential group in the preparation of group counselors. *Journal for Specialists in Group Work, 18*(4), 200–207.

Abstract   Two hundred seventy-two academic units responding to a national survey indicated which of five experiential group models they are using to train group counselors, and which of four safeguards are employed against such unethical practices as invasion of privacy and abuse of power by an instructor. The traditional instructor-led group is the most widely used (39%) of the models. Although this model is one of two in which students are at greatest risk for experiencing adverse dual relationships, 29% of counselor educators using the model did not indicate using any safeguards. The diversity that exists in the way counselor educators are employing alternative models and safeguards translates into considerable variation in the extent to which students are at risk for experiencing dual relationships or receiving poor training. Results indicate that efforts to avoid adverse dual relationships in experiential groups have not significantly reduced the use of this traditional training component.

Newman, J. A., & Lovell, M. (1993). A description of a supervisory group for group counselors. *Counselor Education and Supervision, 33*(1), 22–31.

Abstract   This article describes a case example and evaluation of group supervision of 43 counselors-in-training (two co-leadership pairs) responsible for implementing a 16-week interpersonal skills program. Experiential client-centered and didactic techniques were used to achieve four supervision goals: nurturing effective theory, emphasizing skill development and an understanding of group theory, highlighting counselor investigation, and promoting counselor cultural sensitivity. Following completion of the program, counselors provided open-ended evaluations. Findings indicate that choosing a metaphor to symbolize counselors' leadership role helped to clarify their role, boosted confidence and creativity, and promoted coleader differentiation. The supervisors' ability to be flexible, listen attentively, and validate counselors was cited as both professionally and personally significant.

Omizo, M. M., & Omizo, S. A. (1987). Group counseling with children of divorce: New findings. *Elementary School Guidance and Counseling, 22*(1), 46–52.

Abstract The researchers assigned 60 children of divorce to experimental or control conditions, with experimental subjects participating in group counseling intervention. Comparison of the two groups revealed that participation in group counseling appeared beneficial for enhancing self-concept and internal locus of control among elementary school children experiencing parental divorce.

Oppenheimer, B. T. (1984). Short-term small group intervention for college freshmen. *Journal of Counseling Psychology, 31*(1), 45–53.

Abstract The researcher examined the effectiveness of a short-term small group intervention in facilitating the social adjustment of 99 college freshmen. The social adjustment of vulnerable subjects was significantly enhanced by group participation, whereas nonvulnerable subjects were unaffected, demonstrating the value of a small group experience in facilitating the transition to college for students who needed some assistance in making the transition.

Zimpfer, D., & Waltman, D. (1982). Correlates of effectiveness in group counseling. *Small Group Behavior, 13*(3), 275–290.

Abstract Using multiple groups (N = 9) and multiple counselors (N = 9) to study correlates of effectiveness in group counseling, the researchers found that both counselor and group composition variables related significantly to member interaction, to how much they valued the group, and to changes in member self-images.

Zinck, K., & Littrell, J. M. (2000). Action research shows group counseling effective with at-risk adolescent girls. *Professional School Counseling, 4*(1), 50–59.

Abstract Group counseling appears effective in promoting individual change. At one-week and six-week follow-ups, a majority of the female students reported moderate to strong progress in achieving their primary and secondary goals. Significant reduction in problem severity was reported. In addition, study participants experienced changes in attitudes and relationships with other people. This study indicates that a female adolescent's involvement in group counseling satisfies many of the needs met in individual counseling. Changes made during group counseling tended to endure beyond the termination of the group.

6

Multicultural Counseling

The United States has always been known as a country of considerable population diversity, with many cultures contributing to its greatness. Over the past 40 years, increasing attention has been given to the uniqueness and rights of these minority cultures. The civil and equal rights movements and attending legislation focused attention on racial as well as gender inequalities in the last quarter of the 20th century. Additionally, projected growth in numbers and percentages of America's minority populations in the decades immediately ahead increases the urgency of developing positive helping relationships among all our cultures. This heightened national attention has also been reflected in the counseling profession, in which a noticeable increase in attention to the needs and issues of multicultural counseling has occurred over the past 30 years.

Today, regardless of their setting, counselors must understand that they are functioning in a global village. We must realize that when we talk about culture, we mean a variety of entire peoples, not just minorities. These societies have their own universes or cultures that guide their behaviors, events, and expectations in that culture. In this context, counseling as a human relationship and helping profession must become a significant and positive national influence—and of course, in our specialty area of individual counseling, we must demonstrate consistently and conclusively that we are truly multiculturally oriented in both theory and practice, that we are effective as multicultural counselors.

Additionally, counselors must be actively involved in fighting cultural prejudice and discrimination, especially during children's early school years. Counselors in the elementary school face the tremendous challenge of preventing children from developing attitudes of prejudice and discrimination that could last throughout their lives. By the time children enter elementary school they have already identified with a racial group and have begun accepting the attitudes of that group. In this regard, both their parents as well as their peers are influential. If any of the attitudes the children have learned encourage prejudice, elementary school counseling programs will need to develop activities to counteract this bias. These could include human relations skills training, cultural awareness, and cross-cultural and multicultural encounters and training. The failure of the elementary school to counteract prejudice and discrimination can help perpetuate the view of minorities as less capable.

Counselors and educators at every level must ask themselves why higher percentages of minority youth are dropping out of school; failing to achieve academically; involved in crime, drugs, and violence; and failing to go on to college. Leaders in business and industry and counselors in employee assistance programs (EAPs) may note that although there are increasing numbers of minorities and women in administrative positions, the top-level executive and decision-making positions are overwhelmingly populated by white males. Attention to these needs is mandated by all the major associations that accredit the preparation of counselors (Council for the Accreditation of Counseling and Related Programs, Council on Rehabilitation Education, American Psychological Association, National Council for the Accreditation of Teacher Education, and all the regional accreditation associations).

ETHNIC GROUPS AND MULTICULTURAL COUNSELING

In multicultural counseling, the desired outcomes are not impeded by cultural differences between counselor and client. How the counselor arrives at this higher level of functioning and factors that must be considered are discussed in this chapter.

Certainly, our often stated philosophical assumptions of the inherent worth and dignity of the individual, respect for the individual's uniqueness, the right of the individual to self-actualization, and so forth would indicate our commitment to effective counseling with all clients, regardless of cultural, ethnic, religious, or socioeconomic background. However, as important as commitment must be, counselors must move beyond commitment to an active pursuit of an appropriate theoretical foundation and effective practices if they are to succeed in counseling a multicultural clientele. In our pursuit of positive and meaningful multicultural counseling and guidance we must constantly be aware that the term *multi* means many and that we are sensitizing ourselves to the uniqueness of the many different cultures and backgrounds that make up our population. In so doing, we recognize that many of the traditional characteristics of the mainstream counseling process (e.g., openness, emotional expression, sharing of intimate feelings) may actually inhibit effectiveness with clients of some cultures.

Ridley (1995) has observed that multicultural clients are more likely than White clients to have unfavorable experiences in some of the major aspects of counseling including the following:

- **Diagnosis.** Minority clients tend to receive a misdiagnosis, usually involving more severe psychopathology but occasionally involving less severe psychopathology, more often than is warranted.
- **Staff assignment.** Minority clients tend to be assigned to junior professionals, paraprofessionals, or nonprofessionals for counseling rather than senior and more highly trained professionals.
- **Treatment modality.** Minority clients tend to receive low-cost, less preferred treatment consisting of minimal contact, medication only, or custodial care rather than intensive psychotherapy.
- **Utilization.** Minority clients tend to be represented disproportionately in mental health facilities. Specifically, minority clients are under-represented in private treatment facilities and over-represented in public treatment facilities.
- **Treatment duration.** Minority clients show a much higher rate of premature termination and dropout from therapy, or they are confined to much longer inpatient care.
- **Attitudes.** Minority clients report more dissatisfaction and unfavorable impressions regarding treatment. (p. 9)

Counseling professionals need to remember that there may be language differences between them and their culturally different clients. Although multiculturism has in recent generations been increasingly recognized as a powerful force in the human relationship fabric of our country, we must not let it obscure the absolute necessity for counselors to understand both the culture of their clients and their own cultural background.

It is especially important that counselors in schools be sensitive to the differing cultures represented there. This not only increases their effectiveness as professional counselors and makes them more acceptable and approachable to all students, but it also enables them to serve as adults modeling appropriate behaviors and attitudes toward all ethnic and cultural groups. School counselors must pay particular attention to the problems and needs of minority children and adolescents. It is especially important during the child's developmental years that these youth be assisted in recognizing and understanding in a very positive way the differences that distinguish their culture. Counselors who work with children have an added responsibility because children cannot control their environment. The understanding or lack of understanding demonstrated by others about cultural differences can influence the core of the child's developing personality. Children are in the early stages of cultural awareness and may not recognize that their experiences differ from the experiences of others (Anderson & Cranston-Gingras, 1991, p. 91) and that forms of discrimination may exist.

"Children may internalize the beliefs of the majority about their own cultural group. One of the goals of culturally sensitive counselors is to foster the child's environment so that the emphasis is on the child's uniqueness and not on conformity with the norm" (Anderson & Cranston-Gingras, 1991, p. 91).

Pedersen (1988) recommends that students in counselor preparation programs develop these traits:

- ability to recognize direct and indirect communication styles;
- sensitivity to nonverbal cues;
- awareness of cultural and linguistic differences;
- interest in the culture;
- sensitivity to the myths and stereotypes of the culture;
- concern for the welfare of persons from another culture;
- ability to articulate elements of his or her own culture;
- appreciation of the importance of multicultural teaching;
- awareness of the relationships between cultural groups; and
- accurate criteria for objectively judging "goodness" and "badness" in the other culture. (p. 9)

To stay abreast of multicultural issues and practices in counseling, counselors should be aware of the Association for Multicultural Counseling and Development (AMCD), a division of the American Counseling Association (ACA). This organization publishes a journal of the same name as well as a newsletter, both of which should be on the reading list of informed counselors.

An important way to improve multicultural counseling is to increase the number and ratio of counselors from culturally different or minority backgrounds in our elementary schools. Not only should minority children have access to counselors of similar ethnicity, but all children should have exposure to role models representing the great cultural diversity of our country.

Our country is no longer considered a "melting pot" of many cultures, one in which emphasis is placed on all cultures becoming the same as the majority culture. Rather, the concept of cultural pluralism has been adopted, focusing on retaining and valuing the diverse aspects of every culture that constitutes our nation. In this regard, counselors can advocate the preservation of cultural diversity and model the respect and acceptance that all minorities deserve.

In schools, counselors can ensure that minorities are included in group activities and that classroom guidance activities are utilized to educate the school population about cultural diversity. Counselors must always be mindful that diversity exists within every cultural/racial population. There are no exact profiles for any minority group. The only "stereotype" is that individual differences exist in all populations (Gibson, Mitchell, & Basile, 1993, p. 121).

In further understanding cultures and their impact on clients, note that scholars who study culture seem to agree on several key points:

- Culture includes all aspects of human life and is a process by which groups impose order on and meaning [on] their life experience (Erchak, 1992).
- Culture is verbal, visual, rhythmic, spatial, temporal, and symbolic (Agar, 1994). It involves communications between all the senses in patterns that are recognizable even though members of any given culture may not be able to express an awareness of the patterns to which they are responding.
- An understanding of how the language is used in a specific culture is essential to understanding the language. Language shapes experience, and experience shapes language. It predetermines modes of observation and interpretation, shaping interpretation of experiences, recreating experiences, and empowering members to imagine and create new experiences (Agar, 1994; Goodenough, 1981; Sapir, 1958).
- The most effective method for understanding one's own culture is to compare it to other cultures. This process forces a person to perceive the various systems embedded in different cultures and to use this understanding of systems, which order and impose meaning, to revisit his or her own cultural system.
- Members of a specific culture typically do not experience their culture as a humanly constructed system. They experience their culture as "the way things are and the way things should be." This phenomenon is generally referred to as *ethnocentrism*. Individuals within a culture tend to believe that their ideas about the universe are simply "common sense" (Geertz, 1983) even though what is common sense in one culture may be unheard of or taboo in another. (Okun, Fried, & Okun, 1999, p. 9)

Minority, as a label, implies less than full-time or majority membership in a society. It is important that counselors convey through their attitudes and actions that minority populations are full, equal members of society. Because understanding alone will not accomplish the task, counselors must educate themselves about different ethnic peoples. The counselor must learn to communicate both verbally and nonverbally in a manner and style that is recognizable and comfortable for the client. The counselor must convey his or her own attitude of acceptance and respect for the ethnic client, and the counselor must genuinely feel this respect if he or she is to convey it successfully.

To counsel minority clients successfully, counselors must be able, as in all counseling contacts, to place themselves within the client's frame of reference. This, of course, includes understanding the cultural background and characteristics of the minority client.

In working with minority clients, counselors must understand that many of these clients will have initial anxiety, prejudice, or lack of trust due to cultural differences between counselor and client. It is, therefore, important from the initial interview that counselors be respectful of the cultural traditions and background of the client, recognize the possibility of different value systems, and strive to communicate in a way that is understood and accepted by the client.

African Americans

In 1996 African Americans were the largest minority in the United States with an estimated population of over 33 million. This population has historically been subject to racism, prejudice, and discrimination. Although legislative, educational, and humanitarian efforts have been and are being made to overcome these abusive elements, programs have been slow to develop and not without resistance. Disturbing data even today indicate the high percentage of Black youths in the criminal justice system; high numbers of Blacks unemployed and underemployed, and lack of adequate Black representation in higher education (both as students and faculty), the professions, and supervisory and management positions. The counseling profession cannot address these inequities alone, but this does not excuse us from being proactive as a profession in attempting to right these social wrongs. As individuals, we must prepare ourselves to be effective in working with our African American clients.

The previous chapter discussed the importance of getting off to a good start in the counseling relationship, and this includes integrating an appropriate multicultural dimension when assisting African American clients. Sue and Sue (1990) have offered some suggestions about the elements that are necessary in the first few sessions:

1. Identify the expectations of the Black clients, find out what they believe counseling is, and explore their feelings about counseling.
2. Indicate what you feel counseling is and what you do during counseling. Find out if they feel that will be useful to them.
3. Indicate the limits of confidentiality. If the client was referred, explain your relationship with that agency and the information, if any, that you will share with the agency.
4. If you are not Black, find out how the client feels about working with an individual from a different ethnic group.
5. If there is difficulty with self-disclosure, attempt to identify the reasons for this.
6. Find out information on the history of the problem and the client's perception of the causes. Also, what would the client see as a valuable outcome of counseling?
7. Gather information on the family (nuclear or extended). It is important to determine who helps out and who is living with the family.
8. Identify the strengths of the clients and their families. What resources are available to them? How have they handled problems successfully before?
9. Examine external factors that might be related to the presenting problem, including the impact of racism and concerns for health, education, employment. Identify agencies they come in contact with. Identify any additional stressors.

10. If appropriate, examine issues revolving around racial identity and associated personal conflicts.
11. After information about the problem has been gathered, establish mutually agreed-upon goals.
12. Talk about and consider the means to achieve the goals.
13. Discuss the number of sessions necessary to achieve the goals and the responsibilities of the counselor and the client.
14. Determine whether the client feels the two of you can work together. Also, consider other options that are available. (p. 225)

Of course, these elements can be shifted about and some even omitted on occasion.

It is also important for counselors to recognize that within the African American population there is great diversity. This means that the counselor must be alert and sensitive to individual differences and avoid the trap of cultural stereotyping. Four basic strategies suggested by Exum and Moore (1993) for an "out-of-culture" counselor working with African American clients are as follows:

- Rely on the core conditions.
- Use directive rather than passive or nondirective methods.
- Attend to nonverbal behavior.
- Be available. (McFadden, cited in Exum & Moore, 1993, pp. 204–207).

Latin Americans

Latin Americans represent the fastest growing minority in the United States, with an estimated 35.3 million in 2000. The overwhelming majority (58.5%) of this population is Mexican, with Puerto Rican a distant second at (9.6%) (see Figure 6.1). Not only are Hispanics the fastest growing minority group, but they are also the youngest, which probably means that this sector will continue to grow more rapidly than the rest of the nation's population. The continued very rapid growth of this group, aided by legal immigration influx, further accentuates the need for counselors who can function effectively with Latin American clients.

Counseling professionals need to understand family values and sex roles when they work with Latin Americans (Arredondo, 1991, as cited in Lee & Richardson, 1991). Family is the predominant and most valued of social institutions in Latin cultures. Parental authority is unquestioned and family loyalty is a given. Sex roles are also clearly defined, with males being dominant in the more traditional settings. Males are expected to be the wage earners outside the home, although Latin women in the United States are increasingly entering the workforce. These changing roles and values are often a source of conflict within the Latin family and society.

Respect for the Latin client, as with all clients, is of utmost importance if the counseling process is to succeed. One way to show this respect is to take care in pronouncing the client's name correctly. Another is to be sensitive to the client's particular culture, realizing that there are many Latin subcultures, each with its own characteristics. Like many minority clients, many Latin Americans will have little understanding of counseling and counselors. Counselors will usually be more successful if they use a directive approach with Latin clients. Avoid the use of psychodynamic terminology—a good caveat for use with *all* clients—and assessment measures that might turn the client away.

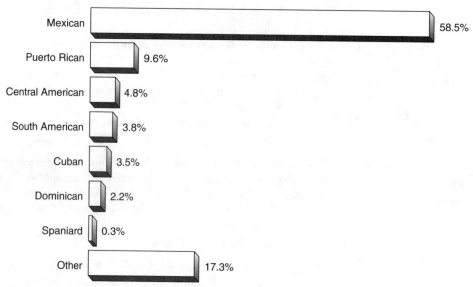

Figure 6-1 Population surges since 1990.
The Hispanic population of the USA grew from 22.4 million in 1990 to 35.3 million in 2000. Percentage of Hispanic population by origin:

Source: Census Bureau, May 2001 report, in *USA Today*, May 10, 2001, p. 3A. Copyright © 2001, USA TODAY. Reprinted with permission.

Asian Americans

Another rapidly growing minority population in the United States is Asian Americans. This population was estimated at 9.5 million in 1995. Within this bloc are numerous distinct national groups, including Japanese Americans, Chinese Americans, Filipino Americans, and Korean Americans. The diversity within this global group again highlights the importance of avoiding broad "include-all" categorizations and characterizations. Even so, there are several areas of commonality that culturally conscientious counselors should be aware of, including family roles and values, control and restraint of emotions, and deference to and respect for authority. The cultural values of the various national groups are also important to recognize.

Counseling and related mental health therapies are not well known or accepted by the vast majority of Asian Americans. It may therefore be appropriate to consider treatment strategies for immigrants and refugees as suggested by Ishisaka, Nguyen, and Okimoto (1985), Lorenzo and Adler (1984), Nidorf (1985), and Tung (1985).

1. Use restraint when gathering information. Because of the stigma against mental illness, the norm against sharing private matters with outsiders, the lack of client knowledge of the mental health field, the therapist should refrain from asking too many questions.

2. Prepare the clients for counseling by engaging in role preparation. Lambert and Lambert (1984) found that Asian immigrants who were told about (a) what happens in therapy, (b) the need for verbal disclosure, (c) problems typically encountered by clients in therapy, (d) the role of the therapist and client, (e) misconceptions of therapy, and (f) the need for attendance adjusted better to counseling than a control group who did not receive role preparation. The clients who were prepared developed more accurate perceptions of therapy, saw their therapist as more interested and respectful, perceived more positive changes on their part, and were more satisfied with their adjustment.

3. Focus on the specific problem brought in by the client, and help the client develop his or her goals for therapy. This allows the concerns of the client to be presented and reduces the chance that the world view of the therapist will be imposed on the client.

4. Take an active and directive role. Because of cultural expectations and a lack of experience with mental health therapy, the clients will rely on the counselor to furnish direction.

5. Do a thorough analysis of current environmental concerns, such as the need for food and shelter. The clients may need help filling out forms, need information on services that are available to them, and help in interacting with agencies. Assess financial and social needs.

6. In working with families, consider intergenerational conflicts especially due to changes in role, culture conflict, and differences in acculturation levels.

7. The therapy should be time limited, focus on concrete resolution of problems, and deal with the present or immediate future. (Sue & Sue, 1990, pp. 199–200).

Arab Americans

An emerging minority of recent decades is Arab Americans. In 1996, an estimated 3 million plus Arabs lived in the United States, in addition to 40,000 students temporarily in this country pursuing higher education. Due to their relatively recent emergence as a recognizable minority, Arab Americans have received little attention from the counseling profession concerning their uniqueness and needs. We are aware of discriminations and stereotypes generated in the public opinion sector by media attention to terrorist activities attributed to individuals of Arabian descent. The hostility and suspicion between many in the two cultures (Arab American/Caucasian American) has handicapped both opportunities and positive outcomes for counseling with this population.

In seeking to assist Arab American clients, counselors must display extra sensitivity to their clients' cultural background. Again, keeping in mind the diversity within this minority population, some generalizations can be made about the beliefs and practices that most Arab Americans share.

1. Marriage and children are essential for a complete and happy adult life.
2. Men are the heads of their families and the designated decision makers. In other words, authority and family identification are patrilineal.
3. The extended family is valued across generations. Young people owe profound respect to their elders, and often even to older siblings.
4. Children are expected to care for their parents and older relatives, usually inviting them to live in their homes, particularly after an older person is widowed.

5. Family honor is most easily damaged by the behavior of women, so they have a great responsibility toward the entire extended family to comport themselves in an honorable way.
6. Family ties and duties have precedence over work or career aspirations.
7. Religious identity and belief in God are essential. (McFadden, 1993 p. 264)

Counselors can test their cultural sensitivity and levels of awareness for counseling Arab American clients by responding to the following questions:

1. Am I able to recognize direct and indirect communication styles?
2. Am I sensitive to nonverbal cues?
3. Am I aware of cultural and linguistic differences among Arab groups?
4. What are some common myths and stereotypes about Arabs?
5. What stereotypes do Arabs have about Americans?
6. Am I aware of my own feelings about Arabs and Arab society and culture? (Pedersen, 1988).

Counselors must constantly strive to improve their therapeutic relationships and effectiveness with this minority, but even more important is our profession's responsibility as human relationship specialists to be active in building positive and productive relationships between our Arab minorities and our mainstream populations. The greatness and idealism of this nation was not built on prejudice and hostilities among our diverse populations. We must join the effort to reverse this undesirable trend.

Native Americans

Native Americans numbered over 2 million in 1996. Though not large in numbers compared to other minorities, the American Indian has suffered long and disgraceful discrimination. This discrimination has been stimulated over the generations by federal government policies and politics, in which tribal welfare was rarely a consideration. Living on desecrated reservations, Native Americans have been isolated from the mainstream American culture and all too frequently have lived in deprivation and poverty.

As with our other minority cultures, counselors must first of all recognize the diversity that exists within the Native American population. Today, the United States government recognizes over 500 tribes, each with its own traditions, values, spiritual beliefs, and family and tribal structure. Complicating this already complex mosaic are various federal legislation enactments and their interpretations.

The would-be counselor of Native Americans must understand that there is no stereotype or cultural profile that is "absolute." Even so, many Native Americans manifest a respect and desire for harmony with nature and their family and tribal systems. Giving, sharing, and cooperation are also common values of long standing. Counselors must approach their Native American clients with sensitivity and the realization that they, the counselors, may be viewed in the same sense as a tribal elder—meaning more talk and advice giving on the part of the counselor. Of course, by explaining the counseling process to the client, this expectation may be somewhat mitigated.

Arredondo (1986) has proposed a systematic model for working with refugees that is also applicable to working with Indian/Native clients. This model is holistic, in that it encompasses six dimensions of the client's life: the historical era, sociopolitical factors, sociocultural factors, individual variables, developmental tasks, and esteem and identity themes.

By using these six dimensions and combining them with social cognitive interventions, the counselor will be using a framework that is considered less culturally biased than other theoretical approaches (LaFromboise & Rowe, 1983). This approach is considered less biased because it recognizes the impact of culture on personal and environmental variables and allows each culture to define its own appropriate behaviors or targets for intervention. It is culturally sensitive in that it provides for the differences across tribes. (Peregoy, 1993, p. 184).

The Culturally Skilled Counselor

The concept of our country as a "melting pot" where all our many cultures become one is no longer appropriate. Rather, we view the strength of our nation as one in which our various cultures, in preserving their own strengths and uniqueness, contribute to our national strength and well-being. Counselors have the opportunity to make significant contributions to the preservation of cultural diversity and the well-being of all cultures; they can also be advocates and role models in their professional practice as effective counselors to culturally diverse populations.

Counselors need a set of principles to guide them in their practice and at the same time help them respect the uniqueness and individuality of every client. These principles will assist counselors in more effectively counseling clients from culturally diverse backgrounds

1. Every client should be understood from his or her unique frame of reference.
2. Nomothetic, normative information does not always fit a particular client.
3. People are a dynamic blend of multiple roles and identities.
4. The idiographic perspective is compatible with the biopsychosocial model of mental health.
5. The idiographic perspective is transtheoretical. (Ridley, 1995, pp. 82–83)

The following therapeutic actions will assist counselors in becoming more effective with minority clients.

1. Develop cultural self-awareness
2. Avoid value imposition
3. Accept your naivete as a multicultural counselor
4. Show cultural empathy
5. Incorporate cultural considerations into counseling
6. Do not stereotype
7. Weigh and determine the relative importance of the client's primary cultural roles
8. Do not blame the victim
9. Remain flexible in your selection of interventions
10. Examine your counseling theories for bias
11. Build on the client's strengths
12. Do not protect clients from emotional pain (Ridley, 1995, pp. 88–100)

Understanding the impact on clients of their cultural values, beliefs, behaviors, and other influences is obviously important when individuals (i.e., counselor and client) from different cultural backgrounds seek to relate and understand each other. For example, cultural differences that may influence cross-cultural counseling might be reflected in manner of speech, personal dress, religious practices, family values, and even leisure practices.

In Appendix D, the multicultural/diversity agenda of the American Counseling Association (1997) is presented.

Ivey, D'Andrea, Ivey, and Simek-Morgan (2002) developed a cube illustrating the various types of multicultural concerns clients can present in therapy (see Figure 6.2). The cube presents a model

> illustrating the various types of multicultural concerns clients can present in therapy. All clients present combinations of many multicultural issues, and different issues may be prepotent at different times. A range of multicultural issues affecting the counseling relationship make up one side of the multicultural cube. Along the left side of the cube is the locus of the issue. Although therapists traditionally tend to locate the concern within the individual, an individual issue may actually be derivative of the family, and the family issue may derive from problems in the group, community, state, or country. This points to the need to engage in family therapy, group work, or even community and political action to promote change. (p. 39)

To conclude, we would note that to serve all cultures counseling programs should

- Have at least one minority counselor.
- Ensure that all professional and staff are multiculturally attuned (use consultants if necessary).

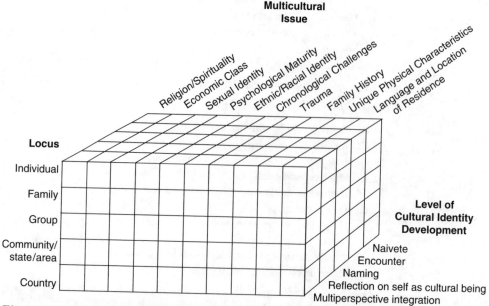

Figure 6-2   The RESPECTFUL cube.

Source: From A. E. Ivey, M. D'Andrea, M. B. Ivey, & L. Simek-Morgan, *Theories of Counseling and Psychotherapy* (5th ed., p. 39). Copyright © 2002. Allyn and Bacon. Reprinted by permission. The RESPECTFUL Cube is reprinted by permission of Allen E. Ivey, 1992, 1995, 2001.

- Address issues that may be the concerns of minorities only.
- Consider whether public announcements of services are appealing and appropriate to *all* populations.
- Involve minority community members in planning.
- Be advocates for all cultures.

Beyond using their multicultural skills in counseling individuals and groups, counselors also have the responsibility for educating others for diversity. This responsibility of educating others, such as workers in the workplace, students in the classroom, and adults in the community in multicultural and diversity perspectives, can be a challenging and at times, frustrating experience. Ridley and Thompson (1999) note that

> classroom instructors, group facilitators, and organizational consultants who offer diversity training, often encounter resistance in their work. In some cases, certain members of the audience harbor serious doubts about the relevance of diversity to their lives or profession. Still others advocate diversity on one level, yet resist making meaningful changes because of what they perceive as the direct cost accompanying change. How well diversity trainers handle the phenomenon of resistance or even recognize it depends largely on their developing expertise in resistance management. Importantly, identifying the various sources of and complexities inherent in resistance is essential to diversity instruction. (p. 3)

Ridley and Thompson (1999) continue,

> In one sense, resistance to diversity training is no different than any type of resistance to positive change and growth; it is an impediment to progress. Thus, by its very nature, diversity training jars the familiarities that people come to know and depend upon. (pp. 3–4)

However, counselors involved in diversity or multicultural sensitivity training should keep in mind that the resistance to this training is no different than other types of resistance to positive change. Resistant management strategies may include the following:

- Create an optimal environment for learning and constructive change
- Take a systems perspective on resistance management
- Identify resistant behavior
- Assertively confront resistance
- Clarify the learning objectives
- Do not react defensively to trainee resistance
- Incorporate exercises that help trainees identify the sources of their resistance (Ridley & Thompson, 1999, pp. 16–21)

Finally, we would note the probability that minorities will become the majority in the workforce over the next several generations. If these minority employees are to be productive and satisfied with their work setting, managers and supervisors must be trained and sensitive to the issues and nuances of cultural differences. Here again, counselors will have an opportunity to make significant contributions for the advancement of cultural harmony.

SUMMARY

America's growing minority population and the emerging national attention to their contributions, rights, influences, and needs is, and should be, reflected in increased attention and response from the counseling profession. Counselors today are functioning in a global village. We must, therefore, not only be culturally aware and respectful in our interactions with our clients, but we must also be active in promoting positive human relationships and fighting cultural prejudice in the larger society. We must recognize the uniqueness of the different minority populations in the United States and to this end, this chapter has discussed the African American, the Latin American, the Asian American, the Arab American, and the Native American. Principles to guide the culturally skilled counselor were presented.

DISCUSSION QUESTIONS

1. How would multicultural issues affect the way you assess a client and arrive at a clinical diagnosis? Do multicultural issues only affect assessment when the client is culturally different from the counselor? Why or why not?
2. Why is multiculturalism the "fourth force" of counseling? How is it similar to the first three forces? How is it different?
3. As a culturally effective counselor, how will you integrate multicultural skills and recommendations into your own personal theory of counseling?
4. When conducting assessments from a multicultural perspective, how will you apply culturally relevant data to your clients without engaging in stereotyping or bias? How will you attend to individual, or idiographic, client data without ignoring cultural norms?

CLASS ACTIVITIES

1. Divide into small groups. In each small group, discuss what cultural biases and assumptions are held and have group members challenge unfounded biases and stereotypes.

2. Consider the following scenario:
   A Korean child is transferred to a predominantly White school. Discuss among the class how the school counselor would help the child adjust to the new environment. What cultural issues should the counselor consider?
3. Divide into small groups. In each group, have each person answer the following questions:
   (a) How would I describe my own ethnicity?
   (b) What would I identify as my race? (c) What do I identify as my culture? Then discuss what one would look for in a client in order to determine the client's ethnicity, race, and cultural background.
4. Divide into pairs. By turn, describe a time when you each exhibited intentional or unintentional racism, and what you could have done differently to avoid exhibiting the racist behavior. Then discuss your own experiences with being a victim of racism. Finally, discuss times you exhibited cultural sensitivity.

SELECTED READINGS

Altarriba, J., & Bauer, L. M. (1998). Counseling the Hispanic client: Cuban Americans, Mexican Americans, and Puerto Ricans. *Journal of Counseling and Development*, 76(4), 389–395.

American Psychological Association, Office of Ethnic Minority Affairs. (1993). Guidelines for providers of psychological services to ethnic, linguistic, and culturally diverse populations. *American Psychologist, 48*, 45–48.

Canino, I. A., & Spurlock, J. (1994). *Culturally diverse children and adolescents: Assessment, diagnosis, and treatment.* New York: Guilford Press.

Coleman, H. L. K. (1995). Cultural factors and the counseling process: Implications for school counselors. *The School Counselor, 42*, 180–185.

Dana, R. H. (1993). *Multicultural assessment perspectives for professional psychology*, Boston: Allyn & Bacon.

Garret, M. T., & Pichette, E. F. (2000). Red as an apple: Native American acculturation and counseling with or without reservation. *Journal of Counseling and Development, 78*(1), 3–13.

Locke, D. C. (1992). *Increasing multicultural understanding: A comprehensive model.* Newbury Park, CA: Sage.

Paniagua, F. A. (1994). *Assessing and treating culturally diverse clients: A practical guide.* Thousand Oaks, CA: Sage.

Pedersen, P. B., Draguns, J. G., Lonner, W. J., & Trimble, J. E. (Eds.). (1996). *Counseling across cultures.* Thousand Oaks, CA: Sage.

Pedersen, P. (1987). Ten frequent assumptions of cultural bias in counseling. *Journal of Multicultural Counseling and Development, 15*(1), 16–24.

Ponterotto, J. G., & Pedersen, P. B. (1993). *Preventing prejudice: A guide for counselors and educators.* Newbury Park, CA: Sage.

Ridley, C. R. (1995). *Overcoming unintentional racism in counseling and therapy.* Thousand Oaks, CA: Sage.

Ridley, C. R., Mendoza, D. W., Kanitz, B. E., Angermeier, L., & Zenk, R. (1994). Cultural sensitivity in multicultural counseling: A perceptual schema model. *Journal of Counseling Psychology, 41,* 125–126.

Robinson, T. L., & Ginter, E. J. (Eds.). (1999). Racism healing its effects. [Special issue]. *Journal of Counseling and Development, 77*(1), 3–53.

Sinacore-Guinn, A. L. (1995). The diagnostic window: Culture and gender sensitive diagnosis and training. *Counselor Education and Supervision, 35,* 18–31.

Sue, D. W., Ivey, A. E., & Pedersen, P. B. (Eds.). (1996). *A theory of multicultural counseling and therapy.* Pacific Grove, CA: Brooks/Cole.

Sue, D. W., Arredondo, P., & McDavis, R. J. (1992). Multicultural counseling competencies and standards: A call to the profession. *Journal of Counseling and Development, 70*(4), 477–486.

Sue, D. W., & Sue, D. (1990). *Counseling the culturally different: Theory and practice.* (2nd ed.). New York: John Wiley.

Thompson, C. E., & Neville, H. A. (1999). Racism, mental health, and mental health practice. *The Counseling Psychologist, 27*(2), 155–223.

Zayes, L. H., Torres, L. R., Malcolm, J., & DesRosiers, F. S. (1996). Clinicians' definitions of ethnically sensitive therapy. *Professional Psychology: Research and Practice, 27,* 78–82.

RESEARCH OF INTEREST

Atkinson, D. R. (1985). A meta-review of research on cross-cultural counseling and psychotherapy. *Journal of Multicultural Counseling and Development, 13,* 138–153.

Abstract   Analyzes four major reviews of the research on the effects of race on counseling and psychotherapy.

Atkinson, D. R. (1990). Minority students' reasons for not seeking counseling and suggestions for improving services. *Journal of College Student Development, 31,* 342–350.

Abstract   In this study, ethnic minority students were surveyed to determine the relationships between cultural commitment and counseling utilization, reasons for not seeking counseling, and suggestions for improving counseling services. Results indicate that past utilization of counseling or psychological services by ethnic minority students is not related to their cultural commitment. Rather, the availability of culturally similar or culturally sensitive counselors is an important determinant of counseling service utilization. Culturally sensitive counselors are most important to ethnic-identified minorities and least important to mainstream-identified minorities.

Counseling Racially Diverse Clients. (2001). [Special issue]. *Journal of Mental Health Counseling, 23*(3).

Abstract   Models of racial and ethnic identity development are presented and their counseling applications explored. These models are useful for understanding the differences and societal experiences among various ethnic groups. Further, they provide a conceptual framework for counselors in understanding the cross-cultural dynamics of counseling relationships. This special issue presents selected models for conceptualization and counseling interventions with clients from varying ethnic groups.

Deffenbacher, J. L., & Swaim, R. C. (1999). Anger expression in Mexican American and White Non-Hispanic adolescents. *Journal of Counseling Psychology, 46*(1), 61–69.

Abstract   This study explored aggressive anger expression in adolescents. A three-factor model proved best (i.e., Expression Through Verbal Assault, Physical Assault Toward People, and Physical Assault Toward Objects). These factors correlated positively with each other and with anger, anxiety, and depression. Correlations of aggressive anger expression styles with anger were larger than their correlations with anxiety and depression. Gender, ethnicity, and developmental effects were found; males reported more physical assault on people than females, and White non-Hispanic and older youths reported more verbal assault than Mexican American and younger students. Both middle and high school students reported greater verbal assault than physical assault on objects which, in turn, was higher than physical assault on people. These findings suggest that adolescent aggressive anger expression is not unidimensional, but is more differentiated and meaningfully related to gender, ethnicity, and developmental status.

Ford, D. Y., Harris, J. J., III, & Schuerger, J. M. (1993). Racial identity development among gifted Black students: Counseling issues and concerns. *Journal of Counseling and Development, 71,* 409–417.

Abstract Discusses a review of the literature regarding the paucity of information pertaining to culture-specific issues of being African American and gifted. Psychological issues of being African American and gifted and perspectives on racial identity development are presented. Components of counseling interventions are indicated.

Multicultural Assessment. (1998). [Special issue.] *The Counseling Psychologist, 26*(6).

Abstract This special issue is introduced by a discussion of multicultural assessment, followed by reactions in three articles challenging practices in assessment from a multicultural viewpoint. The special issue concludes with an article that revisits and refines the multicultural assessment procedure.

Petersen, S. (2000). Multicultural perspective on middle-class women's identity development. *Journal of Counseling and Development, 78*(1), 63–71

Abstract In this qualitative study using grounded theory, Caucasian women and African American women told the story of their identity development across a lifetime. The Difference Model (U. Oleyamade & P. Rosser, 1980) was used to analyze the interviews separately for each cultural group. The pattern of development for each group is explained and comparisons between the groups were explored. The present study provides an explanation of how African American women sustain their identities in the face of oppression and how Caucasian women struggle to emerge from embeddedness in their self-definitions and regain their sense of identity.

Ponterotto, J. G., Rieger, B. P., Barrett, A., & Sparks, R. (1994). Assessing multicultural counseling competence: A review of instrumentation. *Journal of Counseling and Development, 72* (3), 316–322.

Abstract This article reviews four instruments designed to assess multicultural counseling competence in trainees and practicing professionals. The Cross-Cultural Counseling Inventory—Revised (CCCI-R), the Multicultural Counseling Awareness Scale—Form B (MCAS-B), the Multicultural Counseling Inventory (MCI), and the Multicultural Awareness-Knowledge-and-Skills Survey (MAKSS) were each critically reviewed in terms of item development, psychometric properties, and pragmatic utility. Specific research suggestions for continued empirical validation on the instruments are posited, and strong cautions regarding their use in training are leveled.

Ridley, C. R., Li, L. C., & Hill, C. L. (1998). Multicultural assessment: Reexamination, reconceptualization, and practical application. *The Counseling Psychologist, 26*(6), 827–910.

Abstract Current suggestions for assessing clients across cultures fail to adequately aid the average practitioner. This failure arises from unresolved issues and problems, interfering with the ability of most counselors and therapists to render sound clinical judgments. In response to these issues and problems, a procedure is described that sensitizes counselors to cultural data in assessment and case conceptualization. Grounded in a guiding philosophy of assessment, the Multicultural Assessment Procedure (MAP) was developed in consideration of a number of relevant critical issues. The procedure entails identifying cultural data through multiple methods of data collection, interpreting cultural data to formulate a working hypothesis, incorporating cultural data with other relevant clinical information to test the working hypothesis, and arriving at a sound (i.e., comprehensive and accurate) assessment decision. A case illustration demonstrates how to use the proposed procedure.

Utsey, S. O., Ponterotto, J. G., Reynolds, A. L., & Cancelli, A. A. (2000). Racial discrimination, coping, life satisfaction, and self-esteem among African Americans. *Journal of Counseling and Development, 78*(1), 72–80.

Abstract This article reports the results of a study that examined the coping strategies used by African Americans in managing the stressful effects of racism. A total of 213 participants (women, n = 137 men, n = 76) completed the index of Race-Related Stress (S. O. Utsey & J. G. Ponterotto, 1996), the Coping Strategy Indicator (J. H. Amirkhan, 1990), the Satisfaction with Life Scale (E. Diener, R. A. Emmons, R. J. Larsen, & S. Griffin, 1985), and the Rosenberg Self-Esteem Scale (M. Rosenberg, 1965). Results indicated that women preferred avoidance coping for racism experienced on a personal level. For African Americans in general, seeking social support and racism condition were the best predictors of racism-related stress. Life satisfaction and self-esteem were best predicted by avoidance coping. Implications for the provision of counseling services to African Americans are discussed.

Wade, P., & Bernstein, B. L. (1991). Culture sensitivity training and counselor's race: Effects on Black female clients' perceptions and attrition. *Journal of Counseling Psychology, 38,* 9–15.

Abstract Effects of brief culture sensitivity training for counselors and effects of counselors' race on Black female clients' perceptions of counselor characteristics and the counseling relationship and clients' satisfaction with counseling were examined in an actual counseling situation. Client attrition across three sessions was also assessed. Clients assigned to experienced counselors who had received culture sensitivity training rated their counselor higher on credibility and relationship measures, returned for more follow-up sessions, and expressed greater satisfaction with counseling than did clients assigned to experienced counselors who had not received the additional training (control condition). Although same-race counseling dyads resulted in less client attrition, this factor did not influence client perceptions of counselors and the counseling process.

Human Assessment for Counseling

This chapter is designed to acquaint you with the role of assessment for counseling purposes. We initially discuss standardized testing, including some of the controversies attending this practice, and then, in the last section of this chapter, we examine a variety of nonstandardized approaches.

Few activities in education and psychology have remained as consistently controversial over the past 80 years as the standardized testing movement, not only in schools but in government agencies and business and industry as well. From statements in Cubberly's (1934) *Public Education in the United States* and Gross's (1963) *The Brain Watchers*, to "Use and Misuse of Tests in Education: Legal Implications" (Nolte, 1975), "IQ Tests and the Culture Issue" (Ornstein, 1976), and "Standardized Tests: Are They Worth the Cost?" (Herndon, 1976) through Robinson's (1983) "Nader versus ETS [Educational Testing Services]," "America's Test Mania" (Fiske, 1988), and the special issue of *Educational Horizons*, "Assessment: The Winter of Our Discontent" (Fall, 1993), the pros and cons of standardized test usage have been publicly dissected. The controversy has been more recently refueled by the calls of President Bush and others for nationwide standardized achievement testing in the nation's public schools, a program that would have implications for support from federal programs, not to mention local political ramifications. Undoubtedly, in the resulting debate, old social issues will be raised and legal implications are currently being explored.

Many of the criticisms focus on the continued uses and abuses of standardized testing. Prominent psychologists and educators have cautioned counselors and other users of the risks of clients drawing unwarranted conclusions from test results; others have lamented the overemphasis on test scores by individuals, school systems, government agencies, and many businesses and industries. In addition, Anastasi, a leading authority in the field of standardized measurement suggested that tests are also misused because of

> the too human desire for shortcuts, quick solutions, and clear-cut answers to our questions.
> This common human weakness has been capitalized on by soothsayers over the centuries, from
> phrenologists to astrologers and other self-styled expert advisers. People seeking guidance are
> often attracted by the facile promises of charlatans, in contrast to the slower, deliberate considerations and the carefully qualified suggestions of the scientifically trained professional. Similarly, if one or two short tests—whatever their technical limitations and defects—seem to offer

a simple answer to questions about career choice, interpersonal difficulties, emotional problems, or learning deficiencies, many test takers will be temporarily satisfied. At another level, some misuse of tests by a counselor or other test user may arise from time pressure or work overload, which renders shortcuts attractive. (Anastasi, 1992, p. 610)

Other common criticisms are that standardized testing has become increasingly costly in both time and money. Additionally, "coaching" for the test has increased significantly, adding further to the time subtracted from the teaching/learning process. All too frequently the reputation of schools, principals, teachers, and school boards rise and fall with test scores. Too often this leads schools to "teach for the test." Colleges and universities also must share blame for the testing mania as they almost universally rely on standardized scores for student admissions. Recent data indicate that there is a slight decline in the utilization of standardized results for college admission purposes. We would suggest that the tests are not consistently fair to the test-takers themselves. These individuals are not measured against their peers but against norm groups who took the test, at best, several years earlier. They are not measured against what they have had the opportunity to learn through their texts and classroom instruction but against a body of knowledge determined to be appropriate by national surveys or panels of subject-matter experts. Finally, these tests may be formatted in a manner that is unfamiliar to the student test-taker (for example, the time limitations on most standardized tests are much more severe than those on traditionally developed classroom tests).

While recognizing the justifiable criticisms of the overuse and misuse of standardized testing, we should acknowledge the many schools and school systems, as well as a wide variety of agency settings, where tests are used with prudence and caution by adequately trained counselors and psychologists. In most institutional or agency settings where counseling takes place, including schools, standardized tests are the counselor's basic instrument for objective assessment of the personality traits, aptitudes, interests, and other characteristics of individuals. Clearly, individual counseling demands a knowledge and recognition of the individuality of clients. Measurement of individual differences is a part of the mainstream of personnel psychology. Also, two major movements in the 1990s have contributed to improvement in the use and reporting of test results. The accountability movement initiated by the U.S. Office of Education in the 1990s resulted in local school systems being held accountable for achieving educational goals identified by state, and in some instances, federal authorities. Because of the significance of accountability, much effort was expended to ensure that tests measured fairly what was being taught locally.

Also in the 1990s authentic assessment became a major testing development. According to Fisher and King (cited in Whiston, 2000), "The purpose of authentic assessment is to evaluate using a method consistent with the instructional area and to gather multiple indicators of performance. Authentic assessment has had a major influence on teachers' assessments of students' academic progress" (p. 16). It therefore is most appropriate to introduce potential counselors to this important area of counselor understanding and skill, recognizing the continuing debates and issues. Such knowledge plus a basic understanding of these areas of testing will enable you to more effectively discriminate between uses and abuses and to retain in your counseling repertoire a useful analytical tool.

STANDARDIZED TEST SCORES— WHAT DO THEY MEAN?

Whenever we evaluate someone, we do it in terms of some kind of comparison or point of reference. For instance, we may refer to Juan as the most handsome one in the group, Kathy as the best student in the class, and Mariah as the hardest worker in the bookstore. Here, we are comparing Juan to all others in the group, Kathy to the other students in the class, and Mariah to the other workers in the bookstore. Although we might attempt to make some predictions or deduce some other traits for Juan, Kathy, and Mariah from our observation, these would amount to nothing more than speculations, and we could justifiably be accused of unreliable procedures and data. If Kathy, Juan, and Mariah were to seek counseling, their counselor would want more objective and valid data before attempting to describe their traits and performances against the average traits and performances of others with comparable characteristics and experiences. An elementary understanding of statistics and statistically based tests, however, would enable the counselor to do this.

These basic understandings of educational and psychological statistics enable the counselor to (a) describe the characteristics of an individual or group in comparison with a specific group or population, (b) predict the probability of future success or failure in a given area on the basis of present or past behavior, and (c) infer the characteristics of a population from a sample of that population. It therefore follows that a good working knowledge of elementary statistical concepts is important for anyone who uses the various techniques of individual analysis and mandatory for all who use tests and other tools of measurement. This section offers a brief overview of descriptive statistics, the basic statistical terms, and essential computational procedures, beginning with perhaps the most common—and most commonly misunderstood—of all statistical terms, average.

Averages

When Latonya reports to her parents that she scored "70" on her history test, should they be pleased, satisfied, disappointed, or what? Until they have more information, they cannot be sure how to react, because 70 could represent 70% of the questions answered correctly, 70 answered correctly out of 75 asked, a formula score of 70 (i.e., rights minus wrongs), or 70th in a class of 120 taking the examination. In this example, you may note that a score in and of itself is of little value. A score becomes meaningful only when it provides an index of how well or how poorly a person performed in comparison with others taking the same test and, knowing that, what other significance can be interpreted from the results. Latonya's parents are asking what an average performance is on this test and how she differs from the average. Also, they might ask to what does her score relate—what does it mean? Let us begin then by reviewing what is meant by averages.

Most educational and psychological evaluation is based on a person's position in a group compared with others who constitute the group. The average position in a group becomes an important point of mathematical reference in standardized testing for human assessment. There are three distinct statistical types of averages, known as *measures of central tendency:* the mean, the median, and the mode. For most nonstatisticians, the definition of the mean is commonly associated with the term *average,* because the *mean* is defined as the mathematical average of a group of scores. The *median* is the midpoint of a set of scores with 50% of the scores being distributed above and 50% below that point. The *mode* represents the most frequent score in a set of scores. Of these three averages, the mean is the most useful and popular, and the mode, having little statistical value, is the least popular.

Variations from the Average

Once we have determined what is average, we must utilize a statistical methodology to measure the degree to which each person varies from this established average, or *point of central tendency*. Such statistical measures are called *measures of variability*. Two common measures of variability are the range and the standard deviation. The *range* is the spread from the lowest score to the highest score in a distribution. The range is a relatively simple measurement device with limited descriptive value. The *standard deviation,* however, is a statistical process that allows for an exact determination of distances of scores from the mean.

The mean and the standard deviation, when computed for a specific set of test scores, enable a counselor to determine how well an individual performed in relation to the group. This interpretation is made by specifying standard deviation distance from the mean and determining the proportion of the population that will be beyond or will deviate from it, assuming that the scores are normally distributed. This normally distributed population is most popularly viewed as a normal curve, as shown in Figure 7-1. (Note: Rarely are the mean, median, and mode the same.)

In Figure 7-2, the normal curve is, in effect, sliced into bands, one standard deviation wide, with a fixed percentage of cases always falling in each band. Figure 7-2 then illustrates a significant fact: The mean plus and minus one standard deviation encompasses approximately 68% of a normally distributed population; the mean plus and minus two standard deviations encompasses approximately 95% of that population; and the mean plus and minus three standard deviations encompasses 99.7% of that population. This information, which remains constant for any normally distributed set of scores or values, makes possible a meaningful interpretation of any score in a group. As you view the normal curve and its segmentation into standard deviations, note that these facts are handy for interpreting standard

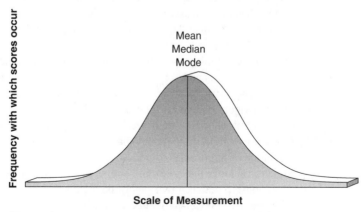

Figure 7-1   The normal curve.

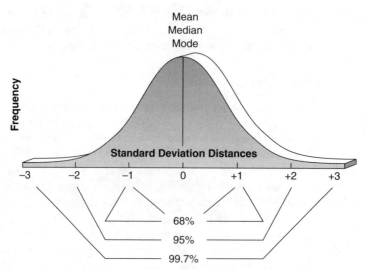

Figure 7-2 Scores in a normal distribution.

scores. Furthermore, whenever you can assume a normal distribution, you can convert standard scores to percentile scores, and vice versa. Thus, three basic facts for deriving a statistical evaluation of a person's performance on a psychological test are the person's raw score, mean, and standard deviation for the group with which the individual is being compared.

Relationships

Once you have determined the meaning of an individual's score in relation to the scores of others who have been administered the same measure, you must ask what are the other relationships or meanings of this score. The score and its comparative standing will take on meaning when it can be related to some meaningful purpose. For example, if students who score high on a college entrance examination actually perform at a high academic level in college, then one can assume that there is a relationship between scores on the examination and performance in college. The test score then becomes meaningful in terms of its prediction of college success, a meaningful purpose.

When you look for a statistical method to express relationships between two variables such as test scores and academic performance, you can compute a *correlation coefficient.* Correlation coefficients range from plus one through zero to minus one. A plus one indicates a perfect positive correlation; that is, the rank order of those taking the college entrance examination and their academic rank order in the college program are identical. A correlation of minus one means that the scores go in exactly the reverse direction. Thus, a correlation of minus one would indicate that persons who score highest on the entrance examination achieve the lowest in college. A zero correlation would represent a complete lack of relationship between two sets of data. A frequently computed coefficient of correlation is the Pearson product-moment coefficient.

Statistical Symbols

The counselor, teacher, or others who read test manuals, interpret test data, or in other ways seek to interpret simple statistical data should be familiar with basic statistical symbols. Although there is no universal statistical language, the following are some of the more commonly recognized symbols and their meanings.

M	Mean
Σ	Sum of
Σfb	The sum of frequencies below the class in which the median will fall
SD	(or S) Standard deviation for a particular set of scores
X	Actual or raw scores obtained
MD	Median
x	Distance (or score difference) of a score from the mean
N	Number of cases
i	Size of a class interval in scale units
M'	Assumed mean
r	Coefficient of correlation
z	Scale value of the standard normal distribution; the standard deviation of distance of a given score from the mean
l	The lower limit of the class in which the median will fall
fw	The total of the frequencies within the class in which the median will fall
f	Frequency; the number of times a particular score occurs
p	Percentage of persons getting a test item correct
q	Percentage of persons getting a test item wrong ($p + q = 100$)

PRESENTING TEST SCORES

Because raw test scores are in themselves meaningless, they have little value for the reporting of individual test results. As previously indicated, a raw score becomes meaningful only when it can be converted into some type of comparative score—one that enables an individual to be compared against others of a group. Most standardized tests, therefore, utilize one or more of the following methods of converting raw scores into a more meaningful method of presenting an individual's test results.

Percentiles

A percentile score represents the percentage of persons in the standardized sample for a given test who fall below a given raw score. A person's percentile ranking indicates his or her relative position in a normative sample. For example, if 60% of the students answer fewer than 30 problems correctly on an English usage test, then a raw score of 30 corresponds to the 60th percentile.

Percentiles are probably the most common method of presenting scores and are relatively easy to interpret. Due to their relative ease of interpretation, however, several cautions should be noted. In working with non-test-sophisticated groups, such as parents, students, and most general populations, it is important to emphasize that percentiles do not represent percentages. Because percentiles represent comparison scores, it is also important to note the population with which an individual is being compared and the valid purposes for which comparisons can be made. It should also be noted that there are inequalities in percentile units.

The reason such distortion occurs is quite simple. When a raw-score distribution approximates the normal curve, there are many more moderate scores, which fall in the middle of the distribution, than either high or low scores, which occur at the ends. Because percentiles are based on the raw-score distance encompassed by a specified percentage of the total group, percentile distances near the median, with its high concentration of cases, will encompass a much smaller raw-score difference than the same percentile distance farther from the median. Hence the 15 points of raw-score difference between the 5th and 10th percentiles may shrink to 5 points of difference between the 40th and 45th.

These distortions make it difficult to use percentiles for profiling and other comparisons of a student's performance on two or more tests. To overcome the limitations in test interpretation resulting from the inequality of percentiles, more and more test publishers are turning to some type of standard score for norming.

Computing Percentiles

To expedite test interpretation, you may want to compute percentiles for a given group. The formula for computing percentiles from a grouped frequency distribution is

$$P_x = l + \left(\frac{PN - \Sigma fb}{fw} \right) i$$

Thus if the 75th percentile is desired, $P_x = 0.75$; if the 40th percentile is desired, $P_x = 0.40$.

A grouped frequency table—once it is properly prepared—can be used for computing most of the elementary statistics a counselor might need for that set of scores. However, the computation of percentiles is made easier by adding to the table a column showing progressive accumulation of frequencies. This is called a *cf* (cumulative frequency) column; it is shown at the left in Table 7-1, which uses the hypothetical Oakwood High School data. The following steps show how one would go about finding the 25th percentile for the Oakwood High School data given in Table 7-2.

1. Multiply *N* by the desired percentile (converted to a decimal) to determine the class in which this percentile falls. For the Oakwood group, *N* is 250 and the desired percentile is 25. The product of 0.25 × 250 is 62.5; the *cf* column indicates that the score value of the individual ranking 62.5 from the bottom is found within the class 50–54, so it is established that P_{25} lies between 49.5 and 54.5.
2. Determine the necessary values for the formula:

$$P_{25}N = 62.5$$
$$\Sigma fb = 40$$
$$fw = 28$$
$$i = 5$$

Table 7-1 Computation of percentiles.

cf	X	f	d	fd
250	95–99	2	7	14
248	90–94	3	6	18
245	85–89	5	5	25
240	80–84	10	4	40
230	75–79	15	3	45
215	70–74	22	2	44
193	65–69	38	1	38
155	60–64	55	0	0
100	55–59	32	−1	−32
68	50–54	28	−2	−56
40	45–49	17	−3	−51
23	40–44	14	−4	−56
9	35–39	5	−5	−25
4	30–34	4	−6	−24
		N = 250		Σfd = −20

3. Insert the values in the formula and perform the indicated computations:

$$P_{25} = 49.5 + \left(\frac{62.5 - 40}{28} \right) 5$$
$$= 49.5 + \frac{22.5 \times 5}{28}$$
$$= 49.5 + 4.02$$
$$= 53.52 \text{ or, rounded, } 53$$

Deciles and Quartiles

Chase (1984) described deciles and quartiles as follows:

Two kinds of figures besides percentiles are also frequently used to show relative standing in a group. These are *deciles* and *quartiles,* both of which are similar to, and indeed can be read from, percentile tables. Deciles are points that divide the distribution of raw scores into segments of 10 percent each. Thus, the first decile $D1$ would be that point on the distribution below which 10 percent of the cases fall, $D2$ the point below which 20 percent of the cases fall, etc. Deciles can be computed in the same manner as percentiles, since $D1$ is $P10$, $D2$ is $P20$, etc.

Deciles, like percentiles, are points on a scale. Therefore, a score can be between the third and the fourth deciles, i.e., in the fourth lowest 10 percent of the group, but it cannot be in the third decile, since that decile is only a point on the scale. Quartiles divide the distribution of raw scores into segments of 25 percent each. Thus, the first quartile, $Q1$ is the point that cuts off the lowest 25 percent, $Q2$ the lowest 50 percent of the group (what is another name for this point? [median], and $Q3$ the lowest 75 percent of the distribution.

It should be emphasized, however, that deciles and quartiles, like percentiles, are points along the scale. They are not segments of that scale. It is wrong to say that case X *is in the third quartile* or something similar. This is an error because the third quartile is only a point on the scale. (p. 77)

Standard Scores

Standard scores have become increasingly popular with standardized test developers. A standard score expresses a person's distance from the mean in terms of the standardized deviation of the distribution. For example, let us return to Kathy, Juan, and Mariah and their scores on a test:

Mean of the test takers	75
Standard deviation	15
Kathy's score	90
Juan's score	65
Mariah's score	45

Using the formula $\dfrac{X(\text{raw score}) - M(\text{mean})}{SD(\text{standard deviation})}$, the following standard scores are obtained

$$\text{Kathy:} \frac{90 - 75}{15} = +1.0$$
$$\text{Juan:} \frac{65 - 75}{15} = -0.7$$
$$\text{Mariah:} \frac{45 - 75}{15} = -2.0$$

Because both decimal points and plus and minus signs may be confusing or easily misplaced, they can be transformed into a more convenient form by multiplying each standard score with some constant. For example, if we multiply these scores by 10, we have +10, −7, and −20. We can then eliminate the plus and minuses by adding a constant of 100. Thus, Kathy's score becomes 110, Juan's 93, and Mariah's 80.

Stanines

Another variation for normalizing standard scores was developed by the United States Air Force in World War II. The name *stanine* is a contraction of standard nine, a 9-point scale having a mean of 5 and a standard deviation of 2. The percentages of a normal distribution that fall within each of the nine stanines are as follows:

Stanine	1	2	3	4	5	6	7	8	9
Percentage	4	7	12	17	20	17	12	7	4

Relationships among various types of test scores and the normal curve may be noted in Figure 7-3.

Norms

A favorite expression of soldiers in the ranks is *snafu* (situation normal—all fouled up). We label people normal or abnormal if they deviate from our concept of normalcy, and we use such expressions as "He would normally do this" or "Under normal conditions you can expect that."

The term *norm* or *normal* is a popular one that most people use frequently to denote the expected or what can be reasonably anticipated. The concept of normal or norm as used in standardized testing terminology also implies normal or average performance on a given test. Norms are derived during the process of standardizing a test. As a basis for determining the norms, a test is administered to a sample (usually large) that is representative of the population for whom the test is designed. This group then comprises the standardization sample to establish the norms for the test. These norms reflect not only the average performances but also the relative frequency of the varying degrees of deviation below and above the average.

Age Norms

The use of age norms or standards is a fairly popular one in the nonscientific sense. We often suggest that Gerardo is as big as a 10-year-old or Janie has the vocabulary of a 6-year-old. The use of this concept in reporting standardized testing results became popular when the term *mental age* was used during the translations and adaptations of the original Binet scales discussed later in this chapter. From this initial usage, age norms were frequently used to measure any trait that showed progressive change with age. For example, in physical development, it would be relatively simple to prepare norms for the height or weight of growing children by years. In testing, age norms represent the test performance of persons grouped and normed according to their chronological age. This type of score is more likely to be noted in the reporting of achievement tests, especially in the elementary school grades.

There are two shortcomings to this concept of scoring and reporting results. First, there is a lack of agreement regarding when children should be introduced to certain basic academic subjects, at what rates, and what comprehension level should normally be expected in these subjects. Also, age norms assume uniform growth from year to year, an assumption of questionable validity.

Grade Norms

Grade norms are similar to age norms inasmuch as they are based on the average score earned by students at a specific grade level. Again, grade norms are popular for reporting achievement test results in terms of grade equivalents. This method of reporting standardized test

Table 7-2 Main types of norms for educational and psychological tests.

Type of Norm	Type of Comparison	Type of Group
Age norms	Individual matched to groups whose performance he equals	Successive age groups
Grade norms	Same as above	Successive grade groups
Percentile norms	Percent of group surpassed by individual	Single age or grade group to which individual belongs
Standard score norms	Number of standard deviations individual falls above or below average of group	Same as above

Source: Measurement and Evaluation in Psychology and Education 4/E by Thorndike/Hagen, © 1955.
Reprinted by permission of Pearson Education, Inc., Upper Saddle River, NJ.

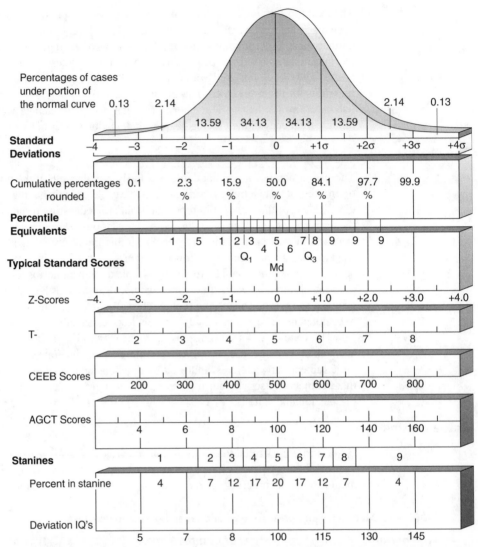

Figure 7-3 Relationships among different types of test scores in a normal distribution.

Source: Measurement and Evaluation in Psychology and Education 4/E by Thorndike/Hagen, © 1955. Reprinted by permission of Pearson Education, Inc., Upper Saddle River, NJ.

results, however, suffers from the same shortcomings as do age norms but is more readily viewed as suggesting standards to which teachers should aspire. Table 7-2 contrasts the main types of norms for educational and psychological tests.

SELECTING A TEST—WHAT CRITERIA?

The numbers and variety of standardized tests available to counselors and other users today require a recognition and application of appropriate criteria in test selection. Furthermore, much of the criticism of standardized testing over the years has focused on poorly designed instruments and poorly prepared users, which implies the need of criteria for both. Certainly, there are clinical as well as research-based reasons for concern about the trustworthiness of the data produced by assessment devices.

For obvious reasons, counselors should not use standardized tests that do not give accurate measures or that they (the counselors) are not competent to interpret. An error in measurement or interpretation can lead to an error in client decision making.

Validity

Validity is traditionally defined as the degree to which an instrument measures what it claims to measure or is used to measure. For example, does the Whiffenpoof Mechanical Aptitude test really measure one's aptitude for mechanical activities, as claimed, or does it simply reflect one's previous experiences in the areas being tested? Or to raise a question of traditional controversy, do IQ tests really measure basic or native intelligence, or do they more appropriately reflect one's cultural and educational experiences? In establishing validity, one must note the appropriateness of test or interview questions and of situational samples to the evaluation objectives. Because it is impossible to include all possible questions or situations in an evaluation tool, those selected for inclusion must be representative of the content areas or behavioral patterns being assessed and appropriate for the individual under study and the given circumstances. When an instrument meets these conditions, it is said to have *content validity*.

When the foregoing types of validity do not or cannot provide sufficient evidence of a test's validity, its construct validity may be cited. *Construct validity* pertains to the adequacy of the theory or concept underlying a specific instrument. In other words, it involves logically ascertaining the psychological attributes that account for variations in test scores or other derived data. Construct validity is reported in terms of the kinds of responses the test should elicit, and the ways in which those responses should be interpreted on the basis of logical inferences about the behavior the test is designed to assess.

Reliability

The second major criterion to be applied in standardized test selection is reliability. *Reliability* represents the consistency with which a test will obtain the same results from the same population but on different occasions. An instrument's reliability enables a counselor or other user to determine the degree to which predictions based on the established consistency of the test can be made.

Two techniques are popularly used to establish reliability. One is the *test-retest method*. When this method is used, timing between the tests is crucial because growth or decline in performance could occur if the interval is too long, whereas recall of original test items might occur if the interval is too short. A second approach for determining reliability is to establish an instrument's *internal consistency.* This consistency is set by comparing test-takers' responses to the odd-numbered questions with the consistency of their responses to the even-numbered questions.

Practicality

A third important, but often overlooked, criterion in the selection of a standardized instrument is *practicality.* First among the practical considerations is whether trained personnel are available to administer, score (if necessary), and interpret the particular standardized test under consideration. The importance of users' understanding the fine points of interpretation cannot be overemphasized.

A second and not unimportant practical consideration is the cost of the instrument and accompanying materials. The expense of scoring is included in this consideration. Additionally, many standardized tests can be used only for one testing, so replacement costs may become another factor. Time required for administration is also a practical consideration, especially, but not exclusively, in school settings.

Finally, counselors should be aware of the invaluable assistance in test selection that may be provided by the utilization of the current edition of the *Mental Measurements Yearbook.* This publication provides a critical review of most of the popular standardized measures currently in use. Counselors also may find the Buros Institute of Mental Measurements Web site helpful: www.unl.edu/buros/.

TYPES OF STANDARDIZED TESTS

Having briefly examined statistical concepts, methods of scoring, and criteria for the selection of standardized tests, let us now consider the specific areas for which standardized tests are available. These include aptitude, achievement, interest, and personality testing. There is admittedly some overlap in these categories, especially in interest and personality, but here we examine them as discrete, though not exclusive, areas for the classification of standardized tests. This discussion focuses on group standardized tests. We recognize the value of individual tests and know that counselors and psychologists in a variety of non-school settings frequently use individual tests; beginning counselors, however, especially in educational settings, work almost exclusively with group tests.

Intelligence or Aptitude?

The terms *aptitude* and *intelligence* are often used synonymously. However, in the discussion of standardized tests, one should examine the subtle differences that distinguish measures of intelligence from measures of aptitude. One distinction is that intelligence tests tend to provide a broad measure of overall or general ability, primarily related to one's potential for learning, whereas aptitude measures tend to focus more narrowly on specific factors. Stating it another way, intelligence tests tend to measure one human characteristic, the intellectual or mental capabilities of the individual; aptitude tests can be used to measure a wide range of primarily career learning and performance potentials. Both intelligence and aptitude measures have been the subject of the nature/nurture debates. Additionally, the overlap between intelligence and scholastic aptitude tests has, at times, blurred the differences between these two areas of standardized psychological measurement.

Intelligence Testing

The most popular area of aptitude or ability testing is the category that includes tests purporting to evaluate general academic ability, mental ability, and intelligence. Of these subsets, intelligence or IQ testing is the oldest and most controversial. Much of this controversy has centered around the various views of what constitutes intelligence, what influences it—heredity versus environment—and whether intelligence changes. These controversies have led to some more popularly accepted labels such as *academic ability, mental maturity, scholastic ability,* or *academic aptitude tests.* Some of these labels are probably more appropriate than others as many of the earlier IQ tests were largely normed on school populations and developed to predict performance in school.

Other shortcomings of general intelligence assessment are that different people arrive at the same end by different intellectual means. The reading level of the test-taker can bias the results. Judgments about intelligence can be linked with judgments about the worth of the individual. Finally, there has been a strong tendency to overlook the cultural and value relativity of intelligence judgments.

The first intelligence tests were designed by a Frenchman, Alfred Binet, to be administered to individual students; in the early 1900s, several American versions were developed. The most popular of these, the Stanford-Binet, based on the work of Lewis Terman at Stanford University, was published in 1916. This test has remained popular to the present, with the most recent revision being the fourth edition (1986, Riverdale Publishing Company). The other popular and perhaps most often administered individual intelligence tests are the various Wechsler scales.

The Wechsler Scales were developed by David Wechsler, a clinical psychologist, and were based on the assumption that intelligence was the sum total of the individual's abilities to think in a rational manner, to act purposefully, and to deal in an effective way with his or her environment. Wechsler Scales were developed for both preschool and primary school children and adult populations. For schoolchildren, tests such as the Wechsler are required nationwide under PL 94-142 in order to identify pupils in need of special services. The scales produce three scores: verbal ability, performance ability, and general ability. The Wechsler Test III (WISC-III, 1991) for ages 6 to 16 also allows for the computing of four index scores of verbal comprehension, perceptual organization, freedom from distractibility, and processing speed.

Another popular individually administered measure of intelligence and achievement for children (ages 2 years, 6 months to 12 years, 6 months) is the Kaufman Assessment Battery for Children. The Kaufman contains 16 subtests of mental and processing skills, which yield five major scores in Sequential Processing, Simultaneous Processing, Mental Processing Composite, Achievement, and Nonverbal. There is also a Kaufman Adolescent and Adult Intelligence Test, which consists of six subtests with two scales. The scales measure ability to solve problems and make decisions based on knowledge, verbal conceptualization, normal and informative education, life experiences, and acculturation. A composite score provides a measure of overall intellectual functioning.

Another intelligence measuring instrument is the Slosson Intelligence Test (1990), which provides an assessment of cognitive abilities for children and adults. Because the 187 items of this instrument are given orally, the examinees' language skills obviously influence their performance.

One of the most popular group intelligence tests over the years has been the Otis, or, as currently labeled, the Otis-Lennon School Ability Test (OLSAT), in its sixth edition. The first Otis test appeared in 1918 as the Otis Group Intelligence Scale and later achieved great popularity in both industry and education as the Otis-Quick Scoring Mental Abilities Tests. The current edition has five levels ranging from grade 1 through grade 12, with working times of 60 or 75 minutes, depending on the level.

Counselors who elect to use intelligence or mental abilities tests must be ever alert to the very sensitive nature of what they are measuring. Intelligence is at the core of the individual's view of his or her self-worth and potential. How does the counselor tell a client that he or she has scored below average on an I.Q. test, or tell parents that their child has a measured IQ below normal? Obviously serious psychological damage can be done, and this has happened in many unfortunate instances over the years.

Counselors should also be aware that many IQ tests have for years been suspected of cultural bias—a bias that would discriminate against minorities and populations in special environments. The use of intelligence tests should, therefore, be approached with extreme caution, if in fact, the tests are to be used at all.

Aptitude Tests

Aptitude may be defined as a trait that characterizes an individual's ability to perform in a given area or to acquire the learning necessary for performance in a given area. It presumes an inherent or native ability that can be developed to its maximum through learning or other experiences. However, it cannot be expanded beyond this certain point, even by learning. Although the idea of limits may be a debatable concept, it is stated here as a basis on which aptitude tests are developed. In theory, then, an aptitude test measures the potential of one to achieve in a given activity or to learn to achieve in that activity.

Aptitude tests would most likely be used by counselors and others because they may (a) identify potential abilities of which the person is not aware; (b) encourage the development of special or potential abilities of a given person; (c) provide information to assist a person in making educational and career decisions or other choices between competing alternatives; (d) help predict the level of academic or vocational success a person might anticipate; and (e) be useful in grouping persons with similar aptitudes for developmental and other educational purposes. Note that these are *potential* advantages and will accrue only under optimal conditions, which include initially the use of appropriate and proper measurement instruments relevant to the client's needs.

Although we usually expect a person to demonstrate considerable differences across a range of aptitudes, we should also be alert to the possibility that a person will not demonstrate or measure at the same level for a given aptitude every time. In other words, a track star may run the 100-yard dash in 10 seconds one day and the same distance under the same conditions in 10.4 seconds the next day. Aptitude measures are thus actuarial rather than absolute.

Special Aptitude Tests

Special aptitude tests usually refer to those tests that seek to measure a person's potential ability to perform or to acquire proficiency in a specific occupation or other type of activity. Tests that measure special aptitudes are sometimes referred to as *single-aptitude tests* or *component ability tests* because they only secure a measure for one specific aptitude or a single special ability. Tests of special aptitude have generally declined in popularity as aptitude batteries have increased in popularity. Counselors must frequently use standardized tests to measure a single aptitude in areas of mechanical, clerical, or artistic abilities. Single-aptitude tests have also been developed for use in various graduate and professional schools. Aptitude tests are also available for particular school subjects, especially in the areas of mathematics and foreign languages.

Vocational Aptitude Batteries

Aptitude batteries are developed on the assumption that different career fields have their own sets of criteria. Further, being able to profile and contrast results for differing careers is an advantage.

Multiple aptitude tests are an outgrowth of factorial studies of intelligence. In discussing the objective of factor analysis, Anastasi (1996) wrote:

> The principal object of factor analysis is to simplify the description of data by reducing the number of necessary variables, or dimensions. Thus, if we find that five factors are sufficient to account for all the common variance in a battery of 20 tests, we can for most purposes substitute five scores for the original 20 without sacrificing any essential information. The usual practice is to retain from among the original tests those providing the best measures of each of the factors. (p. 303)

These batteries typically consist of a series of subtests related in varying combinations to a series of occupations or occupationally related activities. The major advantages of batteries over single-aptitude tests are (a) convenience in administration as a result of having in one package a test that can be used to measure potential in a variety of activities; (b) the norming of all the battery's subtests on the same population, which thus yields comparable subtest norms; and (c) the opportunity to compare potential in a wide variety of areas with one test.

The oldest and most widely used of these multiple aptitude batteries are the General Aptitude Test Battery (GATB), used by the United States Employment Service, and the Differential Aptitude Battery (DAT). The Armed Services Vocational Aptitude Battery (ASVAB) is also extensively used. A brief examination of the characteristics of these tests may help you further understand the nature of aptitude batteries.

General Aptitude Test Battery (GATB)

The General Aptitude Test Battery is administered through the United States Employment Service. However, it is available to nonprofit institutions such as schools for counseling purposes. This battery has 12 subtests, which yield nine scores (see Table 7-3). Note also that these aptitudes are not all independent as some of the subtests are used in determining

Table 7-3 GATB aptitude scores and composite scores.

Aptitude Scores	Composite Scores
General Learning Ability (**G**)	Cognitive = G + V + N
Verbal Aptitude (**V**)	Perceptual = S + P + Q
Numerical Aptitude (**N**)	Psychomotor = K + F + M
Spatial Aptitude (**S**)	
Form Perception (**P**)	
Clerical Perception (**Q**)	
Motor Coordination (**K**)	
Finger Dexterity (**F**)	
Manual Dexterity (**M**)	

Source: From *Principles and Applications of Assessment in Counseling*, 1st edition, by S. Whiston © 2000. Reprinted with permission of Brooks/Cole, an imprint of the Wadsworth Group, a division of Thomson Learning. Fax 800-730-2215

more than one aptitude score. As might be anticipated, this battery is primarily used in career counseling for job placement for individuals 16 years of age or older.

Differential Aptitude Test

The Differential Aptitude Test consists of a battery of eight subtests. The current (1990) edition features two levels. Level 1 is primarily for students in grades 7–9 and level 2 for those in grades 10–12. Both versions may be appropriate to older populations as well. The subtests are verbal reasoning, numerical ability, abstract reasoning, clerical speed and accuracy, mechanical reasoning, space relations, language usage–spelling, and language usage–grammar. This battery has for many years been one of the most popular in schools as an aid in counseling students for vocational and educational decision making.

The Armed Services Vocational Aptitude Battery (ASVAB)

Since 1972 approximately one million high school students per year have taken the Armed Services Vocational Aptitude Battery, a service that is available to local high schools at no cost or obligation to either the school or student. This battery, also used throughout the military services and the Department of Defense, consists of 10 tests: arithmetic reasoning, numerical operations, paragraph comprehension, work knowledge, coding speed, general science, mathematics knowledge, electronics information, mechanical comprehension, and automotive and shop information. Approximately 3 hours of administration time are needed for the current edition of the battery. School counselors should keep in mind that the majority of validation studies of the ASVAB have been with military occupations or military training programs. This may raise caution flags for high school students who are basing nonmilitary career choices primarily on their ASVAB results. There is also some concern about the average score differences between minority and nonminority examinees (Prediger, Swaney & Van Sickle, 1992).

Scholastic Aptitude Tests

Scholastic or academic aptitude tests propose to measure a person's potential for performing in academic situations. Such tests as those that constitute the School and College Ability Test (SCAT) and Scholastic Aptitude Test (SAT) batteries have merit for predicting academic performance at higher educational levels. However, more appropriate labels would be academic achievement or academic predictions, because they tend to predict future academic achievement on the basis of past learning rather than of native ability.

A popular academic aptitude test for the high school level is the advanced level of the School and College Ability Tests (SCAT III), designed for grades 9 to 12. This test yields a verbal, quantitative, and total score. In line with current trends in testing theory, SCAT seeks to measure developed abilities. Thus, the SCAT III draws freely on word knowledge and math processes that test-takers are presumed to have learned in the earlier school grades.

Two popular tests used for the admission, placement, and counseling of college students are the Scholastic Aptitude Test (SAT) of the College Entrance Examinations Board and the American College Testing Program (ACT). The ACT was introduced in 1959 and is also used by many institutions of higher education. It consists of four tests: English usage, mathematical usage, social studies reading, and natural sciences reading.

Many high school counselors and college admissions officials have frequently noted that the best single predictor of a college student's academic performance in college is the student's high school academic grade point average. However, this prediction may be enhanced when combined with scores on a standardized admission test such as the Scholastic Aptitude Test (SAT).

The proponents of such tests for admissions purposes suggest that they measure, in a uniform way, the basic knowledge expected in a field; they compensate for differences in grading practices and differing content emphases among schools. Some critics however, complain that they discriminate against minorities and students attending schools serving lower socioeconomic populations.

Academic Achievement Tests

Academic achievement measurement is an area of standardized testing to which most students have been subject, not on just a single occasion or two, but probably numerous times during their educational programs. Of all the areas of standardized testing, achievement tests are the most popular in terms of numbers administered to numbers of different individuals, as literally hundreds of thousands of achievement tests are administered on an annual basis in the overwhelming majority of schools throughout the country. The accountability movement of recent generations has sparked additional growth in the widespread administration of achievement tests, used in these instances to measure, and all too frequently, evaluate, teachers, schools, and school systems.

This emphasis on achievement testing as an index of educational excellence in school reform movements of the late 1980s and 1990s has stimulated both the use of achievement tests and attention to their results. Renewed calls by elected officials, particularly at the federal level, for national standardized testing to evaluate school performance has further fueled the long-standing controversy over the use and abuse of tests. Despite the widespread popularity of academic achievement tests, they are frequently confused with other measures, especially aptitude tests.

Drummond (1996) identifies the various types of achievement tests as follows:

1. *Survey achievement batteries.* Partially norm-referenced and partially criterion-referenced tests that measure knowledge and skill in reading, mathematics, language arts, social studies, and science
2. *Subject area tests.* Achievement tests in a single subject area, such as math or spelling
3. *Criterion-referenced tests.* Tests that measure knowledge and comprehension of a specific skill or competency, for example, the ability to draw specified inferences from pictorial or written content or the ability to read a metric scale and give the weight of an object in metric and English units of weight
4. *Minimum level skills tests.* Tests that measure objectives or skills identified as the minimum skills to be achieved in order to pass from one level or grade to another
5. *Individual achievement tests.* Tests that are administered individually across a wide age or grade range to measure achievement
6. *Diagnostic tests.* Tests that are used to assess the strengths and weaknesses of individuals in a given subject area by measuring a limited number of skills thoroughly (p. 155)

Academic achievement tests are used to provide measures of (a) the amount of learning, (b) the rate of learning, (c) comparisons with others or with self-achievement in other areas, (d) level of learning in subareas, (e) strengths and weaknesses in a subject matter area, and, in some instances, (f) predictions of future learning. Because of their extensive use and the relatively easy task of identifying appropriate content measures, achievement tests are among the best-designed standardized measures available to counselors. There are, however, certain considerations that users of achievement tests must keep in mind if they are to use such instruments appropriately.

First, it is important that the content of the test be relevant to the subject matter content the student has experienced. In other words, the test should measure what the student has had the opportunity to learn. Further, the emphasis within the test, in terms of topical areas covered, must be appropriate for the emphasis the student has experienced in the subject matter class. Additionally, the level of difficulty of the test items must be appropriate for the age/grade level being tested. A final consideration, one that bears repeating, concerns the norming sample on which the test has been standardized. If this sample is representative of the general population appropriate to the age/grade level being tested, comparison with this general population may be appropriate. If the population of the sample is similar to the population being tested, that would usually be desirable. However, if the norming population is considerably dissimilar, it may not be an appropriate group against which to compare the group being tested.

Although achievement tests that measure only a single subject matter are available, batteries that measure and compare across a series of subject matter areas are far more popular. This popularity results partly because an achievement battery is less expensive than a collection of subject-matter tests and will probably require considerably less time to administer. This advantage occurs because the subject-matter tests within a battery follow uniform procedures for administration of all tests. Too, each subject-matter test has been normed on the same population, making test selection and comparison of students' scores easier.

One of the popular achievement test batteries is the Iowa Test of Basic Skills. This series is available in two forms for kindergarten through grade 8. Depending on which level and form are used, testing time is 60 to 80 minutes. The five major areas tested by this battery are vocabulary, reading comprehension, language skills, work-study skills, and mathematical skills. The test developers point out that this battery measures pupils' abilities to use and acquire skills, for no test or subtest is concerned with only the repetition or identification of facts.

The Iowa Tests of Educational Development are normed for grades 9 through 12 and consist of seven subtests measuring subject-matter areas appropriate for secondary school curricula. Standard scores, grade equivalent scores, national percentile ranks, normal curve equivalent scores, stanines, and large-city norms are available for all tests and for the composites. Local norms are available from the Riverside Scoring Service and the Riverside Publishing Company in Chicago.

The Metropolitan Achievement Test consists of eight battery levels for measuring performance from the beginning of kindergarten through grade 12. This battery consists of single tests for reading comprehension, mathematics, language, social studies, and science. The basic battery consists of the first three tests. The complete battery utilizes all five tests. This battery is available from the Psychological Corporation, a subsidiary of Harcourt Brace Jovanovich, Inc., New York.

Interest Inventories

In a discussion on career planning, one might hear such statements as "I've always been interested in nursing"; "The thought of teaching really turns me off"; "I know I'd enjoy selling cars"; or "Being a flight attendant would be the most exciting career I could imagine!" Such pronouncements of career interests are common among adolescents and young adults. Equally common are statements of uncertainty and frustration regarding career choices, such as "I wish somebody would just tell me what career I should enter"; "I can't make up my mind between engineering or coaching"; or "I'm really upset because I can't think of any job I'm interested in."

Although interest testing has, for many years, been a popular psychometric aid to adolescents and young adults in career planning, recently it has been increasingly used for older populations considering mid-life or other career changes.

Discussions and other explorations of interest are valuable aids for career planning and related career counseling and guidance; even a simple listing in hierarchical order of possible careers may be as valid in some instances as standardized, inventoried interests.

However, certain benefits may result from the use of standardized interest inventories of which counselors, teachers, and others who assist youth and adults in career and related decision making should be aware. Such potential benefits include these:

- A comparative and contrasting inventory of a person's interests
- Verification of a person's claimed interest or tentative choice
- Identification of previously unrecognized interests
- Identification of the possible level of interests for various (usually career) activities
- Contrast of interest with abilities and achievements

- Identification of problems associated with career decision making (no areas of adequate interest; high stated interest versus low inventoried interest in a career field)
- A stimulus for career exploration or career counseling

We would indicate the importance for counselors to remember that interest inventories may measure interests and interests only. Counselors must be aware that, especially with the young, interests change very rapidly and a student's decision to be a professional athlete today may change to being an astronaut tomorrow. Also, counselors should keep in mind that interest inventories measure broad general areas of interest.

The popular development of interest tests evolved from studies indicating that people in a given occupation seemed to be characterized by a cluster of common interests that distinguished them from people in other occupations. Researchers also noted that these differences in interests extended beyond those associated with job performance and that persons in a given occupation also had different nonvocational interests—hobbies and recreational activities that could distinguish them from those in other occupations. Thus, interest inventories could be designed to assess a person's interests and relate them to those of various occupational areas. Two of the earlier and more popular of these inventories, still extensively used today, are the Kuder Preference Record, Vocational (1976) and the Strong Interest Inventory (1994).

The Kuder Preference Record is the original and most popular of the various Kuder interest inventories. It provides a series of interest items arranged in triads, from which the respondents choose the one they would like most and the one they would like least. The results are scored and profiled for the occupational areas of outdoor, mechanical, computational, scientific, persuasive, artistic, literary, music, social service, and clerical. Revision of the original preference record, the Kuder General Interest Survey, extends the use downward to the sixth grade by employing a simpler vocabulary that requires only a sixth-grade reading ability (the original version was usually considered appropriate for use in grades 9 through 12). The Kuder Occupational Interest Survey is still another version that provides scores showing similarities with occupational and college-level areas. This form differs from previous Kuder tests in expressing a person's score on each occupational scale as a correlation between his or her interest pattern and the pattern of a particular occupational group.

The Strong Interest Inventory is a revision of the earlier forms of the Strong Vocational Interest Blank, which was first published in 1933. Its latest edition was published in 1994. The various Strong inventories have been based on the assumption that individuals who are attracted to and enjoy a specific occupation have similar interest profiles and therefore, by assessing and matching the interests of individuals exploring careers against those of workers in the field, counselors can help people make better career decisions.

The various interest inventories have been suggested as usable with older adolescents and adults who may be considering higher level professional or skilled occupations. The Strong Interest Inventory can be scored only by computer. The major and most popular scales for the Strong Vocational Interest series are the 211 occupational scales, plus four personal style scales. Fourteen new growth occupations and contemporary careers have also been added. The Strong Interest Inventory is related to the Pathfinder career decision-making system using interactive video. A microcomputer version is also available. The Strong Interest Inventory is published by the Stanford University Press, Stanford, California, and distributed by Consulting Psychologists Press.

The Ohio Vocational Interest Survey: Second Edition (OVIS-II) is one of a number of somewhat newer interest inventories developed for use with high school students and adults. It was developed after the model on which the Dictionary of Occupational Titles is based (a cubistic model of data, people, and things). The OVIS is separated into three parts: (a) a questionnaire, (b) a local information survey, and (c) the interest inventory. It yields data on 253 job activities that are derived from the interest scales of the survey. An information questionnaire is also provided as well as a report folder and guide to career exploration. The latter is designed to link interests to the world of work. The Ohio Vocational Interest Survey is published by several publishing companies, including The Psychological Corporation.

Another approach to the assessment of career interests is the Self-Directed Search (SDS). This instrument was developed by John Holland, whose hexagonal model of six occupational themes is represented in the six summary scores of Realistic, Investigative, Artistic, Social, Enterprising, and Conventional. The SDS is designed to be self-administered, self-scored, and self-interpreted. When an individual completes the SDS he or she uses a summary code comprising the types that rank first and second across all the subtests. Utilizing this code, one refers to a Job Finder, which presents information about 456 jobs listed in terms of two-letter SDS codes. Once a person gets his or her lists of careers that match a summary code, suggested next steps are listed for organized career planning. Holland's hexagonal model makes it possible to estimate the similarity between an individual and an environment. The shorter the distance between personality type and environmental type, the greater the probability of a good fit; those with the greatest distance suggest job dissatisfaction and lack of stability. This process highlights Holland's popular theory, suggesting that career choices that reinforce one's personality type will be the more satisfying and successful. The Self-Directed Search is marketed by Consulting Psychologists Press, Palo Alto, California.

The Career Maturity Inventory, although not precisely an interest inventory, has been designed to measure the maturity of attitudes and competencies that are involved in career decision making. The attitude scale surveys five attitudinal clusters: (a) involvement in the career choice process, (b) orientation toward work, (c) independence in decision making, (d) preference for career choice factors, and (e) conceptions of the career choice process. In contrast, the competency test measures the more cognitive variables involved in choosing an occupation. The five parts of the competency test are (a) self-appraisal, (b) occupational information, (c) goal selection, (d) planning, and (e) problem solving. The Career Maturity Inventory is available from McGraw-Hill Book Company, New York.

The Career Attitudes and Strategies Inventory (1994) by John Holland and Gary Gottfredson is a self-administered, self-scoring inventory used to measure employed and unemployed adults' beliefs about their career problems, job satisfaction, reaction to change, work strategies, and other career issues. The inventory consists of a checklist for common career obstacles plus 150 multiple-choice items grouped into nine scales: job satisfaction, work involvement, skill development, dominant style, career worries, interpersonal abuse, family commitment, risk-taking style, and geographical barriers.

The Jackson Vocational Interest Survey (1995) is designed for high school, college, and adult age groups. The instrument consists of 289 pairs of statements that describe job-related activities. These statements, when scored, are profiled along 34 basic interest scales. These scales cover career role dimensions relevant to a variety of careers and work style scales indicative of work environment preferences.

Personality Tests

Of all the areas of standardized testing, none is more intriguing to the general public, and perhaps to the counseling profession as well, as personality assessment. From the do-it-yourself personality test in the daily newspaper to sophisticated, projective techniques requiring highly specialized psychological training, personality testing represents a universal quest of the individual to understand what makes him or her and fellow human beings tick. But personality testing is as complex as what it seeks to measure. Let us examine some of the questions or concerns that must be taken into consideration.

What Is Personality?

The term *personality* has many different meanings. You can readily discern the wide variations in viewpoints regarding this topic by asking a group, "What is personality?" and noting the wide range of responses. The concept of personality is a difficult one to treat with the precision usually associated with standardized tests. Thus, constructors of personality tests face the challenge of determining what workable definition of personality they will use and what aspect or aspects of that definition they will measure. Generally speaking, however, in conventional psychometric terminology, "personality tests are instruments for the measurement of emotional, motivational, interpersonal, and attitudinal characteristics, as distinguished from abilities" (Anastasi & Urbina, 1997, p. 348).

What Is Normal Personality?

The question of what constitutes a normal personality would probably elicit a variety of answers from the public. Most people tend to view normal in terms of their own behavioral personality traits and values. Thus, an extremely extroverted person, viewed as normal by one group, may be viewed as abnormal by another group. Even if one is able to objectively identify norms for specific behavioral responses, one still must determine at what point the deviations from those norms become abnormal.

Can Personality Be Measured?

The question of whether personality can be measured has objectively been answered affirmatively by many authors of standardized personality measures and has further been affirmed by many practicing counselors, psychologists, and psychiatrists utilizing observation and other nonstandardized techniques. Some of the difficulties involved in obtaining accurate assessments are client based and must be the concern of the test interpreter:

1. The capability of a person to accurately analyze many aspects of his or her own personality is questionable. In some instances, the client may not possess the insight to respond accurately. Although the client's view of self is important, it may not be appropriate to the intent of the measuring instrument. In other instances, one must recognize that the individual's view of self can be distorted, differ from the perceptions of others, and be misleading to the test interpreter.
2. Some people may deliberately falsify their responses. Most often, deception occurs when a person responds in a manner that he or she views as more socially acceptable than perhaps his or her true response might be. For example, little

children almost inevitably respond that they love their parents, even when they do not know them or when they actively dislike them. Also, one can anticipate that some respondents will project an ideal self rather than the real self in their answers. Some may respond as the friendly and popular person they wish they were, rather than the withdrawn individual with few friends they recognize themselves to be. The intimate nature of a question may dissuade the respondent from answering accurately. Most notable examples in this category are questions dealing with a person's sexual activities, beliefs, and values.

Several of the more popular personality inventories or standardized personality assessment instruments are the Myers-Briggs Type Indicator, the Edwards Personal Preference Schedule, and the Minnesota Multiphasic Personality Inventory (MMPI). The MMPI requires special training and supervised experience for test administrators before they can use it in clinical settings.

The Myers-Briggs Type Indicator is a widely used personality test. The standard Form G contains 126 items that determine preferences on the four scales of (a) extroversion/introversion, (b) sensing/intuition, (c) thinking/feeling, and (d) judging/perceiving. The various combinations of these preferences result in 16 personality types helpful in making career and other decisions.

The Edwards Personal Preference Schedule (EPPS) is a personality inventory based on the theory of personality presented by Henry Murray (Murray, Barrett, & Honburger, 1938). The Edwards Personal Preference Schedule is designed to show the relative importance to the individual of 15 key needs or motives:

Achievement	Affiliation	Nurturance
Deference	Intraception	Change
Order	Succorance	Endurance
Exhibition	Dominance	Heterosexuality
Autonomy	Abasement	Aggression

The Edwards Personal Preference Schedule has a forced-choice format, which means the examinee has a choice between two options on an item.

Another clinically oriented instrument is the Minnesota Multiphasic Personality Inventory. This is a very widely used personality assessment test, especially in clinical settings. Revised in 1992, it is constructed entirely on the basis of clinical criteria. MMPI-II contains 567 statements covering a wide range of subject matters related to the instrument's 10 scales as follows:

Hypochondriasis	Paranoia
Depression	Psychasthenia
Hysteria	Schizophrenia
Psychopathic Deviate	Hypomania
Masculinity-Femininity	Social Introversion

In addition to the 10 clinical scales, the MMPI and MMPI-II contain three validity scales. These are an L or Lie score; an F score, which may indicate the seriousness with which the individual responded to the test items; and a K score, a suppressor variable refining the discrimination of five of the clinical variables. As mentioned earlier, all of the MMPI editions require special training and supervised experience before their utilization.

CRITERION-REFERENCED TESTING

One of the most frequently raised issues in the 1970s and 1980s concerned criterion-referenced testing versus norm-referenced testing. Many educators will suggest that it is not a case of either/or—that, in fact, criterion-referenced testing complements norm-referenced testing and vice versa. One cannot deny the rapid gains in popularity that criterion-referenced testing has made in recent years, but the regeneration of calls for a national standardized testing program suggests that a national preference still exists for norm-referenced testing.

A criterion-referenced test measures whether a person has attained the desired or maximum goal in a learning experience. If we were to contrast criterion-referenced testing with norm-referenced testing by using a practical example, we might note that a sixth-grade class could achieve an average score ahead of 52% of other sixth-grade classes in a representative nationwide sample. This information, however, might not tell those interested, such as teachers, parents, and students, more specifically how well this sixth-grade class reads or what they have learned to read. On the other hand, a typical criterion-referenced test result would indicate how many pupils in this sixth-grade class can read at a certain rate of reading, comprehend at a certain level of comprehension, and recall with reasonable accuracy what they have read after passage of a specific period of time. In the first instance, a class is competing against other classes to demonstrate to what degree pupils have learned or not learned to read. In the latter case, however, pupils are competing against a locally established standard, a learning objective, a criterion.

Rather than noting the range of individual differences in test scores, criterion-referenced tests place persons in one of two groups: those who have attained the criterion and those who have not. Perhaps Hawes (1973) best expressed the popularity of criterion-referenced testing by entitling his article, "Criterion-Referenced Testing—No More Losers, No More Norms, No More Parents Raising Storms."

COMPUTERIZED ADAPTIVE TESTING

Another popular as well as innovative movement in testing is computerized adaptive testing. In this approach a computer selects different questions from an item pool to administer to different students. Worthen, White, and Borg (1993) describe the process:

> The computer selects each question from a pool of items of known difficulty. The question is displayed on a TV screen, and the student either types the letter of the correct multiple-choice response or touches the screen at the location of the correct response. The computer records whether the response is correct or incorrect and selects the next question, based on the student's response to the previous question. If the student's response is correct, the next item selected will be more difficult; if the student's response is incorrect, the next item selected will be easier. As more items are administered, the computer considers the student's performance

on all previous items in estimating his mastery level and selecting the next item to be administered. As a result, the items are adapted to the level of the student. That is, on the whole they
will be neither too easy nor too difficult for the individual. The main advantage of this method
over conventional testing is that in *computer adaptive testing*, because each student is administered a different combination of items, the teacher cannot teach to the test, and the student cannot help his peers by passing on the test items he remembers, because most of the items
administered to other students will be different. (p. 212)

Because each student responds to different sets of questions, the resulting scores of all
the students are not comparable. Counselors need to also be aware that computer-assisted
assessment is different from computer adaptive testing. Computer-assisted assessment
refers to the use of computers for assisting the administration, scoring, and interpretation
of a test. The manner of this assistance can vary from the computer's simply scoring the results to the test-takers taking the test at the computer and then receiving scores and interpretation from the computer and often, a detailed, written report.

DEVELOPING A TESTING PROGRAM

In many school settings, testing programs may be mandated by state legislative bodies or
agencies or set by local school boards with limited input from the schools and their counselors. In nonschool settings, counselors may find that organizational policies dictate, at
least in part, the nature of the organization's utilization of standardized tests. However, in
those more ideal circumstances where counselors and their fellow helping professionals can
determine the nature of the organization's standardized assessment program, it is obviously
desirable to develop a logical, sequential approach that provides for accountability. The following steps present one such procedure that, while appropriate perhaps to school settings,
may also be suitable for some community and business and industrial settings as well:

1. *Determine the needs.* This is obviously the initial and critical step that defines
   the degree to which the testing program will be relevant. Here the key question
   is "What new information do we need to provide good (not just adequate) service to the organization's target population?" The word *new* implies that a specific type of test data should not be a priority if it duplicates information already
   available through other sources. In other words, priority goes to needed data not
   already available. Second priority would be for information that tests can provide for supplementing already existing data.
2. *Determine the program's objectives.* Once the testing needs have been identified, these needs should be translated into the testing program's objectives. For
   accountability purposes, these objectives should be stated in concise, measurable terms.
3. *Select the appropriate instruments.* In determining which tests are best to serve
   the program's objectives, obviously the basic criteria of validity, reliability,
   norming appropriateness, and administrative practicality are applied. In addition,
   the skills needed to administer and interpret the tests must be available. Costs
   are always an important consideration.

4. *Determine the testing schedule.* Tests should be scheduled for specific dates to provide data at the time it is most needed or most appropriate. Spacing is also important to avoid testing overload for both those administering and those taking the tests.

5. *Evaluate the outcomes.* Data indicating the degree to which the objectives have been achieved should be collected and utilized. Appropriateness of the instruments should be examined. Results should lead to continuous program improvement.

In planning a testing program, one must always bear in mind that testing is not an end in itself, but rather, an opportunity to develop a more complete picture of the client—a picture mutually shared by both the client and the counselor.

Multicultural Issues

The controversies associated with standardized testing noted at the beginning of this chapter have almost from the outset of the psychological measurement movement included charges of bias and discrimination based on gender, race, socioeconomic background, and so forth. Legal recognition of these possibilities were recognized in Title VII of the Civil Rights Act of 1964, which included prohibiting the use of tests for employment discrimination. Subsequent court decisions have further refined concepts of bias in tests, with the majority of cases being decided in favor of plaintiffs over test companies.

However, beyond the legal guidelines, counselors and other test administrators and interpreters have the professional responsibility to be sensitive and alert to the multicultural clients they serve. For example, test-taking anxiety may be higher with some populations. Verbal inflections, implied implications of results, and the attitude of the counselor can also appear discriminatory. Economic environments can limit some populations and the verbal directions for some tests may unintentionally bias the test. Also, the client's reading level and rate of reading may be a factor in some instances.

Computerized administering, scoring, and interpretation can be found for a wide selection of specific instruments in all of the major assessment areas. Advocates also point out that clients tend to like computer testing, especially when adaptive testing is programmed.

Another feature of the computerized program is the near-instant feedback of results. Further, the increasing development of narrative interpretations, presented through computer printouts, will obviously speed up the total assessment process. These interpretations are based on the consensus of experts and research and does provide for uniformity in interpretations, lessening the likelihood of counselor error or bias. However, many counselors are concerned because of the limits imposed on counselor/client interactions and the mechanization of the whole process as opposed to the traditional "humanistic" approach.

Other questions have also arisen regarding the application of norms generated on paper-and-pencil tests to computerized versions of the same tests, differing administration procedures, and, for some clients, a deviation from the familiar format of classroom and previously taken standardized tests. Confidentiality and other ethical issues have also been examined. Although these and other questions are being debated and studied, it should be abundantly clear that we must adapt to the new technologies and learn to use these new advances to enhance our own performance as professional counselors.

A Concluding Thought on Standardized Testing

As we conclude this overview on standardized assessment, we note for our readers that the intent of this chapter is to provide only a brief orientation to this very important area of counselor preparation. Subsequent courses in psychological measurement will be required—and should be looked forward to—before a helping professional can ethically and appropriately administer, score, and interpret such tests results.

NONSTANDARDIZED TECHNIQUES
FOR HUMAN ASSESSMENT

Sometimes we are called on to explain, even justify, why one of our close friends acts the way he or she does. The reply may, at least subconsciously, draw on our knowledge of our friend's home and family background; the environment in which he or she grew up or now lives; the cultural background; the physical and psychological characteristics, as we perceive them; or the experiences of the friend. In these instances, a wealth of background information provides insights into the behavior of those we know well. Nor is this knowledge limited by our own particular occupation or discipline. Some of what we know might be classified as cultural or anthropological, some as environmental or sociological, and some as psychological.

In a similar vein, most of us feel more confident with a family physician who has looked after our ailments for years, who knows us as individuals rather than just physical specimens, who understands us totally. It is a situation that an equally competent, but newcomer physician cannot duplicate.

In the world of sporting competition there are frequent references to psyching out the opposition. This psyching out attempts to go beyond understanding the athletic skills of the opponent, implying that the better we know our competition, the better we can compete against them.

These examples suggest this section's objective, namely, to describe nonstandardized assessment techniques for increasing and broadening our understanding of our client population. Thorough assessment increases the potential for maximum treatment efficacy. Interdisciplinary concepts of human assessment are presented, followed by some suggested guidelines or principles of human assessment. We then focus on the nonstandardized techniques commonly employed for individual analysis by counselors in various settings. We should note that standardized techniques, such as psychological testing, are those with a precise and fixed format, set of procedures, and method of scoring that enable the instrument to be used for the same purpose in a variety of settings and times. Standardization suggests uniformity and objectivity. Nonstandardization suggests a broader, variable, and more subjective approach to gathering and interpreting data for human assessment.

CONCEPTS OF HUMAN ASSESSMENT

The most intelligent yet most complicated and difficult to understand living organism known to civilization today is the human being. When we place human beings in their environment, a rapidly changing and complex society, we cannot help but recognize the enormity of the task of those who seek to understand, predict, and assist the development of human behavior. In undertaking this responsibility, we are quick to recognize that no one discipline or area of expertise alone possesses the theoretical or technical basis for a comprehensive understanding of modern people in modern society. To this end, those who study human behavior—whether from an individual or societal viewpoint; whether from the viewpoint of an anthropologist, sociologist, or psychologist; whether from the viewpoint of an American, Japanese, or German—must be willing both to learn and to share with those who have this common interest. It is in this context that we suggest that counselors, regardless of the setting in which they function, can better understand their clients' behavior through the insights gained by studying behavior in the context of other disciplines and cultures. The following is not intended to substitute for such study but only to examine briefly these other perspectives and their implications for counselors.

Sociology

Sociology is a social and behavioral science that focuses on the study of individuals and groups in society and how they behave and interact with one another. The science of sociology contributes to an understanding of the social networks and their impact on individuals, individual roles, and relationships within those networks. Furthermore, sociology is concerned with the study of socialization agents or institutions. These institutions, such as the family, church, school, and government, assume the responsibility of teaching people within that environment what constitutes normal and abnormal behavior for the society. These patterns of normal and abnormal behavior are further shaped by customs, folkways, mores, and laws. Sociology also helps in understanding behavior that deviates from the norms of a group or society. The study of social deviance helps in understanding behaviors, including alcoholism and crime, that are defined as social problems. Such study also helps us to recognize that what is considered normal behavior in one group may be defined as deviant behavior in another group. Furthermore, study in this area can help the counselor recognize the influence of social controls or pressures on the behavior of clients, students, and others. For counselors, it is also important to keep in mind that human beings are social beings, affected by the society of which they are members and, at the same time, expected to contribute to that society.

Counselors will find that knowledge of sociology contributes to their understanding of the groups and structures within the society of which they are a part. It is particularly important to understand the significance of the groupings and roles of clients, the influences on client behavior of the various groups of which they are members, the roles and relationships that are most significant to clients, and the restriction on clients' behavior and behavior change placed on them by the social system of which clients are a part. The counselor must understand the various roles of people and the behavior that occurs or is anticipated as a result of these roles. That also includes an understanding of the significance of status, as already noted in many psychological studies. Some suggest that perhaps there has never been a more status-conscious society than our own. Sociologists help us understand status and its implications through the study of social stratification, which involves social classes, social mobilities, social structures, and, in general, the ranking of social positions within society.

The sociologist, like the psychologist, is also concerned with the study of the development of a person's self-concept. Sociological study focuses on self-concept development through the socialization process. It is especially important for counselors to recognize the impact of significant others and reference groups (both within the domain of sociological study) on the development of a person's self-concept. Who are the people whose judgments, imagined or otherwise, are significant to one's self-concept, and what are the groups that one uses to develop and test attitudes, beliefs, and so forth?

Psychology

As we examine the various scientific disciplines, we should note that psychology has been the one most closely associated with the profession of counseling. Over the years, psychology has made numerous significant contributions to the development and practice of counseling, including counseling theory and processes, individual and group counseling, standardized assessment, and career development and decision-making theories.

Traditionally the discipline of psychology has been closely related to the study of school-age groups and their education. Such fields as educational psychology and human development have been the offspring of these interests. Learning theory has also been extended through work by psychologists. Developmental theorists have assisted counselors and others in understanding why and how humans grow and develop over the life span. Social psychology has provided counselors with insight into the socialization process and social influences, attitudes, attribution, group dynamics, and interpersonal interactions. Ecological theorists have alerted us to the importance of the environment and how it influences individuals and their behavior.

Anthropology

Anthropology is the study of the culture of a society and the characteristics of its social behavior. It involves recording, describing, and analyzing cultures throughout the world and throughout history. In these studies, anthropology identifies the traditions, norms, patterns of learning, coping styles, and other behaviors, from both current and historic perspectives. Among the understandings that counselors can glean from the study of anthropology are recognizing (a) that different cultures have different and similar concepts, (b) the importance of the ethnic and cultural background of the client, (c) the importance of the ethnic and cultural background of the counselor, and (d) the significance of subcultures within the larger societal or cultural context. Anthropology, when applied to counseling, suggests the importance of understanding a culture in order to effectively counsel clients from that culture.

In this context, culture is viewed as the beliefs and practices of people within a society, including guidelines for their behavior in given situations (such as at religious ceremonies, funerals, weddings; on reaching puberty; on attaining maturity, and so forth). Human development is dependent upon environmental characteristics. The characteristics of the environment that have been developed by the past inhabitants of the environment constitute the culture with which a person interacts. That culture provides people with their initial values, behavioral guidelines, and expectancies for the future. As just noted, the self-concept is central to the study of personality and behavior by psychologists and sociologists, and the study of anthropology contributes through an understanding of the nature of self as culturally defined. We also view ourselves as influenced by the perspective we have of self in relation to culture. The study of anthropology alerts us to the fact that personality, as it develops, seeks to prepare the individual for living in his or her culture and, by the same token, that a culture functions only through the personalities of those who constitute it, which thus enables predictions regarding overt behavior on the basis of a knowledge of a culture and its traditions.

Today, we are aware that different subcultures often have different values and life-styles. For example, counselors should be able to understand the lifestyles and values of such populations as African Americans, Native Americans, Asians, Hispanics, Jews, Poles, and others. It is helpful not only to be able to function free of ignorance in helping relationships with clients from various backgrounds, but also to interact without prejudice and bias.

Finally, and related to the study of both anthropology and sociology, we note an increased interest in the field of counseling on cultural and environmental influences on events. In this regard, Blocher and Biggs (1983) described the movement beyond the traditional community mental health approaches to one that examines relationships between human beings and their environment. They suggest that (a) human beings are characterized by a basic and inherent drive toward competence or mastery of an environment, and (b) the development of competence needs to be studied as it occurs in natural settings.

Economics

Economics is a science that studies human production, consumption, and distribution. Its significance in the creation of status and influences on our wants shapes many of our behaviors. Economics is another social science concerned with individual behavior and human relationships. Economists' concern is with people living in various types of economic systems. Economists, like sociologists, are concerned with one's economic position, the socioeconomic status of people in a society. Economic attainment interacts with other factors in a culture to determine status. This socioeconomic status can be significant as a determinant of client feelings, attitudes, behavior, and so forth.

Three major socioeconomic strata have been identified: upper, middle, and lower class. Within each of these levels are three sublevels of upper, middle, and lower (e.g., lower middle class). The most reliable indicators of assignment to a status are income, education, occupation, and geographic location. Because the economic environment in which people live is so closely interwoven with nearly every activity in which counselors engage, we cannot be uninvolved in this area.

C. Gilbert Wrenn (1962) noted the importance of economic learning to counselors when he comments that "the school counselor cannot afford to be a graduate student in psychology and a second-grader in economics" (p. 42). For the counselor, understanding the influences economic systems and theories have on career choices can be meaningful. In addition, the impact of economic systems on human behavior should not go unnoticed by counselors who propose to assess human behavior. The influence of the socioeconomic level of the home on the self-concept of the developing child is also of concern to the counselor.

Interdisciplinary Implications for Counseling

The preceding sections presented a brief overview of perspectives from other disciplines. From these perspectives, implications can be drawn that have relevance to counselors and their functioning in a variety of settings:

1. Counselors must reflect a greater awareness of the various cultures that may be represented within the client population they are hoping to serve.

2. To be effective and relevant, counselors must increase their understanding of the language that is vital to communicating with different cultures, which results from living in one culture and learning in another, the role expectancies of cultures, and cultural biases in schools and other basic institutions that create tensions, hostilities, and distrust among subcultures.

3. Counselors must have an understanding of the social structures of the communities and institutions within which they function. They must also recognize the impact of these and other social structures on how individuals view themselves, their work, education, and other experiences.

4. Counselors must recognize that behavior is a function of an individual's interaction with his or her environment.

5. Counselors must recognize the potential relationships between clients' socioeconomic characteristics and their behaviors and concerns.

6. Counselors should acquire a deeper understanding of the various societal influences on behavior, growth, and development of the individual based on an interdisciplinary approach.

7. Counselors must function more effectively as consultants. In this capacity, the counselor has the opportunity to interpret the social and cultural characteristics of clients and their implications for specific programs and settings.

Guidelines for Human Assessment

Before we examine specific tools and techniques available to counselors for assessing human characteristics, we must first recognize some basic principles or guidelines. These guidelines provide a framework for effectively and professionally functioning in the sometimes delicate task of individual assessment.

1. *Each individual human being is unique, and this uniqueness is to be valued.* Although the principle of individual differences has been eulogized throughout educational and societal circles the better part of the 20th and into the 21st century, in practice, constant pressures encourage conformity and standardization. Counselors must not enlarge this gap between principle and practice but should stress the principle that assessment is a means of increasing understanding of the uniqueness of the individual, a uniqueness that sets everyone apart from all other people, that provides each person with the basis for his or her own personal worth. That uniqueness is to be valued, not standardized.

2. *Variations exist within individuals.* Each person is unique as well as distinct from others. This principle notes that individual assessment seeks to identify, for example, the special talents, skills, and interests of a person and, at the same time, forestall tendencies to generalize from a single or several characteristics of a person, such as "Anyone who excels in math can excel in anything," or "You give me an all-American in one sport and I'll make him all-American in another." Nor do we overlook the shortcomings. Although the emphasis of assessment is on the strengths and positive attributes of a person, all of us have our weaknesses—shortcomings that we must recognize if we are to overcome, bypass, or compensate for them.

3. *Human assessment presumes the direct participation of the person in his or her own assessment.* For human assessment to be as meaningful and accurate as

possible, the person must be willingly and directly involved. This involvement includes input by the client; feedback, clarification, and interpretation, as appropriate, by both the client and counselor; and evaluation by the client. This principle presumes more than the client's one-way feeding in of data, such as taking a standardized test or completing a questionnaire. It assumes her or his right to interpretation and response to that interpretation. It presumes the client's right to clarify and expand his or her response and, as others come to know the client better, to gain better understandings of herself or himself as well.

4. *Accurate human assessment is limited by instruments and personnel.* The effective utilization of assessment techniques is dependent on a recognition of the limitations of instruments and personnel as well as acceptance of their potential. These limitations begin with the human element—ourselves, our knowledge and skill in the techniques we would use. Counselors should not under any circumstances use assessment techniques, including standardized tests, in which they have not been thoroughly trained. Additionally, the limitations of clients in responding to individual items as well as instruments must be taken into account. These limitations may include an unwillingness as well as an inability to respond. In addition to these human elements, there are the limitations of the instruments themselves to consider. These include an awareness of the particular shortcomings unique to a given instrument or technique and the general recognition that any of these provide at best only a sample, only clues, not absolutes, and results that may vary among similar instruments and techniques.

5. *Human assessment accepts the positive.* A goal of human resource assessment is the identification of the potential of each person. It is a positive process that, as noted earlier, seeks to identify the unique worth of each person. Assessment can lead to the identification of worthwhile goals and positive planning. It should be a process clothed in optimism rather than, as so often is the case, fear of outcomes and predictions of doom. The counselor's own attitude becomes important in establishing a positive environment for assessment and in using results for clients' best interests.

6. *Human assessment follows established professional guidelines.* It is important for counselors, and all other helping professionals who use human assessment techniques, to be aware of the relevant ethical guidelines established by their professional organizations. These guidelines are aimed at protecting both the client and the professional practitioner. Ethical standards for counselors, which address assessment as well as other aspects of practice, are presented in Appendices E–J, M, and N.

DOING WHAT COMES NATURALLY— OBSERVATION

On any given day most of us are the subjects of informal analysis by others, and vice versa. These analysts are not among the handful of psychiatrists, psychologists, or counselors with whom we may be acquainted, but they are amateurs doing what comes naturally— observing their fellow human beings, both friend and stranger, and drawing some conclusions about the kinds of persons they are based on what is observed. Depending on what we see and how we interpret it, we may variously categorize people as executive types, models, drifters, untrustworthy, fun-loving, and so on. Furthermore, we are often prone to defend or validate our observations by noting, "I knew there was something that just didn't look right about her," or "You could tell he was a real athlete by the way he walked," and, on other occasions, calling on old cliches (many of which are sexist) as backup evidence, such as "Just another dumb blonde" or "Watch out for those fiery redheads."

When we make observations au naturel, we are, in effect, studying behavior as it is occurring in real life. Although we must recognize—and we will help you to do this—the weakness of the uncontrolled observation method, we must at the same time recognize that many important questions about a person's natural social behavior cannot be determined through a controlled or clinical approach, much less measured by standardized instruments. Counselors are also being encouraged to adopt an ecological perspective that suggests the study of behavior within the natural setting of the person being observed. As we begin an examination of the various techniques counselors use for gaining a better understanding of their clients, let us start with the most natural and popular of all these techniques: observation. As previously noted, we all employ this technique to varying degrees in drawing conclusions about others, but this is not to suggest that all observations are equally useful for human assessment. As a basis for classifying the differing approaches to observation, we make the following points.

Forms of Observation

There are three basic approaches to observation. One, as noted above, is reality observation, when we observe clients' behavior as it is occurring in a natural setting. Two is the sampling approach, when we sample the individual's behavior we wish to assess. Three is the experimental approach, when we impose specified conditions on the client or clients being observed.

Observations may also be classified by the level of sophistication and training required.

Level One: A casual observation, generally unstructured or unplanned, that will give informal impressions. This level requires little or no training.

Level Two: Observation that is planned for a specific purpose. At this level, observation is not only planned but is guided by observation instruments, such as checklists and rating scales. Some training is desired.

Level Three: Clinical level. At this level more sophisticated techniques are utilized and observation is usually under controlled conditions and conducted over a long period of time. Observers are usually trained at the doctoral level. This is usually the level at which mental disorders are diagnosed.

The American Psychiatric Association's most recent effort to categorize mental disorders, *The Diagnostic and Statistical Manual of Mental Disorders (DSM IV-TR)* is frequently used as a guideline for diagnosing mental disorders (APA, 2000). This manual contains authoritative information and "official opinions" about the range of mental problems. It provides counselors with a source of standardized terminology with which they may record assessments and communicate with other mental health specialists. The *DSM-IV-TR* is also frequently used to satisfy the demands of insurance companies. We would point out that the process of differential diagnosis identified with the *DSM-IV-TR* is a complex one that requires extensive study and preferably supervised practice. The *DSM-IV-TR* is discussed in greater detail later in this chapter.

Common Weaknesses of Observation

It has been said, "Anticipation is a wonderful thing. It often ensures that we will see what we want to see whether it is there or not." Because observation is a technique we all use frequently, it is only natural that we assume we are reasonably accurate in our observations. However, this is a misleading assumption. Observation can be one of the most abused techniques in human assessment. Let us therefore proceed to examine some of these abuses or common weaknesses, followed by suggestions for increasing the effectiveness of this valuable assessment technique.

One of the popular questions on the written examinations for drivers' licenses in many states is to ask the applicant to identify, by shape only, the meaning of the various traffic signs. Perhaps you would like to pause and test your recall of these signs, which all of us see every day:

Now compare your responses to the following answers: stop, yield, warning, information, railroad. How did you do? For many at least, this points up one of the glaring weaknesses in undirected observation:

Casual observations do not lend themselves to consistent accurate recall.

Envision yourself on the witness stand in the classical courtroom scene in which you are matching wits with the prosecuting attorney. In a fine "You are guilty" voice, the prosecutor asks, "Who were the first three people you observed on the morning of October 13 a year ago?" Some witnesses might have their recall saved by habit (the wife and kids) or a special event (the minister, a best friend, or my future in-law), but most would have difficulty recalling with accuracy and certainty the first three people they observed on that fateful day and even more difficulty in accurately describing what they were wearing. Although most of us have confidence in our ability to accurately recall what we have observed in the past, courtroom witnesses, witnesses to accidents, observers of historic or sensational events, and even news reporters are so frequently wrong as definitely to suggest that we are not so accurate in our recall of the past, especially the details, as we often assume. Another weakness of undirected observations, then, would be this:

Complete and accurate recall of undirected or casual observations tends to decrease with the passage of time.

Now assume that you are a devout sports fan. Your favorite team is involved in a close game in the final minutes when an official calls a penalty that could conceivably cost your team the game. Regardless of how flagrant that offense or the call, it would be highly predictable that you, and those supporting your team, would have observed the incident differently from the officials and the supporters of the other team. An impartial witness would note that different observers were viewing the same situation differently. Similar illustrations may occur when two different observers describe the same western desert scene as "a beautiful blending by nature of sand, greenery, and lovely hills" and "a wasteland of sand and drab plants running into bleak mountains." All of us have experienced the discrepancies that often occur as someone describes a boyfriend or girlfriend and as the same person appears to us. The point is that people differ in how they view the same event, person, or place, and also in the details they observe. We would note this as another weakness in casual and informal observations for assessment purposes.

> *Similar observations will be viewed differently because each person has his or her own unique frame of reference for interpreting what he or she sees.*

These and other shortcomings suggest that undirected and casual observations of our clients may result in incomplete, misleading, or erroneous assessments. The values and opportunities of observation in client analysis are recognized, but some guidelines and instruments must be developed for increasing the accuracy and effectiveness of this technique. Here are some guiding principles for client analysis through observation, followed by a discussion of some useful instruments for reporting and recording our observations of others.

Guidelines for Client Analysis Through Observation

1. *Observe one client at a time.* Observation for individual analysis is just that; it focuses on the person. We are intent on noticing every observable detail of client behavior that may be meaningful in the counseling context. This is just as desirable an objective for observations of people in external group settings as in the more restricted setting of the counseling office.
2. *Have specific criteria for making observations.* We observe our clients for a purpose. We are watching for characteristics of the person appropriate to this purpose. These provide a basis for the identification of specific criteria, which in effect tell us what to look for. For example, if we are observing young persons for the purpose of determining their relationships with adults, we might decide to specifically observe two criteria or characteristics of this relationship: interactions with teachers and interactions with parents. Of course, it is important that the criteria we use be appropriate to our observational objectives.
3. *Observations should be made over a period of time.* Although there is no specific time span formula for conducting observations, they should take place over a period that is long and frequent enough to establish the reliability of our observation. A single sample of behavior is seldom enough for us to say with certainty that this is characteristic of the person. An illustration of this principle is to recall how your later impressions of people often differ from your first impressions, once you have had the opportunity to observe them over a period of time. Also, although concentrated periods of observation may be appropriate, the

amount of observational time should not be confused with the span of time over which observations take place.

4. *The client should be observed in differing and natural situations.* Natural behavior is most likely to occur in natural situations. Although these situations vary somewhat among persons, for most youth, the school, home, neighborhood, and favorite recreational locales will be natural; with adults, the place one works will replace the school. Even within these natural settings, people will behave differently but naturally in different locales. For example, a student in school may behave differently in the classroom, the cafeteria, the gym, the hallways, and on the playground. If possible, therefore, clients should be observed in those settings and situations that are typical for them. Furthermore, this means a reasonable variety of those settings. For example, a school-age youth may behave one way in a certain class at school, behave another way in other classes, and exhibit completely different behavior in social-recreational settings. An adult may behave differently on the job and at home, and differently again in other social settings. Observing in these different settings may help us determine whether some behaviors are limited to or conditioned by specific environments or situations.

5. *Observe the client in the context of the total situation.* In observation for human analysis, it is important to avoid a tunnel vision approach, or one in which we are so visually intent on observing just the client that we may miss noting those interactions and other factors in the setting that cause the person to behave the way he or she does. An example might be a classroom situation in which we observe that at the conclusion of nearly every math class, Nancy always leaves in tears, but we fail to observe that her classroom neighbors Joseph and Jamal appear to tease her throughout the class every day. We have observed the results but not the cause.

6. *Data from observations should be integrated with other data.* In individual analysis it is important to bring together all that we know about our client. Because we are seeking to see the client as a whole person, we would combine the impressions we gained from our observations with all other pertinent information available to us. The case study technique used by most helping professionals illustrates this point of integrating and relating data before interpretation.

7. *Observations should be made under favorable conditions.* Anyone who has tried to witness a parade three rows back or watch a key play at a game when the crowd jumps up in front can bear witness to the importance of favorable conditions for making observations. In planned observation we want to be in a position to clearly view what we are planning to report. Ideally, we should be able to conduct our observation for a sufficient period of time without either obstructions or distractions. There are also attitudinal considerations in creating favorable conditions for observation. These include an approach that is free from bias toward the client, any projections of expected behavior, or permitting one trait to predict another. It is just as important to have a clear psychological viewpoint as a physical viewpoint for observation for individual analysis. We should also be alert to another form of bias that may occur when the person being observed modifies her or his behavior because she or he is aware of being observed.

OBSERVATION INSTRUMENTS

A variety of instruments are available to counselors for use in recording their observations. Most are designed to eliminate one or more of the common weaknesses of undirected or casual observation. They provide a means of recording and preserving an impression of what was observed—an impression that is as accurate a year later as when it was initially recorded. Additionally, many instruments for reporting observations (checklists, rating scales, observation guides) provide specific directions or traits to guide the observer. Some instruments such as rating scales also provide for some degree of discrimination among the traits observed. Because many of these instruments include definitions or descriptions of their items that users are to accept and follow, they can also form a mutual frame of reference that may promote some consistency among observers viewing the same subject. The most popular of these instruments are rating scales, checklists, inventories, and anecdotal and observation reports.

Rating Scales

Rating scales, as the name implies, are scales for rating each of the characteristics or activities one is seeking to observe or assess. They enable an observer to systematically and objectively observe a person and record those observations. Although such scales are not limited to the recording and evaluating of observations, those are the common and popular uses of the instrument.

Rating scales have long been valued as an observation instrument by counselors. They are useful as a means of focusing on specific characteristics, increasing the objectivity of the rater, and providing for comparability of observations among observers; and they are easy to use.

Designing a Rating Scale

Although commercially designed rating scales are available, counselors may find it more desirable under most circumstances to design their own. A good self-designed scale will be more appropriate for both the situation and the rater or raters, can be revised if needed, and, of course, is economical. The potential of any rating scale, however, is first determined by its design. There are five steps in designing a rating scale.

Determine the Purpose(s).   An obvious initial step is to determine the potential population and the purpose of the observations or ratings. Usually, the purposes or objectives of such an instrument should be limited in both number and scope. This tends to prohibit the development of scales that are too lengthy and overlapping and that discourage user completion. Scales that are clear, concise, and directed toward limited and precise objectives also increase the likelihood of accurate responses.

Identify the Items.   Once the purposes or objectives of the scale have been established, the developer next identifies appropriate criteria or items to be rated. These items should be clearly and directly related to the objectives of the observation. Also, they should be easy to understand, observe, and assess.

Identify the Descriptors.   Although there is often a subtle difference between items and descriptors, it is important to honor this difference. Items may not be ratable, so descriptors are used to effect a transition between an identifying item or statement and an objective description. An example of an item could be "appearance," and an example of a descriptor could be "neat and well-groomed at all times."

Identify Evaluators.   As the label implies, evaluations or ratings in some kind of a scale are an anticipated characteristic of this particular technique for making and reporting observations. A variety of options can be used for this purpose, such as the number of intervals or points on the scale, the defining of the evaluators, and deciding whether to provide space for comments.

Determine the Format.   A part of the format will be determined by the identification of evaluators, as described in the previous step. Additionally, related items are usually grouped together; the length—not too long—and the directions for completion will all be items to attend to in determining the final format for the instrument.

Limitations of the Rating Scale

Limitations in using rating scales are basically those to which all instruments administered and developed by humans are subject—the limitations of the instrument and the limitations imposed by the user. The most common instrument limitations are (a) poor and unclear directions for the scales' use, (b) inadequately defined terms, (c) limited scales for rating, (d) items that tend to prejudice how one responds, (e) overlapping items, and (f) excessive length.

The limitations that raters impose are equally prevalent and can be even more serious, because they can distort or misrepresent the characteristics of a person. The following are common examples:

1. *Ratings made without sufficient observations.* Many raters have an apparent need to complete all the items on a scale and, as a result, will take a stab at items with which they are unfamiliar. Others, in their haste to complete the scale, will make a rating on the basis of limited observation.
2. *Overrating.* There is a growing conviction among those who frequently use rating scales that overrating is a common practice among raters. For example, a recent review of rating scales used in conjunction with admissions to graduate work in a Big Ten university revealed that all 324 candidates were rated "considerably above average" or higher in three categories: appearance, social skills, and leadership.
3. *Middle rating.* Another group of raters appear to play it safe by using only the average or middle categories on a scale, thus avoiding either extremes of high or low assessments. Such ratings tend to misrepresent everyone as being just about average in everything.
4. *Biased ratings.* In addition to personal bias, bias may occur in ratings when raters permit one item that they particularly value or emphasize to set a pattern for the rating of other items.

Although the focus of this discussion has centered on the utilization of rating scales in reporting observations, such scales are not limited to only this application. Rating scales are also used extensively by counselors and others for performance ratings, evaluations (both personal and institutional), and measurement of attitudes, aspirations, and experiences. Example 7-1 is a rating scale for identifying potential school dropouts.

EXAMPLE 7-1 DEVELOPING THE RATING SCALE

The Beatty-Tingley High School has a history of high incidence of pupil dropout before graduation. The problem has become particularly severe in the past 3 years, and various remedial efforts have had little effect. The school board has therefore determined that a concerted effort will be made to identify potential early leavers and then to design possible preventive measures. The counseling staff has been requested to design an instrument that will lead to the identification of these potential early leavers through the observation of certain behavioral traits. They proceeded to develop a rating scale by first stating the purpose as follows:

Purpose

1. To identify potential dropouts

Following a review of relevant research, the counselors agreed on four possible criteria of potential school leavers:

1. Interest in school
2. Relations with peers
3. Relations with teachers
4. Coping styles

Having identified criteria, they next had to agree on descriptors appropriate for the designing of items on the rating scale. These were determined to be as follows:

1. *Interest in school:* attention in class, participation in class activities, preparation for class
2. *Relations with peers:* frequency of interaction with peers, nature of interaction with peers, attitude of peers, friendships with peers
3. *Relations with teachers:* frequency and nature of interaction with teachers, attitudes toward teachers, attitudes of teachers
4. *Coping styles:* problem-solving skills, dealing with frustration and failure, work habits

They then began designing the rating scale. The first items were designed to assess the interest of students in their classes.

Interest in School (check most appropriate category)

Class attention:

Consistent and general alertness to ongoing activities in the subject matter class	Never	Rarely	Sometimes	Usually	Always
	Comments:				

Class participation:

Quality of participation: knowledgeable and appropriate contributions and interactions	Poor	Below Average	Average	Superior	Excellent
	Comments:				

Frequency of participation:

	Never	Seldom	Occasionally	Often	Always
	Comments:				

Preparation for class:

Readiness in terms of reading and other assignments for meaningful participation in class	Never	Seldom	Occasionally	Usually	Always
	Comments:				

Checklists

Another instrument that may be used for recording observations is the observer checklist. This instrument is typically designed to direct the observer's attention to specific, observable personality traits and characteristics. It is relatively easy to use as it not only directs the observer's attention to certain specific traits but also provides a simple means of indicating whether those traits are characteristic to the person being observed. Unlike the rating scale, the observer checklist does not require the observer to indicate the degree or extent to which a characteristic is present. Figure 7-4 shows an example of a simple form of a checklist.

Inventories

Self-report inventories are also a popular technique for acquiring knowledge about clients. Most inventories consist of structured questions or statements to which the respondents will give an objective response. Counselors will then review the client's responses with the client, often asking the question "Why did you respond as you did to this question?" Inventories may be designed to focus on a single aspect of a client's behavior or they may be

Observation Checklist

Personal characteristics of _____
                                                            (name of student)
Observed by (name or code) _____
Periods (dates of observation): from _____ to _____
Conditions under which student was observed: _____

_____

Instructions: Place a check mark in the blanks to the left of any of the following traits you believe to be characteristic of the student.

Positive Traits	Negative Traits
_____ 1. Neat in appearance	_____ 16. Unreliable
_____ 2. Enjoys good health	_____ 17. Uncooperative
_____ 3. Regular in attendance	_____ 18. Domineering
_____ 4. Courteous	_____ 19. Self-centered
_____ 5. Concerned for others	_____ 20. Rude
_____ 6. Popular with other students	_____ 21. Sarcastic
_____ 7. Displays leadership ability	_____ 22. Boastful
_____ 8. Has a good sense of humor	_____ 23. Dishonest
_____ 9. Shows initiative	_____ 24. Resists authority
_____ 10. Industrious	_____ 25. A bully
_____ 11. Has a pleasant disposition	_____ 26. Overly aggressive
_____ 12. Mature	_____ 27. Shy and withdrawn
_____ 13. Respects property of others	_____ 28. Cries easily
_____ 14. Nearly always does his/her best	_____ 29. Deceitful
_____ 15. Adjusts easily to different situations	_____ 30. Oversolicitous

Comments: _____

_____

_____

_____

Figure 7-4   Observation checklist.

broadly constructed to reflect a range of characteristics. For example, self-report inventories are often used to assess self-concept, study habits, and attitudes.

Anecdotal Reports

Anecdotal reports, as the label implies, are descriptions of a client's behavior in a given situation or event. Such reports are subjective and descriptive in nature and are recorded in a narrative form. Often a counselor will collect several of these reports, which then become an anecdotal record of a client's behavior over a period of time or situations.

Design of Anecdotal Records

The format for anecdotal records usually consists of three parts. They are (a) the identifying data recorded, (b) observations reported, and (c) comments of the observer. This format has several variations, as may be noted by examining three different designs for anecdotal records. Figure 7-5 presents a format that follows in sequence the three parts previously identified. Figure 7-6 alters this format to provide space for comments alongside that are appropriate to particular statements of the anecdotal description. Figure 7-7 provides space for comments of additional observers, if desired.

Using the Anecdotal Reporting Method

The first consideration in anecdotal reporting is the selection of incidents that may be significant to report. There may be incidents that are typical of a client's behavior and are relevant for the counselor's or client's better understanding of the client. There may also be incidents so atypical of the client's behavior that their reporting and understanding may be advisable. In some situations, a series of anecdotes reporting similar behaviors over a period of time would increasingly suggest that the observed characteristics are typical of

Anecdotal Report Form
Henry H. Higgins High School

Name ____________________ Observed by ____________________
Where observed ____________________ When: Date ____________________
Time __________ to __________

Description:

Comments:

Figure 7-5 Anecdotal Record: Form A.

Anecdote	Return to: Counseling Offices Basile Elementary School
Student's name	

Description of incident observed	Comments:

Observed by _____

Time _____   Place _____

Figure 7-6   Anecdotal Record: Form B.

Anecdotal report for Name   Date Situation
Description
Comments: Observer:
Comments: Observer:

Figure 7-7   Anecdotal Record: Form C.

the client's behavior. Different observers making similar observations of a client's behavior on a specific occasion, or over time, would have similar implications. Also, anecdotal reporting covering a period of time may identify trends or changes in client behaviors.

In school settings, teachers may be encouraged to use anecdotal reports in calling counselor attention to students who may need their assistance or in contributing to case studies or just a better understanding of individual students. Example 7-2 illustrates uses of anecdotal reporting in school settings, as well as the counselor's interpretations of these reports. Example 7-2 also illustrates how a series of anecdotes can lead to the identification of a student in need of counseling assistance. In some situations, however, even a single anecdote is enough to alert the counselor to a person in need of assistance.

EXAMPLE 7-2   USES OF ANECDOTAL REPORTING IN SCHOOL

Student's Name:	Therese
Incident 1:	Mr. Michael
Reported by:	History teacher
Date:	January 16 (Monday)

Therese was not herself in class today. She usually is very active in the class discussions and always responds to questions when no one else seems to have the answer. However, today she sat quietly in her seat. At one point, when the discussion was bogging down, I called on Therese as always, asking her, "What were some of the factors that kept the United States from joining the League of Nations after World War I?" I could barely hear her response, but I thought she said, "Who cares?" and then in a louder voice that bordered on breaking into tears, "I'm sorry, I don't know the answer."

Teacher's Comments: Therese is one of my more mature and capable students. Something is upsetting her, and it would be helpful if a counselor could talk with her.

Student's Name:	Therese
Incident 2:	Ms. Chevez
Reported by:	Chemistry teacher
Date:	January 18 (Wednesday)

For the first time in the 2 years I have known Therese as a student, she has fallen behind in her work in my class. Furthermore, her behavior has been almost disruptive. For example, today, when one of her best friends, Ann, asked her if she could borrow a test tube from her, Therese snapped back at her, saying, "Don't you ever have enough stuff to do your own assignments? No, I'm not lending you anything anymore!" The exchange obviously was unexpected to Ann, who didn't exchange another word with Therese for the rest of the period, while Therese seemed to spend most of the period simply staring at her lab book.

Teacher's Comments: Something is clearly wrong with this girl. This behavior is not typical at all. She needs to see a counselor.

Student's Name: Therese
Incident 3:   Mrs. Kemp
Reported by: Physical education teacher
Date: January 19 (Thursday)

Today, Therese approached me before my fifth period in which she is enrolled and said, "Mrs. Kemp, I am quitting the gymnastics team and I don't want to talk about it." When I put my arm around her and said, "That's OK, Therese, I hope you're all right," she broke into tears and said, "I'll never be all right again!" and then ran into the locker room. I decided to leave her alone and didn't follow up on our conversation at this time.

Teacher's Comments: I have noted for the past couple of weeks that Therese hasn't seemed to be herself, but today things seemed to explode. I don't know what the difficulty is, but I do intend to follow up on her problem, whatever it may be, when I see her next week. Do you have any suggestions?

In this situation it is obvious that the school counselor, by the end of the week, is able to put together a picture of a young lady who is clearly upset. Although there are no indications of cause in the incidents described, the counselor has sufficient reason to either call in Therese or, through consultation with Mrs. Kemp, attempt to provide her with appropriate help.

The previous discussion illustrates how a series of anecdotes can lead to the identification of a student in need of counseling assistance. In some situations, however, even a single anecdote is enough to alert the counselor to a person in need of assistance.

Advantages Versus Disadvantages

Because anecdotal reports are designed to describe subjectively what has been observed, they become more lifelike than more objective measures. They present a broader, more complete viewpoint of a situation, which at the same time avoids the bleakness of the more quantitative or objective methods of reporting.

The major limitations of anecdotal reporting are those imposed by the observer-reporter. Most common of these are the reporting of feelings about rather than actual behavior of the person observed. The tendency to read in biases or expectancies can result in misleading reports. Overinterpretation and misinterpretation by inexperienced observers are not uncommon. Reporting insignificant, rather than meaningful, behavior can also limit the usefulness of anecdotal reporting.

Situational Observations

Situational observations are utilized to study the behavior of individuals in structured situations. For example, a group might be given a problem situation but no leader is designated. The group is then observed to see how a leader might emerge, who it will be, and also how the different members react. Schoolchildren might be observed in a study situation in which the instructor observes the individual for an announced period of time. Workers on the job might be observed with and without supervision.

Behavioral Charting

Another form of recording and reviewing observed behavior is behavioral charting or tallying. In this technique a particular behavior is observed (e.g., disturbing others, leaves work station, laughs without apparent reason) over specific time periods to determine how frequently it occurs. Figure 7-8 illustrates a reporting format for this technique.

The preceding paragraphs have discussed a variety of observation techniques and instruments. In many situations, counselors and other observers will make a decision about

For:		Ima Hummer		
		(Name of Observed)		
Observed by:	R. Whiner			
Behavior observed:	Attracts attention to herself by making disturbing noises during class work period.			
	_____			
	_____			
	_____			
	_____			
	_____			
Date(s) and time:	April 6 10 A.M.	April 7 10 A.M.	April 8 10 A.M.	April 9 10 A.M.
Place:	English Composition Class (2-hour class)			

	Times Noted	Total
Monday	╫╫	6
Tuesday	|||	3
Wednesday	╫╫ ||	7
Thursday	╫╫	5

Figure 7-8   Behavioral observation form.

which instrument or instruments are most appropriate for the observation task at hand. They may be aided in determining which type or types of instruments to use by considering the following.

1. Is some direction for recording observation(s) for individual analysis desired? (The answer to this is usually yes—or should be.)
2. Is a descriptive or objective report more appropriate?
3. Will more than one observer be reporting observations of the client (or potential client)?
4. Are assessments or evaluations of what has been observed desired?
5. Are comparisons among different clients or between client and other populations likely to be made?
6. Are opinions or impressions—not necessarily facts or factually based information—desired?
7. Does the instrument avoid complex observations and recording methods?
8. Will the instrument make it relatively easy to complete a report in a short time, even if some accuracy or depth of observation may be sacrificed?
9. Will instruments be used by counselors or others who are experienced or trained in their use?

DSM-IV-TR

The most popular diagnostic system in the United States is the *Diagnostic and Statistical Manual of Mental Disorders IV-TR* (2000), published by the American Psychiatric Association. Although the manual itself presents a standardized system of recording, the judgments on which these entries are often made will be subjective.

According to the *DSM-IV-TR,* a mental disorder is characterized as a clinically significant behavioral or psychological syndrome or pattern that occurs in an individual. Further, according to the *DSM IV-TR,* one of the following must be present to diagnose a client as having a mental disorder: distress and/or impairment and/or significant risk. Whether or not clients who present themselves for counseling have mental disorders, the multiaxial diagnosis of the *DSM IV-TR* offers counselors a way to organize the information they have on clients' symptoms, their physical conditions, their levels of coping, and the stressors they are experiencing.

Five categories called axes, are provided as guidelines for organizing client information, symptoms, physical conditions, levels of coping, and stressors being experienced. The axes and their general categories are as follows.

AXIS I	Clinical Disorders
	Other Conditions That May Be a Focus of Clinical Attention
AXIS II	Personality Disorders
	Mental Retardation
AXIS III	General Medical Conditions
AXIS IV	Psychosocial and Environmental Problems
AXIS V	Global Assessment of Functioning

The mental disorders and conditions covered in the *DSM-IV-TR* are divided into 17 categories as follows:

- Disorders usually first diagnosed in infancy, childhood, or adolescence
- Delirium, dementia, and amnestic and other cognitive disorders
- Mental disorders due to a general medical condition
- Substance-related disorders
- Schizophrenia and other psychotic disorders
- Mood disorders
- Anxiety disorders
- Somatoform disorders
- Factitious disorders
- Dissociative disorders
- Sexual and gender identity disorders
- Eating disorders
- Sleep disorders
- Impulse-control disorders not elsewhere classified
- Adjustment disorders
- Personality disorders
- Other conditions that may be a focus of clinical attention

According to the introduction of the *DSM IV-TR* (2000),

Most of the proposed literature-based changes were in the Associated Features and Disorders (which includes Associated Laboratory Findings); Specific Culture, Age, and Gender Features; Prevalence; Course; and Familial Pattern sections of the text. For a number of disorders, the Differential Diagnosis section also was expanded to provide more comprehensive differentials.

Counselors using the *DSM-IV-TR* should have special preparation and supervised experience.

SELF-REPORTING: THE AUTOBIOGRAPHY AND OTHER TECHNIQUES

Up to this point we have been discussing observation techniques for client assessment. In such techniques, clients may be aware of their being observed, but rarely are they direct participants in the process.

Some of the most valuable techniques for human assessment for counseling purposes are those that call for the active involvement of the client. These techniques not only provide special insights for the counselor but also can be valuable to the clients as they engage in a process of guided self-assessment. The use of such techniques as autobiographies, self-expression essays, structured interviews, and questionnaires can facilitate both counselor and client understanding of the client's strengths, weaknesses, and uniqueness.

The Autobiography: A Popular Genre

The autobiography has been one of the most popular forms of literature throughout the ages. Humankind has consistently been interested in the personal view people have of their own life experiences. Additionally, almost everyone, famous or obscure, has at one time jotted down a personal view of his or her life's experiences. Some hope for publication; others write only for personal satisfaction. For the majority of those feeling compelled to examine and set down in writing life's experiences, it is unlikely that the desire will coincide with a need for counseling. Nonetheless, the autobiography, even when it represents a nonvoluntary effort, can be a useful source of information to the skilled counselor. Let us briefly examine its use as a nonstandardized technique in human assessment.

Autobiography: A Different Approach

At this point it is probably appropriate to indicate that counselors should avoid the use of overlapping or similar techniques. For example, there is little to be gained in using both rating scales and observation checklists to report observations of the same type of behavior, or in using three different achievement tests to measure the same area of achievement. A feature of the autobiography is that it is different from any other technique available to the counselor, for it provides clients (or students) with the opportunity to describe their own life as they have experienced it.

The autobiography lets a person express what has been important in his or her life, to emphasize likes and dislikes, identify values, describe interests and aspirations, acknowledge successes and failures, and recall meaningful personal relationships. Such an experience, especially for the mature client, can be thought-provoking, insightful, and a stimulus for action. On occasion, the experience can also relieve tension.

The Autobiography as an Assignment

As previously indicated, there are times in most people's lives when they reach a state of psychological readiness for writing their own life story. However, because this is unlikely to occur at the time such information may be needed by a counselor, the client may be asked to write an autobiography. The counselor should explain the assignment as naturally and straightforwardly as possible, indicating how it will be helpful to both the counselor and the client in the counseling process. The counselor should also emphasize that the contents of the autobiography will at all times (within legal limits) be treated as confidential information. The counselor should indicate possible content and approaches for preparing this assignment as well. Written guidelines may also be prepared for use in such a situation. Example 7-3 is one such set of guidelines that provides the client with three possible options for preparing an autobiography.

In a school setting, the autobiography is often collected through a subject-matter classroom. It is most frequently a written assignment in an English class at the secondary school level, and in the elementary school, as a language assignment or an assignment related to the study of famous historic figures. As a classroom assignment, the autobiography should be treated in such a way that the student will regard it as a worthwhile educational experience. This suggests that it is treated as a regular assignment for a grade, although, if grades are assigned, the teacher must emphasize that one is not receiving an A or F for his or her life thus far, but rather, for the technical manner in which he or she described it in relation to the assignment.

EXAMPLE 7-3   GUIDELINES FOR PREPARING AN AUTOBIOGRAPHY

Purpose

1. To provide you with an opportunity to experience the planning, organizing, and writing of your autobiography
2. To provide you, the writer, and me, the reader, with opportunities for increased understanding, insights, and appreciations of you, the writer

Each writer may develop and work to an outline that suits his or her own style. The emphasis and detail that you give any period, event, or person will be whatever you determine as appropriate. The following are *examples only* of outlines and topics that might be appropriate for inclusion in an autobiography. (Note: I will be the only reader of your autobiography and will, of course, regard its contents as confidential.)

Example A

Part I	My preschool years
	My family, where I lived, early memories, friends, likes and dislikes
Part II	My school years
	Elementary, junior, senior high school, college, teachers, friends, subjects liked and disliked, activities, significant events, experiences, travels, concerns, and decisions
Part III	My adult years
	Where I lived, work experience, friends and family, travels, hobbies, continued education, concerns, and decisions
Part IV	The current me
Part V	My future plans

Example B

1. Significant people in my life
2. Significant events and experiences in my life
3. Significant places in my life

Example C

Start your autobiography as far back as you can remember—your earliest childhood memories. Tell about those things that really made an impression on you, that stood out in your memory, whether happy or sad. Try to include those events that you believe have affected your life, such as moving to another city or entering junior high school. As you write about the event, try to show how the event affected you, what people have truly influenced your life the most, and how they affected the way you feel and act today. Mention your hopes and plans for the future—what you hope to be doing 10 years from now, for example.

When a counselor desires that a client emphasize a certain aspect of his or her life's experiences, that should be indicated to the writer.

Limitations

The autobiography has a number of potential limitations that counselors and other users must take into consideration. For instance, many people may find the writing of an autobiography a chore; thus, it will become a brief, bleak, and usually boring document that contributes little to a better understanding of the writer. The writing ability of the author as well as the conditions under which it is written will influence the potential usefulness. Also, as with any recall-based instrument, the ability of the writer to recall past experiences accurately and in considerable detail is important. Self-insight is another important factor. The reader must also be aware of distortions that overemphasize insignificant happenings or ignore those that are important, or inject falsehoods or fantasies, which very often are descriptive of the ideal or hoped-for life experiences of a writer. Current values may also influence how an author views past experiences and associations, and these may not be consistent with the writer's present set of values; therefore, the writing could be misleading to the reader.

Interpretation

With both the advantages and limitations of the autobiography in mind, let us note possible analyses by the counselor. The counselor-reader may first of all prepare a checklist or summary form for those items that would be particularly relevant to the counseling needs of the client. In other situations, the counselor may simply summarize at the conclusion of the reading the most relevant aspects or, assuming that the copy will be for the counselor's viewing only, may underline or make appropriate notes in the margins.

Autobiographical Excerpts

Two brief excerpts exemplify significant statements that are often found in student autobiographies.

> When I moved from East Park High School to Newry High School I guess I had assumed that things would go on as usual. I had been a big wheel at East Park—you know what I mean—member of the Student Council; president of the "Jokers," the most popular boys' club in school; king of the Sophomore Stomp; member of about half a dozen other clubs; invites to all the parties and social activities that were of any importance. But at Newry, many of the clubs I had belonged to before didn't exist. There were no boys' social clubs and, try as I might, I couldn't seem to make friends that moved in the "popular" circles. A lot of the kids spoke to me and were pleasant enough, but they never thought of me at party time. I found as time went on I missed East Park more and more, and I even began cutting school so I could drive back and visit East Park while school was in session. I had been a "B" student before at East Park, but my grades really took a beating at Newry. In fact, some of the kids at Newry began thinking of me as a "dum-dum," and I know many of the teachers did.

The counselor in this instance found a significant clue in this portion of the client's autobiography to explain his poor grades and the subsequent difficulty he was having in securing college admission.

> I guess I felt like a nobody as far back as I can remember. I think maybe my mother resented me because I wasn't a girl, because when I was born she already had five boys. I know as a

kid I could never seem to do anything right, and my mother used to say I couldn't do anything right because I was a nobody. I remember that she and my Dad both began calling me "Ole No-body." Then my oldest brother, the one with the sense of humor, started calling me "N.B." (for nobody). The rest of the family thought that was real "cute" and so when I started school, and all through school, I have been called "N.B." Actually, my name is James Lucifer Laswich. But I often have to stop to think what my real name is, I'm so used to N.B. I guess one reason I am so used to it is that I just seem to fit the name "Ole Nobody" so well. I sometimes don't think there is a single teacher in this school who remembers me once I leave the class, and I know most of the kids don't. I must be the only kid in school who doesn't have a "best friend."

The case of "Ole Nobody" is another example of a significant statement in a person's autobiography that provides the counselor with clues to the client's seemingly withdrawn behavior and poor self-concept. Figure 7-9 is an example of a format that might be used to assess an autobiography.

Autobiographical Tapes

In recent years, counselors have found an innovative deviation from the usual written au-tobiography—the autobiographical tape—to be useful with some clients. The autobio-graphical tape gives the client an opportunity to describe and discuss his or her life orally. In using this technique, the counselor may first determine whether it is more likely to be useful than the written autobiography. If the tape approach is more appropriate, then the counselor should decide whether to provide the client with a structured outline to respond to or simply describe the client's life as he or she recalls it.

There may be some advantages to the autobiographical tape that will determine the cir-cumstances under which it will be used. For example, some people can express themselves better orally than in writing. Furthermore, because this method requires less preparation and effort on the part of the client, he or she may more freely present details that would other-wise be omitted. Some clients may feel that there is less likelihood that the contents of a tape give away one's secrets than a written document. Voice tone on a taped autobiography may reveal the client's feelings and emotions, and, because of the nature of recording, the autobiography by tape is less likely to be subject to client editing or censoring. Finally, for some clients, taping an autobiography is a more fascinating or innovative approach than the traditional writing experience.

There are, of course, disadvantages to taping. The usual shortcomings of the written autobiography, such as lack of recall, exaggeration, and fantasy, are every bit as probable in this approach. In addition, some clients lack the ability to express themselves clearly orally. Also, for some, the unnaturalness of this approach will be an inhibitor. Nonetheless, the taped autobiography is a tool that the counselor may wish to consider for certain clients under certain circumstances.

Self-Expression Essays

Another useful technique that counselors may want to employ on occasion is the self-expression essay. This technique seeks to solicit the client's response, usually in a short, written essay form, to a particular question or concern. The objective of this technique is to

```
┌─────────────────────────────────────────────────────────────┐
│  Autobiography of _____   │
│  When written (date) _____   │
│  Required assignment _____  Other _____   │
│  Reviewed by (date) _____   │
│  Purpose _____   │
│  _____  │
│  _____  │
│  Significant events _____   │
│  _____  │
│  _____  │
│  Periods or topics omitted _____   │
│  _____  │
│  _____  │
│  Periods or topics overemphasized _____   │
│  _____  │
│  _____  │
│  Possible distortion _____   │
│  _____  │
│  _____  │
│  Other comments _____   │
│  _____  │
│  _____  │
└─────────────────────────────────────────────────────────────┘
```

Figure 7-9   Autobiographical review form.

elicit spontaneous, uncensored responses to a topic or topics relevant to the counseling needs of the client. Examples of appropriate topics would include these:

> My biggest concern is . . .
> I'll bet you don't know that . . .
> I value . . .
> My future plans are . . .
> My job is . . .

It should be emphasized that such documents can elicit positive responses as well as descriptions of possible problems or concerns. Example 7-4 illustrates a positive response.

EXAMPLE 7-4   A SELF-EXPRESSION ESSAY: MY SCHOOL PROBLEM

My school problem is that I have no problem! Look at us! We have a beautiful school and, just my luck, a great faculty. We can't seem to lose more than once or twice a year in any sport. The greatest gang of kids go here and the crowning blow—even the food in the cafeteria is edible. So I have a problem because I'm a natural born griper—I'm at my best when I can complain—I have a feeling of accomplishment when I can point out the weaknesses of others. I used to have a field day before I came to Lee Street High. Now I'm dejected because I'm not rejected.

To help solve my problem I suggest that:

1. The students get busy and deface the school, mark up the restrooms, pull out the shrubbery, and all the other things that make a school more homelike.
2. The faculty get busy telling us how stupid we are, that they quit treating us like humans (I actually feel superior to my dog now), and that they get back in the old game of teacher versus student to the bitter end.
3. Our teams lose a few more games, and that our coaches get rid of their coats and ties and wear baggy sweatshirts and swear loudly at the officials so they won't be mistaken for ladies and gentlemen, and that our student body do something pronto to get rid of that disgraceful "good sportsman-ship" trophy.
4. The students start forming cliques, avoid welcoming newcomers, and in general act more like adolescents than young adults. Oh, yes, we need a few more "kookie" dressers also.
5. Finally, the school cafeteria manager go copy the menus and recipes from some other schools (mashed potatoes should always be served cold, and lumpy gravy should taste like glue, and fried chicken served stringy and dried out).

The Self-Description

The self-description is another client-participation tool that enables the counselor to see the client through the client's eyes. The person is requested to "paint a picture of yourself in words," in one page, if desired.

Such a portrait may share whatever aspects the client wishes to have the reader know. It is usually desirable to do this in the early stages of counseling to give the counselor an additional means of getting to know the client. This differs from the self-expression essay because the self-description is a person's view of himself or herself, as indicated in Example 7-5; conversely, the self-expression essay may describe an individual's attitudes toward activities, events, and beliefs.

EXAMPLE 7-5 EXCERPTS FROM SELF-DESCRIPTION ESSAYS

Sample 1

I would describe myself as a pleasant and amiable person. Others remark about my easygoing manner and happy-go-lucky personality. Honesty is a virtue I hold very dearly, and I perhaps trust others equally, thinking that they have my virtues.

My mother had always taught me that I should be conscious of others' feelings and do my best to please them. I went for many years applying this philosophy, yet found that others were not as conscious of my feelings. This led me to be hurt and used by others emotionally and mentally. I had to almost retrain myself to believe that thinking of myself was not altogether selfish and at times is the only way to think in order to lead a happy life.

Counselor's Notations: The counselor would no doubt notice the section of this self-description that indicates the client has been hurt and used by others emotionally and mentally. Also of interest to the counselor is the client's statement, "I had to almost retrain myself to believe that thinking of myself was not altogether selfish."

Sample 2

I believe that a person should not be too overtly predictable but should possess a consistency of covert thought and feeling. I do not mean to say that I delight in the misconceptions of those who wish to categorize or predict the responses of others. I am not one to purposely masquerade, or, for some reason, to mislead those I work or come in contact with. But oftentimes an unpredictable action, comment, or response will reveal or trigger a surprising reaction on the part of an eager conversationalist. I do not become close to many and am not always patient enough to seek out the best points of my peers or colleagues. My point of view has been said to be too sensitive at times, but I like to think that my increased sensitivity allows me to take a deeper breath of life and enjoy what beauty I may sense.

I am idealistic, serious, extremely concerned about those who need help, and a good listener.

Counselor's Notations: The counselor reading this self-description might note the fact that the client keeps his or her distance from colleagues and is considered at times to be overly sensitive. This self-description is of interest, too, for the writer's description of interactions with his or her peers.

Self-Awareness Exercises

Many people pride themselves on their self-control, their ability to put their feelings aside and deal in a practical manner with the situation at hand. Others simply find it difficult to express their feelings openly to others, as, for example, the often dramatized shy young man who never can work up the courage to tell his true love that he cares for her. At the other extreme we can identify those who may express their feelings openly in such a way as to be harmful to their personal relationships with others. Even in these extremes, they are often unaware of how their expressions of feelings and emotions may be handicapping rather than helping their relationships with others.

Self-awareness exercises are designed to help people become more aware of their feelings, emotions, and values as a step toward more effectively expressing their emotions, feelings, and values. Examples of self-awareness exercises are Exercises 7-1 and 7-2.

EXERCISE 7-1

This exercise is designed to help you increase your awareness of how the expression of feelings/emotions affects your relationships with others. There are no right or wrong answers, so you should react to each statement as honestly as you can, recognizing that "who" and circumstances might alter your response in actual situations.

Use the following scale:

1 = Very annoying
2 = Somewhat bothersome
3 = Doesn't usually bother me
4 = Feel OK
5 = Will probably feel very positive

Indicate in general how you feel about persons who

1. Shout at you in anger   ____
2. Slap you on the back in greeting you   ____
3. Cry in your presence when reading a "sad" book or newspaper item   ____
4. Talk in a very loud voice when they are frustrated or upset   ____
5. Laugh easily and often   ____
6. Are silent and moody when they are mad   ____
7. Are silent and moody when they are sad   ____
8. Are silent when they are disappointed   ____
9. Become emotional whenever things go wrong   ____
10. Become emotional whenever something nice happens to them   ____
11. Never show any emotions   ____
12. Are inconsistent in their open displays of emotion   ____

EXERCISE 7-2

Indicate how you usually manage your emotions using the following scale:

1 = Express my feelings openly
2 = May express my feelings openly to close friends or family
3 = Would modify my expression of feelings so that they would not convey the real intensity of the emotion I'm feeling
4 = Would keep my feelings to myself

1. I think something is funny but I doubt that others may see it that way.
2. I am very disappointed at not achieving a level or a goal I had hoped to.
3. I am very angry as a result of a great inconvenience caused me by the actions of another person.
4. I am frustrated by unnecessary delays and "red tape" in completing an assigned task.
5. I am awarded a great and unexpected honor.
6. I am saddened by a close personal loss.
7. I am a participant in an exciting event or activity.

In reviewing your responses to the items listed in Exercises 7-1 and 7-2, can you identify circumstances under which emotional expressions directed at you by others or your own emotions affect how you interact with others?

Diaries and Daily Schedules

As with the autobiography, many of us have kept a diary from time to time. We may recall how we bared our soul in those secret pages, often protected with a little tin lock, that if reread today might help us better understand some of our present behavior and attitudes. Probably today's clients are no more willing than their predecessors to share such recordings, but when a client willingly maintains and shares diary entries with the counselor, they can provide valuable insights into understanding the client and his or her concerns. Some clients will find it easier to present some aspects of their behavior and experiences in writing than in oral communication and, if so, the counselor may decide to suggest keeping a diary for a period of time.

Another technique for systematically recording the client's daily activities is the daily schedule. This is a simple listing, usually an hour-by-hour accounting of a client's daily activities. This technique can help the counselor and client understand how the latter is organizing her or his time. Whereas the diary is usually a summary of the day's activities, often with feelings and interpretations, the daily schedule is a more objective presentation of the day's activities. Figure 7-10 presents an example of the less familiar of these two instruments, the daily schedule.

Questionnaires

The questionnaire is an extremely popular nonstandardized instrument with which all of us have had many encounters. Questionnaires appear to be a part of the American way of life because they are constantly used to inventory public reactions, solicit opinions, predict needs, and evaluate a wide range of commodities, services, and activities. This popularity does not, however, belittle their importance as an instrument for the economical collection of data from individual clients or groups of clients.

The questionnaire has a variety of uses for the counselor. In a broad way, it obviously provides an easy way to collect a great deal of information that may be useful in further understanding the client. Also, the questionnaire is a client-participation technique that promises opportunities to advance the self-understanding, at least under some circumstances, of those completing it. More specifically, questionnaires may be designed in such a way as to collect specific types of information related to specific needs of the counseling

Diary for _____ Week of _____

Morning	**Afternoon**	**Evening**

Monday:
6:45   Get up
8:00   Leave for school
8:15–12:15   School

12:15–1:00   Lunch in school cafeteria
1:00–3:30   More school
4:00   Get home
4:00–5:00   Loaf around with friends
5:00–5:30   Go to store for Mom
5:30–6:00   Read evening paper, mostly sports

6:00–7:00   Dinner
7:00–8:00   Watch TV
8:00–9:30   Study English and history
9:30–9:45   Take dog for walk
9:45–10:15   Study French
10:45   Bed

Tuesday:
Same as Monday

12:15–12:45   Lunch in school cafeteria
12:45–1:00   Talk to Mr. Leonard
1:00–3:30   Classes
3:30–4:30   Work on chemistry experiment
4:45–6:00   Get home, read paper, listen to CDs

6:00–7:00   Dinner
7:00–8:00   Watch TV
8:00–8:30   Study English and chemistry
8:30–9:00   Watch favorite TV program
9:00–9:30   Study English and chemistry
9:30–9:45   Phone call
9:45–10:15   Study French
10:15   Bed

Wednesday:
Same as Monday

12:15–1:00   Bring lunch; eat in Mr. Leonard's class and watch experiment
1:00–3:30   Classes
4:00   Get home
4:00–4:45   Study trig
4:45–5:30   Loaf around with guys who come by

6:00–6:30   Dinner
6:30–8:00   Study for history test
8:00–8:30   Watch TV
8:30–9:45   Study for history test
9:45–10:00   Walk dog
10:00–10:30   Study French
10:30   Bed

Figure 7-10   Daily schedule.

clientele. Questionnaires may also seek information that validates other data already available to the counselor. Additionally, questionnaires can help identify problems of individuals or groups, as well as their opinions, attitudes, or values. Questionnaires are a good way to collect needs assessment data as a basis for establishing program objectives and evaluation data as a basis for program improvement.

The usefulness of the instrument, however, will be determined, at least in part, by the kind of information it seeks to collect, the appropriateness of the questionnaire's design, and the skill of the person who administers it.

In questionnaire design there are certain basic considerations to keep in mind.

1. *Directions:* Indicate the purpose of the instrument and give clear, concise directions for its completion.
2. *Item design:* Design items that are clear, concise, and uncomplicated. Items should solicit only one response and should be stated in such a way that the responder will not be biased or influenced in how he or she responds. Questionnaire items should also reflect the language level of the anticipated respondents.
3. *Item content:* Questions should be designed to collect the kinds of information appropriate to the assessment purpose of the instrument. However, caution must be taken in eliciting socially sensitive, culturally restricted, or other personal-private information. Even a few such items (e.g., " Would you engage in sexual activity outside of marriage?" "Have you ever thought of committing a crime?") can arouse resentment or suspicions of some respondents that will affect their response to the total questionnaire as well. Although unsigned questionnaires may secure reasonably accurate group responses to a sensitive topic, the counselor will find such unidentified responses of considerably less value in individual counseling.
4. *Length:* A final consideration, obvious but important, is the length of the questionnaire. Often, we receive questionnaires of such length that we are discouraged from even beginning them. Clients and student populations are no exceptions in their reactions to lengthy questionnaires. Such instruments must be of reasonable length if they are to facilitate the data collection for which they are designed.

Structured Interviews

Another basic and popular technique for increasing a counselor's understanding of the client is the structured interview. This approach not only provides opportunities for client observation under certain controlled conditions, but, equally important, enables the counselor to obtain specific information and to explore in-depth behavior or responses. Interviews that are structured are usually planned to serve a particular purpose. Once the purpose has been clearly specified, questions are designed that are suitable to achieve the goal or purpose of the interview. These questions are usually arranged in some sort of a logical sequence, although the interviewer must be so flexible as to alter both the nature and sequence of the questions as circumstances suggest.

Although the basic principles of counseling apply to the one-to-one interview (see Chapter 4), it is appropriate at this point to note that the interviewing process and setting, to be successful, should be as natural as possible, not anxiety producing. Because the interviewing setting and process may be comfortable to counselors, they may, on occasion, forget that for the interviewee unfamiliar with either, it can be a frightening experience. Perhaps if you recall your own experiences when called in for an income tax audit by the Internal Revenue Service or when interviewed for a first job, you can appreciate a client's wariness. One must also recognize the possible existence of such human qualities as client forgetfulness, exaggeration, or trying too hard to give the right answer as limitations in some structured interviews.

For an example of a structured interview, let us go again to the Beatty-Tingley High School (Example 7-1) and its high school dropout problem. Once potential dropouts had been identified through combining the rating scale with other data, the counseling staff decided to conduct structured interviews with those students who were willing to participate. The purpose of these interviews was to further explore students' views and attitudes about school in relation to their educational and career planning. The counselors then proceeded to structure the interview as follows:

Structured Interview

(Give an introduction and explain the purpose of the interview, describe how we will proceed, and answer any questions.)

1. First, tell me how it has been going for you in school this year.
   What have been the best things about school this year?
2. What have you disliked the most about school?
   How do you spend your time when you're not in school?
3. Have you ever thought of dropping out? If so, what would you plan to do then?
   How could school be made more enjoyable for you?
4. Let's talk a little about your future—what are your job or career plans? (Follow up with questions regarding reasons of choice: long-range goals and further education.)
   Are there any questions you'd like to ask me? Anything else you'd like to say?
5. (Conclude.)

You will note that an initial explanation is made of the purpose and procedures of the interview. Also, the questions are structured in such a way as to elicit discussion rather than a yes or no response. Of course, the interviewee is given the opportunity to ask questions or make additional comments before the interview is terminated.

In many agency or clinical settings this process may be referred to as a *diagnostic interview*. In these settings the large number of individuals served often necessitates some form of diagnostic workup. Many agencies will use a separate diagnostic interview, removing the diagnostic from the counseling process. As noted earlier in this chapter, clinical guidelines such as the *Diagnostic and Statistical Manual of Mental Disorders-IV-TR* may be used for this purpose.

Intake Interviews

Initial interviews with clients in agency and most other counselor settings are usually referred to as "intake interviews"—or sometimes history interviews. (History interviews are designed to collect facts about the client's life in a systematic way.) The intake interview is a part of the assessment process, when the counselor is seeking information regarding the client's concerns, current status, and perhaps certain personal traits. An assumption behind the intake interview, according to Cormier and Hackney (1999),

> is that the client is coming to counseling for more than one interview and intends to address problems or concerns that involve other people, other settings, and the future, as well as the present. Most counselors try to limit intake interviews to an hour. In order to do this, the counselor must assume responsibility and control over the interview. (p. 66)

A suggested outline by Cormier and Hackney (1999) covers the following major data-gathering topics:

- Personal identifying data
- Presenting problems, both primary and secondary
- Client's current life setting
- Family inventory
- Personal history
- Description of the client during the interview
- Summary and recommendations (pp. 66–68)

GROUP ASSESSMENT TECHNIQUES

Group guidance and counseling techniques were discussed in greater detail in Chapter 5, but it is appropriate in this chapter dealing with nonstandardized assessment techniques to review briefly the techniques for assessing the roles and relationships of individuals in groups. The understanding of our clients as total beings is heavily dependent on understanding their group associations. Groups are a natural form of human association. In today's world, the hermit is an almost extinct species; persons are no longer rugged individualists, going it alone. Group associations are natural, and all of us belong to many different and diverse groups. For example, some of us may, within a brief period of 24 hours, associate with our family group, our work group, our social recreation group, a civic group, political group, and church group. In each of these settings, the roles and relationships are significant in shaping our behavior, both within and without the group.

Also, in many of these groups, an outsider would find it difficult to assess roles and relationships accurately by only a casual observation of the group. Probably you have experienced going to a party, a class, or some activity where there are in-group jokes, a history of previous group activities that precluded you, and apparent roles and relationships that you did not understand. Even experienced group observers such as teachers and counselors find it helpful to use structured assessment instruments on occasion to facilitate accurate understandings of persons in the group setting as well as group interactions themselves. The more popular of these techniques include sociograms, Guess Who? questionnaires, communigrams, and social distance scales.

Sociometric Techniques

Sociometric techniques are basic approaches for the study of social relationships, such as degrees of acceptance, roles, and interactions within groups. Sociometric instruments provide a means for assessing and displaying such information as interpersonal choices made by group members.

Although sociometric devices appear to be relatively easy to devise, administer, and interpret, these impressions are deceiving. In fact, extreme caution and careful planning and analysis should be prerequisites to the use of these methods. In determining the appropriateness of conditions for using sociometric analyses, consider the following.

1. *The length of time the group has been together.* The longer the group has existed, the more likely it is that the data collected will be meaningful.
2. *The age level of the group.* A general rule of thumb is that the older the participants, the more likely it is that the information provided will be reliable. J. L. Moreno, the acknowledged founder of modern sociometry, hypothesized that social cohesion develops with age (Moreno, 1960). He reports the cohesion of groups of children up to the age of 6 or 7 to be poor and weak; the cohesion of groups formed by children from 7 to 8 years to age 14 to be relatively high; and the cohesion of groups formed by youths between the ages of 14 and 18 to have become stabilized.
3. *The size of the group.* Groups that are too large or too small will provide less valid information. It is also important to remember that all members of a group must be included in any sociometric studies.
4. *The activity provides a natural opportunity to secure responses.* In order for group members to participate willingly and honestly in sociometric analysis, the group activities should appear logical and meaningful to the members. "What gives every sociometrically defined group its momentum is the 'criterion,' the common motive that draws persons together spontaneously, for a certain end" (Moreno, 1960, p. 97).
5. *The group chosen for study should be appropriate to the informational needs of the counselor.* For example, if it is a school counselor seeking to identify the causes of behavior problems in a given classroom, the observation of this same group of students in, for example, a recreational setting outside the classroom would not be as appropriate.

Constructing and Administering the Sociometric Test

From a construction standpoint, the sociometric test or inventory is a very simple instrument. The basic and most important aspect of its construction is the nature of the grouping situation, or criterion, on which it is based; unless the criterion is appropriate to the participants' ages, activities, and actual opportunities for association, the elicited responses will have little sociometric value. More specifically, a criterion or situation must be selected to elicit participants' choices that, when applied, will have practical significance, and to maintain the confidence of those participating, as previously noted, the results must be applied. Examples of school situations that lend themselves well to sociometric studies include assigning students to various committees, setting up small study groups, and organizing class projects. In these cases, and in many others, the selection of associates could appropriately be made by the participants themselves.

When the criterion has been determined, attention must next be directed to the number of choices the participant should make. Although the optimum number of choices has not been determined, it would appear that too few choices would not have the practical values of five or six where, for example, group assignments are to follow. It is recommended that sociometric techniques to be used with school groups contain only positive choices.

Much of the success of a sociometric test hinges upon how well it is administered. The person administering it must be respected and be on good terms with the group members. The actual administration of a sociometric test should be kept highly informal; any resemblance to a typical test situation should be avoided. The instrument itself should never be referred to as a test, nor should the group members be forewarned of its administration (in keeping with sociometric theory, which emphasizes spontaneity as an important aspect of response). For example, in a school setting, sociometric studies are more effective when the teacher merely states without prior or subsequent discussion that the class is going to engage in an activity (e.g., forming committees to give special reports) that requires small groups to be established, and that students' choice of associates is to be used as much as possible as a basis for grouping. The teacher then adds a statement about confidentiality and about the impossibility of honoring every choice of every student. Finally, the students are instructed to write their name at the top of the blank paper or card they will be given, number their paper from one to five, and list in order of preference the names of the students with whom they would like to work.

Cautions in Interpretation

The responses to sociometric questions first should be tabulated and then used to construct a *sociogram*—a graphic depiction of the interpersonal relationships existing in a group at the time a sociometric test is given to its members. A sociometric analysis of group structure requires that a sociogram be constructed. However, if each participant's relative degree of social acceptance is all that is desired, a simple count of the total responses each one receives is sufficient.

As previously noted, sociometric data must be interpreted with a great deal of caution. Sociometric techniques do not analyze or provide interpretations in themselves but rather initiate or contribute to the assessment or understanding of persons. It is also important to remember that in many group settings the choices of group members may say more about the chooser than the chosen. Finally, we should recognize that some group members may not want to be chosen; they may prefer to be alone or with a few friends in certain group settings.

Perhaps the easiest of the different kinds of sociograms to make is the one shown in Figure 7-11. This sociogram uses concentric circles in a targetlike pattern, with each student represented by a number. Only mutual positive choices are shown, and preferential rank is not considered. The highly chosen individuals, or sociometric stars, are placed in the small center circle; the sociometric isolates, students not chosen and who choose no one, are placed in the large outer circle; and all other students are placed in the area between the inner and outer circles, those more frequently chosen being placed closer to the inner circle. Sex is indicated by different geometric designs: the males' numbers are placed within a triangle; the females' numbers are encircled. For even clearer differentiation, males are confined to one side of the figure, females to the other.

The "Guess Who?" Technique

Another useful sociometric technique is the "Guess Who?" questionnaire. This technique is best used with relatively well-established groups in which members have had the opportunity to become reasonably well acquainted. It is also most effective when the questions are positive in nature rather than negative. For example, "Who is most friendly?" is a better Guess Who? than "Who is the least friendly?" The Guess Who? questionnaire provides

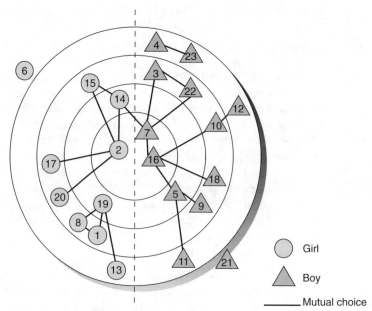

Figure 7-11 Sociogram depicting mutual choices.

for the association of characteristics or activities with individuals. It can help us understand why some members of the group receive attention, behave in certain ways, or function in certain roles. We may also be able to identify those who are popular with group members and those who receive little, if any, recognition. The Guess Who? instrument is usually designed to collect specific information that counselors, teachers, or other group observers believe would be helpful in working with the group and its individual members. Figure 7-12 presents an example of a short Guess Who? instrument.

The directions for this technique may be altered to permit participants to list all group members they believe are, for example, funny, friendly, helpful, and so on. The teachers or other group observers may use a simple tally system that notes the total number of times each group member was mentioned for each item. A popular variation in school settings is one in which pupils are asked to assume that the class is going to put on a play. They are provided with a list of characters and asked to nominate classmates who could best portray the roles described. Examples of such characters might be as follows:

> This person is known as "the arbitrator." He or she is always ready to try to prevent arguments from growing serious by suggesting compromises. He or she usually can see both sides of an argument and as a result rarely take sides.
>
> This person is known as the good humor person. She or he is always pleasant and good-natured. She or he smiles a lot, laughs easily, and rarely shows anger.

One other variation is to tell a story or describe a situation, real or fictional, in which group members are asked to assign their peers as the different characters. Consider Example 7-6.

Group _____   Date _____

Directions: Write the name of at least one but no more than two persons whom you would identify as most outstanding in your group for the trait or activity listed. Your teacher (counselor, group leader) will use the results from your responses for planning group activities. If you cannot identify a group member for an item, you may leave it blank. It is not necessary to sign your name.

1. Tells the funniest jokes or stories   _____

2. Enjoys funny jokes and stories the most   _____

3. Is the most friendly   _____

4. Is the most helpful   _____

5. Is the most sincere   _____

6. Can always be depended on   _____

7. Has the best imagination   _____

8. Is a good organizer   _____

9. Is optimistic   _____

10. Is a good leader   _____

11. Has special talents   _____

12. Is generous   _____

Figure 7-12   Guess who? instrument.

EXAMPLE 7-6   THE GUESS WHO? TECHNIQUE

Ron Bakersfield is a new student who has just enrolled in Snow Deep High School. In his previous school, Ron was an outstanding and all-round athlete, a good student, and popular with his fellow students. He is a handsome young man who dresses neatly and cleanly, but on this day he is a bit unsure of himself. He wonders whether his new schoolmates will accept him, how long it will take him to get acquainted, who his new friends will be, what his new teachers will be like, and whether he will make the teams.

The school counselor, recognizing Ron as a new student, has called in two of the more popular students in the school to meet Ron and show him around. The first to arrive is Marie Shafer, an attractive, personable girl, who greets Ron with a handshake and a big smile. The counselor suggests to Ron that Marie is known as the sunshine girl in the school because she is always smiling and has a friendly word for everyone. The next arrival is Craig Brewer, whom the counselor introduces as one of the most popular students in the school and whose hobby is photography. Craig appears also to be pleasant but a bit more reserved than Marie. With an assurance that "We'll see that Ron gets around," Craig and Marie usher him out of the counselor's office.

On the way to his first class, Ron is introduced in quick succession to Raquél, whom they refer to as "Miss Energy"; Tom, a serious student who is taking pilot lessons; Rex, who was introduced as the most interesting storyteller in the school; and Denzel, to whom they gave the label, "Mr. Reliable." At this point, Ron is beginning to feel more at home and more welcome in his new school and already sees the prospect of making some good friends with fine qualities.

After reading this brief scenario, to whom would you assign the roles of Ron, Marie, Craig, Raquél, Rex, Denzel, and Tom?

As you may have noted, the Guess Who? technique is relatively easy to use. Scoring is not complicated because a simple counting of the number of individual nominations received for each description will suffice. If both positive and negative descriptors are used, you may subtract the number of negatives from the number of positives received for each characteristic.

Communigrams

Another aspect of group observation and the group process is an assessment of the verbal participation of its members. This is perhaps the easiest communication pattern to observe and record because, in its simplest form, we are recording who talks and how often they talk over a given period of time. Figure 7-13 charts the number of participations of each member of the group with a tally mark. Each mark represents one communication, usually defined as an uninterrupted statement.

In Figure 7-14, the direction of communication among members is depicted.

Social Distance Scales

Another client participation technique that counselors may find useful is social distance scales. Most of the existing social distance or social acceptance scales devised for use with classroom or other school groups are patterned after the scale devised in 1925 by E. S. Bogardus. The Bogardus scale was designed for measuring and comparing attitudes toward different nationalities—specifically, to determine the degree to which various racial and nationality groups were accepted or rejected. Thus, social distance is usually defined by social psychologists as the distance a person indicates to exist between other persons and himself or herself. This distance is usually identified through the reaction to statements that measure and compare attitudes of acceptance or rejection of other people. The statements assessing Tommy Rott provide an example of a social distance scale.

Figure 7-13
Communigram: Participation of individuals.

Maria	~~THL~~ III	Heather	~~THL~~
Bill	II	Eduardo	III
Amy	I		

Figure 7-14
Communigram: Direction of
communication among
members.

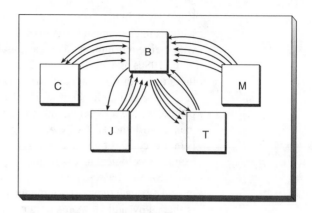

EXAMPLE 7-7   SOCIAL DISTANCE SCALE

Tommy Rott

	I would like him as a close friend	I would like him as a friend	I would like him as an acquaintance	I am indifferent toward him as a friend or acquaintance	I would prefer not to have him as a friend or acquaintance

---

Other social distance items may be built around choices such as with whom one would like to take trips, study, or go to a dance. The results from social distance scales may indicate a self social distance and group social distance. The degree of acceptance of the group by a person may be an index of self score and the degree of acceptance of the person by the group would be the group score. Many studies of social distance scales in classrooms have tended to lead to the conclusion that the greatest contribution of social distance scales is in revealing the wide range of acceptance and rejection of any one student in a group. Again, as with many other client participation techniques, there is frequently a tendency to overuse or misinterpret them because of their simplicity of administration. Counselors and other users should be aware that such information does not reveal the why of a person's acceptance or rejection of others. Furthermore, the users of this instrument must determine how they can use negative data, such as indicated group rejection, to the client's advantage.

ECOLOGICAL ASSESSMENT

In recent generations many people have become environmentally conscious. We are concerned with the preservation of our natural resources and environments, the air we breathe, the water we drink, the fruit and vegetables we eat, and so forth. Too, we note the frequency of publications suggesting the best communities in which to live, the best retirement areas, and the most healthy states. All these examples suggest what we already know: that there is an ongoing relationship between individuals and their environments. As early as 1936

Kurt Lewin, in his *Principles of Topological Psychology*, presented the field of psychology with his mathematical formula of $B = F(PXE)$ or behavior is a result of persons interacting with their environment. Whereas this formula would seem to be beyond question, it is only in the 1980s and 1990s that we have noted significant attention being given in counseling literature to this concept and the growing importance of ecological psychology.

Thus, although our traditional models of assessment have led us to focus only on people, we are now recognizing that people cannot be studied as complete entities outside their environments. As Lewin suggested, behavior always occurs in a specific setting. It is in this context then, and in this chapter discussing nonstandardized assessment, that we examine ecological assessment.

Ecological assessment is concerned with assessing how individuals orient to, operate in, and evaluate their environments. It is interested in how the individual perceives, shapes, is shaped by, and views his or her environments. In this process, counselors would seek to understand the characteristics of such significant settings as the home, school, community, and workplace and their impact on the individual, and for certain purposes (e.g., prevention programs, minority relationships), groups of individuals.

All of us seek to optimize our environmental experiences—to find the best environments that fulfill our needs and enable us to achieve our goals. The degree to which we fail to do this will, of course, influence our satisfaction with our lives and mental health. Counselors must become aware of the aspirations of their clients and the degree to which their environments are facilitating or handicapping their achievement.

In assessing an environment, counselors should note such ecological variables as the physical, geographic, and meteorological characteristics. They should become aware of the characteristics of the general population as reflected in its norms, values, attitudes, relationships, traditions, and other personal traits.

Counselors should also understand those behavior settings (institutions and agencies) that have control over the behavior occurring within them as well as those that influence external behavior. Ecological assessment would seem to stress the importance of the counselors getting out of the office and into the physical community. This will facilitate an understanding of the environments—the people, agencies, and institutions—with which her or his clients interact.

RECORDS

Someone has suggested that the first slabs of stone our prehistoric ancestors carved out of the mountains were for the purpose of setting up personnel files. It appears that systems of recording are as old as civilization and that the primary object of much that has been recorded over the ages has been the individual. Record keeping is a reflection of humans' historic curiosity to understand to the fullest extent possible their fellow humans (and just so we will not forget what we have already learned, we record it). Records are important to counselors and other helping professionals in understanding and working effectively and efficiently with their clients. It is in this context that records are discussed in the following sections.

Basic Considerations

If records or a record system are to serve their potential for client understanding and assistance, certain basic considerations need to be examined before determining the nature and characteristics of the record and its attending system. These include the following.

The Extent of Record Keeping

The ever-increasing and seemingly never-ending preoccupation with record keeping may give all of us cause to wonder how many records we actually have in our name, where they are located, for what purposes, and so on. Extensive records have been maintained by the educational institutions that we attended, for even as students we become aware of the extensive and varied recorded data that the school maintains to understand us better. Figure 7-15 rather accurately (but not too seriously) depicts the varying views to which the many records or types of data might, on occasion, seem to lend themselves.

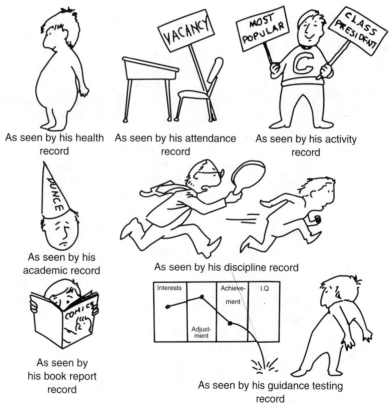

As seen by his health record — As seen by his attendance record — As seen by his activity record

As seen by his academic record — As seen by his discipline record — As seen by his book report record — As seen by his guidance testing record

Figure 7-15 "Harry High School" as seen through a multirecord system.

The advent of the computer and other technological advances have, if anything, seemed to stimulate a challenge to gather and record data in a manner befitting these new developments in data storage, manipulation, and retrieval. Nor can school counselors belittle the importance of the decisions made on the basis of such recorded data—decisions that most frequently influence career directions and educational opportunities. Counselors working with school-age clients through community agencies and other nonschool settings must also be aware of the extent and impact of school-maintained records. Additionally, counselors must be alert to the invasions created by computer hackers that threaten the security of computerized record systems in nearly all settings.

Who Will Use the Client's Record?

The answer to who will use the records varies across the many places in which counselors function. For example, counselors in private practice may, subject to legal limitations, have exclusive access to a client's records, whereas, at the other end of the continuum, many school counselors may be expected to share client records with school administrative and supervisory personnel, teachers, parents, and, of course, the client. Counselors, ever concerned with client confidentiality, must at the outset determine who legally and ethically will have access to any data recorded in a systematic or institutional manner.

The use of student and client records also raises the question of record security. The increased utilization of computerized record systems requires the exercise of appropriate precautions and restrictions to safeguard client data. Although students and parents may exercise the right to examine a student's records, that does not lessen the counselor's duty in the school, or any setting, to provide proper security for those records that are the responsibility of the counseling program. These responsibilities include provisions for the lock and key security of client records at all times, instructions and policies for nonprofessional (clerical) handling of data, and stated policies including ethical and legal guidelines for access to and review of data by clients, parents, and others. In determining access to school records, it must be noted that certain records of students are at least quasi-public in nature. The questions that arise are who may inspect such records, for what purposes, and when?

What Are Other Legal and Ethical Considerations?

Practicing counselors, as well as those in preparation, may be confused somewhat by the apparent proliferation of statements by professional organizations providing ethical guidelines for the maintenance and use of client records. However, an examination of statements by the American Counseling Association and the American Psychological Association would indicate little that is in conflict and much in general agreement. These standards are presented in Appendices F and G.

The primary legal concerns of counselors insofar as records and recording are concerned continue to focus on the confidentiality of the counseling records and the right of privileged communications. Although attorneys have possessed this right by common law over the centuries and statutory law has extended this privilege to physicians, clergy, and sometimes, psychologists, counselors have limited legal guarantee in terms of statutory provisions. School counselors must be particularly aware of the provisions of the Family Educational Rights and Privacy Act of 1974. Key statements from this act presented by Flygare (1975) point out the following:

- A student (or his parents) must be given access to his records within 45 days from the time a request is made.
- A student (or his parents) must be granted a hearing by the institution upon request to determine the validity of any document in the student's file.
- Confidential letters or statements placed in the file prior to January 1, 1975, need not be disclosed under the law.
- A student may waive his right of access to confidential letters regarding admissions, honors, or employment.
- An educational institution cannot, with certain exceptions, release personally identifiable information about students.
- Educational institutions must notify students and parents of their rights under the law. (p. 15)

The detailed provisions of this act are presented in Appendix K.

Furthermore, counselors must be aware of the implications of Title IX of the Education Amendments of 1972, effective July 1975, which provides that "no person . . . shall on the basis of sex be excluded from participation in, be denied the benefits of, or be subjected to discrimination under any education program receiving federal financial assistance" (p. 85). The implications for record keeping are clear; sexual discrimination must not be maintained. That includes standardized test results based on male/female norms, and career exploration activities and counseling that reflect sex-role stereotyping. Counselors must also avoid multicultural discriminations as well in client record keeping.

School counselors should also be aware of other kinds of unacceptable statements often found in student records. These include statements that may be libelous, slanderous, biased, negative, unverifiable, or confusing.

Counselors must bear in mind that privileged communication is for the benefit of the client. Thus, only clients have the option to waive that right and they may do so if they choose, even if protected legally. It should also be noted that privileged communications are subject to legal limitations.

Privileged communication and *confidentiality* have often been used interchangeably, even though there is a significant distinction between the two terms. *Privileged communications* refers to the right of the counselor to refuse to divulge confidential information in a court of law. *Confidentiality* represents an ethical guideline in terms of counselors' decisions that they should not and will not divulge what has been revealed to them in contacts with their clients. In this context, we should also note the probability that client and student records will be computerized. As numerous incidents have proven, the confidentiality of so-called secure computerized record and data systems has been violated time and time again. It is obviously a necessity that counselors ensure the security of all client records and record systems.

What Purposes Will the Client's Record Serve?

The use of the client's records will, of course, be determined to a large extent by the answer to the question previously raised—who are the users? There are certain traditional uses appropriate for almost all types of personnel records:

1. They provide an available pool of basic information about the person.
   - Provide a means for recording and preserving meaningful information about the person for later use

- Assist the users of the information in gaining a better understanding of the person with whom they will be interacting
- Assist the person on whom the record is maintained to gain new insights and perspectives

2. In addition, counselors use records in
   - Preparation for the counseling interview
   - The development of case studies
   - Client placement or referral
   - Consultation with other therapists, medical personnel, parents
   - Follow-up and research studies

3. School counselors also use records to identify students who
   - May be in need of counseling assistance
   - Possess special talents or interests
   - May have special needs—because of physical disabilities, for example

4. School records assist faculty and parents in gaining a better understanding of the individual student, which, it is hoped, may contribute to positive student-parent and student-teacher relationships.
   - Assist the individual student to gain self-understanding
   - Contribute to school and community needs assessments of school-age populations
   - Facilitate the orientation of new pupils.

These listings are meant to be illustrative only and not exclusive, as any practicing counselor could readily expand on them.

Record Interpretation

The interpretation of any kind of counseling or personnel record will obviously be limited by the data recorded and the skill and understanding of the user. Some guidelines or safeguards include the following:

- Records provide only clues to behavior—no more—and some clues are relevant whereas others are not.
- Does the present (the time at which you are examining the record data) compare to the past (the time when the data were originally recorded)?
- Look for trends or significant changes, but beware of the fact that many people have unique patterns of growth and development.
- Feelings, attitudes, and intensity of emotions seldom show in recorded information.
- Distinguish between symptoms and causes.
- Determine whether record data are based on substantial facts or merely represent opinions.
- Remember that records present only a small sample of the client's behavior.
- School records, especially, can also provide opportunities to examine certain habitual performance measures, such as attendance, grades, and health.

SUMMARY

Initially in this chapter standardized testing and related computerized testing programs were discussed. It was noted that these programs have become popular benchmarks for measuring the educational attainment of individuals and schools. Most of us have experienced at least the receiving end of this phenomenon. Standardized testing is also a traditional and important tool in the counselor's array of techniques for understanding the client. Despite the historic and extensive use of standardized tests, counselors and other users must be aware of the many criticisms and concerns that have been voiced regarding their use for diagnostic purposes. An understanding of these criticisms and concerns and the degree to which they are valid will enable users to administer standardized tests effectively but safely in their practices.

The importance of comprehending basic statistical processes should not be underestimated. An understanding of averages and variations from the average, as expressed in statistical terminology, and relationships as computed mathematically, is basic to the interpretation of standardized tests. The user of standardized tests also must be aware of and be able to apply the criteria for test selection. These basic criteria are the validity, reliability, and practical characteristics of the test under consideration. Strengths and weaknesses of the common areas of standardized testing should be understood. It is also important that the user recognize the limitations as well as the strengths of a given instrument if it is to be intelligently used in practice. Counselors and others may also want to consider criterion-referenced tests as a substitute or supplement to their programs of standardized testing. Counselors should be aware of the contributions other disciplines make to the understanding of human behavior. In addition, a wide variety of nonstandardized techniques for human assessment, utilized across many disciplines, is available to the counselor who is knowledgeable about their construction and usage. The last section of the chapter provided an overview of these possibilities.

The last portion of this chapter has presented an overview of nonstandardized techniques that may be used in human assessment. Although many nonstandardized techniques cannot lay claim to either the validity or reliability of standardized instruments, they nonetheless provide the counselor with a wide range of data collection options from which to choose, according to the dictates of the counseling situation and the assessment needs of the clients.

Observation was noted as the most popular of the techniques usually used to assess others; however, in order that it be as accurate and meaningful as possible, we suggested the use of some forms for recording observation such as anecdotal records and forms for further directing observations toward specific characteristics such as rating scales and checklists. In this regard, the popularity (and sophistication) of the *DSM-IV-TR* in clinical settings was noted.

Questionnaire and autobiographies were suggested as techniques in which useful information can be collected. Assessing behavior and roles in groups by techniques such as sociograms, communigrams, social distance scales, and role playing were suggested. The growing interest in ecological assessment was also discussed. There followed an examination of the role of records in human assessment and some of the legal and ethical considerations in record keeping. Assessment, both standardized and nonstandardized, can play an important role in career planning and decision making. Chapter 8 examines this important activity.

DISCUSSION QUESTIONS

1. What standardized tests have you taken? (Poll the class.) Did the results ever influence your planning or decision making?
2. How many of you have taken courses in sociology, anthropology, economics, political science, and the like, that you felt helped you understand others better? What were these courses? How were they helpful?
3. How do you feel about being "measured" by standardized tests? How do you feel about the use of standardized tests to "measure" traits of your clients?
4. Have you ever found your observations of a situation, scene, or person differing from those of

other observers present at the same time? How do you account for these differences?

5. Under what circumstances would you recommend standardized (norm-referenced) testing over criterion-referenced testing and vice versa?

6. Are you aware of or have you been involved in public controversies regarding standardized testing? If so, describe and analyze the situation.

7. What autobiographies have you read by famous people? Did any of these provide you with special insights into the writer? Why?

8. What standardized tests would you recommend, if any, to screen potential candidates seeking admission to a counselor training program? Defend your answer.

9. Have you ever kept a diary? What prompted you to keep one? Did it help you understand yourself better in any way? Discuss your responses.

10. Are there any measurement voids—areas of performances, behaviors, circumstances, and so on— for which it would be helpful to have standardized tests developed?

11. In assessment, would you prefer to have your own traits assessed by standardized tests or rating scales? Why?

12. What would you do in the following situations? (Briefly)
    a. An "honor" student makes a score of 90 on a group intelligence test.
    b. A problem and failing student makes scores at the 95th percentile on an achievement battery.
    c. Several parents call you and want to know their child's college placement test scores— also those of their neighbor's children.
    d. A student breaks his or her pencil in the middle of a timed standardized test.

13. What traits or characteristics do you observe when you meet someone for the first time?

14. What are examples of customs, folkways, mores, and laws that influence patterns of normal and abnormal behavior?

15. If you were to write your autobiography for publication, what title would you use?

CLASS ACTIVITIES

1. Develop a profile of the "normal" personality.

2. Identify someone in the class with whom you are barely acquainted. Design an observation instrument to guide your observations and observe this person for the next week. At the end of the week, discuss how your instrument has increased your understanding of the individual.

3. Develop an interest checklist that might distinguish potential counselors from those who would not enjoy careers as counselors.

4. In small groups, develop a checklist that might be used to evaluate candidates applying for admission to a master's-level counselor preparation program. Share and discuss with the class.

5. Develop test items for a standardized test designed to measure an individual's potential for entering a counselor preparation program. Administer the test to students, score in class, and discuss the process.

6. In small groups, design a rating scale to assess individual personal relationship skills. Share and discuss.

7. In small groups, members are instructed to share learnings from working, living near, and/or contacts with people from minority cultures.

SELECTED READINGS

Achenback, T. M., & McConaughy, S. H. (1997). *Empirically based assessment of child and adolescent psychopathology: Practical applications* (2nd ed.). Thousand Oaks, CA: Sage.

Duckworth, J. C., & Anderson, W. P. (1995). *MMPI & MMPI-2: Interpretation manual for counselors and clinicians* (4th ed.). Bristol, PA: Accelerated Development.

Elliott, T. R. (1993). Training psychology graduate students in assessment for rehabilitation settings. In R. L. Glueckauf, L. B. Sechrest, G. R. Bond, & E. C. McDonel (Eds.), *Improving assessment in rehabilitation and health* (pp. 196–211). Newbury Park, CA: Sage.

Ickes, W. J. (Ed.). (1997). *Empathic accuracy*. New York: Guilford Press.

Ivey, A. (1982). Towards less of the same: Rethinking the assessment process. *Measurement and Evaluation in Guidance, 15*(1), 82–86.

Miller, G. (1982). Deriving meaning from standardized tests: Interpreting test results to clients. *Measurement and Evaluation in Guidance, 15*(1), 87–94.

Ridley, C. R., Hill, C. L., Thompson, C. E., & Ormerod, A. J. (2001). Clinical practice: Guidelines in assessment. In D. B. Pope-Davis & H. L. K. Coleman (Eds.), *The intersection of race, class, and gender in multicultural counseling.* Thousand Oaks, CA: Sage.

Sodowsky, G. R., Kuo-Jackson, P. Y., & Loya, G. J. (1997). Outcome of training in the philosophy of assessment: Multicultural counseling competencies. In D. B. Pope-Davis & H. L. K. Coleman (Eds.), *Multicultural counseling competencies: Assessment, education and training and supervision* (pp. 3–42). Thousand Oaks, CA: Sage.

Vacc, N. A., Juhnke, G. A., & Nilsen, K. A. (2001). Community mental health service providers' codes of ethics and the *Standards for Educational and Psychological Testing. Journal of Counseling and Development, 79*(2), 217–224.

RESEARCH OF INTEREST

Bernstein, D. P., Kasapis, C., Bergman, A., & Weld, E. (1997). Assessing Axis II disorders by informant interview. *Journal of Personality Disorders, 11*(2), 158–167.

Abstract This study determined the diagnostic agreement between the assessment methods of obtaining diagnostic data directly through patients and through interviews with knowledgeable informants, as well as their relative contribution to the formulation of consensus diagnoses. Sixty-two psychiatric subjects were assessed directly with the Structured Interview for *DSM-III* Personality Disorders (SIDP), and were asked to nominate an informant—either a family member or friend—to provide information about the subject in an interview with the same instrument. Diagnostic agreement between subject-based and informant-based personality disorder interviews was poor, confirming the findings of two previous studies. Information obtained from subjects tended to be given greater weight in formulating consensus diagnoses than information provided by informants. However, about one quarter of diagnostic disagreements were resolved in favor of informant-based information. In contrast to a previous study, the inclusion of informant information did not appear to reveal greater psychopathology in subjects. Supplementing direct patient interviews with data provided by a knowledgeable informant appears to enhance the resolution of some personality disorder diagnoses.

Mead, M. A., Hohenshil, T. H., & Singh, K. (1997). How the *DSM* system is used by clinical counselors: A national study. *Journal of Mental Health Counseling, 19*(4), 383–401.

Abstract A mailed questionnaire was used to investigate Certified Clinical Mental Health Counselors' use and opinions of the *Diagnostic and Statistical Manual of Mental Disorders (Third Edition, Revised) (DSM-III-R).* Data collected for the study indicate that respondents use the diagnostic system for billing insurance, case conceptualization, treatment planning, communication with other professionals, meeting requirements of employers and external entities such as courts, and educational and evaluative functions. Disadvantages for using the system cited by respondents included possible negative results of its use, bias and labeling, difficulty in usage, and difficulty applying the *DSM* in marriage and family counseling. Findings of the study also indicated that respondents believe clients are deliberately misdiagnosed using the system.

Morran, D. K., Kurpius, D. J., Brack, G., & Rozecki, T. G. (1994). Relationship between counselors' clinical hypotheses and client ratings of counselor effectiveness. *Journal of Counseling and Development, 72*(6), 655–660.

Abstract A total of 27 graduate counseling students participated as counselors and clients. Counselors completed a Clinical Hypotheses Exercise Form. Clients completed the Counselor Rating Form—Short Version following sessions. Counselors able to formulate more multidimensional and comprehensive clinical hypotheses (accounting for a broader spectrum of client data dimensions) and who were able to present multiple options for testing hypotheses were judged more effective. Higher ratings were associated with more hypothesis dimensions within the clinical hypothesis statement, a higher frequency of supportive information units to substantiate the hypothesis, higher quality of the hypothesis and supportive statements, and a higher frequency of questions listed to test the validity of the hypothesis.

Ornduff, S. R. (1997). TAT assessment of object relations: Implications for child abuse. *Bulletin of the Menninger Clinic, 61*(1), 1–15.

Abstract Several recent empirical studies have documented impaired object relations in victims of childhood maltreatment. The consistency of these findings, despite sampling and other methodological differences, highlights the applicability of object relations theory to the study of abuse sequelae. This article illustrates the use of the Social Cognition and Object Relations Scales in the clinical assessment of maltreated children by applying it to selected TAT stories of a sexually abused girl, a physically abused girl, and a distressed but nonabused peer. The stories were randomly selected from a data archive that includes a social history and psychological testing data on some 300 children, all of whom were outpatients at a child guidance clinic. Results revealed impairments in object relations among maltreated children and demonstrated the applicability of the TAT and the Social Cognition and Object Relations Scales in child assessment.

Parker, G., Hadzi-Pavlovic, D., Sengoz, A., & Boyce, P. (1994). A brief self-report depression measure assessing mood state and social impairment. *Journal of Affective Disorders*, 30(2), 133–142.

Abstract A brief self-report measure of depression severity was developed that assesses mood state and functional impairment and is independent of features weighted to any one depressive type. Analyses were undertaken among 360 psychiatric patients. Mood severity and functional impairment scores demonstrated some independence among subjects. Subjects with a "melancholic" depressive type (categorized by four differing systems) differed from residual "non-melancholic" depressed patients by having higher impairment scores, but the assigned groups did not differ by mood severity scores. Advantages of the measure were summarized.

Prediger, D. J. (1994). Multicultural assessment standards: A compilation for counselors. *Measurement and Evaluation in Counseling and Development*, 27, 68–73.

Abstract This article presents a compilation of standards relevant to multicultural populations drawn from source documents of the American Counseling Association (ACA). Thirty-nine standards were identified in the five source documents. These standards are divided into four groups by assessment tasks: (a) content considerations in the selection of assessment instruments (AI's); (b) norming, reliability, and validity considerations in the selection of AI's; (c) administration and scoring of AI's; and (d) use/interpretation of assessment results. The source documents are the Code of Fair Testing Practices in Education, the Ethical Standards of the ACA, "Multicultural Counseling Competencies and Standards," Responsibility of Users of Standardized Tests, and Standards for Educational and Psychological Testing.

Ridley, C. R., Li, L. C., & Hill, C. L. (1998). Multicultural assessment. *The Counseling Psychologist*, 26(6), 827–910.

Abstract Current suggestions for assessing clients across cultures fail to adequately aid the average practitioner. This failure arises from unresolved issues and problems, interfering with the ability of most counselors and therapists to render sound clinical judgments. In response to these issues and problems, a procedure is described that sensitizes counselors to cultural data in assessment and case conceptualization. Grounded in a guiding philosophy of assessment, the Multicultural Assessment Procedure (MAP) was developed in consideration of a number of relevant critical issues. The procedure entails identifying cultural data through multiple methods of data collection, interpreting cultural data to formulate a working hypothesis, incorporating cultural data with other relevant clinical information to test the working hypothesis, and arriving at a sound (i.e., comprehensive and accurate) assessment decision. A case illustration demonstrates how to use the proposed procedure.

Sandhu, D. S., Poetes, P. R., & McPhee, S. A. (1996). Assessing cultural adaptation: Psychometric properties of the Cultural Adaptation Pain Scale. *Journal of Multicultural Counseling and Development*, 24(1), 15–25.

Abstract This article explores the psychometric properties of a newly developed Cultural Adaptation Pain Scale, using a sample of 1,932 college students. This scale is designed to assess the degree of subjective pain, social distance, and discouragement that may be related to cultural adaptation. Factor analyses revealed four factors in the scale that had an overall Cronbach's alpha of .85: Pain, Learned Helplessness, Positive Adaptation, and Bigoted. The scale was generally reliable and had face validity. Implications for multicultural counseling are discussed.

Spengler, P. M., Strohmer, D. C., Dixon, D. N., & Shivy, V. A. (1995). A scientist-practitioner model of psychological assessment: Implications for training, practice, and research. *Counseling Psychologist*, 23(3), 506–534.

Abstract This article proposes a prototype for a scientist-practitioner model of psychological assessment that integrates theory and research on human inference, judgment, and decision making; threats to accurate clinical prediction; and counselor characteristics associated with effective judgment processes. Issues related to counseling psychologists' application of research findings and use of scientific reasoning in counseling practice are explored, including implications for training, research, and practice.

Tinsley, D. J., Tinsley, H. E., Boone, S., & Shim-Li, C. (1993). Prediction of scientist-practitioner behavior using personality scores obtained during graduate school. *Journal of Counseling Psychology, 40*(4), 511–517.

Abstract   This study investigated the usefulness of personality measures obtained during graduate training in predicting the scientist-practitioner behavior of counseling psychologists. Personality scale scores on the Self-Directed Search, Strong-Campbell Interest Inventory (General Occupational Theme scores), Minnesota Importance Questionnaire, Omnibus Personality Inventory, Tennessee Self-concept Scale, and MMPI obtained during students' first semester of graduate study were used as predictors. Scientist-practitioner orientation scores calculated for participants reflected their scientist-practitioner interests, preferred job, and publication record. Only scores on the Independence scale of the Minnesota Importance Questionnaire and on the Social Extraversion scale of the Omnibus Personality Inventory were statistically significant predictors of actual scientist-practitioner orientation.

Counseling for Career Planning and Decision Making

As noted in Chapter 1, the counseling movement in the United States has had a long association with and concern for career development and decision making. This chapter introduces you to this traditional area of counselor activity. The chapter's objectives are to (a) describe specific interests in and influences on career planning, (b) present popular theories of career decision making, and (c) examine career planning and counseling in various settings.

During its early years, organized counseling efforts consisted primarily of vocational guidance. This interest, originating with Parsons, was an outgrowth of a concern for the complexity of the world of work and the resultant difficulty in career planning, a concept that is still viable today. As originally practiced by Parsons and his associates, the concept of matching youths with jobs, based on the characteristics of both, has also had a long and traditional association with the counseling movement.

As this concept was broadened and other basic activities were added in the 1920s and 1930s, vocational guidance became a service activity most frequently identified with the provision of occupational and educational information. In the late 1950s and 1960s, with the original impetus from the National Defense Education Act of 1958, placement and follow-up also became significant activities of the vocational or career guidance phase of counseling programs. Thus, for nearly 60 years the counseling movement had been the caretaker for career planning in U.S. schools and agencies.

In 1971, however, the United States Office of Education, through the Commissioner of Education at that time, Sidney P. Marland, Jr., committed more than $9 million of discretionary funds to research and development projects focusing on the establishment of comprehensive career education models. With this act, the concept of career education as an all-school responsibility was launched, and counselors were no longer the sole designated professionals for providing career counseling and guidance for students in schools.

In the 1990s, a trend emerged toward once again recognizing counselors as the priority professionals in the providing of career guidance and counseling. For example, in 1994, the U.S. Congress recognized the role of counselors in providing career assistance with the passage of the School-to-Work Opportunities Act. This act provided a framework for creating school-to-work opportunity systems in all states, with career counseling a high priority. Additional trends have included the development and recognition of career counseling specialists and the establishment of career centers serving special populations such as college students, women, minorities, and retirees. Additionally, we are seeing the extension of counseling services to the poor and the homeless, as well as to management and professional specialists who are being "downsized." Projected changes in the workplace in the immediate future will bring about further demands for career counseling in all settings.

DEFINITIONS AND CLARIFICATIONS

An outgrowth of the increased attention to career needs and the attending emphasis on career counseling and guidance has been a proliferation of definitions, with attending confusion, seeking to differentiate among such terms as *career education, career development, career guidance, vocational education,* and *human development.* In this chapter and elsewhere in this text, the following definitions apply:

- *Career:* The sum total of one's work experiences in a general occupational category such as teaching, accounting, medicine, or sales.
- *Occupation:* A specific job or work activity.
- *Career development:* That aspect of one's total development that emphasizes learning about, preparation for, entry into, and progression in the world of work.
- *Career education:* Those planned-for educational experiences that facilitate a person's career development and preparation for the world of work. The totality of experiences through which one learns about and prepares for engaging in work as part of a way of living. A primary responsibility of the school with an emphasis on learning about, planning for, and preparing to enter a career.
- *Career guidance:* Those activities that are carried out by counselors in a variety of settings for the purpose of stimulating and facilitating career development in persons over their working lifetimes. These activities include assistance in career planning, decision making, and adjustment.
- *Occupational information:* Data concerning training and related educational programs, careers, career patterns, and employment trends and opportunities.
- *Vocation:* A trade or occupation.
- *Vocational education:* Education that is preparatory for a career in a vocational or technical field.

These rather limited definitions are perhaps at one end of the continuum. For example, a career is sometimes defined as the sum total of a person's life experiences and lifestyles, whereas career education is frequently viewed as consisting of all activities and experiences, planned or otherwise, that prepare the person for work. However, straightforward and concise—although limited—definitions are most practical in specific planning for programs of career counseling development, or education.

It should also be noted, that, though differing in definition, career development, career education, and career counseling are interrelated. One without the other is ineffective and meaningless. As career education stimulates career development, career counseling provides direction for career education and development.

Counselors must also recognize that career education and complementary programs of career counseling should be developmental in nature and thus not limited to a particular age group. Career development across the life span is the appropriate theme for now and the foreseeable future.

CURRENT INTERESTS IN CAREER PLANNING

The present high level of interest in career planning was initiated when Sidney Marland made his plea for "career education now" in a speech to the National Association of Secondary School Principals at its convention in Houston in 1971. Since then, the concept has gained widespread acceptance in the educational establishment in the United States. Educators from every field and discipline have been involved in the movement. Additionally, many state legislatures passed career education legislation, and career education became a mandate of the U.S. Congress when Public Law 93-380 was signed by former President Ford in August 1974. In less than a decade, more than 10 major national associations endorsed career education, hundreds of publications on career education were published and distributed, and an astounding array of proponents and interpreters of the career education concept emerged.

Continued interest in career guidance and counseling programs was reflected in the Carl D. Perkins Vocational Education Act (Public Law 98-524) of 1984, which mandated programs designed to assist individuals in developing self-assessment, career-planning, career decision making, and employability skills. Two federal acts indicate the government's continuing interest in providing career assistance to youth preparing to enter the labor force: (a) the amendments in 1992 to the Job Training Partnerships Act, a partnership of federal, state and local agencies, with school systems, employers and their communities to help youth acquire the skills and knowledge they need to assume full participation in society; and (b) as previously noted, the School-to-Work Transition Act of 1994, which provided funding to bring together schools and their pupils, parents, communities, and their businesses to fashion America's future workforce. The latter act includes career counseling and a mandate for career exploration in schools to make the connection from school to work a realistic one. The major purpose of the act is to link what students learn in school to what they will need to know to succeed in the world of work.

In 1990, the U.S. Congress passed the Americans with Disabilities Act, which extended the prohibition of job-related discrimination (initially in the Rehabilitation Act of 1973) to all firms that employ 15 or more people. Also, the act appears to encourage equal access to counseling services for workers with disabilities.

Significant national conferences attracting professional counselors have reflected the interest and commitment of the counseling profession in a continued and major involvement in career development, counseling, and guidance. Among these convocations are the 20/20 Conference: Building Strong School Counseling Programs, held in Washington, D.C., in 1987; the National Career Development Association's Diamond Jubilee Conference, Orlando, Florida, in January 1988; and the first Association for Counselor Education and Supervision national conference in St. Louis in October 1988, which established three national task forces, including one chaired by Dr. Kenneth Hoyt, to examine national concerns in the world of work. There has also been a series of national conferences sponsored or cosponsored by the National Career Development Association including the Daytona Beach Conference of 1997 examining "Careers and Technology."

The need for this focus on career counseling became increasingly apparent in the late 1980s and early 1990s as career-related problems—youth unemployment, underemployment, mid-life career changes, and discrimination in the workplace—became major societal issues. The need for planned programs of career assistance for all ages has been further reflected in the establishment of career counseling centers on many campuses, women's (career) centers, and other community centers focusing on the special career needs of individuals as we moved into a new century.

Career development has also changed its focus. In the 1940s, 1950s, 1960s, and early 1970s, emphasis was on stage theories, in which individuals explored, made decisions about, prepared for, and entered careers by early adulthood and stayed until retirement. In recent decades, the prevailing concept has become career development across the life span. The current and projected demands of the workplace, plus the lifelong working potential of the individual, have established new career variables that include workers experiencing a variety of jobs and related educational experiences across an increasingly healthier and longer lifetime. The career development of the individual promises to be continuous and ongoing; thus, career counseling and assistance programs must be available to all ages from elementary schoolchildren to the elderly. By the same token, counselors may assist client populations in settings ranging from elementary schools to senior citizen centers to meet the needs of career development throughout life.

THE CHANGING NATURE OF THE WORLD OF WORK

In addition to the needs that prompted the career education movement and have more recently created a renewed interest in career counseling and guidance, other needs also have been generated by significant changes in some of our traditional concepts of careers and work. Symptomatic of these changes are the following points.

- **No longer one career—one's lifetime work**

    Our ancestors, perhaps even our parents, could, on identifying their life's work, enter a career that would last for life. Unlike them, more and more persons entering the workforce in the late 1990s and early generations of the 21st century will have three to seven different and significant careers over the span of their life's work. We are now living in an age in which the rapidity of technological development can affect what we do and how we do it almost overnight. Additionally, the trend toward employment of temps (employees labeled as temporary) has furthered destabilized the workforce and individual careers. Among the major disadvantages to these workers is that temps have no job security and no benefits such as health insurance and pensions—a distinct and significant departure from worker expectations in the past. Counselors are being more frequently reminded that such changes can result in increasing numbers of adults who, either by choice or necessity, will be making career decisions throughout their working life span.

- **Going, going, gone! Men-only, women-only, White-only careers**

    The influx of women into the workplace since World War II has changed "who" is working. "Where" they are working has also changed as recent generations have witnessed the elimination of many barriers that in the past limited certain professions and occupations exclusively to certain populations or sexes. Career exclusiveness, for example, excluded women from traditional male occupations such as engineering, airline piloting, and taxicab and truck driving, to mention but a few. These once male-dominated careers (and some for women, such as nursing) have been effectively challenged not only in the courts, but, more important, in the world of work.

Additionally, the antidiscrimination and antipoverty movements have further challenged the exclusiveness of certain careers that were once limited to only racial majority members of upper socioeconomic income populations.

All projections point to the early years of this new century as a time when the percentage of adult women in the workforce will equal that of the male population. Further, although the invisible glass ceiling restricting the advancement of women and minorities into managerial and supervisory positions still subtly exists, progress has and will continue to be made, especially in the new and emerging industries.

Youth unemployment among minorities continues to be of national concern and the projected immigration influx from Central and South America could further inflate these numbers in the years ahead. Immigrants along with women and minorities are also underrepresented in those career areas experiencing the greatest growth. Too, minority youth and women single parents are often handicapped in the job market by their poverty status.

So, although progress has and will continue to be made, much remains to be done to ensure equality of career opportunity for all regardless of gender, race, or socioeconomic status. This presents a major challenge to counselors and the counseling profession.

- **Globalization of the marketplace**

    As we enter the 21st century, we are experiencing a rapid expansion of businesses and industries worldwide. International mergers have become more common as corporations seek to remain competitive and profitable. American workers have seen their jobs moving to South and Central America, and Asia. Even when given the opportunity to move with their jobs, few Americans want to leave home and country, unlike workers in many other countries. Whereas this trend will undoubtedly continue and increase as we move further into the new century, there is little evidence at this point that the American worker is ready to become a worker in another country.

- **Here today—gone tomorrow! No longer can the future be predicted by the present**

    In other times people interested in charting their future could make many appropriate preparations and predictions based on their knowledge of the present, even the past. However, changing technology affecting the workplace, plus drastic changes in the international marketplace and changes in the makeup of our workforce have made it increasingly difficult, if not almost impossible, in recent years to adequately predict the future by examining only the present and the past.

    As a matter of fact, the last half of the 20th century has witnessed the virtual disappearance of the small mom-and-pop family-run business, the locally owned corner service station, the owner-on-the-premises "we deliver" grocery store, and the neighborhood drug store—soda fountain and all! These are now memories of the older generation, replaced by the corporate-run supermarket, chain drug store, and mega-corporate oil company. Many employees now work for distant owners or corporate boards and have declining input into the operation of the business or industry of which they are a part. All of this serves as a reminder that changes in the way America earns its living brings about changes in how Americans live. We live in an interactive society where work influences not only how we earn our living, but also how we live our lives.

This accelerated rate of change in modern society prevents us from assuming, as we might have in the past, that the future will be similar to the present. In fact, we must recognize that much present planning is being based on what is anticipated in the future. Furthermore, this science of future predicting has become an increasingly precise and accurate one. Even without the scientific evidence, the one certainty we can predict for the future is that it will be different.

- **No longer is one in charge of one's own destiny.**

It is clear that the day of the rugged individualist—one who would achieve his or her own destiny—is but a memory. In today's complicated society with its many interacting forces, countless variables affect the destiny of people, and most people have little or no control over them. Often they are unaware of the factors shaping their lives. Although people can plan and chart their futures, they must also consider alternatives. Not the least of these is the reality of the international marketplace, which has resulted in the replacement of a national labor market by a global one. International competition has severe implications for the American worker in terms of wages and benefits, job security, and place of employment. With these changes has come a dramatic increase in the employment of "temps" and a transitory workforce moving from geographic locale to locale. Because these and other factors will lessen people's control over their career destiny, the need for qualified career counselors will continue to be unprecedented.

THEORIES OF CAREER DEVELOPMENT AND DECISION MAKING

One of the more fascinating aspects of the study of careers, both formally and informally, is the never-ending attempt to identify why people end up in certain careers. In history we may read about the factors that resulted in a lifetime of politics for Franklin D. Roosevelt; the multicareer talents of Benjamin Franklin, Thomas Jefferson, or George Washington Carver; the cowboy who became O. Henry, the famous author; Elizabeth Cady Stanton, who became a dazzling patriot and activist; and more recently, the actor who became president of the United States, Ronald Reagan. At one time or another we have probably been curious about the career decisions of friends and acquaintances. But to become more personal, why are you in your present career? What influenced your career planning and decision making?

You probably have been asked this question before, and as you reflected and responded, you may have analyzed a set of facts or reasons that appeared relevant to your decisions. You presented some plausible explanation. Many of us have also offered career advice to others, based on our own personal career experiences or personal theory of career development. Even so, we must recognize the biases and limitations of our own experiences. To develop a theory to a usable state, it is necessary to gather data that are relevant, study the relationships between the data, and finally, speculate on what these mean. These speculations are stated as hypotheses, explanations, or predictions, which can be tested. If a theory proves to have some validity, it will be built on and developed further through research and application activities.

To help youth and adults in their career development, planning, and adjustment, counselors and others who work as helping professionals must have some understanding of the better recognized and researched theories of career development that emerged in the last half of the 20th century. An understanding of such theories gives the practicing counselor a knowledge of the studies of others, usually specialists in the field. They provide a rationale for counselor action that goes beyond personal experience and intuition.

Because many disciplines (education, economics, psychology, sociology) are actively engaged in investigating various career questions, a multitude of theories have emerged. Both the numbers of theories and the extensiveness of their investigation preclude any attempt here to analyze the various major theories in detail. The diversity that exists among human beings and the constantly changing nature of work, life, and our environments make theoretical conception difficult and less than absolute, to say the least. We would further note that in recent years the relevancy of many of the traditional theories of career choice have been examined for their appropriateness for the high-tech information-processing work world of the 1990s and 2000s and for a workforce with a significant female and minority population. Further, the drastic changes in career stability for the future generations will continually challenge the traditional career theories. However, we suggest that proven theories, though in need of ongoing updating, can still provide us with some appropriate guidelines. With these limitations in mind, let us explore several of the more popular categories for illustrative purposes only, without any intent to suggest or recommend a particular theoretical approach.

Trait-Factor Theory

The initial theory to emerge for career counseling and development was labeled trait-factor. This label was devised from the assumptions that assessing of the individual's traits through objective measures and then matching these traits to those typically required for successful performance in a given career area would enable the counselor to provide objective assistance to their clients seeking career direction. This trait-factor approach was based on Frank Parsons's concept of vocational guidance described in his book, *Choosing a Vocation*, published in 1909. In this publication Parsons suggested three steps for enhancing the individual's career decision making. In abbreviated form, these steps were as follows:

1. A clear and objective understanding of one's self, including abilities, interests, attitudes, and so forth.
2. A knowledge of the requirements and characteristics of specific careers.
3. A recognition and application of the relationships between one and two above for successful career planning.

The trait-factor approach to career decision making is the oldest and perhaps the most durable of the many theoretical approaches available for career counseling.

The Developmental Theories

The developmental theories relevant to career planning view career development as one aspect of a person's total development. Further, developmental theorists assume that career development is a process that takes place over an individual's life span. As a result, most theories have tended to focus on developmental stages that are related to age. In this regard, recent generations have seen increased interest and research in adults, including older adulthood. Ginzberg, Ginsburg, Axelrad, and Herma (1951) were early pioneers in creating a theory of occupational choice from a developmental perspective. This team analyzed the process of occupational decision making in terms of three periods: fantasy choices, tentative choices, and realistic choices. This theory suggests a process that moves increasingly toward realism in career decision making as one becomes older.

In 1972, Ginzberg modified the original theory to suggest that the process of vocational choice and development is lifelong and open-ended. In this process, achieving the optimum is more appropriate to describe the ongoing efforts of persons as they seek to find the most suitable job. Originally, Ginzberg and colleagues suggested that the crystallization of occupational choice inevitably had the quality of compromise. Ginzberg's revised theory also places considerable weight on constraints such as family income and situation, parental attitudes and values, opportunities in the world of work, and value orientations. Both the early theory and Ginzberg's later revision suggest the importance of the early school years in influencing later career planning.

Blau, Gustad, Jessor, Parnes, and Wilcock (1956) conceived of occupational choice as a process of compromise, continually modified, between preferences for and expectations of being able to get into various occupations. They identify eight factors determining entry into an occupation. Four of these characterize the occupation: demand, technical (functional) qualifications, personal (nonfunctional) qualifications, and rewards. Those characterizing the person were information about an occupation, technical skills, social characteristics, and value orientations. Ginzberg's revisions seem cognizant of the changes emerging in the world of work (i.e., career decision making across the life span and the need to repeatedly assess career goals in light of the changing world of work).

Perhaps the most influential of the developmental career researchers and writers was Donald E. Super. In the development of his theory, Super emphasized the important role played by vocational maturity. The major concepts in Super's theory were (a) vocational stages, (b) developmental tasks to achieve if one is to successfully pass through a particular stage, (c) implementation of the self-concept in developing a career identity, (d) development of career maturity, and (e) career patterns.

More recently, Super (1990) has presented a life span development theory based on 14 propositions, as follows.

1. People differ in their abilities, and personalities, needs, values, interests, traits, and self-concepts.
2. People are qualified, by virtue of these characteristics, each for a number of occupations.
3. Each occupation requires a characteristic pattern of abilities and personality traits—with tolerances wide enough to allow both some variety of occupations for each individual and some variety of individuals in each occupation.

4. Vocational preferences and competencies, the situations in which people live and work, and, hence, their self-concepts, change with time and experience, although self-concepts, as products of social learning, are increasingly stable from late adolescence until late maturity, providing some continuity in choice and adjustment.

5. This process of change may be summed up in a series of life stages (a "maxicycle") characterized as a sequence of growth, exploration, establishment, maintenance, and decline, and these stages may in turn be subdivided into (a) the fantasy, tentative, and realistic phases of the exploratory stage and (b) the trial and stable phases of the establishment stage. A small (mini) cycle takes place in transitions from one stage to the next or each time an individual is destabilized by a reduction in force, changes in type of personnel needs, illness or injury, or other socioeconomic or personal events. Such unstable or multiple-trial careers involve new growth, re-exploration, and reestablishment (recycling).

6. The nature of the career pattern—that is, the occupational level attained and the sequence, frequency, and duration of trial and stable jobs—is determined by the individual's parental socioeconomic level, mental ability, education, skills, personality characteristics (needs, values, interests, traits, and self-concepts), and career maturity and by the opportunities to which he or she is exposed.

7. Success in coping with the demands of the environment and of the organism in that context at any given life-career stage depends on the readiness of the individual to cope with these demands (that is, on his or her career maturity).

8. Career maturity is a hypothetical construct. Its operational definition is perhaps as difficult to formulate as is that of intelligence, but its history is much briefer and its achievements even less definite.

9. Development through the life stages can be guided partly by facilitating the maturing of abilities and interests and partly by aiding in reality testing and in the development of self-concepts.

10. The process of career development is essentially that of developing and implementing occupational self-concepts. It is a synthesizing and compromising process in which the self-concept is a product of the interaction of inherited aptitudes, physical makeup, opportunity to observe and play various roles, and evaluations of the extent to which the results of role playing meet the approval of superiors and fellows (interactive learning).

11. The process of synthesis of or compromise between individual and social factors, between self-concepts and reality, is one of role playing and of learning from feedback, whether the role is played in fantasy, in the counseling interview, or in such real-life activities as classes, clubs, part-time work, and entry jobs.

12. Work satisfactions and life satisfactions depend on the extent to which the individual finds adequate outlets for abilities, needs, values, interests, personality traits, and self-concepts. They depend on establishment in a type of work, a work situation, and a way of life in which one can play the kind of role that growth and exploratory experiences have led one to consider congenial and appropriate.

13. The degree of satisfaction people attain from work is proportional to the degree to which they have been able to implement self-concepts.

14. Work and occupation provide a focus for personality organization for most men and women, although for some persons this focus is peripheral, incidental, or even

nonexistent. Then other foci, such as leisure activities and homemaking, may be central. (Social traditions, such as gender-role stereotyping and modeling, racial and ethnic biases, and the opportunity structure, as well as individual differences, are important determinants of preferences for such roles as worker, student, leisurite, homemaker, and citizen.) (Super, 1990, pp. 206–208)

Another popular theory, very often referred to as classic was Havighurst's developmental tasks theory. Havighurst (1964) discusses vocational development as a lifelong process consisting of six stages from childhood to old age. Each age period has characteristic tasks that must be successfully achieved if a person is to attain happiness and success with tasks appropriate to the vocational stages that follow. The developmental stages are outlined in Table 8-1.

Table 8-1   Vocational development: A lifelong process.

Stages of Vocational Development	Age
I. Identification with a worker	5–10
Father, mother, other significant persons. The concept of working becomes an essential part of the ego-ideal.	
II. Acquiring the basic habits of industry	10–15
Learning to organize one's time and energy to get a piece of work done. School work, chores. Learning to put work ahead of play in appropriate situations.	
III. Acquiring identity as a worker in the occupational structure	15–25
Choosing and preparing for an occupation. Getting work experience as a basis for occupational choice and for assurance of economic independence.	
IV. Becoming a productive person	25–40
Mastering the skills of one's occupation.	
Moving up the ladder with one's occupation.	
V. Maintaining a productive society	40–70
Emphasis shifts toward the societal and away from the individual aspect of the worker's role. The individual sees himself as a responsible citizen in a productive society. He pays attention to the civic responsibility attached to his job. The individual is at the peak of his occupational career and has time and energy to adorn it with broader types of activity. He pays attention to inducting younger people into stages III and IV.	
VI. Contemplating a productive and responsible life	70+
This person is retired from work or is in the process of withdrawing from the worker's role. He looks back over his work life with satisfaction, sees that a personal social contribution has been made, and is pleased with it. While he may not have achieved all of his ambitions, he accepts life and believes in himself as a productive person.	

Another classic theory developed by E. H. Erickson identified eight psychosocial stages from birth through death. Each of these stages consists of a developmental crisis that must be resolved. Depending on the reactions of individuals, a conflict is involved with each crisis, that will be resolved in a positive or negative way. The successful accomplishments in early stages will contribute to the individual's ability to resolve future crises, thus creating an interdependence among the stages. However, an undesirable or unhealthy resolution of a psychosocial crisis can result in difficulties throughout one's later life. It is possible, however, that an unsatisfactory resolution may later be altered to satisfactory outcomes when proper conditions present themselves. The importance of meeting the personal, cultural, cognitive, and social-emotional needs of individuals as they develop has obvious implications for the individual's career development and later adjustments. Erickson's stages are presented in Table 8-2.

Personality Theories

Personality theories view vocational preferences as expressions of personality. They suggest that much career-seeking behavior is an outgrowth of efforts to, in effect, match one's individual characteristics with those of a specific occupational field.

Table 8-2   Erikson's stages of personal and social development.

As people grow, they face a series of psychosocial crises that shape personality, according to Erik Erikson. Each crisis focuses on a particular aspect of personality and each involves the person's relationship with other people.

	Approximate ages	*Psychosocial crises*	*Significant relationships*	*Psychosocial emphasis*
I	Birth to 18 mo.	Trust vs. mistrust	Maternal person	To get To give in return
II	18 mo. to 3 yr.	Autonomy vs. doubt	Parental persons	To hold on To let go
III	3 to 6 yr.	Initiative vs. guilt	Basic family	To make (= going after) To "make like" (= playing)
IV	6 to 12 yr.	Industry vs. inferiority	Neighborhood, school	To make things To make things together
V	12 to 18 yr.	Identity vs. role confusion	Peer groups and models of leadership	To be oneself (or not to be) To share being oneself
VI	Young adulthood	Intimacy vs. isolation	Partners in friendship, sex, competition, cooperation	To lose and find oneself in another
VII	Middle adulthood	Generativity vs. self-absorption	Divided labor and shared household	To take care of
VIII	Late adulthood	Integrity vs. despair	"Mankind" "My kind"	To be, through having been To face not being

Source: From *Educational Psychology*, 3rd ed. (p. 40) by R. E. Slavin. Reprinted with permission as adapted from *Identity and the Life Cycle* by Erik H. Erikson. Copyright © 1980 by W. W. Norton & Co., Inc. Copyright © 1959 by International Universities Press, Inc. Reprinted by permission of W. W. Norton & Company, Inc.

A current, popular approach representing personality theory is John Holland's theory of personality types and environmental models. This theory is based on major assumptions regarding personality types, their determination and relation to various outcomes and vocational choices. In other words, individuals express themselves, their values and interests, and so forth, through their career choices—their work environments. The concepts and assumptions that underlie the theory are as follows:

- The choice of vocation is an expression of personality.
- Interest inventories are personality inventories.
- Vocational stereotypes have reliable and important psychological and sociological meanings.
- The members of a vocation have similar personalities and similar histories of personal development.
- Because people in a vocational group have similar personalities, they will respond to many situations and problems in similar ways, and they will create characteristic interpersonal environments.
- Vocational satisfaction, stability, and achievement depend on the congruence between one's personality and environment (composed largely of other people) in which one works.

The following statements summarize the major assumptions of Holland's (1966, 1973, 1985a) theory:

- In our culture, most persons can be categorized as one of six types: realistic, intellectual, social, conventional, enterprising, and artistic.
- There are six kinds of environments: realistic, intellectual, social, conventional, enterprising, and artistic.
- People search for environments and vocations that will permit them to exercise their skills and abilities, to express their attitudes and values, to take on agreeable problems and roles, and to avoid disagreeable ones.
- A person's behavior can be explained by the interaction of his personality and his environment. (Holland, 1973, pp. 2–4)

Table 8-3 summarizes Holland's (1985b) theory, describing the personality characteristics of the six categories and the work environments related to each. Holland has developed a popular assessment instrument based on his theory, *The Self-Directed Search*, accompanied by an *Occupational Finder*. Holland does not suggest his categories as mutually exclusive, as noted in the *Occupational Finder*, which suggests that a work setting would be a combination of three environments. It is also equally rare for an individual to fit into only one of the six psychological types.

Another popular personality theory developed by Anne Roe (1956) was based on Maslow's classic theory of basic needs. These needs, in order of their importance, from high to low were stated as follows:

- Physiological needs
- Safety needs
- Need for belongingness and love
- Need for self-esteem and respect

Table 8-3 Holland's personality types.

The **Realistic** type likes realistic jobs such as automobile mechanic, aircraft controller, surveyor, farmer, electrician. Has mechanical abilities but may lack social skills. Is described as

Asocial	Inflexible	Practical
Conforming	Materialistic	Self-effacing
Frank	Natural	Thrifty
Genuine	Normal	Uninsightful
Hardheaded	Persistent	Uninvolved

The **Investigative** type likes investigative jobs such as biologist, chemist, physicist, anthropologist, geologist, medical technologist. Has mathematical and scientific ability but often lacks leadership ability. Is described as

Analytical	Independent	Rational
Cautious	Intellectual	Reserved
Complex	Introspective	Retiring
Critical	Pessimistic	Unassuming
Curious	Precise	Unpopular

The **Artistic** type likes artistic jobs such as composer, musician, stage director, writer, interior decorator, actor/actress. Artistic abilities: writing, musical, or artistic, but often lacks clerical skills. Is described as

Complicated	Imaginative	Intuitive
Disorderly	Impractical	Nonconforming
Emotional	Impulsive	Open
Expressive	Independent	Original
Idealistic	Introspective	Sensitive

The **Social** type likes social jobs such as teacher, religious worker, counselor, clinical psychiatric case worker, speech therapist. Has social skills and talents but often lacks mechanical and scientific ability. Is described as

Ascendant	Helpful	Responsible
Cooperative	Idealistic	Sociable
Empathic	Kind	Tactful
Friendly	Patient	Understanding
Generous	Persuasive	Warm

The **Enterprising** type likes enterprising jobs such as salesperson, manager, business executive, television producer, sports promoter, buyer. Has leadership and speaking abilities but often lacks scientific ability. Is described as

Acquisitive	Energetic	Flirtatious
Adventurous	Excitement-	Optimistic
Agreeable	seeking	Self-confident
Ambitious	Exhibitionistic	Sociable
Domineering	Extroverted	Talkative

Table 8-3   *(continued)*

The **Conventional** type likes conventional jobs such as bookkeeper, stenographer, financial analyst, banker, cost estimator, tax expert. Has clerical and arithmetic ability but often lacks artistic abilities. Is described as

Careful	Inflexible	Persistent
Conforming	Inhibited	Practical
Conscientious	Methodical	Prudish
Defensive	Obedient	Thrifty
Efficient	Orderly	Unimaginative

Source: Adapted and reproduced by special permission of the Publisher, from the Self-Directed Search Professional Manual by John L. Holland, Ph.D. Copyright © 1985, 1987, 1994 by Psychological Assessment Resources, Inc. Further reproduction is prohibited without permission from PAR, Inc. The SDS materials are available from PAR by calling (800) 331-8378.

- Need for information
- Need for understanding
- Need for beauty
- Need for self-actualization

Maslow's concept suggests that until the higher needs are met, the need or needs that follow will not be attended to. For example, those needs for maintaining life (i.e., the first two indicated) must be satisfied before the needs for love and respect (the third and fourth indicated) can be addressed.

Roe's research led her to believe that the needs structure of the individual would be greatly influenced by early childhood experiences. This needs structure would in turn influence occupational categories the individual would select. Roe's extensive research into occupations led her to the development of eight occupational groups (Roe & Klas, 1972):

- Service
- Business contact
- Organization
- Technology
- Outdoors
- Science
- Culture
- Arts and entertainment

These eight occupational categories were then subdivided into six classification levels as determined by degree of responsibility and abilities needed.

- Professional and managerial (1), independent responsibility
- Professional and managerial (2), less independence of important responsibility
- Semiprofessional and small business
- Skilled
- Semiskilled
- Unskilled

Roe's system of classification and categorization has proved useful as a framework for organizing a multitude of occupations in a meaningful way, and her work has had an impact on interest test development and career research.

Social Learning Theory

Social learning theory is an outgrowth of efforts by John Krumboltz and C. Nichols (1990) and his associates to adapt Bandura's (1997) behavioral theory to career decision making. In 1996, Mitchell and Krumboltz added to their earlier social-learning theory approach to include the suggestion that the entire theory be referred to as a learning theory of career counseling (LTCC). This theory suggests that four categories of factors are influential in the career development and decision making of individuals. These factors are as follows.

1. Genetic endowment and special abilities
2. Environmental conditions and events
3. Learning experiences
4. Task approach skills

Sociological Theories

Popular among the sociological views of careers is one suggesting that people arrive at a particular occupation more by chance than through deliberate planning or steady progress toward an earlier defined goal. Newspapers and television reports constantly remind us of persons who seem to be in the right place at the right time and for no other reason end up in an unanticipated career. In a broad sense, we might include the chance one has for career choice as influenced by the environment, social class, culture, and other conditions one is born into or raised in; opportunities for education; observation of role models; and so forth. More narrowly, we may note that chance factors result in occupational choice by an impulse or sudden emotional reaction in which unconscious forces appear to determine a person's behavior and occupation choice. Consider, for example, the person who on apparent impulse walks out of a good office job to work as a missionary in an African jungle. Perhaps you have decided to enter the counseling field based at least in part on chance or unanticipated influences. In any event, accident theory contends that because people may make decisions or be influenced by unforeseen or accidental circumstances, it is not possible to evaluate all the decisive factors in their choices.

Many sociologists and psychologists have expressed the opinion that chance encounters play prominent roles in changing the life course of countless individuals. Herr and Cramer (1996) have synthesized Bandura's (1982) perspectives (see Table 8-4). Sociological theory also notes the influences of home, school, social class, communities, and peer groups.

Economic Theories

Economic theories suggest the importance of economic factors in career choice. Prominent among these are the availability of types of jobs versus the availability of qualified workers for these jobs. Too, as many studies have indicated, a major factor in career choice is "What kind of job can I get?" In these instances, the most important consideration is being able to provide at least the basic necessities for oneself and family. Job security has also

Table 8-4 A synthesis of Bandura's perspectives of factors influencing chance encounters.

Personal Determinants of the Effect of Chance Encounters	Social Determinants of the Effect of Chance Encounters
Entry Skills Interest, skills, personal knowledge likely to gain acceptance or sustain contact with another	*Milieu Rewards* The types of rewards and sanctions an individual or group provides if a chance encounter alters a life path
Emotional Ties Interpersonal attractiveness tending to sustain chance encounters so that certain social determinants might operate	*Symbolic Environment and Information* Images of reality provided by other than direct experience; different individuals or groups furnish different symbolic environments
Values and Personal Standards Unintended influences more likely to be important if persons involved share similar standards and value systems	*Milieu Reach and Closedness* Chance encounters with a relatively closed milieu—e.g., cults, communal groups—have the greatest potential for abruptly reordering life paths
	Psychological Closedness Belief systems provide structure, directions, and purpose in life. Once persons, through chance encounter, get caught up in the belief system of a particular group, it can exert selective influence on the course of development and erect a psychological closedness to outside influence. Beliefs channel social interactions in ways that create their own validating realities

Source: From E. L. Herr and S. H. Cramer, *Career Guidance and Counseling Through the Life-span: Systematic Approaches* (5th ed.), p. 208. Copyright © 1996. Reprinted by permission by Allyn & Bacon.

become an important consideration in career choice in the 1990s and beyond, and worker benefits, especially medical insurance and retirement plans, can also be factors in where one seeks employment.

Decision-making theory has its origins in the field of economics and implies that careers are selected from alternatives on the basis of which choice promises to be the most rewarding or of most value to the individual (and not necessarily in a monetary sense).

Other Theories

A number of other perspectives further broaden the concepts of influence on career development. For example, Brown (1996) developed a value-based theory of career development suggesting that individuals act and make decisions that are influenced by their values. We may note that the rules by which societies live tend to be value-based. These societal values in turn become rules that many individuals use to judge their own behaviors. Values are also influential in rationalizing the goals we establish for ourselves including career goals.

In recent years increasing attention has been given to examining how the differing career theories might converge or could be made to bridge with each other. In the Savickas and Lent (1994) publication, *Convergence in Career Development Theories*, five prominent career theorists representing the theories of development (Super), psychodynamic (Bordin), personality (Holland), social learning (Krumboltz), and work adjustment (Davis) examined how their theories might converge with others. This publication was the outgrowth of a project on convergence stimulated by a series of articles written on the occasion of the 20th anniversary of the *Journal of Vocational Development* in 1990. The initial thrust toward exploration of convergence of theories appears to have been stimulated by a career convergence project with contributions from prominent theorists (John Krumboltz, Rene Davis, John Holland, Edward Bordin, and Donald Super.) Although no appreciable progress was reported on convergence, useful distinctions among the major theories were reaffirmed and theoretical deficiencies and features needing renovation were noted. Samuel Osipow and Donald Super were early leaders in encouraging the exploration of convergence theories that led to the career convergence project and a conference on the topic attended by your authors at The Ohio State University in the spring of 1994.

IMPLICATIONS OF CAREER THEORIES FOR COUNSELORS

A review of the previously discussed major theories would note in brief that the trait-factor approach suggests the importance of the individual's abilities and interest in career choice. Personality theories suggest a relationship between career decisions and personality traits such as self-concept. Developmental theories have emphasized the importance of human development and maturity in readiness and reality in career decision making. Social-learning theory recognizes the influences of heredity, special abilities, environment, learning experiences, and task approach skills. The most prominent sociological theory emphasizes the role that chance plays in the career decisions of individuals. Economic theories obviously underscore the importance of economic factors in career choices. Values theory believes that individuals' values and the values of their society are important in establishing career goals.

These theories can lead us to conclude that career development is a process leading to a decision; there are stages through which one passes en route to career maturity and decision making; one must accomplish certain tasks at each stage; and personality traits and values are related to career decision making. Furthermore, environmental constraints may limit the careers to which one aspires; and finally, the individual's best-laid plans may be altered by chance factors.

The characteristics of these theories have certain implications for counseling clients with career development or adjustment needs.

- Counselors must understand the process and characteristics of human development, including readiness to learn and successfully complete particular tasks at certain developmental stages.

- Counselors must understand the basic human needs as well as the special needs of persons and their relationship to career development and decision making.
- Counselors must be able to assess and interpret individual traits and characteristics and to apply these assessments to a variety of client career-related needs.
- Counselors must assist clients to recognize that unforeseen or chance factors may, on occasion, alter career planning.
- Counselors must recognize that the rapid changes in the way people work and live in this high-tech era require a constant examination and updating of the theory and research we use as a basis for our career counseling efforts.

Counselors must themselves recognize, as well as assist clients in recognizing, that yesterday's world of work no longer exists. Frequent career changes, environmental changes—including the possibility of international employment—and work as temporaries are among the realistic probabilities facing workers today.

CAREER COUNSELING AND THE DEVELOPMENT OF HUMAN POTENTIAL

Beyond the various career choice theories is the recognition that all aspects of human development, whether they be social, physical, emotional, or educational, are but parts of one's total development—parts that are usually interwoven and often difficult to distinguish from the other aspects of human development. Career development is, of course, no exception. A recognition of these relationships and the application of certain basic principles of human development are significant in the design and implementation of programs providing counseling over the life span for the development of human potential.

Five concepts of development related to career counseling and the development of human potential are noted as follows.

1. Development occurs across the life span of the individual. Significant in this development is the maturing process, which is related to the mastery of developmental tasks at each life stage. Career counseling should reflect an awareness of this process and the developmental tasks to provide those experiences and information that enable the individual to master these tasks at the highest level of one's potential.
2. Environment is a significant factor influencing the development of one's potential. Career counseling seeks to accent the favorable factors in an individual's environment and compensate for or intervene with those unfavorable factors that might limit one's capacity to develop to the fullest.
3. Career development should recognize the different age-stages through which the individual progresses and provide the experiences and learnings that are appropriate for each.
4. As individuals develop, the aptitudes and interests in which they excel should be enhanced by experiences and other strategies designed to assist them in developing their full potential.
5. Programs designed to optimize the development of the individual must also work to inhibit factors that might prevent such full development. This suggests

that prevention and early intervention programs should be designed to compensate for negative factors that could possibly influence the individual's development in a negative way.

Of course, we do not have to examine developmental theory to understand the capabilities that exist within the human being. The achievements of humankind from the discovery of fire to walking on the moon are testimony to the ever-present undetermined potential of human beings. Although we must presume that the multiple potentials of most people will never be fully exploited, the challenge nonetheless remains to achieve and develop to the optimum possible.

As countries prepare to compete in the global marketplace, a resource that will be examined more and more with a view to promoting the advancement and well-being of societies will be the most valuable of all, the human resource. Too, as disadvantaged populations seek to overcome their inequalities, they will continue to call, with public support, for increased equal opportunities for their own optimum development.

Although we have historical examples of counselors being called on to assist in the identification and development of human potential in limited ways (e.g., encouraging students to take more science and math courses, identifying students for gifted programs), we are now moving into an era when the development of every individual's full capability becomes that person's right and society's hope. Three phases for a human resource development program are these:

1. Assessment for the identification of the individual's aptitudes and interests
2. Planning for appropriate experiences to assist the individual's full development and enhancement
3. Placement in educational and/or career settings in which the individual's developed capabilities can be realized for the benefits of the individual and society

Although the identification and development of individual human potential should be initiated in the early years of schooling, it is appropriate to continue to assess, monitor, and assist the individual across the life span. Postsecondary educational institutions, adult education programs, career centers and employment offices, community mental health agencies, and private practitioners can all play significant roles in this process. They cannot afford to do less. Society cannot afford to let them do less.

A career may offer the greatest opportunity for a person to achieve much that he or she is capable of accomplishing. Career counseling for human development may include a focus on encouraging clients to challenge the limitations of their present self-concept; to, in a manner of speaking, redefine themselves and stimulate their vitality. Let us next examine groups that traditionally represent populations in our society that are underdeveloped: women, minorities, the poor, people with disabilities, and dual-career couples.

Women

A prime example of the development of human potential through the world of work is the large-scale movement of women into the workforce during and since World War II. Not only are more women entering the labor pool, but they are entering a wide range of occupations far beyond such traditional women's careers as nursing, teaching, waitressing, and clerical work that represented the limits of their realistic aspirations in the first generation of the 20th century. Today, women seek careers in the medical, legal, law enforcement, military, construction, sales, and transportation fields, to name but a few that have long been bastions of male employment. Further, women are being increasingly appointed to managerial and supervisory positions and high judicial offices, are being elected to governorships and legislative bodies, and, in general, are making significant advances up the career ladder in all areas. All this is happening as we note projections that anticipate nearly as high a percentage of adult women in the workforce as adult men in the early 2000s.

Despite this optimistic note on women's progress, we must recognize the many barriers that still prevent women from achieving their full potential. High among these restrictors is the age-old problem of prejudice. Prejudice is reflected in numerous ways, but two specific examples are salaries and opportunities.

Additionally, we have noted increased media attention in recent years to the old problem of sexual harassment of the female worker; home and workplace demands on the dual-career couple's working females when males fail to be equal partners at home; and increasing numbers of female single parents. The majority of women in today's workforce are there because of economic necessity—and this includes the nearly 60% of single-parent families headed by women. Because of these and other circumstances, women often accept lower wages than their male counterparts. There are serious salary discrepancies at every career level and women are far more frequently underemployed in low-wage jobs than men of comparable qualifications.

Thus, although laudable progress has been made in women's development, much remains to be done. Career counselors have the opportunity to facilitate this development. The female client must be aided in looking beyond stereotypes and other restrictions. Some may need assistance in appropriately balancing family life and work and accepting their rights to be both a mother and a worker.

Frequent surveys of working women have noted the demands placed on them to balance their family life and their work life. As corporate America has failed to be sufficiently responsive to the needs of female workers, mothers are beginning to seek or develop opportunities to work out of their homes, do contract jobs, or opt for employment as "temporaries." Counselors must also help female clients identify alternatives to traditional work opportunities as well as recognize educational opportunities that may increase their opportunities and enhance their earning power. With some, assertiveness training, job search skills, and positive self-concept development may also be helpful.

Minorities

Minorities in the United States throughout the country's history have represented a tragic loss through ignored and undeveloped human resources. Although progress has been made in recent generations to eliminate barriers and open opportunities to minority populations, the work is not finished. The nation's shortcomings are recognizable in the underrepresentation of minorities in professions, managerial and supervisory positions, government offices of leadership, and preparatory programs in higher education. At the opposite end of the career ladder, minorities are overrepresented in lower paying and lower prestige jobs, underemployment and unemployment, and school attrition. As we look to our future, it is especially disturbing to note that more of our African American youth are in the criminal justice system than are gainfully employed, and that high percentages of minority girls are single parents, heads of households, and poor. Obviously, our societal future is not a healthy one if tomorrow's minority adults are already seriously disadvantaged in developing their full capabilities. They truly have been neglected and underserved.

Counselors and counseling programs have both a significant challenge and a significant opportunity to assist minority populations in achieving career equity and attaining optimum development. To even entertain the promise of effectiveness in this regard, counselors must be sure that they themselves do not hold or reinforce educational or career stereotypes for minorities, do not use biased assessment instruments, and are at all times culturally aware and sensitive.

It is also important for counselors assisting minority career clients to inform their clients of possible prejudices and to work with them and employers to eliminate these barriers. Counselors must also be aware of increasing minority ownership of businesses and the opportunities here for minority employment. Counselors at all times should be advocates for the employment of minorities based not on their ethnic cultural background, but on their personal qualifications.

The Poor

Although we are frequently reminded that the United States is the richest country on earth, not all of our population shares in the wealth. Certainly, a glaring tarnish on our image is the significant numbers of our population who exist in poverty. As noted in chapter 4 (Individual Counseling), over 34 million people in the United States were living below the poverty line in 1998. The figures are even greater for minority populations, and when we consider that children represent the largest population living in poverty, we must ask how this can happen in the United States of America. Often overlooked or uncountable are the estimated one million-plus homeless people, a group that represents the ultimate in ignored human resources. The challenges these groups present to counseling and the other helping professions are complex and difficult.

High numbers of children from preschool through adolescence live in poverty. In San Francisco, for example, an estimated 5,000 youth were homeless in the mid-1990s. Although the Homeless Assistance Act (1987) was designed to aid school systems in developing programs that reconnect homeless children with schools, the results have often been discouraging as schools frequently fail to understand how life on the streets can affect homeless youth. School counselors will be especially challenged to keep homeless children in school and to prevent them from being stigmatized, discouraged, and bored with school. Schools should be a haven and a hope for homeless children, but, to date, not all schools and their counselors appear to have made sufficient strides in dealing with this population.

From a programmatic standpoint, three concerns must be addressed. First, schools in poverty areas *must* have *good* counseling programs, staffed by competent, caring, and environmentally aware counselors. Second, community career assistance programs must be located in those areas where the need is greatest—where the poor reside. Finally, adult education programs with strong counseling components must be made much more accessible and convenient to these populations.

In terms of individual counseling, Isaacson and Brown (1993) noted that

Personal counseling may be needed by disadvantaged individuals to clarify self-concept as well as to understand their circumstances. Several authors have emphasized the devastating impact that job loss has on feelings of self-worth. The chronically poor are likely to carry an even heavier feeling of worthlessness. The so-called American dream suggests that one's success in life is the product of hard work—the harder one works, the more one reaps in material rewards, status, and self-satisfaction. One frequent product is the feeling of guilt and failure by those without jobs or with only marginal jobs. Marshall (1983) and Shifron, Dye, and Shifron (1983) describe ways to help such clients deal with feelings and values that may interfere with everyday life and often result from forces outside the individual's control.

Realistic and practical information about the world of work can be used to help the disadvantaged to see potential opportunities to break out of what is frequently viewed as a hopeless morass. Interviews with workers, work samples, plant visits, and synthetic work situation may help the person to understand the job, to relate that job to self, to see attainable goals, and perhaps to acquire usable role models. (Isaacson & Brown, 1993, pp. 314–315)

People with Disabilities

Another population whose human capabilities are often underdeveloped is individuals with disabilities. The Americans with Disabilities Act (ADA), a comprehensive law, identifies individuals with disabilities as follows:

- An individual with a disability is a person who has a physical or mental impairment that substantially limits one or more "major life activities," or has a record of such an impairment, or is regarded as having such an impairment.
- Examples of physical or mental impairments include, but are not limited to, such contagious and noncontagious diseases and conditions as orthopedic, visual, speech, and hearing impairments; cerebral palsy, epilepsy, muscular dystrophy, multiple sclerosis, cancer, heart disease, diabetes, mental retardation, emotional illness, specific learning disabilities, HIV disease (whether symptomatic or asymptomatic), tuberculosis, drug addiction, and alcoholism. Homosexuality and bisexuality are not physical or mental impairments under the ADA.
- "Major life activities" include functions such as caring for oneself, performing manual tasks, walking, seeing, hearing, speaking, breathing, learning, and working.
- Individuals who currently engage in the illegal use of drugs are not protected by the ADA when an action is taken on the basis of their current illegal use of drugs. (*Americans with Disabilities Act Handbook,* 1991, pp. 3–4)

State rehabilitation agencies provide individual counseling to disabled clients who meet the eligibility requirements of having a disability that is a significant handicap to employment. The rehabilitation services must reasonably be expected to benefit the disabled individual in terms of the person's employability.

In counseling clients with disabilities for career assistance, counselors must (a) have an understanding of various disabilities and their career implications; (b) be knowledgeable regarding appropriate resources, training, and career opportunities; and (c) be sensitive, supportive, and, at the same time, realistic. Counselors must be prepared to help clients with disabilities in personal adjustment, self-concept development, career development, and job placement. Counselors may also play the role of advocates for such clients seeking access to education or other training or the workplace itself. In other instances, counselors may find themselves facilitating family support for the efforts of people with disabilities. The family support system is important at all ages, of course, and with children—especially those with disabilities—it is important in many ways, not the least of which is influencing how they feel about themselves.

Counselors can also help clients connect to peer support groups of other individuals with disabilities. As with so many other services, minorities have not proportionally availed themselves of rehabilitation counseling. Dziekan and Okocha (1993) comment:

> It is only possible to speculate about reasons for lower acceptance rates for minority clients, and a number of factors might have contributed. Lower proportions of minority individuals applying for services may have actually met agency eligibility criteria. Lower proportions of minority clients may have chosen not to follow through with the acceptance process because of their frustrations with the steps and delays involved. Alternatively, biases in the perceptions of rehabilitation counselors determining eligibility for services may have resulted in inaccurate assessments and underestimations of rehabilitation potential. (p. 1987)

Although much progress has been made through legislative enactments and increased public awareness, counselors can play a vital role in the still-needed advancements of people with disabilities toward their greatest possible development.

Dual-Career Couples

Dual career couples are becoming the norm rather than the exception. This development is already affecting both family life and corporate life and is leading to reexamination of models of family functioning and corporate policies. Certainly, the issue of human development will be a challenging one. Will one partner have priority? Can both be equally developed? And what about children? How will they be cared for and by whom? These and other issues loom large as we approach a dramatically changing world of work with its new challenges. These challenges will include (a) readjusting family roles so that husbands share in previously traditional women's roles in the home; (b) child-rearing practices, especially necessary to avoid the pitfalls of latchkey children; (3) priority decisions—whose career has precedence and what happens when one partner has the opportunity for promotion with transfer to another community.

The continued growth of dual-career couples has presented counselors with relatively new and unexplored challenges in career, and marriage and family counseling. Certainly, the traditional theories of career counseling were not developed with the dual-career couple in mind. New conceptual frameworks must be researched and developed. Individual counseling must be interspersed with cojoint counseling. Open communications and compromise must be encouraged. A multitude of issues regarding the shared responsibilities of child rearing should be explored before they become major issues.

Because society looks at the school as an agency for helping youth develop, let us examine how career planning and decision-making programs in schools contribute to this development.

CAREER PLANNING AND DECISION MAKING IN SCHOOLS

Nearly all human beings can anticipate three common experiences. The first of these, development or growth, begins at birth and is especially attended to through much of an individual's youth. The second is education, in an informal sense, this also starts at birth and continues throughout life, with a special societal emphasis during most of a person's youth when formal schooling is provided. The third common experience is work, beginning in youth and continuing through most of adulthood.

These three experiences are significantly shaped by one common setting—the school. It is here that a person's development is stimulated and shaped for the three great experiences of his or her life: learning, living with others, and working. Thus, the role of the school in what the person may become and, in turn, what society itself may become, is critical. Counselors in any setting have an interest in the impact the school experience has on their clients.

The counseling program's role in the school setting must be one of facilitating and enhancing the school's contributions to the learning, growth and development, and preparation for work of youths. In this chapter we are particularly concerned with the last: preparation for the world of work, including attending to a person's career development, planning, and decision making within the educational context.

In order to emphasize the opportunities for the student's career development, certain guiding principles are suggested as appropriate objectives for the school counseling program in general and the career guidance phase in particular. The following principles are stated within a developmental framework:

1. *All students should be provided with an opportunity to develop an unbiased base from which they can make their career decisions.* The shrinking of students' occupational choices as they proceed through the school years is an educational tragedy. First-graders seem to regard most familiar occupations in a positive light. By the time they reach the seventh or eighth grade, pupils have begun to make decisions based on at least some general occupational considerations. Many have developed or have been educated toward biases that automatically eliminate many possibilities from further consideration. The large percentage of students who enter college preparatory courses at the ninth-grade level and never enter college or even fail to complete their secondary schooling is but one evidence of this fact. Students should not be led to believe that only certain occupations are desirable or that only certain avenues—such as a four-year degree program—lead to meaningful work. In this regard, the school counseling program, in effective cooperation with the classroom teacher, should develop in each pupil positive attitudes and respect for all honest work. This is a formidable task, for many students are almost constantly bombarded with the biases of the adult world surrounding them. If these students are to benefit from a true freedom of choice, the career counseling and guidance programs have a vital mission in the schools.

2. *The early and continuous development of positive pupil attitudes toward education is critical.* The deterioration of the elementary pupil's occupational choices

is unfortunate, but the failure to maintain the pupil's continuing interest in an optimum educational development is disastrous. For objective evidence, one need only turn to the various dropout studies and the equally countless studies concerning the lack of pupil motivation and achievement commensurate with ability. In short, career development has limited meaning without parallel educational development. Any program of pupil career counseling and guidance must have as a major objective the stimulation of the student's educational development.

3. *As a corollary to these previous points, the student must be taught to view a career as a way of life and an education as a preparation for life.* Frequently pupils arrive at the educational decision-making stage of life viewing careers only in terms of job descriptions. At all educational levels the opportunity exists to develop, not only widen, occupational horizons. This broader approach to the eventual career choice is based on the realization that one's way of work is one's way of life. Similarly, there must be attention to the concept of education itself, keeping in mind the idea of education for life rather than education only for one's eventual career. This approach—one of education for the fuller life—also has obvious implications for education's continuing efforts to reduce the percentage of school dropouts.

4. *Students must be assisted in developing adequate understanding of themselves and must be prepared to relate this understanding to both social-personal development and career-educational planning.* These understandings are significant in the fulfillment of the individual's need for self-actualization. In this context, both career guidance and pupil appraisal seek to further enrich their meaning and value to students by preparing them to look at themselves realistically in terms of continuing educational opportunities, career requirements, and the demands and relationships of society.

5. *Students at all levels must be provided with an understanding of the relationship between education and careers.* If pupils are to develop an attitude and belief that education is relevant, they must understand how it is relevant. Pupils need an awareness of the relationships between levels of education and related career possibilities. They should also be made aware of both the vocations and avocations that stem directly from certain subjects.

6. *Pupils need an understanding of both where and why they are at a given point on the educational continuum at a given time.* It is not enough for pupils to know they will be in the third grade this year and in the fourth grade next year if all goes well. If they are to gain an increased appreciation of current educational programs as well as future educational possibilities, pupils must be provided specific opportunities to gain insights into the educational process, its sequence, and its integrating of knowledge.

7. *Pupils at every stage of their educational program should have career-oriented experiences that are appropriate for their levels of readiness and simultaneously meaningful and realistic.* This means that opportunities for participation and observation will frequently take precedence over discussions and teacher or counselor lectures.

8. *Students must have opportunities to test concepts, skills, and roles to develop values that may have future career application.* The school career counseling

and guidance program takes advantage of natural school groupings in providing secure opportunities for the pupil to experience and develop human relationships and other skills, a variety of roles, and a system of values and concepts that are related to everyday living.

9. *The school career counseling and guidance program is centered in the classroom, with coordination and consultation by the school counselor, participation by parents, and resource contributions from the community.* The pupil's career counseling and guidance team needs the involvement of all those concerned with the student's development, with the teacher, counselor, and parent playing key roles.

10. *The school's program of career counseling and guidance is integrated into the functioning counseling and guidance and total educational programs of the institution.* The complete development of the individual is vital; therefore, the career aspects should not be separated from the whole. In fact, it is only within the total educational program framework that each segment can be strengthened by and in turn strengthen every other segment.

11. *Students must be prepared to cope with the dramatic changes in the world of work that have eliminated many of the traditional characteristics of careers from the past.* These include such changes as the global marketplace, the international workforce, computer searches for jobs, the Internet, and other new technologies.

12. *Students must be assisted in developing the maturity necessary for making effective career decisions and entering the world of work.* This maturity is especially vital in view of the significant changes reshaping the world of work to the point that the past no longer provides pathways to the present and future.

The School Counselor's Role in Student Career Development

The need for career guidance and counseling is increasingly evident in the mass of data pointing to difficulties in career decision making, the underutilization of human resources, dissatisfaction with chosen careers, and such perennial problems as the hard-core unemployed. Career guidance programs are designed, in cooperation with programs of career education, to cope with such needs. To satisfactorily plan such programs, which will increase students' planning and decision-making skills, counselors must understand how career decisions are made and the possible consequences of certain kinds of decisions. This approach implies an understanding of theories and related research in career decision making and the counselor's role in the career development of youth.

Because the career movement in schools has been viewed as primarily a developmental and educational process, the school counselor has, at last, the opportunity to function in a developmental and, in a sense, a preventive capacity. Although the teacher is clearly the key person on the career education team, the school counselor, by virtue of special understandings and skills, can make a valuable contribution to the school's total effort. These contributions may be categorized under the following activities.

Career Counseling

Programs of career education are designed to prepare persons for the eventual selection of a career, but many adolescents and young adults will be unable to cope adequately with this critical decision making without the assistance of a professional counselor. Parental counseling, group counseling, and group guidance activities represent contributions of the counselor to the career development of the individual and the school's career education program.

Career Assessment

An important aspect of the career education program provides students the opportunities to assess their personal characteristics in relation to career planning and decision making. The counselor can make a significant contribution to the development of appropriate self-understandings of youth through the employment of both standardized and nonstandardized assessment techniques. However, it is important that these instruments are free of gender or cultural biases.

Resource Person and Consultant

The school counselor has been traditionally active in acquiring materials appropriate to career decision making and planning. The counselor is also aware of computerized information programs and media aids such as films, filmstrips, and audio- and videotapes. Although the counselor cannot collect all materials, it is reasonable to expect that he or she will be aware of the sources from which such materials may be obtained. In this capacity, the counselor serves as a resource person to the individual teachers involved in the career education program.

The counselor also serves in a consulting capacity, utilizing her or his understanding of the pupil population and career development resources and opportunities to complement the career education program.

Linkage Agent

Increasingly, the counselor will be active in collaborative efforts, not only with teachers and others in the school setting but with community agencies and employers as well. Local government employment counselors and their agencies are especially important contacts. The School-to-Work Opportunities Act of 1994 emphasizes the linkage role of the school counselor as a key individual in helping students make the transition from school to work. Such traditional career activities as job shadowing, work-based learning, and relating academic tasks to careers are common components of school-to-work programs.

In addition to the activities previously indicated in this section, the counselor has an important role to play in implementing and strengthening career education programs. This role does not, however, diminish the importance of the career guidance function in career planning and decision making. Let us, therefore, move on to examine some techniques for this activity.

Techniques for Career Planning and Decision Making

In counseling youths for their career development and eventual placement, counselors may employ a variety of facilitative techniques to increase self-awareness, educational awareness, career awareness, career exploration, and planning and decision making.

Self-Awareness

From a very early age onward, people must become aware of and respect their uniqueness as human beings. Learning about one's aptitudes, interests, values, and personality traits is important in the development of concepts related to self and the utilization of these concepts in career exploration. Counselors may use such techniques as values clarification exercises, group guidance activities, written assignments (such as autobiographies), films and videotapes, and standardized tests. Individual or group counseling should follow if circumstances warrant.

Educational Awareness

Awareness of the relationships between self, educational opportunities, and the world of work is an important aspect of career planning. Counselors may use films as well as printed materials for this purpose. Group guidance activities (such as orientation days), presentations by school alumni, and the use of educational awareness inventories can be useful. Games that relate hobbies and recreational activities to courses and careers can be stimulating for grade school and middle school pupils. Guided activities can also educate school-age youth to the relationships between desirable school habits (e.g., responsibility, punctuality, effort, positive human relationships) and good worker traits.

Career Awareness

Counselors and counseling programs in schools should, at all educational levels, assist the pupil in the continuous expansion of knowledge and awareness of the world of work. This must include a developing recognition of the relationships between values, lifestyles, and careers. Many excellent films and printed materials are available for this purpose, but of course these must be integrated into a planned, developmental program appropriate to the student's age or grade level. Specialized programs (e.g., career days, career shadowing, junior partners, closed circuit television trips, and actual field trips) are useful if well planned. Excellent computer programs (noted later in this chapter) are available, and an extensive variety of Web sites can also assist students.

Career Exploration

Career exploration represents a movement toward a systematic, planned inquiry and analysis of careers that are of interest. Comparisons, reality testing, and standardized testing may be useful. Computerized programs, to be discussed later, can also be helpful. Classes in career exploration and decision making are not uncommon.

A variety of techniques are available for career exploration in schools. Integrating career information into classroom instruction enhances the meaning of both as the relationship between learning in school and living out of school becomes more evident to the pupil. The relation of subject matter to careers, hobbies, everyday living needs, and the accomplishments of well-known personalities exemplifies this integration. Many excellent published materials are also available for facilitating career exploration.

Career Planning and Decision Making

Students eventually need to narrow their career possibilities and then proceed to examine and test these options as critically as possible. Here again, such established techniques as values clarification activities, standardized testing, job shadowing, career days, and other group guidance activities are helpful. Many students will need to learn the process of decision making, including choosing between competing alternatives, examining the consequences of specific choices, learning the value of compromise, and implementing a decision. At this point, students must recognize the impact of their current planning and decision making on their future lives. It should also be a time when students are assisted to take control of their lives and become active agents in shaping of their own futures.

Placement and Follow-up

Career placement and follow-up services are significant to the success of career counseling programs. The high rate of youth unemployment has highlighted the need for a greater emphasis on career placement for youth. Assistance to young people by both school and employment counselors is important if they are to avoid unnecessary difficulties and frustrations in their career search activities. Also, counselors are aware that unsatisfactory career entry can have long-term effects for youth. They need to recognize that the current TV generations are often unrealistic in their expectations of career opportunities and their viewpoints of specific careers. Preemployment counseling may be necessary to assist these young people in obtaining a more realistic understanding of the world of work.

As we examine an increasingly complex and changing career world, it is clear that the career placement service has the potential for assisting many, perhaps most, youth in the school setting. Such programs should be designed to assist both in-school and out-of-school youth, both school dropouts and school graduates. Such programs are typically involved in the following activities:

1. Assessing the needs of students regarding part-time and full-time employment, training, employability skills, and further educational desires.
2. Establishing a working relationship with business, industry, and labor representatives in order to facilitate effective cooperation and communication between these groups and educators.
3. Providing avenues and assistance to students seeking part-time or full-time employment that are compatible with their abilities and interests.
4. Establishing an efficient, participatory communication-feedback network among all involved—students, business, industry, labor personnel, community leaders, parents, media, and school personnel.

Many communities have well-established local governmental employment programs that often give special attention to the needs of local youth. Counselors should explore these as they develop a placement program. The school guidance program should work cooperatively and in a complementary manner with local government employment personnel to provide the best possible assistance for youthful job seekers. Even when such local programs exist, however, the important developmental aspects of school placement programs are not the responsibility of other agencies or institutions. School placement programs, therefore, must include activities that develop or enhance the student's skills, attitudes, and knowledge needed for job acquisition and retention. Programs developed under the School-to-Work Transition Act of 1994 would be expected to include many of these elements.

Placement program activities may be viewed as three-dimensional. The primary activity, of course, is student development; however, this will obviously be handicapped if job development is not also a planned program activity, and both of these activities will be less than effective without plans for program maintenance and operation. Because placement in its broader context includes the placement of clients in a variety of settings (i.e., work, educational, environmental) for a variety of reasons and benefits, let us now examine educational and environmental placement.

Educational Placement

In general, educational placement differs little from other forms of placement as it represents an organized effort to match the qualifications of individuals plus personal interests and resources with the requirements of institutions and programs. Typically, school counselors, with responsibilities for college and other postsecondary educational placement, provide students with information regarding institutional entrance requirements, expenses, characteristics of the institution, and program content. They also frequently will assist students in completing the necessary application forms. Today's technology also provides students with easy access via the Web to extensive information about collegiate institutions and all aspects of higher education. An example of a form that counselors may use with high school students interested in college placement is the college checklist (see Figure 8-1).

Many school counselors are also involved in educational placement within their schools. In this capacity they are concerned with placing students in appropriate curricula and specific courses. However, scheduling activities that consist largely of a mechanical process designed to get all pupils into all slots at a given time, with a total disregard of individual differences, is not considered a guidance responsibility, even though counselors report that they spend many hours doing such tasks.

In the literature, at least, if not always in practice, placement within educational institutions has been viewed as more than just career, college, and educational placement. In its broadest sense, placement is an activity that places or facilitates the self-placement of persons in situations or settings that will enable them to benefit from needed experiences, make satisfactory adjustments, gain useful information, and, in general, contribute to their total development. As an example of this broader concept of placement, let us look at placement that focuses on giving a person experiences in different roles and environments.

Role placement assumes that experiencing different and significant roles is important for all developing pupils. Although many will experience some of these roles naturally and without planning, for the majority these developmental opportunities would be missed unless specific provisions are made. This is another opportunity for the school counselor and classroom teacher to work cooperatively in planning meaningful experiences that enhance both the instructional programs and the student's personal development. Significant role experiences would include opportunities to function periodically as a leader, a team member, an individual (isolated) worker, a teacher, an achiever, a responsible person, a social being, a person of authority and decision making, or one who serves others. A role assignment sheet, as illustrated in Figure 8-2, is a method for recording these experiences.

Environmental Placement

Environmental placement can be another developmental activity. The major focus of this type of placement is to provide students with the opportunities to experience other significant, yet distinctly different, environments from their own. An example is giving city youth opportunities to spend time in rural areas as part of farm days or country cousins programs.

	Name of College		Name of College		Name of College	
I. Entrance Requirements and General Information						
	Yes	**No**	**Yes**	**No**	**Yes**	**No**
1. Does this college offer major preparation in the field of _____ (student's planned major)?	___	___	___	___	___	___
2. Will I be eligible for admission upon completion of my currently planned program for high school graduation?	___	___	___	___	___	___
3. Are entrance examinations required?	___	___	___	___	___	___
4. Must I take a physical examination?	___	___	___	___	___	___
5. Are there other entrance requirements? (If so, list in Section VII, under Notes and Comments.)	___	___	___	___	___	___
6. Is this a coeducational college?	___	___	___	___	___	___
7. Is this a state- or city-supported college?	___	___	___	___	___	___
8. Are the offerings of this college accredited by a regional accrediting association?	___	___	___	___	___	___
9. Does this college have an ROTC program?	___	___	___	___	___	___
10. What is the average enrollment?	___	___	___	___	___	___
II. Expenses (per school year)						
11. Room	___	___	___	___	___	___
12. Board	___	___	___	___	___	___
13. Tuition	___	___	___	___	___	___
14. Activity fees	___	___	___	___	___	___
15. Any other special expenses:						
(item) _____	___	___	___	___	___	___
(item) _____	___	___	___	___	___	___
16. Total basic cost per year	$___	___	$___	___	$___	___
III. Room and Board						
17. Are dormitory facilities available for men and women?	___	___	___	___	___	___
18. Are noncommuting freshmen required to live in the dormitory?	___	___	___	___	___	___
19. May you select your own roommate if you desire?	___	___	___	___	___	___
20. Are dining facilities available (three meals per day) for students?	___	___	___	___	___	___

Figure 8-1   College checklist.

	Name of College		Name of College		Name of College	
	Yes	No	Yes	No	Yes	No

IV. *Student Services and Aids*

21. Are scholarships available?

22. Are part-time jobs available?

23. Are guidance services provided?

24. Is there a freshman orientation program?

25. Are placement services available for

    (a) graduating seniors?

    (b) summertime jobs?

26. Are health services provided?

    (a) Dispensary care?

    (b) Dental care?

    (c) Hospitalization plan?

27. Can I get special scholastic help
    (such as tutoring) if I need it?

V. *Student Activities*

28. Fraternities and sororities?

29. Honorary organizations?

30. Social dancing permitted?

31. Are campus recreational facilities available?

32. Is there an intramural program?

33. Major varsity sports?

34. A convocation series?

35. Dramatic opportunities?

36. Music (band and glee club)?

37. Any others you are particularly interested in:
    (item)_____

VI. Any questions you want to ask? _____

_____

VII. Notes and comments _____

_____

(Student's name) _____

Figure 8-1   *(continued)*

_____ Grade   Class of _____ Period _____ to _____

B. D. Lewis Elementary School

Role Assignments	Leader	Team Member	Individual Worker	Achiever	Responsibility	Social Leader	Decision Maker	Server
Pupils' Names								
1. Marie Adams								
2. Alyssa Debrovitz								
3. Marc Collins								
4. Chester Dent								
5. Charles James								
6. Kathryn James								
7. Liona Chan								
8. Archie Leedy								
9. Paul Lewis								
10. Katherine Louise								
11. Daniel Kim								
12. Matt Nuzrem								
13. Jack Smith								
14. Alex Wagner								
15. Heather Watson								

* Dates are entered where role is assigned.

✓ indicates student has assumed or experienced this role and further assignment is not needed at this time.

Figure 8-2   Role assignments.

Urban youth may exchange places with farm youth for several days or weeks. Another example is a blend of educational preparation and environmental placement in which students spend some time in diverse collegiate settings.

Regardless of the nature of client placement, follow-up should also be planned. In the following section, reasons that clients are not placed and forgotten are set forth.

Follow up

Programs of placement activities, regardless of setting, must provide evidence of the effectiveness of their practices for both accountability and program improvement purposes. A large measure of supporting evidence for these purposes may be secured through carefully planned follow-up activities. As a complement to the guidance placement program, follow-up activities focus on effectiveness in placing persons for a variety of purposes and settings, as viewed not only by the clients but also by those to whom the client is responsible in such settings as job placement.

Follow-up data may be obtained through questionnaires, checklists, interviews, and phone calls. Placement follow-up with those placed usually focuses on how satisfied the persons are with their placement and the process, progress they believe they are making in their situation, adequacy of their previous preparation experience, and future plans and recommendations. Employers may be asked to respond concerning the adequacy of preparation and experience of the employee, adaptation to work, ability to work with others, progress anticipated by employee, and recommendations for improving the placement process.

In college placement, follow-up may seek to identify how adequately prepared for college the entering student is and areas of strength and weakness, the degree to which the student appears to be adjusting to college, and recommendations for improving the placement process. As follow-up data are collected, it is equally important to anticipate and plan for systematic utilization of the data.

In recognizing the importance of planning for career placement and follow-up, we would also be cognizant of the complexities and variables involved. In an effort to assist counselors and their clients to deal more effectively with those complexities and variables, computerized assistance systems have been and continue to be developed. Several of these systems will be described in a later section in this chapter.

CAREER COUNSELING IN NONSCHOOL SETTINGS

The initial out-of-school career contacts of many youths will be made through the assistance of their state employment services. In these offices, career guidance activities may be based on a review and discussion of the applicant's qualifications and interests in relation to available employment opportunities. Appraisal instruments, such as the General Aptitude Test Battery, may be used to further assist the client and the counselor in career planning. Counselors in these settings are usually especially well versed in their knowledge of local job opportunities and characteristics and usually have access to computerized job bank systems. These employment office counselors often work closely with high school counselors in facilitating the career planning and transitions of youths from school to work.

The young adult entering the workforce for the first time can encounter a number of challenges including the following:

- The individual discovers discrepancies between what he or she anticipated upon entry into the workplace and what is actually encountered. This initial letdown or disillusionment can affect the individual's initial attitude and achievements.
- Adjusting to supervision and direction from superiors as well as adhering to company policies can be frustrating to those who were recently free-spirited students.
- The assumption of complete responsibility, especially financially, for their life and lifestyle can be a burden if the individual is unprepared.
- The possibility of marriage brings another major responsibility and dramatic change in the individual's lifestyle to mesh with his or her initial career entry.
- The individual may suddenly have less free time and may encounter changes in the types of leisure activities he or she engages in.

Career counseling can function at the pre-entry level to assist the individual in realistically entering the workplace as well as locating a first job commensurate, to the degree possible, with the client's interests and expectations. Counselors can also assist clients in their initial adjustments to the demands of the workplace, marriage, and changing lifestyle. Counselors in community mental health agencies, community career centers, employment offices, EAPs (employee assistance programs), and private practice may be called on to provide young clients with career assistance.

Career counseling and placement, however, can no longer be considered an activity that focuses on youth alone. A variety of factors have resulted in significant changes in the careers of adult populations. Those changes, some of which were noted earlier in this chapter, in turn, have influenced the career counseling and placement efforts in governmental and business settings. Contributing factors include the impact of technological and social change, shifts in societal and consumer values, a population that is growing older and capable of working longer, economic necessity, and international market influences.

Moreover, technological change has resulted in related societal changes such as population shifts, altered consumer demands, and major new government policies regarding health, education, and welfare. These changes have had an impact on other occupations not directly affected by changing technologies. Human service occupations are a good example. Thousands of young adults entered educational programs in these fields. When they graduated several years later, they frequently found the labor market quite different from what it was when they began their schooling. Many could not find jobs in their career areas; others took jobs for which they were overqualified and underpaid.

Americans preparing for jobs in several other occupations have encountered similar difficulties. As technological and social changes become more rapid, predicting the state of the workforce becomes increasingly difficult.

During recent generations, social and cultural changes have also altered traditional concepts and expectations that resulted in sex-role stereotyping in the world of work. As noted earlier in this chapter, this situation has led not only to more female engineers, construction workers, airplane pilots (and more male nurses and elementary school teachers) but also to increasing numbers of women who, in the process of combining careers and marriage, interrupt their careers for child rearing before returning to the labor force.

In short, midlife career changes and entries are becoming commonplace for both men and women.

Every occupation is represented, but some are more visible than others. Classic cases of midlife career change can be found in the ranks of those who put in twenty years or so in the military or in municipal activities, such as fire and police protection and then retire at a relatively young age, free to pursue a second career. In the 1970s, thousands of engineers and scientists became unemployed because of substantial cuts in space and defense spending; these workers in declining industries were often forced to seek unrelated types of employment, or to take lesser paying jobs in the same occupation. More recently, the field of education has experienced cutbacks, causing teachers and other educational personnel to switch career paths. Whether voluntary or involuntary, it is clear that midlife career change is a visible phenomenon and that a significant proportion of workers will not fit the one life–one occupation mode. (Herr & Cramer, 1996, pp. 535–536)

Though midlife career changes may be commonplace, even anticipated by many workers, such changes can bring adjustment as well as decision-making difficulties. Some adjustments will be the result of adapting to a new work routine with new skills, new work associates, and possible movement to a new environment and new way of life. Also, some will view the necessity or desirability of career change as a reflection on their status as valued workers and an indication that they have erred in their earlier career planning. Marital relationships can be threatened, even when one of the spouses is not facing career change, and existing problems are often agitated further.

In counseling this more mature and work-experienced group, the career counselor will want to consider the following counseling goals (many of which involve reassurance and immediate assistance) outlined by Herr and Cramer (1996):

1. Provide support in building and maintaining positive attitudes toward one's worth and dignity. Is the individual confusing temporary rejection as a worker with rejection as a human being? Does the individual have a work history of rejection? Does the person express feelings of hopelessness, worthlessness, obsolescence, despair? Is confidence shattered?

2. Explore possible retraining and other avenues for improving employment opportunities.

3. Provide any and all geographic information. Does the individual know where the best markets for employment are? Is mobility a problem?

4. Assess the actual reasons for employment difficulties. For example, is the person coming for assistance because of layoff, resignation, sickness, retirement, or firing?

5. Assist individuals in accurately gauging their present state of motivation, the expectations they hold for future employment, and their perceptions of themselves as workers.

6. Especially with managerial, professional, and technical occupations, help the individual to consider the relative importance of such factors as salary, use of abilities, status, amount of responsibility, security, opportunities for advancement, chance to make a contribution, and so on. Also important is the need to explore the possibilities and consequences of occupational downgrading and salary decrease.

7. Assist in developing job-seeking behaviors, if necessary.

8. Provide placement and follow-up services if no other opportunities exist in the area served; refer to appropriate agencies and institutions if placement services are available. (Herr & Cramer, 1996, p. 546).

Many of those seeking new careers will probably again seek the assistance of counselors in the Employment Security Division of the U.S. Department of Labor. The Comprehensive Employment and Training Act of 1982 is an example of federal assistance to state and local governments for the purpose of developing training programs to meet local job needs. This program has a wide range of training activities aimed at economically disadvantaged youth and adults.

More recently, the School-to-Work Opportunities Act was passed by Congress and was enacted into law in May, 1994. This act is administered by the National School-to-Work Office under the joint direction of the U.S. Departments of Labor and Education. The act encourages educational and career opportunities for all students by creating a framework for business and educational partnerships at the state and local levels. It is anticipated that these partnerships help students make the vital connection between what they learn in school and in the workplace and prepare them for good careers and advanced education and training.

Other state and/or federal government programs include provisions for school-to-work transition programs, senior community service employment, job corps, and work incentive programs. State rehabilitation agencies provide career counseling and other services to those eligible.

Although ideally much midlife career change and career retirement counseling would take place in the workplace, some obstacles still impede this development. However, career development programs that provide supporting counseling services are also beginning to emerge in business and industry. A 2001 survey by the National Employment Counselors Association noted how employers rate the importance of experience as follows:

Relevant work experience	4.00
Internship experience	3.85
Any work experience	3.79
Co-op experience	3.21

(5-point scale: 1 = not important and 5 = extremely important)

Source: NACE (National Association of Colleges and Employers) *Job Outlook 2001*, Cam report, P. O. Box 1862, E. Lansing, MI 48826, April 1, 2001, as seen in *NECA* (National Employment Counseling Association) *Newsletter*, Summer 2001, p. 7.

Additionally, employers also rated the importance of candidate qualities as follows:

Communications skills (verbal and written)	4.69
Honesty/integrity	4.66
Teamwork skills (works well with others)	4.55
Interpersonal skills (relates well to others)	4.52
Motivation/initiative	4.52
Strong work ethic	4.50
Analytical skills	4.37
Flexibility/adaptability	4.33
Computer skills	4.25
Self-confidence	4.08
Leadership skills	4.04
Organized	4.00
Detail oriented	4.00

Friendly/outgoing personality	3.91
Tactfulness	3.79
Well mannered/polite	3.79
Creative	3.71
Entrepreneurial skills/risk taker	3.45
Sense of humor	3.39

(5-point scale: 1 = not important and 5 = extremely important)

Source: NACE (National Association of Colleges and Employers) *Job Outlook 2001*, Cam report, P. O. Box 1862, E. Lansing, MI 48826, April 1, 2001, as seen in *NECA* (National Employment Counseling Association) *Newsletter*, Summer 2001, p. 7.

Moving along the maturity continuum, the aging of America is another phenomenon that is increasingly challenging those responsible for providing career counseling in institutional and agency settings. As people marvel at the artistic accomplishments of Grandma Moses at 100 and Pablo Picasso at 90, or George Burns's Academy Award-winning performance in *The Sunshine Boys*, one must be aware that age is not an inevitable barrier to career accomplishments. This is further underscored when we note that the Queen Mother (England) reached her 101st birthday and Senator Strom Thurmond is approaching the century mark. Coupled with this is also an awareness that life expectancy is increasing at the same time that human physical well-being and vigor are steadily improving for all age groups. It can be anticipated that increasing numbers of older and healthier citizens will be capable and desirous of work.

As with other age groups, the older American worker is entering a changing era highlighted by the virtual abolition of mandatory retirement. Age-based mandatory retirement was eliminated for all but a few special circumstances by the 1986 Amendments to the 1967 Age Discrimination in Employment Act. Although on the surface this would appear to ensure that older workers could work as long as they wish, the restructuring of the world of work and its labor economy has resulted in older workers being prematurely forced into early retirement. This, at a time when more and more of the elderly are living longer, healthier lives, is a source of concern. As a result, counselors in corporate employee assistance programs are being called upon with increasing frequency to assist older employees to prepare psychologically as well as economically for retirement or alternate career possibilities. Counselors in other nonschool settings, including Older American Centers, churches, YWCAs and YMCAs and elderhostels, are noting that many older retirees want to continue in or return to the workforce. Some wish to do so for economic reasons; for others there may be feelings of a loss of worth, status, or belonging; a sense of loneliness; and the lack of opportunity to associate with others. Some retirees report boredom, saying that they have no meaningful leisure time activities.

In assisting this client population, counselors must identify the expectancies and desires of the individual. In some instances, clients may be assisted in examining part-time or full-time reemployment options or they may be given a more realistic view of retirement and retirement living.

In some situations the exploration of meaningful leisure time and volunteer activities may be helpful. Elderly support groups may assist in coping with the loss of a spouse, a close friend's changing lifestyle associated with aging and retirement, or leisure planning and reentry into the job market.

COMPUTERIZED CAREER ASSISTANCE SYSTEMS

The 1990s have brought continued rapid development and public acceptance of the computer. Computers, already popular in business, industry, and higher education, are now becoming commonplace in schools at all levels, and the current boom in home computers appears likely to continue. Young people's fascination with this technological marvel is reflected not only in their patronage of video arcades and purchase of computerized video games but also in their quest for knowledge and use of even the most sophisticated of computers. In fact, youth may have become the most computer-literate group.

The attraction of students at all age levels to the computer has given schools unprecedented opportunities for its utilization in motivation and learning. This potential exists for school counseling programs as well, especially in providing career information and assistance.

Computer usage in counseling programs in educational settings is not new, having been around since the 1960s, but the introduction of the microcomputer in the 1970s promoted major changes as well as opportunities for the utilization of computer-assisted career guidance systems. The economic and technical advantages of microcomputers continue to be a major stimulus to their use in school settings for career counseling and guidance purposes.

TYPES OF SYSTEMS

In this section, two types of systems will be briefly described: (a) information systems and (b) guidance systems.

Information Systems

Information systems are generally designed to provide users with a structured search scheme for occupations and to disseminate occupational and educational information to users. These procedural steps may be used separately or in sequence. In the former, the user may complete exercises or provide ratings, even test scores, indicating interests and aptitudes as a basis for the computer's search for compatible occupations. In the information accessing process, the user can access general information regarding specific occupations. The computer may also be programmed to respond to certain specific questions the user may ask about the occupation.

The development of information systems was greatly stimulated by grants provided by the Department of Labor and the National Occupational Information Coordinating Committee, which enabled states to develop statewide career information systems. Many of these, labeled career information systems (CIS), emphasize local and regional information. The components of the CIS systems include an initial questionnaire, labeled QUEST, for providing self-estimates of various areas including aptitudes, interests, and physical limitations. Users then receive a printout briefly describing occupations related to their QUEST responses. Many CIS systems also use a file identifying ways to prepare for an occupation and a file identifying sources for additional information on each occupation.

Another information system, identified as the guidance information system (GIS), provides access to various kinds of national data regarding careers, educational opportunities, and the armed services. Several interest inventory systems are available as options.

This system is marketed through the Educational Software Division of Houghton Mifflin Company, which reported use in 1990 at more than 4,500 locations. Information in this system is arranged according to groups of characteristics related to occupations and four-year colleges.

Another popular system, the C-LECT, offers three modules: an occupational module, an educational module, and a financial aids–apprenticeship module. In addition, the system provides a report writer that allows the user to get a report on his or her inputs at any time during the session. C-LECT is marketed by Chronicle Guidance Publications, Inc.

Guidance Systems

Guidance systems are broader in scope and more instructional than information systems, providing in addition to the organized search and dissemination functions of information systems modules such as self-assessment, instruction in decision making, and future planning. The two most popular of these are the System of Interactive Guidance and Information (SIGI), now updated as SIGI PLUS, developed and marketed through the Educational Testing Service, Princeton, New Jersey; and the Discover System, developed by JoAnn Harris-Bowlsbey and marketed through Discover, Inc., Hunt Valley, Maryland, and the American College Testing Program.

The SIGI system was designed originally to assist college and college-bound students and out-of-school adults. It is now applied to four-year schools and adults in a wide range of settings as well. SIGI PLUS consists of nine modules: (a) Introduction (orientation to the process), (b) Self-assessment, (c) Search (of possible preferred occupations), (d) Information (regarding possible occupations), (e) Skills, (f) Preparation, (g) Coping (can the individual do what is required), (h) Deciding (decision making), and (i) Next Steps (putting a plan into action).

The DISCOVER system offers different programs for junior/middle school, high school, adults in transition, employees and organizations, and those approaching retirement. The junior/middle school version consists of three modules: (a) You and the World of Work, (b) Exploratory Occupations, and (c) Planning for High School. The popular high school version has seven modules:

Module 1: *Beginning the Career Journey*

Administers and scores a career maturity inventory and suggests parts of DISCOVER to be used.

Module 2: *Learning About the World of Work*

Helps users understand American College Testing's World-of-Work Map.

Module 3: *Learning About Yourself*

Administers and scores on-line assessment and inventories and accepts results of paper and pencil versions.

Module 4: *Finding Occupations*

Generates occupation lists from the results of Module 3.

Module 5: *Learning About Occupations*

Provides national details about hundreds of occupations and includes local or state information if customized.

Module 6: *Making Educational Choices*

Helps users select a training pathway.

Module 7: *Planning Next Steps*

Provides details about educational opportunities and develops job-seeking skills. (DISCOVER is published by American College Testing: Iowa City, IA).

Planning Next Steps

Provides details about educational opportunities and develops job-seeking skills. (American College Testing, 2001)

The college versions add modules in career planning and transitions. The organizational and retirement versions consist of four modules, each unique to organizational settings or retirement planning.

Beginning in the mid-1990s and continuing into the new century, the need for adult counseling and career placement services dramatically increased. This need was brought about by downsizing in many of the nation's industries, the merging of others, and an emphasis throughout industry on cutting production costs. The result was not only pools of unemployment but also large numbers of temporary or transitional employees. The rise in temporary employment, while beneficial to business and industry, provided the temporarily hired individual with limited retirement funding and often no health insurance—and of course, no guarantee of future employment.

Career Information and the Internet

The Internet has made available huge volumes of information on any given research topic. Indicated below are a number of Web sites related to career awareness. The reader needs to keep in mind that it is not possible to list everything. One may, by following links from the sites indicated, find other interesting sites (Cutshall, 2001, p. 32).

About.com: Career Planning
<www.careerplanning.about.com>

America's Career Info Net
<www.acinet.org/acinet>

America's Job Bank
<www.ajb.dni.us>

Best Jobs USA
<www.bestjobsusa.com>

Campus Career Center Worldwide
<www.campuscareercenter.com>

Career Builder
<www.careerbuilder.com>

Career Consulting Corner
<www.careercc.com>

CareerExplorer.net
<www.careerexplorer.net>

Career Interests Game
    <career.missouri.edu/holland>

Career/Life Skills
    <www.career-lifeskills.com>

Career Magazine
    <www.careermag.com>

Career Management International
    <www.cmi-lmi.com/kingdomality.html>

I Could Be
    <www.icouldbe.org>

JobBank USA
    <www.jobbankusa.com>

Job Profiles
    <www.jobprofiles.com>

Jobtrak Corporation
    <www.jobtrak.com>

Mapping Your Future
    <www.mapping-your-future.org>

Monster.com
    <www.monster.com>

My Future
    <www.myfuture.com>

Princeton Review Career Quiz
    <www.review.com/career>

Salary.com
    <www.salary.com>

Vocational Research Institute
    <www.vri.org>

ETHICAL CONSIDERATIONS

The rapid growth of computer usage in the field of counseling and its anticipated increased usage in the future have raised certain ethical questions related to the use of computers in counseling. Potential problems in client confidentiality, misinterpretation of tests results and other data by clients, and lack of appropriate counselor interaction with clients are but a few examples. Sampson and Pyle (1983) suggest 14 principles in response to ethical issues involved with the use of computer-assisted counseling, testing, and guidance systems:

1.   Ensure that confidential data maintained on a computer are limited to information that is appropriate and necessary for the services being provided.
2.   Ensure that confidential data maintained on a computer are destroyed after it is determined that the information is no longer of any value in providing services.

3. Ensure that confidential data maintained on a computer are accurate and complete.

4. Ensure that access to confidential data is restricted to appropriate professionals by using the best computer security methods available.

5. Ensure that it is not possible to identify, with any particular individual, confidential data maintained in a computerized data bank that is accessible through a computer network.

6. Ensure that research participation release forms are completed by an individual who has automatically collected individually identifiable data as a result of using a computer-assisted counseling, testing, or guidance system.

7. Ensure that computer-controlled test scoring equipment and programs function properly thereby providing individuals with accurate test results.

8. Ensure that generalized interpretations of test results presented by microcomputer-controlled audiovisual devices accurately reflect the intention of the test author.

9. Ensure that a client's needs are assessed to determine if using a particular system is appropriate before using a computer-assisted counseling, testing, or guidance system.

10. Ensure that an introduction to using a computer-assisted counseling, testing, and guidance system is available to reduce possible anxiety concerning the system, misconceptions about the role of the computer, and misunderstandings about basic concepts or the operation of the system.

11. Ensure that a follow-up activity to using a computer-assisted counseling, testing, and guidance system is available to correct possible misconceptions, misunderstandings, or inappropriate use as well as assess subsequent needs of the client.

12. Ensure that the information contained in a computer-assisted career counseling and guidance system is accurate and up-to-date.

13. Ensure that the equipment and programs that operate a computer-assisted counseling, testing, and guidance system function properly.

14. Determining the need for counselor intervention depends on the likelihood that the client would experience difficulties that would in turn limit the effectiveness of the system or otherwise exacerbate the client's problem. It is the counselor's responsibility to decide whether the best approach to avoiding the above problems for a specific client population is direct intervention or indirect intervention through the use of workbooks, self-help guides, or other exercises. (pp. 285–286)

Certainly, we must hope that rapid developments in computer technology will not "outrun" careful consideration of the ethical issues involved.

Counselors also have an ethical responsibility to be aware of and strive to meet the career counseling competencies as identified by the National Career Development Association. These competencies may be seen in Appendix O. These are especially significant for those specializing in career counseling or whose job descriptions require significant attention to the career needs of their clients.

SUMMARY

Dramatic changes in the world of work and the increased need for career assistance among all ages has resulted in a new impetus for career counseling and placement in both school and agency settings in recent decades. In the past, career counseling was a recognized activity of most school counseling programs, but it received little curricular emphasis and, as a result, was less than effective in many settings. The career education movement of the 1970s, however, led schools to recognize the inseparability of career education and career counseling and guidance. Career counseling programs were also encouraged to provide increased attention to placement and follow-up as a planned program activity. This emphasis has been prompted by legislative funding and recognition that career development without placement is an incomplete process. In this area, significant developments in computerized career assistance programs have been noted.

The concern over career planning and decision making has focused attention on why people make the decisions they do and with what results. To help develop an understanding of these issues, a number of the traditional theories were reviewed in this chapter. Some investigators are challenging these theories as inappropriate for today's populations and careers.

Agencies and other noneducational institutions that, in the past, were primarily concerned with career placement of first-time job seekers are now recognizing the probability and importance of midlife career changes, the possibility of employment in a new field after retirement, and the elimination of many traditional barriers to the employment of women, minorities, and older adults. Additionally, attention is being focused on increased recognition of the career needs of workers with disabilities and the career concerns of dual-career couples. These and other factors have led to a renewed interest in and examination of influences on career planning and decision making of adults. Also, the unique career assistance needs of older, retiring Americans is receiving increased attention. Career counseling across the lifetime is becoming a reality.

Historically, career counseling has been a concern and activity of counselors. The next chapter discusses a comparatively recent development in our profession—the counselor's role as a developmental and educational consultant.

DISCUSSION QUESTIONS

1. What are the differences among career education, vocational education, and business education?
2. If we anticipate that many adults will have as many as seven major career changes during their working lifetimes, what are the implications for counseling in all settings? Identify five different careers you might consider. What alternate careers would you consider if required to do so?
3. Discuss this multipotentiality of individuals and the implications of this for career planning and decision making.
4. What significant changes have occurred in careers and the world of work as you have observed it in recent generations? What changes may be anticipated in the remainder of this century?
5. Discuss a career in counseling as "a way of life."
6. Why have you decided to enter the career that you are in? What do you expect to give to this career? What do you anticipate that you will receive from it?
7. Discuss the impact of significant career development experiences in your life.
8. How are technological developments affecting the way we work?
9. Discuss relationships between leisure time and work time.
10. Identify and discuss the relationship between basic needs and career decisions.

CLASS ACTIVITIES

1. Have each member of the class identify the significant influences on his or her career planning and decision making. Following a discussion of these with other members (in small groups) have each individual identify the theory of career choice that seems most appropriate for his or her career development and choice. Place individuals in groups according to the theories they have identified and allow time for comparison of influencing factors among group members.
2. Draw a career map (using newsprint and felt pens, with stick figures and simple drawings going from lower left to upper right) that depicts significant events and influencing factors in your career development and experiences.
3. Organize small groups to investigate career-oriented societal problems of a career nature and recommend national and/or local solutions. Problems might include concerns such as unemployment for a special population (i.e., minorities,

youth, women), underemployment for a special population, substance abuse in the workplace, dual career families and latchkey children, and school dropouts and career failures.

4. Discuss your personal experiences with career assessment instruments or take a career interest or aptitude test and report your impressions of the results.

5. Interview individuals either entering the workforce for the first time or approaching retirement regarding their experiences for the coming year.

6. If you had to identify an alternate career, indicate what that career might be and why.

7. Discuss the implications of the suggestion that "a career is a way of life" as it applies to a career in counseling.

SELECTED READINGS

Bundy, M., & Boser, J. (1987). Helping latchkey children: A group guidance approach. *The School Counselor, 35*(1), 58–65.

Cochran, L. (1997). *Career counseling: A narrative approach.* Thousand Oaks, CA: Sage.

Feller, R., & Gluckman, N. (1986). The unemployed and counselors: An analysis of responses to a complex social issue. *Counseling and Human Development, 18*(6), 1–11.

Gerstein, L., & Bayer, G. (1988). Employee assistance programs: A system's investigation of their use. *Journal of Counseling and Development, 66*(6), 294–297.

Gianakos, I. (1999). Career counseling with battered women. *Journal of Mental Health Counseling, 21*(1), 1–14.

Gilbert, L. A. (Ed.). (1987). Special edition: Dual-career families in perspective. *The Counseling Psychologist, 15*(1), 3–145.

Holland, J. L. (1996). Integrating career theory and practice: The current situation and some potential remedies. In M. L. Savickas & W. B. Walsh (Eds.), *Handbook of career counseling theory and practice* (pp. 1–11). Palo Alto, CA: Davies-Black.

McCarthy, C. J., & Lambert, R. G. (1999). Structural model of coping and emotions produced by taking a new job. *Journal of Employment Counseling, 36*(2), 50–66.

Myers, S. L., Jr. (1986). Black unemployment and its link to crime. *Urban League Review, 10*(1), 98–105.

Phillips, S. D., & Imhoff, A. R. (1997). Women and career development: A decade of research. *Annual Review of Psychology, 48,* 31–59.

Pope, M. (2000). A brief history of career counseling in the United States. *The Career Development Quarterly, 48*(3), 194–211.

Frank Parson's continuing legacy to career development interventions. (2001). [Special Section]. *The Career Development Quarterly, 50*(1), 56–88.

Raskin, P. M. (1994). Identity and the career counseling of adolescents: The development of vocational identity. In S. L. Archer (Ed.), *Interventions for adolescent identity development* (pp. 155–173). Thousand Oaks, CA: Sage.

Repp, A. C., Favell, J., & Munk, D. (1996). Cognitive and vocational interventions for school-age children and adolescents with mental retardation. In J. W. Jacobson & J. A. Mulick (Eds.), *Manual of diagnosis and professional practice in mental retardation* (pp. 265–276). Washington, DC: American Psychological Association.

RESEARCH OF INTEREST

Emmett, J. D. (1997). The preparation of elementary school counselors for career development: What exists—what is needed. *Journal of Career Development, 23*(3), 177–187.

Abstract Forty directors of accredited programs in school counseling responded to a survey. Participants were asked whether they had modified the requirements of their career development courses for students preparing to work in career development at the elementary school level. Those answering in the affirmative were asked which of six course areas they had modified and to describe the modifications made. The six course areas were career development theories, career assessment, career information resources, career development programming, field experiences, and career interviewing/career counseling competencies. Participants were also asked to describe the modifications to their career development courses they believed to be most successful. Eighteen of the respondents reported modifying their career courses for elementary school counselors-in-training. Many of the modifications occurred in the areas of career theory, information resources, and development programming.

Fleenor, J. (1986). The personal career development profile: Using the 16 PF for vocational exploration. *Measurement and Evaluation in Counseling Development, 18*(4), 185–189.

Abstract This article reviews the Sixteen Personality Factor Questionnaire and the Personal Career Development Profile as tools for vocational exploration and career development. Reliability and validity problems are reported, followed by a recommendation to use the Strong-Campbell Interest inventory instead.

Juntunen, C. (1996). Relationship between a feminist approach to career counseling and career self-efficacy beliefs. *Journal of Employment Counseling, 33*(3), 130–143.

Abstract To determine whether liberal feminist and conventional approaches to career counseling might differentially affect women's career self-efficacy beliefs, 40 college women heard audiotapes of career counseling and provided ratings of their own career self-efficacy. Results show that a feminist approach to career counseling can have a significantly more positive effect on career self-efficacy than a conventional approach. This was true for ratings on the category of nontraditional careers as well as for overall career self-efficacy ratings.

Luzzo, D. A., James, T., & Luna, M. (1996). Effects of attributional retraining on the career beliefs and career exploration behavior of college students. *Journal of Counseling Psychology, 43*(4), 415–422.

Abstract Two studies were conducted to evaluate the efficacy of attributional retraining as a career counseling technique for college students. Participants who received the attributional retraining treatment viewed an 8-minute videotape designed to foster internal, controllable, and unstable attributions for career decision making. Participants in the control groups viewed a similar videotape that lacked any reference to career-related attributions. Results revealed that participants who received attributional retraining exhibited significant changes in career beliefs and attributional style and engaged in significantly more career exploration behavior than the participants in the control groups. An evaluation of attributional retraining as a career-counseling technique for college students was provided, and ideas for further research were suggested.

Mau, W., & Kopischke, A. (2001). Job search methods, job search outcomes, and job satisfaction of college graduates: A comparison of race and sex. *Journal of Employment Counseling, 38*, 141–149.

Abstract A nationally representative sample of college graduates (N = 11,152) were surveyed regarding their job-seeking behaviors and outcomes. Race and sex differences among the job search strategies used, number of job interviews, number of job offers, annual salary, and job satisfaction were examined. Results indicated significant race and sex differences in job search methods used. There were significant differences in underemployment and job satisfaction as a function of race, and in underemployment and annual salary as a function of sex. There were no significant differences in number of job interviews or job offers regardless of race or sex.

Niles, S. G. (1997). Annual review: Practice and research in career counseling and development—1996. *The Career Development Quarterly, 46*(2), 115–141.

Abstract The National Career Development Association's (NCDA) Professional Standards Committee (1997) has recently identified 11 competency areas (career development theory, individual and group counseling skills, individual and group assessment, information resources, program management and implementation, consultation, diverse populations, supervision, ethical legal issues, research evaluation, and technology). These competencies were used as categories for classifying research on career development and counseling published in 1996. Two primary areas of research activity were identified: making career counseling theory useful for more clients, and emphasizing the role of contextual factors in shaping career development. Four competency areas not addressed sufficiently by researchers were also identified: consultation, supervision, technology, and ethics. Implications for practice and future research were discussed.

Olson, T. F., & Matkin, R. E. (1992). Student and counselor perceptions of career counselor work activities in a community college. *Career Development Quarterly, 40*(4), 324–333.

Abstract This study examined whether differences exist between student and counselor perceptions of work activities performed by counselors in a community college. Three hundred twenty-two students and eleven counselors responded to a 40-item questionnaire indicating whether tasks were actually performed and whether they ought to be performed by counselors when providing career guidance. Students indicated they did not believe counselors were actually performing the majority of tasks commonly and ideally associated with career counseling services. Although students and counselors agreed on ideal career counselor work activities, counselor responses revealed no differences between their actual and ideal duties.

Patton, W., & Creed, P. A. (2001). Developmental issues in career maturity and career decision status. *The Career Development Quarterly, 49*(4), 336–351.

Abstract There is considerable diversity in the literature regarding age and gender differences on career maturity and career decision status. There is also a dearth of data on high school samples. The present study reports cross-sectional data from 1,971 Australian adolescents, ages 12.51 to 17.99 years, who completed the Career Decision Scale (S. H. Osipow, C. G. Carney, J. Winer, B. Yanico, & M. Koschier, 1976) and the Career Development Inventory (Australian; J. Lokan, 1984). Results illustrated a developmental progression in career maturity, although a less uniform pattern emerged with gender differences. Findings regarding career indecision also presented a complex picture and highlight the need to focus on other demographic and contextual factors.

Smith, M., & Glass, G. (1977). Meta-analysis of psychotherapy outcome studies. *American Psychologist, 32*(9), 752–760.

Abstract   Results of nearly 400 controlled evaluations of psychotherapy and counseling were coded and integrated statistically. The findings provide convincing evidence of the efficacy of psychotherapy. Few important differences in effectiveness could be established among many quite different types of psychotherapy. More generally, virtually no difference in effectiveness was observed between the class of all behavioral therapies (systematic desensitization, behavior modification) and the nonbehavioral therapies (Rogerian, psychodynamic, rational-emotive, transactional analysis, etc.).

Sumerel, M. B., & Borders, L. D. (1995). Supervision of career counseling interns. *Clinical Supervisor, 13*(1), 91–100.

Abstract   This study examined data concerning career counseling internships and compared supervision practices in various internship sites. Thirty-four supervisors of career counseling interns in three settings (college/university career planning centers, college/university counseling centers, community colleges) described their supervisory approach, format, and focus, and indicated which career counseling competencies they emphasized. Results indicate that supervision practices were similar in the three settings: supervision occurred weekly and was based on self-report given by the intern in individual sessions. Supervisors emphasized the career counseling competencies of counseling skills and career information most often and consultation least often.

Wiener, K. K. K., Oei, T. P. S., & Creed, P. A. (1999). *Journal of Employment Counseling, 36*(2), 67–81.

Abstract   Unemployed ($n = 118$) and employed ($n = 120$) people were contrasted on variables of well-being, confidence, and employment commitment. The unemployed scored lower on the General Health Questionnaire (Goldberg, 1972) and the General Self-Efficacy Scale (Sherer et al., 1982). No differences were identified on levels of employment commitment. For the unemployed sample, predictors of job-seeking behavior and well-being were then examined. Intention to seek work predicted job-seeking behavior, while self-efficacy, employment commitment, and intentions to seek work predicted well-being. Results are discussed in light of current theories of job-seeking behavior, and recommendations are made for practice.

The Counselor as Developmental and Educational Consultant

A network television news program recently carried a report that a group of big business executives were going to offer their consulting services to small businesses to aid their survival chances. These businesspeople were referred to as consultants—a term so common that the newscaster did not bother to define it. Consultation as an activity and consultant as a career label became increasingly prevalent in the last generations of the 20th century. Although generally recognized as originating in the medical profession in the 19th century, today many career areas use the label *consultant*. This includes such common examples as loan consultant, landscape consultant, travel consultant, tax consultant, automotive sales consultant, and on and on.

A *consultant* is usually an expert in a field who consults with or offers her or his expertise to others both within and outside the career area. In fact, the activity is so ubiquitous in the business world that we frequently hear humorous definitions of a consultant, such as "anyone 50 miles from home with a briefcase" or "one who pulls in, pops off, and pulls out."

Consultation as a mental health and educational activity is less well recognized and understood, although mental health consultation has a long tradition in the healing arts. The objective of this chapter is to introduce and describe the activity of consulting and the counselor's role as a consultant.

The label *consultant* usually refers to an individual possessing extra expertise, knowledge and/or skill in a specific field. The individual engages in consultation when her or his expertise is requested by another party or organization, usually to enable the requesting party or organization to assist another—a third party or organization.

The consultant is the helper in a triad that includes a consultee and the object of the consultation. For example, a mental health counselor may serve as a consultant to parents who want to improve their children's social skills; unlike counseling, this is not a therapeutic relationship. It is also important to keep in mind that the consultant's role is an advising or enhancing one, not a supervisory one. Remember too that these distinctive roles are maintained throughout the consultation experience and that their identities are not blurred or distorted in any way.

Consultation in its application to counseling as a mental health activity in schools has been even less widely recognized and defined. Most of the attention given to consultation as a school counseling activity before the 1970s seemed to suggest that it was primarily appropriate for the elementary school only. Articles such as "Consultation to a School Guidance Program" (Abbe, 1961), "Depth Consultation with Parents" (Crocker, 1964),

"Elementary School Guidance: The Consultant" (Eckerson & Smith, 1962), and "The Counselor as a Consultant to Teachers" (Faust, 1967) dealt with consultation in elementary school guidance programs. No mention at all of consultation as a school counseling activity was made in some of the popular basic guidance texts of the 1950s and 1960s, such as *Principles of Guidance* (Jones, 1963), *The Guidance Function in Education* (Hutson, 1958), *An Introduction to Guidance* (Crow & Crow, 1960), *Guidance: An Introduction* (Ohlsen, 1955), and *Guidance Services in Schools* (Froelich, 1958).

In discussing consultation in his early landmark publication *The Counselor-Consultant in the Elementary School*, Faust (1967) noted:

> Although counseling has been described and researched for many years, this is not true of consultation. The latter has been practiced for as many years as counseling, if not longer, but the literature is strangely sparse in its treatment of this role. (p. 32)

Although these early discussions focused on mental health consultation in community agencies, industrial settings, and the elementary school, in the past decade consultation as an appropriate counselor activity in any setting, including secondary schools and higher education institutions, has developed rapidly.

For example, the American Counseling Association (then called the American Personnel and Guidance Association) devoted two consecutive special issues of its journal, *Personnel and Guidance Journal* to the counselor's role and function as a consultant at all educational levels as well as in community and other mental health settings. Kurpius and Robinson were the editors of these two special issues: "Consultation I: Definition-Models-Programs" (volume 56, number 6, February 1978); and "Consultation II: Topical Issues and Features in Consultation" (volume 56, number 7, March 1978).

In July 1985, *The Counseling Psychologist* produced its own special issue (volume 13, number 3, July 1985) that examined the counselor as consultant (Brown & Kurpius, 1985). In 1988 the Association for Counselor Education and Supervision published two monographs focusing on consultation (Kurpius & Brown, 1988; Brown, Kurpius, & Morris, 1988). In 1993, the American Counseling Association devoted two special issues of the *Journal of Counseling and Development* to this topic (Kurpius & Fuqua, 1993a; Kurpius & Fuqua, 1993c). The interest that consulting holds for the profession is evident and worthy of our attention. Next, we examine the process as well as some of the roles and models for consultation.

THE CONSULTATION PROCESS

When counselors function as consultants, they must keep in mind certain assumptions that are basic to the consultation process:

- The need that exists cannot be adequately met by the individual or organization requesting consultation.
- The consultant possesses the special expertise to appropriately assist the requestor.
- The requesting party (the consultee) has the capacity to implement the consultant's recommendations.

- The consultant understands the organizational and environmental context within which his or her suggestions will be applied and is aware of the possible consequences of these suggestions beyond problem solutions.

Woody, Hansen, and Rossberg (1989), after an extensive review of the literature on consulting, consolidated their conceptualizations of the consultation process into five stages: "(1) pre-entry, (2) initial contact and establishment of a relationship, (3) assessment and diagnosis, (4) intervention, and (5) termination" (p. 179).

Even though the process of consultation is initiated by the consultee in need of assistance, the consultant must keep in mind that consultation is not primarily therapeutic in nature. In other words, those seeking consultative assistance do not usually come to the counselor-consultant for personal counseling; rather, they come for assistance with a usually well-defined professional problem.

Another view of the consultation process might be to examine the stages through which the process moves, as listed here:

1. Description of the situation
2. Analysis of the problem
3. Selection of the solution
4. Application of the solution
5. Evaluation of the process and outcome.

CONSULTATION MODELS

The increase in popularity and demand for consultation services has led to the development or identification of several models or styles appropriate to the consultation process. Authorities on consultation differ somewhat in the organization or categorization of theories or systems for providing consultation services, but their similarities far exceed their differences.

The traditional historic model that highlights the basic consultation process is a triadic model, as suggested by Tharp and Wetzel (1969). In this model, consultation services are offered indirectly through an intermediary to a target client or clients. The consultation process is illustrated in Figure 9-1. This figure displays the activities of all participants in the consulting process.

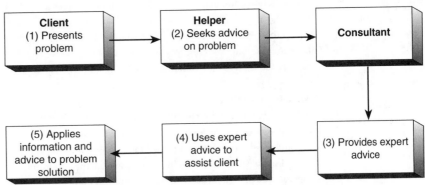

Figure 9-1   The consultation process.

Four popular consultation models suggest that the counselor-consultant can function effectively by (a) providing a direct service to a client identified by another party, (b) prescribing a solution to a specific problem identified by a consultee, (c) assisting others in developing a plan for problem solution, and (d) taking direct responsibility for defining a problem and proposing a solution. Kurpius (1978) and Kurpius and Fuqua (1993b) organized these functions into four consulting modalities as follows:

Provision Mode

The provision mode of consultation is commonly used when a potential consultee finds himself confronted with a problem for which he or she may not have the time, interest, or competence to define objectively, to identify possible solutions, or to implement and evaluate the problem-solving strategy. Consequently, a consultant is requested to provide a direct service to the client, with little or no intervention by the consultee after the referral is accepted.

Prescriptive Mode

Sometimes consultees experience unusual work-related problems for which they request special help. Even though competent and motivated to solve the problem directly, the consultees may lack confidence in their own intervention strategy or may lack certain specific knowledge and skills for carrying out a given problem-solving plan.

In these situations, the consultee is often in need of a resource person (consultant) to support the diagnosis and treatment plan already developed by the consultee or to explore additional alternatives for defining and solving a specific problem.

There are other times, however, when a consultee is looking for an exact "prescription" to ameliorate a specific problem. While the prescriptive mode is quite appropriate for many situations, there are four questions that should be answered jointly by the consultant and consultee: (a) Has all the information needed to define and solve the problem been shared and is [it] accurate? (b) Has the plan prescribed by the consultant been accepted by the consultee and will it be implemented as designed? (c) Who will evaluate the "process" and "outcomes" associated with the prescriptive plan—the consultant, the consultee, or both? (d) Will adjustments in the prescription, if needed, be requested by the consultee?

Collaboration Mode

When following the collaboration mode the consultant's goal is to facilitate the consultee's self-direction and innate capacity to solve problems. As a result, the consultant serves more as a generalist than a technical expert. His major efforts are directed toward helping people develop a plan for solving problems. Hence he acts as a catalyst and "reality tapper," helping consultees to share observations, concepts, and proven practices. He also helps consultees examine forces that are facilitative or debilitative in both the immediate and larger environments.

Mediation Mode

Mediation is uniquely different from the other three modes of consultation in which the consultee initiates the contact and requests help for solving a problem. In mediation, it is the consultant who recognizes a persisting problem, gathers, analyzes, and synthesizes existing information, defines the problem, decides on the most appropriate intervention, and then calls together the persons who have direct contact with the problem and have the greatest potential to influence a desired change. (Kurpius, 1978, p. 335)

Schein (1978, 1991) organized the consultation process into three models. The assumptions of these models are as follows:

Model I: Purchase of Expertise

The core characteristic of this model is that the client has made up his or her mind on what the problem is, what kinds of help are needed, and to whom to go for this help. The client expects expert help and expects to pay for it, but not to get involved in the process of consultation itself.

In order for this model to work successfully, the following assumptions have to be met, however.

1. That the client has made a correct diagnosis of his or her own problem.
2. That the client has correctly identified the consultant's capabilities to solve the problem.
3. That the client has correctly communicated the problem.
4. That the client has thought through and accepted the potential consequences of the help that will be received.

In summary, this model of consultation is appropriate when clients have diagnosed their needs correctly, have correctly identified consultant capabilities, have done a good job of communicating what problem they are actually trying to solve, and have thought through the consequences of the help they have sought. As can be seen, this model is "client intensive," in that it puts a tremendous load on the client to do things correctly if the problem is to be solved. If problems are complex and difficult to diagnose, it is highly likely that this model will not prove helpful.

Model 2: Doctor-Patient

The core of this model is that the client experiences some symptoms that something is wrong but does not have a clue as to how to go about figuring out what is wrong or how to fix it. The diagnostic process itself is delegated completely to the consultant along with the obligation to come up with a remedy. The client becomes dependent upon the consultant until such time as the consultant makes a prescription, unless the consultant engages the client in becoming more active on his or her own behalf. Several implicit assumptions are the key to whether or not the doctor-patient model will in fact provide help to the client.

1. That the client has correctly interpreted the symptoms and the sick "area."
2. That the client can trust the diagnostic information that is provided by the consultant.
3. That the "sick" person or group will reveal the correct information necessary to arrive at a diagnosis and cure, i.e., will trust the doctor enough to "level" with him or her.
4. That the client has thought through the consequences, i.e., is willing to accept and implement whatever prescription is given.
5. That the patient/client will be able to remain healthy after the doctor/consultant leaves.

In summary, the doctor-patient model of consultation highlights the dependence of the client on the consultant both for diagnosis and prescription and thus puts a great burden on the client to correctly identify sick areas, accurately communicate symptoms, and think through the consequences of being given a prescription.

Model 3: Process Consultation

The core of this model is the assumption that for many kinds of problems that clients face, the only way to locate a workable solution, one that the client will accept and implement, is to involve the client in the diagnosis of the problem and the generating of that solution. The focus shifts from the content of the problem to the process by which problems are solved, and the consultant offers "process expertise" in how to help and how to solve problems, not expertise on the particular content of the client's problem. The consultant does not take the problem onto his or her own shoulders in this model. The "monkey always remains on the client's back," but the consultant offers to become jointly involved with the client in figuring out what the problem is, why it is a problem, why it is a problem right now, and what might be done about it. This consulting model is not a panacea appropriate to all problems and all situations. It also rests on some specific assumptions that have to be met if the model is to be viewed as the appropriate way to work with a client.

1. That the nature of the problem is such that the client not only needs help in making an initial diagnosis but would benefit from participation in the process of making that diagnosis.
2. That the client has constructive intent and some problem-solving ability.
3. That the client is ultimately the only one who knows what form of solution or intervention will work in his or her own situation.
4. That if the client selects and implements his or her own solution, the client's problem-solving skills for future problems will increase.

How does the consultant implement the process consultation model? The basic principle is to get into the client's world and see it initially from the client's perspective. This usually means paying attention to the task process—and how the problem is defined, how the agenda is set, how information is gathered, how decisions are made, all the activities that make up the "problem-solving process." (Schein, 1978, pp. 340–342)

It has become a principle in education and psychology that it is far better in the long run to teach others to be effective problem solvers than it is merely to solve a given problem for them. Thus, the more effective organizational consultants will leave the organization with a model that has been learned and can be independently implemented. (Fuqua & Kurpius, 1993, p. 607)

Fuqua and Kurpius (1993) developed the five conceptual models presented Table 9-1. Blocher (1987) identified seven models of consultation:

1. *Triadic consultation*—three distinct roles characterize this model. They are the consultant who provides the expertise, the mediator who applies what he or she receives from the consultant and the client who is the object or recipient of the service.
2. *Technical consultation*—a more narrow and focused intervention in which a consultant's expertise is sought in relation to a specific situation or problem.
3. *Collaborative consultation*—suggests a cooperative relationship in which information and resources are pooled and the consultant and consultee work together as equal partners in the process.
4. *Facilitative consultation*—the consultant facilitates the consultee's access to a variety of new resources. In this model both parties recognize the consultant's legitimate interest in the broad aspects of the functioning of the consultee system.
5. *Mental health consultation*—the consultant assists a consultee (therapist) to gain a better understanding of one's interaction with a client through such means as analyz-

Table 9-1 Integrating conceptual models.

Conceptual Model	Operating Frames			
	Reactive	*Responsive*	*Proactive*	*High Performing*
Systems Theory	Where is the breakdown? What subsystem is causing the problem?	Who's responsible for what?	How do we refine our system for the long term?	How does a system achieve flexibility?
Organizational Culture	Who is causing us pain and why?	How do we resolve conflict?	How is our culture affecting us?	How do we manage our culture for improving the quality of life?
Strategic Planning	How do we alleviate the pain in the short term?	What needs to work better? How do we correct it?	How do we develop a plan for moving forward?	How does strategic planning become part of our system?
Organizational Change Cycles	How did we "bottom out" developmentally?	How do we cope with these circumstances?	How do we get to the developmental phase?	How do we monitor and influence normal developmental cycles?
Paradigm Shift Thinking	How can we relieve stress without changing our thinking?	What thoughts need to be adjusted?	Is our thinking congruent with our purposes?	How can we continually update our knowledge and our thinking in a changing world?

Source: Reprinted from D. R. Fuqua & D. K. Kurplus, "Conceptual Models in Organizational Consultation," *Journal of Counseling and Development, 71,* 1993, p. 617. © American Counseling Association. Reprinted with permission. No further reproduction authorized without written permission of the American Counseling Association.

ing the treatment approach, consideration of their (consultee's) responses to their client and in general, providing support to the consultee.

6. *Behavioral consultation*—focused on the use of behavioral management techniques as suggested or taught by the consultant to a consultee in order to influence or shape the behavior of the consultee's clients in a systematic way.

7. *Process consultation*—the consultant delivers services to an organization in order to increase the effectiveness of a work group in reaching its goals. This consultation addresses the interactions among groups of individuals who work with each other in face-to-face relationships. (pp. 264–270)

Regardless of which approach or model may be selected, certain characteristics appear to be common in the consultation process.

1. The service is indirect.
2. The solution and its application are a collaborative effort.
3. The consultant and the client collaborate in planning for problem solution.
4. The desired outcome is the resolution of the problem.

CONSULTATION SKILLS

As with all counseling and guidance activities, if the counselor is to function effectively as a consultant in either agency or school settings, he or she will need certain special skills:

- The special expertise needed to provide effective consultation for the identified need, knowledge of, and experience in the consultation process
- The recognition and understanding of differing environments and their impacts on populations and organizations

Of course, the counselor who is functioning in a consultation role should possess and employ the skills essential in the counseling process. Certainly communication and other interpersonal skills such as attending, listening, questioning, and feedback are critical. Respect and understanding should be exhibited. Consultants should possess expertise in systematic problem-solving techniques and evaluation procedures as well. The counselor's skills in facilitating groups can be very helpful. Counselors must also possess the ability to effectively assume different roles as needed during the consultation process. These include roles as facilitators, coordinators, mediators, planners, educators, and motivators.

CONSULTATION IN SCHOOL SETTINGS

In school settings, counselors who function in a consulting role are in effect giving their special expertise to teachers, school administrators, and other appropriate personnel. In this role, they become a resource professional for the developmental or adjustment needs involving third parties, usually students. To function effectively as a consultant in the educational setting, the counselor must possess special knowledge or skills appropriate to the consulting need. Among the relevant skills the counselor can bring to consulting with teachers and other educational providers and planners are the following:

1. An understanding of human growth and development, the problems and processes of adjustment, and the needs of the individual as one goes through those processes
2. An understanding of psychological or affective education in the classroom, and a concern for its importance
3. An understanding of and skills in promoting communications and other desirable human relationship skills
4. Training in the assessment of individual characteristics and skills in relating these assessments to the development of the individuals' potential
5. Special knowledge of educational and career development and opportunities
6. An ability to communicate, counsel, and consult with parents, fellow educators, and the community
7. An understanding of group processes and skills useful in facilitating group motivation and change

In addition, the effective counselor-consultant must have an understanding of the person or group with whom he or she is consulting, the target population for the consulting, and the characteristics of the school in which the consulting is taking place. The counselor-consultant should also be knowledgeable regarding contributing external environmental factors.

As a consultant, the school counselor has the potential to engage in a wide range of activities or roles, which we will look at next.

Consulting with Teachers

As mentioned previously, the teacher is the key person in school settings at any level. In consultation in schools, then, the counselor must assume that he or she will most frequently consult with teachers individually or in groups. Teachers have the most frequent contacts with pupils and the developmental and adjustment needs of their pupils are often expressed in classroom groups. Counselors may effectively assist teachers as consultants to individualize classroom instruction.

School counselors are also experienced in collecting, organizing, and synthesizing data on individual students and in interpreting this information to identify individual differences. Through these activities, they sharpen their own understanding of the individual and share these insights in consultation with the classroom teacher.

Additionally, the counselor's expertise in human behavior and development theory combined with the teacher's knowledge of instructional methods and materials is the basis for an excellent team effort in the crucial task of planning and establishing a productive learning environment.

> The classroom teacher is obviously the most knowledgeable about resources appropriate to his or her subject matter, but the counselor can nonetheless be profitably consulted on those occasions when specialized career and educational information is needed to make a class more meaningful. He or she can also be consulted to identify out-of-school resources and experiences relevant to students' learning needs. The counselor's insights can be helpful in the development of materials and methodologies that will enable counselors and teachers to work together in special educational activities with vocational students (Gibson, 1973, p. 51).

The counselor's role as a curriculum consultant to the classroom teacher has been further underscored with the passage of Public Law 94-142. This law requires all children categorized as disabled to be placed in regular educational programs to the fullest extent possible, resulting in a wider diversity in the characteristics and abilities of classroom groups. Of course, pupil guidance is a responsibility of everyone and will be most effective when it is treated as an integral and important part of every segment of the school curriculum. In other words, guidance should be infused into the daily instruction in all subject-matter classrooms. In this regard, counselors must be willing to assist their teacher colleagues in planning appropriate classroom activities. In the elementary schools, where teachers, for the most part, teach by grade levels, counselors should meet with these teachers by grade levels to assist them in planning for the appropriate activities and the integration of these into the classroom instruction. Counselors will continue to play a significant consultant role in assisting teachers specifically and the educational system generally in implementing Public Law 94-142.

Again, a basic principle of effective consultation is that the recipients must believe they need it. Teachers and others will neither seek out nor be receptive to the counselor as a consultant if they see no value or rationale for such assistance. In each situation, therefore, the counselor must communicate and demonstrate his or her role as an effective consultant.

The Counselor as a Consultant to the School Administrator

The school counselor can also make significant consultation contributions to the educational leadership of the school and the school system. The counselor has the capacity to gather data that describe the characteristics of the student population and their needs; this information can be useful for educational planning and management.

The counselor's understanding of the process and characteristics of human growth and development enables him or her to relate and provide special counsel regarding the special needs of individuals and groups of pupils.

The counselor can also provide valuable consulting experience to the school administrator on the school climate or environment. A mentally healthy school environment facilitates not only learning but also positive social interactions and good citizenship. Because this aspect of school life seems often overlooked (or ignored, as accountability models stress standardized measured academic achievements), counselors may have to become advocates for a healthy school environment with their school administrators. In this capacity, counselors may help administrators understand the counselor's role in planning and implementing schoolwide programs that have a good impact on the school's psychological environment. Finally, the counselor does not overlook the morale needs of his or her colleagues—the teachers. Stress management workshops, working to establish better and more open communication between teachers and administrators, and "jelly bean" days (i.e., special compliment-giving times) are all helpful ways counselors can, through consultation, assist school administrators and the school environment.

Consulting with Parents

The counselor can effectively consult with parents on various occasions to promote understanding of pupil characteristics and their relationships to pupil behavior. Consultation can assist parents in coping with or modifying student behaviors, improving interpersonal relationship skills, and adjusting attitudes. Parents may also consult with the school counselor in regard to their children's academic planning, progress, or problems. High school parents will frequently consult with school counselors about their child's career-planning needs. The counselor may also serve as a consultant to interpret school programs to parents and to explain the mainstreaming of students with disabilities.

Most parents expect and want to be informed by the school regarding their child's needs and accomplishments. The school's public relations program in general and their counseling program in particular will be enhanced by an active program of consultation with parents.

When counselors consult with parents

regarding maladaptive behavior, first and foremost the counselor must communicate concern for the child and for his or her success in school. It is critically important that the counselor and teacher both communicate explicitly to the parents that they are not blaming them or their child-raising techniques for any problem behaviors their child may be exhibiting. Simply stating an awareness of the presence of difficulties and that they are interfering with the child's success in school may be sufficient. At this point the counselor may go on to inform parents of specific behaviors or attitudes that may be thwarting their child's success. Parents are usually aware that a problem exists prior to their coming in for the consultation process. With encouragement and a positive attitude from the counselor, parents typically contribute background knowledge and are helpful. (Gibson, Mitchell, & Basile, 1993, pp. 244–245)

The school counselor-consultant must keep in mind that many behavioral issues in the school may be a product of other environments including the home.

The Counselor as a Curriculum Consultant

The counselor can play an important role in curriculum consultation. Additionally, federal legislation specifies the counselor's importance in implementing programs of career education and education of children with disabilities. In an instructional sense, the school counselor is not, of course, a curriculum specialist. However, when the curriculum is viewed as the sum of educational experiences the school proposes to provide, it follows that the counselor, because of his or her professional commitment to each student's total development, should be actively involved, regardless of legislative mandates, in curriculum planning.

As a consultant in matters related to the career interests and concerns of students, a counselor may conduct comprehensive assessments of student career interests to provide a basis for expanded and relevant curriculum offerings. Nor should the important area of avocational interests be overlooked. A combination of educational and avocational opportunities often serves to maintain student interest and motivation. The counselor should assume major responsibility to identify and interpret these interests and concerns to all educators involved. Assessment of student interest must be translated into action, however, and it is at that point that many opportunities for curriculum development are left to flounder in the sea of academic indifference.

School counselors and curriculum planners have a joint responsibility to see that these important aspects of the student's total development are not left to chance. Curricular consultation frequently points out the need for curricular change, and because the school counselor's responsibilities involve him or her with both teachers and administrators, the counselor is in a position to facilitate their cooperation and interaction in promoting the needed change. For change to occur, (a) need for the change must be identified, (b) those involved must be willing to consider the change, and (c) the plan for change must be developed, accepted, and implemented.

CONSULTATION SERVICES TO COMMUNITY AND BUSINESS ORGANIZATIONS

Counselors in community mental health centers and private agencies have been offering consultation services to community groups and businesses and industries for well over 30 years. Community agencies have offered consulting assistance to clergy and religious organizations, in criminal justice settings, in business and industry, in schools, in hospitals and other health settings, and to other groups such as youth organizations, senior citizens' groups, and professional sports organizations. As described earlier in this chapter, the consultant or consulting organization works with an intermediary rather than directly with the population that is targeted by the process. We would emphasize again that consulting is not a therapeutic relationship; rather, it is a guidance or problem-solving relationship. Consulting in the community with business, industrial, and other organizations provides community mental health centers with a major opportunity for community outreach and for informing the community at large of their goals and services.

Community mental health organizations and counselors employed in EAP (employee assistance programs) programs are aware of significant increases in the opportunities for consultation in business and industrial organizations due to the dramatic changes in the world of work (briefly noted in chapters 1 and 8. These changes, among other things, mean that both the employing organization and their employees need to be looked at in a new light.

It is especially important that the consulting counselor or consulting team be aware of organizational characteristics, including the following:

- Organizational goals and outcomes
- Relationships, responsibilities, opportunities, and the personnel hierarchy
- Special skills and knowledge needed at all levels
- The work environment including physical factors (safety, comfort, attractiveness of the workplace) and psychological factors (security and benefits, opportunities for advancement, fair treatment and the feeling of belonging)
- The values of the organization and the values of the employees
- The fiscal health of the organization
- Policies of the organization and their impact on employees
- How change is facilitated within the organization

Once a collaborative arrangement is agreed on, the consultant or consulting team might well proceed as follows.

1. Identify the people with whom you are dealing (and where they are in the organizational chart)
2. Identify the problem and its dimensions, and what the consultees expect from you (and vice versa)
3. Develop a collaborative plan to address the problem or issues
4. Apply and, if necessary, modify the plan
5. Review and evaluate the outcome

Counselor-consultants should keep in mind the importance of needs assessment in almost every circumstance. Sometimes it is important to remind organizational chiefs that productivity is produced by people. Finally, we would note that counselors employed in business and industrial settings in employee assistance programs may be called on as the resident expert to provide consultation to management and other executive decision makers in such areas as employee relationships, stress management, environmental manipulation, employee absenteeism, and so forth. These counselors may also use their group skills to help managers and supervisors lead employee groups focusing on employee or management programs. Regardless of the setting, counselors are being increasingly recognized and appreciated for their consultation skills and services.

SUMMARY

In almost any Sunday issue of a major metropolitan newspaper, such as the *New York Times* or the *Chicago Tribune*, the classified business section has advertisements seeking either to employ consultants or to utilize their consulting services. Usually, these consulting services focus on planning and strategies, economic and technical reviews, marketing assistance, material development, and evaluations. Certainly the business and industrial world has used consulting services for generations.

Consultation has also been a recognized mental health activity for a number of years, although not nearly so well publicized as its business counterpart. There are also consulting firms that specialize in educational matters, and consultation contracts are becoming increasingly popular.

However, consultation as an activity of counselors has led to an examination of various models appropriate to the consultation process and their adaptation to counselor use. Kurpius (1978) describes four modalities of consultation as provision, prescription, collaboration, and remediation. Schein (1978) organizes the process into three models: purchase of expertise, doctor-patient, and process consultation. Werner (1978) describes six possible agency models as client-centered case consultation, consultee-centered case consultation, program-centered administration consultation, consultee-centered administrative consultation, community-centered ad hoc consultation, and consultee-centered ad hoc consultation.

Regardless of model choice, counselor-consultants must recognize that they are involved in a process that provides structure and direction for their consultation efforts. It is naive to think that knowledge or experience in itself qualifies one to consult. An understanding of the process of consultation and the acquisition of the skills for consultation are prerequisites to success as a consultant. These are usually acquired through special courses in consultation.

The qualified counselor will have opportunities to consult. It is important to keep in mind, however, that consultation must be wanted—must be requested—if it is to take place. Even when requested, the counselor-consultant should proceed with tact and understanding. After all, no one likes to be "told off," even by experts!

Counselors have utilized consultation more and more to enhance the delivery of their services. Since the 1990s another trend has been increasingly emphasized in our profession. Prevention and wellness have caught the public's fancy, and serious efforts to prevent many of the disorders that have handicapped individuals and society are under way. The helping professions are responding, and the next chapter discusses how the counseling profession is doing just that.

DISCUSSION QUESTIONS

1. In your opinion, how is the title "consultant" generally viewed by the public?

2. Discuss any experience that you, your family, or a close friend has had involving a consultant. What were the circumstances leading to the use of the consultant? What were his or her special skills or knowledge? How had the consultant acquired these special skills or knowledge? Describe the consultation process.

3. Describe circumstances in which you as a practitioner-counselor might call on the services of a consultant. Describe the setting of your envisioned employment and how you might utilize consultation assistance.

4. What is the consultation expertise that a counselor can offer to
   a. Schools
   b. Business or industry
   c. Other settings

5. Give examples in which each of the following models of consultation might be used:
   a. Purchase of expertise
   b. Doctor-patient
   c. Process consultation

CLASS ACTIVITIES

1. Organize the class into small groups of three or four people. Groups are to discuss the following situation. Assume that you are the newly hired counseling staff of North Rogerian High School. Your predecessors were terminated, in the words of the school principal, because "they were too

much into therapy—spent all their time in one-to-one!" You have been advised to avoid even a hint of this image in your first year on the job. The director of pupil services for the school system has suggested the consultation approach for this coming year. Discuss and outline a consultation approach for this 3-year high school of 57 teachers and 1,400 students in an affluent midwestern setting. What would be your rationale and how would you describe your "model" in a presentation to the school's faculty meeting and later to the school's parents' association? Compare and discuss the differing approaches among the small groups.

2. Organize the class into three groups (one group per each of three topics). Groups are to develop a rationale for one of the following topics they are assigned.
   a. A major role for consultation in community mental health agencies
   b. Consultation on the college campus
   c. A private practice mental health consulting firm
3. Organize into groups of three or four. Assess the strengths of your group from the perspective of a consultation team. Report to the class the special consultation expertise (counseling or noncounseling) of your group.
4. Identify several consultants or consulting firms in your community and invite them to participate on a class panel discussing their qualifications, role, and function as consultants.

SELECTED READINGS

Dougherty, A. M. (2000). *Psychological consultation and collaboration in school and community settings* (3rd ed.). Belmont, CA: Wadsworth.

Dustin, D., & Ehly, S. (1992). School consultation in the 1990s. *Elementary School Guidance and Counseling, 26,* 165–175.

Henning-Stout, M. (1993). Theoretical and empirical bases of consultation. In J. E. Zins, T. R. Kratochwill, & S. N. Elliott (Eds.), *Handbook of consultation services for children: Applications in educational and clinical settings* (pp. 15–45). San Francisco: Jossey-Bass.

Kurpius, D., & Brown, D. (Eds.). (1985). Consultation [Special issue]. *The Counseling Psychologist, 13*(3), 333–476.

Martin, R. (1983). Consultant, consultee, and client explanations of each other's behavior in consultation. *School Psychology Review, 12*(1), 35–41.

Meyer, E. C., DeMasso, D. R., & Koocher, G. P. (1996). Mental health consultation in the pediatric intensive care unit. *Professional Psychology: Research and Practice, 27,* 130–136.

Schmidt, J. J., & Medl, W. A. (1983). Six magic steps of consulting. *The School Counselor, 30*(3), 212–216.

RESEARCH OF INTEREST

Alderman, G. L., & Gimpel, G. A. (1996). The interaction between type of behavior problem and type of consultant: Teachers' preferences for professional assistance. *Journal of Educational and Psychological Consultation, 74*(4), 305–313.

Abstract   In this study, 122 teachers responded to a survey regarding the type of classroom behavior problems for which they would be most likely to seek assistance from another school professional (consultant) and the effectiveness of different school-based consultants. Results indicated that teachers are most likely to seek assistance outside the classroom for aggressive behavior problems and are most likely to handle inattentiveness, disruptive (but not aggressive) behaviors, and excessive talking on their own. Overall, teachers indicated only a moderate level of effectiveness for all types of consultants. Handling the problem in the classroom without assistance from a consultant had a higher mean effectiveness rating than consulting with various professionals. Teachers also responded to open-ended questions addressing behaviors contributing to effective consultation and behaviors leading to ineffective consultation. Implications of these results are discussed with respect to consulting in the school system.

Buetens, K. K., & Sullivan, E. (1996). Team consultation model: Alcoholism and drug abuse training for Head Start staff. *Child and Youth Care Forum, 25*(6), 393–402.

Abstract   This study presents two training approaches used in assisting Head Start staff to increase their knowledge and skills in identifying and intervention with substance abuse issues among families. The first phase of the project, the Workshop Model, provided formalized education of substance abuse to all staff that was essential to developing a solid foundation and common framework in substance abuse and related issues. The second phase of the project, the Team

Consultation Model, used a case consultation format. This model was successful in creating a more collaborative and interactive approach to training staff in substance abuse identification and intervention; sample cases are provided. The process by which the training approaches evolve and the willingness of consultant and staff to find a solution to training needs are discussed.

Buysse, V., Shulte, A. C., Pierce, P. P., & Terry, D. (1994). Models and styles of consultation: Preferences of professionals in early intervention. *Journal of Early Intervention, 18*(3), 302–310.

Abstract This study examined the consultation model and style preferences of 67 professionals from Colorado early intervention programs. Subjects viewed two simulated consultations and rated each in terms of the consultant's perceived effectiveness. Results show that a collaborative approach involving shared responsibility across all stages of the consultation process was preferred. Results also indicate a marked preference for a directive style that involved sharing specific strategies to address the concerns of a consultee over a nondirective style that consisted merely of facilitating the consultee's own problem-solving abilities. These results are consistent with the findings of consumer preference studies.

Henning-Stout, M. (1994). Consultation and connected knowing: What we know is determined by the questions we ask. *Journal of Educational and Psychological Consultation, 5*(1), 5–21.

Abstract This article explores an alternative epistemology from which the practice of consultation can be considered. The alternative, described as connected knowing, characterizes the ways that many women make sense of the world. Connected knowers explore academic and practical questions in the context of the human relationships involved. They ask questions and attempt to understand the positions and interests of the other people whose lives are touched by those questions. This way of knowing, available both to women and men, has immediate relevance for consultation research, practice, and training.

Ikeda, M. J., Tilly, W. D., Stumme, J., & Volmer, L. (1996). Agency-wide implementation of problem solving consultation: Foundations, current implementation, and future directions. *School Psychology Quarterly, 11*(3), 228–243.

Abstract This article describes steps taken and the support needed for large-scale implementation of a consultative service delivery model. The foundation of a problem-solving consultation model used at Heartland Area Educational Agency 11 in Iowa is presented. Case examples are used to illustrate various components within problem-solving consultation. Efforts to evaluate perceptions of problem-solving consultation and to guide further implementation of consultation at the systems level are summarized. Areas in which additional resources would enhance problem-solving consultation are discussed. Shifts in the philosophy of service delivery that are fundamental for successful implementation of problem-solving consultation are described.

Taylor, I., O'Reilly, M., & Lancioni, G. (1996). An evaluation of an ongoing consultation model to train teachers to treat challenging behavior. *International Journal of Disability, Development and Education, 43*(3), 203–218.

Abstract This study investigated the use of functional assessment techniques to develop a multicomponent intervention for a male primary school student with high levels of self-injury and aggression. An in-depth functional assessment, as outlined by the *Diagnostic and Statistical Manual of Mental Disorders-IV*, identified the operant function of these behaviors. This information allowed for the development of an extensive behavior support plan. The classroom teacher was then trained to implement the support plan and received ongoing consultation from a psychologist regarding her adherence to the behavioral techniques. The intervention resulted in significant decreases in challenging behavior.

10

Prevention
and Wellness

Although the old saying "an ounce of prevention is worth a pound of cure" would seem to be particularly appropriate to the health professions, until recently, these professions, including the mental health professions, have given little more than lip service to prevention. However, recent generations have witnessed the pursuit of wellness through prevention by millions of Americans with near revolutionary zeal. At times, our whole country seems to be waking up to Jazzercize, washing down vitamin pills with instant stay-trim breakfasts, practicing relaxation techniques on the job, jogging after work, attending stress management workshops, following the Pritikin diet, and so forth. These signs of the times point to our growing concern with the prevention of health disorders, including disorders of mental health. This concern represents, if not a shift in emphases, a sharing of emphasis between remediation and prevention. Traditionally, in the not-too-distant past, when prevention has been discussed, it has been in the context of avoiding something undesirable. For example, societal prevention efforts have usually focused on

- Prevention of wars (treaties, strong armed services)
- Prevention of illnesses (immunizations)
- Prevention of financial loss (tariffs, import taxes, personal insurance)

The significance or importance of the prevention activity has been usually determined by the degree to which the undesirable threatens life and healthy living or threatens the security of large numbers of the society. This chapter's objectives are, therefore, to (a) present the role of prevention in counseling programs and (b) introduce prevention through stress management, attention to nutrition, and the wise use of recreation and leisure time.

PREVENTION

In the mental health field, a substantial increase in reported prevention activities, research, and professional literature appropriate for counselors is evident. These include a broad range of studies reported in early publications such as *Preventive Psychology* (Felner, Jason, Moritsugu, & Farber, 1983); special issues of the *Personnel and Guidance Journal* (now entitled the *Journal of Counseling and Development* (Shaw & Goodyear, 1984a and Goodyear & Shaw, 1984b); a special issue of the *Journal of Counseling and Development*, focusing on wellness throughout the life span (Myers, Emmerling, & Leafgren, 1992); and more recently the *Journal of Mental Health Counseling* (Robinson & Roth, 1992) special issue on women and health; and later, the *American Psychologist* (Vol. 51, no. 11, 1996), with five excellent articles on prevention. Also of interest is the April 1997 issue of the *American Journal of Community Psychology* (Vol. 25, no. 2) which contains five articles on prevention; and the *American Psychologist* special issue on positive psychology, published in January 2000 (Vol. 55, no. 1).

The prevention model adopted by counselors and other mental health workers is in large part the prevention model adopted by psychology, which in turn was borrowed from the field of public health. Within this context it was determined that to succeed, prevention programs must (a) address social ailments that can result in disastrous consequences; (b) address ailments that threaten large numbers of the society; (c) address these ailments **before** their onset; (d) treat large, preferably captive or mandated, populations; and (e) identify those characteristics that place individuals (groups) "at risk."

Prevention, then, may be viewed as an effort that seeks to avoid the occurrence of something undesirable. Within this definition, three levels of prevention are identified as primary, secondary, and tertiary. *Primary prevention* generally refers to programs designed to impact specific and sizable populations who are not presently affected by a disorder for the purpose of keeping them free of the disorder. It is similar to the medical profession's immunization of populations to prevent a disease that often has epidemic possibilities. *Secondary prevention* represents efforts to identify and intervene with affected individuals at the early onset of the disorder, because treatment is clearly more effective at the early stages than later when the disorder is more firmly established. *Tertiary prevention* is preventive only in the sense that it is seeking to prevent the growth of the disorder, reduce the effects, and rehabilitate the individual.

Acknowledging that prevention is the effort to avoid the undesirable, we would again recognize that the priority prevention activities of societies have been on prevention of that which threatens life and/or healthy living. In the area of physical health, prevention has always been recognized by both the public and the medical professions as the more valued approach and millions of dollars have been spent to develop vaccines and other preventive measures. In the field of mental health, however, the public (and often the profession itself) has until recently appeared to give a higher priority to remediation and treatment. For example, the public seems to consistently support building bigger and better jails, developing substance abuse treatment programs, and establishing rape crisis centers; at the same time, in many locales, it has opposed such preventive efforts by schools as sex education and values clarification techniques.

Obviously, individuals do not want to spend time in the best hospital or the best jail or have the best artificial tooth. Prevention is clearly preferred when the alternative is undesirable; we, therefore, work at it and are willing to pay for it. Thus, prevention programs are in demand when life or security is threatened. These demands are further underlined when large numbers are victims or potential victims of the threat. Such current social problems as substance abuse, people abuse, AIDS, crime and delinquency, teen pregnancies, and school dropouts certainly meet the criteria of affecting or threatening large numbers. The counseling profession, with counselors strategically positioned in schools and influentially located in community, health, business and industry, religious, and armed services settings, must respond with prevention programs. Here too is another area of opportunity to develop our uniqueness as a helping profession, as a profession distinct from other helping professions.

There are obvious reasons that primary prevention is both critically important and desirable. These include the following:

- The major problems of society can never be eliminated through treatment alone.
- The financial costs to society is exorbitant for those diseases and social disorders that are not prevented.
- The cost of these disorders go far beyond the financial cost as we note the personal suffering and emotional disorders resulting.

In planning for prevention, some obvious needs may exist. Preventive programs in substance abuse are popular in schools. Premarital counseling is commonplace. Also, many counseling agencies have programs to help married couples avoid some of the anticipated problems and adjustments of marriage. All prevention programs will experience more success when the following conditions are considered.

1. The prevention program must begin before the onset of the advance indicators or symptoms of the disorder.
2. It must be aimed at populations rather than individuals.
3. The design of the program must recognize the uniqueness of the population and their environments. This includes an assessment of the wide range of forces that influence the lives of the target population.
4. Program planners should review appropriate research to identify proven or promising prevention procedures.
5. Organizational support for the program must be strong. This includes a willingness to support long-term goals (even though the quick fix approach is easier to sell).

Despite the obstacles, counselors and other mental health professionals are being urged, even mandated by legislation in some instances, to broaden the scope of their prevention activities in order to identify and thus intervene with even larger populations at risk. This approach recognizes the importance of significant settings and experiences that influence individual adjustment and development. The home, school, workplace, church, and community are obviously relatively stable settings over periods of time that have a significant impact on large numbers of people. It is in these settings that prevention programs should flourish.

For programs to succeed, however, prevention planning must be based on some systematic approach for identifying the needs of specific client populations. This involves the study of factors associated with the characteristics of particularly susceptible people, including important interrelationships, especially in the family.

Counselors must communicate and work with parents as parents have many opportunities to foster healthy lifestyles for their children's emotional and interpersonal development from infancy. Children are taught ethical values and responsibility through what social scientists call "modeling" or demonstrating acceptable behaviors for children to follow. Parents are models whose habits and attitudes are significant influences on their children's values and actions. Counselors in both community and school settings may offer parenting groups to assist parents (Soska, 1997).

The importance of parents as the primary influence on the child's developmental well-being demands that counselors work with parents on an ongoing basis in which we mutually share, learn, and plan together for the benefit of the child. Again, we would emphasize the importance of parents having a systematic plan for involvement in their child's preventive and positive mental health development.

Environment is also a major factor influencing the development of behaviors that put populations at risk; at the positive extreme, the environment inhibits the development of undesirable behaviors. It is important to understand how people adapt in a given environment, and the significant events in the environment that signify success or positive developmental outcomes. As a major influence on behavior, counselors and other helping professionals engaged in preventive efforts must understand the environment in order to predict, control, modify, or prevent human behaviors that occur within it. Significant environments such as the home, school, workplace, and community are behavioral settings that not only influence and control behavior within them but also condition behavior beyond these settings. This includes the imposition of limits on deviant behaviors and coping styles. Environments are not just physical in nature; they also have a psychological dimension. Although the latter may be more complex and difficult to identify, its impact must not be underestimated, and its significance must be addressed in successful prevention programs.

Environments are also assessed to determine what specific characteristics they have that place populations at risk for certain disorders. This means that the individuals' transactions with their environments may provide critical clues for successful programs. To discover these characteristics, experts suggest that environmental assessment using the field survey method is the most reliable technique, and Public Law 88-169 has mandated needs assessments for community mental health centers. In examining environments and their impacts on populations, special attention should be given to (a) high-impact environments such as the home, school, and workplace; (b) the ways normal developmental tasks are facilitated or impeded by the environment; (c) significant life events in the environment, and (d) the quality of everyday life for the inhabitants of the environment. An environmental needs assessment also gives counselors the opportunity to assess the readiness of a population for a given type of prevention program.

A list of environmental factors that impact us personally would include these:

- Privacy
- Space/territory
- Density/spaciousness
- Appearance/aesthetic qualities
- Architecture/design
- Geographics and nature trails
- Noise
- Safety

The quality of life of the individual is obviously a factor, often unrecognized, in planning for prevention. Much has been written by Carl R. Rogers and others regarding the importance of unconditional positive regard in counseling clients, but counselors should look beyond this rather limited focus to recognize the significance of unconditional positive regard in preventing the pathologies that occur when life appears to be meaningless. Counselors must become more aware of the importance of contentment, happiness, and self-satisfaction as a prevention vaccine. We must note the importance of recognizing those environmental variables—and the degree to which counselors can manipulate them—that result in individual happiness, the development of human potential, and the prevention of pathology.

A common goal for nearly all people is happiness (including freedom from fear, hunger, and physical discomfort). Certainly happiness is a key criterion in determining the quality of individual life, which has relevance to those problems and issues that bring individuals to counseling. The importance of human relationships in happiness leads us to a further preventive goal of developing appropriate interpersonal skills and values for helping young people learn to value and respect their diversity and the diversity of others and to learn nonviolent approaches to dealing with everyday conflicts.

Prevention programs are usually complex because they must be designed to deal with multiple factors. Some disorders are associated with many risk factors, and some risk factors are also associated with many disorders. Additionally, some risk factors appear to vary in their impact at different stages of the individual's development. Too, certain disorders may result from a specific chain of events. All of these factors may heighten the public's wariness of prevention programs. Although prevention programs are receiving increasing public acceptance today, counselors in all settings must continue to lobby for prevention.

As an obvious and crucial starting point, the elementary school can play a significant role in any community or school system's preventive efforts, and evidence indicates that schools are increasingly responding to this challenge. As noted earlier in chapter 3, a study by Gibson (1989) indicates that prevention was a major emphasis of elementary school counseling and guidance programs in 85% of the 114 elementary programs surveyed. The primary objectives of these programs are noted in Table 3-9.

Among the popular activities used in elementary school prevention programs were group counseling for self-concept improvement, a guidance curriculum for the classroom to develop interpersonal and social relationship skills and avoid personal conflicts, and facilitation of problem solving and decision making. Self-concept development was also enhanced through consultation and training with parents. Attendance was improved and dropouts prevented through tutoring, career guidance, and group guidance activities. Substance abuse prevention was initiated through a wide range of activities including Just Say No clubs, peer intervention, behavioral self-management groups, drug education, and use of local celebrities as advisers.

Many schools have successfully initiated comprehensive safety programs for the prevention of sexual abuse and child abuse and the promotion of personal safety using drama, games, films, and classroom guidance programs.

Successful prevention programs in schools appear to share a number of common features.

- Assistance in developing coping skills
- Self-esteem and values development
- The building of support groups
- Parental involvement
- The involvement of older peers as role models and mentors
- Environmental assessment and, to the extent possible, environmental manipulation
- Elements that reflect the uniqueness of the target population, the setting, and the problem
- Instruction in basic life skills aimed at helping individuals resist peer and social pressures
- A futures element, including a commitment to the time necessary to obtain results
- An evaluation component

- Program planning involving counselors and other helping professionals, parents, students, teachers, and community leaders
- Group counseling
- Behavior and attitude modification education
- Individual counseling
- Training programs for teachers, parents, counselors, and school administrators.

Sprinthall (1990) reported that

the evidence for both primary prevention and developmental interventions has been remarkable. Baker, Swisher, Nadenichek, and Popowitz (1984) reviewed a large number of empirical evaluations of prevention strategies and, using meta-analytic techniques to combine the results of these studies, concluded that the treatment effect size was larger for such interventions than that found in meta-analytic analyses of the results of psychotherapy. In addition to such research on primary prevention strategies, there are now an ever increasing number of studies of all sorts of outreach endeavors which continue to yield significant results for their target populations. For two very different examples, consider the work of Taylor and colleagues (1986) showing that social support groups for persons suffering from cancer led to significantly decreased depression and the work of Burnette, Williams, and Law (1987) suggesting that, for Vietnam veterans who participated in discussion groups, self-management effectiveness increased and expression of anger scores decreased. (p. 506)

Whereas the focus of prevention programs through much of the 1990s was on substance (especially drug) abuse, recent years have shown a rapidly escalating interest in smoking prevention, as statistics indicate a continuing increase in preteen and teenage use of tobacco products. The prevention of teen pregnancies and sexually transmitted diseases have also increasingly become the subject of school prevention programs.

Prevention in Nonschool Settings

Prevention activities are logically and justifiably present in school settings due to their before-the-onset nature and also because the near-total pre-adolescent populations can be impacted, but they are not by any means limited to these settings. Many of the prevention programs in nonschool settings are classified as secondary or tertiary prevention efforts, but there are some examples of primary prevention programs as well. For example, in many communities programs such as those represented by Alcoholics Anonymous and Koala are not only engaged in treatment at secondary and tertiary levels, but at the primary level as well with youth preventive programs. Community mental health agencies, private practitioners, and residential and daytime treatment centers are very active in the prevention arena. Many employee assistance programs (EAPs) are also involved in prevention programs. Here again, drug abuse, alcohol abuse, and tobacco are the focus of many of these programs. In addition, however, programs dealing with spouse abuse, sexual abuse, and stress management and wellness have become increasingly popular, as have programs seeking to prevent such disorders.

Of course, prevention of the undesirable in both mental and physical health must include a commitment and effort to total wellness. The sections that conclude this chapter briefly examine wellness and two important contributors to it: stress management and the enjoyable and prudent use of leisure time.

Wellness

Nowhere has the craze for wellness and prevention manifested itself more than in the growth in popularity of health foods and healthy eating plans, exercise books, fitness equipment, and clubs. The United States has jogged its way through the 1990s and is continuing into the new millennium, munching alfalfa sprouts and drinking mineral water. The individual's concern for his or her well-being cannot and should not be ignored by today's counselor. Counselors must be aware of the relationship between individual experiences and individual health, both mental and physical. Counselors need to understand the psychological consequences of illness and accidents.

A special issue of the *Journal of Counseling and Development* (Myers, Emmerling, & Leafgren, 1992) focused on the theme of "Wellness Throughout the Lifespan." In this issue, one of the editors, Myers, indicates that

> Remley (1991) noted that the counseling profession has rejected the medical-illness-oriented model as the basis for our services. In defining what differentiates us as a separate and distinct mental health profession, he stated, "We do not believe that people must first be diagnosed with an illness before they can be treated with counseling services. Instead, we believe that all people can benefit from counseling. . . . Fully functioning people who experience everyday stress in their lives and those who are seriously mentally ill can benefit from a counseling philosophy that offers help for a better tomorrow." The philosophy described by Remley is grounded in a developmental approach that focuses on prevention and wellness. (p. 138)

Counselors in community, school, business, and industrial settings are being increasingly involved in programs promoting lifestyle change for health living. These efforts have focused on health concerns such as smoking, alcohol and drug abuse, eating disorders, and sexually transmitted diseases. Nor should this concern be limited to our clients. As fully functioning counselors, we must also be concerned with our own physical well-being.

A popular phrase is that "you are what you eat." Now, scientific inquiry seems to be further emphasizing this point as research has increasingly highlighted the relationships between nutrition and behavior, between our emotions and our diet. Although counselors are not expected to be experts in nutrition, dieting, and exercise, they should be aware of basic factors and their possible link with the client's mental health.

Promoting concepts of wellness cannot begin too early. Omizo, Omizo, and D'Andrea (1992) report a program promoting wellness among elementary school children. The results of the study

> seem to support the use of classroom guidance activities in promoting wellness among elementary school children. Children who participated in the guidance activities had significantly higher levels of self-esteem and knowledge of wellness information than did children who did not participate in the guidance activities. Although the anxiety measure did not reach a level of significance, children in the experimental group had lower levels of stress subsequent to the treatment. The class allowed the children to participate in the activities that focused on prevention as opposed to remediation. They had opportunities to share, receive and give feedback, receive guidance and information, and apply what they had learned. The teacher was an excellent role model and practiced good health habits. She also incorporated the material into other areas of the curricula. (p. 197)

Nelson (1992), a choice-awareness counseling theorist, suggests that there are three levels of counseling: spa, learning, and relearning.

A place may be made in nearly every counseling session for *spa*: uplifting, positive experiences in which the focus is placed directly on helping clients feel good about themselves. With many clients, a few minutes at the end of each interview may be saved for these positive experiences; with some clients the entire effort of an individual session may be that of spa. The simplest of the several examples of spa in counseling offered in Nelson's article is the activity "Things I Can Do," in which the counselor helps the client focus on and savor some of the most often-repeated actions of which he or she is capable: breathe, walk, talk, eat, sleep, think, and so on. All counseling clients can benefit from the emerging sense of wellness that can come from spa in counseling. (p. 214)

As we consider counseling across the life span, Ponzo (1992), among others, encourages counselors to become more active in promoting successful aging. He stresses that

prime-time living is possible to the end. People need to know and believe this. So imbued, and given the skills to translate vision into reality, we should find larger numbers of people dying at the prime of their life. Consequently, there will be reductions in health care costs and increases in the productivity of elderly persons. Accomplishing this, the huge waves of people soon to be old need not be seen as a potentially destructive force, but as a dynamically productive opportunity for society. These people can view their elder years as a time for continued growth and fulfillment. Counselors can play a key role in helping people better prepare for living out a long and vital life. As many have said, "If I knew I was going to live this long, I would have prepared better." Regardless of how good the preparation, it will not restore Woody Allen's desired immortality, but it will assure mortal beings of more prime-time living. Promoting successful aging is a lifetime process. The time to start is now. (p. 213)

Appropriate exercise, a good diet, and a stress-free lifestyle are recognized as important considerations in any program of client wellness. Perhaps not so well recognized is the importance of managing the daily stressors of today's living by wise and enjoyable leisure and recreational activities in prevention and wellness.

Stress Management

The U.S. workforce has become aware that millions of its members are "going up in smoke"—that their effectiveness is handicapped by the psychological symptom labeled *burnout*. Although we must assume that many workers across all careers have, over the centuries, felt that their job is getting them down, the pressures are getting to them, the boss is driving them to drink, and so forth, it was not until the 1970s that a popular label, *burnout,* was commonly used to describe various psychological conditions associated with stress and adjustment needs. In fact, today, we recognize that the term *burnout* can refer to one or a combination of factors that psychologists say contribute to a person's inability to cope with the expectancies and demands of everyday living. Counselors in all settings must be prepared to prevent or intervene with clients threatened by or actually under stress.

Synonymous with the labeling of the disorder was the increasing awareness at management and supervisory levels that employee health is as important as other job-related concerns to the effectiveness of the organization and a further recognition that employee illness can be psychological as well as physical. As a result, one of the large-scale preventive efforts of the 1980s and 1990s was the stress management movement. Not unexpectedly, counselors have been increasingly called on to develop prevention and early intervention programs in stress prevention and management. Counselors involved in these efforts have been quick to recognize the value of such prevention efforts because of the dangerously cumulative phenomenon of psychosocial stress.

Although the causes for burnout or stress may vary significantly from person to person, counselors need to be cognizant of the more common factors, such as the following.

- Too many demanding, frustrating, or otherwise stressful situations
- Constant pressure to do more than can be done
- Too much time-consuming yet unrewarding work (e.g., paperwork)
- Constant conflicts between competing alternatives for time and effort (e.g., home and work)
- Persistent demands for skills or knowledge that appear to be beyond that possessed by the individual
- Constant interference or interruptions of planned or anticipated activities
- Lack of positive feedback, recognition, reward, or notice of efforts or accomplishments
- Lack of clarity or direction regarding work expectancies
- Depressing work environment
- Poor interpersonal relationships
- Constant disillusions or disappointments
- All work and no play, failure to lead a balanced lifestyle

Counselors may also recognize that candidates for burnout may be identified by the level, stage, or degree of burnout. Here is a view of a possible sequence to burnout:

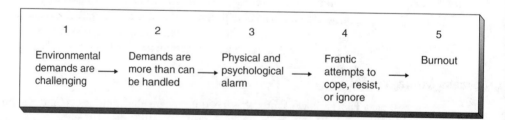

Counselors working in business and industrial settings should be aware of the extent and impact of stress in these settings.

In working for stress prevention or reduction, initially the counselor and client need to identify the stressors in the client's situation, their relative significance, whether they can be dealt with, and possible preventive or coping strategies. Among the general strategies that may be helpful to clients (and even yourself on occasion) are the following:

1. Bring burnout into the open; talk about it, especially with others sharing the same situation and concerns.
2. Build a support system with a small group of colleagues (including at least one optimist); help others in stress, be positive, be mutually supportive.

3. Practice time management; organize your time and stick with it. This includes planning for and protection of your free time on and off the job.
4. Develop leisure time pursuits or hobbies.
5. Get away from it all, especially when you feel the pressure beginning to build. Take real vacations regularly.
6. Shape up, both physically and psychologically; feel good about yourself!

A prime candidate for burnout and prognosis for stress management is the workaholic—a "species" who has become all too commonplace in today's often stressful and uncertain workplace. To the casual observer, workaholics seem addicted to their jobs. Their work profile usually reflects a number of the following characteristics:

1. Get to work early and leave late.
2. Work at workstation while eating lunch.
3. Work during the commute to and from the office, and have a car phone for business purposes.
4. Take work home most evenings and weekends.
5. Rarely take vacations, and when one does, take work along and keep in touch with the office.
6. Use recreational pursuits, if any, for business purposes (e.g., golf with a client, dinner with clients, a trip to Florida to attend a convention).
7. Ration strictly the time for children and family. (Rationale: I'm doing what I must to be a good provider!)
8. Have irregular eating and sleeping habits. Personal health becomes a concern only when it threatens work schedule.
9. Be unable to say no when asked to do a job; often volunteer for extra duties.

When counselors encounter burned out or nearly burned out workaholics as their clients, they need to understand the reasons for the behavior. Among those commonly encountered are fear of job loss, failure to advance, an effort to gain control of their lives, or as compensation for their shortcomings. In addition to stress and time management, the enjoyable use of leisure time is an important and often overlooked variable in clients' stress management and general well-being. Let us examine the topic a little further.

Recreation and Leisure

We recognize that in one sense, the United States is very leisure conscious. Americans watch more television and listen to more radio than anyone else in the world. We are the most traveled nation in the world. We are enthusiastic sports fans from Little League to big leagues. We idolize our entertainment and sports figures almost, and at times, above all others. Swimming pools, golf courses, tennis courts, and sports clubs are prevalent and we avidly read both fiction and nonfiction publications, attend movies, rent videos, buy compact discs in voluminous quantities, and so on. In another sense, however, real, high-quality leisure time is proportionately distributed according to socioeconomic status, meaning that those of the upper levels of the socioeconomic scale tend to participate in a variety of meaningful leisure activities; those at the lower end of the socioeconomic scale frequently spend the majority of their leisure time watching television and listening to the radio. We do have an increasing population of workaholics to whom we must give more attention, as well as individuals working two or more jobs. We have, again at the other extreme, what might be labeled "free time drifters." These are usually youths hesitant about their career direction or in some instances simply unable to secure full-time or even adequate part-time employment. The latter, of course, become prime candidates for substance abuse and youthful criminal activity. Further, our educational system has not been responsive in preparing us for meaningful leisure time activity. Typical physical education and recreational activities in schools are group-oriented, facility-bound (limited to gyms, swimming pools, golf courses, and tracks) and youth-limited. They have little carryover for many, especially in adulthood. In one sense they are not educational inasmuch as they do not prepare us for leisure time activities that most individuals can pursue throughout their adult lives.

If you could spend three days doing whatever you wished, how would you spend your time? What do you plan to do with your vacation time this year? Chances are, your answers to these questions indicate the recreational and leisure time activities that are important to you. We need to be reminded of how important this time is to us and that recreation and leisure are important activities in American society. We need to pause to consider the amount of time, money, and effort we expend in these pursuits to recognize their significance in our lives. The interrelationships between a career and a way of life cannot ignore the role of recreation and leisure in the latter. Counselors concerned with the total well-being of their clients must, therefore, become more sensitive to the role and potential of leisure time activities for enhancing their clients' quality of life and meeting their unmet or partially fulfilled needs.

Juliet Schor (1993), in her interesting publication *The Overworked American: The Unexpected Decline of Leisure*, suggests that there are forces, some conscious, some unconscious, mitigating against the increased use of leisure time. She notes that many workers themselves are not sold on leisure time and that critics of more leisure time feel that it would probably be used for more part-time work, more time watching television, and probably more family time, but not really time in the pursuit of meaningful leisure. She concludes that it is possible to reclaim and effectively use more leisure time, but contends that

> corporations remain the most significant obstacle. Most will be vociferous opponents to my ideas. At last count, the Conference Board reports that fewer than fifty firms nationwide have comprehensive programs for work and family issues. But, as always, enlightened, forward-looking companies do exist. Wells Fargo gives personal-growth leaves, Xerox offers social-service sabbaticals. Job sharing is possible at a growing number of companies, including Hewlett Packard, Black & Decker, TRY Vidar, and Levi-Strauss. Control Data has a vibrant part-time program which includes benefits. Anna Roddick, founder of the rapidly expanding Body Shop, gives her employees a half-day off each week with pay to engage in volunteer activities. While the number of innovative corporations is still small, it is growing. And apparently awareness of time-related personnel problems is increasing as well. In the last few years, at least some corporate executives have been waking up to the realities of their employees' lives. (Schor, 1993, p. 163).

At this point, it may be helpful to distinguish between free time and leisure time. We might define free time as unencumbered time that the individual can use or not use in any way he or she may decide. Leisure time is that time spent in the pursuit of specific activities anticipated to be enjoyable. Although some free or unencumbered time is desirable, large amounts of free time can result in boredom, frustration, anger, low self-esteem, anxiety, and stress. Enjoyable leisure time, however, has a number of potential benefits such as stimulation and motivation (which often carries over into work), feelings of rejuvenation (also important to work), relaxation and stress reduction, personal growth, opportunities for exploration, and the development of new horizons.

A rationale for leisure counseling may be based on the following:

1. Many individuals do not utilize, in an enjoyable and consistent manner, their leisure time.
2. The interaction between an individual's work experiences and his or her leisure and recreational experiences clearly impact his or her mental health.
3. Self-fulfillment includes the development of all the individual's potentials, including those that might be labeled avocational or recreational.
4. Therefore, planning for the wise and fulfilling use of leisure time is essential if the individual is to use her or his time in rewarding, enriching, and stress-reducing ways.
5. Leisure counseling can facilitate this planning by assisting individuals in identifying possible options consistent with their lifestyles and interests, making appropriate choices, and, when needed, securing the necessary education.

We have become increasingly aware of the lack of recreational facilities and positive leisure time activities for large segments of our youth population today, especially poor, inner-city and rural youth. We are also aware that too much time on their hands frequently leads these young people to youth gangs, substance abuse, delinquency, and crime. Perhaps school counselors should develop programs to assist youth in exploring and developing avocational interests as well as vocational interests.

Much of the adult population also needs assistance in expanding their leisure time activities beyond visiting relatives and watching television. Growth groups focusing on the discovery of meaningful recreational pursuits can be helpful. Special-interest groups in which individuals can explore and learn more about specific leisure activities (e.g., travel, ballroom dancing, square dancing, eating out, bowling, playing tennis, swimming) can arouse interests, as can play fairs.

Counselors who provide counseling and guidance services to our senior citizens must be aware that many preparing to enter retirement have no adequate alternative to their work to fill this void when retirement occurs. This involuntary isolation from their working colleagues leaves many an individual lonely, depressed, and physically as well as mentally stagnated. This population must be assisted in identifying enjoyable, meaningful, and doable leisure time activities. In working with older citizens, counselors may use assessment techniques, including standardized interest inventories, values clarification techniques, exploratory and growth groups, and special educational programs.

As counselors we are seeking to assist our clients in improving their quality of life—to live life to the fullest, to optimize their human potential. In this context, then, the professional counselor is sensitive to the contributions that leisure counseling may make to their clientele in achieving these outcomes. In so doing, we are once again seeking to help clients become the best they've ever been; to view counseling not as just a restorative process but as an experience that advances the individual toward his or her true human fulfillment.

In concluding this brief examination of leisure counseling, we suggest that the demands for counseling in this area will increase rapidly in the years ahead. We also believe that continued research into the role of leisure and its relationship to work will increase our knowledge and skills not only for life adjustment counseling but, perhaps more important, for preventive and developmental purposes as well.

SUMMARY

This chapter has presented, in a sense, a beginning to important new directions for counselors and the counseling profession that promise to raise the profession to heretofore unanticipated heights of societal service. To what more lofty goals can counselors aspire than the prevention of mental illness and the promotion of a happy, productive life through wellness and wise, enjoyable use of leisure time?

Whereas other helping professions may concentrate on remediation or, at best, restoring the client to a previous status quo, counseling, of all the helping professions, has the prospects to advance clients to the level of the best they can become! This potential does not mean a deemphasis on our traditional skills and knowledge discussed in earlier chapters (e.g., counseling, assessment, career development) but rather suggests applying these skills to new opportunities that optimistically view the positive, the possible.

The success of prevention and the other activities of counseling programs will be influenced to a large degree by how effectively programs are planned, managed, and led. The next chapter will discuss the important contribution of program development and management to the delivery of counseling services.

DISCUSSION QUESTIONS

1. What major societal/mental health concerns would appear to be most effectively treatable by prevention programs?
2. What can be done nationally, that may not be currently undertaken, to more effectively prevent such social ills as substance abuse, child/spouse abuse, AIDS, homelessness, and teen pregnancies? What can counselors do at the local community level?
3. What are the implications of the current interest in health and wellness for the counseling profession?

4. How important is leisure time in your life? Explain. How do you like to spend your leisure time? (Discuss and compare with your classmates.)
5. Discuss the relationship between nutrition and mental health.
6. Discuss ways in which you have personally adapted to your environment.

CLASS ACTIVITIES

1. In small groups, discuss and compare the healthy living efforts of class members. Each group will identify a member to briefly report their discussion to the class.
2. (To be done by each class member) Share (a) two or three of your favorite recreational or leisure time activities with the class, (b) your favorite vacation, and/or (c) a new leisure activity you would like to explore
3. In small groups, identify a mental health problem and design a prevention program or activity for a specific organizational setting. Share with the group.
4. Read one prevention article in a professional journal. Summarize this article in a professional journal. Summarize this article in an oral presentation to the class.

SELECTED READINGS

Buss, D. M. (2000). The evolution of happiness. *American Psychologist, 55*(1), 15–23.

Corney, R. (1996). Counselling psychology in the context of health and illness. In R. Woolfe & W. Dryden (Eds.), *Handbook of counselling psychology* (pp. 401–418). London: Sage.

Lightsey, O. R. (1996). What leads to wellness? The role of psychological resources in well-being. *Counseling Psychologist, 24,* 689–759.

Prevention in counseling psychology (2000). [Special issue]. *The Counseling Psychologist, 28*(6).

Robinson, B. E. (2000). Workaholism: Bridging the gap between workplace, sociocultural, and family research. *Journal of Employment Counseling, 37*(1), 31–47.

Seligman, M. E. P., & Csikszentmihalyi, M. (Eds.). (2001). Positive psychology [Special issue]. *American Psychologist, 55*(1).

RESEARCH OF INTEREST

Baker, S. B., Swisher, J. D., Nadenichek, R. E., & Popowitz, C. L. (1984). Measured effects of primary prevention strategies. *Personnel and Guidance Journal, 62*(8), 459–464.

Abstract These researchers conducted a meta-analysis of more than 40 primary prevention studies to investigate the measured effects of primary prevention strategies. Studies selected were those that were controlled experiments with empirical comparisons between treatment and controlled conditions and studies in which the treatment conditions had goals and involved participants; this allowed the studies to be classified as primary prevention. Fifteen of the studies utilized or included elementary school populations. The researchers concluded that, considering the difficulties that limit opportunities to conduct successful primary prevention programs in the school, the results are encouraging.

Bunce, D. (1997). What factors are associated with the outcome of individual-focused worksite stress management interventions? *Journal of Occupational and Organizational Psychology, 70*(1), 1–17.

Abstract This article examines research contrasting different approaches to individual-focused stress management interventions (SMIs). SMIs target individual workers and generally seek to enhance their ability to cope with occupational strain. Several issues regarding SMIs are addressed including the efficacy of SMIs relative to one another, the active ingredients of SMIs, and the extent to which research has considered individual differences including their impact on outcome variance. Many of the comparative studies found that SMIs are outcome equivalent and that both nonspecific factors and factors related to the technical content of the intervention are associated with outcome. Very little research was available regarding individual differences, and none was located that examined potential mediators of change. Bunce concluded that due to design and methodological limitations in the majority of studies, a new generation of research is needed that, among other things, clearly delineates between interventions of differing technical content and includes session process measures to help distinguish the degree of outcome variance associated with specific and nonspecific factors.

Carlso, K. A. (1994). Prevention in its social context: Student views. *Journal of Alcohol and Drug Education, 40*(1), 26–35.

Abstract This study surveyed 2,791 students in 4th through 12th grade concerning prevention programming and substance use. Subjects evaluated the helpfulness of their school's prevention programs, including punitive sanctions, and gave their views on the adequacy and fairness of school and legal punishments for common drug and alcohol offenses. The most favorable evaluated prevention activities were those providing support and skills for nonuse. Punitive sanctions delivered at the school or through external legal authorities received more variable responses; those directed at the most serious drug offenses were strongly supported, whereas punishments for common alcohol violations were seen as inappropriate. As grade level increased, the attitude toward such sanctions shifted from a judgment of these as helpful to the view that they were not helpful.

Elliott, T. R., & Marmarosh, C. L. (1994). Problem-solving appraisal, health complaints, and health-related expectancies. *Journal of Counseling and Development, 72*(5), 531–537.

Abstract This study examined the relation of problem-solving appraisal to health complaints and health-related expectancies among 251 undergraduates. Subjects completed measures of problem-solving ability, health expectancies, and health complaints. Self-appraised effective problem solvers (EPSs) reported fewer physical symptoms 3 weeks before, during, and 3 months after assessment than did ineffective problem solvers (IPSs). EPSs also had greater internal and lower chance expectancies for health outcomes than did IPSs. Self-appraised personal control over emotional experiences when engaging in problem solving was significantly predictive of health perceptions. Behavioral health and wellness interventions with college students may be improved by incorporating problem-solving perspectives.

Glasgow, R. E., Terborg, J. R., Hollis, J. F., & Severson, H. H. (1995). Take heart: Results from the initial phase of a worksite wellness program. *American Journal of Public Health, 85*(2), 209–216.

Abstract This study evaluated the short-term effects of a low-intensity worksite (WS) heart disease risk-reduction program using a matched pair design in 26 heterogeneous WSs assigned to early intervention and delayed intervention conditions. WSs did not differ on changes in smoking prevalence, dietary fat intake, and serum cholesterol. The intervention did not produce improvements beyond secular trends observed in control WSs and did not improve employee health behaviors related to nutrition and tobacco use more than repeated assessments alone. Six potential explanations for the lack of effects are offered.

Myers, D. G. (2000). The funds, friends, and faith of happy people. *American Psychologist, 55*(1), 56–67.

Abstract New studies are revealing predictors of subjective well-being, often assessed as self-reported happiness and life satisfaction. Worldwide, most people report being at least moderately happy, regardless of age and gender. As part of their scientific pursuit of happiness, researchers have examined possible associations between happiness and (a) economic growth and personal income, (b) close relationships, and (c) religious faith.

Phillips-Miller, D. L., Campbell, N. J., & Morrison, C. R. (2000). Work and family: Satisfaction, stress, and spousal support. *Journal of Employment Counseling, 37*(1), 16–30.

Abstract Married veterinarians (*N* = 242) provided information regarding work satisfaction, work-related stress, marital-family stress, and spousal support for career. Female veterinarians reported significantly greater effect of marital/family stress on career and less perceived spousal support for career than did their male counterparts. Areas of greatest work dissatisfaction for both genders were income and time required at work. No differences emerged between men and women on various measures of work satisfaction. In addition, no difference was found between the genders in the effect of work-related stress on career.

Smith, M. U., & Katner, H. P. (1995). Quasi-experimental evaluation of three AIDS prevention activities for maintaining knowledge, improving attitudes, and changing risk behaviors of high school seniors. *AIDS Education and Prevention, 7*(5), 391–402.

Abstract Seven hundred and twenty-eight 12th-grade students participated in one of three AIDS interventions: a question and answer (QA) session, a presentation by a person with AIDS (PWA), or a role-play activity (RP). A pre-intervention questionnaire assessed AIDS-related knowledge and attitudes. Immediate postintervention questionnaires assessed knowledge and the intervention, and, 5 weeks later, a questionnaire reassessed knowledge and attitudes in addition to changes in risk behaviors. Knowledge gains were similar in the three groups; forgetting was greatest among PWA students. The attitudes of the RP group toward persons with AIDS tended to be the most positive, but differences among the groups were not statistically significant. The proportion of RP students who reported changing their sexual activities after the intervention was significantly greater than that proportion of the other groups.

Counseling Program Development and Management

Through the centuries, a great deal has been written about the importance of management, development, and leadership to success in the worlds of business and government. The business world has long studied the successes and failures of corporations large and small and the styles of management that have accounted for their achievements or lack of them. Management is also important in government effectiveness and fiscal soundness. Development is crucial to many countries, geographic areas, and companies, the success or failure of armies, the winning of athletic championships, and so forth. Leadership has played a major role in the rise and fall of nations. Management is important to government effectiveness and fiscal soundness, and development is crucial in many countries, even in these modern times.

In this century, school administration in education, hospital administration in medicine, and personnel administration in business and the armed services have become areas for specialization. Beginning in the 1980s, business books such as *In Search of Excellence* by Peters and Waterman (1982), *The One-Minute Manager* by Blanchard (1982), *A Passion for Success* by Inamori (1995) and *Iacocca: An Autobiography* by Iacocco and Novack (1984) are examples of publications in this area that appeared with regularity on the best-seller lists.

Additionally, by the 1990s, the taxpaying public became increasingly interested in how efficiently and effectively human service organizations were serving their designated publics. As inflation deflated personal incomes—as well as real dollars available to tax-supported organizations, including school systems and mental health agencies—these organizations were called upon to give good value. This good value in turn meant that counseling programs were expected to be responding to client needs in an effective (proven results) and efficient (maximizing services, minimizing costs) manner. Thus, prospective counselors should know how to develop, manage, and lead counseling and guidance programs. This chapter's objectives are to provide an introduction to some guiding principles and practices of counseling program development, management, and leadership.

Lewis, Lewis, and Souflee, Jr. (1993), state that

> given the turbulent environments in which most of today's human service organizations find themselves—environments characterized by scarcity, ambiguity, and uncertainty—one of the issues revealed to the manager in the move up the managerial tiers is that of organizational survival. Demands for accountability, demands to do more with less, shifting political and economic priorities—all of these factors constitute an additional challenge to management and to contemporary human service organizations. (p. 21)

Thus, despite a general recognition of the importance of management, development, and leadership to organized enterprise, little attention has been given (in terms of formal preparation, at least) to the art of developing and managing counseling programs in various settings. Today, the complex, multiple goals required of most public agencies, institutions, and schools and school systems emphasize the need for development and management of counselor programs and accountability to the public. From a program management standpoint, *accountability* means the provision of objective evidence to prove that counselors are successfully responding to identified needs. Such evidence can be records, written reports, and perhaps computations and tables. All too often those preparing to enter the profession naively assume that the practice of therapy precludes any involvement with mundane matters such as program management, including administration. This is not to suggest that paperwork should replace people work or that it should be an equal priority. However, prospective counselors should be aware of the significance of their other responsibilities as well. Let us first define these terms.

- *Management:* Those activities that facilitate and complement the daily, ongoing functions of the counseling staff. These include such administrative activities as recording and reporting, budgetary planning and control, facility management, and provisions for support personnel resources.
- *Development:* Includes needs assessment for program planning, research, evaluation, and the establishment of program accountability. Also presumes planning for program improvement.
- *Leadership:* The providing of positive direction and motivation for personnel and program improvement. Primarily, but not exclusively, the responsibility of the professional designated as the chief management person for a specified unit (program, office, department, clinic).

DEVELOPING THE ACCOUNTABLE PROGRAM

All of us like to be members of winning teams. We would also probably agree that talent alone is not enough; winning teams require teamwork and a winning game plan. On joining a counseling staff, a counselor becomes not only a team member but also is committed to and involved in the continuous process of program development and improvement—the implementation of a game plan. The effective development of any counseling program, regardless of setting, depends first on an accurate and continuous assessment of the needs of the target population to be served. Such needs assessment is the key to successful planning for goals and objectives. The accurate assessment of potential client needs is critical in establishing and maintaining program relevance and fostering program accountability and evaluation.

Needs assessment, then, is the foundational activity for the development of accountable programs. This needs assessment is not a speculative, opinion-dominated process but a fact-seeking activity, which in turn enables programs to develop activities to meet the real needs of their clientele. The needs assessment activity, which can range from a simple to a complex process, is concerned with two databases:

1. *Target population assessment:* This data gathering seeks to establish factually the needs of the target population that the counseling program has been created to serve. These data will also influence priorities among these needs.

2. *Environmental assessment:* This is the gathering of factual data that facilitate the counseling program's understanding of the setting from which the target population comes and within which the program functions. Also, it is important that counselors understand the environment in which behavior occurs.

Target population assessment provides a factual basis for a program's goals and objectives, and environmental assessment provides a factual basis for the procedures by which a program achieves its goals and objectives. The personal needs are the internal factors that initiate, direct, and sustain the program's activities, whereas the environmental characteristics provide the depth of understanding for more effectively responding to the needs.

Lewis and Lewis (1991), writing from a community agency perspective, identify the generic planning process as one using the following basic steps: (a) needs assessment, (b) definition of goals and objectives, (c) identification of alternative methods for meeting goals, (d) decision making, and (e) development of plans for implementation and evaluation. "Each of these steps involves a major commitment both from agency personnel and from community members. Each step also depends on the effective completion of the previous task, beginning with the all-important process of needs assessment" (p. 35).

Counselors must not only be skilled in observing and assessing the characteristics of the individual and his or her behavior, but they must also be skilled at assessing and understanding the environment that influences the behavior of their clients. Influential environmental factors might include such characteristics as the weather, cleanliness of the surroundings, population density, ethnic diversity, leisure facilities, aesthetic factors, natural resources, accessibility, and noise. Environmental assessment would also include such social/personal data as marriage and divorce rates; membership in religious, civic, and service organizations; crime rate; and political characteristics. Also important in environmental assessment are such economic factors as tax rates, employment rate, and business trends. Of course, environmental assessment must also take into account the educational characteristics of the area.

The Needs Assessment

The development of accountable and relevant programs begins with the assessment of the needs of the target population (see Figure 11-1). In this process, developmental, preventive, and enhancement needs of the population are considered as well as those that have intervention and remediation implications. This is a technique for factually establishing program

Step 1	Step 2	Step 3	Step 4	Step 5	Step 6
Assessment of Needs Through Data Collection	Interpretation of Data	Priority Needs	Program Objectives	Program Procedures (activities developed based on program resources available)	Planning for Program Improvement (based on evaluation of outcomes and procedures)

Figure 11-1   Sequence of procedures for developing an accountable program of counseling and guidance.

Source: From Gibson, Robert L., Mitchell, Marianne H., and Basile, Sherry K., *Counseling in the Elementary School: A Comprehensive Approach*, p. 272. Copyright © 1993 by Allyn and Bacon. Reprinted by permission.

goals and objectives. Such an assessment directly involves the target population or a sampling of it, as well as critical support populations. For example, a school guidance program would not only gather data from students but would also survey parents, teachers, and others who had frequent and direct contact with the student population.

The direct involvement of these populations is usually secured through questionnaires or structured interviews. Figure 11-2 presents an example of a simple questionnaire used in student needs assessment and completed by not only students but by support populations as well.

In addition to questionnaire and interview data, other sources such as school and community records will provide data that substantiate or identify the needs of potential clients. Environmental assessment seeks to establish the characteristics of program and population setting through identifying the characteristics of the environment's population, economics, and geography. Community assessment may be facilitated through the use and development of certain data planning instruments, as noted in Figures 11-3 and 11-4. Typical sources from which the previously suggested data may be gathered are noted in Figure 11-4, a checklist designed to guide the information seeker to common sources of community information. The form is not intended to record data but only to provide a guide to possible sources.

Data Analysis and Interpretation

Once data have been collected through the needs assessment process, the important task of data interpretation is a crucial next step to give meaning and relevance to the collected information. This data interpretation initially requires the categorization and summarization of data according to the categories established. Although the data may be manipulated statistically to maximize its meaning and significance, ultimately four basic questions must be asked for each data category.

- What do the data mean?
- What are the implications of this interpretation that can, within reason, be assumed?
- What is the importance of this information in (a) broad general terms and (b) in terms of program responsibility?
- What priorities should be assigned to these data as interpreted?

Considerations in determining priorities include appropriateness to the mission of the program, staff expertise, recognition by the public as a need, percentage of clients who would benefit from the addressing of this need, and any other factors that might be unique to the program. Counselors should keep in mind that programs in most settings are not designed to be just remedial. Prevention, development, and enhancement are also justifiable priorities for programs.

Identifying Program Priorities and Goals

Once gathered, the needs assessment data provide direction for determining goals and priorities and for developing counseling program objectives that are relevant and meaningful to the target population and setting. The initial procedure is a simple listing of goals and priorities, first as perceived by the target population. These then may be slightly reordered, as verified by the immediate support population, and then slightly reordered again, once these

Person filling out form:	Rankings: Check one for each question below					Additional Response
____ Student ____ Parent ____ Teacher ____ Businessperson	Very Important	Quite Important	Moderately Important	Somewhat Important	Not Important at All	In your opinion is this service being provided? (check one)
1. How important is it for students to be able to discuss personal problems with the school couselor?						yes__ no__
2. How important is it for the school counselor to provide career information?						yes__ no__
3. How important is it for the school counselor to provide information concerning colleges, trade schools, or the armed services?						yes__ no__
4. How important is it for the counselor to show the relationship between education and careers?						yes__ no__
5. How important is it for the counselor to provide assistance to the student in job placement upon graduation?						yes__ no__

Figure 11-2 Needs identification questionnaire.

	Very Important	Quite Important	Moderately Important	Somewhat Important	Not Important at All	In your opinion is this service being provided? (check one)
6. How important is it for the counselor to discuss with students which courses they will take in school?						yes__ no__
7. How important is it for the counselor to work with students who are failing or dropping out?						yes__ no__
8. How important is it for the counselor to lead small-group discussions on current student problems?						yes__ no__
9. How important is a counseling and guidance program in a high school?						yes__ no__
10. What other services for students do you think the school counselor should provide? (Please write in the space below and on the back.)						yes__ no__

Figure 11-2 (continued)

Community: _____

Survey dates: _____

Survey team: _____

_____

_____ 1. Political leadership

_____

_____ 2. Governmental (nonpolitical) leadership

_____

_____ 3. Educational leadership (school board members, superintendents, principals,
_____   education association or union officials)
_____ 4. Major religious denominations (ministers, priests, rabbis)

_____

_____ 5. Minority group (or groups) leadership

_____

_____ 6. Judicial system (chief of police, juvenile judge, lawyers, county sheriff, probationary
_____   officials)
_____ 7. Business/commercial/industrial leadership (presidents [in residence] of local
_____   corporations, plant managers, owners of prominent local businesses)
_____ 8. Labor organization leadership

_____

_____ 9. Youth leadership (student council members, athletic standouts, social club or gang
_____   leadership)
_____ 10. Civic leadership (officials of civic clubs, volunteer organizations)

_____

_____ 11. Other (indicate status and representation)

_____   _____

_____   _____

_____   _____

Note: Be sure all interviewees meet the criteria for "significant contributors" as indicated in interviewing
instructions. Structured interview guides should be adhered to insofar as possible. Exceptions should
be noted and reasons for deviations explained.

Figure 11-3   Community survey checklist: Interview schedule.

Community: _____

Survey dates: _____

Survey team: _____

_____

_____

_____ 1. Census data

_____ 2. News media analysis

_____ 3. Boards of education (minutes of) meetings

_____ 4. Annual reports of schools

_____ 5. County government data

_____ 6. City government data

_____ 7. Employment agencies

_____ 8. Church board reports

_____ 9. Chamber of Commerce data

_____ 10. Geographic data

_____ 11. Ecological-environmental data

_____ 12. Other significant data (list sources)

_____

_____

_____

_____

_____

Note: If data are not available, place notation "NA" in blank at left of item.
Otherwise, when data are collected, place a "✓."

Figure 11-4 Community survey checklist: Data collection.

base data are supplemented by information from secondary populations and sources. In the school setting, the students would represent the target population; teachers and parents would be the immediate support population. Supplementary or secondary population would include community personnel and data from student and other relevant records. This process leads to a tentative prioritizing of needs. A final reordering is established by eliminating any needs that may not be the professional responsibility of the counseling program or may require resources beyond those available to the counseling program. The outcome of this process is the establishment of working priorities in a hierarchical order; these are then translated into goals and objectives.

The translation of priorities into goals and objectives requires their being stated in writing. The program goals are typically described in broad, general terms that may not be tied to specific time constraints. The program objectives must be stated in objective, measurable terms and related to a time frame. Objectives are designed to describe desired performances and should contribute to the achievement of a program goal and the meeting of one or more specially identified needs. Of course, the assessment of needs and the establishment of related goals and objectives are not in themselves a guarantee of program relevancy. A needs assessment only establishes an awareness of what a counseling program should consider in planning the utilization of its resources. The real criteria of program relevancy will result from the degree of understanding and concern and the appropriateness of the plan of action developed and executed by the counseling staff. An effective plan of action will reflect many, if not all, of the following characteristics:

1. *It should be developmental.* Program planning should be developmental, indicating immediate, intermediate, and long-range program goals. As a starting point, it may be appropriate to envision an ultimate, utopian program for the setting for which it will be designed and having established these long-range goals, determine those priorities that should be given immediate attention, those that may need attention within the next several years, and those that the program ultimately hopes to accomplish. Programs should at all times be developmental, for development implies continuous growth and improvement.

2. *It should have a logical, sequential plan of development.* The development of any program usually proceeds from a foundation that seems appropriate to subsequent development. This foundation is its needs and readiness assessment and their relationship to the resources at hand.

3. *It should be flexible.* Counseling programs must be flexible in order to meet the changing needs of youth and other client populations. This suggests also that initial planing for program development must be limited to what can reasonably be achieved. Programs that are overly ambitious in their design allow little room for unexpected opportunities. A part of flexibility in planning should be the identification of possible problems and alternate procedures for goal achievement.

4. *It should give a high priority to communication, coordination, and cooperation.* Like the other components of program development, these activities should not be left to chance. It is important, for example, to have a plan for communicating the development of the school guidance program to faculty members individually and in groups, as well as to students, parents, and others. Cooperation with other programs and persons is important if the program is to receive reciprocal cooperation. In communicating with the various relevant groups and people in the community, different approaches must be used that recognize the uniqueness and differences of these individuals and groups. For example, techniques for communicating with youths would certainly be different in many ways from those that are effective with adults and related professionals. Often, counseling programs fail to communicate their mission clearly and effectively to others; as a result, many question the need for such programs. Coordination and cooperation failures have also adversely affected the positive image that counseling programs seek to portray.

5. *It should provide a basis for resource employment.* An adequate plan for program development provides a logical basis for personnel assignment, budget development, and resource allocation and utilization. This means that the plan must be a clear and concise one in which the relationships between program

goals, the activities for achieving these goals, and the personnel and other resources needed to accomplish them can be readily recognized. The program director must be a resource coordinator. Program planning must, therefore, take into account those resources that may be available for program development and goal accomplishment. An inventory of possible resources becomes an important activity in planning for program development.

Identifying Processes for the Achievement of Program Goals

After program goals are identified and specified in objective or measurable terminology, the logical next step in program development is identifying the appropriate processes for achieving each goal. In this step it is important to treat each goal separately even though one procedural activity may serve several goals. What is desired is the identification of the one or more most efficient and effective procedures for goal achievement in a timely manner. Initially, it may be desirable to list all the possible ways in which a goal might be attained and then to eliminate those that seem the least effective or efficient. In the identification of processes one must continually keep in mind the number of staff available and their qualifications for implementing the procedure and the time commitment that would be required for effective implementation. It is also important to keep in mind the "big picture" so that the combination of procedures does not overtax the staff or overload the program.

Once the appropriate procedures have been identified for each of the goals, it is not only important but also helpful to plot these into a time frame. This is frequently referred to as the developmental plan for X program in X year (e.g., Counseling Program for Year 2003). A typical developmental plan will list the program's objectives vertically; then horizontally, it will display the months of the year and in the resulting frames, will list the program's procedures, month-by-month, for achieving each of the program's specified objectives.

Communications: An Important Part of Procedural Planning

An important element in any plan for program development is an effective means of communicating the program's goals, activities, and outcomes to all appropriate audiences. Accountable organizations must, by their very nature, collect, organize, maintain, and utilize a large and varied amount of information. Members of organizations must have ready access to key data for day-to-day operations, required reporting, public communications, and future planning. It is this public communication that is the most neglected by counseling program planners. Basic professional skills are an assumed prerequisite for appointment to counseling positions, but interpersonal competence outside the counseling relationship is an often-neglected requirement for program success. All business and industries and most other health services have marketing plans; counseling programs, however, frequently fail to "market their product." In the development of effective programs that will, in turn, achieve the necessary public support, it is important to include a communications plan—a plan that will inform and influence the supporting publics, including those clientele potentially eligible to utilize the services. In the development of the communications segment of a counseling program, it is often helpful to develop a communications plan that identifies (a) the audiences to be addressed, (b) what information they should receive, (c) what the purpose of providing this information is, (d) how the information is to be communicated,

(e) by whom it is to be communicated, and (f) when it is to be communicated. Keep in mind that communication is an ongoing, continuous activity that involves not only sending but also receiving. Knowledge acquisition is mandatory for keeping counselors relevant.

EVALUATING THE COUNSELING PROGRAM

Everyone constantly seeks ways to improve many routine chores, whether it involves trying a new toothpaste or a different breakfast cereal or taking a new route to work. In a sense, people constantly evaluate many daily decisions and activities. People are also involved, usually unofficially, in many external evaluations of such things as the local newspaper; a current TV program; the decisions of Congress; and the teachers, courses, and textbooks with which children come in contact. Just as these evaluations are a part of the process of improving daily living or exercising a right to express one's opinions, the more formal, structured evaluations of one's professional activities and organizations should also receive daily attention.

As the critics of counseling have constantly pointed out in recent years, justifiably or not, evaluative evidence and activities appear, all too frequently, to be either missing or, at best, misleading. Certainly, counseling programs are under closer scrutiny and increased accountability from a variety of sources as demands for counseling services and programs have expanded.

A Process for Professional and Program Improvement

One often reads or hears about a public office holder, a salesperson, or a teacher with 30 years of experience but with no mention of the quality of that experience. Experience does not, in and of itself, guarantee improvement and quality. Professionals must have as their own personal-ethical goal the constant and critical evaluation of their professional performance. A lack of evaluation often leads to mediocrity or failure to reach one's full potential in terms of what professionals might accomplish for the clients they serve. Evaluation for counselors in a variety of settings is foremost a process for professional improvement, a process in which one gathers objective, performance-oriented data on a systematic and nonbiased basis. These data are then used to constantly improve, upgrade, and update one's professional performance.

Amid the changing concepts of evaluation in recent decades, one of the most popular among evaluation experts is the view of evaluation as a process for providing information for decision makers. This information should be objective data that will assist decision makers in determining the relative value of competing alternatives and that will immeasurably improve their probability of making the right decisions for program improvement.

In this context of evaluation as a process for program improvement, two distinctions are important: *formative* evaluation and *summative* evaluation. Worthen, White, and Borg (1993) note that

> formal evaluation studies can serve either a *formative* purpose (such as helping to improve a mathematics curriculum) or a *summative* purpose (such as deciding whether that curriculum should be continued). Although these distinctions may blur somewhat in practice, they are useful nonetheless.

Formative evaluation is conducted during the planning and operation of a school program to provide those involved with evaluative information they can use in improving the program. For example, assume a school district is attempting to develop a local curriculum package on the history of their particular county. During development of the new curriculum unit, formative evaluation might involve content inspection by history experts' early tryouts with small numbers of children in one school in the district, and so forth. Each step would provide immediate feedback to the curriculum developers, who could use such information to make necessary revisions.

Summative evaluation occurs after a curriculum or program is considered ready for regular use, and provides potential consumers evidence about the program's worth. In our example, after the local history program was developed, a summative evaluation might determine how effective the program was in teaching local history, using a broad sample of the schools, teachers, and students in the district for which it was developed. The findings of that summative evaluation could be made available to all schools in the district who could then better determine whether to use the history unit in their schools. Summative evaluation is also used to make "go/no go" decisions, such as whether to continue or terminate a particular curriculum.

Formative and summative evaluation are both essential because decisions are needed early in the development of a program, to improve it, as well as when it has stabilized, to judge its final worth. (p. 625)

Other Functions of Evaluation

The wide range of evaluation purposes may seem to rival that of the political party platforms of promising something for everybody. Although that is not the intent, it is important to recognize some of the values of this activity. Examples of these additional functions of evaluation are as follows:

- Verifies or rejects practices by providing evidence for what works and what does not, or the degree to which an activity seems to be effective. This also helps to avoid meaningless innovations and unproven fads.
- Measures improvement by providing evidence on a continuous basis so that both rate and level of progress may be ascertained.
- Enhances probability of growth by providing a basis for improvements in the operation and its activities.
- Builds credibility. By the very nature of the activity, evaluation suggests a continuous search for better ways of doing things; a constant quest for improvement; a willingness to put efforts on the line and take a look at how we're doing.
- Provides for increased insights. By the fact of examining our own or an organization's functioning, we become more knowledgeable and understanding about this functioning, more aware of influencing factors and potential consequences.
- Increases and improves participation in decision making. Because evaluation involves everyone within the organization structure, the process, by necessity, involves them in the outcomes, which in turn should bring about the participation of all such personnel in planning new directions and implementing the findings.
- Places responsibilities. By identifying who is responsible for what and when, evaluation stimulates links between specific persons and specific activities. It decreases the probability that everyone will claim credit for the successes and no one will accept responsibility for the failures.

- Provides a rationality for the enterprise by improving overall accountability, including evidence of accomplishments and growth.

Lewis, Lewis, and Souflee (1993) state that evaluators may use

research techniques, but they apply them to the needs of specific agencies. Evaluation can be used to aid in administrative decision making, to improve currently operating programs, to provide for accountability, to build increased support for effective programs, and, in some instances, to make generalizations about the connections between specific activities and their effects. (p. 234)

Principles of Evaluation

Because evaluation is a process for appraising the effectiveness of a program or activity, it is most beneficial when conducted within a framework of guiding principles. Seven of these are discussed in the following list.

1. *Effective evaluation requires a recognition of program goals.* Before any meaningful program of evaluation can be undertaken, it is essential that the goals of that program be clearly identified. These objectives provide indications of program intent, which form the basis for subsequent planning and procedures. The objectives of the program should be stated in clear and measurable terminology. This principle suggests that counseling programs be evaluated on the basis of how well they are doing what they set out to do.

2. *Effective evaluation requires valid measuring criteria.* Once program goals are clearly defined, valid criteria for measuring progress toward those goals must be identified. The development of such criteria is crucial if the evaluation is to be both valid and meaningful. For example, if an annual program goal for a junior community college counseling program would be to provide each entering student with a series of three career interviews with a counselor, the measuring criteria could be a simple count indicating the percentage of students who did, in fact, have such an opportunity. If, however, the program goal was to provide each student with a broadening of his or her career understanding, the measuring criteria would be less obvious and might depend on a further refinement of what is meant by career understanding. In other words, vaguely stated goals and vaguely stated criteria lessen the effectiveness of program evaluation.

3. *Effective program evaluation depends on valid application of the measuring criteria.* As discussed in the previous paragraph, valid criteria for measuring progress toward the program's stated goals must be established. It is not sufficient, however, merely to establish criteria. Their ultimate validity will depend on their valid application. This implies that effective evaluation of all counseling programs should involve, in each instance, persons who are professionally competent in both evaluation techniques and the understanding of such counseling programs. Too often, effective evaluation criteria are dissipated in the hands of evaluators who have, at best, only a superficial knowledge of the appropriate role and functions of counseling programs.

4. *Program evaluation should involve all who are affected.* Evaluation of a counseling program should involve those who are participants in or who are affected

by the program. This would include, in addition to the counseling staff, program administrators, users of the services, and, on appropriate occasions, members of the community or supporting agencies. The major contribution to effective evaluation must come from those who have firsthand knowledge or involvement in the program. External evaluators from governmental agencies, accrediting associations, or other educational institutions can, of course, be helpful, but those should not be the sole bases of evaluation.

5. *Meaningful evaluation requires feedback and follow-through.* The evaluation process and the evaluation report are not in and of themselves of great value. Only when the results are used for program improvement and development does the evaluation process take on meaning. This presumes, then, that the results of any program evaluation are made available to those concerned with program management and development. It also presumes that the program manager and his or her staff will use these results for future program planning, development, and decision making.

6. *Evaluation is most effective as a planned, continuous process.* This approach may enable the program staff to identify at any time weaknesses that need correcting immediately or accomplishments that should be capitalized on. This means that there are specific plans and designated responsibilities for both the ongoing evaluation of a program's progress and the more extensive annual or semiannual reviews.

7. *Evaluation emphasizes the positive.* Frequently, evaluation is viewed as a threatening process aimed at ferreting out hidden weaknesses and spotlighting goofs. If program evaluation is to produce the most meaningful results possible, it must be conducted in a spirit that is positive, be aimed at facilitating program improvement, and emphasize strengths as well as weaknesses.

Methods of Evaluation

Before-and-After Method

The before-and-after method of evaluation seeks to identify the progress that takes place in a program's development as a result of specific program activities over a given period. For example, a school counseling program's objective might be to provide each student with a weekend work experience during her or his junior year. At the beginning of the school year, before the program, it could be presumed that none had had this experience. At the end of the year, after the program, the number who actually participated would give some indication of goal achievement. An example of a community agency's program might be to provide three stress management workshops over the course of the calendar year for employees in the local Mushy Mattress Factory. At the end of the calendar year, it could be noted that the workshops were actually conducted and that the goal has therefore been achieved.

Comparison Methods

The how-do-we-compare process makes evaluations on the basis of comparing one group against another or against the norm of a number of groups. Different techniques for achieving the same goal can also be evaluated by this comparative method. For example, a secondary school in Bloomington, Indiana, might note that it has a counselor/pupil ratio of 1 to 258, compared with the norm for 200 midwestern secondary schools of 1 to 418. Such a comparison would indicate, of course, that the Bloomington school system is making more adequate provisions for high school counseling personnel than most other school systems in the Midwest.

The How-Do-We-Stand Method

The how-do-we-stand method is based on identifying desirable program outcomes and related characteristics and criteria. From these criteria, rating scales, checklists, and questionnaires may be developed and used to indicate the degree to which a program measures up. For example, evaluative criteria or checklists used by most accrediting associations and many state government agencies and departments reflect this approach. Although this evaluation method may ignore appropriate objectives and sometimes unique and innovative practices on a local level, it does provide guidelines that enable programs to be compared with generally accepted standards.

Procedures for Evaluation

The evaluation process usually involves a series of activities in a sequence, which approximates the following:

1. *Identifying goals to be assessed.* The first step establishes the variables, or limits, for the evaluation. Evaluation can focus on the total counseling program or on only one or several particular objectives. These program objectives should be stated in clear, concise, specific, and measurable terms. Broadly stated goals are much more difficult to measure than a specifically stated goal.
2. *Developing an evaluation plan.* Once the objectives for evaluation have been established, the identification and validation of criteria appropriate for measuring the program's progress toward these objectives follow. The overall evaluation plan, in addition to specifying the kinds of data to be collected, should also specify how it will be collected, when, and by whom. This plan must also give attention to how the data will be organized and reported and to whom. Finally, such a plan should conclude with provisions for using the findings for future program development.
3. *Applying the evaluation plan.* After an acceptable evaluation plan has been designed, its validity is then dependent on the manner in which it is carried out. Once again, we stress the importance of adequate planning and a positive approach, utilizing evaluators who possess the necessary understanding and competency. Timing is also important because some aspects of a program can only be appropriately evaluated in a "longitudinal" sense, whereas other specific activities need an "immediately after" assessment.
4. *Using the findings.* Evaluation as an activity is in itself of little value. It is in the application of the findings that the real worth of evaluation lies. Through the process of evaluation, programs can ascertain their strengths and weaknesses. The resulting insights may then provide directions for future program improvement. The utilization of these findings, however, cannot be left to mere chance.

There must be planning, with specific responsibilities for the utilization of the findings, and subsequent follow-up to establish the degree to which the evaluation recommendations have been fulfilled.

External Evaluation Associations

Schools

The major evaluation associations for elementary and secondary schools and of significance to university programs, both undergraduate and graduate, are the various regional accreditation associations (e.g., North Central, Southern). These associations have developed evaluative criteria that are translated into checklists and other instrumentation or techniques; these are used by both participating schools and association evaluation teams that conduct accreditation visits to educational institutions seeking accreditation. Additionally, there are accreditation bodies representing most of the major higher education disciplines. For example, NCATE (the National Council for the Accreditation of Teacher Education) is the accreditation body specializing in accrediting schools, colleges, or departments of education.

Community Agencies

A number of external evaluation associations accredit various types of agencies. These include the (a) Joint Commission on Accreditation of Healthcare Organizations (JCAHO), (b) Commission on Accreditation of Rehabilitation Facilities (CARF), (c) Council on Accreditation of Services for Families and Children (COA), and (d) National Committee for Quality Assurance (NCQA). Typically these associations specify standards and then indicate criteria by which each standard is measured or evaluated. For example, the Joint Commission on Accreditation of Healthcare Organizations organizes the standards to be met under two sections: (1) individually focused functions; and (2) organization functions. Specifically, the individually focused functions are (a) rights, responsibilities, and ethics; (b) assessment; (c) care; (d) education; and (e) continuum. The organization functions are (a) improving organization performance; (b) leadership; (c) management of the environment of care; (d) management of human resources; (e) management of information; (f) surveillance, prevention, and control of infection; (g) behavioral health promotion; and (h) foster care. Each of these standards has specified criteria for satisfactorily meeting the standard.

Community mental health center programs have also felt increased pressures to conduct systematic program evaluations, partly as the result of the increasing demands of the federal government to verify program efficiency and effectiveness in community mental health centers. For example, the landmark Public Law 94-63, the Community Mental Health Centers Amendments of 1975, required community mental health centers to conduct program evaluations and mandated three general types of evaluation, as follows:

1. *Quality assurance of clinical services.* Each center is to establish an ongoing quality assurance of its clinical services.
2. *Self-evaluation.* Each center will collect data and evaluate its services in relation to program goals and values and to catchment area needs and resources. The data shall consist of (a) cost of center operations; (b) patterns of use of services; (c) availability, awareness, acceptability, and accessibility of services; (d) impact

of services upon the mental health of residents of the catchment area; (e) effectiveness of consultation and education services; and (f) impact of the center on reducing inappropriate institutionalization.

3. *Residents' review.* Each center will at least annually publicize and make available all evaluation data of the type listed above to residents of the catchment area. In addition, it will organize and publicize an opportunity for citizens to review the center's program of services to assure that services are responsive to the needs of residents of the catchment area.

UNDERSTANDING PROGRAM MANAGEMENT AND DEVELOPMENT

Beginning counselors might view the prospects of program management and development responsibilities and the likelihood of being involved in administering an ongoing program as not only remote but also as potentially undesirable. Let us therefore advance some of the reasons that counselors should possess a minimal understanding of management, development, and leadership.

Administration and Your Job

A common complaint throughout all organizations today and perhaps throughout history concerns the inroads made on professional time by nonprofessional or administrative activities. Administrative obligations, however, are a fact of life for all functioning professionals, including counselors in all settings. Because one cannot avoid all responsibilities for program administration, management, and development at any level, it will be beneficial if from the beginning of your professional activities as a counselor you have a minimal understanding of these matters and how you may best respond.

Recognizing the inevitability of administrative responsibilities, what can one do to discharge these duties as expeditiously and effectively as possible? The following are suggestions gleaned from informal interviews with successful program managers and administrators in various settings.

1. *Be organized.* To be organized means, among other things, having a place for everything and everything in its place. This keeps you from wasting time in search-and-find operations. Being organized also means planning the use of your time. This includes maintaining a daily calendar that allows sufficient time for each task for which you are responsible. Because it is not always possible to estimate the exact amount of time a counseling interview may consume, it is better to allocate too much rather than too little time on one's calendar. Implicit in organization is an efficient filing and record-keeping system that allows ready access to items as needed. Files should contain all necessary and relevant information but should be periodically purged of outdated and nonuseful materials. Although neatness is not necessarily a guarantee of organization, there appears to be a relationship between a neat office and a well-organized one.

2. *Do it right the first time.* Much administration seems to focus on preparing reports, maintaining records, and organizing data. As previously indicated,

increasing emphasis on accountability, plus requirements mandated by state or federal statutes, has further accentuated the necessity of gathering objective data supporting the counseling enterprise. It is important to take time to understand exactly what it is you have to report and how it is to be reported. If you do not understand it, do not hesitate to ask for help if you need it. Do not waste your time and someone else's by doing it wrong the first time. You must also demand accuracy of yourself in completing any report or record and in organizing data. Long, cumbersome documents encourage guessing on the part of respondents. Other reports, especially those of an evaluative nature, may tempt one to fake or fudge a bit on the responses. The single word of advice is *don't*. In addition to the risk of being embarrassed by someone noting your inaccuracies, you risk the more dangerous possibility that important decisions will be made on the basis of inaccurate and irresponsible data.

3. *Do it on time.* Assuming that you have been convinced to do your reporting and recording accurately, do not detract from your administrative responsibilities by being late. Usually, there is a reason that certain data are required at certain times for certain decisions. Your delays can handicap this process, especially when your colleagues have all responded on time. On those rare occasions when an emergency prevents you from discharging a responsibility on time, you must give it the highest priority and complete it at the earliest opportunity to avoid a domino effect in which every activity down the line will also be subject to tardiness.

4. *Plan your own time.* All of us on occasion will come up against constraints on our time. Walking down the halls in almost any setting, we can hear comments such as "All I ever do is to go meetings," or "All I get done is answer the phone," or "If people would just stop dropping in unannounced," or "I don't seem to have any time to myself anymore." Time frustration seems to occur with all of us. Thus, the use and control of time are critical in one's efficient functioning, in both administration and in counseling; they also have an impact on one's morale. The objective of planning your time is to make the most of it and, at the same time, leave you enough freedom and flexibility so you do not feel that the clock is your boss. In order to do this, there are several considerations. One is to do the things you do at the times you do them best. For example, some may find they prepare reports most efficiently if they do so first thing in the morning. Others may find it desirable to use the first hour or so at work to complete the waking-up process with a second cup of coffee. It is also important to do the things we do where we do them best, perhaps getting away to some private little corner where we are uninterrupted for certain administrative responsibilities. We may also wish an informal setting for conferences with colleagues. In planning the use of time, it is important that we understand ourselves in relation to where and how we function best. We adapt our time commitment to our working style.

5. *Do it neatly.* The effects of doing it right and doing it on time may still be lost if an interpreter is needed to translate what you have done. If your handwriting is sloppy, try typing or printing reports for others. Lack of neatness can also detract from the impact of reports. A report that looks as if it has been done and redone a dozen times may also be more subject to scrutiny and questions by superiors.

Suggestions for functioning effectively also include the following don'ts:

1. *Don't let it spoil your day.* Although not everyone may enjoy the challenges of recording and reporting, such tasks should be accepted as inevitable responsibilities that will not be facilitated by constant complaints. The frequent suggestions of many administrators is that you do it and forget it.
2. *Don't expect to understand the need for every report.* Frustrations frequently occur when one fails to see a rationale for the kind of data that are needed. Allied with this is the fact that we may also not understand why it has to be done "their" way instead of our "better" way. When something is requested by your immediate supervisor, you are more likely to understand the need than if it is requested by the upper management, several layers removed. However, inevitably there will be occasions when reports are requested from afar that will challenge all that is rational. Again, do it and forget it.
3. *Don't be tempted to become an administrator.* In some settings, counselors appear to receive their largest number of "brownie points" from their superiors by meeting their administrative responsibilities. It therefore becomes a natural temptation to overemphasize that aspect of the job. Many counselors commonly complain that they spend too much time in administrative activities; even many program administrators agree. A counselor's major responsibility in any setting, with the possible exception of a program director, is to counsel. This should be the counselor's primary, time-consuming activity. Although it is important to meet one's administrative responsibilities efficiently and effectively, that does not imply they overshadow in importance or time the main reason for which one is hired as a counselor.

As an aid to help those who may be reluctant to move from disorganization to organization, the following score pad (Table 11-1) will enable you to play the time game. It may help persons develop an awareness of their personal time management styles.

Program Management

Program management as it is perceived in recent generations can obviously be described in a variety of different ways. Regardless of labels, nearly all programs must provide for the management of (a) personnel, (b) budgeting, (c) facilities, and (d) activities. The program manager must, of course, be responsible for the development of a plan that logically structures and coordinates all of these elements. Program management also involves the development of policies that guide practice. Program management may also provide job descriptions that guide staff members of the program in their activities and responsibilities. Program management also recognizes differing levels of responsibility and management. For example, Figure 11-5 depicts such levels as they might exist in educational systems.

The responsibilities and activities of program management may vary according to levels and settings, but it is possible to identify two basic areas of functioning. The first deals with the managing of basic resources, such as personnel, budget, and facilities. The second focuses on organizing and facilitating such basic activities as coordination, communication, cooperation, decision making, and evaluation. The emphasis of discussions here will be on what is involved rather than on how one should do it. Following are some suggestions

Table 11-1   The time game score pad (Object: To improve your score on a daily, weekly, or monthly basis).

Hour	What did I do?	Had I planned to do it?[a]	How well did I do it?[b]	Did I do it with a positive attitude?[c]	Comments to self[d]
8 A.M.					
9 A.M.					
10 A.M.					
11 A.M.					
12 noon					
1 P.M.					
2 P.M.					
3 P.M.					
4 P.M.					
5 P.M.					

[a] 5 points if you had planned to do it.

   3 points if you had planned to do it because it was overdue.

   0 points if you hadn't planned to do it.

   −3 points if you hadn't planned to do it but it was an unexpected requirement that had a higher priority than what you had planned.

[b] Score yourself on a scale of 0 to 5.

[c] 3 points if you did it with enthusiasm.

   2 points if you did it with a positive attitude.

   1 point if you did it and then forgot about it.

   0 points if you did it and then worried about it.

−1 point if you did it with frustration and/or anger.

−5 points if you did it and it drove you to distraction.

[d] 1 point for each constructive suggestion.

−1 point for statements using profanity.

Totals:

   1. Subtotal A + B + C + D.

   2. Subtract 5 points if you didn't take a lunch break.

   3. Subtract 10 points if you didn't take a lunch break for a second day in a row.

appropriate for entry-level counselors, who should also be aware that as one moves into management responsibilities, one's own style and techniques tend to emerge.

Managing Personnel

Of all the resources that a program manager is called on to use, the human resource is by far the most important. The manner in which this resource is managed will largely determine the success or failure of the program and also whether the manager is a program leader or simply a program administrator. Program managers, on the one hand, view themselves as facilitators—leaders who function in such a manner that it enables their staff to operate

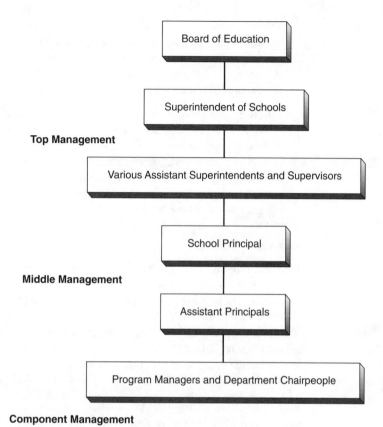

Component Management

Figure 11-5 Levels of educational management.

more effectively, and yes, more easily, in meeting their assigned responsibilities. Program administrators, on the other hand, often view themselves as overseers—policy enforcers and performance evaluators—hardly ones to inspire performance. The program manager's initial responsibility in many instances will begin with staffing, which will be a consistent consideration as long as there is staff turnover. Staff selection should minimally involve three factors: (1) qualifications; (2) versatility; and (3) adaptability. These factors are discussed in the paragraphs that follow.

Qualifications

An individual's qualifications are primarily but not exclusively based on training and experience in relation to the expectancies of the position. In viewing an applicant's training background, consideration should be given not only to the content of the training program but also to when, where, and areas of specialization. Although academic achievements in themselves are not the sole criterion for performance on the job, a person's academic achievements should not be completely ignored. There may be little difference in performance between the A and B student, but one should not anticipate that the C student will perform as well on the job as the A student.

When examining experience, program managers usually compare the type, amount, and success of previous experiences. Experience may not always be a factor, for many program managers are anxious to hire recent graduates who can bring new ideas, more up-to-date concepts, and, perhaps, needed youthful enthusiasm to their programs.

In school settings, Gysbers and Henderson (2000) note:

> Effective performance in a position is a shared responsibility of the position holder and the school district. Counselor applicants have a responsibility to define themselves adequately so that prospective employers can evaluate whether they are "right" for the jobs available. Employers have the responsibility for clearly and specifically defining the positions available. Counselors have a professional responsibility to be competent in what the district has the right to expect—that is, the educational areas defined as minimum standards for certification by the state and the ethical standards defined by the profession. (p. 231).

Staff Versatility

When the program manager has a staff of at least one to manage, providing for program versatility enters into staff selection. Differing backgrounds should provide a wider range of specialty skills. Also, it has frequently been noted that staffs of two or more should include one member of each sex and minority or cultural representation, as appropriate. Some range in age representation is important, especially in institutional and community settings, and the old schoolboy network (hire all graduates from the same school) should not be perpetuated at the expense of program versatility.

Adaptability

Another consideration that is often overlooked in staffing is the adaptability of a staff member to both the job setting and the community or area environment. The person must not only like the job, but the job must like the person. A staff member will function more effectively when there are congenial relationships among the staff as well as those with whom they come in frequent contact. This, of course, would include the clients that the staff is serving. It is not suggested that one form friendships with clients, but it is important to be able to relate to the client population, whether it is inner city, suburban society, Appalachian poor, or Alaskan Eskimo.

Staff members must also be able to adapt to the community or area environment that supports the job setting. It is highly unlikely that people can be unhappy in their community or home life and happy in their work life. The inability to adapt to a community environment can also have adverse effects on the public relations aspect of the counseling program.

Managing Personnel

Once staffing decisions have been made and personnel are functioning on a job, management's responsibilities continue to be important. These include the following:

1. *Assignment of responsibility.* Staff members should have specific activities for which they are responsible and for which each staff member knows she or he is answerable. In assigning these responsibilities, the program manager seeks to capitalize on the special skills, experience, and personal characteristics of the

staff member. In some instances this will involve the delegation of some un-desirable or less-favored tasks. Staff members must anticipate these as well as their share of the more rewarding activities. A good program manager will not delegate all the "donkey work" and keep only the "goodies" for himself or her-self. It is of utmost importance that every staff member have some duties that are enjoyable, challenging, and motivating. To paraphrase an old saying "All dull work and no fun work, makes Jack or Jill an unmotivated professional!"

2. *Provisions for staff support.* The fact that counselors are providing helping ser-vices and human support to others does not mean that counselors should or can function without the support of others. A program manager must see that staff members help and support each other and, additionally, receive help and support from beyond the counseling offices. Ways in which this may be accomplished include meaningful group work or committee assignments in which members share their interest in a common problem or topic with other personnel outside the counseling staff. Obviously, part of this human support system is the pro-gram manager's personal interaction with each staff member.

3. *Provisions for staff development.* The effective program manager is ever alert to the ongoing need for the professional development of all staff members. Com-pleting a degree provides entry into the professional workforce but it does not signify an end to the development of a counselor's professional competencies. In fact, it should signal the beginning of such development. Clients have the right to expect that their counselors will be up to date—aware of the latest advance-ments, significant research, and promising practices in the field. Thus, profes-sional development is to be anticipated and sought after by the professional counselor throughout his or her active career. Program leaders have the responsi-bility of providing opportunities, motivation, and, if possible, resources. This topic is discussed later in this text in a section entitled "The Counselor's Profes-sional Development."

Budget Management

The importance of budget and budget management in any setting can hardly be over-emphasized. A budget's significance in any system of accountability is paramount. In effect, it enables the supporting public, whether they are taxpayers or donators, to see what they are paying for or whether they are getting their money's worth. To the individual staff member, budgeting is often a mysterious, misunderstood, maddening, and far-removed process that has a direct and undeniable relationship to staff morale. It is therefore impor-tant that staff members recognize the level at which their immediate program manager is involved and the extent of that involvement.

It is also helpful to understand the level at which budgeting decisions, especially those affecting staff members, are made. In many settings, lower-level managers may be limited in their budget responsibilities to recommending or requisitioning from budgets established elsewhere. Crucial budget decisions, such as salaries and salary increments, staffing addi-tions, and equipment purchases, tend to be made at middle and upper-management levels. These real budget managers are usually involved in budgeting for personnel, including both professional and support staff, and services, such as consultants, communications, supplies, equipment, and travel. Budget decisions for capital improvements, such as new buildings or significant remodeling, are usually made at only the highest level of management.

One form of budgeting that has become increasingly prevalent at even the lower levels of management involves program activities supported by federal or state grants. These are usually developed in response to mandated federal or state programs. These programs have specific objectives and procedures and a budget that is directly related and accountable to those procedures and objectives.

Beginning counselors are unlikely to be involved in budget management, but they probably will be involved in budget expenditures. Because mismanagement or misspent monies may become your personal expense, the following suggestions are pertinent.

1. Each budget item is related to an activity, which in turn is related to a specific goal or objective of the organization. It is important to understand the reason for an expenditure, which also suggests spending only for those categories that are budgeted; for example, if professional travel is not provided for in a budget, you do not travel to a professional meeting by taking $500 from the supply item in the budget, even if it is not being spent elsewhere.

2. Spend only what you have. Although you may occasionally overdraw a bank account, you are usually reminded quickly and make amends before it becomes a bankruptcy disaster. However, all too frequently, when spending someone else's money, there is an inclination to be less concerned until it is too late. Remember, any spending you do that is beyond the available budget will probably end up being your own personal expense.

3. Spend economically. The fact that you have a budget does not mean that the sky is the limit as long as you spend it for items in the budget and as long as you do not exceed the budget. Budget managers are expected to be good shoppers. This does not mean that you sacrifice quality for economy but that you get the most for your budgetary dollar. For example, on major purchases, such as computers or video and electronic equipment, it is customary to obtain two or three estimates including those provided by traditional discount houses before determining the place of purchase. If the expenditure is for travel, recipients are usually expected to be aware of the various bargain travel fares and travel regular or tourist class on common carriers. If private vehicles are used, mileage rates are usually established by federal, state, or local agencies.

4. Secure receipts. If you spend budgeted funds in any amount, you will be reimbursed only when there is proof of purchase. The only acceptable proof of purchase is a receipt for the goods or service obtained (showing the item, even if it is an elephant, is not considered proof of purchase).

5. Keep a running account. Anyone who has responsibility for any budget or segment of one must know exactly what has been expended and what remains at any given point during the duration of the budget. This means keeping a daily, if necessary, running account of debits, credits, and balances.

6. Be aware of any unusual (or usual) legal or contract restraints. This point is perhaps most appropriate when persons have budgetary responsibilities emanating from special contracts or grants. In such instances, budget managers, when in doubt, should consult the appropriate legal or contract authority before authorizing an expenditure.

Managing Facilities

The management of facilities takes on appropriate importance when one considers that people spend more of their waking hours in their place of work than in their home or anywhere else. Facilities are important in determining whether individuals will have the opportunity to do their job in a manner in which they are capable of doing it. In large, complex institutions, facilities are often viewed as symbols that reflect the importance with which the operation is viewed. (It is thus inevitable that a school principal's office will always be a shade larger, at least, than the school counselor's; that the college president's office and decor will be considerably larger and more luxurious than that of the institution's most distinguished professor.) Facility concerns of program managers include the following:

- *Adequacy*. Size, furnishings, general decor, cleanliness, and above all for counselors, privacy are determinants of the adequacy of one's work space. These factors tend to determine the atmosphere in which one works. Those who have ever worked in dingy, dreary, ill-equipped, or dirty facilities can recall the impact of these on one's morale and subsequent performance. Obviously, the more attractive one's work space is, the more positive an impact it will have on the individual's performance.

- *Accessibility*. A person should not feel that she or he has already done a half day's work just by getting to the office. Accessibility is also important in terms of clients. Countless studies have noted that when university counseling centers or community agencies are situated in locations far from the main populations they are intended to serve, their clientele does not materialize.

- *Individuality*. Have you ever viewed the administrative offices of large-scale enterprises or business corporations, where dozens of employees have been provided identical cubicles and furnishing as so many similar mechanical parts in a precision machine? Such facilities provide little opportunity for the individual worker to assert any individuality. In other words, each individual counselor should have enough flexibility in planning their personal office facilities to express their own individuality.

- *Supplementary space*. Program managers also are responsible for securing and managing supplementary facilities, such as conference rooms, resource or staff rooms, filing areas (security can be important here), storage and supply areas, reception areas, and support staff facilities.

Developing and Managing the Basic Activities

The program manager must also guide the organization through the basic activities of the counseling program. This does not mean the professional activities but rather the basic supporting activities that complement the professional services of the organization. These include the following:

- *Coordination*. In the even less-than-complex organizations, some degree of coordination is necessary to prevent overlapping, conflicting, or duplicating of activities. Coordination is necessary among activities and programs, both internally and externally.

- *Cooperation.* Cooperation is a vital ingredient in both coordination and public relations. Program managers must encourage and demonstrate a willingness to work with others in such vital counselor activities as case studies, conferences, referrals, and consultation. As suggested previously, counselors should be willing to give help when called on by fellow professional colleagues or support personnel in other fields as well. Cooperation is one of the basic functions in establishing and maintaining positive professional connections.

- *Effective communications.* Communications often determine whether a program is managed efficiently. Counselors are usually well trained in the art of personal communication, but it is surprising how frequently the communication process breaks down within a program as well as with higher-level management and external agencies and organizations. Guidelines for effective communication in management suggest that care must be taken so the personal touch is not lost as a result of using impersonal means to communicate, such as memos, policy statements, and directives. When such impersonal means are necessary, there must be adequate personal follow-up to ensure that these communications are understood. In addition, communication must provide for some sort of feedback. Oral communication to large groups such as staff or faculty meetings must justify the time it consumes for the number of people present.

- *Evaluation.* A program manager is responsible for ensuring the gathering of data that provide for systematic, ongoing evaluation of the program's activities. A program manager also coordinates periodic and accreditation types of planning. At the individual staff member level, a program manager is responsible for evaluating each member of the organization and communicating this evaluation to both the individual staff member and higher management.

- *Decision making.* Effective program management requires that someone be in charge. As the one in charge, a program manager must have decision-making authority commensurate with the responsibilities of the decision. Program managers can share the decision thinking, but they cannot be expected to share all the decision making.

In concluding this section we would comment that there are two equally important aspects of program management. One deals with being efficient in the coordination of the various components of the program to ensure goal achievement. The second is the humanistic responsibilities of management. This involves applying the basic skills of human relationships (in which counselors are obviously trained) to staff relationships and the development of an environment conducive to staff motivation and achievement. It includes helping individuals achieve their potential and enjoy doing so.

RESEARCH FOR PROGRAM IMPROVEMENT

In introducing this topic we recognize that research does not always project a popular image. Some of the reasons for this lack of popularity are the following:

- Most research seems to ignore the common problems and everyday needs of practitioners.

- Most research reports are written in a manner that limits their interpretation and hence their application by practitioners.
- Research activities and resulting research reports rarely excite the imagination.
- The research monies made available by federal and state agencies are cornered by universities and private research and development corporations.
- Research is too time-consuming and has very few rewards for most practitioners.

Notwithstanding the usually exaggerated misconceptions about research, the helping profession of counseling and its membership have a responsibility to advance the knowledge and practice of the profession by, at the very least, using research findings and, one hopes, becoming involved in such studies as well. Research becomes another valuable tool that counselors can use in this era of accountability to prove that what they do can make a positive difference in the lives of individuals, groups, and the function of organizations. Let us now examine some of the positive outcomes you can anticipate from research.

Positive Outcomes of Research

For general practitioners in counseling and other helping professions, the most positive general outcome of practitioner research is the improvement of one's professional skills and understanding. Research can answer professional questions, solve dilemmas, and explain failures. Research enables practitioners to become better at their art. It can enable us to verify what works and what does not and, if pursued, why. It can eliminate much of the guesswork and uncertainty from practice. Engaging in practical research can increase our insights and deepen understandings of ourselves, the counseling profession, and the relationships between the two. Our own research can help us as individual professionals become better at what we do.

Also, practitioners' research tends to focus on local problems or concerns and may, therefore, have opportunities to provide results that are immediately applicable. The occasion to make a positive difference in one's job environment can be challenging. Furthermore, even if practitioners tend to focus on local concerns in their research activities, that still gives them opportunities to make contributions to their profession; to exchange their ideas and findings with other similar local settings and other interested professionals. Presentations and discussions at local, state, and national conferences give the researcher further chances to share findings, explore with other professionals the implications of the results, and possibly expand the interpretation of the research findings.

Finally, research can be interesting. Any new experience, learning new knowledge, or finding an answer to an old problem can be stimulating. Research only becomes dull and meaningless to researchers when they investigate topics or problems that are to them dull and meaningless. Identify a professional question (problem or concern) that you would personally like answered and set out to find the answer. You may discover that it is a surprisingly exciting quest, and you may then agree that research can be one of the most rewarding of all professional activities.

Some Definitions

Basic Research

Basic research is concerned with or conducted solely for the purpose of developing theories or establishing general principles. In educational and other settings, basic research provides the theory that, in turn, produces implications for solving problems.

Applied Research

Applied research provides data to support a theory through applying or testing the theory and evaluating its usefulness in problem solving.

Action Research

Action research is designed to solve problems through the application of the scientific method. For example, a counselor may utilize a systematic and scientifically appropriate process to determine whether a new approach is effective in decreasing cigarette smoking among adolescents.

Historical Research

As the label implies, historical research involves studying, understanding, and explaining events that occurred in the past. The purpose of historical research is to investigate causes, effects, or trends of past occurrences that may, in turn, help to explain present events and predict future ones. By necessity, most historical studies rely on documentary resources and, in some instances, personal recall.

Descriptive Research

Descriptive research seeks to test hypotheses or answer questions concerning the present. There are two major classifications of descriptive research: qualitative and quantitative. In quantitative research the investigator will observe events, probably using some coding scheme and then will draw inferences based on what has been observed. The goal of quantitative research is to describe cause and effect relationships. On the other hand, the qualitative researcher attempts to retain the viewpoint of the individual(s) being studied. This may, for example, involve the study of video or audio recordings and an analysis of field or observational notes. The qualitative researcher, then, attempts to understand the ways that individuals give meaning to the behavior of themselves and others and to describe these understandings.

Experimental Research

This sort of research experiments with different variables to predict what will occur in the future under a given set of conditions.

Experimental research provides stronger support for inferences about causal relationships among variables than does any other research approach. Four essential features of experiments follow:

- The mission includes the idea of cause.
- The researcher manages or manipulates one or more independent variables.
- Measures are taken of one or more dependent variables.
- The research plan controls extraneous factors that might contaminate the results to minimize unwanted influences of such factors and strengthen the inferences made about causal relationships between independent and dependent variables.

Experimental approaches frequently used in counseling research include analogue research, traditional group experiments, and time series experiments. Sometimes circumstances do not permit controlling extraneous factors to the degree that true experiments require. Quasi-experiments represent a compromise in such instances. (Hadley & Mitchell, 1995, p. 43)

Pilot Study

A pilot study is a preliminary trial of research methods and instruments before the development of the final research plan.

Hypotheses

Hypotheses are predictions regarding the probable outcome of a research study that, in turn, form a basis for goals and procedures to achieve these goals.

Sampling

Sampling is a research technique for selecting a specified number of people from a defined population as representative of that specific population.

The Research Process

Some research undoubtedly requires complex, sophisticated research skills. However, much valuable information can be obtained through research that meets the requirements of scientific inquiry but does not require a high level of research skill. Thus, the following examination of research procedures is not intended to provide a basis for undertaking research but rather to provide a better understanding of the basic factors involved in conducting research. It allows—and should encourage—practitioners to consider and become involved in relatively unsophisticated research investigations.

The first step in undertaking research is to identify a researchable problem—a need for information. Whatever stimulates your interest or curiosity or arouses doubts may be the basis for a research problem. Most of us experience a constant and continuing need for information in our daily jobs. We wonder about the adequacy or effectiveness of our techniques, the various characteristics of our clients, and the nature of client needs. If we decide to initiate research in the area of techniques, we might simply seek to determine the kinds of information needed for justifying present practices or developing more effective and functional ones.

A second step in most research is to review or survey previous research and writings relevant to the possible research topic. The purposes of this review are to (a) see whether adequate answers have already been found to the questions the researcher has in mind, (b) gain a better understanding of the nature of the problem, and (c) gain insights regarding approaches that might be used to efficiently attain the outcomes desired. Although in the past this particular step may have been one that discouraged many from considering research activities, the computer capacities of libraries with their various information retrieval systems enable even the neophyte researcher to have in hand, quickly, a computerized printout of relevant research and writings, usually summarized for convenience. Of course, for those with personal computers, searches over the Internet bring nearly instantaneous results.

The third step is to identify specifically the nature of the information desired or formulate the specific research problem. The problem should be stated fully and precisely in objective terminology in a complete grammatical sentence. It should be written so that others can understand it without the prompting of the researcher. The beginning researcher should also be aware that within the main problem there may be logical subcomponents, identified as subproblems.

The fourth step in the research process is to determine the kinds of information needed to permit sound conclusions about the issue (or issues) in question. In this step, the previously stated problem and related subproblems are now viewed through questions or logical constructs, called *hypotheses*. Hypotheses are assumptions made regarding the problem or its solution that steer the researcher in some direction to gather facts that will provide the most valid answers. For example, a research investigation may be attempting to determine why a school has an unusually high dropout rate. Several possibilities for this dropout rate could be hypothesized: (a) students are not interested in school; (b) students lack the ability to continue in school; (c) students are under economic pressure to leave school and obtain a job. Each of these assumptions or hypotheses provides some direction or basis for identifying facts that would enable the investigator to determine objectively why the majority of students are leaving school.

Having identified the kinds of information needed, the researcher determines what procedures are most appropriate for collecting and analyzing the data. In this fifth step, the population or sample to be used and the means by which it is to be selected are determined, as are instruments and other data-collecting tools appropriate for the questions or hypotheses that have been stated. In this stage, the researcher seeks to determine the most appropriate sampling procedures and the most efficient, effective instruments or techniques for gathering the data needed in order to respond to the hypotheses as completely and as validly as possible.

Once the types of information and the procedures and instruments needed for collecting this information have been determined, the sixth step is the actual collection of the data. A data collection plan should be developed indicating the data needed, probable source of the data, how it is to be collected (e.g., questionnaires, surveys, interviews, reading of reports), who is to collect the data, and the deadlines for collection.

In the seventh step, the collected data are systematically organized and analyzed. The method of data analysis should be determined before collecting data to ensure that the suggested treatment is appropriate to the data collected and the manner in which it is organized. Depending on the research design developed in step five of this sequence, the analysis may be no more than a simple mathematical or elementary statistical one.

Beginning practitioners can still engage profitably in research activities by simply recognizing their limitations in the design of their study. In the final step, the research findings are interpreted and conclusions drawn, which may lead to resolving or answering the problems. Here the previously stated hypotheses are either confirmed or rejected and answers are provided to the questions that initiated the research activity. Figure 11-6 depicts the research process.

Utilizing Research Reports

Findings from research studies can be important to counselors in all settings. Research findings can provide factual data to reinforce or guide their professional judgment and improve their practice. Whether one is an active researcher or not, a counseling professional cannot afford to gloss over the important research in the field. We must, for example, be aware of both the reservoir of accumulated knowledge dealing with human behavior and the results of cur-

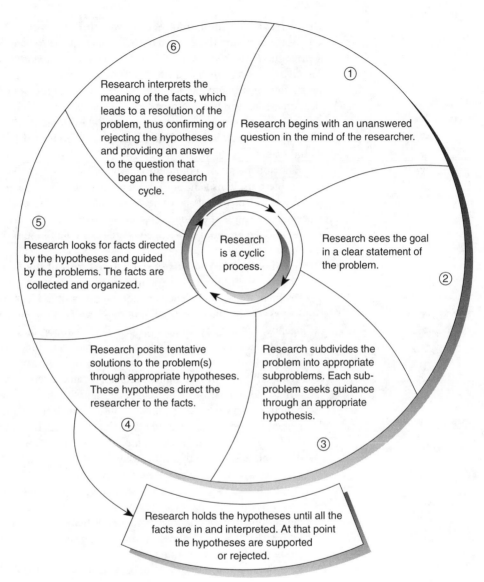

Figure 11-6   The research process.

Source: Practical Research, 6e: Planning and Design by Paul D. Leedy, © 1997. Reprinted by permission of Pearson Eduction, Inc., Upper Saddle River, NJ.

rent research studies that broaden, deepen, or perhaps alter our understanding of this behavior. As research technology continues to improve, we can anticipate an increase in research studies, more sophistication in their methodology and validity in their outcomes, as well as more relevance and application of the findings. Thus, all practicing counselors must not only recognize the importance of research but also be cognizant of what we might label guidelines for identifying research of potential significance. Your authors suggest the following guidelines.

- **Be Aware of Common Sources of Research Reporting in Your Field**

    Some common indices and abstracts such as the *Review of Educational Research*, the *Education Index*, *Social Science Index*, *Sociology Index*, *Index Medicus*, *Psychological Abstracts*, and *Dissertation Abstracts* are good starting points in which to broadly identify reports of recent research investigations. Publications representing the professional organizations in counseling and related fields are rich sources of recent research studies in the field.

- **Identify Research Studies That Appear to Be Relevant to Your Own Professional Needs**

    The abundance of reported research, past and present, is enough to overwhelm the most conscientious researcher. Any user of research findings must learn to be selective lest she or he drown in the ever-growing tidal waves of research reporting. Therefore, it is important that we identify as specifically as possible the kind of knowledge we are seeking and focus our search on this topic.

- **Review the Studies You Have Selected in Terms of the Following:**

    1. The design of the study: (You may need the assistance of a competent researcher at this point. They are not too difficult to locate if you are close to a large school system, institution of higher education, large mental health agency, or state government office.) This is important in determining the probable accuracy of the findings, their generalizability to your situation, and the conclusions or implications that can be drawn from them.

    2. Readability: Some research reports are technical reports written primarily for other researchers. Both the vocabulary and the statistical methods through which the data are presented may confuse, mislead, or simply confound the reader. Unsophisticated attempts to figure out what the report is saying should not be undertaken. If you cannot understand the report you should select a different report to study or you may again seek the help of a competent researcher who can interpret the study to you.

    3. Originality of the research: A firsthand report of a study by the researcher(s) who was the principal investigator is more desirable than secondhand reporting, summaries, or citations by others. Whereas secondary sources can be useful, they are usually more brief than the original source and may inadvertently misrepresent the findings.

    4. Reputation of the author/researcher: Established researchers/authors have achieved their preeminence through previous studies that have been endorsed by their peers as sound in design, addressing important needs, and significant in their findings.

Writing Research Grant Applications

Millions of dollars are made available to agencies, institutions, and school systems annually from federal and state agencies and private foundations. These monies, usually earmarked for specific purposes, are most frequently allocated or awarded on the basis of a competitive review of proposals or grant applications received. Because many of the funding opportunities are in the areas of counseling interest and expertise, counselors must possess the necessary application skills to competitively pursue such funding as may be of interest to and appropriate for their organizations. The following general guidelines are suggested:

1. Read thoroughly the published announcements and other information that describe the guidelines to follow in preparing and submitting a grant application. This will, among other things, help you to determine your organization's eligibility.
2. Follow to the letter the guidelines for the preparation and submission of the grant proposal. The appropriate format is expected, and the dates or submission deadlines must be met.
3. Know, to the extent possible, the funding agency or foundation.

Personal contacts by visit or phone are, of course, very useful in clarifying, explaining, or elaborating on purposes, procedures, and guidelines. Some agencies will provide, on request, examples of exemplary projects and lists of previous recipients. Foundations will send you their annual reports and publications such as the *Commerce Business Daily*, *Federal Register*, *The Education Daily*, and *Federal Grants and Contracts Weekly*. Descriptions of private foundations and their research priorities are indicated in *The Taft Foundation Reporter* (published by the Taft Group in Washington, DC) and *The Foundation Directory* (published by the Foundation Center, New York). Many of these plus additional resources are now readily available via the Internet.

All specified sections of a proposal format are important, but the four that are briefly explained in the following discussion require special attention.

Statement of the Problem

This section of the proposal should contain a well-defined, specific statement of the problem; the need for such a study (its educational significance); and concisely stated, measurable objectives. Conceptual and research literature should be cited to stress the significance of, or the need for, the study, but the literature cited should be specifically relevant to the proposed study.

Procedures

This section of the proposal must present the design of the study and a fully detailed description of the procedures to be utilized. It should be apparent to a reader that the stipulated procedures will enable the achievement of the project's stated objectives. It should describe the sample to be used and how the sample is to be selected, the instruments and other data-collecting tools or approaches to be utilized, the statistical treatments to be applied, and the evaluational procedures to be employed. If the objectives were definitely stated—as they should be—the evaluational procedures should evolve from them. Although this section must be concise, it must also be complete. A basic criterion for evaluating most proposals is the soundness of the methodology employed.

Personnel and Facilities

This, too, is a most important section, especially in proposals for federal funding. As the purpose of this section is to enable a determination of the research capabilities, care must be taken to identify the personnel involved and to show that by training and experience, these individuals have the research competencies required for the implementation of the proposed study. Similarly, the facilities required for the research endeavor should be described and their availability assured.

Budget

The cost estimates for the proposed project must be accurate, detailed, justifiable, and reasonable. It must be clearly evident how the anticipated expenditures relate to each of the specific procedural steps.

Reporting Research Results

Obviously, conducting research is not enough—unless you intend to keep the results selfishly to yourself! Reporting your study enables you to advance not only yourself professionally but the profession as well. This can either be an oral report—through presentations at professional conferences, workshops, and such—or a written report—in professional journals, newsletters, or monographs. Oral reports have the advantage of enabling the audience to directly question and interact with the presenter. Written reports have the advantage of reaching a wider audience. Heppner, Kivlighan, and Wampold (1992) present some general principles for writing research reports: " (1) be informative, (2) be forthright, (3) do not overstate or exaggerate, (4) be logical and organized, (5) have some style, (6) write and rewrite, and (7) if all else fails, just write!" (p. 376).

These authors note that in writing for publication, the exact organization

of a research report varies depending on the publication for which it is intended and the nature of the study. Nevertheless, a perusal of counseling journals reveals a model organization, roughly as follows:

Title
Abstract
Introduction
Method
- Subjects
- Measures (or Variables or Instruments)
- Materials
- Design (or Design and Analysis)
- Procedures

Results
Discussion (or Conclusions)
References
Tables
Figures

The nature of each of these components depends on the publication and the readership. Nevertheless, there are some aspects of each of these components that are critical to a well-written research report. (p. 376)

Ethical Issues in Human Research

By its very nature, counseling research, with rare exceptions, must involve human beings. Growing concern for the rights of human subjects has resulted in increased efforts by professional organizations and research institutions and agencies, including the U.S. government, to safeguard the rights and dignity of individuals who are involved as subjects of research.

In this regard, attention must be given to protecting subjects' right to privacy, determining whether the research puts subjects at risk in any way, obtaining informed consent of subjects, and not involving subjects in research that challenges or threatens their morals or values.

PROGRAM LEADERSHIP

Although discussed in brief earlier, we would once again emphasize that perhaps no single characteristic beyond the professional qualifications of the counseling staff is more significant to the success of the counseling operation than the quality of program leadership. It is desirable that counselors at least recognize those characteristics that tend to identify leaders and distinguish them from program administrators or managers. Most people recognize the individual who is a true leader. A real leader is one who leads, not directs; real leadership gives priority to the benefit of the program and those who are led, rather than to the leader. Some of the characteristics of program leadership include the following:

- *Is successful:* Program leaders have good track records. They justify the old concept that success breeds success. Included in the program leader's win column is previous recognition as a successful and resourceful counselor. Also, the program leader is an extra-competent professional. Program leadership for counseling programs can be provided only by professional counselors. Program leaders will contribute their competence and expert knowledge to the successful functioning of the counseling program, including an awareness of professional, ethical, and legal guidelines for the profession.
- *Inspires confidence:* A program leader inspires confidence in herself and individual staff members. She does this by being supportive and also realistic. She expects the possible, but not the impossible. She gives and shares credit publicly so that others know of the successes of individual staff members.
- *Shares:* The program leader shares the ownership of the operation and develops a feeling of us rather than me and you. Active ownership does not mean that the staff runs the operation. It means that the staff shares in the running of it. Sharing the ownership of the operation creates a feeling of belonging, of being on the team. Real leadership sees that no one feels left out. There are no in-groups and out-groups.
- *Motivates:* All studies of leadership indicate that a common ingredient of leaders in nearly every setting is an ability to motivate others to achieve their potential and, perhaps at times, even exceed it. Although each leader has a different and

unique style, the evidence is present when one observes hardworking, achieving staff members.

- *Creates a positive atmosphere:* A leader understands what makes life at the office livable or makes people happy in their work, and creates professional atmospheres conducive to accomplishment. This includes effective program organization, management, and administration.
- *Is visible:* One cannot lead in absentia. Successful program leaders at all levels are those who are frequently and clearly visible to and available for interaction with their supporting staff.
- *Is forward-looking:* Leadership demands planning for the future. Program leaders are insightful and future-oriented in their planning.
- *Is a decision maker:* Effective leadership not only accepts the decision-making responsibility and will make the hard decisions but will also make the appropriate decisions.

These characteristics can provide a checklist to identify potential counseling program leaders. Program leaders are not likely to be chosen when the top management position is viewed as a consolation prize, a stepping stone for someone tagged to proceed up the organization, a political position to shore up support for top management, or proof that the Peter Principle (Peter & Hull, 1959) really operates. (This principle suggests that one is eventually promoted to his or her level of incompetence.)

SUMMARY

This chapter has introduced the reader to perhaps the most significant activities in determining the individual counselor's success and the success of the program of which he or she is a part. These activities are (a) developing an accountable and efficient program, (b) managing this program in a way that optimizes both human and program resources, and (c) the consistent improvement of programs through ongoing research activities. The chapter concluded with a brief but important discussion of the significance of leadership in both individual and program achievement.

DISCUSSION QUESTIONS

1. Do you find such activities as writing letters, managing your finances, and handling personal management items—such as insurance, food planning, and study planning—challenging, boring, or something you put off?
2. What is meant by the term *accountability?* Why has it become so popular in education in recent years?
3. What differences do you see between the manager of a business (e.g., auto dealer, grocer, insurance agent) and the manager of a counseling program?
4. How can counselors become more accountable?
5. Identify some well-known leaders (past or present) whom you have admired. What have you admired about them?
6. What are the differences between accountability and evaluation?
7. What kind of a program leader would you like to work for?
8. Have you ever had an idea that you would have liked to research? If so, what did you do about it?
9. What is the relationship between needs assessment and program relevancy?
10. What are some of the relationships between evaluation and research?
11. Comment on the suggestions given when budgeting is of concern in program management.
12. What objective evidence could you provide a potential employer as to your excellence in counseling?

CLASS ACTIVITIES

1. Examine the leadership characteristics offered as being significant to the success of counseling and compare those to your personal characteristics. How do you size up?
2. In small groups, discuss the pros and cons of your experiences of being evaluated as a student over the years of your schooling.
3. Compare the leadership qualities desired in counselors to leadership qualities typically identified with other fields of endeavor (e.g., the military, business and industry, and politics). Discuss in small groups and compare answers.
4. Students are currently evaluated (graded) on certain performance criteria (i.e., tests, papers, projects). How might this change if students were asked to become accountable? Discuss in small groups.
5. Read a recent research report (periodical article) in the field of counseling and present this research to the class. Discuss its implications for practice.
6. In dyads, share your professional and personal ethical standards in the counseling practice you intend to make your career.

SELECTED READINGS

Barker, C., Pistrang, N., & Elliot, R. (1994). *Research methods in clinical and counselling psychology*. Chichester, England: Wiley.

Barkham, M., & Barker, C. (1996). Evaluating counseling psychology practice. In R. Woolfe & W. Dryden (Eds.), *Handbook of counselling psychology* (pp. 87–110). London: Sage.

Cunningham, G. (1994). *Effective employee assistance programs: A guide for EAP counselors and managers*. Thousand Oaks, CA: Sage.

Fairchild, T. N. (1986). Time analysis: Accountability tool for counselors. *The School Counselor, 34*(1), 36–43.

Fish, L. (1988). Why multivariate methods are unusually vital. *Measurement and Evaluation in Counseling and Development, 21*, 130–137.

Gelso, C. J. (1996). Applying theories in research: The interplay of theory and research in science. In F. T. L. Leong & J. T. Austin (Eds.), *The psychology research handbook: A guide for graduate students and research assistants* (pp. 359–368). Thousand Oaks, CA: Sage.

Hadley, R. G., & Mitchell, L. K. (1995). *Counseling research and program evaluation*. Pacific Grove, CA: Brooks/Cole.

Hannaford, M. J. (1987). Balancing the counseling program to meet school needs. *National Association of Secondary School Principals Bulletin, 71*(499), 3–9.

Hughey, K. E. (2001). Comprehensive guidance and counseling programs: Theory, policy, practice, and research [Special issue]. *Professional School Counseling, 4*(4).

Kotter, J. P. (1988). *The Leadership Factor*. New York: The Free Press.

MacDevitt, M., & MacDevitt, J. (1987). Low cost needs assessment for a rural mental health center. *Journal of Counseling and Development, 65*(9), 505–507.

Newman, J., & Scott, T. (1988). The construct problem in measuring counseling performance. *Counselor Education and Supervision, 28*, 71–79.

Ponterotto, J. (1988). Racial/ethnic minority research in the *Journal of Counseling Psychology*: A content analysis and methodological critique. *Journal of Counseling and Development, 35*(4), 410–418.

Sapp, M. (1997). *Counseling and psychotherapy: Theories, associated research, and issues*. Landham, MD: University Press.

Wampold, B. E. (1996). Designing a research study. In F. T. L. Leong & J. T. Austin (Eds.), *The psychology research handbook: A guide for graduate students and research assistants* (pp. 59–72). Thousand Oaks, CA: Sage.

Wampold, B. E. (1997). Methodological problems in identifying efficacious psychotherapies. *Psychotherapy Research, 7*(1), 21–43.

Wilson, N. S., & Remley, T. P., Jr. (1987). Leadership in guidance: A survey of school counseling supervisors. *Counselor Education and Supervision, 26*(3), 213–230.

RESEARCH OF INTEREST

Aspenson, D. O., Gersh, T. L., Perot, A. R., & Galassi, J. P. (1993). Graduate psychology students' perceptions of the scientist-practitioner model of training. *Counseling Psychology Quarterly, 6*(3), 201–215.

Abstract   Ten clinical, nine counseling, and five school psychology graduate students participated in a qualitative and quantitative study to assess perceptions of the scientist-practitioner model for training professional psychologists. Subjects participated in semistructured interviews and were administered the Vocational Preference Inventory and a scientist-practitioner inventory. Data were analyzed using a combination of grounded theory and additional qualitative data analytic approaches. Reported experiences ranged from subjects with a zeal for the model to those who considered it impractical, unnecessary, and irrelevant to their career goals. Most interpreted the model to mean that psychologists are trained as producers/consumers of research and as practicing clinicians.

Carter, M. F., Crosby, C., Geertshuis, S., & Startup, M. (1996). Developing reliability in client-centered mental health needs assessment. *Journal of Mental Health UK*, *5*(3), 233–243.

Abstract   This article provides a method for conceptualizing and assessing the expressed needs of people with a long-term mental illness. Based on a study involving 57 patients with long-term mental illness, client-key informant agreement, and test-retest reliability are reported for the Bangor Assessment of Need Profile. The results suggest poor client-key worker agreement and fair to very good test-retest reliability. The paper discusses the meaning and objective of indices of agreement in relation to the presence or absence of need. It concludes that a clearer understanding of what the mental health service user has to say concerning her or his own needs is required in relation to individual client mental state and quality of life outcome measures.

Delaney, J. T., & Huselid, M. A. (1996). The impact of human resource management practices on perceptions of organizational performance. *Academy of Management Journal*, *39*(4), 949–969.

Abstract   This study examined 727 for-profit and nonprofit firms from the National Organizations Survey to determine whether human resource management practices affect firms' perceptual measures of organizational performance. Results show positive associations between human resource management (HRM) practices, such as training and staffing selectivity, and perceptual firm performance measures. Results also suggest methodological issues for consideration in examinations of the relationship between HRM systems and firm performance.

Hillenbrand, E., & Claiborn, C. D. (1990). Examining reasoning skill differences between expert and novice counselors. *Journal of Counseling and Development*, *68*, 684–691.

Abstract   The cognitive reasoning of expert and novice counselors involved in a diagnostic activity is examined. Cases experienced variation according to the extent to which problem-relevant information was clear and apparent. The

conclusion is that the structure of the problem being diagnosed is likely to be a significant variable influencing reasoning.

Hinkle, J. S. (1992). Computer-assisted career guidance and single-subject research: A scientist-practitioner approach to accountability. *Journal of Counseling and Development*, *70*, 391–395.

Abstract   An overview of computer-assisted career guidance is presented. The author describes how use of intensive research designs can promote further accountability among computer-assisted career counselors. Applicable single-subject research, alternating treatment designs, and replication information is described.

Huselid, M. A., Jackson, S. E., & Schuler, R. S. (1997). Technical and strategic human resource management effectiveness as determinants of firm performance. *Academy of Management Journal*, *40*(1), 171–188.

Abstract   This study evaluated the impact of human resource (HR) managers' capabilities on HR management effectiveness and the latter's impact on corporate financial performance. For 293 U.S. firms, effectiveness was associated with capabilities and attributes of HR staff. Also found were relationships between HR management effectiveness and productivity, cash flow, and market value.

McLennan, J. (1996). Improving our understanding of therapeutic failure: A review. *Counseling Psychology Quarterly*, *9*(4), 379–391.

Abstract   This article reviews the literature concerning therapeutic failure and offers a general conceptual account of therapeutic failure in individual counseling and psychotherapy. The literature suggests that there are large individual differences in therapists' overall effectiveness. A conceptual model of therapeutic failure is proposed, organized around the assumption that failure results from a therapist's inability to meet the needs of a particular client. Suggestions aimed at reducing the likelihood of therapeutic failure are offered, and implications for training and practice are presented.

Plake, B. S., Conoley, J. C., Kramer, J. J., & Murphy, L. U. (1991). The Buros Institute of Mental Measurements: Commitment to the tradition of excellence. *Journal of Counseling and Development*, *69*, 449–455.

Abstract   This article reviews the history of the Buros Institute of Mental Measurement by highlighting origins of the

Mental Measurements Yearbook. Bibliographic reference series, Tests in Print, and specialized monographed series are described through a historic perspective. Plans for the 1990s are discussed.

Sedlacek, W. E., & Adams-Gaston, J. (1992). Predicting the academic success of student-athletes using SAT and noncognitive variables. *Journal of Counseling and Development, 70,* 724–727.

Abstract This study compares the reliability of the Noncognitive Questionnaire (NCQ) and the Scholastic Aptitude Test (SAT) in predicting academic success for student-athletes at the collegiate level. It suggests that noncognitive variables are better predictors of grades and academic success for athletes than are SAT scores. It concludes that athletes need to be considered nontraditional student-athletes rather than student-athletes.

Segal, N. L. (1990). The importance of twin studies for individual differences research. *Journal of Counseling and Development, 68,* 612–622.

Abstract Ten research methodology designs related to twin research are described. Findings focus on personality and temperament issues, learning disabilities, attitudes, behavior disorders, and social behavior. Implications for mental health practitioners and counselors are discussed.

Seligman, L., & Kelly, S. C. (1990). Writing and publishing books in counseling: A survey of authors. *Journal of Counseling and Development, 68,* 42–45.

Abstract This article provides data from 74 authors of books published in the field of counseling. It reviews the process of writing and publishing books and presents information regarding time tables, choosing publishers, and obtaining and negotiating contracts. Authors' suggestions for prospective authors are provided.

Spreitzer, G. M., & Quinn, R. E. (1996). Empowering middle managers to be transformational leaders. *Journal of Applied Behavioral Science, 32*(3), 237–261.

Abstract This article describes a field study of a large-scale management development program in a manufacturing corporation, designed to stimulate middle managerial change. Three thousand middle managers participated in the program, entailing a one-week core session and a six-month follow-up. Subjects with low levels of self-esteem, job affect, and social support tended to limit their efforts to changing themselves and thus had little impact on the organization. Subjects with high levels of self-esteem, job affect, and social support were more likely to make transformational changes. Implications for change mastery and resistance to change are discussed.

Stavros, D., & Moore, J. E. (1985, March 31–April 4). *Two perspectives on school climate: Do staff and students see a school the same way?* Paper presented at the Annual Meeting of the American Educational Research Association, Chicago, IL.

Abstract Two studies of school climate were conducted at Detroit's Boulevard High School in 1984, three years after the institution of a school improvement program. One study measured students' perceptions, the other assessed staff perceptions. Based on the findings of this research, it became clear that in order to get a good picture of the school climate, data from both students and staff were needed. Staff and students had convergent opinions in many areas. The school's academic program was viewed positively by both groups. Students were positive about guidance and counseling, the curriculum, and the instruction. The staff were positive about related areas: frequent monitoring of student progress and opportunity to learn and time-on-task. They viewed the department head, especially in the role of instructional leader, in a positive light. The staff did not feel safe in the school (and students did not participate in activities that would cause them to remain at school after hours). Both students and staff were generally satisfied with the school but had negative perceptions concerning Boulevard's administration. The staff viewed the principal as accessible but as a poor instructional leader. Students felt that the administration was not accessible, and they were not involved in the decision-making process. And finally, although staff tended to have low expectations of student performance, students felt they were learning almost all they could and learning a lot in most or all classes.

Whiston, S. C. (1996). Accountability through action research: Research methods for practitioners. *Journal of Counseling and Development, 74*(6), 616–623.

Abstract This article summarizes how outcome research methodologies can be incorporated into counseling practice in many settings. Findings reveal that performing an outcome study can assist counselors in evaluating their own effectiveness. In addition, more field-based studies can contribute to the empirical knowledge base. An overview of the steps involved in an outcome or evaluative study is discussed, and a summary of the instruments and techniques for research in mental health counseling, career counseling, and school counseling is provided.

White, A. S., & Hernandez, N. R. (1991). Trends in article citations in three counseling journals, 1952-1988. *Journal of Counseling and Development, 69,* 419–422.

Abstract These authors examine article citations in the *Personnel and Guidance Journal, Journal of Counseling and Development, Journal of Counseling Psychology,* and *Counselor Education and Supervision Journal.* Results demonstrate that citations gradually became more numerous while also coming from increasingly distinct sources. The authors conclude that the focus of each journal fills a special function while also contributing to the field of research as a whole.

Counseling and Technology

As we initiate this discussion of the new technology and its impact on counselors and the counseling profession, we might pause for a moment to recall some significant technological events of the recent century that changed forever the way we live. Certainly the availability of electricity to the overwhelming majority of our population; the tremendous improvements in transportation, such as the automobile, the train, and the jet plane that made America a mobile society; the advent of both the radio and television, which brought live entertainment into the homes of America; and the significant advances in personal communication, paced by the telephone; and more recently, and the jumping off place for this chapter, the rapid development of the computer and related technology—all are indicators of the technological marvels that impacted the lives of our grandparents, our parents, and last, ourselves.

THE NEW TECHNOLOGY AND ITS IMPACT

Today, the union of the computer with communications technology is resulting in major social transformations that bid to reshape our society and our economy. By most projections, networks will determine the electronic products we use in the coming generations. Erbium-doped optical fibers are revolutionizing the way signals are regenerated and then transmitted. New video screens cannot only be hung on a wall but will soon be popularly worn on the wrist. All in all, computer networks will greatly affect the structure of all organizations and how they conduct their work, how the workers carry out their tasks, and how management functions. We are also recognizing the advantages of worldwide access to a broad range of useful information and seeing many clients react positively to the new technology. Further, the new technology is obviously speeding up as well as increasing the accuracy of such activities as individual assessment, career searches, scholarship and college entrance information, and job searches. We can view cyberspace as the new frontier for our century, an electronic frontier where the law is in doubt.

As we reflect on the amazing technological advances of the recent century and their impacts on our daily living, we can look forward with anticipation and, we suppose, a certain amount of trepidation to the technological advances that will impact us all in this new millennium. No doubt, we are only on the threshold of discovering the full possibilities of computers, the Internet and Web sites, teleconferencing, distance learning, simulation games, and electronic marketing. At the same time, we are also becoming increasingly aware of the depersonalization that much of this technology has brought. We have all made telephone inquiries to be shunted aside to a series of prerecorded menus, and personal phone calls when we were asked by a recorded message to leave a recorded message. Many of us have learned to make purchases online for which, after a certain number of keystrokes we will be sent a product billed to our credit card and never speak to a human being during the transaction. Many will argue, and rightfully so, that these advances have speeded up the process of communication, but we would note that these are not personal voice-to-voice or face-to-face communications and this is our concern as counselors, who believe in the benefits of interpersonal relationships. In fact, some in our profession view this trend toward impersonalization as a threat to the profession and its activities. In support, they cite instances of Web site and computerized counseling programs in which the individual seeking assistance never leaves home and, in fact, may never have a personal discussion with a counselor. Other potential pitfalls that the new technology may present to us and our clients include (a) expense, (b) the effect on client motivation, and (c) the potential for client misinterpretation if the counselor's role is diminished.

However, despite the doubts and disadvantages, online counseling is becoming more prevalent. *USA Today* published an article in its May 22, 2001, issue entitled "Online Therapy Clicks," written by Marilyn Elias. The author of the article noted that online counseling is the hottest and certainly the most controversial new trend in therapy, according to many experts. Five years ago, six therapists were online. Now, there are more than 500, says consumer advocate Martha Ainsworth. NetCounseling is also done in "chats," which permit clients and their therapists to message back and forth for the usual hour of therapy, Obviously, a concern of the counseling profession is the possibility for intrusion by untrained individuals whose only qualification is that they own a computer. Concern must also be evidenced for individuals with severe mental disorders who may opt for computerized treatment rather than face-to-face interaction with a counselor.

At this point, we would recognize that the Information Highway provides counselors with a potent marketing tool. Counselors will be able to display not only their qualifications but also their specialized expertise and other relevant criteria for the perusal of potential clients. Counselors utilizing this media should, of course, indicate whether they counsel clients using the new media technology or whether their practice is limited to the traditional face-to-face interaction in a counseling facility.

Thus, in the counseling profession, we must be prepared not to ignore the new technology but to take advantage of it and use it to advance our profession and to better serve our clients. We would conclude this section by simply noting that while there are, at this point, some undesirables in our new technological advancements, the advantages and promises far outweigh these and we must look to the future and not live in the past.

THE NEW TECHNOLOGY AND THE COUNSELORS' BASIC ACTIVITIES

The new technology has brought with it a whole new vocabulary and new definitions for old terms. For example, "Web" is no longer exclusively associated with a spider's activity, and distance education does not refer to the mileage one travels to attend one's classes. Popular definitions associated with the new technology would include the following:

Internet: The interconnection of existing commercial and noncommercial computer networks to transfer information electronically between two or more computer users. Networks connect computers that allow individuals to share resources and exchange information easily. The Internet represents a network of networks. It permits individuals at sites literally all over the world to communicate with each other simultaneously. E-mail (electronic mail) is the most common way to exchange personal, written messages between individuals or even groups of individuals. Listservers are discussion groups on the Internet that carry on ongoing conversations via e-mail by groups of individuals sharing a common interest.

Web site: The total collection of www information resources, including a home page and links for an organization or individual.

World Wide Web (www): An interconnected system of information on the Internet that allows text, graphics, video, and audio as mediums for access and transmission.

Distance education: The delivery of self-assessment, information, and instructions to remote locations, with or without practitioner assistance, for the purpose of assisting individuals in making informed decisions. In distance learning, instructors and at least a significant number of learners are separated by geographic distance. Audio-video communications and other electronic resources are used to bridge the gap. Distance learning activities seek to increase client access to information and even people.

CD-ROMs: Compact discs for the storage and later utilization of data. They can store text, audio, video, animation, and graphics information. DVDs are similar to CD-ROMs, but have much greater storage capacity.

The Information Highway: The Information Highway represents an integration of computers, cable television, telephones, and the Internet to provide an interactive communications and information source.

Listservers: Listservers provide for the worldwide distribution of electronic journals and discussions through e-mail software.

"Search Engines: A function built into certain Web sites that allows the user to search the world wide web by keywords" (Sampson, Kolodinsky, & Greeno, 1997, p. 204).

E-Mail: "Electronic mail is a process by which text messages are transmitted between two or more individuals via the Internet" (Sampson, Kolodinsky, & Greeno, 1997, p. 204).

Electronic mail is also becoming a resource for individuals with personal concerns seeking assistance from mental health professionals. For example, an individual might send an e-mail about a personal relationship problem with his or her supervisor. The counselor might respond requesting more detailed information regarding the nature of the problem, and the individual client would provide the requested information, again via e-mail. The counselor might then reply with information that could include the scheduling of an interview in the counselor's office.

Potential clients may also be oriented to the counseling process, including their responsibilities, through the Internet, and they may possibly provide intake data online prior to an initial face-to-face session with the counselor. At this point, we would caution users that the security of electronic mail and the Internet may limit its use and effectiveness in the delivery of counseling services.

In viewing this new technology and its potential for enhancing counseling services, we would begin with the client's initial contact with the counselor. Most frequently, especially in agency settings and private practice, this initial contact is characterized by an intake interview in which the client's characteristics and the characteristics of his or her concerns are identified. Obviously, the ease of not only recording but retrieving these data by computer facilitates this initial step in the counseling process. The ready availability of these data also enhances the analysis of the client's concern.

Following the client's initial interview, some sort of assessment process may be anticipated. This process frequently includes computer-assisted testing, accessing information appropriate to the client's needs and concerns, comparative data where appropriate, and, in some instances, even the evaluation of proposed interventions are other examples of computer assistance. In this regard, we would note that the wide range of client assessments available today include computer-assisted testing and computer-assisted scoring of traditional tests as well as new and emerging instruments covering a wide range of topics.

For the counselor, the computer and related technology and their capacity for providing more information, more accurately and quickly, can free up valuable time to work with clients. For clients, technology not only links them rapidly to many sources of information but also helps them to visualize problems and solutions.

Perhaps nowhere in the counseling profession has the new computer technology been more noticeable or effective than in the area of career counseling. We have previously noted major advances in computer-assisted career guidance and information systems in chapter 8. Beyond that, a variety of Web sites now offer instant access to employment opportunities, educational and occupational information, college scholarships, and other types of career information. Many Web sites are available to assist counselors and their clients. These may be categorized under such major service areas as interests, abilities, careers, educational opportunities (including financial information), and job openings. Counselors may be assisted in identifying Web sites to search by such publications as *The Insider's Guide to Mental Health Resources Online* by John M. Grohol (2000/2001). Also useful may be the American Counseling Association Web site: *www.counseling.org*. Other Web sites useful to counselors are Find Your Careers—*www4.usnews.com/usnews/edu/beyond/bccguide.htm*; Education and Training Information: United States Universities and Community Colleges—*www.utexas.edu/world/univ/*; Career and Vocational Education, Yahoo—*www.yahoo.com/education/career and vocational/*.

Many states have created technological centers where counselors and other professional helpers, as well as knowledgeable individuals may secure desired information using such technological means as the Internet, e-mail, Web sites and toll-free telephones. An excellent example is ICPAC (Indiana Career and Postsecondary Advancement Center), which serves the State of Indiana and the world, created in 1986 by the Indiana General Assembly. Its mission is informing, encouraging, and supporting the education and career development of the people of Indiana. For detailed information concerning ICPAC, one may visit the Web site at *icpac.indiana.edu*. ICPAC also operates a toll-free telephone hot line, staffed by informational specialists who can answer questions and provide resources on education and career options.

Counselors should be aware that their clients can have access to academic and non-academic course offerings through the Internet. In the former instance, they may even earn academic credit. This opportunity will undoubtedly become increasingly popular and important in future generations as we witness people's frequent transition from one career to another across their working life span.

Counselors will also find technology useful for offering flexibility in scheduling testing for clients, for facilitating student enrollment in schools, for providing practice tests with feedback for clients seeking to qualify for admission to educational institutions, or for seeking occupations that require a license based on an examination. Technology allows counselors to acquire and manipulate data to identify factors that contribute to certain undesirable client behaviors and decisions. Counselors then have a basis for developing effective preventive programs designed to eliminate or modify the causative factors.

In addition to the broad-based searches, Web sites may be accessed more narrowly for specific assessment purposes. For example, interest inventories may be reached through the *Career Interests Game*, which may be found at *www.missouri.edu/~cppcwww/holland. shtml*. Abilities/skill inventories may be identified through the *University of Waterloo Career Services Career Development Manual* (Web site address: *www.adm.uwaterloo. ca/infocecs/crc/manual-home.html* and career descriptions may be accessed through the *Occupational Outlook Handbook*: *http://stats.bls.gov/ocohome.htm*.

The Beach Boys' popular rendition of "Surfing, U.S.A." several decades ago, with a few changes, could be an appropriate Web site theme song today. The vast amount of data available today on the Internet, even though mind-boggling, is certainly worth singing about! It is therefore important that counselors recognize the sources that can help them in "surfing the Net." One extremely helpful source for career Web assistance is NOICC (National Occupational Information Coordinating Committee): *www.noicc.gov*. Also, nearly every state has a career exploration Web site. An exemplary model is the Career Explorer, available through the State of North Carolina. This is a very extensive program designed to help school counselors. The content of the Career Explorer is written to appeal to adolescents. The program also offers a variety of interactive services with which users can access information.

COUNSELING AND THE INTERNET

We are aware of the valuable assistance provided to those in need in recent decades by crisis lines, videotapes, and self-help audiotapes. We also know that in many instances computer therapy may be the only help available for individuals who cannot readily access human help because of their location, their financial situation, or physical disabilities. However, because these and other technological aids are helpful on occasion to individuals does not lessen the importance of the counselor in personally assisting clients in addressing their needs. We must remember that the most effective counseling is, as it always has been, an interactive, face-to-face process between the client and his or her counselor.

We also acknowledge that there are many appropriate circumstances in which counselors can refer and assist their clients in the use of the Internet. This may be especially appropriate for gathering information and data that may facilitate decision making. However, remember that not all clients will be skillful in computer use or have access to the Internet. Also, caution has to be observed in evaluating the worth of information found on the Internet. In some instances, the Internet sites may encourage decision making by the client. Here the counselor must suggest that the most beneficial results are more likely to occur when both the client and counselor are involved in the client's decision making. With this in mind, we would suggest that the sequence of events for effective use of the Internet in individual counseling might proceed as follows:

1. Identification and clarification of the client's problem or concern.
2. Identification of potential Internet sites for securing information that may be appropriate for the client's needs.
3. Evaluation of the information secured through the Internet searches.
4. Application of the information to the client's concern.
5. Evaluation of the outcomes in terms of client satisfaction and resolution of the client's needs or concerns. (Bowlsbey, Dikel & Sampson, Jr., 1998)

The practice of technologically assisted distance counseling is summed up in a taxonomy of face-to-face and technologically assisted distance counseling presented in Table 12-1. A more detailed description of this taxonomy may be noted in Appendix N."

Counselors should also be aware of the World Wide Web. According to Altekruse and Brew (2000),

The web offers easy access to images and sound (even motion pictures!) as well as text, and powerful links within documents to specific places in other documents. For example, many national organizations such as the American Counseling Association (*www.counseling.org*),

Table 12-1   A taxonomy of face-to-face and technology-assisted distance counseling.

Counseling
- Face-To-Face Counseling
  - Individual Counseling
  - Couple Counseling
  - Group Counseling
- Technology-Assisted Distance Counseling
  - Telecounseling
    - Telephone-Based Individual Counseling
    - Telephone-Based Couple Counseling
    - Telephone-Based Group Counseling
  - Internet Counseling
    - E-Mail-Based Individual Counseling
    - Chat-Based Individual Counseling
    - Chat-Based Couple Counseling
    - Chat-Based Group Counseling
    - Video-Based Individual Counseling
    - Video-Based Couple Counseling
    - Video-Based Group Counseling

Source: The Practice of Internet Counseling. (2001). National Board for Certified Counselors, Inc.; and Center for Credentialing and Education, Inc.; Greensboro, NC 27403-3660. p. 2. Reprinted with the permission of the National Board for Certified Counselors and Affiliates, 3 Terrace Way, Suite D, Greensboro, NC 27403-3660.

the National Association of Social Workers (*www.naswdc.org*), and the American Psychological Association (*www.apa.org*) have web sites with information on purchasing books, accessing electronic journals, membership, and ethical guidelines. (p. 131)

However, counselors need to be aware that the unregulated status of the Internet means that there are no restrictions on who may access assessment instruments, since many are available to whoever has the means of accessing them. Further, in the absence of any enforced standards, it would not be surprising to find instruments that have neither established validity nor reliability.

Many counseling programs will find it desirable to design a management information system for their computers to collect and analyze on an ongoing basis the degree to which services are delivered as well as outcome information. Such a system can also provide timely access to information required to meet the needs of program management and evaluation.

Clearly, the computer is the tool of choice for processing data for research projects, even though the data itself must be usually entered by hand. In conducting research, computers can be programmed to select random samples automatically. Randomization can be conducted manually, but this seems unnecessarily laborious, especially when selecting large samples. Also in research, content analysis is a way to process data for the systematic, objective, and quantitative measuring of different variables. This process may include classifying, counting, rating, or some combination of these processes. Care must be taken to define exactly the boundaries of the various categories of the variables to be rated, but computers can perform much of the routine work.

DISTANCE EDUCATION

Distance education is another technological development that has become popular in recent years as a means of transmitting education beyond the classroom. In its simplest form, Dr. Boring can teach his class in Snoozology 101 from his home-based classroom on the campus of Insomniac Tech and through an interactive hook-up, also teach this same class simultaneously at other off-campus locations.

As distance learning can occur at many places where guidance and counseling services are not available, distance learning will become increasingly important in assisting individuals to make informed decisions. Note that distance guidance and learning obviously expands the opportunities for counselors and counseling programs to extend their outreach activities into rural areas, inner-city poverty pockets, and geographically isolated environments. The expansion of these services for career assistance alone would appear to be almost a necessity in an era of frequent career change for the majority of the workforce.

Two landmark documents on distance education were issued in April 1999. One, *What's the Difference*, was prepared for the American Federation of Teachers and the National Education Association by Phipps and Merisotis, staff members at the Institute for Higher Education Policy. The Phipps and Merisotis document focused on a review of contemporary research on the effectiveness of distance education in higher education. The second document, *The Virtual University and Educational Opportunity*, authored by Gladieux and Swail (1999) of the College Board, discussed issues of equity and access. Both documents have implications for counselor educators who are wrestling with the changing environment of electronically enhanced instruction. (Peterson, 2000, p. 144)

THE COUNSELOR'S PROFESSIONAL DEVELOPMENT

Technology can also be invaluable to counselors' ongoing professional development by providing access to libraries without walls or virtual libraries. Virtual libraries through technology bring together the resources of many libraries. Of particular interest to counselors is the ERIC/CASS (Educational Resources Information Center/Counseling and Student Services Clearinghouse) network developed in 1997. ERIC/CASS designed a series of virtual libraries that were especially responsive to informational needs of counselors. Walz and Reedy (2000) compiled seven distinguishing characteristics of this virtual library:

- Resources are available in full text and can be easily downloaded.
- The libraries target critical, high-priority counseling topics.
- The libraries require no special skills to search and use.
- Libraries are regularly updated.
- Each library includes a frequently asked questions (FAQ) section.
- Virtual libraries for counselors are introduced on the basis of a clear demonstrated need.
- New acquisitions for the virtual libraries are aggressively sought from multiple sources. (pp. 162–164)

At this point, you may be asking, "What do I need to know to function competently as a professional in the technological age?" The ACES (Association for Counselor Education and Supervision) Technology Interest Network recommended that at the completion of a counselor education program students should have acquired the following technical competencies.

- Be able to use productivity software to develop Web pages, group presentations, letters, and reports;
- Be able to use such audiovisual equipment as video recorders, audio recorders, projection equipment, videoconferencing equipment, and playback units;
- Be able to use computerized statistical packages;
- Be able to use computerized testing, diagnostic, and career decision-making programs with clients;
- Be able to use e-mail;
- Be able to help clients search for various types of counseling-related information via the Internet, including information about careers, employment opportunities, educational and training opportunities, financial assistance/scholarships, treatment procedures, and social and personal information;
- Be able to subscribe, participate in, and sign off counseling-related listservers;
- Be knowledgeable of the legal and ethical codes that relate to counseling services via the Internet;
- Be knowledgeable of the strengths and weaknesses of counseling services provided via the Internet;
- Be able to use the Internet for finding and using continuing education opportunities in counseling;
- Be able to evaluate the quality of Internet information. (Bloom & Walz, 2000, pp. 429–430)

LEGAL AND ETHICAL ISSUES

Legal and ethical issues related to technology tend to center on online ethics, illegal access, safeguarding client confidences, and copyright infringements (e.g., with standardized testing). The question must be asked as to whether services delivered to a client via technology are at least as good as the in-person services one would receive otherwise.

SUMMARY

This chapter, on counseling and technology, covers a topic that was rarely if ever mentioned in counseling textbooks published prior to 1990. Yet today, as we enter the new century, we recognize the transformation of our society, its education, economy, and governmental structures by the fusion of the technologies of computing and communications. Initially this chapter recognizes the impact of the new technology not only on our society but also on the profession of counseling. We examined this technology in the context of the work counselors do and how they do it. We briefly explored new directions such as counseling on the Internet and distance education and concluded the chapter by examining technological competencies that will be needed by counselors in the new technological age.

DISCUSSION QUESTIONS

1. What use do you personally make of the computer? The Internet? The World Wide Web? Distance education?
2. How have computerized information or information systems assisted you personally?
3. In view of the current, as well as predicted, technological advancements in the near future, how do you envision your functioning in the "counselor's office of tomorrow"?
4. Hackers have been successful in breaking into information sources from the Pentagon to medical and other institutions. In view of hackers' skill and zeal for obtaining private information, how do you propose to protect your clients from such infringements of their privacy?
5. In view of the suggested technological competencies suggested by ACES (the Association for

Counselor Education and Supervision), discuss your own level of preparation to function as a technologically competent counselor.
6. Should technological competency be a requirement for counselor licensure or certification?

CLASS ACTIVITIES

1. Many articles are being published predicting startling scientific and technological breakthroughs in the generations immediately ahead. Identify and report on one or more of these predictions.
2. Identify and visit a class on your campus involved in distance learning either as a receiver or sender. Report your experience to the class.
3. Organize an interactive hook-up (audio, visual, or both) with some comparable course being offered on another campus. Identify topics to be discussed. Report outcomes.
4. Organize into groups and make scheduled visits to local industries, government offices, hospitals, local community agencies, and schools to identify and observe their use of technology in the everyday operations of their organization. Share your findings with the other groups in the class.

SELECTED READINGS

Harris-Bowlsbey, J., & Sampson, J. P., Jr. (2001). Computer-based career planning systems: Dreams and realities. *The Career Development Quarterly, 49*(3), 250–260.

Key technologies for the 21st century. (1995). *Scientific American, 273*(3).

Rivlin, G. (2001). They are changing our world. *Parade Magazine*, November 25, 2001, 4–5.

Roblyer, M. D., & Edwards, J. (2000). *Integrating educational technology into teaching* (2nd ed.). Upper Saddle River, NJ: Merrill/Prentice Hall.

Sabella, R. (2001). E-ducate yourself. *ASCA School Counselor, 39*(1), 14–15.

Sampson, J. P., Jr. (1999). Integrating Internet-based distance guidance with services provided in career centers. *The Career Development Quarterly, 47*(3), 243–254.

Schack, M. B. (1998). Choosing the right college: New software for counselors and students. *Professional School Counseling, 1*(4), 66.

Wireless wonders. (1999). *U. S. News and World Report.* December 13, 1999. [Special issue.].

RESEARCH OF INTEREST

Harris-Bowlsbey, J., & Sampson, J. P., Jr. Computer-based career planning systems: Dreams and realities. *The Career Development Quarterly, 49*(3), 250–260.

Abstract   The authors look back more than 30 years to those who introduced the use of the computer as an important new tool to assist students in the area of career development. To what extent have dreams been realized and concerns allayed? Rapid advances in technology, not included in the authors' vision, have transformed the world into a different place. How have these advances affected the use of computers in counseling? The article concludes with a list of current concerns, along with recommendations for further action and research.

Knouse, S. B. (2001) Virtual mentors: Mentoring on the Internet. *Journal of Employment Counseling, 38*(4), 162–169.

Abstract   Mentoring is an increasingly important function for career success. Many special groups, however, including minorities and women, have difficulty finding a mentor. One solution is virtual mentoring—selecting and interacting with mentors on the Internet. The author discusses advantages of virtual mentoring over other forms of mentoring, describes examples of Internet mentoring for various special groups and purposes, and suggests future directions for Internet mentoring.

Luzzo, D. A., & MacGregor, M. W. (2001). Practice and research in career counseling and development—2000. *The Career Development Quarterly, 50*(2), 98–139.

Abstract   The authors summarize the career counseling and development literature that appeared during 2000 in refereed journals, book chapters, and full-length books. The review of literature is divided into five major categories: (a) theoretical and conceptual advances, (b) career counseling and development of identified populations, (c) assessment in career counseling and development, (d) career counseling programs and interventions, and (e) resources for the professional development of career counselors and vocational psychologists.

This article also discusses the technological advances that the authors believe will influence the career assessment field. The article reviews discussions by several authors of the role of the Internet as a career intervention strategy.

Sampson, J. P., Jr. (1999). Integrating Internet-based distance guidance with services provided in career centers. *The Career Development Quarterly, 47*(3), 243–254.

Abstract   The Internet has evolved so rapidly that there is little information on integrating Internet-based distance guidance opportunities with resources and services provided by existing career centers. In this article, the author describes career centers and then explores the need for career centers in the information age, the types of Internet Web sites, the functions of an integrated Web site in promoting cost-effectiveness, options for integrating user needs, the role of instructional design in Web site development, cost-effectiveness and staff collaboration, Web master responsibilities, Internet Web site implementation, staff training, and ethical issues. This article is based on a paper presented at a seminar titled, "Guidance in Open Learning Environments in the Finnish Polytechnics" at Espoo-Vantaa Polytechnic, Vantaa, Finland, 1998.

Zhu, S. H., Tedeschi, G. J., Anderson, C. M., & Pierce, J. P. (1996). Telephone counseling for smoking cessation: What's in a call? *Journal of Counseling and Development, 75*(2), 93–102.

Abstract   Telephone counseling for smoking cessation has been gaining popularity as studies have demonstrated its efficacy. What comprises a successful program, however, has not yet been detailed in the literature. In this article, an innovative telephone counseling intervention for smoking cessation is described, with attention to the clinical issues of client assessment, motivation, self-efficacy, planning, coping, relapse-sensitive call scheduling, and self-image. Counselor training and supervision issues, ethical and legal considerations regarding this form of service delivery, and suggestions for future direction also are outlined.

13 Ethical and Legal Guidelines

The final chapter focuses on the responsibilities that you incur as you enter the career world of the professional counselor. It emphasizes the importance of practicing within the ethical guidelines established by your professional associations and the guidelines established by law. In fact, the very labeling of counseling as a helping profession suggests that we have assumed the responsibilities of our profession in providing for our clientele and serving the public. These responsibilities include acceptable standards of performance or competence, an accepted code of personal conduct in relationships with clients and the public, and a commitment to contribute to the public well-being that transcends monetary gain.

A profession also takes responsibility for regulating or policing its membership to ensure that ethical and legal guidelines are adhered to and that legal enactments are sought where desirable to protect the public. A profession's commitment to appropriate ethical and legal standards is critical to the profession's earning, maintaining, and deserving the public's trust. Without this trust, a profession ceases to be a profession. Ethical guidelines, then, are designed to cultivate and enhance the public's trust in the profession. Adhering to such guidelines is, therefore, the responsibility of all members of the profession. Such headlines as "Minister Runs Off with Choir Director's Wife"; "College Professor Robs Liquor Store"; and "Lawyer Blackmails Client" are examples of headlines describing an isolated action by a single member of a profession that tarnishes all members of the profession and the profession itself. We must also keep in mind that the clients we serve may be vulnerable, as they are entrusting to counselors their intimate thoughts and the personal issues affecting their lives.

THE NATURE OF ETHICS

A code of ethics represents the values of a profession translated into standards of conduct for the membership. Codes of ethics provide structure or guidelines for a profession's membership to follow in their professional practice and also for the public to anticipate in their interactions with the profession and its membership.

For counselors at least two basic statements of ethical practice and behavior apply to work in the profession: (a) *Code of Ethics and Standards of Practice* of the American Counseling Association, 1995 (see Appendix F), and (b) *Ethical Principles of Psychologists and Code of Conduct* of the American Psychological Association (1992) (see Appendix G). The members of these associations are expected to follow these codes of ethics and professional standards. Failure to abide by these standards may result in expulsion from the profession.

ETHICAL ISSUES

Competence

The ethical issue of competence begins when the counselor accepts a position as a professional counselor. The counselor must determine, along with the potential employer, whether she or he is qualified by virtue of training and, where appropriate, experience for the position. The counselor-applicant must indicate qualifications for licensure or certification where appropriate and also special interests and/or values that might influence on-the-job functioning. Obviously, from the outset, counselors should not apply for positions in which they are not interested or for which they are not qualified.

On the job, the counselor is professionally responsible to practice within his or her limitations. Although competence is often difficult to determine, training and experience can provide useful guidelines in indicating what we are qualified to do. Consultation with supervisors and/or more experienced professional colleagues can help identify the limits of one's professional competence.

Degrees, licenses, and certificates may convey levels of competence to the public; yet, in actuality, we must recognize variations in competencies among practitioners with the same credentials. We would also again note the responsibility of the professional counselor to continuously update his or her competence through participation in various professional educational opportunities, reading the professional literature, and attending professional meetings.

When counselors determine that a client's needs may be beyond their competencies, they should promptly arrange for an appropriate referral. This responsibility includes helping the client identify a suitable professional.

Confidentiality and Privileged Communication

Trust is an essential cornerstone in the counseling relationship, and central to the development and maintenance of trust is the principle of confidentiality. The obligation of counselors to maintain confidentiality in their relationships with their clients is not absolute, however, and counselors need to be aware of both the ethical and legal guidelines that apply.

In distinguishing between confidentiality and privileged communication, it is important to remember that confidentiality is primarily an *ethical* concept whereas privileged communication is a *legal* concept.

Confidentiality is defined as

an ethical responsibility and professional duty that demands that information learned in private interaction with a client not be revealed to others. Professional ethical standards mandate this behavior except when the counselors commitment to uphold client confidences must be set aside due to special and compelling circumstances or legal mandate. (Arthur & Swanson, 1993, p. 3)

Questions surrounding confidentiality can be very complex and often involve legal as well as ethical considerations. A useful starting place may be to clarify the distinctions among three terms—privacy, confidentiality, and privileged communication. These terms are sometimes used interchangeably by counselors, but the concepts have important differences. Both confidentiality and privileged communication arise from our societal belief that individuals have a right to privacy. *Privacy* is the broadest of the three concepts and refers to the right of persons to decide what information about themselves will be shared with or withheld from others. Confidentiality and privileged communication both apply more specifically to the professional relationship between counselors and clients. *Confidentiality* is primarily an ethical concept that refers to the counselor's obligation to respect the client's privacy, and to our promise to clients that the information they reveal during counseling will be protected from disclosure without their consent. *Privileged communication* is the narrowest of the three terms and is a legal concept. Privileged communication laws protect clients from having confidential communications with their counselors disclosed in a court of law without their permission (Shuman & Weiner, 1987). For a communication to be privileged, a statute must have been enacted that grants privilege to a category of professionals and those whom they serve. (Remley & Herlihy, 1987, p. 80)

Sometimes counselors may be working with life-endangering clients in situations involving child abuse, possible homicide, or suicide threats. State laws require that suspected cases of child abuse be reported. Legally, counselors are also required to breach confidentiality to protect the life of a third party. The ethical codes of both the American Counseling Association and the American Psychological Association allow counselors to breach confidentiality if necessary to protect the life of a suicidal client. Additional discussion concerning the legal aspects of privileged communication will be presented in the section entitled "Legal Concerns of Counselors." Arthur and Swanson (1993) note exemptions cited by Bissell and Royce (1992) to the ethical principle of confidentiality:

1. The client is a danger to self or others. The law places physical safety above considerations of confidentiality or the right of privacy. Protection of the person takes precedence and includes the duty to warn.
2. The client requests the release of information. Privacy belongs to the client and may be waived. The counselor should release information as requested by the client.
3. A court orders the release of information. The responsibility under the law for the counselor to maintain confidentiality is overridden when the court determines that the information is needed to serve the cause of justice.
4. The counselor is receiving systematic clinical supervision. The client gives up the right to confidentiality when it is known that session material will be used during supervision.
5. Clerical assistants process information and papers relating to the client. The client should be informed that office personnel will have access to the records for routine matters such as billing and record keeping.
6. Legal and clinical consultation are needed. Again, the client should be informed of the (ethical) right of the counselor to obtain other professional opinions about progress and the name(s) of those used as a consultant(s).
7. Clients raise the issue of their mental health in a legal proceeding. In a custody suit, for example, parents introduce their mental condition into the suit, whereupon they authorize release of the counselor's records.
8. A third party is present in the room. Clients are (presumably) aware a person other than the counselor is present and therefore waive their right of privacy in permitting the third person to be present.
9. Clients are below the age of 18. Parents or guardians have the legal right to communication between the minor and the counselor.

10. Intra-agency or institutional sharing of information is part of the treatment process. Otherwise confidential material may be shared among professional staff when it is in the interest of the client to do so. However, the client must be aware that this is being done.

11. Sharing of information is required within a penal system. Information obtained from prisoners that may otherwise be considered confidential may be shared within the system in the interest of the operation of the system and disposition of the case.

12. The client's purpose in disclosing information was to seek advice in the furtherance of a crime or fraud. The obligation here changes from one of maintaining confidentiality to one of protecting society from further criminal activity.

13. The counselor has reason to suspect child abuse. All states now legally require the reporting of suspected abuse. (Arther & Swanson, 1993, pp. 20–21)

Remley and Herlihy (2001) presented exceptions to confidentiality and privileged communications organized as seen in Figure 13-1.

Personal Relationships with Clients

In examining the personal relationships between counselors and their clients, professional organizations have sought to define the ethical limits of the professional relationship. A major concern of the mental health professions, in this regard, has been the sexual exploitation of clients by their therapists. Although the codes of ethics of all major professional organizations unequivocally condemn such activities, counselors should be aware that one of the most frequently identified violations of professional ethics involves sexual relationships with clients. Counselors who engage in sexual relations with clients are at risk for lawsuits, loss of license, and possible criminal charges. In many states sexual conduct with a client is prohibited, regardless of the client's consent. When minor clients are involved, helping professionals, including counselors, can be prosecuted for statutory rape.

In addition, relationships with clients that may impair the counselor's professional judgments or the client's responses must be avoided. This means avoiding counseling relationships with relatives, close friends, and employers, among others. Counselors must, at all times, avoid exploiting clients for financial gain, social status, research data, or other motives.

Finally, the counselor must at all times be aware of the human rights of clients. Even the severely mentally ill have legal and ethical rights that the counselor must be guided by in practice. This includes clients' right to participate in decision making regarding their treatment, the use of psychological tests, and any participation in research studies.

THE COUNSELOR AND THE LAW

During recent decades, few aspects of the counselor's role and function in any setting have remained untouched by judicial and legislative activities. For example, an early guideline was presented by the Community Mental Health Centers Act of 1980, which defined the community to be served in terms of geographic and topographic characteristics.

Many other services that counselors and their fellow helping professionals must provide in community agency settings are also specified by law. These include drug abuse treatment as well as treatment for the chronically mentally ill and severely disturbed children

Sharing information with subordinates or fellow professionals is permissible under the following circumstances:

- Clerical or other assistants handle confidential information.
- A counselor consults with colleagues or experts.
- The counselor is working under supervision.
- Other professionals are involved in coordinating client care.

Protecting someone who is in danger may require disclosure of confidential information when the following conditions exist:

- The counselor suspects abuse or neglect of children or other persons presumed to have limited ability to care for themselves.
- A client poses a danger to others.
- A client poses a danger to self (is suicidal).
- A client has a fatal, communicable disease and the client's behavior is putting others at risk.

Confidentiality is compromised when counseling multiple clients, including the following:

- Group counseling
- Counseling couples or families

There are unique confidentiality and privileged communication considerations when working with minor clients:

- Counseling minor clients

Certain exceptions are mandated by law, including the following:

- Disclosure is court ordered.
- Clients file complaints against their counselors.
- Clients claim emotional damage in a lawsuit.
- Civil commitment proceedings are initiated.

Figure 13-1   Exceptions to confidentiality and privileged communication.
Source: Ethical, Legal, and Professional Issues in Counseling by Remley/Herlihy, © 2001. Reprinted by permission of Pearson Education, Inc., Upper Saddle River, NJ.

and adolescents. Further, most states have enacted legislation that provides a legal basis for those who may practice or designate themselves as counselors and social workers.

Increasingly, managers of counseling programs and counselors themselves have become aware of the legal implications of their activities, the legal restrictions, and even legal conflicts with their professional conscience. This increased legal intervention is an outgrowth of a dramatic increase in litigation and attending legislation during the past 25 years.

In performing their professional duties, counselors must not put themselves in jeopardy for either civil or criminal liability. Thus, counselors must exercise due care or face liability in a civil suit for failing to perform their duties as required by law. Civil liability, stated simply, means that one can be sued for acting wrongly toward another, or for failing to act when there was a recognized duty to do so. Judicial relief is usually in the form of money damages awarded to the injured party. (Hopkins & Anderson, 1990, p. 23)

Certainly few counselors ever anticipate that they might become defendants in a criminal action simply by practicing their profession. Fortunately, very few ever do. But counselors should be aware of certain occupational hazards that could lead to criminal liability. The ideal for professional counselors is to maintain a certain distance between themselves and their clients so they may advise the clients in a professional way. Occasionally, however, situations arise that might lead counselors to go much further than the law literally allows in protecting their clients or in providing emotional support and comfort. In such cases, the counselor may unwittingly risk criminal liability.

Criminal liability resulting from the professional practice of counseling might result in a variety of criminal charges such as these:

- accessory to a crime;
- failure to report suspected child abuse;
- contributing to the delinquency of a minor;
- sexual misconduct. (Hopkins & Anderson, 1990, p. 49)

Contributing to the delinquency of a minor is of special concern to school counselors and those whose practice includes children and families. However, counselors in all settings where the potential exists for juvenile clients should be aware of actions that could lead to prosecution for contributing to the delinquency of a minor. All states have enacted legislation designed to protect children from acts or relationships deemed injurious. However, as Hopkins and Anderson (1990) point out,

> Unfortunately, most state legislatures have not defined the specific conduct that constitutes the crime, and many jurisdictions leave it to the jury to determine whether a defendant's conduct was criminal. A broad definition of the offense might include any actions that tend to injure the health, morals, or welfare of juveniles, or that encourage juveniles to participate in such actions. There is no certainty as to what constitutes this immoral conduct from state to state, however. (p. 52)

Counselors in all settings cannot afford to be legally ignorant. They must understand the law and its implications in arenas of counselor concern and function. These include acts or practices that might be viewed as discriminatory, compromising the constitutional and other legal rights of, and prejudicing the opportunities of individuals. In this regard, note some of the legal implications for counselors of Title IX, the Buckley Amendment, and the Education for All Handicapped Children Act.

The Counselor and Title IX

Title IX of the Education Amendments of 1972, which took effect in July, 1975, provides that

> no person . . . shall on the basis of sex, be excluded from participation in, be denied the benefits of, or be subjected to discrimination under any education program receiving federal financial assistance.

Some implications of this act for practicing counselors are as follows. First, adequate counseling services must not only provide for the needs, interests, and abilities of clients but also must consider the changing nature of society and how such changes affect their working with clients. Counselors must help clients in self-understanding and sorting through varying options and what their decisions may imply.

Second, counselors must be aware that differential sex socialization is often subtly perpetuated in the language and impressions of the media (e.g., textbooks, newspapers, magazines, television). Although not justifiable, it is not surprising that such biases appear in career and other counseling materials.

The Counselor and the Buckley Amendment

Few legislative actions have had a greater impact on the practice of counseling and attendant record keeping than the Buckley Amendment. Before the passage in 1974 of the Family Educational Rights and Privacy Act (FERPA) as it is titled (or the Buckley Amendment as it is commonly called), counselors derived most of their directions for their professional functioning from the ethical guidelines provided by their professional associations. In this regard, the *Code of Ethics and Standards of Practice* (1995) of the American Counseling Association has an entire section devoted to confidentiality (Section B) and a subsection regarding records (Section B4). (See Appendix F).

Although ethical standards are not, in themselves, legally binding, there are numerous instances, beginning with the case of *Cherry v. the Board of Regents of the State of New York* in 1942, that suggested courts might use professional ethical codes as guidelines for making judicial decisions. In the case of record keeping and confidentiality, however, the passage of the Buckley Amendment became the single most important guideline for professional conduct with regard to student records and related activities.

The Buckley Amendment

> basically says that parents of minor students (and students who are 18 or older or who are in college) have two rights: (a) to inspect and review their education records and to challenge the contents to ensure the records are not inaccurate or misleading, and (b) to have their written authorization obtained before copies of their education records can be transferred to any third party. (Remley & Herlihy, 2001, p. 120).

Because school counselors as well as counselors in other educational settings are frequently called on to write letters of recommendation for college admissions or employment, it should be noted that the Buckley Amendment implications are clear that

> unless the educator is specifically informed otherwise, he or she should assume that the student may have access to letters of recommendation. The student can be requested to sign a waiver, so that he or she will not have such access. However, unless such a waiver is signed, the student can be defended, both factually and professionally. In general educators are on relatively safe ground when writing letters of recommendation if the following conditions are met:
>
> 1. Letters of recommendation are an expected, normal, and integral part of one's duties and responsibilities.
> 2. Letters are sent only to second parties (not published), who can be expected to have a reasonable interest in and concern for the person in question.
> 3. Letters are factual, free of malice, and reasonably objective.
> 4. Letters are in response to a request. (St. John & Walden, 1976, p. 683)

It should be obvious at this point that counselors regardless of their setting, should confer with the legal counsel retained by their employing organization for guidance regarding confidential communication. Program managers may want, again with the assistance of their legal counsel, to develop detailed guidelines to assist counselors and other staff members in protecting the confidentiality of communications, consistent with state and federal statutes.

School Counselors and Public Law 94-142

Another act of importance to school counselors is the Education for All Handicapped Children Act (PL 94-142) of November 1975. This law guarantees the rights of all children, regardless of the severity of the disability, to a free, appropriate education. The law further establishes a formula for providing financial aid to states and local school districts, based on the number of children with disabilities receiving special education plus related services. It is this latter activity—related services—that provides for counseling by a certified counselor. In noting the implications of this act for counselors, we would suggest that counselors in schools in almost any situation would have a role to play in the implementation of the act, even though this implementation will undoubtedly vary from school district to school district. It would appear obvious that parent counseling, related to Public Law 94-142, should occur in a school setting as would such activities as classroom consulting, extracurricular planning, development of the student's individual education plan, and monitoring student progress.

An important provision of the Education for All Handicapped Children's Act of 1975 was mandating equity for children categorized as exceptional. Exceptional children were those identified with physical, emotional, or intellectual characteristics that placed them outside the normal range causing them to be categorized as having a disability. An important concept resulting from this act was the process known as mainstreaming. This process provides for the education of the handicapped in the same environment as able students. Mainstreaming is implemented through annual individual educational plans (IEPs) that are developed for each individual child. These IEPs include information about the individual child's current level of functioning; annual goals; measurable, short-term objectives; and an inventory of specific educational services required for each individual child. Parents and a team of teachers, administrators, and pupil service professionals, including counselors, prepare the IEPs. The Act was amended in 1986 to include the development of individual family service plans (IFSPs)

The Counselor and the Americans with Disabilities Act

Although noted previously in chapter 8, it is appropriate to discuss the Americans with Disabilities Act, which became law in 1990, further in this chapter. This act prohibits discrimination on the basis of disabilities. Its provisions cover discrimination under titles dealing with (a) employment, (b) accessibility, (c) accommodations in public facilities, (d) telecommunications, and (e) miscellaneous provisions. This act has implications for counselors assisting clients with disabilities. These include the following:

- Counselors at all levels and in all settings must become familiar with the provisions of the act.
- In many settings, counselors should work with local businesses and industries to facilitate the employment of disabled individuals.

- Counselors should help disabled clients understand their rights as specified by the act.
- In counseling the disabled, the focus is on what the client can do, on the client's potential, not his or her limitations. In this regard, counselors must examine and ensure that their own attitudes are not discriminatory.
- The counselor's office and organization must be physically accessible to disabled clients.

LEGAL CONCERNS OF COUNSELORS

Confidentiality

Earlier in this chapter, we defined and discussed the issues of confidentiality and privileged communication for counselors. These continue to be issues confronting the counseling profession. Herlihy, Glosoff and others have, from time to time, surveyed the existence of privileged communication statutes and rules of evidence in the 50 states and the District of Columbia. In the fall of 2000, Glosoff, Herlihy, and Spence reported the results of their study seeking to determine the status of privileged communication for counselors throughout the nation. Included in their analysis were all jurisdictions that have legislated credentials for professional counselors. The results of their study found that statutes or rules of evidence granting privileged communication to the counselor-client relationship existed in 44 states and the District of Columbia. Swenson noted (1993) the trend toward expanding privilege to include a wider variety of professional relationships, while weakening the privilege by creating exceptions.

Glosoff, Herlihy, and Spence's finding (2000) that

> some type of privilege exists in 98% of the jurisdictions that license counselors lends support to counselors' contention that they are bona fide mental health providers, along with psychologists and other mental health professionals who have established that their relationships with clients are "special" and therefore deserving of privilege. (p. 460)

Determining the status of privileged communications between counselors and clients is a complex task. We strongly urge counselors to seek the assistance of an attorney regarding legal obligations.

Fischer and Sorenson (1996) cite Wigmore, the leading authority on the Anglo-American law of evidence, as indicating four requirements.

1. The communications must originate in confidence that they will not be disclosed.
2. The confidentiality must be essential to full and satisfactory maintenance of the relationship between the parties.
3. The relationship must be one which, in the opinion of the community, should be sedulously fostered.
4. The injury to that relation, caused by disclosure, would be greater than the benefit gained to the process of litigation.

These criteria are generally accepted by modern scholars of the law of evidence as the appropriate test for what qualifies as privileged communication.

> Judges have been very reluctant to grant or acknowledge such a privilege and more reluctant still to extend it to new relationships. Even with long-recognized exemptions, such as the lawyer-client relationship, courts have demanded that certain conditions be met. (pp. 19–20)

Competence and Malpractice

As previously noted, counselors are expected to function within the limits of their professional expertise. This is not only ethically expected but also legally desirable. The dramatic increase in malpractice suits across all the helping professions indicates that our competence may be under legal scrutiny at any time. The governing legal principle in such cases is pointed out by Fischer and Sorenson (1996) as follows:

> One who undertakes, gratuitously or for consideration, to render services to another which he should recognize as necessary for the protection of the other person or things, is subject to liability to the other for physical harm resulting from his failure to exercise reasonable care to perform his undertaking, if:
>
> a.   His failure to exercise such care increases the risk of harm, or
> b.   The harm is suffered because of the other's reliance upon the undertaking. (p. 42)

They also note that the most common situations in which legal problems are most likely to occur are these:

- Administering drugs
- Giving birth control advice
- Giving abortion-related advice
- Making statements that might be defamatory
- Assisting in searches of students' lockers
- Violating confidentiality and the privacy of records (Fischer & Sorenson, 1996, p. 51)

Counselors as Expert Witnesses

Counselors are increasingly making court appearances as expert witnesses. Depending on the counselor's work setting, she or he may be called on to testify in cases of child abuse and neglect, sexual abuse, child custody, divorce, and addictions, to name but a few. Being an expert witness and deporting oneself well as a professional cannot be dealt with casually. We, therefore, recommend that practicing counselors review the American Counseling Association Legal Series monograph *The Counselor as an Expert Witness* (1993) by William Weikel and Paula Hughes, edited by Theodore P. Remley, Jr. In addition, if the counseling organization retains a lawyer for legal advice, it is also advisable to consult with this individual. It may also be helpful to observe other experts offering their testimony and to read, where permitted, transcripts of trials where expert witnesses have testified.

Third-Party Payments

A legal issue for many counselors, especially those in private practice or employed by agencies dependent on client payments, is the issue of third-party payments. This is the practice of reimbursement from a third party, usually an insurance company, for services that a counselor (the second party) renders to a client (the first party). Remley and Herlihy (2001) indicate that

> HMOs, PPOs, and health insurance companies can voluntarily acknowledge counselors as qualified mental health care providers, and most do. However, these health care organizations have a legal right to refuse to give their clients access to counselors unless there is legislation to the contrary. This type of legislation, called "freedom of choice legislation," requires health care providers to give access to licensed counselors for mental health care if they give access to other mental health care providers such as psychologists or social workers. Many states have passed freedom of choice legislation. In states that have not, counselors are active in trying to get freedom of choice legislation passed. (p. 43)

SUMMARY

This chapter has reminded readers of ethical guidelines and expectancies for the profession of counseling. Special attention has been paid to the issues of competence, confidentiality, and personal relationships with clients. This chapter has also noted the importance to counselors of being informed about the legal implications and restrictions on their professional activities.

Whether our profession of counseling advances and achieves noble goals will depend very little on textbook writers, past and present, but on you, our readers, who will represent our profession in the future. You are our future. We wish you well!

DISCUSSION QUESTIONS

1. Identify and discuss the lack of or questionable ethics in activities such as sales, advertising, politics, and government.
2. What are the differences and similarities between ethics and values?
3. Why are codes of ethics important to the counseling profession?
4. Are warranties or guarantees for products indications that manufacturers want to treat customers ethically?
5. Are there any legal concerns you would have as a practicing counselor?
6. Are you aware of any recent court decisions or pending legislation that could have implications for counselors in schools? In nonschool settings?
7. How do you intend to keep abreast of legal enactments or court decisions affecting the counseling profession?

CLASS ACTIVITIES

1. Examine current newspapers and magazines for examples of ethical and legal violations that betray a public trust. Share your findings in class or small groups.
2. In small groups, share and discuss situations in which you feel you were treated unethically.
3. Ask a local lawyer to address the class on the topic of professional malpractice.
4. Arrange to attend a trial or court session where an expert witness is scheduled to testify.

SELECTED READINGS

Bratina, T. G., & Bratina, T. A. (1998). Electronic career search. *Journal of Employment Counseling, 35*(1), 17–25.

Ibrahim, F. A. (1996). A multicultural perspective on principle and virtue ethics. *Counseling Psychologist, 24,* 74–85.

Kitchener, K. S. (1996). There is more to ethics than principles. *Counseling Psychologist, 24,* 92–97.

Krieshok, T. (1987). Psychologists and counselors in the legal system: A dialogue with Theodore Blau. *Journal of Counseling and Development, 66*(2), 69–72.

Mabe, A. R., & Rollin, S. A. (1986). The role of a code of ethical standards in counseling. *Journal of Counseling and Development, 64,* 294–297.

McCarthy, M. M., & Sorenson, G. P. (1993). School counselors and consultants: Legal duties and liabilities. *Journal of Counseling and Development, 72*(2), 159–167.

Neukrug, E., Lovell, C., & Parker, R. J. (1996). Employing ethical codes and decision-making models: A developmental process. *Counseling and Values, 40,* 98–106.

Psychology and the Internet. (2000). *Monitor on Psychology, 31*(4). [Special issue].

Remley, T., & Herlihy, B. (2001). *Ethical, legal, and professional issues in counseling.* Upper Saddle River, NJ: Prentice Hall.

Ridley, C. R., Liddle, M. C., Hill, C. L., & Li, L. C. (2001). Ethical decision making in multicultural counseling. In J. G. Ponterotto, J. M. Casar, L. A. Suzuki, & C. M. Alexander (Eds.), *Handbook of multicultural counseling* (2nd ed.). (pp. 165–188). Thousand Oaks, CA: Sage.

Rowley, W. J., & MacDonald, D. (2001). Counseling and the law: A cross-cultural perspective. *Journal of Counseling and Development, 79*(4), 422–429.

Shilloto-Clarke, C. (1996). Ethical issues in counselling psychology. In R. Woolfe & W. Dryden (Eds.), *Handbook of counselling* (pp. 555–580). London: Sage.

RESEARCH OF INTEREST

Borders, L. D., Cashwell, C. S., & Rotter, J. C. (1995). Supervision of counselor licensure applicants: A comparative study. *Counselor Education and Supervision, 35*(1), 54–69.

Abstract This article provides baseline information about supervision being given to counselor licensure applicants and investigates the impact of regulations on the conduct of this supervision. A comparison study of supervisors was conducted with 107 subjects from South Carolina and 83 from Missouri, the former with recommended supervisor and supervision regulations and the latter without it. Subjects completed questionnaires regarding their supervision practices and rated their supervision knowledge skills. Supervisors in both states were experienced counselors from a variety of fields and indicated altruistic and humanitarian reasons for working with counselor licensure applicants. More of South Carolina supervisors had aligned with counselor education and reported more training experiences. Regulations did not have adverse effects on supervision.

Geisler, J. S. (1995). The impact of the passage of a counselor licensure law: One state's experience. *Journal of Mental Health Counseling, 17*(2), 188–198.

Abstract Responses to a questionnaire completed by 764 Licensed Professional Counselors (LPCs) revealed that the majority of LPCs are holding their licenses in reserve waiting to use them at a later date. Fifty-nine percent of LPCs were women, and the mean age of all LPCs was 47 years. Fifty-nine percent of counselors received their undergraduate degrees in the social sciences or education. For those in a fee-for-service setting, the mean fee per session was $69.91 (range $20–138). Only 9% of LPCs had requested reimbursement. They report having difficulty receiving third-party payments. Those who had been successful had been assertive in marketing their services and had been proactive with HMOs, employee assistance programs, and insurance companies, and had contracts with businesses and managed health care organizations.

Navin, S., Beamish, P., & Johanson, G. (1995). Ethical practices of field-based mental health counselor supervisors. *Journal of Mental Health Counseling, 17*(2), 243–253.

Abstract This study examined current ethical supervisory practices of 321 field-based mental health supervisors in Ohio as they relate to the Supervisory Role section of the Association for Counselor Education and Supervision ethical standards. Sixty-one percent of respondents held licenses in more than one area. The standards more consistently followed were participating in professional organizations, reviewing legal and ethical responsibilities, establishing procedures for crisis intervention, meeting regularly with and providing ongoing feedback to counseling students, conducting remedial referral, and avoiding sexual contact with students. The standard least consistently followed was training in supervision, suggesting that little formal course work had been completed by clinical supervisors. The standard that produced the most mixed results involved multiple roles.

Appendix A
National Standards for School Counseling Programs

OVERVIEW

The purpose of a counseling program in a school setting is to promote and enhance the learning process. To that end, the School Counseling Program facilitates Student Development in three broad areas: Academic Development, Career Development, and Personal/Social Development. The following chart describes the standards for each area.

I. Academic Development

Standard A: Students will acquire the attitudes, knowledge, and skills that contribute to effective learning in school and across the life span.

Standard B: Students will complete school with the academic preparation essential to choose from a wide range of substantial post-secondary options, including college.

Standard C: Students will understand the relationship of academics to the world of work, and to life at home and in the community.

II. Career Development

Standard A: Students will acquire the skills to investigate the world of work in relation to knowledge of self and to make informed career decisions.

Standard B: Students will employ strategies to achieve future career success and satisfaction.

Standard C: Students will understand the relationship between personal qualities, education and training, and the world of work.

III. Personal/Social Development

Standard A: Students will acquire the attitudes, knowledge, and interpersonal skills to help them understand and respect self and others.

Standard B: Students will make decisions, set goals, and take necessary action to achieve goals.

Standard C: Students will understand safety and survival skills.

The standards for each content area are intended to provide guidance and direction for states, school systems and individual schools to develop quality and effective school counseling programs. The emphasis is on success for *all students,* not only those students who are motivated, supported, and ready to learn. The school counseling program based upon national standards enables *all students* to achieve success in school and to develop into contributing members of our society.

Source: From the American School Counselor Association. (1997). Campbell, C. A. & Dahir, C. A. *National Standards for School Counseling Programs* (pp. 17–19). Copyright © 1997. American School Counselor Association. Reprinted with permission.

School success requires that students make successful transitions from elementary school to middle/junior high school to high school. Graduates from high school have acquired the attitudes, skills, and knowledge that are essential to the competitive workplace of the 21st century.

A school counseling program based upon national standards provides the elements for all students to achieve success in school. School counselors continuously assess their students' needs to identify barriers and obstacles that may be hindering success and also advocate for programmatic efforts to eliminate these barriers.

Each standard is followed by a list of student competencies which articulate desired student learning outcomes. Student competencies define the specific knowledge, attitudes and skills that students should obtain or demonstrate as a result of participating in a school counseling program. These listings are not meant to be all inclusive, nor is any individual program expected to include all of the competencies in the school counseling program. The competencies offer a foundation for what a standards-based program should address and deliver. These can be used as a basis to develop measurable indicators of student performance.

The program standards for **academic development** *guide the school counseling program to implement strategies and activities to support and maximize each student's ability to learn.* Academic development includes acquiring skills, attitudes, and knowledge which contribute to effective learning in school and across the life span; employing strategies to achieve success in school; and understanding the relationship of academics to the world of work, and to life at home and in the community. Academic development standards and competencies support the premise that all students meet or exceed the local, state, and national academic standards.

The purpose of a counseling program in a school setting is to promote and enhance the learning process.

The program standards for **career development** *guide the school counseling program to provide the foundations for the acquisition of skills, attitudes, and knowledge that enable students to make a successful transition from school to the world of work, and from job to job across the life span.* Career development includes the employment of strategies to achieve future career success and job satisfaction as well as fostering understanding of the relationship between personal qualities, education and training, and the world of work. Career development standards and competencies ensure that students develop career goals as a result of participation in a comprehensive plan of career awareness, exploration, and preparation activities.

The program standards for **personal/social development** *guide the school counseling program to provide the foundation for personal and social growth as students progress through school and into adulthood.* Personal/social development contributes to academic and career success. Personal/social development includes the acquisition of skills, attitudes, and knowledge which help students understand and respect self and others, acquire effective interpersonal skills, understand safety and survival skills, and develop into contributing members of our society. Personal/social development standards and competencies ensure that students have learned to successfully and safely negotiate their way in the increasingly complex and diverse world of the 21st century.

The professional school counselor is a certified/licensed educator trained in school counseling. Professional school counselors address the needs of students through the implementation of a comprehensive, standards-based, developmental school counseling program. They are employed in elementary, middle/junior high, and senior high schools, and in post-secondary settings. Their work is differentiated by attention to age-specific developmental stages of student growth, and the needs, tasks and student interests related to those stages. School counselors work with all students, including those who are considered at-risk and those with special needs. They are specialists in human behavior and relationships who provide assistance to students through four primary interventions: counseling (individual and group), large group guidance, consultation, and coordination.

COUNSELING is a confidential relationship which the counselor conducts with students individually and in small groups to help them resolve or cope constructively with their problems and developmental concerns.

LARGE GROUP GUIDANCE is a planned, developmental program of guidance activities designed to foster students' academic, career, and personal/social development. It is provided for all students through a collaborative effort by counselors and teachers.

CONSULTATION is a collaborative partnership in which the counselor works with parents, teachers, administrators, school psychologists, social workers, visiting teachers, medical professionals and community health personnel in order to plan and implement strategies to help students be successful in the education system.

COORDINATION is a leadership process in which the counselor helps organize, manage and evaluate the school counseling program. The counselor assists parents in obtaining needed services for their children through a referral and follow-up process and serves as liaison between the school and community agencies so that they may collaborate in efforts to help students. Professional school counselors are responsible for developing comprehensive school counseling programs that promote and enhance student learning. By providing prevention and intervention services within a comprehensive program, school counselors focus their skills, time and energies on direct services to students, staff, and families. In the delivery of direct services, the American School Counselor Association (ASCA) recommends that professional school counselors spend at least 70% of their time in direct services to students. The ASCA considers a realistic counselor-student ratio for effective program delivery to be a maximum of 1:250.

Above all, school counselors are student advocates who work cooperatively with other individuals and organizations to promote the academic, career, and personal/social development of children and youth. School counselors, as members of the educational team, consult and collaborate with teachers, administrators and families to assist students to be successful. They work on behalf of students and their families to insure that all school programs facilitate the educational process and offer the opportunity for school success for each student. School counselors are an integral part of all school efforts to insure a safe learning environment and safeguard the human rights of all members of the school community.

Professional school counselors meet the state certification/licensure standards and abide by the laws of the states in which they are employed. To assure high quality practice, school counselors are committed to continued professional growth and personal development. They are proactively involved in professional organizations which foster and promote school counseling at the local, state and national levels. They uphold the ethical and professional standards of these associations and promote the development of the school counseling profession.

Delegate Assembly, June 1999

Source: From the American School Counselor Association (1999). *The Role of the Professional School Counselor.* Copyright © 1999. American School Counselor Association. Reprinted with permission.

AMERICAN SCHOOL COUNSELOR ASSOCIATION (ASCA) POSITION

It is the professional school counselor's responsibility to report suspected cases of child abuse/neglect to the proper authorities. Recognizing that the abuse of children is not limited to the home and that corporal punishment by school authorities might well be considered child abuse, ASCA supports any legislation that specifically bans the use of corporal punishment as a disciplinary tool within the schools.

THE RATIONALE

The incidence of reported child abuse and child neglect has increased significantly during the past several years. Although there are societal beliefs and values that parents have the right to discipline their children as they choose, it becomes a public issue of child protection when that discipline becomes abusive. Research shows that a large percentage of abusive parents were abused children, perpetuating the cycle of abuse. The consequences of abuse are physical and/or emotional harm, which include the inability to build healthy relationships, increased likelihood of being abused by another perpetrator of abuse and lowered self-esteem.

Definitions

Abuse: The infliction of physical harm upon the body of a child by other than accidental means, continual psychological damage or denial of emotional needs (e.g., extensive bruises/patterns; burns/patterns; lacerations, welts or abrasions; injuries inconsistent with information offered; sexual

abuse involving molestation or exploitation, including but not limited to rape, carnal knowledge, sodomy or unnatural sexual practices; emotional disturbance caused by continuous friction in the home, marital discord or mentally ill parents; cruel treatment).

Neglect: The failure to provide necessary food, care, clothing, shelter, supervision or medical attention for a child (e.g., malnourished, ill-clad, dirty, without proper shelter or sleeping arrangements, lacking appropriate health care; unattended, lacking adequate supervision; ill and lacking essential medical attention; irregular/illegal absences from school; exploited, overworked; lacking essential psychological/emotional nurturing; abandonment.

Corporal Punishment: Any act of physical force upon a pupil for the purpose of punishing that pupil. This definition specifically excludes any reasonable force exercised by a school employee that is used in self-defense, in defense of other persons or property or to restrain or remove a pupil who is disrupting school functions and who refuses to comply with a request to stop.

THE PROFESSIONAL SCHOOL COUNSELOR'S ROLE

Generally, state laws require people in the helping professions who have reasonable cause to believe that a child is suffering physical or emotional injury to report this situation as directed by state law to the appropriate authorities. School counselors are mandated reporters and need policies, referral procedures and essential knowledge. It is a legal, moral and ethical responsibility to report child abuse.

Source: From the American School Counselor Association (1999). *Position Statement: Child Abuse.* Copyright © 1999. American School Counselor Association. Reprinted with permission.

ASCA recognizes that it is the absolute responsibility of school counselors to report suspected cases of child abuse/neglect to the proper authorities. Responsible action by the counselor can be achieved through the recognition and understanding of the problem, knowing the reporting procedures and participating in available child abuse information programs. Professional school counselors aid in early detection of abuse. The association also recognizes that the abuse of children is not limited to the home and that corporal punishment by school authorities can be considered child abuse.

School counselors commit themselves to providing strategies to help break the cycle of child abuse. It is the school counselors' responsibility to help children and adults cope with abusive behavior, facilitate behavioral changes and develop positive interpersonal relationships as well as to prepare for parenting styles. Professional school counselors coordinate team efforts on behalf of the child; provide support to staff and other school personnel; work to re-establish trust and to provide brief, educational counseling or to refer to ongoing counseling services outside of the school community; provide developmental workshops and/or support groups enhancing parenting skills; and provide programs and inservices designed to help prevent child abuse.

SUMMARY

Professional school counselors are a key link in the child abuse prevention network. It is their responsibility to report suspected cases of child abuse or neglect to the proper authorities. The professional school counselor must be able to guide and help abused and neglected students by providing appropriate services during crisis situations. Up-to-date information, and intervention, can sometimes mean a turning point in the life and behavior of an abusive family.

Appendix D
American Counseling Association
Multicultural/Diversity Agenda

CORE VALUES

- The phenomenon of multiculturalism and diversity are the essence of all that we do as a profession and as professionals. They are core competencies of the American Counseling Association and stepping stones on the path to social justice.
- Valuing diversity and multiculturalism is an obligation of a competent professional counselor, an association leader, all counselor educators, students and counselor education programs, and institutions that deliver consulting services in the public and private sector.
- Addressing the dynamics of oppression and privilege are key to institutional and individual change.
- Advocating for diversity and multiculturalism to the society at large is an obligation of professional counselors, counselor educators and the American Counseling Association.
- Achieving multicultural/diversity outcomes has no end point but is an ongoing process both for the association and for the members.
- People need to feel safe and be welcome wherever they are in their own developmental process throughout the association and its stakeholders.
- The profession exists to serve multicultural/diverse populations.
- The terms multiculturalism and diversity are evolving in their meanings and applications but encompass inclusivity and the celebration of human differences.

PRINCIPLES AND GOALS

Principle I

ACA will foster an appreciation of diversity and multiculturalism and has an obligation to work toward creating conditions in which leaders and members are encouraged to engage in issues of multiculturalism and diversity.

Goal 1

To ensure that ACA's Code of Ethics, Standards of Practice, credentialing, and accreditation standards reflect diversity and multiculturalism as core competencies.

Goal 2

To engage in political processes, public policy, and advocacy to uphold the core values of diversity and multiculturalism.

Goal 3

For ACA leaders, members, and staff to actively model and advocate for the core values of multiculturalism and diversity.

Goal 4

To ensure the leadership and membership throughout ACA reflects a multicultural and diverse society.

Source: From American Counseling Association (1997), *Multicultural/Diversity Agenda.* Copyright © 1997 American Counseling Association. Reprinted by permission. No further reproduction authorized without written permission of the American Counseling Association.

Goal 5

To identify and promulgate the attributes of counselor education programs and continuing education initiatives that successfully promote the development of diversity and multiculturalism core values.

Goal 6

To encourage ACA members to provide pro bono counseling services to people in need.

Principle II

ACA values and respects the development, recruitment, retention, and involvement of a multiculturally diverse membership.

Goal 1

To develop ACA as a multiculturally competent association.

Goal 2

To increase the number of leaders from under-represented groups.

Goal 3

To expand and retain the membership of ACA to reflect a multicultural and diverse society.

Goal 4

To ensure an organizational environment that is safe, inviting, and nurturing to individuals from varied backgrounds/cultures.

Goal 5

To ensure that opportunities for acquiring diversity/multicultural competencies are available to all ACA members.

Principle III

ACA values and encourages professional counselors who integrate multicultural diversity knowledge and skills into their practices. Therefore, it is the responsibility of ACA members to be professional and competent in multicultural/diversity issues.

Goal 1

To provide multicultural diversity education and training to ACA members.

Goal 2

To identify and recognize counselors, who have demonstrated exemplary competencies in the area of multiculturalism and/or diversity.

Goal 3

To provide a wide range of professional resources on multicultural diversity issues for counselors.

Goal 4

To provide electronic access to multicultural/diversity resources.

Goal 5

To build bridges internationally.

Principle IV

ACA values and respects a joyful expansion of leadership that is diverse across the membership and the practice of counseling.

Goal 1

To develop a cadre of emerging leaders.

Goal 2

To promote diversity in all fields of counseling practice.

Goal 3

To expand leadership opportunities within ACA.

Goal 4

To reflect diversity, interest, *and* expertise in national, divisional, and branch committee membership.

RUST Statement Revised (AACD/AMECD Policy Statement) Responsibilities of Users of Standardized Tests

I. INTRODUCTION

Background

At the 1976 AACD (then APGA) Convention, the Board of Directors requested the development of a statement on the responsible use of standardized tests to promote proper test use, reflecting the advantages of assessment along with concerns about negative effects, and to help its members employ safeguards against misuse of tests. A committee representing all AACD Divisions and Regions spent two years studying the issues and developed a statement, published in the October 1978 issue of *Guidepost*, entitled "Responsibilities of Users of Standardized Tests." The Association for Measurement and Evaluation in Counseling and Development was charged with maintaining ongoing review of the so-called RUST Statement. The present statement has grown out of that review.

Target Audience

The statement is intended to address the needs of the members of AACD and its Divisions, Branches, and Regions, including counselors and other human service workers. Although it may interest test developers, teachers, administrators, parents, the press, or the general public, it is not specifically designed for these audiences.

Organization and Focus

The statement is organized into eight sections: Introduction, Test Decisions, Qualification of Test Users, Test Selection, Test Administration, Test Scoring, Test Interpretation, and Communicating Test Results. Basic to the statement is the assumption that test data are merely numbers and that guidelines can help to promote their constructive use. The statement specifies general principles and activities which constitute responsible practice. These are grouped around similar issues and are indexed for ease of reference.

II. TEST DECISIONS

Decisions should be based on data. In general, test data improve the quality of decisions. However, deciding whether or not to test creates the possibility of three kinds of errors. First, a decision not to test can result in misjudgments that stem from inadequate or subjective data. Second, tests may produce data which could improve accuracy in decisions affecting the client, but which are not used in counseling. Third, tests may be misused. The responsible practitioner will determine, in advance, the purpose for administering a given test, considering protections and benefits for the client, practitioner, and agency.

A. Define purposes for testing by developing specific objectives and limits for the use of test data in relation to the particular assessment purpose:

1. Placement: If the purpose is selection or placement, the test user should understand the programs or institutions into which the client may be placed and be able to judge the consequences of inclusion or exclusion decisions for the client.

2. Prediction: If the purpose is prediction, the test user should understand the need for predictive data as well as possible negative consequences (e.g., stereotyping).

3. Description: If the purpose is diagnosis or description, the test user should understand the general domain being measured and be able to identify those aspects which are adequately measured and those which are not.

4. Growth: If the purpose is to examine growth or change, the test user should understand the practical and theoretical difficulties associated with such measurement.

5. Program Evaluation: If the purpose of assessment is the evaluation of an agency's programs, the test user should be aware of the various information needs for the evaluation and of the limitations of each instrument used to assess those needs, as well as how the evaluation will be used.

B. Determine Information Needs and Assessment Needs:

1. Determine whether testing is intended to assess individuals, groups, or both.

2. Identify the particular individual and/or group to be tested with regard to the agency's purposes and capabilities.

3. Determine the limitations to testing created by an individual's age; racial, sexual, ethnic, and cultural background; or other characteristics.

4. Avoid unnecessary testing by identifying decisions which can be made with existing information.

5. Assess the consequences for clients of deciding either to test or not to test.

6. Limit data gathering to the variables that are needed for the particular purpose.

7. Cross-validate test data using other available information whenever possible.

III. QUALIFICATIONS OF TEST USERS

While all professional counselors and personnel workers should have formal training in psychological and educational measurement and testing, this training does not necessarily make one an expert, and even an expert does not have all the knowledge and skills appropriate to some particular situations or instruments. Questions of user qualifications should always be addressed when testing is being considered.

Lack of proper qualifications can lead to errors and subsequent harm to clients. Each professional is responsible for making judgements on this in each situation and cannot leave that responsibility either to clients or to others in authority. It is incumbent upon the individual test user to obtain appropri-

ate training or arrange for proper supervision and assistance when engaged in testing. Qualifications for test users depend on four factors:

A. Purposes of Testing: Technically proper testing for ill-understood purposes may constitute misuse. Because the purposes of testing dictate how the results are used, qualifications of test users are needed beyond general testing competencies to interpret and apply data.

B. Characteristics of Tests: Understanding the nature and limitations of each instrument used is needed by test users.

C. Settings and Conditions of Test Use: Assessment of the quality and relevance of test user knowledge and skill to the situation is needed before deciding to test or to participate in a testing program.

D. Roles of Test Selectors, Administrators, Scorers, and Interpreters: Test users must be engaged in only those testing activities for which their training and experience qualify them.

IV. TEST SELECTION

The selection of tests should be guided by information obtained from a careful analysis of the characteristics of the population to be tested; the knowledge, skills, abilities, or attitudes to be assessed; the purposes for testing; and the eventual use and interpretation of the test scores. Use of tests should also be guided by criteria for technical quality recommended by measurement professionals (i.e., the APA/AERA/NCME "Standards for Educational and Psychological Tests" and the APA/AERA/NCME/AACD/ASHA "Code of Fair Testing Practices in Education").

A. Relate Validity to Usage:

1. Determine the validity of a test (whether the test measures what is meant to be measured) through evidence of the constructs used in developing the test, the correlation of the test performance with other appraisals of the characteristics being measured, and/or the predictions of specified behaviors from the test performance.

2. Determine whether a test is congruent with the users' definition of the characteristics of human performance to be appraised.

3. Use tests for selection purposes only when they show predictive validity for the specific tasks or competencies needed in an educational or employment experience and when they maintain legal and ethical prescriptions for non-discriminatory practices in program selection, employment, or placement.

B. Use Appropriate Tests:

1. Document tests as appropriate for the characteristics of the population to be tested.

2. Only use tests within the level of skills of the practitioner.

3. Use tests consistent with local needs:

   a. Give attention to how the test is designed to handle variation of motivation, working speed, language facility, and experiential background among persons taking it; bias in response to its content; and effects of guessing in response to its questions.

   b. Determine whether a common test or different tests are required for accurate measurement of groups with special characteristics.

      i. Recognize that the use of different tests for cultural, ethnic, and racial groups may constitute ineffective means for making corrections for differences.

      ii. Determine whether persons or groups that use different languages should be tested in either or both languages and in some instances, tested first for bilingualism or language dominance.

C. Consider Technical Characteristics:

1. Select only tests that have documented evidence of reliability or consistency.

2. Select only tests that have adequate documented evidence of the effectiveness of the measure for the purpose to be served and justification of the inferences based on the results.

3. Scrutinize standardization and norming procedures for relevance to the local population and use of the data.

4. Use separate norms for men and women or other subgroups when empirical evidence indicates they are appropriate.

5. Determine the degree of technical quality demanded of a test on the basis of the nature of the decisions to be made.

6. Include ease and accuracy of the procedures for scoring, summarizing, and communicating test performance among the criteria for selecting a test.

7. Consider practical constraints of cost, conditions, and time for testing as secondary test selection criteria.

D. Employ User Participation in Test Selection: Actively involve everyone who will be using the assessments (administering, scoring, summarizing, interpreting, making decisions) as appropriate in the selection of tests so that they are congruent with local purposes, conditions, and uses.

V. TEST ADMINISTRATION

Test administration includes procedures to ensure that the test is used in the manner specified by the test developers and that the individuals being tested are working within conditions which maximize opportunity for optimum, comparable performance.

A. Provide Proper Orientation:

1. Inform testing candidates, parents, and institutions or agencies in the community as appropriate about the testing procedures. The orientation should make the test meaningful for the individual or group being tested, and should include the purposes of the test, the kinds of tasks it involves, how it is administered and how the scores will be reported and used.

2. Provide persons being tested sufficient practice experiences prior to the test.

3. Prior to testing, check all test takers' ability to record their responses adequately (e.g., in the use of machine-scorable answer sheets).

4. Provide periodic training by qualified personnel for test administrators within agencies or institutions using tests.

5. Review test materials and administration sites and procedures prior to the time for testing to ensure standardized conditions and appropriate response to any irregularities which may occur.

B. Use Qualified Test Administrators:

1. Acquire any training required to administer the test.

2. Ensure that individuals taking self-administered or self-scored instruments have the necessary understanding and competencies.

C. Provide Appropriate Testing Conditions:

1. Ensure that the testing environment (seating, work surfaces, lighting, heating, freedom from distractions, etc.) and psychological climate are conducive to the best possible performance of the test takers.

2. Carefully observe, record, and attach to the test record any deviation from prescribed test administration procedures.

3. Use a systematic and objective procedure for observing and recording environmental, health, or emotional factors, or other elements which may invalidate test performance. This record should be attached to the test scores of the persons tested.

4. Use sufficiently trained personnel to provide uniform conditions and to observe the conduct of the examinees when large groups of individuals are tested.

D. Give Proper Directions:

1. Present each test in the manner prescribed in the test manual to ensure that it is fair to each test taker.

2. Administer standardized tests with the verbatim instructions, exact sequence and timing, and identical materials that were used in the test standardization.

E. Demonstrate Professional Collaboration: In settings where skill and knowledge are pooled and responsibility shared, consider the qualifications of the testing team as a whole as more important than those of individuals. However, coordination and consistency of responsibilities with expertise must be maintained.

VI. TEST SCORING

Accurate measurement of human performance necessitates adequate procedures for scoring the responses of examinees. These procedures must be audited as necessary to ensure consistency and accuracy of application.

A. Consider Accuracy and Interpretability: Select a test scoring process that maximizes accuracy and interpretability.

B. Rescore Samples: Routinely rescore samples of examinee responses to monitor the accuracy of the scoring process.

C. Screen Test Results: Screen reports of test results using personnel competent to recognize unreasonable or impossible scores.

D. Verify Scores and Norms: Verify the accuracy of computation of raw scores and conversion to normative scales prior to release of such information to examinees or users of test results.

E. Communicative Deviations: Report as part of the official record any deviation from normal conditions and examinee behaviors.

F. Label Results: Clearly label the date of test administration along with the scores.

VII. TEST INTERPRETATION

Test interpretation encompasses all the ways that meaning is assigned to the scores. Proper interpretation requires knowledge about the test which can be obtained by studying its manual and other materials along with current research literature with respect to its use; no one should undertake the interpretation of scores on any test without such study.

A. Consider Reliability: Reliability is important because it is a prerequisite to validity and because the degree to which a score may vary due to measurement error is an important factor in its interpretation.

1. Estimate test stability using a reliability (or other appropriate) coefficient.

2. Use the standard error of measurement to estimate the amount of variation due to random error in individual scores and to evaluate the precision of cut-scores in selection decisions.

3. Consider, in relationship to the uses being made of the scores, variance components attributed to error in the reliability index.

4. Evaluate reliability estimates with regard to factors that may have artificially raised or lowered them (e.g., test speededness, biases in population sampling).

5. Distinguish indices of objectivity (i.e., scorer reliability) from rest reliability.

B. Consider Validity: Proper test interpretation requires knowledge of the validity evidence available for the intended use of the test. Its validity for other uses is not relevant. Indeed, use of a measure for a purpose for which it was not designed may constitute misuse. The nature of the validity evidence required for a test depends upon its use.

1. Use for Placement: Predictive validity is the usual basis for valid placement.

   a. Obtain adequate information about the programs or institutions in which the client may be placed to judge the consequences of such placement.

   b. Use all available evidence to infer the validity of an individual's score. A single test score should not be the sole basis for a placement or selection recommendation. Other items of information about an individual (e.g., teacher report, counselor opinion) frequently improve the likelihood that proper judgments and decisions will be made.

   c. Consider validity for each alternative (i.e., each placement option) when interpreting test scores and other evidence.

   d. Examine the possibility that a client's group membership (socioeconomic status, gender, subculture, etc.) may affect test performance and, consequently, validity.

   e. Estimate the probability of favorable outcomes for each possible placement before making recommendations.

   f. Consider the possibility that outcomes favorable from an institutional point of view may differ from those that are favorable from the individual's point of view.

2. Use for Prediction: The relationship of the test scores to an independently developed criterion measure is the basis for predictive validity.

   a. Consider the reliability and validity of the criterion measure(s) used.

b. Consider the validity of a measure in the context of other predictors available (i.e., does the test make a valid contribution to prediction beyond that provided by other measures).

c. Use cross-validation to judge the validity of prediction processes.

d. Consider the effects of labeling, stereotyping, and prejudging people (e.g., self-fulfilling prophecies that may result from labeling are usually undesirable).

e. If a statistically valid predictor lacks both construct and content validity, analyze the mechanism by which it operates to determine whether or not its predictive validity is spurious.

3. Use for Description: Comprehensiveness of information is fundamental to effective description, since no set of test scores completely describes an individual.

a. Clearly identify the domain assessed by any measure and the adequacy of the content sampling procedures used in developing items.

b. Clarify the dimensions being measured when multiple scores from a battery or inventory are used for description.

   i. Examine the content and/or construct validity of each score separately.

   ii. Consider the relative importance of each of the separate elements for interpretation.

   iii. Give appropriate weights to reflect the variabilities (e.g., standard deviations) and relationships (e.g., correlations) of scores which are to be combined.

c. Distinguish characteristics that can be validated only empirically and those for which content specifications exist.

4. Use for Assessment of Growth: Assessment of growth or change requires valid tests as well as a valid procedure for combining them.

a. Specifically evaluate the reliability of differences between scores as measures of change.

b. Establish the validities of the measures used to establish change in relation to one another as well as individually.

c. Consider comparability of intervals in scales used to assess change.

   i. Evaluate derived or extrapolated scores (e.g., grade equivalents) for possible different meanings at different score levels.

   ii. Consider problems in interpretation and comparability of tests (e.g., floor or ceiling effects, content changes from level to level, poor articulation

in multilevel tests, lack of comparability of alternate forms, inadequacy of score-equating across forms, and differences in administration and timing of tests from that of their norming).

d. Assess potential for undesirable correlations of difference scores with the measures entering into their calculations (e.g., regression toward the mean).

e. Recognize the potential lack of comparability between norms for differences derived from norms and norms for differences derived from differences (i.e., mathematically derived norms for differences are not necessarily equivalent to norms based on distributions of actual differences).

5. Use for Program Evaluation: Assessments of group differences (between groups or within groups over time) are based on research designs which to varying degrees admit competing interpretations of the results.

a. Use procedures in the evaluation which ensure that no factors other than those being studied have major influence on the results (i.e., internal validity).

b. Use statistical procedures which are appropriate and have all assumptions met by the data being analyzed.

c. Evaluate the generalizability (external validity) of the results for different individuals, settings, tests, and variables.

C. Scores, Norms, and Related Technical Features: The result of scoring a test or subtest is usually a number called a raw score which by itself is not interpretable. Additional steps are needed to translate the number directly into either a verbal description (e.g., pass or fail) or into a derived score (e.g., a standard score). Less than full understanding of these procedures is likely to produce errors in interpretation and ultimately in counseling or other uses.

1. Examine appropriate test materials (e.g., manuals, handbooks, users' guides, and technical reports) to identify the descriptions or derived scores produced and their unique characteristics.

a. Know the operational procedures for translating raw scores into descriptions or derived scores.

b. Know specific psychological or educational concepts or theories before interpreting the scores of tests based on them.

c. Consider differential validity along with equating error when different tests, different test forms, or scores on the same test administered at different times are compared.

2. Clarify arbitrary standards used in interpretation (e.g., mastery or nonmastery for criterion-referenced tests).

a. Recognize that when a score is interpreted based on a proportion score (e.g., percent correct), its elements are being given arbitrary weights.

b. Recognize that the difficulty of a fixed standard (e.g., 80 percent right) varies widely and thus does not have the same meaning for different content areas and for different assessment methods.

c. Report the number (or percentage) of items right in addition to the interpretation when it will help others understand the quality of the examinees' performance.

3. Employ derived scores based on norms which fit the needs of the current use of the test.

a. Evaluate whether available norm groups are appropriate as part of the process of interpreting the scores of clients.

  i. Use norms for the group to which the client belongs.

  ii. Recognize that derived scores based on different norm groups may not be comparable.

  iii. Use local norms and derived scores based on them whenever possible.

b. Choose a score based on its intended use.

  i. Consider relative standing scores (e.g., percentile ranks) for comparison of individuals to the norm or reference group.

  ii. Consider standard or scaled scores whenever means and variances or other arithmetic operations are appropriate.

  iii. When using a statistical technique, use the test's derived score which best meets the assumptions of the analysis.

D. Administration and Scoring Variation: Stated criteria for score interpretation assume standard procedures for administering and scoring the test. Departures from standard conditions and procedures modify and often invalidate these criteria.

1. Evaluate unusual circumstances peculiar to the administration and scoring of the test.

a. Examine reports from administrators, proctors, and scorers concerning irregularities or unusual conditions (e.g., excessive anxiety) for possible effects on test performance.

b. Consider potential effects of examiner-examinee differences in ethnic and cultural background, attitudes, and values based on available relevant research.

c. Consider any reports of examinee behavior indicating the responses were made on some basis other than that intended.

d. Consider differences among clients in their reaction to instructions about guessing and scoring.

2. Evaluate scoring irregularities (e.g., machine scoring errors) and bias and judgment effects when subjective elements enter into scoring.

VIII. COMMUNICATING TEST RESULTS

The responsible counselor or other practitioner reports test data with a concern for the individual's need for information and the purposes of the information. There must also be protection of the right of the person tested to be informed about how the results will be used and what safeguards exist to prevent misuse (right to information) and about who will have access to the results (right to privacy).

A. Decisions about Individuals: Where test data are used to enhance decisions about an individual, the practitioner's responsibilities include:

1. Limitations on Communication:

a. Inform the examinee of possible actions that may be taken by any person or agency who will be using the results.

b. Limit access to users specifically authorized by the law or by the client.

c. Obtain the consent of the examinee before using test results for any purpose other than those advanced prior to testing.

2. Practitioner Communication Skills:

a. Develop the ability to interpret test results accurately before attempting to communicate them.

b. Develop appropriate communication skills, particularly with respect to concepts that are commonly misunderstood by the intended audience, before attempting to explain test results to clients, the public, or other recipients of the information.

3. Communication of Limitations of the Assessment:

a. Inform persons receiving test information that scores are not perfectly accurate and indicate the degree of inaccuracy in some way, such as by reporting score intervals.

b. Inform persons receiving test information of any circumstances that could have affected the validity or reliability of the results.

c. Inform persons receiving test information of any factors necessary to understand potential sources of bias for a given test result.

d. Communicate clearly that test data represent just one source of information and should rarely, if ever, be used alone for decision making.

4. Communication of Client Rights:

   a. Provide test takers or their parents or guardians with information about any rights they may have to obtain test copies and/or their completed answer sheets, to retake tests, to have tests rescored, or to cancel test scores.

   b. Inform test takers or their parents or guardians, about how long the test scores will remain on file along with the person to whom, and circumstances under which, they may be released.

   c. Describe the procedures test takers or their parents or guardians may use to register complaints or have problems resolved.

B. Decisions about Groups: Where standardized test data are being used to describe groups for the purpose of evaluation, the practitioner's responsibilities include:

   1. Background Information:

      a. Identify the purposes for which the reported data are appropriate.

      b. Include additional information (e.g., population characteristics) if it can improve accuracy of understanding.

   2. Averages and Norms:

      a. Clarify the amount of meaning that can be attached to differences between groups (e.g., statistical significance should not be taken as a judgment of importance).

      b. Qualify norms based on their appropriateness for the group being tested.

   3. Use obsolescence schedules so that stored data are systematically relocated to historic files or destroyed.

   4. Process data used for research or program evaluation to assure individual anonymity (e.g., released only in aggregated form).

5. Political Usage:

   a. Emphasize that test data should be used only for the test's stated purposes.

   b. Public release of test information provides data for many purposes. Take steps to minimize those which may be adverse to the interests of those tested.

6. Agency Policies:

   a. Advocate agency test-reporting policies designed to benefit the groups being measured.

   b. Advocate the establishment of procedures for periodic review of test use.

IX. EXTENSIONS OF THESE PRINCIPLES

This statement is intended to address current and emerging problems and concerns that are generic to all AACD divisions, branches, and regions by formulating principles that are specific enough to serve as a template for more closely focused statements addressed to specific situations. Individual divisions, branches, and regions are encouraged to elaborate upon this statement to reflect principles, procedures, and examples appropriate to their members.

This revision of the 1978 RUST Statement was prepared by a standing committee of AMECD chaired by William D. Schafer. Participating in the revision were Esther E. Diamond, Charles G. Eberly, Patricia B. Elmore, Jo-Ida C. Hansen, William A. Mehrens, Jane E. Myers, Larry Rawlins, and Alan G. Robertson.

Additional copies of the RUST Statement may be obtained from the American Counseling Association, 5999 Stevenson Avenue, Alexandria, VA 22304. Single copies are free.

Appendix F
ACA Code of Ethics
and Standards of Practice

New: Ethical Standards for Internet Online Counseling

- *ACA Code of Ethics*
- ACA Standards of Practice
- References
- *Policy And Procedures For Processing Complaints Of Ethical Violations*

ACA CODE OF ETHICS PREAMBLE

The American Counseling Association is an educational, scientific, and professional organization whose members are dedicated to the enhancement of human development throughout the life-span. Association members recognize diversity in our society and embrace a cross- cultural approach in support of the worth, dignity, potential, and uniqueness of each individual.

The specification of a code of ethics enables the association to clarify to current and future members, and to those served by members, the nature of the ethical responsibilities held in common by its members. As the code of ethics of the association, this document establishes principles that define the ethical behavior of association members. All members of the American Counseling Association are required to adhere to the Code of Ethics and the Standards of Practice. The Code of Ethics will serve as the basis for processing ethical complaints initiated against members of the association.

ACA CODE OF ETHICS

Section A: The Counseling Relationship

Section B: Confidentiality

Section C: Professional Responsibility

Section D: Relationships with Other Professionals

Section E: Evaluation, Assessment, and Interpretation

Section F: Teaching, Training, and Supervision

Section G: Research and Publication

Section H: Resolving Ethical Issues

Section A: The Counseling Relationship

A.1. Client Welfare

a. Primary Responsibility. The primary responsibility of counselors is to respect the dignity and to promote the welfare of clients.

b. Positive Growth and Development. Counselors encourage client growth and development in ways that foster the clients' interest and welfare; counselors avoid fostering dependent counseling relationships.

c. Counseling Plans. Counselors and their clients work jointly in devising integrated, individual counseling plans that offer reasonable promise of success and are consistent with abilities and circumstances of clients. Counselors and clients regularly review counseling plans to ensure their continued viability and effectiveness, respecting clients' freedom of choice. (See A.3.b.)

d. Family Involvement. Counselors recognize that families are usually important in clients' lives and strive to enlist family understanding and involvement as a positive resource, when appropriate.

e. Career and Employment Needs. Counselors work with their clients in considering employment in jobs and circumstances that are consistent with the clients' overall abilities, vocational limitations, physical restrictions, general temperament, interest and aptitude patterns, social skills, education, general qualifications, and other relevant characteristics and needs. Counselors neither place nor participate in placing clients in positions that will result in damaging the interest and the welfare of clients, employers, or the public.

A.2. Respecting Diversity

a. Nondiscrimination. Counselors do not condone or engage in discrimination based on age, color, culture, disability, ethnic group, gender, race, religion, sexual orientation, marital status, or socioeconomic status. (See C.5.a., C.5.b., and D.1.i.)

b. Respecting Differences. Counselors will actively attempt to understand the diverse cultural backgrounds of the clients with whom they work. This includes, but is not limited to, learning how the counselor's own cultural/ethnic/racial identity impacts her or his values and beliefs about the counseling process. (See E.8. and F.2.i.)

A.3. Client Rights

a. Disclosure to Clients. When counseling is initiated, and throughout the counseling process as necessary, counselors inform clients of the purposes, goals, techniques, procedures, limitations, potential risks, and benefits of services to be performed, and other pertinent information. Counselors take steps to ensure that clients understand the implications of diagnosis, the intended use of tests and reports, fees, and billing arrangements. Clients have the right to expect confidentiality and to be provided with an explanation of its limitations, including supervision and/or treatment team professionals; to obtain clear information about their case records; to participate in the ongoing counseling plans; and to refuse any recommended services and be advised of the consequences of such refusal. (See E.5.a. and G.2.)

b. Freedom of Choice. Counselors offer clients the freedom to choose whether to enter into a counseling relationship and to determine which professional(s) will provide counseling. Restrictions that limit choices of clients are fully explained. (See A.1.c.)

c. Inability to Give Consent. When counseling minors or persons unable to give voluntary informed consent, counselors act in these clients' best interests. (See B.3.)

A.4. Clients Served by Others

If a client is receiving services from another mental health professional, counselors, with client consent, inform the professional persons already involved and develop clear agreements to avoid confusion and conflict for the client. (See C.6.c.)

A.5. Personal Needs and Values

a. Personal Needs. In the counseling relationship, counselors are aware of the intimacy and responsibilities inherent in the counseling relationship, maintain respect for clients, and avoid actions that seek to meet their personal needs at the expense of clients.

b. Personal Values. Counselors are aware of their own values, attitudes, beliefs, and behaviors and how these apply in a diverse society, and avoid imposing their values on clients. (See C.5.a.)

A.6. Dual Relationships

a. Avoid When Possible. Counselors are aware of their influential positions with respect to clients, and they avoid exploiting the trust and dependency of clients. Counselors make every effort to avoid dual relationships with clients that could impair professional judgment or increase the risk of harm to clients. (Examples of such relationships include, but are not limited to, familial, social, financial, business, or close personal relationships with clients.) When a dual relationship cannot be avoided, counselors take appropriate professional precautions such as informed consent, consultation, supervision, and documentation to ensure that judgment is not impaired and no exploitation occurs. (See F.1.b.)

b. Superior/Subordinate Relationships. Counselors do not accept as clients superiors or subordinates with whom they have administrative, supervisory, or evaluative relationships.

A.7. Sexual Intimacies with Clients

a. Current Clients. Counselors do not have any type of sexual intimacies with clients and do not counsel persons with whom they have had a sexual relationship.

b. Former Clients. Counselors do not engage in sexual intimacies with former clients within a minimum of 2 years after terminating the counseling relationship. Counselors who engage in such relationship after 2 years following termination have the responsibility to examine and document thoroughly that such relations did not have an exploitative nature, based on factors such as duration of counseling, amount of time since counseling, termination circumstances, client's personal history and mental status, adverse impact on the client, and actions by the counselor suggesting a plan to initiate a sexual relationship with the client after termination.

A.8. Multiple Clients

When counselors agree to provide counseling services to two or more persons who have a relationship (such as husband and wife, or parents and children), counselors clarify at the outset which person or persons are clients and the nature of the relationships they will have with each involved person. If it becomes apparent that counselors may be called upon to perform potentially conflicting roles, they clarify, adjust, or withdraw from roles appropriately. (See B.2. and B.4.d.)

A.9. Group Work

a. Screening. Counselors screen prospective group counseling/therapy participants. To the extent possible, counselors select members whose needs and goals are compatible with goals of the group, who will not impede the group process, and whose well-being will not be jeopardized by the group experience.

b. Protecting Clients. In a group setting, counselors take reasonable precautions to protect clients from physical or psychological trauma.

A.10. Fees and Bartering (See D.3.a. and D.3.b.)

a. Advance Understanding. Counselors clearly explain to clients, prior to entering the counseling relationship, all financial arrangements related to professional services including the use of collection agencies or legal measures for nonpayment. (A.11.c.)

b. Establishing Fees. In establishing fees for professional counseling services, counselors consider the financial status of clients and locality. In the event that the established fee structure is inappropriate for a client, assistance is provided in attempting to find comparable services of acceptable cost. (See A.10.d., D.3.a., and D.3.b.)

c. Bartering Discouraged. Counselors ordinarily refrain from accepting goods or services from clients in return for counseling services because such arrangements create inherent potential for conflicts, exploitation, and distortion of the professional relationship. Counselors may participate in bartering only if the relationship is not exploitative, if the client requests it, if a clear written contract is established, and if such arrangements are an accepted practice among professionals in the community. (See A.6.a.)

d. Pro Bono Service. Counselors contribute to society by devoting a portion of their professional activity to services for which there is little or no financial return (pro bono).

A.11. Termination and Referral

a. Abandonment Prohibited. Counselors do not abandon or neglect clients in counseling. Counselors assist in making appropriate arrangements for the continuation of treatment, when necessary, during interruptions such as vacations, and following termination.

b. Inability to Assist Clients. If counselors determine an inability to be of professional assistance to clients, they avoid entering or immediately terminate a counseling relationship. Counselors are knowledgeable about referral resources and suggest appropriate alternatives. If clients decline the suggested referral, counselors should discontinue the relationship.

c. Appropriate Termination. Counselors terminate a counseling relationship, securing client agreement when possible, when it is reasonably clear that the client is no longer benefiting, when services are no longer required, when counseling no longer serves the client's needs or interests, when clients do not pay fees charged, or when agency or institution limits do not allow provision of further counseling services. (See A.10.b. and C.2.g.)

A.12. Computer Technology

a. Use of Computers. When computer applications are used in counseling services, counselors ensure that (1) the client is intellectually, emotionally, and physically capable of using the computer application; (2) the computer application is appropriate for the needs of the client; (3) the client understands the purpose and operation of the computer applications; and (4) a follow-up of client use of a computer application is provided to correct possible misconceptions, discover inappropriate use, and assess subsequent needs.

b. Explanation of Limitations. Counselors ensure that clients are provided information as a part of the counseling relationship that adequately explains the limitations of computer technology.

c. Access to Computer Applications. Counselors provide for equal access to computer applications in counseling services. (See A.2.a.)

Section B: Confidentiality

B.1. Right to Privacy

a. Respect for Privacy. Counselors respect their clients right to privacy and avoid illegal and unwarranted disclosures of confidential information. (See A.3.a. and B.6.a.)

b. Client Waiver. The right to privacy may be waived by the client or his or her legally recognized representative.

c. Exceptions. The general requirement that counselors keep information confidential does not apply when disclosure is required to prevent clear and imminent danger to the client or others or when legal requirements demand that confidential information be revealed. Counselors consult with other professionals when in doubt as to the validity of an exception.

d. Contagious, Fatal Diseases. A counselor who receives information confirming that a client has a disease commonly known to be both communicable and fatal is justified in disclosing information to an identifiable third party, who by his or her relationship with the client is at a high risk of contracting the disease. Prior to making a disclosure the counselor should ascertain that the client has not already informed the third party about his or her disease and that the client is not intending to inform the third party in the immediate future. (See B.1.c and B.1.f.)

e. Court-Ordered Disclosure. When court ordered to release confidential information without a client's permission, counselors request to the court that the disclosure not be required due to potential harm to the client or counseling relationship. (See B.1.c.)

f. Minimal Disclosure. When circumstances require the disclosure of confidential information, only essential information is revealed. To the extent possible, clients are informed before confidential information is disclosed.

g. Explanation of Limitations. When counseling is initiated and throughout the counseling process as necessary, counselors inform clients of the limitations of confidentiality and identify foreseeable situations in which confidentiality must be breached. (See G.2.a.)

h. Subordinates. Counselors make every effort to ensure that privacy and confidentiality of clients are maintained by subordinates including employees, supervisees, clerical assistants, and volunteers. (See B.1.a.)

i. Treatment Teams. If client treatment will involve a continued review by a treatment team, the client will be informed of the team's existence and composition.

B.2. Groups and Families

a. Group Work. In group work, counselors clearly define confidentiality and the parameters for the specific group being entered, explain its importance, and discuss the difficulties related to confidentiality involved in group work. The fact that confidentiality cannot be guaranteed is clearly communicated to group members.

b. Family Counseling. In family counseling, information about one family member cannot be disclosed to another member without permission. Counselors protect the privacy rights of each family member. (See A.8., B.3., and B.4.d.)

B.3. Minor or Incompetent Clients

When counseling clients who are minors or individuals who are unable to give voluntary, informed consent, parents or guardians may be included in the counseling process as appropriate. Counselors act in the best interests of clients and take measures to safeguard confidentiality. (See A.3.c.)

B.4. Records

a. Requirement of Records. Counselors maintain records necessary for rendering professional services to their clients and as required by laws, regulations, or agency or institution procedures.

b. Confidentiality of Records. Counselors are responsible for securing the safety and confidentiality of any counseling records they create, maintain, transfer, or destroy whether the records are written, taped, computerized, or stored in any other medium. (See B.1.a.)

c. Permission to Record or Observe. Counselors obtain permission from clients prior to electronically recording or observing sessions. (See A.3.a.)

d. Client Access. Counselors recognize that counseling records are kept for the benefit of clients, and therefore provide access to records and copies of records when requested by competent clients, unless the records contain information that may be misleading and detrimental to the client. In situations involving multiple clients, access to records is limited to those parts of records that do not include confidential information related to another client. (See A.8., B.1.a., and B.2.b.)

e. Disclosure or Transfer. Counselors obtain written permission from clients to disclose or transfer records to legitimate third parties unless exceptions to confidentiality exist as listed in Section B.1. Steps are taken to ensure that receivers of counseling records are sensitive to their confidential nature.

B.5. Research and Training

    a.   Data Disguise Required. Use of data derived from counseling relationships for purposes of training, research, or publication is confined to content that is disguised to ensure the anonymity of the individuals involved. (See B.1.g. and G.3.d.)

    b.   Agreement for Identification. Identification of a client in a presentation or publication is permissible only when the client has reviewed the material and has agreed to its presentation or publication. (See G.3.d.)

B.6. Consultation

    a.   Respect for Privacy. Information obtained in a consulting relationship is discussed for professional purposes only with persons clearly concerned with the case. Written and oral reports present data germane to the purposes of the consultation, and every effort is made to protect client identity and avoid undue invasion of privacy.

    b.   Cooperating Agencies. Before sharing information, counselors make efforts to ensure that there are defined policies in other agencies serving the counselor's clients that effectively protect the confidentiality of information.

Section C: Professional Responsibility

C.1. Standards Knowledge

Counselors have a responsibility to read, understand, and follow the Code of Ethics and the Standards of Practice.

C.2. Professional Competence

    a.   Boundaries of Competence. Counselors practice only within the boundaries of their competence, based on their education, training, supervised experience, state and national professional credentials, and appropriate professional experience. Counselors will demonstrate a commitment to gain knowledge, personal awareness, sensitivity, and skills pertinent to working with a diverse client population.

    b.   New Specialty Areas of Practice. Counselors practice in specialty areas new to them only after appropriate education, training, and supervised experience. While developing skills in new specialty areas, counselors take steps to ensure the competence of their work and to protect others from possible harm.

    c.   Qualified for Employment. Counselors accept employment only for positions for which they are qualified by education, training, supervised experience, state and national professional credentials, and appropriate professional experience. Counselors hire for professional counseling positions only individuals who are qualified and competent.

    d.   Monitor Effectiveness. Counselors continually monitor their effectiveness as professionals and take steps to improve when necessary. Counselors in private practice take reasonable steps to seek out peer supervision to evaluate their efficacy as counselors.

    e.   Ethical Issues Consultation. Counselors take reasonable steps to consult with other counselors or related professionals when they have questions regarding their ethical obligations or professional practice. (See H.1.)

    f.   Continuing Education. Counselors recognize the need for continuing education to maintain a reasonable level of awareness of current scientific and professional information in their fields of activity. They take steps to maintain competence in the skills they use, are open to new procedures, and keep current with the diverse and/or special populations with whom they work.

    g.   Impairment. Counselors refrain from offering or accepting professional services when their physical, mental, or emotional problems are likely to harm a client or others. They are alert to the signs of impairment, seek assistance for problems, and, if necessary, limit, suspend, or terminate their professional responsibilities. (See A.11.c.)

C.3. Advertising and Soliciting Clients

    a.   Accurate Advertising. There are no restrictions on advertising by counselors except those that can be specifically justified to protect the public from deceptive practices. Counselors advertise or represent their services to the public by identifying their credentials in an accurate manner that is not false, misleading, deceptive, or fraudulent. Counselors may only advertise the highest degree earned which is in counseling or a closely related field from a college or university that was accredited when the degree was awarded by one of the regional accrediting bodies recognized by the Council on Postsecondary Accreditation.

    b.   Testimonials. Counselors who use testimonials do not solicit them from clients or other persons who, because of their particular circumstances, may be vulnerable to undue influence.

c. Statements by Others. Counselors make reasonable efforts to ensure that statements made by others about them or the profession of counseling are accurate.

d. Recruiting Through Employment. Counselors do not use their places of employment or institutional affiliation to recruit or gain clients, supervisees, or consultees for their private practices. (See C.5.e.)

e. Products and Training Advertisements. Counselors who develop products related to their profession or conduct workshops or training events ensure that the advertisements concerning these products or events are accurate and disclose adequate information for consumers to make informed choices.

f. Promoting to Those Served. Counselors do not use counseling, teaching, training, or supervisory relationships to promote their products or training events in a manner that is deceptive or would exert undue influence on individuals who may be vulnerable. Counselors may adopt textbooks they have authored for instruction purposes.

g. Professional Association Involvement. Counselors actively participate in local, state, and national associations that foster the development and improvement of counseling.

C.4. Credentials

a. Credentials Claimed. Counselors claim or imply only professional credentials possessed and are responsible for correcting any known misrepresentations of their credentials by others. Professional credentials include graduate degrees in counseling or closely related mental health fields, accreditation of graduate programs, national voluntary certifications, government-issued certifications or licenses, ACA professional membership, or any other credential that might indicate to the public specialized knowledge or expertise in counseling.

b. ACA Professional Membership. ACA professional members may announce to the public their membership status. Regular members may not announce their ACA membership in a manner that might imply they are credentialed counselors.

c. Credential Guidelines. Counselors follow the guidelines for use of credentials that have been established by the entities that issue the credentials.

d. Misrepresentation of Credentials. Counselors do not attribute more to their credentials than the credentials represent, and do not imply that other counselors are not qualified because they do not possess certain credentials.

e. Doctoral Degrees from Other Fields. Counselors who hold a master's degree in counseling or a closely related mental health field, but hold a doctoral degree from other than counseling or a closely related field, do not use the title "Dr." in their practices and do not announce to the public in relation to their practice or status as a counselor that they hold a doctorate.

C.5. Public Responsibility

a. Nondiscrimination. Counselors do not discriminate against clients, students, or supervisees in a manner that has a negative impact based on their age, color, culture, disability, ethnic group, gender, race, religion, sexual orientation, or socioeconomic status, or for any other reason. (See A.2.a.)

b. Sexual Harassment. Counselors do not engage in sexual harassment. Sexual harassment is defined as sexual solicitation, physical advances, or verbal or nonverbal conduct that is sexual in nature, that occurs in connection with professional activities or roles, and that either (1) is unwelcome, is offensive, or creates a hostile workplace environment, and counselors know or are told this; or (2) is sufficiently severe or intense to be perceived as harassment to a reasonable person in the context. Sexual harassment can consist of a single intense or severe act or multiple persistent or pervasive acts.

c. Reports to Third Parties. Counselors are accurate, honest, and unbiased in reporting their professional activities and judgments to appropriate third parties including courts, health insurance companies, those who are the recipients of evaluation reports, and others. (See B.1.g.)

d. Media Presentations. When counselors provide advice or comment by means of public lectures, demonstrations, radio or television programs, prerecorded tapes, printed articles, mailed material, or other media, they take reasonable precautions to ensure that (1) the statements are based on appropriate professional counseling literature and practice; (2) the statements are otherwise consistent with the Code of Ethics and the Standards of Practice; and (3) the recipients of the information are not encouraged to infer that a professional counseling relationship has been established. (See C.6.b.)

e. Unjustified Gains. Counselors do not use their professional positions to seek or receive unjustified personal gains, sexual favors, unfair advantage, or unearned goods or services. (See C.3.d.)

C.6. Responsibility to Other Professionals

    a. Different Approaches. Counselors are respectful of approaches to professional counseling that differ from their own. Counselors know and take into account the traditions and practices of other professional groups with which they work.

    b. Personal Public Statements. When making personal statements in a public context, counselors clarify that they are speaking from their personal perspectives and that they are not speaking on behalf of all counselors or the profession. (See C.5.d.)

    c. Clients Served by Others. When counselors learn that their clients are in a professional relationship with another mental health professional, they request release from clients to inform the other professionals and strive to establish positive and collaborative professional relationships. (See A.4.)

Section D: Relationships with Other Professionals

D.1. Relationships with Employers and Employees

    a. Role Definition. Counselors define and describe for their employers and employees the parameters and levels of their professional roles.

    b. Agreements. Counselors establish working agreements with supervisors, colleagues, and subordinates regarding counseling or clinical relationships, confidentiality, adherence to professional standards, distinction between public and private material, maintenance and dissemination of recorded information, work load, and accountability. Working agreements in each instance are specified and made known to those concerned.

    c. Negative Conditions. Counselors alert their employers to conditions that may be potentially disruptive or damaging to the counselor's professional responsibilities or that may limit their effectiveness.

    d. Evaluation. Counselors submit regularly to professional review and evaluation by their supervisor or the appropriate representative of the employer.

    e. In-Service. Counselors are responsible for in-service development of self and staff.

    f. Goals. Counselors inform their staff of goals and programs.

    g. Practices. Counselors provide personnel and agency practices that respect and enhance the rights and welfare of each employee and recipient of agency services. Counselors strive to maintain the highest levels of professional services.

    h. Personnel Selection and Assignment. Counselors select competent staff and assign responsibilities compatible with their skills and experiences.

    i. Discrimination, Counselors, as either employers or employees, do not engage in or condone practices that are inhumane, illegal, or unjustifiable (such as considerations based on age, color, culture, disability, ethnic group, gender, race, religion, sexual orientation, or socioeconomic status) in hiring, promotion, or training. (See A.2.a. and C.5.b.)

    j. Professional Conduct. Counselors have a responsibility both to clients and to the agency or institution within which services are performed to maintain high standards of professional conduct.

    k. Exploitative Relationships. Counselors do not engage in exploitative relationships with individuals over whom they have supervisory, evaluative, or instructional control or authority. 1. Employer Policies. The acceptance of employment in an agency or institution implies that counselors are in agreement with its general policies and principles. Counselors strive to reach agreement with employers as to acceptable standards of conduct that allow for changes in institutional policy conducive to the growth and development of clients.

D.2. Consultation (See B.6.)

    a. Consultation as an Option. Counselors may choose to consult with any other professionally competent persons about their clients. In choosing consultants, counselors avoid placing the consultant in a conflict of interest situation that would preclude the consultant being a proper party to the counselor's efforts to help the client. Should counselors be engaged in a work setting that compromises this consultation standard, they consult with other professionals whenever possible to consider justifiable alternatives.

    b. Consultant Competency. Counselors are reasonably certain that they have or the organization represented has the necessary competencies and resources for giving the kind of consulting services needed and that appropriate referral resources are available.

    c. Understanding with Clients. When providing consultation, counselors attempt to develop with their clients a clear understanding of problem definition, goals for change, and predicted consequences of interventions selected.

    d. Consultant Goals. The consulting relationship is one in which client adaptability and growth toward self-direction are consistently encouraged and cultivated. (See A.1.b.)

D.3. Fees for Referral

    a. Accepting Fees from Agency Clients. Counselors refuse a private fee or other remuneration for rendering services to persons who are entitled to such services through the counselor's employing agency or institution. The policies of a particular agency may make explicit provisions for agency clients to receive counseling services from members of its staff in private practice. In such instances, the clients must be informed of other options open to them should they seek private counseling services. (See A.10.a., A.11.b., and C.3.d.)

    b. Referral Fees. Counselors do not accept a referral fee from other professionals.

D.4. Subcontractor Arrangements

When counselors work as subcontractors for counseling services for a third party, they have a duty to inform clients of the limitations of confidentiality that the organization may place on counselors in providing counseling services to clients. The limits of such confidentiality ordinarily are discussed as part of the intake session. (See B.1.e. and B.1.f.)

Section E: Evaluation, Assessment, and Interpretation

E.1. General

    a. Appraisal Techniques. The primary purpose of educational and psychological assessment is to provide measures that are objective and interpretable in either comparative or absolute terms. Counselors recognize the need to interpret the statements in this section as applying to the whole range of appraisal techniques, including test and nontest data.

    b. Client Welfare. Counselors promote the welfare and best interests of the client in the development, publication, and utilization of educational and psychological assessment techniques. They do not misuse assessment results and interpretations and take reasonable steps to prevent others from misusing the information these techniques provide. They respect the client's right to know the results, the interpretations made, and the bases for their conclusions and recommendations.

E.2. Competence to Use and Interpret Tests

    a. Limits of Competence. Counselors recognize the limits of their competence and perform only those testing and assessment services for which they have been trained. They are familiar with reliabil-

ity, validity, related standardization, error of measurement, and proper application of any technique utilized. Counselors using computer-based test interpretations are trained in the construct being measured and the specific instrument being used prior to using this type of computer application. Counselors take reasonable measures to ensure the proper use of psychological assessment techniques by persons under their supervision.

    b. Appropriate Use. Counselors are responsible for the appropriate application, scoring, interpretation, and use of assessment instruments, whether they score and interpret such tests themselves or use computerized or other services.

    c. Decisions Based on Results. Counselors responsible for decisions involving individuals or policies that are based on assessment results have a thorough understanding of educational and psychological measurement, including validation criteria, test research, and guidelines for test development and use.

    d. Accurate Information. Counselors provide accurate information and avoid false claims or misconceptions when making statements about assessment instruments or techniques. Special efforts are made to avoid unwarranted connotations of such terms as IQ and grade equivalent scores. (See C.5.c.)

E.3. Informed Consent

    a. Explanation to Clients. Prior to assessment, counselors explain the nature and purposes of assessment and the specific use of results in language the client (or other legally authorized person on behalf of the client) can understand, unless an explicit exception to this right has been agreed upon in advance. Regardless of whether scoring and interpretation are completed by counselors, by assistants, or by computer or other outside services, counselors take reasonable steps to ensure that appropriate explanations are given to the client.

    b. Recipients of Results. The examinee's welfare, explicit understanding, and prior agreement determine the recipients of test results. Counselors include accurate and appropriate interpretations with any release of individual or group test results. (See B.1.a. and C.5.c.)

E.4. Release of Information to Competent Professionals

    a. Misuse of Results. Counselors do not misuse assessment results, including test results, and interpretations, and take reasonable steps to prevent the misuse of such by others. (See C.5.c.)

b. Release of Raw Data. Counselors ordinarily release data (e.g., protocols, counseling or interview notes, or questionnaires) in which the client is identified only with the consent of the client or the client's legal representative. Such data are usually released only to persons recognized by counselors as competent to interpret the data. (See B.1.a.)

E.5. Proper Diagnosis of Mental Disorders

a. Proper Diagnosis. Counselors take special care to provide proper diagnosis of mental disorders. Assessment techniques (including personal interview) used to determine client care (e.g., locus of treatment, type of treatment, or recommended follow-up) are carefully selected and appropriately used. (See A.3.a. and C.5.c.)

b. Cultural Sensitivity. Counselors recognize that culture affects the manner in which clients' problems are defined. Clients' socioeconomic and cultural experience is considered when diagnosing mental disorders.

E.6. Test Selection

a. Appropriateness of Instruments. Counselors carefully consider the validity, reliability, psychometric limitations, and appropriateness of instruments when selecting tests for use in a given situation or with a particular client.

b. Culturally Diverse Populations. Counselors are cautious when selecting tests for culturally diverse populations to avoid inappropriateness of testing that may be outside of socialized behavioral or cognitive patterns.

E.7. Conditions of Test Administration

a. Administration Conditions. Counselors administer tests under the same conditions that were established in their standardization. When tests are not administered under standard conditions or when unusual behavior or irregularities occur during the testing session, those conditions are noted in interpretation, and the results may be designated as invalid or of questionable validity.

b. Computer Administration. Counselors are responsible for ensuring that administration programs function properly to provide clients with accurate results when a computer or other electronic methods are used for test administration. (See A.12.b.)

c. Unsupervised Test Taking. Counselors do not permit unsupervised or inadequately supervised use of tests or assessments unless the tests or assessments are designed, intended, and validated for self-administration and/or scoring.

d. Disclosure of Favorable Conditions. Prior to test administration, conditions that produce most favorable test results are made known to the examinee.

E.8. Diversity in Testing

Counselors are cautious in using assessment techniques, making evaluations, and interpreting the performance of populations not represented in the norm group on which an instrument was standardized. They recognize the effects of age, color, culture, disability, ethnic group, gender, race, religion, sexual orientation, and socioeconomic status on test administration and interpretation and place test results in proper perspective with other relevant factors. (See A.2.a.)

E.9. Test Scoring and Interpretation

a. Reporting Reservations. In reporting assessment results, counselors indicate any reservations that exist regarding validity or reliability because of the circumstances of the assessment or the inappropriateness of the norms for the person tested.

b. Research Instruments. Counselors exercise caution when interpreting the results of research instruments possessing insufficient technical data to support respondent results. The specific purposes for the use of such instruments are stated explicitly to the examinee.

c. Testing Services. Counselors who provide test scoring and test interpretation services to support the assessment process confirm the validity of such interpretations. They accurately describe the purpose, norms, validity, reliability, and applications of the procedures and any special qualifications applicable to their use. The public offering of an automated test interpretations service is considered a professional-to-professional consultation. The formal responsibility of the consultant is to the consultee, but the ultimate and overriding responsibility is to the client.

E.10. Test Security

Counselors maintain the integrity and security of tests and other assessment techniques consistent with legal and contractual obligations. Counselors do not appropriate, reproduce, or modify published tests or parts thereof without acknowledgment and permission from the publisher.

E.11. Obsolete Tests and Outdated Test Results

Counselors do not use data or test results that are obsolete or outdated for the current purpose. Counselors make every effort to prevent the misuse of obsolete measures and test data by others.

E.12. Test Construction

Counselors use established scientific procedures, relevant standards, and current professional knowledge for test design in the development, publication, and utilization of educational and psychological assessment techniques.

Section F: Teaching, Training, and Supervision

F.1. Counselor Educators and Trainers

a. Educators as Teachers and Practitioners. Counselors who are responsible for developing, implementing, and supervising educational programs are skilled as teachers and practitioners. They are knowledgeable regarding the ethical, legal, and regulatory aspects of the profession, are skilled in applying that knowledge, and make students and supervisees aware of their responsibilities. Counselors conduct counselor education and training programs in an ethical manner and serve as role models for professional behavior. Counselor educators should make an effort to infuse material related to human diversity into all courses and/or workshops that are designed to promote the development of professional counselors.

b. Relationship Boundaries With Students and Supervisees. Counselors clearly define and maintain ethical, professional, and social relationship boundaries with their students and supervisees. They are aware of the differential in power that exists and the student's or supervisee's possible incomprehension of that power differential. Counselors explain to students and supervisees the potential for the relationship to become exploitive.

c. Sexual Relationships. Counselors do not engage in sexual relationships with students or supervisees and do not subject them to sexual harassment. (See A.6. and C.5.b)

d. Contributions to Research. Counselors give credit to students or supervisees for their contributions to research and scholarly projects. Credit is given through coauthorship, acknowledgment, footnote statement, or other appropriate means, in accordance with such contributions. (See G.4.b. and G.4.c.)

e. Close Relatives. Counselors do not accept close relatives as students or supervisees.

f. Supervision Preparation. Counselors who offer clinical supervision services are adequately prepared in supervision methods and techniques. Counselors who are doctoral students serving as practicum or internship supervisors to master's level students are adequately prepared and supervised by the training program.

g. Responsibility for Services to Clients. Counselors who supervise the counseling services of others take reasonable measures to ensure that counseling services provided to clients are professional.

h. Endorsement. Counselors do not endorse students or supervisees for certification, licensure, employment, or completion of an academic or training program if they believe students or supervisees are not qualified for the endorsement. Counselors take reasonable steps to assist students or supervisees who are not qualified for endorsement to become qualified.

F.2. Counselor Education and Training Programs

a. Orientation. Prior to admission, counselors orient prospective students to the counselor education or training program's expectations, including but not limited to the following: (1) the type and level of skill acquisition required for successful completion of the training, (2) subject matter to be covered, (3) basis for evaluation, (4) training components that encourage self-growth or self-disclosure as part of the training process, (5) the type of supervision settings and requirements of the sites for required clinical field experiences, (6) student and supervisee evaluation and dismissal policies and procedures, and (7) up-to-date employment prospects for graduates.

b. Integration of Study and Practice. Counselors establish counselor education and training programs that integrate academic study and supervised practice.

c. Evaluation. Counselors clearly state to students and supervisees, in advance of training, the levels of competency expected, appraisal methods, and timing of evaluations for both didactic and experiential components. Counselors provide students and supervisees with periodic performance appraisal and evaluation feedback throughout the training program.

d. Teaching Ethics. Counselors make students and supervisees aware of the ethical responsibilities and standards of the profession and the students' and supervisees' ethical responsibilities to the profession. (See C.1. and F.3.e.)

e. Peer Relationships. When students or supervisees are assigned to lead counseling groups or provide clinical supervision for their peers, counselors take steps to ensure that students and supervisees placed in these roles do not have personal or adverse relationships with peers and that they understand they have the same ethical obligations as counselor educators, trainers, and supervisors. Counselors make every effort to ensure that the rights of peers are not compromised when students or supervisees are assigned to lead counseling groups or provide clinical supervision.

f. Varied Theoretical Positions. Counselors present varied theoretical positions so that students and supervisees may make comparisons and have opportunities to develop their own positions. Counselors provide information concerning the scientific bases of professional practice. (See C.6.a.)

g. Field Placements. Counselors develop clear policies within their training program regarding field placement and other clinical experiences. Counselors provide clearly stated roles and responsibilities for the student or supervisee, the site supervisor, and the program supervisor. They confirm that site supervisors are qualified to provide supervision and are informed of their professional and ethical responsibilities in this role.

h. Dual Relationships as Supervisors. Counselors avoid dual relationships such as performing the role of site supervisor and training program supervisor in the student's or supervisee's training program. Counselors do not accept any form of professional services, fees, commissions, reimbursement, or remuneration from a site for student or supervisee placement.

i. Diversity in Programs. Counselors are responsive to their institution's and program's recruitment and retention needs for training program administrators, faculty, and students with diverse backgrounds and special needs. (See A.2.a.)

F.3. Students and Supervisees

a. Limitations. Counselors, through ongoing evaluation and appraisal, are aware of the academic and personal limitations of students and supervisees that might impede performance. Counselors assist students and supervisees in securing remedial assistance when needed, and dismiss from the training program supervisees who are unable to provide competent service due to academic or personal limitations. Counselors seek professional consultation

and document their decision to dismiss or refer students or supervisees for assistance. Counselors ensure that students and supervisees have recourse to address decisions made to require them to seek assistance or to dismiss them.

b. Self-Growth Experiences. Counselors use professional judgment when designing training experiences conducted by the counselors themselves that require student and supervisee self-growth or self-disclosure. Safeguards are provided so that students and supervisees are aware of the ramifications their self-disclosure may have on counselors whose primary role as teacher, trainer, or supervisor requires acting on ethical obligations to the profession. Evaluative components of experiential training experiences explicitly delineate predetermined academic standards that are separate and do not depend on the student's level of self-disclosure. (See A.6.)

c. Counseling for Students and Supervisees. If students or supervisees request counseling, supervisors or counselor educators provide them with acceptable referrals. Supervisors or counselor educators do not serve as counselor to students or supervisees over whom they hold administrative, teaching, or evaluative roles unless this is a brief role associated with a training experience. (See A.6.b.)

d. Clients of Students and Supervisees. Counselors make every effort to ensure that the clients at field placements are aware of the services rendered and the qualifications of the students and supervisees rendering those services. Clients receive professional disclosure information and are informed of the limits of confidentiality. Client permission is obtained in order for the students and supervisees to use any information concerning the counseling relationship in the training process. (See B.1.e.)

e. Standards for Students and Supervisees. Students and supervisees preparing to become counselors adhere to the Code of Ethics and the Standards of Practice. Students and supervisees have the same obligations to clients as those required of counselors. (See H.1.)

Section G: Research and Publication

G.1. Research Responsibilities

a. Use of Human Subjects. Counselors plan, design, conduct, and report research in a manner consistent with pertinent ethical principles, federal and state laws, host institutional regulations, and scientific standards governing research with human subjects. Counselors design and conduct research that reflects cultural sensitivity appropriateness.

b. Deviation From Standard Practices. Counselors seek consultation and observe stringent safeguards to protect the rights of research participants when a research problem suggests a deviation from standard acceptable practices. (See B.6.)

c. Precautions to Avoid Injury. Counselors who conduct research with human subjects are responsible for the subjects' welfare throughout the experiment and take reasonable precautions to avoid causing injurious psychological, physical, or social effects to their subjects.

d. Principal Researcher Responsibility. The ultimate responsibility for ethical research practice lies with the principal researcher. All others involved in the research activities share ethical obligations and full responsibility for their own actions.

e. Minimal Interference. Counselors take reasonable precautions to avoid causing disruptions in subjects' lives due to participation in research.

f. Diversity. Counselors are sensitive to diversity and research issues with special populations. They seek consultation when appropriate. (See A.2.a. and B.6.)

G.2. Informed Consent

a. Topics Disclosed. In obtaining informed consent for research, counselors use language that is understandable to research participants and that (1) accurately explains the purpose and procedures to be followed; (2) identifies any procedures that are experimental or relatively untried; (3) describes the attendant discomforts and risks; (4) describes the benefits or changes in individuals or organizations that might be reasonably expected; (5) discloses appropriate alternative procedures that would be advantageous for subjects; (6) offers to answer any inquiries concerning the procedures; (7) describes any limitations on confidentiality; and (8) instructs that subjects are free to withdraw their consent and to discontinue participation in the project at any time. (See B.1.f.)

b. Deception. Counselors do not conduct research involving deception unless alternative procedures are not feasible and the prospective value of the research justifies the deception. When the methodological requirements of a study necessitate concealment or deception, the investigator is required to explain clearly the reasons for this action as soon as possible.

c. Voluntary Participation. Participation in research is typically voluntary and without any penalty for refusal to participate. Involuntary participation is appropriate only when it can be demonstrated that participation will have no harmful effects on subjects and is essential to the investigation.

d. Confidentiality of Information. Information obtained about research participants during the course of an investigation is confidential. When the possibility exists that others may obtain access to such information, ethical research practice requires that the possibility, together with the plans for protecting confidentiality, be explained to participants as a part of the procedure for obtaining informed consent. (See B.1.e.)

e. Persons Incapable of Giving Informed Consent. When a person is incapable of giving informed consent, counselors provide an appropriate explanation, obtain agreement for participation, and obtain appropriate consent from a legally authorized person.

f. Commitments to Participants. Counselors take reasonable measures to honor all commitments to research participants.

g. Explanations after Data Collection. After data are collected, counselors provide participants with full clarification of the nature of the study to remove any misconceptions. Where scientific or human values justify delaying or withholding information, counselors take reasonable measures to avoid causing harm.

h. Agreements to Cooperate. Counselors who agree to cooperate with another individual in research or publication incur an obligation to cooperate as promised in terms of punctuality of performance and with regard to the completeness and accuracy of the information required.

i. Informed Consent for Sponsors. In the pursuit of research, counselors give sponsors, institutions, and publication channels the same respect and opportunity for giving informed consent that they accord to individual research participants. Counselors are aware of their obligation to future research workers and ensure that host institutions are given feedback information and proper acknowledgment.

G.3. Reporting Results

a. Information Affecting Outcome. When reporting research results, counselors explicitly mention all variables and conditions known to the investigator that may have affected the outcome of a study or the interpretation of data.

b. Accurate Results. Counselors plan, conduct, and report research accurately and in a manner that minimizes the possibility that results will be misleading. They provide thorough discussions of the limitations of their data and alternative hypotheses. Counselors do not engage in fraudulent research, distort data, misrepresent data, or deliberately bias their results.

c. Obligation to Report Unfavorable Results. Counselors communicate to other counselors the results of any research judged to be of professional value. Results that reflect unfavorably on institutions, programs, services, prevailing opinions, or vested interests are not withheld.

d. Identity of Subjects. Counselors who supply data, aid in the research of another person, report research results, or make original data available take due care to disguise the identity of respective subjects in the absence of specific authorization from the subjects to do otherwise. (See B.1.g. and B.5.a.)

e. Replication Studies. Counselors are obligated to make available sufficient original research data to qualified professionals who may wish to replicate the study.

G.4. Publication

a. Recognition of Others. When conducting and reporting research, counselors are familiar with and give recognition to previous work on the topic, observe copyright laws, and give full credit to those to whom credit is due. (See F.1.d. and G.4.c.)

b. Contributors. Counselors give credit through joint authorship, acknowledgment, footnote statements, or other appropriate means to those who have contributed significantly to research or concept development in accordance with such contributions. The principal contributor is listed first and minor technical or professional contributions are acknowledged in notes or introductory statements.

c. Student Research. For an article that is substantially based on a student's dissertation or thesis, the student is listed as the principal author. (See F.1.d. and G.4.a.)

d. Duplicate Submission. Counselors submit manuscripts for consideration to only one journal at a time. Manuscripts that are published in whole or in substantial part in another journal or published work are not submitted for publication without acknowledgment and permission from the previous publication.

e. Professional Review. Counselors who review material submitted for publication, research, or other scholarly purposes respect the confidentiality and proprietary rights of those who submitted it.

Section H: Resolving Ethical Issues

H.1. Knowledge of Standards

Counselors are familiar with the Code of Ethics and the Standards of Practice and other applicable ethics codes from other professional organizations of which they are members, or from certification and licensure bodies. Lack of knowledge or misunderstanding of an ethical responsibility is not a defense against a charge of unethical conduct. (See F.3.e.)

H.2. Suspected Violations

a. Ethical Behavior Expected. Counselors expect professional associates to adhere to the Code of Ethics. When counselors possess reasonable cause that raises doubts as to whether a counselor is acting in an ethical manner, they take appropriate action. (See H.2.d. and H.2.e.)

b. Consultation. When uncertain as to whether a particular situation or course of action may be in violation of the Code of Ethics, counselors consult with other counselors who are knowledgeable about ethics, with colleagues, or with appropriate authorities.

c. Organization Conflicts. If the demands of an organization with which counselors are affiliated pose a conflict with the Code of Ethics, counselors specify the nature of such conflicts and express to their supervisors or other responsible officials their commitment to the Code of Ethics. When possible, counselors work toward change within the organization to allow full adherence to the Code of Ethics.

d. Informal Resolution. When counselors have reasonable cause to believe that another counselor is violating an ethical standard, they attempt to first resolve the issue informally with the other counselor if feasible, providing that such action does not violate confidentiality rights that may be involved.

e. Reporting Suspected Violations. When an informal resolution is not appropriate or feasible, counselors, upon reasonable cause, take action such as reporting the suspected ethical violation to state or national ethics committees, unless this action conflicts with confidentiality rights that cannot be resolved.

f. Unwarranted Complaints. Counselors do not initiate, participate in, or encourage the filing of ethics complaints that are unwarranted or intend to harm a counselor rather than to protect clients or the public.

H.3. Cooperation with Ethics Committees

Counselors assist in the process of enforcing the Code of Ethics. Counselors cooperate with investigations, proceedings, and requirements of the ACA Ethics Committee or ethics committees of other duly constituted associations or boards having jurisdiction over those charged with a violation. Counselors are familiar with the ACA Policies and Procedures and use it as a reference in assisting the enforcement of the Code of Ethics.

ACA STANDARDS OF PRACTICE

All members of the American Counseling Association (ACA) are required to adhere to the Standards of Practice and the Code of Ethics. The Standards of Practice represent minimal behavioral statements of the Code of Ethics. Members should refer to the applicable section of the Code of Ethics for further interpretation and amplification of the applicable Standard of Practice.

Section A: The Counseling Relationship

Section B: Confidentiality

Section C: Professional Responsibility

Section D: Relationship With Other Professionals

Section E: Evaluation, Assessment and Interpretation

Section F: Teaching, Training, and Supervision

Section G: Research and Publication

Section H: Resolving Ethical Issues

Section A: The Counseling Relationship

Standard of Practice One (SP-1): Nondiscrimination. Counselors respect diversity and must not discriminate against clients because of age, color, culture, disability, ethnic group, gender, race, religion, sexual orientation, marital status, or socioeconomic status. (See A.2.a.)

Standard of Practice Two (SP-2): Disclosure to Clients. Counselors must adequately inform clients, preferably in writing, regarding the counseling process and counseling relationship at or before the time it begins and throughout the relationship. (See A.3.a.)

Standard of Practice Three (SP-3): Dual Relationships. Counselors must make every effort to avoid dual relationships with clients that could impair their professional judgment or increase the risk of harm to clients. When a dual relationship cannot be avoided, counselors must take appropriate steps to ensure that judgment is not impaired and that no exploitation occurs. (See A.6.a. and A.6.b.)

Standard of Practice Four (SP-4): Sexual Intimacies with Clients. Counselors must not engage in any type of sexual intimacies with current clients and must not engage in sexual intimacies with former clients within a minimum of 2 years after terminating the counseling relationship. Counselors who engage in such relationship after 2 years following termination have the responsibility to examine and document thoroughly that such relations did not have an exploitative nature. (See A.7.b.)

Standard of Practice Five (SP-5): Protecting Clients During Group Work. Counselors must take steps to protect clients from physical or psychological trauma resulting from interactions during group work. (See A.9.b.)

Standard of Practice Six (SP-6): Advance Understanding of Fees. Counselors must explain to clients, prior to their entering the counseling relationship, financial arrangements related to professional services. (See A.10. a.-d. and A.11.c.)

Standard of Practice Seven (SP-7): Termination. Counselors must assist in making appropriate arrangements for the continuation of treatment of clients, when necessary, following termination of counseling relationships. (See A.11.a.)

Standard of Practice Eight (SP-8): Inability to Assist Clients. Counselors must avoid entering or immediately terminate a counseling relationship if it is determined that they are unable to be of professional assistance to a client. The counselor may assist in making an appropriate referral for the client. (See A.11.b.)

Section B: Confidentiality

Standard of Practice Nine (SP-9): Confidentiality Requirement. Counselors must keep information related to counseling services confidential unless disclosure is in the best interest of clients, is required for the welfare of others, or is required by law. When disclosure is required, only information that is essential is revealed and the client is informed of such disclosure. (See B.1. a.+f.)

Standard of Practice Ten (SP-10): Confidentiality Requirements for Subordinates. Counselors must take measures to ensure that privacy and confidentiality of clients are maintained by subordinates. (See B.1.h.)

Standard of Practice Eleven (SP-11): Confidentiality in Group Work. Counselors must clearly communicate to group members that confidentiality cannot be guaranteed in group work. (See B.2.a.)

Standard of Practice Twelve (SP-12): Confidentiality in Family Counseling. Counselors must not disclose information about one family member in counseling to another family member without prior consent. (See B.2.b.)

Standard of Practice Thirteen (SP-13): Confidentiality of Records. Counselors must maintain appropriate confidentiality in creating, storing, accessing, transferring, and disposing of counseling records. (See B.4.b.)

Standard of Practice Fourteen (SP-14): Permission to Record or Observe. Counselors must obtain prior consent from clients in order to record electronically or observe sessions. (See B.4.c.)

Standard of Practice Fifteen (SP-15): Disclosure or Transfer of Records. Counselors must obtain client consent to disclose or transfer records to third parties, unless exceptions listed in SP-9 exist. (See B.4.e.)

Standard of Practice Sixteen (SP-16): Data Disguise Required. Counselors must disguise the identity of the client when using data for training, research, or publication. (See B.5.a.)

Section C: Professional Responsibility

Standard of Practice Seventeen (SP-17): Boundaries of Competence. Counselors must practice only within the boundaries of their competence. (See C.2.a.)

Standard of Practice Eighteen (SP-18): Continuing Education. Counselors must engage in continuing education to maintain their professional competence. (See C.2.f.)

Standard of Practice Nineteen (SP-19): Impairment of Professionals. Counselors must refrain from offering professional services when their personal problems or conflicts may cause harm to a client or others. (See C.2.g.)

Standard of Practice Twenty (SP-20): Accurate Advertising. Counselors must accurately represent their credentials and services when advertising. (See C.3.a.)

Standard of Practice Twenty-One (SP-21): Recruiting Through Employment. Counselors must not use their place of employment or institutional affiliation to recruit clients for their private practices. (See C.3.d.)

Standard of Practice Twenty-Two (SP-22): Credentials Claimed. Counselors must claim or imply only professional credentials possessed and must correct any known misrepresentations of their credentials by others. (See C.4.a.)

Standard of Practice Twenty-Three (SP-23): Sexual Harassment. Counselors must not engage in sexual harassment. (See C.5.b.)

Standard of Practice Twenty-Four (SP-24): Unjustified Gains. Counselors must not use their professional positions to seek or receive unjustified personal gains, sexual favors, unfair advantage, or unearned goods or services. (See C.5.e.)

Standard of Practice Twenty-Five (SP-25): Clients Served by Others. With the consent of the client, counselors must inform other mental health professionals serving the same client that a counseling relationship between the counselor and client exists. (See C.6.c.)

Standard of Practice Twenty-Six (SP-26): Negative Employment Conditions. Counselors must alert their employers to institutional policy or conditions that may be potentially disruptive or damaging to the counselor's professional responsibilities, or that may limit their effectiveness or deny clients' rights. (See D.1.c.)

Standard of Practice Twenty-Seven (SP-27): Personnel Selection and Assignment. Counselors must select competent staff and must assign responsibilities compatible with staff skills and experiences. (See D.1.h.)

Standard of Practice Twenty-Eight (SP-28): Exploitative Relationships With Subordinates. Counselors must not engage in exploitative relationships with individuals over whom they have supervisory, evaluative, or instructional control or authority. (See D.1.k.)

Section D: Relationship With Other Professionals

Standard of Practice Twenty-Nine (SP-29): Accepting Fees From Agency Clients. Counselors must not accept fees or other remuneration for consultation with persons entitled to such services through the counselor's employing agency or institution. (See D.3.a.)

Standard of Practice Thirty (SP-30): Referral Fees. Counselors must not accept referral fees. (See D.3.b.)

Section E: Evaluation, Assessment and Interpretation

Standard of Practice Thirty-One (SP-31): Limits of Competence. Counselors must perform only testing and assessment services for which they are competent. Counselors must not allow the use of psychological assessment techniques by unqualified persons under their supervision. (See E.2.a.)

Standard of Practice Thirty-Two (SP-32): Appropriate Use of Assessment Instruments. Counselors must use assessment instruments in the manner for which they were intended. (See E.2.b.)

Standard of Practice Thirty-Three (SP-33): Assessment Explanations to Clients. Counselors must provide explanations to clients prior to assessment about the nature and purposes of assessment and the specific uses of results. (See E.3.a.)

Standard of Practice Thirty-Four (SP-34): Recipients of Test Results. Counselors must ensure that accurate and appropriate interpretations accompany any release of testing and assessment information. (See E.3.b.)

Standard of Practice Thirty-Five (SP-35): Obsolete Tests and Outdated Test Results. Counselors must not base their assessment or intervention decisions or recommendations on data or test results that are obsolete or outdated for the current purpose. (See E.11.)

Section F: Teaching, Training, and Supervision

Standard of Practice Thirty-Six (SP-36): Sexual Relationships with Students or Supervisees. Counselors must not engage in sexual relationships with their students and supervisees. (See F.1.c.)

Standard of Practice Thirty-Seven (SP-37): Credit for Contributions to Research. Counselors must give credit to students or supervisees for their contributions to research and scholarly projects. (See F.1.d.)

Standard of Practice Thirty-Eight (SP-38): Supervision Preparation. Counselors who offer clinical supervision services must be trained and prepared in supervision methods and techniques. (See F.1.f.)

Standard of Practice Thirty-Nine (SP-39): Evaluation Information. Counselors must clearly state to students and supervisees in advance of training the levels of competency expected, appraisal methods, and timing of evaluations. Counselors must provide students and supervisees with periodic performance appraisal and evaluation feedback throughout the training program. (See F.2.c.)

Standard of Practice Forty (SP-40): Peer Relationships in Training. Counselors must make every effort to ensure that the rights of peers are not violated when students and supervisees are assigned to lead counseling groups or provide clinical supervision. (See F.2.e.)

Standard of Practice Forty-One (SP-41): Limitations of Students and Supervisees. Counselors must assist students and supervisees in securing remedial assistance, when needed, and must dismiss from the training program students and supervisees who are unable to provide competent service due to academic or personal limitations. (See F.3.a.)

Standard of Practice Forty-Two (SP-42): Self-Growth Experiences. Counselors who conduct experiences for students or supervisees that include self-growth or self-disclosure must inform participants of counselors' ethical obligations to the profession and must not grade participants based on their nonacademic performance. (See F.3.b.)

Standard of Practice Forty-Three (SP-43): Standards for Students and Supervisees. Students and supervisees preparing to become counselors must adhere to the Code of Ethics and the Standards of Practice of counselors. (See F.3.e.)

Section G: Research and Publication

Standard of Practice Forty-Four (SP-44): Precautions to Avoid Injury in Research. Counselors must avoid causing physical, social, or psychological harm or injury to subjects in research. (See G.1.c.)

Standard of Practice Forty-Five (SP-45): Confidentiality of Research Information. Counselors must keep confidential information obtained about research participants. (See G.2.d.)

Standard of Practice Forty-Six (SP-46): Information Affecting Research Outcome. Counselors must report all variables and conditions known to the investigator that may have affected research data or outcomes. (See G.3.a.)

Standard of Practice Forty-Seven (SP-47): Accurate Research Results. Counselors must not distort or misrepresent research data, nor fabricate or intentionally bias research results. (See G.3.b.)

Standard of Practice Forty-Eight (SP-48): Publication Contributors. Counselors must give appropriate credit to those who have contributed to research. (See G.4.a. and G.4.b.)

Section H: Resolving Ethical Issues

Standard of Practice Forty-Nine (SP-49): Ethical Behavior Expected. Counselors must take appropriate action when they possess reasonable cause that raises doubts as to whether counselors or other mental health professionals are acting in an ethical manner. (See H.2.a.)

Standard of Practice Fifty (SP-50): Unwarranted Complaints. Counselors must not initiate, participate in, or encourage the filing of ethics complaints that are unwarranted or intended to harm a mental health professional rather than to protect clients or the public. (See H.2.f.)

Standard of Practice Fifty-One (SP-51): Cooperation with Ethics Committees. Counselors must cooperate with investigations, proceedings, and requirements of the ACA Ethics Committee or ethics committees of other duly constituted associations or boards having jurisdiction over those charged with a violation. (See H.3.)

REFERENCES

The following documents are available to counselors as resources to guide them in their practices. These resources are not a part of the Code of Ethics and the Standards of Practice.

American Association for Counseling and Development/Association for Measurement and Evaluation in Counseling and Development. (1989). The responsibilities of users of standardized tests (rev.). Washington, DC: Author.

American Counseling Association. (1988) (Note: This is ACA's previous edition of its ethics code). Ethical standards. Alexandria, VA: Author.

American Psychological Association. (1985). Standards for educational and psychological testing (rev.). Washington, DC: Author.

Joint Committee on Testing Practices. (1988). Code of fair testing practices in education. Washington, DC: Author.

National Board for Certified Counselors. (1989). National Board for Certified Counselors code of ethics. Alexandria, VA: Author.

Prediger, D. J. (Ed.). (1993, March). Multicultural assessment standards. Alexandria, VA: Association for Assessment in Counseling.

Appendix G
American Psychological Association Ethical Principles of Psychologists and Code of Conduct

CONTENTS

INTRODUCTION

PREAMBLE

GENERAL PRINCIPLES

Principle A: Competence
Principle B: Integrity
Principle C: Professional and Scientific Responsibility
Principle D: Respect for People's Rights and Dignity
Principle E: Concern for Others' Welfare
Principle F: Social Responsibility

ETHICAL STANDARDS

1.   General Standards

1.01   Applicability of the Ethics Code
1.02   Relationship of Ethics and Law
1.03   Professional and Scientific Relationship
1.04   Boundaries of Competence
1.05   Maintaining Expertise
1.06   Basis for Scientific and Professional Judgments
1.07   Describing the Nature and Results of Psychological Services
1.08   Human Differences
1.09   Respecting Others
1.10   Nondiscrimination
1.11   Sexual Harassment
1.12   Other Harassment
1.13   Personal Problems and Conflicts
1.14   Avoiding Harm
1.15   Misuse of Psychologists' Influence
1.16   Misuse of Psychologists' Work
1.17   Multiple Relationships
1.18   Barter (with Patients or Clients)
1.19   Exploitative Relationships
1.20   Consultations and Referrals
1.21   Third-Party Requests for Services
1.22   Delegation to and Supervision of Subordinates
1.23   Documentation of Professional and Scientific Work
1.24   Records and Data
1.25   Fees and Financial Arrangements
1.26   Accuracy in Reports to Payors and Funding Sources
1.27   Referrals and Fees

2.   Evaluation, Assessment, or Intervention

2.01   Evaluation, Diagnosis, and Interventions in Professional Context
2.02   Competence and Appropriate Use of Assessments and Interventions
2.03   Test Construction
2.04   Use of Assessment in General and with Special Populations
2.05   Interpreting Assessment Results
2.06   Unqualified Persons
2.07   Obsolete Tests and Outdated Test Results
2.08   Test Scoring and Interpretation Services
2.09   Explaining Assessment Results
2.10   Maintaining Test Security

Source: From American Psychological Association (1992), *Ethical Principles of Psychologists and Code of Conduct.* Copyright © 1992 by the American Psychological Association. Reprinted by permission.

INTRODUCTION

The American Psychological Association's (APA's) Ethical Principles of Psychologists and Code of Conduct (hereinafter referred to as the Ethics Code) consists of an Introduction, a Preamble, six General Principles (A–F), and specific Ethical Standards. The Introduction discusses the intent, organization, procedural considerations, and scope of application of the Ethics Code. The Preamble and General Principles are *aspirational* goals to guide psychologists toward the highest ideals of psychology. Although the Preamble and General Principles are not themselves enforceable rules, they should be considered by psychologists in arriving at an ethical course of action and may be considered by ethics bodies in interpreting the Ethical Standards. The Ethical Standards set forth *enforceable* rules for conduct as psychologists. Most of the Ethical Standards are written broadly, in order to apply to psychologists in varied roles, although the application of an Ethical Standard may vary depending on the context. The Ethical Standards are not exhaustive. The fact that a given conduct is not specifically addressed by the Ethics Code does not mean that it is necessarily either ethical or unethical.

Membership in the APA commits members to adhere to the APA Ethics Code and to the rules and procedures used to implement it. Psychologists and students, whether or not they are APA members, should be aware that the Ethics Code may be applied to them by state psychology boards, courts, or other public bodies.

The Ethics Code applies only to psychologists' work-related activities, that is, activities that are part of the psychologists' scientific and professional functions or that are psychological in nature. It includes the clinical or counseling practice of psychology, research, teaching, supervision of trainees, development of assessment instruments, conducting assessments, educational counseling, organizational consulting, social intervention, administration, and other activities as well. These work-related activities can be distinguished from the purely private conduct of a psychologist, which ordinarily is not within the purview of the Ethics Code.

The Ethics Code is intended to provide standards of professional conduct that can be applied by the APA and by other bodies that choose to adopt them. Whether or not a psychologist has violated the Ethics Code does not by itself determine whether he or she is legally liable in a court action, whether a contract is enforceable, or whether other legal consequences occur. These results are based on legal rather than ethical rules. However, compliance with or violation of the Ethics Code may be admissible as evidence in some legal proceedings, depending on the circumstances.

In the process of making decisions regarding their professional behavior, psychologists must consider this Ethics Code, in addition to applicable laws and psychology board regulations. If the Ethics Code establishes a higher standard of conduct than is required by law, psychologists must meet the higher ethical standard. If the Ethics Code standard appears to conflict with the requirements of law, then psychologists make known their commitment to the Ethics Code and take steps to resolve the conflict in a responsible manner. If

This version of the APA Ethics Code was adopted by the American Psychological Association's Council of Representatives during its meeting, August 13 and 16, 1992, and is effective beginning December 1, 1992. Inquiries concerning the substance or interpretation of the APA Ethics Code should be addressed to the Director, Office of Ethics, American Psychological Association, 750 First Street, NE, Washington, DC 20002-4242.

This Code will be used to adjudicate complaints brought concerning alleged conduct occurring on or after the effective date. Complaints regarding conduct occurring prior to the effective date will be adjudicated on the basis of the version of the Code that was in effect at the time the conduct occurred, except that no provisions repealed in June 1989, will be enforced even if an earlier version contains the provision. The Ethics Code will undergo continuing review and study for future revisions; comments on the Code may be sent to the above address.

The APA has previously published its Ethical Standards as follows:

American Psychological Association. (1953). *Ethical standards of psychologists*. Washington, DC: Author.

American Psychological Association. (1958). Standards of ethical behavior for psychologists. *American Psychologist, 13,* 268–271.

American Psychological Association. (1963). Ethical standards of psychologists. *American Psychologist, 8,* 56–60.

American Psychological Association. (1968). Ethical standards of psychologists. *American Psychologist, 23,* 357–361.

American Psychological Association. (1977, March). Ethical standards of psychologists. *APA Monitor*, pp. 22–23.

American Psychological Association. (1979). *Ethical standards of psychologists*. Washington, DC. Author.

American Psychological Association. (1981). Ethical principles of psychologists. *American Psychologist, 36,* 633–638.

American Psychological Association. (1990). Ethical principles of psychologists (amended June 2, 1989). *American Psychologist, 45,* 390–395.

NOTE: Request copies of the APA's Ethical Principles of Psychologists and Code of Conduct from the APA Order Department, 750 First Street, NE, Washington, DC 20002-4242, or phone (202) 336–5510.

[1]Professional materials that are most helpful in this regard are guidelines and standards that have been adopted or endorsed by professional psychological organizations. Such guidelines and standards, whether adopted by the American Psychological Association (APA) or its Divisions, are not enforceable as such by this Ethics Code, but are of educative value to psychologists, courts, and professional bodies. Such materials include, but are not limited to, the APA's *General Guidelines for Providers of Psychological Services* (1987), *Specialty Guidelines for the Delivery of Services for Clinical Psychologists, Counseling Psychologists, Industrial/Organizational Psychologists, and School Psychologists* (1981), *Guidelines for Computer Based Tests and Interpretations* (1987), *Standards for Educational and Psychological Testing* (1985), *Ethical Principles in the Conduct of Research with Human Participants* (1982), *Guidelines for Ethical Conduct in the Care and Use of Animals* (1986), *Guidelines for Providers of Psychological Services to Ethnic, Linguistic, and Culturally Diverse Populations* (1990), and *Publication Manual of the American Psychological Association* (3rd ed., 1983). Materials not adopted by APA as a whole include the APA Division 41 (Forensic Psychology)/American Psychology—Law Society's *Specialty Guidelines for Forensic Psychologists* (1991).

neither law nor the Ethics Code resolves an issue, psychologists should consider other professional materials[1] and the dictates of their own conscience, as well as seek consultation with others within the field when this is practical.

The procedures for filing, investigating, and resolving complaints of unethical conduct are described in the current Rules and Procedures of the APA Ethics Committee. The actions that APA may take for violations of the Ethics Code include actions such as reprimand, censure, termination of APA membership, and referral of the matter to other bodies. Complainants who seek remedies such as monetary damages in alleging ethical violations by a psychologist must resort to private negotiation, administrative bodies, or the courts. Actions that violate the Ethics Code may lead to the imposition of sanctions on a psychologist by bodies other than APA, including state psychological associations, other professional groups, psychology boards, other state or federal agencies, and payors for health services. In addition to actions for violation of the Ethics Code, the APA Bylaws provide that APA may take action against a member after his or her conviction of a felony, expulsion or suspension from an affiliated state psychological association, or suspension or loss of licensure.

PREAMBLE

Psychologists work to develop a valid and reliable body of scientific knowledge based on research. They may apply that knowledge to human behavior in a variety of contexts. In doing so, they perform many roles, such as researcher, educator, diagnostician, therapist, supervisor, consultant, administrator, social interventionist, and expert witness. Their goal is to broaden knowledge of behavior and, where appropriate, to apply it pragmatically to improve the condition of both the individual and society. Psychologists respect the central importance of freedom of inquiry and expression in research, teaching, and publication. They also strive to help the public in developing informed judgments and choices concerning human behavior. This Ethics Code provides a common set of values upon which psychologists build their professional and scientific work.

The Code is intended to provide both the general principles and the decision rules to cover most situations encountered by psychologists. It has as its primary goal the welfare and protection of the individuals and groups with whom psychologists work. It is the individual responsibility of each psychologist to aspire to the highest possible standards of conduct. Psychologists respect and protect human and civil rights, and do not knowingly participate in or condone unfair discriminatory practices.

The development of a dynamic set of ethical standards for a psychologist's work-related conduct requires a personal commitment to a lifelong effort to act ethically; to encourage ethical behavior by students, supervisees, employees, and colleagues, as appropriate; and to consult with others, as needed, concerning ethical problems. Each psychologist supplements, but does not violate, the Ethics Code's values and rules on the basis of guidance drawn from personal values, culture, and experience.

GENERAL PRINCIPLES

Principle A: Competence

Psychologists strive to maintain high standards of competence in their work. They recognize the boundaries of their particular competencies and the limitations of their expertise. They provide only those services and use only those techniques for which they are qualified by education, training, or experience. Psychologists are cognizant of the fact that the competencies required in serving, teaching, and/or studying groups of people vary with the distinctive characteristics of those groups. In those areas in which recognized professional standards do not yet exist, psychologists exercise careful judgment and take appropriate precautions to protect the welfare of those with whom they work. They maintain knowledge of relevant scientific and professional information related to the services they render, and they recognize the need for ongoing education. Psychologists make appropriate use of scientific, professional, technical, and administrative resources.

Principle B: Integrity

Psychologists seek to promote integrity in the science, teaching, and practice of psychology. In these activities psychologists are honest, fair, and respectful of others. In describing or reporting their qualifications, services, products, fees, research, or teaching, they do not make statements that are false, misleading, or deceptive. Psychologists strive to be aware of their own belief systems, values, needs, and limitations and the effect of these on their work. To the extent feasible, they attempt to clarify for relevant parties the roles they are performing and to function appropriately in accordance with those roles. Psychologists avoid improper and potentially harmful dual relationships.

Principle C: Professional and Scientific Responsibility

Psychologists uphold professional standards of conduct, clarify their professional roles and obligations, accept appropriate responsibility for their behavior, and adapt their methods to the needs of different populations.

Psychologists consult with, refer to, or cooperate with the other professionals and institutions to the extent needed to serve the best interests of their patients, clients, or other recipients of their services. Psychologists' moral standards and conduct are personal matters to the same degree as is true for any other person, except as psychologists' conduct may compromise their professional responsibilities or reduce the public's trust in psychology and psychologists. Psychologists are concerned about the ethical compliance of their colleagues' scientific and professional conduct. When appropriate, they consult with colleagues in order to prevent or avoid unethical conduct.

Principle D: Respect for People's Rights and Dignity

Psychologists accord appropriate respect to the fundamental rights, dignity, and worth of all people. They respect the rights of individuals to privacy, confidentiality, self-determination, and autonomy, mindful that legal and other obligations may lead to inconsistency and conflict with the exercise of these rights. Psychologists are aware of cultural, individual, and role differences, including those due to age, gender, race ethnicity, national origin, religion, sexual orientation, disability, language, and socioeconomic status. Psychologists try to eliminate the effect on their work of biases based on those factors, and they do not knowingly participate in or condone unfair discriminatory practices.

Principle E: Concern for Others' Welfare

Psychologists seek to contribute to the welfare of those with whom they interact professionally. In their professional actions, psychologists weigh the welfare and rights of their patients or clients, students, supervisees, human research participants, and other affected persons, and the welfare of animal subjects of research. When conflicts occur among psychologists' obligations or concerns, they attempt to resolve these conflicts and to perform their roles in a responsible fashion that avoids or minimizes harm. Psychologists are sensitive to real and ascribed differences in power between themselves and others, and they do not exploit or mislead other people during or after professional relationships.

Principle F: Social Responsibility

Psychologists are aware of their professional and scientific responsibilities to the community and the society in which they work and live. They apply and make public their knowledge of psychology in order to contribute to human welfare. Psychologists are concerned about and work to mitigate the causes of human suffering. When undertaking research, they strive to advance human welfare and the science of psychology. Psychologists try to avoid misuse of their work. Psychologists comply with the law and encourage the development of law and social policy that serve the interests of their patients and clients and the public. They are encouraged to contribute a portion of their professional time for little or no personal advantage.

ETHICAL STANDARDS

1. General Standards

These General Standards are potentially applicable to the professional and scientific activities of all psychologists.

1.01 Applicability of the Ethics Code

The activity of a psychologist subject to the Ethics Code may be reviewed under these Ethical Standards only if the activity is part of his or her work-related functions or the activity is psychological in nature. Personal activities having no connection to or effect on psychological roles are not subject to the Ethics Code.

1.02 Relationship of Ethics and Law

If psychologists' ethical responsibilities conflict with law, psychologists make known their commitment to the Ethics Code and take steps to resolve the conflict in a responsible manner.

1.03 Professional and Scientific Relationship

Psychologists provide diagnostic, therapeutic, teaching, research, supervisory, consultative, or other psychological services only in the context of a defined professional or scientific relationship or role. (See also Standards 2.01, Evaluation, Diagnosis, and Interventions in Professional Context, and 7.02, Forensic Assessments.)

1.04 Boundaries of Competence

(a) Psychologists provide services, teach, and conduct research only within the boundaries of their competence, based on their education, training, supervised experience, or appropriate professional experience.

(b) Psychologists provide services, teach, or conduct research in new areas or involving new techniques only after first undertaking appropriate study, training, supervision, and/or consultation from persons who are competent in those areas or techniques.

(c) In those emerging areas in which generally recognized standards for preparatory training do not yet exist, psychologists nevertheless take reasonable steps to ensure the competence of their work and to protect patients, clients, students, research participants, and others from harm.

1.05 Maintaining Expertise

Psychologists who engage in assessment, therapy, teaching, research, organizational consulting, or other professional activities maintain a reasonable level of awareness of current scientific and professional information in their fields of activity, and undertake ongoing efforts to maintain competence in the skills they use.

1.06 Basis for Scientific and Professional Judgments

Psychologists rely on scientifically and professionally derived knowledge when making scientific or professional judgments or when engaging in scholarly or professional endeavors.

1.07 Describing the Nature and Results of Psychological Services

(a) When psychologists provide assessment, evaluation, treatment, counseling, supervision, teaching, consultation, research, or other psychological services to an individual, a group, or an organization, they provide, using language that is reasonably understandable to the recipient of those services, appropriate information beforehand about the nature of such services and appropriate information later about results and conclusions. (See also Standard 2.09, Explaining Assessment Results.)

(b) If psychologists will be precluded by law or by organizational roles from providing such information to particular individuals or groups, they so inform those individuals or groups at the outset of the service.

1.08 Human Differences

Where differences of age, gender, race, ethnicity, national origin, religion, sexual orientation, disability, language, or socioeconomic status significantly affect psychologists' work concerning particular individuals or groups, psychologists obtain the training, experience, consultation, or supervision necessary to ensure the competence of their services, or they make appropriate referrals.

1.09 Respecting Others

In their work-related activities, psychologists respect the rights of others to hold values, attitudes, and opinions that differ from their own.

1.10 Nondiscrimination

In their work-related activities, psychologists do not engage in unfair discrimination based on age, gender, race, ethnicity, national origin, religion, sexual orientation, disability, socioeconomic status, or any basis proscribed by law.

1.11 Sexual Harassment

(a) Psychologists do not engage in sexual harassment. Sexual harassment is sexual solicitation, physical advances, or verbal or nonverbal conduct that is sexual in nature, that occurs in connection with the psychologist's activities or roles as a psychologist, and that either: (1) is unwelcome, is offensive, or creates a hostile workplace environment, and the psychologist knows or is told this; or (2) is sufficiently severe or intense as to be abusive to a reasonable person in the context. Sexual harassment can consist of a single intense or severe act or of multiple persistent or pervasive acts.

(b) Psychologists accord sexual-harassment complainants and respondents dignity and respect. Psychologists do not participate in denying a person admittance or advancement, employment, tenure, or promotion, based solely upon their having made, or their being the subject of, sexual harassment charges. This does not preclude taking action based upon the outcome of such proceedings or consideration of other appropriate information.

1.12 Other Harassment

Psychologists do not knowingly engage in behavior that is harassing or demeaning to persons with whom they interact in their work based on factors such as those persons' age, gender, race, ethnicity, national origin, religion, sexual orientation, disability, language, or socioeconomic status.

1.13 Personal Problems and Conflicts

(a) Psychologists recognize that their personal problems and conflicts may interfere with their effectiveness. Accordingly, they refrain from undertaking an activity when they know or should know that their personal problems are likely to lead to harm to a patient, client, colleague, student, research participant, or other person to whom they may owe a professional or scientific obligation.

(b) In addition, psychologists have an obligation to be alert to signs of, and to obtain assistance for, their personal problems at an early stage, in order to prevent significantly impaired performance.

(c) When psychologists become aware of personal problems that may interfere with their performing work-related duties adequately, they take appropriate measures, such as obtaining professional consultation or assistance, and determine whether they should limit, suspend, or terminate their work-related duties.

1.14 Avoiding Harm

Psychologists take reasonable steps to avoid harming their patients or clients, research participants, students, and others with whom they work, and to minimize harm where it is foreseeable and unavoidable.

1.15 Misuse of Psychologists' Influence

Because psychologists' scientific and professional judgments and actions may affect the lives of others, they are alert to and guard against personal, financial, social, organizational, or political factors that might lead to misuse of their influence.

1.16 Misuse of Psychologists' Work

(a) Psychologists do not participate in activities in which it appears likely that their skills or data will be misused by others, unless corrective mechanisms are available. (See also Standard 7.04, Truthfulness and Candor.)

(b) If psychologists learn of misuse or misrepresentation of their work, they take reasonable steps to correct or minimize the misuse or misrepresentation.

1.17 Multiple Relationships

(a) In many communities and situations, it may not be feasible or reasonable for psychologists to avoid social or other nonprofessional contacts with persons such as patients, clients, students, supervisees, or research participants. Psychologists must always be sensitive to the potential harmful effects of other contacts on their work and on those persons with whom they deal. A psychologist refrains from entering into or promising another personal, scientific, professional, financial, or other relationship with such persons if it appears likely that such a relationship reasonably might impair the psychologist's objectivity or otherwise interfere with the psychologist's effectively performing his or her functions as a psychologist, or might harm or exploit the other party.

(b) Likewise, whenever feasible, a psychologist refrains from taking on professional or scientific obligations when preexisting relationships would create a risk of such harm.

(c) If a psychologist finds that, due to unforeseen factors, a potentially harmful multiple relationship has arisen, the psychologist attempts to resolve it with due regard for the best interests of the affected person and maximal compliance with the Ethics Code.

1.18 Barter (with Patients or Clients)

Psychologists ordinarily refrain from accepting goods, services, or other nonmonetary remuneration from patients or clients in return for psychological services because such arrangements create inherent potential for conflicts, exploitation, and distortion of the professional relationship. A psychologist may participate in bartering *only* if (1) it is not clinically contraindicated, *and* (2) the relationship is not exploitative. (See also Standards 1.17, Multiple Relationships, and 1.25, Fees and Financial Arrangements.)

1.19 Exploitative Relationships

(a) Psychologists do not exploit persons over whom they have supervisory, evaluative, or other authority such as students, supervisors, employees, research participants, and clients or patients. (See also Standards 4.05–4.07 regarding sexual involvement with clients or patients.)

(b) Psychologists do not engage in sexual relationships with students or supervisees in training over whom the psychologist has evaluative or direct authority, because such relationships are so likely to impair judgment or be exploitative.

1.20 Consultations and Referrals

(a) Psychologists arrange for appropriate consultations and referrals based principally on the best interests of their patients or clients, with appropriate consent, and subject to other relevant considerations, including applicable law and contractual obligations. (See also Standards 5.01, Discussing the Limits of Confidentiality, and 5.06, Consultations.)

(b) When indicated and professionally appropriate, psychologists cooperate with other professionals in order to serve their patients or clients effectively and appropriately.

(c) Psychologists' referral practices are consistent with law.

1.21 Third-Party Requests for Services

(a) When a psychologist agrees to provide services to a person or entity at the request of a third party, the psychologist clarifies to the extent feasible, at the outset of the service, the nature of the relationship with each party. This clarification includes the role of the psychologist (such as therapist, organizational consultant, diagnostician, or expert witness), the probable uses of the services provided or the information obtained, and the fact that there may be limits to confidentiality.

(b)   If there is a foreseeable risk of the psychologist's being called upon to perform conflicting roles because of the involvement of a third party, the psychologist clarifies the nature and direction of his or her responsibilities, keeps all parties appropriately informed as matters develop, and resolves the situation in accordance with this Ethics Code.

1.22   Delegation to and Supervision of Subordinates

(a)   Psychologists delegate to their employees, supervisees, and research assistants only those responsibilities that such persons can reasonably be expected to perform competently, on the basis of their education, training, or experience, either independently or with the level of supervision being provided.

(b)   Psychologists provide proper training and supervision to their employees or supervisees and take reasonable steps to see that such persons perform services responsibly, competently, and ethically.

(c)   If institutional policies, procedures, or practices prevent fulfillment of this obligation, psychologists attempt to modify their role or to correct the situation to the extent feasible.

1.23   Documentation of Professional and Scientific Work

(a)   Psychologists appropriately document their professional and scientific work in order to facilitate provision of services later by them or by other professionals, to ensure accountability, and to meet other requirements of institutions or the law.

(b)   When psychologists have reason to believe that records of their professional services will be used in legal proceedings involving recipients of or participants in their work, they have a responsibility to create and maintain documentation in the kind of detail and quality that would be consistent with reasonable scrutiny in an adjudicative forum. (See also Standard 7.01, Professionalism, under Forensic Activities.)

1.24   Records and Data

Psychologists create, maintain, disseminate, store, retain, and dispose of records and data relating to their research, practice,

and other work in accordance with law and in a manner that permits compliance with the requirements of this Ethics Code. (See also Standard 5.04, Maintenance of Records.)

1.25   Fees and Financial Arrangements

(a)   As early as if feasible in a professional or scientific relationship, the psychologist and the patient, client, or other appropriate recipient of psychological services reach an agreement specifying the compensation and the billing arrangements.

(b)   Psychologists do not exploit recipients of services or payors with respect to fees.

(c)   Psychologists' fee practices are consistent with law.

(d)   Psychologists do not misrepresent their fees.

(e)   If limitations to services can be anticipated because of limitations in financing, this is discussed with the patient, client, or other appropriate recipient of services as early as is feasible. (See also Standard 4.08, Interruption of Services.)

(f)   If the patient, client, or other recipient of services does not pay for services as agreed, and if the psychologist wishes to use collection agencies or legal measures to collect, the fees, the psychologist first informs the person that such measures will be taken and provides that person an opportunity to make prompt payment. (See also Standard 5.11, Withholding Records for Nonpayment.)

1.26   Accuracy in Reports to Payors and Funding Sources

In their reports to payors for services or sources of research funding, psychologists accurately state the nature of the research or service provided, the fees or charges, and where applicable, the identity of the provider, the findings, and the diagnosis. (See also Standard 5.05, Disclosures.)

1.27   Referrals and Fees

When a psychologist pays, receives payment from, or divides fees with another professional other than in an employer-employee relationship, the payment to each is based on the services (clinical, consultative, administrative, or other) provided and is not based on the referral itself.

2.   Evaluation, Assessment, or Intervention

2.01   Evaluation, Diagnosis, and Interventions in Professional Context

(a)   Psychologists perform evaluations, diagnostic services, or interventions only within the context of a defined professional relationship. (See also Standard 1.03, Professional and Scientific Relationship.)

(b) Psychologists' assessments, recommendations, reports, and psychological diagnostic or evaluative statements are based on information and techniques (including personal interviews of the individual when appropriate) sufficient to provide appropriate substantiation for their findings. (See also Standard 7.02, Forensic Assessments.)

2.02 Competence and Appropriate Use of Assessments and Interventions

(a) Psychologists who develop, administer, score, interpret, or use psychological assessment techniques, interviews, tests, or instruments do so in a manner and for purposes that are appropriate in light of the research on or evidence of the usefulness and proper application of the techniques.

(b) Psychologists refrain from misuse of assessment techniques, interventions, results, and interpretations and take reasonable steps to prevent others from misusing the information these techniques provide. This includes refraining from releasing raw test results or raw data to persons, other than to patients or clients as appropriate, who are not qualified to use such information. (See also Standards 1.02, Relationship of Ethics and Law, and 1.04, Boundaries of Competence.)

2.03 Test Construction

Psychologists who develop and conduct research with tests and other assessment techniques use scientific procedures and current professional knowledge for test design, standardization, validation, reduction or elimination of bias, and recommendations for use.

2.04 Use of Assessment in General and with Special Populations

(a) Psychologists who perform interventions or administer, score, interpret, or use assessment techniques are familiar with the reliability, validation, and related standardization or outcome studies of, and proper applications and uses of, the techniques they use.

(b) Psychologists recognize limits to the certainty with which diagnoses, judgments, or predictions can be made about individuals.

(c) Psychologists attempt to identify situations in which particular interventions or assessment techniques or norms may not be applicable or may require adjustment in administration or interpretation

because of factors such as individuals' gender, age, race, ethnicity, national origin, religion, sexual orientation, disability, language, or socioeconomic status.

2.05 Interpreting Assessment Results

When interpreting assessment results, including automated interpretations, psychologists take into account the various test factors and characteristics of the person being assessed that might affect psychologists' judgments or reduce the accuracy of their interpretations. They indicate any significant reservations they have about the accuracy or limitations of their interpretations.

2.06 Unqualified Persons

Psychologists do not promote the use of psychological assessment, techniques by unqualified persons. (See also Standard 1.22, Delegation to and Supervision of Subordinates.)

2.07 Obsolete Tests and Outdated Test Results

(a) Psychologists do not base their assessment or intervention decisions or recommendations on data or test results that are outdated for the current purpose.

(b) Similarly, psychologists do not base such decisions or recommendations on tests and measures that are obsolete and not useful for the current purpose.

2.08 Test Scoring and Interpretation Services

(a) Psychologists who offer assessment or scoring procedures to other professionals accurately describe the purpose, norms, validity, reliability, and applications of the procedures and any special qualifications applicable to their use.

(b) Psychologists select scoring and interpretation services (including automated services) on the basis of evidence of the validity of the program and procedures as well as on other appropriate considerations.

(c) Psychologists retain appropriate responsibility for the appropriate application, interpretation, and use of assessment instruments, whether they score and interpret such tests themselves or use automated or other services.

2.09 Explaining Assessment Results

Unless the nature of the relationship is clearly explained to the person being assessed in advance and precludes provision of an explanation of results (such as in some organizational consulting, preemployment or security screenings, and forensic evaluations), psychologists ensure that an explanation of the results is provided using language that is reasonably understandable to the person assessed or to another legally authorized person on behalf of the client. Regardless of whether the scoring and interpretation are done by the psychologist, by assistants, or by automated or other outside services, psychologists take reasonable steps to ensure that appropriate explanations of results are given.

2.10   Maintaining Test Security

Psychologists make reasonable efforts to maintain the integrity and security of tests and other assessment techniques consistent with law, contractual obligations, and in a manner that permits compliance with the requirements of this Ethics Code. (See also Standard 1.02, Relationship of Ethics and Law.)

3.   Advertising and Other Public Statements

3.01   Definition of Public Statements

Psychologists comply with this Ethics Code in public statements relating to their professional services, products, or publications or to the field of psychology. Public statements include but are not limited to paid or unpaid advertising, brochures, printed matter, directory listings, personal resumes or curricula vitae, interviews or comments for use in media, statements in legal proceedings, lectures and public oral presentations, and published materials.

3.02   Statements by Others

(a)   Psychologists who engage others to create or place public statements that promote their professional practice, products, or activities retain professional responsibility for such statements.

(b)   In addition, psychologists make reasonable efforts to prevent others whom they do not control (such as employers, publishers, sponsors, organizational clients, and representatives of the print or broadcast media) from making deceptive statements concerning psychologists' practice or professional or scientific activities.

(c)   If psychologists learn of deceptive statements about their work made by others, psychologists make reasonable efforts to correct such statements.

(d)   Psychologists do not compensate employees of press, radio, television, or other communication media in return for publicity in a news item.

(e)   A paid advertisement relating to the psychologist's activities must be identified as such, unless it is already apparent from the context.

3.03   Avoidance of False or Deceptive Statements

(a)   Psychologists do not make public statements that are false, deceptive, misleading, or fraudulent, either because of what they state, convey, or suggest or because of what they omit, concerning their research, practice, or other work activities or those of persons or organizations with which they are affiliated. As examples (and not in limitation) of this standard, psychologists do not make false or deceptive statements concerning (1) their training, experience, or competence; (2) their academic degrees; (3) their credentials; (4) their institutional or association affiliations; (5) their services; (6) the scientific or clinical basis for, or results or degree of success of their services; (7) their fees; or (8) their publications or research findings. (See also Standards 6.15, Deception in Research, and 6.18, Providing Participants with Information about the Study.)

(b)   Psychologists claim as credentials for their psychological work, only degrees that (1) were earned from a regionally accredited educational institution or (2) were the basis for psychology licensure by the state in which they practice.

3.04   Media Presentations

When psychologists provide advice or comment by means of public lectures, demonstrations, radio or television programs, prerecorded tapes, printed articles, mailed material, or other media, they take reasonable precautions to ensure that (1) the statements are based on appropriate psychological literature and practice, (2) the statements are otherwise consistent with this Ethics Code, and (3) the recipients of the information are not encouraged to infer that a relationship has been established with them personally.

3.05   Testimonials

Psychologists do not solicit testimonials from current psychotherapy clients or patients or other persons who because of their particular circumstances are vulnerable to undue influence.

3.06   In-Person Solicitation

Psychologists do not engage, directly or through agents, in uninvited in-person solicitation of business from actual or potential psychotherapy patients or clients or other persons who because of their particular circumstances are vulnerable to undue influence. However, this does not preclude attempting to implement appropriate collateral contacts with significant others for the purpose of benefiting an already engaged therapy patient.

4. Therapy

4.01 Structuring the Relationship

(a) Psychologists discuss with clients or patients as early as is feasible in the therapeutic relationship appropriate issues, such as the nature and anticipated course of therapy, fees, and confidentiality. (See also Standards 1.25, Fees and Financial Arrangements, and 5.01, Discussing the Limits of Confidentiality.)

(b) When the psychologist's work with clients or patients will be supervised, the above discussion includes that fact, and the name of the supervisor, when the supervisor has legal responsibility for the case.

(c) When the therapist is a student intern, the client or patient is informed of that fact.

(d) Psychologists make reasonable efforts to answer patients' questions and to avoid apparent misunderstandings about therapy. Whenever possible, psychologists provide oral and/or written information, using language that is reasonably understandable to the patient or client.

4.02 Informed Consent to Therapy

(a) Psychologists obtain appropriate informed consent to therapy or related procedures, using language that is reasonably understandable to participants. The content of informed consent will vary depending on many circumstances; however, informed consent generally implies that the person (1) has the capacity to consent, (2) has been informed of significant information concerning the procedure, (3) has freely and without undue influence expressed consent, and (4) consent has been appropriately documented.

(b) When persons are legally incapable of giving informed consent, psychologists obtain informed permission from a legally authorized person, if such substitute consent is permitted by law.

(c) In addition, psychologists (1) inform those persons who are legally incapable of giving informed consent about the proposed interventions in a manner commensurate with the persons' psychological capacities, (2) seek their assent to those interventions, and (3) consider such persons' preferences and best interests.

4.03 Couple and Family Relationships

(a) When a psychologist agrees to provide services to several persons who have a relationship (such as husband and wife or parents and children), the psychologist attempts to clarify at the outset (1) which of the individuals are patients or clients and (2) the relationship the psychologist will have with each person. This clarification includes the role of the psychologist and the probable uses of the services provided or the information obtained. (See also Standard 5.01, Discussing the Limits of Confidentiality.)

(b) As soon as it becomes apparent that the psychologist may be called on to perform potentially conflicting roles (such as marital counselor to husband and wife, and then witness for one party in a divorce proceeding), the psychologist attempts to clarify and adjust, or withdraw from roles, appropriately. (See also Standard 7.03, Clarification of Role, under Forensic Activities.)

4.04 Providing Mental Health Services to Those Served by Others

In deciding whether to offer or provide services to those already receiving mental health services elsewhere, psychologists carefully consider the treatment issues and the potential patient's or client's welfare. The psychologist discusses these issues with the patient or client, or another legally authorized person on behalf of the client, in order to minimize the risk of confusion and conflict, consults with the service providers when appropriate, and proceeds with caution and sensitivity to the therapeutic issues.

4.05 Sexual Intimacies with Current Patients or Clients

Psychologists do not engage in sexual intimacies with current patients or clients.

4.06 Therapy with Former Sexual Partners

Psychologists do not accept as therapy patients or clients persons with whom they have engaged in sexual intimacies.

4.07 Sexual Intimacies with Former Therapy Patients

(a) Psychologists do not engage in sexual intimacies with a former therapy patient or client for at least two years after cessation or termination of professional services.

(b) Because sexual intimacies with a former therapy patient or client are so frequently harmful to the patient or client, and because such intimacies undermine public confidence in the psychology profession and thereby deter the public's use of needed services, psychologists do not engage in sexual intimacies with former therapy patients and clients even after a two-year interval except in the most unusual circumstances. The psychologist who engages in such activity after the two years following cessation or termination of treatment bears the burden of demonstrating that there has been no exploitation, in light of all relevant factors, including (1) the amount of time that has passed since therapy terminated, (2) the nature and duration of the therapy, (3) the circumstances of termination, (4) the patient's or client's personal history, (5) the patient's or client's current mental status, (6) the likelihood of adverse impact on the patient or client or others, and (7) any statements or actions made by the therapist during the course of therapy suggesting or inviting the possibility of a post-termination sexual or romantic relationship with the patient or client. (See also Standard 1.17, Multiple Relationships.)

4.08 Interruption of Services

(a) Psychologists make reasonable efforts to plan for facilitating care in the event that psychological services are interrupted by factors such as the psychologist's illness, death, unavailability, or relocation or by the client's relocation or financial limitations. (See also Standard 5.09, Preserving Records and Data.)

(b) When entering into employment or contractual relationships, psychologists provide for orderly and appropriate resolution of responsibility for patient or client care in the event that the employment or contractual relationship ends, with paramount consideration given to the welfare of the patient or client.

4.09 Terminating the Professional Relationship

(a) Psychologists do not abandon patients or clients. (See also Standard 1.25e, under Fees and Financial Arrangements.)

(b) Psychologists terminate a professional relationship when it becomes reasonably clear that the patient or client no longer needs the service, is not benefiting, or is being harmed by continued service.

(c) Prior to termination for whatever reason, except where precluded by the patient's or client's conduct, the psychologist discusses the patient's or client's views and needs, provides appropriate pretermination counseling, suggests alternative service providers as appropriate, and takes other reasonable steps to facilitate transfer of responsibility to another provider if the patient or client needs one immediately.

5. Privacy and Confidentiality

These Standards are potentially applicable to the professional and scientific activities of all psychologists.

5.01 Discussing the Limits of Confidentiality

(a) Psychologists discuss with persons and organizations with whom they establish a scientific or professional relationship (including, to the extent feasible, minors and their legal representatives) (1) the relevant limitations on confidentiality, including limitations where applicable in group, marital, and family therapy or in organizational consulting, and (2) the foreseeable uses of the information generated through their services.

(b) Unless it is not feasible or is contraindicated, the discussion of confidentiality occurs at the outset of the relationship and thereafter as new circumstances may warrant.

(c) Permission for electronic recording of interviews is secured from clients and patients.

5.02 Maintaining Confidentiality

Psychologists have a primary obligation and take reasonable precautions to respect the confidentiality rights of those with whom they work or consult, recognizing that confidentiality may be established by law, institutional rules, or professional or scientific relationships. (See also Standard 6.26, Professional Reviewers.)

5.03 Minimizing Intrusions on Privacy

(a) In order to minimize intrusions on privacy, psychologists include in written and oral reports, consultations, and the like, only information germane to the purpose for which the communication is made.

(b) Psychologists discuss confidential information obtained in clinical or consulting relationships, or evaluative data concerning patients, individual or organizational clients, students, research participants, supervisees, and employees, only for appropriate scientific or professional purposes and only with persons clearly concerned with such matters.

5.04 Maintenance of Records

Psychologists maintain appropriate confidentiality in creating, storing, accessing, transferring, and disposing of records under their control, whether these are written, automated, or in any other medium. Psychologists maintain and dispose of records in accordance with law and in a manner that permits compliance with the requirements of this Ethics Code.

5.05 Disclosures

(a) Psychologists disclose confidential information without the consent of the individual only as mandated by law, or where permitted by law for a valid purpose, such as (1) to provide needed professional services to the patient or the individual or organizational client, (2) to obtain appropriate professional consultations, (3) to protect the patient or client or others from harm, or (4) to obtain payment for services, in which instance disclosure is limited to the minimum that is necessary to achieve the purpose.

(b) Psychologists also may disclose confidential information with the appropriate consent of the patient or the individual or organizational client (or of another legally authorized person on behalf of the patient or client), unless prohibited by law.

5.06 Consultations

When consulting with colleagues, (1) psychologists do not share confidential information that reasonably could lead to the identification of a patient, client, research participant, or other person or organization with whom they have a confidential relationship unless they have obtained the prior consent of the person or organization or the disclosure cannot be avoided, and (2) they share information only to the extent necessary to achieve the purposes of the consultation. (See also Standard 5.02, Maintaining Confidentiality.)

5.07 Confidential Information in Databases

(a) If confidential information concerning recipients of psychological services is to be entered into databases or systems of records available to persons whose access has not been consented to by the recipient, then psychologists use coding or other techniques to avoid the inclusion of personal identifiers.

(b) If a research protocol approved by an institutional review board or similar body requires the inclusion of personal identifiers, such identifiers are deleted before the information is made accessible to persons other than those of whom the subject was advised.

(c) If such deletion is not feasible, then before psychologists transfer such data to others or review such data collected by others, they take reasonable steps to determine that appropriate consent of personally identifiable individuals has been obtained.

5.08 Use of Confidential Information for Didactic or Other Purposes

(a) Psychologists do not disclose in their writings, lectures, or other public media, confidential, personally identifiable information concerning their patients, individual or organizational clients, students, research participants; or other recipients of their services that they obtained during the course of their work, unless the person or organization has consented in writing or unless there is other ethical or legal authorization for doing so.

(b) Ordinarily, in such scientific and professional presentations, psychologists disguise confidential information concerning such persons or organizations so that they are not individually identifiable to others and so that discussions do not cause harm to subjects who might identify themselves.

5.09 Preserving Records and Data

A psychologist makes plans in advance so that confidentiality of records and data is protected in the event of the psychologist's death, incapacity, or withdrawal from the position or practice.

5.10 Ownership of Records and Data

Recognizing that ownership of records and data is governed by legal principles, psychologists take reasonable and lawful steps so that records and data remain available to the extent needed to serve the best interests of patients, individual or organizational clients, research participants, or appropriate others.

5.11 Withholding Records for Nonpayment

Psychologists may not withhold records under their control that are requested and imminently needed for a patient's or client's treatment solely because payment has not been received, except as otherwise provided by law.

6. Teaching, Training Supervision, Research, and Publishing

6.01 Design of Education and Training Programs

Psychologists who are responsible for education and training programs seek to ensure that the programs are competently designed, provide the proper experiences, and meet the requirements for licensure, certification, or other goals for which claims are made by the program.

6.02 Descriptions of Education and Training Programs

(a) Psychologists responsible for education and training programs seek to ensure that there is a current and accurate description of the program content, training goals and objectives, and requirements that must be met for satisfactory completion of the program. This information must be made readily available to all interested parties.

(b) Psychologists seek to ensure that statements concerning their course outlines are accurate and not misleading, particularly regarding the subject matter to be covered, bases for evaluating progress, and the nature of course experiences. (See also Standard 3.03, Avoidance of False or Deceptive Statements.)

(c) To the degree to which they exercise control, psychologists responsible for announcements, catalogs, brochures, or advertisements describing workshops, seminars, or other non-degree-granting educational programs ensure that they accurately describe the audience for which the program is intended, the educational objectives, the presenters, and the fees involved.

6.03 Accuracy and Objectivity in Teaching

(a) When engaged in teaching or training, psychologists present psychological information accurately and with a reasonable degree of objectivity.

(b) When engaged in teaching or training, psychologists recognize the power they hold over students or supervisees and therefore make reasonable efforts to avoid engaging in conduct that is personally demeaning to students or supervisees. (See also Standards 1.09, Respecting Others, and 1.12, Other Harassment.)

6.04 Limitation on Teaching

Psychologists do not teach the use of techniques or procedures that require specialized training, licensure, or expertise, including but not limited to hypnosis, biofeedback, and projective techniques, to individuals who lack the prerequisite training, legal scope of practice, or expertise.

6.05 Assessing Student and Supervisee Performance

(a) In academic and supervisory relationships, psychologists establish an appropriate process for providing feedback to students and supervisees.

(b) Psychologists evaluate students and supervisees on the basis of their actual performance on relevant and established program requirements.

6.06 Planning Research

(a) Psychologists design, conduct, and report research in accordance with recognized standards of scientific competence and ethical research.

(b) Psychologists plan their research so as to minimize the possibility that results will be misleading.

(c) In planning research, psychologists consider its ethical acceptability under the Ethics Code. If an ethical issue is unclear, psychologists seek to resolve the issue through consultation with institutional review boards, animal care and use committees, peer consultations, or other proper mechanisms.

(d) Psychologists take reasonable steps to implement appropriate protections for the rights and welfare of human participants, other persons affected by the research, and the welfare of animal subjects.

6.07 Responsibility

(a) Psychologists conduct research competently and with due concern for the dignity and welfare of the participants.

(b) Psychologists are responsible for the ethical conduct of research conducted by them or by others under their supervision or control.

(c) Researchers and assistants are permitted to perform only those tasks for which they are appropriately trained and prepared.

(d) As part of the process of development and implementation of research projects, psychologists consult those with expertise concerning any special population under investigation or most likely to be affected.

6.08 Compliance with Law and Standards

Psychologists plan and conduct research in a manner consistent with federal and state law and regulations, as well as professional standards governing the conduct of research, and particularly those standards governing research with human participants and animal subjects.

6.09 Institutional Approval

Psychologists obtain from host institutions or organizations appropriate approval prior to conducting research, and they provide accurate information about their research proposals.

They conduct the research in accordance with the approved research protocol.

6.10 Research Responsibilities

Prior to conducting research (except research involving only anonymous surveys, naturalistic observations, or similar research), psychologists enter into an agreement with participants that clarifies the nature of the research and the responsibilities of each party.

6.11 Informed Consent to Research

(a) Psychologists use language that is reasonably understandable to research participants in obtaining their appropriate informed consent (except as provided in Standard 6.12, Dispensing with Informed Consent). Such informed consent is appropriately documented.

(b) Using language that is reasonably understandable to participants, psychologists inform participants of the nature of the research; they inform participants that they are free to participate or to decline to participate or to withdraw from the research; they explain the foreseeable consequences of declining or withdrawing; they inform participants of significant factors that may be expected to influence their willingness to participate (such as risks, discomfort, adverse effects, or limitations on confidentiality, except as provided in Standard 6.15, Deception in Research); and they explain other aspects about which the prospective participants inquire.

(c) When psychologists conduct research with individuals such as students or subordinates, psychologists take special care to protect the prospective participants from adverse consequences of declining or withdrawing from participation.

(d) When research participation is a course requirement or opportunity for extra credit, the prospective participant is given the choice of equitable alternative activities.

(e) For persons who are legally incapable of giving informed consent, psychologists nevertheless (1) provide an appropriate explanation, (2) obtain the participant's assent, and (3) obtain appropriate permission from a legally authorized person, if such substitute consent is permitted by law.

6.12 Dispensing with Informed Consent

Before determining that planned research (such as research involving only anonymous questionnaires, naturalistic observations, or certain kinds of archival research) does not require the informed consent of research participants, psychologists consider applicable regulations and institutional review board requirements, and they consult with colleagues as appropriate.

6.13 Informed Consent in Research Filming or Recording

Psychologists obtain informed consent from research participants prior to filming or recording them in any form, unless the research involves simply naturalistic observations in public places and it is not anticipated that the recording will be used in a manner that could cause personal identification or harm.

6.14 Offering Inducements for Research Participants

(a) In offering professional services as an inducement to obtain research participants, psychologists make clear the nature of the services, as well as the risks, obligations, and limitations. (See also Standard 1.18, Barter [with Patients or Clients].)

(b) Psychologists do not offer excessive or inappropriate financial or other inducements to obtain research participants, particularly when it might tend to coerce participation.

6.15 Deception in Research

(a) Psychologists do not conduct a study involving deception unless they have determined that the use of deceptive techniques is justified by the study's prospective scientific, educational, or applied value and that equally effective alternative procedures that do not use deception are not feasible.

(b) Psychologists never deceive research participants about significant aspects that would affect their willingness to participate, such as physical risks, discomfort, or unpleasant emotional experiences.

(c) Any other deception that is an integral feature of the design and conduct of an experiment must be explained to participants as early as is feasible, preferably at the conclusion of their participation, but no later than at the conclusion of the research. (See also Standard 6.18, Providing Participants with Information about the Study.)

6.16 Sharing and Utilizing Data

Psychologists inform research participants of their anticipated sharing or further use of personally identifiable research data and of the possibility of unanticipated future uses.

6.17 Minimizing Invasiveness

In conducting research, psychologists interfere with the participants or milieu from which data are collected only in a manner that is warranted by an appropriate research design and that is consistent with psychologists' roles as scientific investigators.

6.18 Providing Participants with Information about the Study

(a) Psychologists provide a prompt opportunity for participants to obtain appropriate information about the nature, results, and conclusions of the research, and psychologists attempt to correct any misconceptions that participants may have.

(b) If scientific or humane values justify delaying or withholding this information, psychologists take reasonable measures to reduce the risk of harm.

6.19 Honoring Commitments

Psychologists take reasonable measures to honor all commitments they have made to research participants.

6.20 Care and Use of Animals in Research

(a) Psychologists who conduct research involving animals treat them humanely.

(b) Psychologists acquire, care for, use, and dispose of animals in compliance with current federal, state, and local laws and regulations, and with professional standards.

(c) Psychologists trained in research methods and experienced in the care of laboratory animals supervise all procedures involving animals and are responsible for ensuring appropriate consideration of their comfort, health, and humane treatment.

(d) Psychologists ensure that all individuals using animals under their supervision have received instruction in research methods and in the care, maintenance, and handling of the species being used, to the extent appropriate to their role.

(e) Responsibilities and activities of individuals assisting in a research project are consistent with their respective competencies.

(f) Psychologists make reasonable efforts to minimize the discomfort, infection, illness, and pain of animal subjects.

(g) A procedure subjecting animals to pain, stress, or privation is used only when an alternative procedure is unavailable and the goal is justified by its prospective scientific, education, or applied value.

(h) Surgical procedures are performed under appropriate anesthesia; techniques to avoid infection and minimize pain are followed during and after surgery.

(i) When it is appropriate that the animal's life be terminated, it is done rapidly, with an effort to minimize pain, and in accordance with accepted procedures.

6.21 Reporting of Results

(a) Psychologists do not fabricate data or falsify results in their publications.

(b) If psychologists discover significant errors in their published data, they take reasonable steps to correct such errors in a correction, retraction, erratum, or other appropriate publication means.

6.22 Plagiarism

Psychologists do not present substantial portions or elements of another's work or data as their own, even if the other work or data source is cited occasionally.

6.23 Publication Credit

(a) Psychologists take responsibility and credit, including authorship credit, only for work they have actually performed or to which they have contributed.

(b) Principal authorship and other publication credits accurately reflect the relative scientific or professional contributions of the individuals involved, regardless of their relative status. Mere possession of an institutional position, such as Department Chair, does not justify authorship credit. Minor contributions to the research or to the writing for publications are appropriately acknowledged, such as in footnotes or in an introductory statement.

(c) A student is usually listed as principal author on any multiple-authored article that is substantially based on the student's dissertation or thesis.

6.24 Duplicate Publication of Data

Psychologists do not publish, as original data, data that have been previously published. This does not preclude republishing data when they are accompanied by proper acknowledgment.

6.25 Sharing Data

After research results are published, psychologists do not withhold the data on which their conclusions are based from other competent professionals who seek to verify the substantive claims through reanalysis and who intend to use such data only for that purpose, provided that the confidentiality of the participants can be protected and unless legal rights concerning proprietary data preclude their release.

6.26 Professional Reviewers

Psychologists who review material submitted for publication, grant, or other research proposal review respect the confidentiality of and the proprietary rights in such information of those who submitted it.

7. Forensic Activities

7.01 Professionalism

Psychologists who perform forensic functions, such as assessments, interviews, consultations, reports, or expert testimony, must comply with all other provisions of this Ethics Code to the extent that they apply to such activities. In addition, psychologists base their forensic work on appropriate knowledge of and competence in the areas underlying such work, including specialized knowledge concerning special populations. (See also Standards 1.06, Basis for Scientific and Professional Judgments; 1.08, Human Differences; 1.15, Misuse of Psychologists' Influence; and 1.23, Documentation of Professional and Scientific Work.)

7.02 Forensic Assessments

(a) Psychologists' forensic assessments, recommendations, and reports are based on information and techniques (including personal interviews of the individual, when appropriate) sufficient to provide appropriate substantiation for their findings. (See also Standards 1.03, Professional and Scientific Relationship; 1.23, Documentation of Professional and Scientific Work; 2.01, Evaluation, Diagnosis, and Interventions in Professional Context; and 2.05, Interpreting Assessment Results.)

(b) Except as noted in (c), below, psychologists provide written or oral forensic reports or testimony of the psychological characteristics of an individual only after they have conducted an examination of the individual adequate to support their statements or conclusions.

(c) When, despite reasonable efforts, such an examination is not feasible, psychologists clarify the impact of their limited information on the reliability and validity of their reports and testimony, and they appropriately limit the nature and extent of their conclusions or recommendations.

7.03 Clarification of Role

In most circumstances, psychologists avoid performing multiple and potentially conflicting roles in forensic matters. When psychologists may be called on to serve in more than one role in a legal proceeding—for example, as consultant or expert for one party or for the court and as a fact witness—they clarify role expectations and the extent of confidentiality in advance to the extent feasible, and thereafter as changes occur, in order to avoid compromising their professional judgment and objectivity and in order to avoid misleading others regarding their role.

7.04 Truthfulness and Candor

(a) In forensic testimony and reports, psychologists testify truthfully, honestly, and candidly and, consistent with applicable legal procedures, describe fairly the bases for their testimony and conclusions.

(b) Whenever necessary to avoid misleading, psychologists acknowledge the limits of their data or conclusions.

7.05 Prior Relationships

A prior professional relationship with a party does not preclude psychologists from testifying as fact witnesses or from testifying to their services to the extent permitted by applicable laws. Psychologists appropriately take into account ways in which the prior relationship might affect their professional objectivity or opinions and disclose the potential conflict to the relevant parties.

7.06 Compliance with Law and Rules

In performing forensic roles, psychologists are reasonably familiar with the rules governing their roles. Psychologists are aware of the occasionally competing demands placed upon them by these principles and the requirements of the court system, and attempt to resolve these conflicts by making known their commitment to this Ethics Code and taking steps to resolve the conflict in a responsible manner. (See also Standard 1.02, Relationship of Ethics and Law.)

8. Resolving Ethical Issues

8.01 Familiarity with Ethics Code

Psychologists have an obligation to be familiar with this Ethics Code, other applicable ethics codes, and their application to psychologists' work. Lack of awareness or misunderstanding of an ethical standard is not itself a defense to a charge of unethical conduct.

8.02 Confronting Ethical Issues

When a psychologist is uncertain whether a particular situation or course of action would violate this Ethics-Code, the psychologist ordinarily consults with other psychologists knowledgeable about ethical issues, with state or national psychology ethics committees, or with other appropriate authorities in order to choose a proper response.

8.03 Conflicts Between Ethics and Organizational Demands

If the demands of an organization with which psychologists are affiliated conflict with this Ethics Code, psychologists clarify the nature of the conflict, make known their commitment to the Ethics Code, and to the extent feasible, seek to resolve the conflict in a way that permits the fullest adherence to the Ethics Code.

8.04 Informal Resolution of Ethical Violations

When psychologists believe that there may have been an ethical violation by another psychologist, they attempt to resolve the issue by bringing it to the attention of that individual if an informal resolution appears appropriate and the intervention does not violate any confidentiality rights that may be involved.

8.05 Reporting Ethical Violations

If an apparent ethical violation is not appropriate for informal resolution under Standard 8.04 or is not resolved properly in that fashion, psychologists take further action appropriate to the situation, unless such action conflicts with confidentiality rights in ways that cannot be resolved. Such action might include referral to state or national committees on professional ethics or to state licensing boards.

8.06 Cooperating with Ethics Committees

Psychologists cooperate in ethics investigations, proceedings, and resulting requirements of the APA or any affiliated state psychological association to which they belong. In doing so, they make reasonable efforts to resolve any issues as to confidentiality. Failure to cooperate is itself an ethics violation.

8.07 Improper Complaints

Psychologists do not file or encourage the filing of ethics complaints that are frivolous and are intended to harm the respondent rather than to protect the public.

Appendix H
Code of Ethics of the American Mental Health Counselors Association 2000 Revision

PREAMBLE

Mental health counselors believe in the dignity and worth of the individual. They are committed to increasing knowledge of human behavior and understanding of themselves and others. While pursuing these endeavors, they make every reasonable effort to protect the welfare of those who seek their services, or of any subject that may be the object of study. They use their skills only for purposes consistent with these values and do not knowingly permit their misuse by others. While demanding for themselves freedom of inquiry and community, mental health counselors accept the responsibility this freedom confers: competence, objectivity in the application of skills, and concern for the best interest of clients, colleagues, and society in general. In the pursuit of these ideals, mental health counselors subscribe to the following principles:

CLINICAL ISSUES

Principle 1   Welfare of the Consumer

A) Primary Responsibility

1. The primary responsibility of the mental health counselor is to respect the dignity and integrity of the client. Client growth and development are encouraged in ways that foster the client's interest and promote welfare.

2. Mental health counselors are aware of their influential position with respect to their clients, and avoid exploiting the trust and fostering dependency of their clients.

3. Mental health counselors fully inform consumers as to the purpose and nature of any evaluation, treatment, education or training procedure and they fully acknowledge that the consumer has the freedom of choice with regard to participation.

B) Counseling Plans

Mental health counselors and their clients work jointly in devising integrated, individual counseling plans that offer reasonable promise of success and are consistent with the abilities and circumstances of the client. Counselors and clients regularly review counseling plans to ensure their continued viability and effectiveness, respecting the client's freedom of choice.

C) Freedom of Choice

Mental health counselors offer clients the freedom to choose whether to enter into a counseling relationship and determine which professionals will provide the counseling. Restrictions that limit clients' choices are fully explained.

D) Clients Served by Others

1. If a client is receiving services from another mental health professional or counselor, the mental health counselor secures consent from the client, informs that professional of the arrangement, and develops a clear agreement to avoid confusion and conflicts for the client.

2. Mental health counselors are aware of the intimacy and responsibilities inherent in the counseling relationship. They maintain respect for the client and avoid actions that seek to meet their personal needs at the expense of the client. Mental health counselors are aware of their own values, attitudes, beliefs and behaviors, and how these apply in a diverse society. They avoid imposing their values on the consumer.

E) Diversity

1. Mental health counselors do not condone or engage in any discrimination based on age, color, culture, disability, ethnic group, gender, race, religion, sexual orientation, marital status or socioeconomic status.

2. Mental health counselors will actively attempt to understand the diverse cultural backgrounds of the clients with whom they work. This includes learning how the counselor's own cultural/ethical/racial/religious identity impacts his or her own values and beliefs about the counseling process. When there is a conflict between the client's goals, identity and/or values and those of the mental health counselor, a referral to an appropriate colleague must be arranged.

F) Dual Relationships

Mental health counselors are aware of their influential position with respect to their clients and avoid exploiting the trust and fostering dependency of the client.

1. Mental health counselors make every effort to avoid dual relationships with clients that could impair professional judgement or increase the risk of harm. Examples of such relationships may include, but are not limited to: familial, social, financial, business, or close personal relationships with the clients.

2. Mental health counselors do not accept as clients individuals with whom they are involved in an administrative, supervisory, and evaluative nature. When acting as supervisors, trainers, or employers, mental health counselors accord recipients informed choice, confidentiality and protection from physical and mental harm.

3. When a dual relationship cannot be avoided, counselors take appropriate professional precautions such as informed consent, consultation, supervision and documentation to ensure that judgement is not impaired and no exploitation has occurred.

G) Sexual Relationships

Sexual relationships with clients are strictly prohibited. Mental health counselors do not counsel persons with whom they have had a previous sexual relationship.

H) Former Clients

Counselors do not engage in sexual intimacies with former clients within a minimum of two years after terminating the counseling relationship. The mental health counselor has the responsibility to examine and document thoroughly that such relations did not have an exploitative nature based on factors such as duration of counseling, amount of time since counseling, termination circumstances, the client's personal history and mental status, adverse impact on the client, and actions by the counselor suggesting a plan to initiate a sexual relationship with the client after termination.

I) Multiple Clients

When mental health counselors agree to provide counseling services to two or more persons who have a relationship (such as husband and wife, or parents and children), counselors clarify at the outset which person or persons are clients, and the nature of the relationship they will have with each involved person. If it becomes apparent that counselors may be called upon to perform potentially conflicting roles, they clarify, adjust, or withdraw from roles appropriately.

J) Informed Consent

Mental health counselors are responsible for making their services readily accessible to clients in a manner that facilitates the clients' abilities to make an informed choice when selecting a provider. This responsibility includes a clear description of what the client can expect in the way of tests, reports, billing, therapeutic regime and schedules, and the use of the mental health counselor's statement of professional disclosure. In the event that a client is a minor or possesses disabilities that would prohibit informed consent, the mental health counselor acts in the client's best interest.

K)   Conflict of Interest

Mental health counselors are aware of possible conflicts of interests that may involve the organization in which they are employed and their client. When conflicts occur, mental health counselors clarify the nature of the conflict and inform all parties of the nature and direction of their loyalties and responsibilities, and keep all parties informed of their commitments.

L)   Fees and Bartering

1. Mental health counselors clearly explain to clients, prior to entering the counseling relationship, all financial arrangements related to professional services, including the use of collection agencies or legal measures for nonpayment.

2. In establishing fees for professional counseling services, mental health counselors consider the financial status of their clients and locality. In the event that the payment of the mental health counselor's usual fees would create undue hardship for the client, assistance is provided in attempting to find comparable services at an acceptable cost.

3. Mental health counselors ordinarily refrain from accepting goods or services from clients in return for counseling service because such arrangements create inherent potential for conflicts, exploitation and distortion of the professional relationship. Participation in bartering is only used when there is no exploitation, if the client requests it, if a clear written contract is established, and if such an arrangement is an accepted practice among professionals in the community.

M)   Pro Bono Service

Mental health counselors contribute to society by devoting a portion of their professional activity to services for which there is little or no financial return.

N)   Consulting

Mental health counselors may choose to consult with any other professionally competent person about a client. In choosing a consultant, the mental health counselor should avoid placing the consultant in a conflict of interest situation that would preclude the consultant from being a proper party to the mental health counselor's effort to help the client.

O)   Group Work

1. Mental health counselors screen prospective group counseling/therapy participants. Every effort is made to select members whose needs and goals are compatible with goals of the group, who will not impede the group process, and whose well being will not be jeopardized by the group experience.

2. In the group setting, mental health counselors take reasonable precautions to protect clients from physical and psychological harm or trauma.

3. When the client is engaged in short term group treatment/training programs, i.e. marathons and other encounter type or growth groups, the members ensure that there is professional assistance available during and following the group experience.

P)   Termination and Referral

Mental health counselors do not abandon or neglect their clients in counseling. Assistance is given in making appropriate arrangements for the continuation of treatment, when necessary, during interruptions such as vacation and following termination.

Q)   Inability to assist clients

If the mental health counselor determines that their services are not beneficial to the client, they avoid entering or terminate immediately a counseling relationship. Mental health counselors are knowledgeable about referral sources and appropriate referrals are made. If clients decline the suggested referral, mental health counselors discontinue the relationship.

R)   Appropriate Termination

Mental health counselors terminate a counseling relationship, securing a client's agreement when possible, when it is reasonably clear that the client is no longer benefiting, when services are no longer required, when counseling no longer serves the needs and interests of the client, when clients do not pay fees charged, or when agency or institution limits do not allow provision of further counseling services.

Principle 2   Clients' Rights

The following apply to all consumers of mental health services, including both in- and out-patients and all state, county, local, and private care mental health facilities, as well as clients of mental health practitioners in private practice.

The client has the right:

A)   To be treated with dignity, consideration and respect at all times;

B)   To expect quality service provided by concerned, trained, professional and competent staff;

C)   To expect complete confidentiality within the limits of the law, and to be informed about the legal exceptions to confidentiality; and to expect that no information will be released without the client's knowledge and written consent;

D)   To a clear working contract in which business items, such as time of sessions, payment plans/ fees, absences, access, emergency procedures, and third-party reimbursement procedures are discussed;

E)   To a clear statement of the purposes, goals, techniques, rules of procedure and limitations, as well as the potential dangers of the services to be performed, and all other information related to or likely to affect the ongoing mental health counseling relationship;

F)   To appropriate information regarding the mental health counselor's education, training, skills, license and practice limitations and to request and receive referrals to other clinicians when appropriate;

G)   To full, knowledgeable, and responsible participation in the ongoing treatment plan to the maximum extent feasible;

H)   To obtain information about their case record and to have this information explained clearly and directly;

I)   To request information and/or consultation regarding the conduct and progress of their therapy;

J)   To refuse any recommended services and to be advised of the consequences of this action;

K)   To a safe environment free of emotional, physical and sexual abuse;

L)   To a client grievance procedure, including requests for consultation and/or mediation; and to file a complaint with the mental health counselor's supervisor, and/or the appropriate credentialing body; and

M)   To a clearly defined ending process, and to discontinue therapy at any time.

Principle 3   Confidentiality

Mental health counselors have a primary obligation to safeguard information about individuals obtained in the course of practice, teaching, or research. Personal information is communicated to others only with the person's written consent or in those circumstances where there is clear and imminent danger to the client, to others or to society. Disclosure of counseling information is restricted to what is necessary, relevant and verifiable.

A)   At the outset of any counseling relationship, mental health counselors make their clients aware of their rights in regard to the confidential nature of the counseling relationship. They fully disclose the limits of, or exceptions to, confidentiality, and/or the existence of privileged communication, if any.

B)   All materials in the official record shall be shared with the client, who shall have the right to decide what information may be shared with anyone beyond the immediate provider of service and be informed of the implications of the materials to be shared.

C)   Confidentiality belongs to the clients. They may direct the mental health counselor, in writing, to release information to others. The release of information without the consent of the client may only take place under the most extreme circumstances. The protection of life, as in the case of suicidal or homicidal clients, exceeds the requirements of confidentiality. The protection of a child, an elderly person, or a person not competent to care for themselves from physical or sexual abuse or neglect requires that a report be made to a legally constituted authority. The mental health counselor complies with all state and federal statutes concerning mandated reporting of suicidality, homicidality, child abuse, incompetent person abuse and elder abuse. The protection of the public or another individual from a contagious condition known to be fatal also requires action that may include reporting the willful infection of another with the condition.

The mental health counselor (or staff member) does not release information by request unless accompanied by a specific release of information or a valid court order. Mental health counselors will comply with the order of a court to release information but they will inform the client of the receipt of such an order. A subpoena is insufficient to release information. In such a case, the counselor must inform his client of the situation and, if the client refuses release, coordinate between the client's attorney and the requesting attorney so as to protect client confidentiality and one's own legal welfare.

In the case of all of the above exceptions to confidentiality, the mental health counselor will release only such information as is necessary to accomplish the action required by the exception.

D)   The anonymity of clients served in public and other agencies is preserved, if at all possible, by withholding names and personal identifying data. If external conditions require reporting such information, the client shall be so informed.

E)   Information received in confidence by one agency or person shall not be forwarded to another person or agency without the client's written permission.

F) Service providers have the responsibility to ensure the accuracy and to indicate the validity of data shared with their parties.

G) Case reports presented in classes, professional meetings, or publications shall be so disguised that no identification is possible unless the client or responsible authority has read the report and agreed in writing to its presentation or publication.

H) Counseling reports and records are maintained under conditions of security, and provisions are made for their destruction when they have outlived their usefulness. Mental health counselors ensure that all persons in his or her employ, volunteers, and community aides maintain privacy and confidentiality.

I) Mental health counselors who ask that an individual reveal personal information in the course of interviewing, testing or evaluation, or who allow such information to be divulged, do so only after making certain that the person or authorized representative is fully aware of the purposes of the interview, testing or evaluation, and of the ways in which the information will be used.

J) Sessions with clients may be taped or otherwise recorded only with their written permission or the written permission of a responsible guardian. Even with a guardian's written consent, one should not record a session against the expressed wishes of a client. Such tapes shall be destroyed when they have outlived their usefulness.

K) Where a child or adolescent is the primary client, or the client is not competent to give consent, the interests of the minor or the incompetent client shall be paramount. Where appropriate, a parent(s) or guardian(s) may be included in the counseling process. The mental health counselor must still take measures to safeguard the client's confidentiality.

L) In work with families, the rights of each family member should be safeguarded. The provider of service also has the responsibility to discuss the contents of the record with the parent and/or child, as appropriate, and to keep separate those parts, which should remain the property of each family member.

M) In work with groups, the rights of each group member should be safeguarded. The provider of service also has the responsibility to discuss the need for each member to respect the confidentiality of each other member of the group. He must also remind the group of the limits on and risk to confidentiality inherent in the group process.

N) When using a computer to store confidential information, mental health counselors take measures to control access to such information. When such information has outlived its usefulness, it should be deleted from the system.

Principle 4　Utilization of Assessment Techniques

A)　Test Selection

1. In choosing a particular test, mental health counselors should ascertain that there is sufficient evidence in the test manual of its applicability in measuring a certain trait or construct. The manual should fully describe the development of the test, the rationale, and data pertaining to item selection and test construction. The manual should explicitly state the purposes and applications for which the test is intended, and provide reliability and validity data about the test. The manual should furthermore identify the qualifications necessary to properly administer and interpret the test.

2. In selecting a particular combination of tests, mental health counselors need to be able to justify the logic of those choices.

3. Mental health counselors should employ only those tests for which they judge themselves competent by training, education, or experience. In familiarizing themselves with new tests, counselors thoroughly read the manual and seek workshops, supervision, or other forms of training.

4. Mental health counselors avoid using outdated or obsolete tests, and strive to remain current regarding test publication and revision.

5. Tests selected for individual testing must be appropriate for that individual in that appropriate norms exist for variables such as age, gender, and race. The test form must fit the client. If the test must be used in the absence of available information regarding the above subsamples, the limitations of generalizability should be duly noted.

B)　Test Administration

1. Mental health counselors should faithfully follow instructions for administration of a test in order to ensure standardization. Failure to consistently follow test instructions will result in test error and incorrect estimates of the trait or behavior being measured.

2. Tests should only be employed in appropriate professional settings or as recommended by instructors or supervisors for training purposes. It is best to avoid giving tests to relatives, close friends or business associates, in that doing so constructs a dual professional/personal relationship, which is to be avoided.

3. Mental health counselors should provide the test taker with appropriate information regarding the reason for assessment, the approximate length of time required, and to whom the report will be distributed. Issues of confidentiality must be addressed, and the client must be given the opportunity to ask questions of the examiner prior to beginning the procedure.

4. Care should be taken to provide an appropriate assessment environment in regard to temperature, privacy, comfort, and freedom from distractions.

5. Information should be solicited regarding any possible handicaps, such as problems with visual or auditory acuity, limitations of hand/eye coordination, illness, or other factors. If the disabilities cannot be accommodated effectively, the test may need to be postponed or the limitations of applicability of the test results noted in the test report.

6. Professionals who supervise others should ensure that their trainees have sufficient knowledge and experience before utilizing the tests for clinical purposes.

7. Mental health counselors must be able to document appropriate education, training, and experience in areas of assessment they perform.

C) **Test Interpretation**

1. Interpretation of test or test battery results should be based on multiple sources of convergent data and an understanding of the tests' foundations and limits.

2. Mental health counselors must be careful not to make conclusions unless empirical evidence is present to justify the statement. If such evidence is lacking, one should not make diagnostic or prognostic formulations.

3. Interpretation of test results should take into account the many qualitative influences on test-taking behavior, such as health, energy, motivation, and the like. Description and analysis of alternative explanations should be provided with the interpretations.

4. One should not make firm conclusions in the absence of published information that estab-

lishes a satisfactory degree of test validity, particularly predictive validity.

5. Multicultural factors must be considered in test interpretation and diagnosis, and formulation of prognosis and treatment recommendations.

6. Mental health counselors should avoid biased or incorrect interpretation by assuring that the test norms reference the population taking the test.

7. Mental health counselors are responsible for evaluating the quality of computer software interpretations of test data. Mental health counselors should obtain information regarding validity of computerized test interpretation before utilizing such an approach.

8. Supervisors should ensure that their supervisees have had adequate training in interpretation before entrusting them to evaluate tests in a semi-autonomous fashion.

9. Any individual or organization offering test scoring or interpretation services must be able to demonstrate that their programs are based on sufficient and appropriate research to establish the validity of the programs and procedures used in arriving at interpretations. The public offering of an automated test interpretation service will be considered a professional-to-professional consultation. The formal responsibility of the consultant is to the consultee, but his or her ultimate and overriding responsibility is to the client.

10. Mental health counselors who have the responsibility for making decisions about clients or policies based on test results should have a thorough understanding of counseling theory, assessment techniques, and test research.

11. Mental health counselors do not represent computerized test interpretations as their own and clearly designate such computerized results.

D) **Test Reporting**

1. Mental health counselors should write reports in a clear fashion, avoiding excessive jargon or clinical terms that are likely to confuse the lay reader.

2. Mental health counselors should strive to provide test results in as positive and nonjudgmental manner as possible.

3. Mindful that one's report reflects on the reputation of oneself and one's profession, reports are

carefully proofread so as to be free of spelling, style, and grammatical errors as much as is possible.

4. Clients should be clearly informed about who will be allowed to review the report and, in the absence of a valid court order, must sign appropriate releases of information permitting such release. Mental health counselors must not release the report or findings in the absence of the aforementioned releases or order.

5. Mental health counselors are responsible for ensuring the confidentiality and security of test reports, test data, and test materials.

6. Mental health counselors must offer the client the opportunity to receive feedback about the test results, interpretations, and the range of error for such data.

7. Transmissions of test data or test reports by fax or e-mail must be accomplished in a secure manner, with guarantees that the receiving device is capable of providing a confidential transmission only to the party who has been permitted to receive the document.

8. Mental health counselors should train his or her staff to respect the confidentiality of test reports in the context of typing, filing, or mailing them.

9. Mental health counselors (or staff members) do not release a psychological evaluation by request unless accompanied by a specific release of information or a valid court order. A subpoena is insufficient to release a report. In such a case, the counselor must inform his/her client of the situation and, if the client refuses release, coordinate between the client's attorney and the requesting attorney so as to protect client confidentiality and one's own legal welfare.

Principle 5   Pursuit of Research Activities

Mental health counselors who conduct research must do so with regard to ethical principles. The decision to undertake research should rest upon a considered judgment by the individual counselor about how best to contribute to counseling and to human welfare. Mental health counselors carry out their investigations with respect for the people who participate and with concern for their dignity and welfare.

1. The ethical researcher seeks advice from other professionals if any plan of research suggests a deviation from any ethical principle of research with human subjects. Such deviation must still protect the dignity

and welfare of the client and places on the researcher a special burden to act in the subject's interest.

2. The ethical researcher is open and honest in the relationship with research participants.

a) The ethical researcher informs the participant of all features of the research that might be expected to influence willingness to participate and explains to the participant all other aspects about which the participant inquires.

b) Where scientific or human values justify delaying or withholding information, the investigator acquires a special responsibility to assure that there are no damaging consequences for the participants.

c) Following the collection of the data, the ethical researcher must provide the participant with a full clarification of the nature of the study to remove any misconceptions that may have arisen.

d) As soon as possible, the participant is to be informed of the reasons for concealment or deception that are part of the methodological requirements of a study.

e) Such misinformation must be minimized and full disclosure must be made at the conclusion of all research studies.

f) The ethical researcher understands that failure to make full disclosure to a research participant gives added emphasis to the researcher's abiding responsibility to protect the welfare and dignity of the participant.

3. The ethical researcher protects participants from physical and mental discomfort, harm and danger. If the risks of such consequences exist, the investigator is required to inform the participant of that fact, secure consent before proceeding, and take all possible measures to minimize the distress.

4. The ethical researcher instructs research participants that they are free to withdraw their consent and from participation at any time.

5. The ethical researcher understands that information obtained about research participants during the course of an investigation is confidential. When the possibility exists that others may obtain access to such information, the participant must be made aware of the possibility and the plans for protecting confidentiality as a part of the procedure for obtaining informed consent.

6. The ethical researcher gives sponsoring agencies, host institutions, and publication channels the same respect and opportunity for informed consent that they accord to individual research participants.

7. The ethical researcher is aware of his or her obligation to future research workers and ensures that host institutions are given feedback information and proper acknowledgement.

Principle 6   Consulting

A) Mental health counselors acting as consultants must have a high degree of self-awareness of their own values, knowledge, skills and needs in entering a helping relationship that involves human and/or organizational change. The focus of the consulting relationship should be on the issues to be resolved and not on the personal characteristics of those presenting the consulting issues.

B) Mental health counselors should develop an understanding of the problem presented by the client and should secure an agreement with the consultation client, specifying the terms and nature of the consulting relationship.

C) Mental health counselors must be reasonably certain that they and their clients have the competencies and resources necessary to follow the consultation plan.

D) Mental health counselors should encourage adaptability and growth toward self-direction. Mental health counselors should avoid becoming a decision-maker or substitute for the client.

E) When announcing consultant availability for services, mental health counselors conscientiously adhere to professional standards.

F) Mental health counselors keep all proprietary information confidential.

G) Mental health counselors avoid conflicts of interest in selecting consultation clients.

PROFESSIONAL ISSUES

Principle 7   Competence

The maintenance of high standards of professional competence is a responsibility shared by all mental health counselors in the best interests of the public and the profession. Mental health counselors recognize the boundaries of their particular competencies and the limitations of their expertise. Mental health counselors only provide those services and use only those techniques for which they are qualified by education, techniques or experience. Mental health counselors maintain knowledge of relevant scientific and professional information related

to the services they render, and they recognize the need for on-going education.

A) Mental health counselors accurately represent their competence, education, training and experience.

B) As teaching professionals, mental health counselors perform their duties based on careful preparation in order that their instruction is accurate, up to date and educational.

C) Mental health counselors recognize the need for continued education and training in the area of cultural diversity and competency. Mental health counselors are open to new procedures and sensitive to the diversity of varying populations and changes in expectations and values over time.

D) Mental health counselors and practitioners recognize that their effectiveness depends in part upon their ability to maintain sound and healthy interpersonal relationships. They are aware that any unhealthy activity would compromise sound professional judgement and competency. In the event that personal problems arise and are affecting professional services, they will seek competent professional assistance to determine whether they should limit, suspend or terminate services to their clients.

E) Mental health counselors have a responsibility both to the individual who is served and to the institution within which the service is performed to maintain high standards of professional conduct. Mental health counselors strive to maintain the highest level of professional services offered to the agency, organization or institution in providing the highest caliber of professional services. The acceptance of employment in an institution implies that the mental health counselor is in substantial agreement with the general policies and principles of the institution. If, despite concerted efforts, the member cannot reach an agreement with the employer as to acceptable standards of conduct that allows for changes in institutional policy conducive to the positive growth and development of counselors, then terminating the affiliation should be seriously considered.

F) Ethical behavior among professional associates, mental health counselors and non-mental health counselors is expected at all times. When information is possessed that raises serious doubts as to the ethical behavior of professional colleagues, whether association members or not, the mental health counselor is obligated to take action to attempt to rectify such a condition. Such action shall utilize the institution's channels first and then utilize procedures established by the state licensure board.

G) Mental health counselors are aware of the intimacy of the counseling relationship, maintain a healthy respect for the integrity of the client, and avoid engaging in activities that seek to meet the mental health counselor's personal needs at the expense of the client. Through awareness of the negative impact of both racial and sexual stereotyping and discrimination, the member strives to ensure the individual rights and personal dignity of the client in the counseling relationship.

Principle 8   Professional Relationships

Mental health counselors act with due regard for the needs and feelings of their colleagues in counseling and other professions. Mental health counselors respect the prerogatives and obligations of the institutions or organizations with which they associate.

A) Mental health counselors understand how related professions complement their work and make full use of other professional, technical, and administrative resources that best serve the interests of consumers. The absence of formal relationships with other professional workers does not relieve mental health counselors from the responsibility of securing for their clients the best possible professional services; indeed, this circumstance presents a challenge to the professional competence of mental health counselors, requiring special sensitivity to problems outside their areas of training, and foresight, diligence, and tact in obtaining the professional assistance needed by clients.

B) Mental health counselors know and take into account the traditions and practices of other professional groups with which they work and cooperate fully with members of such groups when research, services and other functions are shared, or in working for the benefit of public welfare.

C) Mental health counselors treat professional colleagues with the same dignity and respect afforded to clients. Professional discourse should be free of personal attacks.

D) Mental health counselors strive to provide positive conditions for those they employ and to spell out clearly the conditions of such employment. They encourage their employees to engage in activities that facilitate their further professional development.

E) Mental health counselors respect the viability, reputation, and proprietary rights of organizations that they serve. Mental health counselors show due regard for the interest of their present or perspective employers. In those instances where they are critical of policies, they attempt to effect change by constructive action within the organization.

F) In pursuit of research, mental health counselors are to give sponsoring agencies, host institutions, and publication channels the same respect and opportunity for giving informed consent that they accord to individual research participants. They are aware of their obligation to future research workers and insure that host institutions are given feedback information and proper acknowledgement.

G) Credit is assigned to those who have contributed to a publication, in proportion to their contribution.

H) Mental health counselors do not accept or offer referral fees from other professionals.

I) When mental health counselors violate ethical standards, mental health counselors who know firsthand of such activities should, if possible, attempt to rectify the situation. Failing an informal solution, mental health counselors should bring such unethical activities to the attention of the appropriate state licensure board committee on ethics and professional conduct. Only after all professional alternatives have been utilized will mental health counselors begin legal action for resolution.

Principle 9   Supervisee, Student and Employee Relationships

Mental health counselors have an ethical concern for the integrity and welfare of supervisees, students, and employees. They maintain these relationships on a professional and confidential basis. They recognize the influential position they have with regard to both current and former supervisees, students and employees. They avoid exploiting their trust and dependency.

A) Mental health counselors do not engage in ongoing counseling relationships with current supervisees, students and employees.

B) All forms of sexual behavior with supervisees, students and employees are unethical. Further, mental health counselors do not engage in sexual or other harassment of supervisees, students, employees or colleagues.

C) Mental health counselor supervisors advise their supervisees, students and employees against offering or engaging in or holding themselves out as competent to engage in professional services beyond their training, level of experience and competence.

D) Mental health counselors make every effort to avoid dual relationships with supervisees, students and employees that could impair their judgment or increase the risk of personal or financial exploitation. When a dual relationship can not be avoided, mental health counselors take appropriate professional precautions to make sure that judgment is not impaired. Examples of such dual relationships include, but are not limited to, a supervisee who receives supervision as a benefit of employment, or a student in a small college where the only available counselor on campus is an instructor.

E) Mental health counselors do not disclose supervisee confidences except:

1. To prevent clear and eminent danger to a person or persons.

2. As mandated by law.

    a) As in mandated child or senior abuse reporting.

    b) Where the counselor is a defendant in a civil, criminal or disciplinary action.

    c) In educational or training settings where only other professionals who will share responsibility for the training of the supervisee are present.

    d) Where there is a waiver of confidentiality obtained in writing prior to such a release of information.

F) Supervisees must make their clients aware in their informed consent statement that they are under supervision and they must provide their clients with the name and credentials of their supervisor.

G) Mental health counselors require their supervisees, students and employees to adhere to the Code of Ethics. Students and supervisees have the same obligations to clients as those required of mental health counselors.

Principle 10 Moral and Legal Standards

Mental health counselors recognize that they have a moral, legal and ethical responsibility to the community and to the general public. Mental health counselors should be aware of the prevailing community standards and the impact of professional standards on the community.

A) To protect students, mental health counselors/teachers will be aware of diverse backgrounds of students and will see that material is treated objectively and fairly to reflect the multicultural community in which they live.

B) Providers of counseling services conform to the statutes relating to such services as established by their state and its regulating professional board(s).

C) As employees, mental health counselors refuse to participate in an employer's practices that are inconsistent with the moral and legal standards established by federal or state legislation regarding the treatment of employees. In particular and for example, mental health counselors will not condone practices that result in illegal or otherwise unjustified discrimination on the basis of race, sex, religion or national origin in hiring, promotion or training.

D) In providing counseling services to clients, mental health counselors avoid any action that will violate or diminish the legal and civil rights of clients or of others that may be effected by the action.

E) Sexual conduct, not limited to sexual intercourse, between mental health counselors and clients is specifically in violation of this Code of Ethics. This does not, however, prohibit the use of explicit instructional aids including films and videotapes. Such use is within excepted practices of trained and competent sex therapists.

Principle 11 Professional Responsibility

In their commitment to the understanding of human behavior, mental health counselors value objectivity and integrity, and in providing services they maintain the highest standards. They accept responsibility for the consequences of their work and make every effort to ensure that their services are used appropriately.

A) Mental health counselors accept ultimate responsibility for selecting appropriate areas for investigation and the methods relevant to minimize the possibility that their finding will be misleading. They provide thorough discussion of the limitations of their data and alternative hypotheses, especially where their work touches on social policy or might be misconstrued to the detriment of specific age, sex, ethnic, socioeconomic, or other social categories. In publishing reports of their work, they never discard observations that may modify the interpretation of results. Mental health counselors take credit only for the work they have actually done. In pursuing research, mental health counselors ascertain that their efforts will not lead to changes in individuals or organizations unless such changes are part of the agreement at the time of obtaining informed consent. Mental health counselors clarify in advance the expectations for sharing and utilizing research data. They avoid dual relationships that may limit objectivity, whether theoretical, political, or monetary, so that interference with data, subjects, and milieu is kept to a minimum.

B) As employees of an institution or agency, mental health counselors have the responsibility to remain alert to institutional pressures that may distort reports of counseling findings or use them in ways counter to the promotion of human welfare.

C) When serving as members of governmental or other organizational bodies, mental health counselors remain accountable as individuals to the Code of Ethics of the American Mental Health Counselors Association.

D) As teachers, mental health counselors recognize their primary obligation to help others acquire knowledge and skill. They maintain high standards of scholarship and objectivity by presenting counseling information fully and accurately, and by giving appropriate recognition to alternative viewpoints.

E) As practitioners, mental health counselors know that they bear a heavy social responsibility because their recommendations and professional actions may alter the lives of others. They therefore remained fully cognizant of their impact and alert to personal, social, organizational, financial or political situations or pressures that might lead to the misuse of their influence.

F) Mental health counselors provide reasonable and timely feedback to employees, trainees, supervisors, students, clients, and others whose work they may evaluate.

Principle 12   Private Practice

A) A mental health counselor should assist, where permitted by legislation or judicial decision, the profession in fulfilling its duty to make counseling services available in private settings.

B) In advertising services as a private practitioner, mental health counselors should advertise the services in such a manner so as to accurately inform the public as to services, expertise, profession, and techniques of counseling in a professional manner. Mental health counselors who assume an executive leadership role in the organization shall not permit their name to be used in professional notices during periods when not actively engaged in the private practice of counseling. Mental health counselors advertise the following: highest relevant degree, type and level of certification or license, and type and/or description of services or other relevant information. Such information should not contain false, inaccurate, misleading, partial, out of context, descriptive material or statements.

C) Mental health counselors may join in partnership/corporation with other mental health counselors and/or other professionals provided that each mental health counselor of the partnership or corporation makes clear his/her separate specialties, buying name in compliance with the regulations of the locality.

D) Mental health counselors have an obligation to withdraw from an employment relationship or a counseling relationship if it is believed that employment will result in violation of the Code of Ethics, if their mental capacity or physical condition renders it difficult to carry out an effective professional relationship, or if the mental health counselor is discharged by the client because the counseling relationship is no longer productive for the client.

E) Mental health counselors should adhere and support the regulations for private practice in the locality where the services are offered.

F) Mental health counselors refrain from attempts to utilize one's institutional affiliation to recruit clients for one's private practice. Mental health counselors are to refrain from offering their services in the private sector when they are employed by an institution in which this is prohibited by stated policy that reflects conditions of employment.

Principle 13   Public Statements

Mental health counselors in their professional roles may be expected or required to make public statements providing counseling information or professional opinions; or supply information about the availability of counseling products and services. In making such statements, mental health counselors take into full account the limits and uncertainties of present counseling knowledge and techniques. They represent, as accurately and objectively as possible, their professional qualifications, expertise, affiliations, and functions, as well as those of the institutions or organizations with which the statements may be associated. All public statements, announcements of services, and promotional activities should serve the purpose of providing sufficient information to aid the consumer public in making informed judgements and choices on matters that concern it. When announcing professional counseling services, mental health counselors may describe or explain those services offered but may not evaluate as to their quality or uniqueness and do not allow for testimonials by implication. All public statements should be otherwise consistent with this Code of Ethics.

Principle 14   Internet On-Line Counseling

Mental health counselors engaged in delivery of services that involves the telephone, teleconferencing and the Internet in which these areas are generally recognized, standards for preparatory training do not yet exist. Mental health counselors take responsible steps to ensure the competence of their work and protect patients, clients, students, research participants and others from harm.

A)   Confidentiality

Mental health counselors ensure that clients are provided sufficient information to adequately address and explain the limitations of computer technology in the counseling process in general and the difficulties of ensuring complete client confidentiality of information transmitted through electronic communications over the Internet through on-line counseling. Professional counselors inform clients of the limitations of confidentiality and identify foreseeable situations in which confidentiality must be breached in light of the law in both the state in which the client is located and the state in which the professional counselor is licensed. Mental health counselors shall become aware of the means for reporting and protecting suicidal clients in their locale. Mental health counselors shall become aware of the means for reporting homicidal clients in the client's jurisdiction.

B)   Mental Health Counselor Identification

Mental health counselors provide a readily visible notice advising clients of the identities of all professional counselor(s) who will have access to the information transmitted by the client. Mental health counselors provide background information on all professional communications, including education, licensing and certification, and practice information.

C)   Client Identification

Professional counselors identify clients, verify identities of clients, and obtain alternative methods of contacting clients in emergency situations.

D)   Client Waiver

Mental health counselors require clients to execute client waiver agreements stating that the client acknowledges the limitations inherent in ensuring client confidentiality of information transmitted through on-line counseling and acknowledge the limitations that are inherent in a counseling process that is not provided face-to-face. Limited training in the area of on-line counseling must be explained and the client's informed consent must be secured.

E)   Electronic Transfer of Client Information

Mental health counselors electronically transfer client confidential information to authorized third-party recipients only when both the professional counselor and the authorized recipient have "secure" transfer and acceptance communication capabilities; the recipient is able to effectively protect the confidentiality of the client's confidential information to be transferred; and the informed written consent of the client, acknowledging the limits of confidentiality, has been obtained.

F)   Establishing the On-Line Counseling Relationship

1. Appropriateness of On-Line Counseling

Mental health counselors develop an appropriate in-take procedure for potential clients to determine whether on-line counseling is appropriate for the needs of the client. Mental health counselors warn potential clients that on-line counseling services may not be appropriate in certain situations and, to the extent possible, inform the client of specific limitations, potential risks, and/or potential benefits relevant to the client's anticipated use of on-line counseling services. Mental health counselors ensure that clients are intellectually, emotionally, and physically capable of using on-line counseling services, and of understanding the potential risks and/or limitations of such services.

2. Counseling Plans

Mental health counselors develop individual on-line counseling plans that are consistent with both the client's individual circumstances and the limitations of on-line counseling. Mental health counselors who determine that on-line counseling is inappropriate for the client should avoid entering into or immediately terminate the on-line counseling relationship and encourage the client to continue the counseling relationship through a traditional alternative method of counseling.

3. Boundaries of Competence

Mental health counselors provide on-line counseling services only in practice areas within their expertise. Mental health counselors do not provide services to clients in states where doing so would violate local licensure laws or regulations.

G)   Legal Considerations

Mental health counselors confirm that the provision of on-line services are not prohibited by or otherwise violate any applicable state or local statutes, rules, regulations or ordinances, codes of professional membership organizations and certifying boards, and/or codes of state licensing boards.

Principle 15   Resolution of Ethical Problems

Neither the American Mental Health Counselors Association, its Board of Directors, nor its National Committee on Ethics investigate or adjudicate ethical complaints. In the event a member has his or her license suspended or revoked by an appropriate state licensure board, the AMHCA Board of Directors may then act in accordance with AMHCA's National By-Laws to suspend or revoke his or her membership.

Any member so suspended may apply for reinstatement upon the reinstatement of his or her licensure.

Appendix I
AAMFT Code of Ethics
Effective July 1, 2001

PREAMBLE

The Board of Directors of the American Association for Marriage and Family Therapy (AAMFT) hereby promulgates, pursuant to Article 2, Section 2.013 of the Association's By-laws, the Revised AAMFT Code of Ethics, effective July 1, 2001.

The AAMFT strives to honor the public trust in marriage and family therapists by setting standards for ethical practice as described in this Code. The ethical standards define professional expectations and are enforced by the AAMFT Ethics Committee. The absence of an explicit reference to a specific behavior or situation in the Code does not mean that the behavior is ethical or unethical. The standards are not exhaustive. Marriage and family therapists who are uncertain about the ethics of a particular course of action are encouraged to seek counsel from consultants, attorneys, supervisors, colleagues, or other appropriate authorities.

Both law and ethics govern the practice of marriage and family therapy. When making decisions regarding professional behavior, marriage and family therapists must consider the AAMFT Code of Ethics and applicable laws and regulations. If the AAMFT Code of Ethics prescribes a standard higher than that required by law, marriage and family therapists must meet the higher standard of the AAMFT Code of Ethics. Marriage and family therapists comply with the mandates of law, but make known their commitment to the AAMFT Code of Ethics and take steps to resolve the conflict in a responsible manner. The AAMFT supports legal mandates for reporting of alleged unethical conduct.

The AAMFT Code of Ethics is binding on Members of AAMFT in all membership categories, AAMFT-Approved Supervisors, and applicants for membership and the Approved Supervisor designation (hereafter, AAMFT Member). AAMFT members have an obligation to be familiar with the AAMFT Code of Ethics and its application to their professional services. Lack of awareness or misunderstanding of an ethical standard is not a defense to a charge of unethical conduct.

The process for filing, investigating, and resolving complaints of unethical conduct is described in the current Procedures for Handling Ethical Matters of the AAMFT Ethics Committee. Persons accused are considered innocent by the Ethics Committee until proven guilty, except as otherwise provided, and are entitled to due process. If an AAMFT Member resigns in anticipation of, or during the course of, an ethics investigation, the Ethics Committee will complete its investigation. Any publication of action taken by the Association will include the fact that the Member attempted to resign during the investigation.

PRINCIPLE I   RESPONSIBILITY TO CLIENTS

Marriage and family therapists advance the welfare of families and individuals. They respect the rights of those persons seeking their assistance, and make reasonable efforts to ensure that their services are used appropriately.

1.1 Marriage and family therapists provide professional assistance to persons without discrimination on the basis of race, age, ethnicity, socioeconomic status, disability, gender, health status, religion, national origin, or sexual orientation.

1.2 Marriage and family therapists obtain appropriate informed consent to therapy or related procedures as early as feasible in the therapeutic relationship, and use language that is reasonably understandable to clients. The content of informed consent may vary depending upon the client and treatment plan; however, informed consent generally necessitates that the client: (a) has the capacity to consent; (b) has been adequately informed of significant information concerning treatment processes and procedures; (c) has been adequately informed of potential risks and benefits of treatments for which generally recognized standards do not yet exist; (d) has freely and without undue influence expressed consent; and (e) has provided consent that is appropriately documented. When persons, due to age or mental status, are legally incapable of giving informed consent, marriage and family therapists obtain informed permission from a legally authorized person, if such substitute consent is legally permissible.

1.3 Marriage and family therapists are aware of their influential positions with respect to clients, and they avoid exploiting the trust and dependency of such persons. Therapists, therefore, make every effort to avoid conditions and multiple relationships with clients that could impair professional judgment or increase the risk of exploitation. Such relationships include, but are not limited to, business or close personal relationships with a client or the client's immediate family. When the risk of impairment or exploitation exists due to conditions or multiple roles, therapists take appropriate precautions.

1.4 Sexual intimacy with clients is prohibited.

1.5 Sexual intimacy with former clients is likely to be harmful and is therefore prohibited for two years following the termination of therapy or last professional contact. In an effort to avoid exploiting the trust and dependency of clients, marriage and family therapists should not engage in sexual intimacy with former clients after the two years following termination or last professional contact. Should therapists engage in sexual intimacy with former clients following two years after termination or last professional contact, the burden shifts to the therapist to demonstrate that there has been no exploitation or injury to the former client or to the client's immediate family.

1.6 Marriage and family therapists comply with applicable laws regarding the reporting of alleged unethical conduct.

1.7 Marriage and family therapists do not use their professional relationships with clients to further their own interests.

1.8 Marriage and family therapists respect the rights of clients to make decisions and help them to understand the consequences of these decisions. Therapists clearly advise the clients that they have the responsibility to make decisions regarding relationships such as cohabitation, marriage, divorce, separation, reconciliation, custody, and visitation.

1.9 Marriage and family therapists continue therapeutic relationships only so long as it is reasonably clear that clients are benefiting from the relationship.

1.10 Marriage and family therapists assist persons in obtaining other therapeutic services if the therapist is unable or unwilling, for appropriate reasons, to provide professional help.

1.11 Marriage and family therapists do not abandon or neglect clients in treatment without making reasonable arrangements for the continuation of such treatment.

1.12 Marriage and family therapists obtain written informed consent from clients before videotaping, audio recording, or permitting third-party observation.

1.13 Marriage and family therapists, upon agreeing to provide services to a person or entity at the request of a third party, clarify, to the extent feasible and at the outset of the service, the nature of the relationship with each party and the limits of confidentiality.

PRINCIPLE II   CONFIDENTIALITY

Marriage and family therapists have unique confidentiality concerns because the client in a therapeutic relationship may be more than one person. Therapists respect and guard the confidences of each individual client.

2.1 Marriage and family therapists disclose to clients and other interested parties, as early as feasible in their professional contacts, the nature of confidentiality and possible limitations of the clients' right to confidentiality. Therapists review with clients the circumstances where confidential information may be requested and where disclosure of confidential information may be legally required. Circumstances may necessitate repeated disclosures

2.2 Marriage and family therapists do not disclose client confidences except by written authorization or waiver, or where mandated or permitted by law. Verbal authorization will not be sufficient except in emergency situations, unless prohibited by law. When providing couple, family or group treatment, the therapist does not disclose information outside the treatment context without a written authorization from each individual competent to execute a waiver. In the context of couple, family or group treatment, the therapist may not reveal any individual's confidences to others in the client unit without the prior written permission of that individual.

2.3 Marriage and family therapists use client and/or clinical materials in teaching, writing, consulting, research, and public presentations only if a written waiver has been obtained in accordance with Sub-principle 2.2, or when appropriate steps have been taken to protect client identity and confidentiality.

2.4 Marriage and family therapists store, safeguard, and dispose of client records in ways that maintain confidentiality and are in accord with applicable laws and professional standards.

2.5 Subsequent to the therapist moving from the area, closing the practice, or upon the death of the therapist, a marriage and family therapist arranges for the storage, transfer, or disposal of client records in ways that maintain confidentiality and safeguard the welfare of clients.

2.6 Marriage and family therapists, when consulting with colleagues or referral sources, do not share confidential information that could reasonably lead to the identification of a client, research participant, supervisee, or other person with whom they have a confidential relationship unless they have obtained the prior written consent of the client, research participant, supervisee, or other person with whom they have a confidential relationship. Information may be shared only to the extent necessary to achieve the purposes of the consultation.

PRINCIPLE III PROFESSIONAL COMPETENCE AND INTEGRITY

Marriage and family therapists maintain high standards of professional competence and integrity.

3.1 Marriage and family therapists pursue knowledge of new developments and maintain competence in marriage and family therapy through education, training, or supervised experience.

3.2 Marriage and family therapists maintain adequate knowledge of and adhere to applicable laws, ethics, and professional standards.

3.3 Marriage and family therapists seek appropriate professional assistance for their personal problems or conflicts that may impair work performance or clinical judgment.

3.4 Marriage and family therapists do not provide services that create a conflict of interest that may impair work performance or clinical judgment.

3.5 Marriage and family therapists, as presenters, teachers, supervisors, consultants and researchers, are dedicated to high standards of scholarship, present accurate information, and disclose potential conflicts of interest.

3.6 Marriage and family therapists maintain accurate and adequate clinical and financial records.

3.7 While developing new skills in specialty areas, marriage and family therapists take steps to ensure the competence of their work and to protect clients from possible harm. Marriage and family therapists practice in specialty areas new to them only after appropriate education, training, or supervised experience.

3.8 Marriage and family therapists do not engage in sexual or other forms of harassment of clients, students, trainees, supervisees, employees, colleagues, or research subjects.

3.9 Marriage and family therapists do not engage in the exploitation of clients, students, trainees, supervisees, employees, colleagues, or research subjects.

3.10 Marriage and family therapists do not give to or receive from clients (a) gifts of substantial value or (b) gifts that impair the integrity or efficacy of the therapeutic relationship.

3.11 Marriage and family therapists do not diagnose, treat, or advise on problems outside the recognized boundaries of their competencies.

3.12 Marriage and family therapists make efforts to prevent the distortion or misuse of their clinical and research findings.

3.13 Marriage and family therapists, because of their ability to influence and alter the lives of others, exercise special care when making public their professional recommendations and opinions through testimony or other public statements.

3.14 To avoid a conflict of interests, marriage and family therapists who treat minors or adults involved in custody or visitation actions may not also perform forensic evaluations for custody, residence, or visitation of the minor. The marriage and family therapist who treats the minor may provide the court or mental health professional performing the evaluation with information about the minor from the marriage and family therapist's perspective as a treating marriage and family therapist, so long as the marriage and family therapist does not violate confidentiality.

3.15 Marriage and family therapists are in violation of this Code and subject to termination of membership or other appropriate action if they: (a) are convicted of any felony; (b) are convicted of a misdemeanor related to their qualifications or functions; (c) engage in conduct which could lead to conviction of a felony, or a misdemeanor related to their qualifications or functions; (d) are expelled from or disciplined by other professional organizations; (e) have their licenses or certificates suspended or revoked or are otherwise disciplined by regulatory bodies; (f) continue to practice marriage and family therapy while no longer competent to do so because they are impaired by physical or mental causes or the abuse of alcohol or other substances; or (g) fail to cooperate with the Association at any point from the inception of an ethical complaint through the completion of all proceedings regarding that complaint.

PRINCIPLE IV   RESPONSIBILITY TO STUDENTS AND SUPERVISEES

Marriage and family therapists do not exploit the trust and dependency of students and supervisees.

4.1 Marriage and family therapists are aware of their influential positions with respect to students and supervisees, and they avoid exploiting the trust and dependency of such persons. Therapists, therefore, make every effort to avoid conditions and multiple relationships that could impair professional objectivity or increase the risk of exploitation. When the risk of impairment or exploitation exists due to conditions or multiple roles, therapists take appropriate precautions.

4.2 Marriage and family therapists do not provide therapy to current students or supervisees.

4.3 Marriage and family therapists do not engage in sexual intimacy with students or supervisees during the evaluative or training relationship between the therapist and student or supervisee. Should a supervisor engage in sexual activity with a former supervisee, the burden of proof shifts to the supervisor to demonstrate that there has been no exploitation or injury to the supervisee.

4.4 Marriage and family therapists do not permit students or supervisees to perform or to hold themselves out as competent to perform professional services beyond their training, level of experience, and competence.

4.5 Marriage and family therapists take reasonable measures to ensure that services provided by supervisees are professional.

4.6 Marriage and family therapists avoid accepting as supervisees or students those individuals with whom a prior or existing relationship could compromise the therapist's objectivity. When such situations cannot be avoided, therapists take appropriate precautions to maintain objectivity. Examples of such relationships include, but are not limited to, those individuals with whom the therapist has a current or prior sexual, close personal, immediate familial, or therapeutic relationship.

4.7 Marriage and family therapists do not disclose supervisee confidences except by written authorization or waiver, or when mandated or permitted by law. In educational or training settings where there are multiple supervisors, disclosures are permitted only to other professional colleagues, administrators, or employers who share responsibility for training of the supervisee. Verbal authorization will not be sufficient except in emergency situations, unless prohibited by law.

PRINCIPLE V   RESPONSIBILITY TO RESEARCH PARTICIPANTS

Investigators respect the dignity and protect the welfare of research participants, and are aware of applicable laws and regulations and professional standards governing the conduct of research.

5.1 Investigators are responsible for making careful examinations of ethical acceptability in planning studies. To the extent that services to research participants may be compromised by participation in research, investigators seek the ethical advice of qualified professionals not directly involved in the investigation and observe safeguards to protect the rights of research participants.

5.2 Investigators requesting participant involvement in research inform participants of the aspects of the research that might reasonably be expected to influence willingness to participate. Investigators are especially sensitive to the possibility of diminished consent when participants are also receiving clinical services, or have impairments which limit understanding and/or communication, or when participants are children.

5.3 Investigators respect each participant's freedom to decline participation in or to withdraw from a research study at any time. This obligation requires special thought and consideration when investigators or other members of the research team are in positions of authority or influence over participants. Marriage and family therapists, therefore, make every effort to avoid multiple relationships with research participants that could impair professional judgment or increase the risk of exploitation.

5.4   Information obtained about a research participant during the course of an investigation is confidential unless there is a waiver previously obtained in writing. When the possibility exists that others, including family members, may obtain access to such information, this possibility, together with the plan for protecting confidentiality, is explained as part of the procedure for obtaining informed consent.

PRINCIPLE VI   RESPONSIBILITY TO THE PROFESSION

Marriage and family therapists respect the rights and responsibilities of professional colleagues and participate in activities that advance the goals of the profession.

6.1   Marriage and family therapists remain accountable to the standards of the profession when acting as members or employees of organizations. If the mandates of an organization with which a marriage and family therapist is affiliated, through employment, contract or otherwise, conflict with the AAMFT Code of Ethics, marriage and family therapists make known to the organization their commitment to the AAMFT Code of Ethics and attempt to resolve the conflict in a way that allows the fullest adherence to the Code of Ethics.

6.2   Marriage and family therapists assign publication credit to those who have contributed to a publication in proportion to their contributions and in accordance with customary professional publication practices.

6.3   Marriage and family therapists do not accept or require authorship credit for a publication based on research from a student's program, unless the therapist made a substantial contribution beyond being a faculty advisor or research committee member. Coauthorship on a student thesis, dissertation, or project should be determined in accordance with principles of fairness and justice.

6.4   Marriage and family therapists who are the authors of books or other materials that are published or distributed do not plagiarize or fail to cite persons to whom credit for original ideas or work is due.

6.5   Marriage and family therapists who are the authors of books or other materials published or distrib-

uted by an organization take reasonable precautions to ensure that the organization promotes and advertises the materials accurately and factually.

6.6   Marriage and family therapists participate in activities that contribute to a better community and society, including devoting a portion of their professional activity to services for which there is little or no financial return.

6.7   Marriage and family therapists are concerned with developing laws and regulations pertaining to marriage and family therapy that serve the public interest, and with altering such laws and regulations that are not in the public interest.

6.8   Marriage and family therapists encourage public participation in the design and delivery of professional services and in the regulation of practitioners.

PRINCIPLE VII   FINANCIAL ARRANGEMENTS

Marriage and family therapists make financial arrangements with clients, third-party payors, and supervisees that are reasonably understandable and conform to accepted professional practices.

7.1   Marriage and family therapists do not offer or accept kickbacks, rebates, bonuses, or other remuneration for referrals; fee-for-service arrangements are not prohibited.

7.2   Prior to entering into the therapeutic or supervisory relationship, marriage and family therapists clearly disclose and explain to clients and supervisees: (a) all financial arrangements and fees related to professional services, including charges for canceled or missed appointments; (b) the use of collection agencies or legal measures for nonpayment; and (c) the procedure for obtaining payment from the client, to the extent allowed by law, if payment is denied by the third-party payor. Once services have begun, therapists provide reasonable notice of any changes in fees or other charges.

7.3   Marriage and family therapists give reasonable notice to clients with unpaid balances of their intent to seek collection by agency or legal recourse. When such action is taken, therapists will not disclose clinical information.

7.4   Marriage and family therapists represent facts truthfully to clients, third-party payors, and supervisees regarding services rendered.

7.5   Marriage and family therapists ordinarily refrain from accepting goods and services from clients in return for services rendered. Bartering for professional services may be conducted only if: (a) the supervisee or client requests it, (b) the relationship is not exploitative, (c) the professional relationship is not distorted, and (d) a clear written contract is established.

7.6 Marriage and family therapists may not withhold records under their immediate control that are requested and needed for a client's treatment solely because payment has not been received for past services, except as otherwise provided by law.

PRINCIPLE VIII   ADVERTISING

Marriage and family therapists engage in appropriate informational activities, including those that enable the public, referral sources, or others to choose professional services on an informed basis.

8.1 Marriage and family therapists accurately represent their competencies, education, training, and experience relevant to their practice of marriage and family therapy.

8.2 Marriage and family therapists ensure that advertisements and publications in any media (such as directories, announcements, business cards, newspapers, radio, television, Internet, and facsimiles) convey information that is necessary for the public to make an appropriate selection of professional services. Information could include:
(a) office information, such as name, address, telephone number, credit card acceptability, fees, languages spoken, and office hours; (b) qualifying clinical degree (see subprinciple 8.5);
(c) other earned degrees (see subprinciple 8.5) and state or provincial licensures and/or certifi-

cations; (d) AAMFT clinical member status; and (e) description of practice.

8.3 Marriage and family therapists do not use names that could mislead the public concerning the identity, responsibility, source, and status of those practicing under that name, and do not hold themselves out as being partners or associates of a firm if they are not.

8.4 Marriage and family therapists do not use any professional identification (such as a business card, office sign, letterhead, Internet, or telephone or association directory listing) if it includes a statement or claim that is false, fraudulent, misleading, or deceptive.

8.5 In representing their educational qualifications, marriage and family therapists list and claim as evidence only those earned degrees: (a) from institutions accredited by regional accreditation sources recognized by the United States Department of Education; (b) from institutions recognized by states or provinces that license or certify marriage and family therapists; or (c) from equivalent foreign institutions.

8.6 Marriage and family therapists correct, wherever possible, false, misleading, or inaccurate information and representations made by others concerning the therapist's qualifications, services, or products.

8.7 Marriage and family therapists make certain that the qualifications of their employees or supervisees are represented in a manner that is not false, misleading, or deceptive.

8.8 Marriage and family therapists do not represent themselves as providing specialized services unless they have the appropriate education, training, or supervised experience.

This Code is published by:
American Association for Marriage and Family Therapy
1133 15th Street, NW, Suite 300
Washington, DC 20005-2710
TEL: (202) 452-0109
FAX: (202) 223-2329
www.aamft.org

Violations of this Code should be submitted in writing to the attention of:
AAMFT Ethics Committee
1133 15th Street, NW, Suite 300
Washington, DC 20005-2710
TEL: (202) 452-0109
E-mail: ethics@aamft.org

Appendix J
NBCC's Code of Ethics
Amended October 31, 1997

The following information is copyrighted by the National Board for Certified Counselors, Inc. (NBCC®). It cannot be distributed or reproduced without permission from NBCC®. Questions concerning the NBCC® Code of Ethics should be sent to *ethics@nbcc.org*.

Table of Contents

NATIONAL BOARD FOR CERTIFIED COUNSELORS CODE OF ETHICS

Preamble

The National Board for Certified Counselors (NBCC) is a professional certification board which certifies counselors as having met standards for the general and specialty practice of professional counseling established by the Board. The counselors certified by NBCC may identify with different profes-sional associations and are often licensed by jurisdictions which promulgate codes of ethics. The NBCC code of ethics provides a minimal ethical standard for the professional behavior of all NBCC certificants. This code provides an expectation of and assurance for the ethical practice for all who use the professional services of an NBCC certificant. In addition, it serves the purpose of having an enforceable standard for all NBCC certificants and assures those served of some resource in case of a perceived ethical violation.

The NBCC Ethical Code applies to all those certified by NBCC regardless of any other professional affiliation. Persons who receive professional services from certified counselors may elect to use other ethical codes which apply to their counselor. Although NBCC cooperates with professional associations and credentialing organizations, it can bring actions to discipline or sanction NBCC certificants only if the provisions of the NBCC Code are found to have been violated.

The National Board for Certified Counselors, Inc. (NBCC) promotes counseling through certification. In pursuit of this mission, the NBCC:

- Promotes quality assurance in counseling practice
- Promotes the value of counseling
- Promotes public awareness of quality counseling practice
- Promotes professionalism in counseling
- Promotes leadership in credentialing

Section A: General

1. Certified counselors engage in continuous efforts to improve professional practices, services, and research. Certified counselors are guided in their work by evidence of the best professional practices.

Source: Reprinted with the permission of the National Board for Certified Counselors and Affiliates, 3 Terrace Way, Suite D., Greensboro, NC 27403-3660.

2. Certified counselors have a responsibility to the clients they serve and to the institutions within which the services are performed. Certified counselors also strive to assist the respective agency, organization, or institution in providing competent and ethical professional services. The acceptance of employment in an institution implies that the certified counselor is in agreement with the general policies and principles of the institution. Therefore, the professional activities of the certified counselor are in accord with the objectives of the institution. If the certified counselor and the employer do not agree and cannot reach agreement on policies that are consistent with appropriate counselor ethical practice that is conducive to client growth and development, the employment should be terminated. If the situation warrants further action, the certified counselor should work through professional organizations to have the unethical practice changed.

3. Ethical behavior among professional associates (i.e., both certified and non-certified counselors) must be expected at all times. When a certified counselor has doubts as to the ethical behavior of professional colleagues, the certified counselor must take action to attempt to rectify this condition. Such action uses the respective institution's channels first and then uses procedures established by the NBCC or the perceived violator's profession.

4. Certified counselors must refuse remuneration for consultation or counseling with persons who are entitled to these services through the certified counselor's employing institution or agency. Certified counselors must not divert to their private practices, without the mutual consent of the institution and the client, legitimate clients in their primary agencies or the institutions with which they are affiliated.

5. In establishing fees for professional counseling services, certified counselors must consider the financial status of clients. In the event that the established fee status is inappropriate for a client, assistance must be provided in finding comparable services at acceptable cost.

6. Certified counselors offer only professional services for which they are trained or have supervised experience. No diagnosis, assessment, or treatment should be performed without prior training or supervision. Certified counselors are responsible for correcting any misrepresentations of their qualifications by others.

7. Certified counselors recognize their limitations and provide services or use techniques for which they are qualified by training and/or supervision.

Certified counselors recognize the need for and seek continuing education to assure competent services.

8. Certified counselors are aware of the intimacy in the counseling relationship and maintain respect for the client. Counselors must not engage in activities that seek to meet their personal or professional needs at the expense of the client.

9. Certified counselors must insure that they do not engage in personal, social, organizational, financial, or political activities which might lead to a misuse of their influence.

10. Sexual intimacy with clients is unethical. Certified counselors will not be sexually, physically, or romantically intimate with clients, and they will not engage in sexual, physical, or romantic intimacy with clients within a minimum of two years after terminating the counseling relationship.

11. Certified counselors do not condone or engage in sexual harassment, which is defined as unwelcome comments, gestures, or physical contact of a sexual nature.

12. Through an awareness of the impact of stereotyping and unwarranted discrimination (e.g., biases based on age, disability, ethnicity, gender, race, religion, or sexual orientation), certified counselors guard the individual rights and personal dignity of the client in the counseling relationship.

13. Certified counselors are accountable at all times for their behavior. They must be aware that all actions and behaviors of the counselor reflect on professional integrity and, when inappropriate, can damage the public trust in the counseling profession. To protect public confidence in the counseling profession, certified counselors avoid behavior that is clearly in violation of accepted moral and legal standards.

14. Products or services provided by certified counselors by means of classroom instruction, public lectures, demonstrations, written articles, radio or television programs or other types of media must meet the criteria cited in this code.

15. Certified counselors have an obligation to withdraw from the practice of counseling if they violate the Code of Ethics, or if the mental or physical condition of the certified counselor renders it unlikely that a professional relationship will be maintained.

Section B: Counseling Relationship

1. The primary obligation of certified counselors is to respect the integrity and promote the welfare of clients, whether they are assisted individually, in

family units, or in group counseling. In a group setting, the certified counselor is also responsible for taking reasonable precautions to protect individuals from physical and/or psychological trauma resulting from interaction within the group.

2. Certified counselors know and take into account the traditions and practices of other professional disciplines with whom they work and cooperate fully with such. If a person is receiving similar services from another professional, certified counselors do not offer their own services directly to such a person. If a certified counselor is contacted by a person who is already receiving similar services from another professional, the certified counselor carefully considers that professional relationship as well as the client's welfare and proceeds with caution and sensitivity to the therapeutic issues. When certified counselors learn that their clients are in a professional relationship with another counselor or mental health professional, they request release from the clients to inform the other counselor or mental health professional of their relationship with the client and strive to establish positive and collaborative professional relationships that are in the best interest of the client. Certified counselors discuss these issues with clients and the counselor or professional so as to minimize the risk of confusion and conflict and encourage clients to inform other professionals of the new professional relationship.

3. Certified counselors may choose to consult with any other professionally competent person about a client and must notify clients of this right. Certified counselors avoid placing a consultant in a conflict-of-interest situation that would preclude the consultant serving as a proper party to the efforts of the certified counselor to help the client.

4. When a client's condition indicates that there is a clear and imminent danger to the client or others, the certified counselor must take reasonable action to inform potential victims and/or inform responsible authorities. Consultation with other professionals must be used when possible. The assumption of responsibility for the client's behavior must be taken only after careful deliberation, and the client must be involved in the resumption of responsibility as quickly as possible.

5. Records of the counseling relationship, including interview notes, test data, correspondence, audio or visual tape recordings, electronic data storage, and other documents are to be considered professional information for use in counseling. Records should contain accurate factual data. The physical records are property of the certified counselors or

their employers. The information contained in the records belongs to the client and therefore may not be released to others without the consent of the client or when the counselor has exhausted challenges to a court order. The certified counselors are responsible to insure that their employees handle confidential information appropriately. Confidentiality must be maintained during the storage and disposition of records. Records should be maintained for a period of at least five (5) years after the last counselor/client contact, including cases in which the client is deceased. All records must be released to the client upon request.

6. Certified counselors must ensure that data maintained in electronic storage are secure. By using the best computer security methods available, the data must be limited to information that is appropriate and necessary for the services being provided and accessible only to appropriate staff members involved in the provision of services. Certified counselors must also ensure that the electronically stored data are destroyed when the information is no longer of value in providing services or required as part of clients' records.

7. Any data derived from a client relationship and used in training or research shall be so disguised that the informed client's identity is fully protected. Any data which cannot be so disguised may be used only as expressly authorized by the client's informed and uncoerced consent.

8. When counseling is initiated, and throughout the counseling process as necessary, counselors inform clients of the purposes, goals, techniques, procedures, limitations, potential risks and benefits of services to be performed, and clearly indicate limitations that may affect the relationship as well as any other pertinent information. Counselors take reasonable steps to ensure that clients understand the implications of any diagnosis, the intended use of tests and reports, methods of treatment and safety precautions that must be taken in their use, fees, and billing arrangements.

9. Certified counselors who have an administrative, supervisory and/or evaluative relationship with individuals seeking counseling services must not serve as the counselor and should refer the individuals to other professionals. Exceptions are made only in instances where an individual's situation warrants counseling intervention and another alternative is unavailable. Dual relationships that might impair the certified counselor's objectivity and professional judgment must be avoided and/or the counseling relationship terminated through referral to a competent professional.

10. When certified counselors determine an inability to be of professional assistance to a potential or existing client, they must, respectively, not initiate the counseling relationship or immediately terminate the relationship. In either event, the certified counselor must suggest appropriate alternatives. Certified counselors must be knowledgeable about referral resources so that a satisfactory referral can be initiated. In the event that the client declines a suggested referral, the certified counselor is not obligated to continue the relationship.

11. When certified counselors are engaged in intensive, short-term counseling, they must ensure that professional assistance is available at normal costs to clients during and following the short-term counseling.

12. Counselors using electronic means in which counselor and client are not in immediate proximity must present clients with local sources of care before establishing a continued short or long-term relationship. Counselors who communicate with clients via Internet are governed by NBCC standards for Web Counseling.

13. Counselors must document permission to practice counseling by electronic means in all governmental jurisdictions where such counseling takes place.

14. When electronic data and systems are used as a component of counseling services, certified counselors must ensure that the computer application, and any information it contains, is appropriate for the respective needs of clients and is non-discriminatory. Certified counselors must ensure that they themselves have acquired a facilitation level of knowledge with any system they use including hands-on application, and understanding of the uses of all aspects of the computer-based system. In selecting and/or maintaining computer-based systems that contain career information, counselors must ensure that the system provides current, accurate, and locally relevant information. Certified counselors must also ensure that clients are intellectually, emotionally, and physically compatible with computer applications and understand their purpose and operation. Client use of a computer application must be evaluated to correct possible problems and assess subsequent needs.

15. Certified counselors who develop self-help/stand-alone computer software for use by the general public, must first ensure that it is designed to function in a stand-alone manner that is appropriate and safe for all clients for which it is intended. A manual is required. The manual must provide the user with intended outcomes, suggestions for using the software, descriptions of inappropriately used applications, and descriptions of when and how other forms of counseling services might be beneficial. Finally, the manual must include the qualifications of the developer, the development process, validation date, and operating procedures.

16. The counseling relationship and information resulting from it remains confidential, consistent with the legal and ethical obligations of certified counselors. In group counseling, counselors clearly define confidentiality and the parameters for the specific group being entered, explain the importance of confidentiality, and discuss the difficulties related to confidentiality involved in group work. The fact that confidentiality cannot be guaranteed is clearly communicated to group members. However, counselors should give assurance about their professional responsibility to keep all group communications confidential.

17. Certified counselors must screen prospective group counseling participants to ensure compatibility with group objectives. This is especially important when the emphasis is on self-understanding and growth through self-disclosure. Certified counselors must maintain an awareness of the welfare of each participant throughout the group process.

Section C: Measurement and Evaluation

1. Because many types of assessment techniques exist, certified counselors must recognize the limits of their competence and perform only those assessment functions for which they have received appropriate training or supervision.

2. Certified counselors who utilize assessment instruments to assist them with diagnoses must have appropriate training and skills in educational and psychological measurement, validation criteria, test research, and guidelines for test development and use.

3. Certified counselors must provide instrument specific orientation or information to an examinee prior to and following the administration of assessment instruments or techniques so that the results may be placed in proper perspective with other relevant factors. The purpose of testing and the explicit use of the results must be made known to an examinee prior to testing.

4. In selecting assessment instruments or techniques for use in a given situation or with a particular client, certified counselors must carefully evaluate the specific theoretical bases and

characteristics, validity, reliability and appropriateness of the instrument.

5. When making statements to the public about assessment instruments or techniques, certified counselors must provide accurate information and avoid false claims or misconceptions concerning the meaning of the instrument's reliability and validity terms.

6. Counselors must follow all directions and researched procedures for selection, administration and interpretation of all evaluation instruments and use them only within proper contexts.

7. Certified counselors must be cautious when interpreting the results of instruments that possess insufficient technical data, and must explicitly state to examinees the specific limitations and purposes for the use of such instruments.

8. Certified counselors must proceed with caution when attempting to evaluate and interpret performances of any person who cannot be appropriately compared to the norms for the instrument.

9. Because prior coaching or dissemination of test materials can invalidate test results, certified counselors are professionally obligated to maintain test security.

10. Certified counselors must consider psychometric limitations when selecting and using an instrument, and must be cognizant of the limitations when interpreting the results. When tests are used to classify clients, certified counselors must ensure that periodic review and/or retesting are made to prevent client stereotyping.

11. An examinee's welfare, explicit prior understanding, and consent are the factors used when determining who receives the test results. Certified counselors must see that appropriate interpretation accompanies any release of individual or group test data (e.g., limitations of instrument and norms).

12. Certified counselors must ensure that computer-generated test administration and scoring programs function properly thereby providing clients with accurate test results.

13. Certified counselors who develop computer-based test interpretations to support the assessment process must ensure that the validity of the interpretations is established prior to the commercial distribution of the computer application.

14. Certified counselors recognize that test results may become obsolete, and avoid the misuse of obsolete data.

15. Certified counselors must not appropriate, reproduce, or modify published tests or parts thereof without acknowledgment and permission from the publisher, except as permitted by the fair educational use provisions of the U.S. copyright law.

Section D: Research and Publication

1. Certified counselors will adhere to applicable legal and professional guidelines on research with human subjects.

2. In planning research activities involving human subjects, certified counselors must be aware of and responsive to all pertinent ethical principles and ensure that the research problem, design, and execution are in full compliance with any pertinent institutional or governmental regulations.

3. The ultimate responsibility for ethical research lies with the principal researcher, although others involved in the research activities are ethically obligated and responsible for their own actions.

4. Certified counselors who conduct research with human subjects are responsible for the welfare of the subjects throughout the experiment and must take all reasonable precautions to avoid causing injurious psychological, physical, or social effects on their subjects.

5. Certified counselors who conduct research must abide by the basic elements of informed consent:
   a. fair explanation of the procedures to be followed, including an identification of those which are experimental
   b. description of the attendant discomforts and risks
   c. description of the benefits to be expected
   d. disclosure of appropriate alternative procedures that would be advantageous for subjects with an offer to answer any inquiries concerning the procedures
   e. an instruction that subjects are free to withdraw their consent and to discontinue participation in the project or activity at any time

6. When reporting research results, explicit mention must be made of all the variables and conditions known to the investigator that may have affected the outcome of the study or the interpretation of the data.

7. Certified counselors who conduct and report research investigations must do so in a manner that minimizes the possibility that the results will be misleading.

8. Certified counselors are obligated to make available sufficient original research data to qualified others who may wish to replicate the study.

9. Certified counselors who supply data, aid in the research of another person, report research results, or make original data available, must take due care to disguise the identity of respective subjects in the absence of specific authorization from the subjects to do otherwise.

10. When conducting and reporting research, certified counselors must be familiar with and give recogni-

tion to previous work on the topic, must observe all copyright laws, and must follow the principles of giving full credit to those to whom credit is due.

11. Certified counselors must give due credit through joint authorship, acknowledgment, footnote statements, or other appropriate means to those who have contributed to the research and/or publication, in accordance with such contributions.

12. Certified counselors should communicate to other counselors the results of any research judged to be of professional value. Results that reflect unfavorably on institutions, programs, services, or vested interests must not be withheld.

13. Certified counselors who agree to cooperate with another individual in research and/or publication incur an obligation to cooperate as promised in terms of punctuality of performance and with full regard to the completeness and accuracy of the information required.

14. Certified counselors must not submit the same manuscript, or one essentially similar in content, for simultaneous publication consideration by two or more journals. In addition, manuscripts that have been published in whole or substantial part should not be submitted for additional publication without acknowledgment and permission from any previous publisher.

Section E: Consulting

Consultation refers to a voluntary relationship between a professional helper and a help-needing individual, group, or social unit in which the consultant is providing help to the client(s) in defining and solving a work-related problem or potential work-related problem with a client or client system.

1. Certified counselors, acting as consultants, must have a high degree of self awareness of their own values, knowledge, skills, limitations, and needs in entering a helping relationship that involves human and/or organizational change. The focus of the consulting relationship must be on the issues to be resolved and not on the person(s) presenting the problem.

2. In the consulting relationship, the certified counselor and client must understand and agree upon the problem definition, subsequent goals, and predicted consequences of interventions selected.

3. Certified counselors acting as consultants must be reasonably certain that they, or the organization represented, have the necessary competencies and resources for giving the kind of help that is needed or that may develop later, and that appropriate referral resources are available.

4. Certified counselors in a consulting relationship must encourage and cultivate client adaptability and growth toward self-direction. Certified counselors must maintain this role consistently and not become a decision maker for clients or create a future dependency on the consultant.

Section F: Private Practice

1. In advertising services as a private practitioner, certified counselors must advertise in a manner that accurately informs the public of the professional services, expertise, and techniques of counseling available.

2. Certified counselors who assume an executive leadership role in a private practice organization do not permit their names to be used in professional notices during periods of time when they are not actively engaged in the private practice of counseling unless their executive roles are clearly stated.

3. Certified counselors must make available their highest degree (described by discipline), type and level of certification and/or license, address, telephone number, office hours, type and/or description of services, and other relevant information. Listed information must not contain false, inaccurate, misleading, partial, out-of-context, or otherwise deceptive material or statements.

4. Certified counselors who are involved in a partnership/corporation with other certified counselors and/or other professionals, must clearly specify all relevant specialties of each member of the partnership or corporation.

Certification Examination

Applicants for the NBCC Certification Examinations must have fulfilled all current eligibility requirements, and are responsible for the accuracy and validity of all information and/or materials provided by themselves or by others for fulfillment of eligibility criteria.

Approved on July 1, 1982

Amended on February 21, 1987, January 6, 1989, and October 31, 1997

Reference documents, statements, and sources for the development of the NBCC Code of Ethics were as follows:

The Ethical Standards of the American Counseling Association (ACA), Responsible Uses for Standardized Testing (AMECD), codes of ethics for the American Psychological Association, and the National Career Development Association, Handbook of Standards for Computer-Based Career Information Systems (ACSCI); and Guidelines for the Use of Computer-Based Career Information and Guidance Systems (ACSCI).

Appendix K
Public Law 93-380
Protection of the Rights and Privacy of Parents and Students—Family Educational Rights and Privacy Act of 1974

Sec. 513.(a) Part C of the General Education Provisions Act is further amended by adding at the end thereof the following new section:

PROTECTION OF THE RIGHTS AND PRIVACY OF PARENTS AND STUDENTS

Sec. 438.(a)(1) No funds shall be made available under any applicable program to any State or local educational agency, any institution of higher education, any community college, any school, any agency offering a preschool program, or any other educational institution which has a policy of denying, or which effectively prevents, the parents of students attending any school of such agency, or attending such institution of higher education, community college, school, preschool, or other educational institution, the right to inspect and review any and all official records, files, and data directly related to their children, including all material that is incorporated into each student's cumulative record folder, and intended for school use or to be available to parties outside the school or school system, and specifically including, but not necessarily limited to, identifying data, academic work completed, level of achievement (grades, standardized achievement test scores), attendance data, scores on standardized intelligence, aptitude, and psychological tests, interest inventory results, health data, family background information, teacher or counselor ratings of serious or recurrent behavior patterns. Where such records or data include information on more than one student, the parents of any student shall be entitled to receive, or be informed of, that part of such record or data as pertains to their child. Each recipient shall establish appropriate procedures for the granting of a request by parents for access to their child's school records within a reasonable period of time, but in no case more than forty-five days after the request has been made.

(2) Parents shall have an opportunity for a hearing to challenge the content of their child's school records, to insure that the records are not inaccurate, misleading, or otherwise in violation of the privacy or other rights of students, and to provide an opportunity for the correction or deletion of any such inaccurate, misleading, or otherwise inappropriate data contained therein.

(b)(1) No funds shall be made available under any applicable program to any State or local educational agency, any institution of higher education, any community college, any school, any agency offering a preschool program, or any other educational institution which has a policy of permitting the release of personally identifiable records or files (or personal information contained therein) of students without the written consent of their parents to any individual, agency, or organization, other than to the following—

(A) other school officials, including teachers within the educational institution or local educational agency who have legitimate educational interests;

(B) officials of other schools or school systems in which the student intends to enroll, upon condition that the student's parents be notified of the transfer, receive a copy of the record if desired, and have an opportunity for a hearing to challenge the content of the record;

(C) authorized representatives of (i) the Comptroller General of the United States, (ii) the Secretary, (iii) an ad-

Source: Reprinted with permission from *United States Code Congressional and Administrative News—1974*, Vol. 1, pp. 541–697. Copyright © 1975 by West Publishing Company.

ministrative head of an educational agency (as defined in section 409 of this Act), or (iv) State educational authorities, under the conditions set forth in paragraph (3) of this subsection; and

(D) in connection with a student's application for, or receipt of, financial aid.

(2) No funds shall be made available under any applicable program to any State or local educational agency, any institution of higher education, any community college, any school, agency offering a preschool program, or any other educational institution which has a policy of practice of furnishing, in any form, any personally identifiable information contained in personal school records, to any persons other than those listed in subsection (b)(1) unless—

(A) there is written consent from the student's parents specifying records to be released, the reasons for such release, and to whom, and with a copy of the records to be released to the student's parents and the student if desired by the parents, or

(B) such information is furnished in compliance with judicial order, or pursuant to any lawfully issued subpoena, upon condition that parents and the student are notified of all such orders or subpoenas in advance of the compliance therewith by the educational institution or agency.

(3) Nothing contained in this section shall preclude authorized representatives of (A) the Comptroller General of the United States, (B) the Secretary, (C) an administrative head of an educational agency or (D) State educational authorities from having access to student or other records which may be necessary in connection with the audit and evaluation of Federally-supported education programs, or in connection with the enforcement of the Federal legal requirements which relate to such programs: *Provided* that, except when collection of personally identifiable data is specifically authorized by Federal law, any data collected by such officials with respect to individual students shall not include information (including social security numbers) which would permit the personal identification of such students or their parents after the data so obtained has been collected.

(4)(A) With respect to subsections (c)(1) and (c)(2) and (c)(3), all persons, agencies, or organizations desiring access to the records of a student shall be required to sign a written form which shall be kept permanently with the file of the student, but only for inspection by the parents or student, indicating specifically the legitimate educational or other interest that each person, agency, or organization has in seeking this information. Such form shall be available to parents and to the school official responsible for record maintenance as a means of auditing the operation of the system.

(B) With respect to this subsection, personal information shall only be transferred to a third party on the condition that such party will not permit any other party to have access to such information without the written consent of the parents of the student.

(c) The Secretary shall adopt appropriate regulations to protect the rights of privacy of students and their families in connection with any surveys or data-gathering activities conducted, assisted, or authorized by the Secretary or an administrative head of an education agency. Regulations established under this subsection shall include provisions controlling the use, dissemination, and protection of such data. No survey or data-gathering activities shall be conducted by the Secretary, or an administrative head of an education agency under an applicable program, unless such activities are authorized by law.

(d) For the purpose of this section, whenever a student has attained eighteen years of age, or is attending an institution of postsecondary education the permission or consent required of and the rights accorded to the parents of the student shall thereafter be required of and accorded to the student.

(e) No funds shall be made available under any applicable program unless the recipient of such funds informs the parents of students, or the students, if they are eighteen years of age or older, or are attending an institution of postsecondary education, of the rights accorded them by this section.

(f) The Secretary, or an administrative head of an education agency, shall take appropriate actions to enforce provisions of this section and to deal with violations of this section, according to the provisions of this Act, except that action to terminate assistance may be taken only if the Secretary finds that there has been a failure to comply with the provisions of this section, and he has determined that compliance cannot be secured by voluntary means.

(g) The secretary shall establish or designate an office and review board within the Department of Health, Education, and Welfare for the purpose of investigating, processing, reviewing, and adjusting violations of the provisions of this section and complaints which may be filed concerning alleged violations of this section, according to the procedures contained in sections 434 and 437 of this Act.

(b)(1)(i) The provisions of this section shall become effective ninety days after the date of enactment of section 438 of the General Education Provisions Act.

(2)(i) This section may be cited as the "Family Educational Rights and Privacy Act of 1974."

PROTECTION OF PUPIL RIGHTS

Sec. 514.(a) Part C of the General Education Provisions Act is further amended by adding after section 438 the following new section:

Protection of Pupil Rights

Sec. 439.(a) All instructional material, including teacher's manuals, films, tapes, or other supplementary instructional material which will be used in connection with any research or experimentation program or project shall be available for inspection by the parents or guardians of the children engaged in such program or project. For the purpose of this section "research or experimentation program or project" means any program or project in any applicable program designed to explore or develop new or unproven teaching methods or techniques.

(b) The amendment made by subsection (a) shall be effective upon enactment of this Act.

Appendix L
American School Counselor Association
The School Counselor and Comprehensive
School Counseling Programs

THE POSITION STATEMENT OF THE AMERICAN SCHOOL COUNSELOR ASSOCIATION (ASCA)

ASCA endorses comprehensive school counseling programs that promote and enhance student learning. The focus of the program is on the three broad and interrelated areas of student development: academic, career, and personal/social development. Each encompasses a variety of desired student learning competencies, which form the foundation of the developmental school counseling program. The school counselor uses a variety of activities and resources to promote the desired student development. School counselor responsibilities include organization, implementation, and coordination of the program.

THE RATIONALE

A comprehensive school counseling program is developmental in nature. It is systematic, sequential, clearly defined, and accountable. The foundation of the program is developmental psychology, educational philosophy, and counseling methodology. Proactive and preventative in focus, the school counseling program is integral to the educational program. It assists students in acquiring and using life-long skills through the development of academic, career, self-awareness, and interpersonal communication skills. The goal of the comprehensive school counseling program is to provide all students with life success skills.

The school counseling program has characteristics similar to other educational programs, including a scope and se-

quence; student competencies or outcomes; activities and processes to assist students in achieving the outcomes; professionally credentialed personnel; materials and resources; and national standards for evaluation.

We recognize that our educational system is being challenged by the increasing needs of today's students and the rising expectations of society. Many of our children enter school with emotional, physical, and interpersonal barriers to learning. Although comprehensive school counseling programs include necessary crisis-oriented responsive services, the emphasis is on the developmental skill building for all students beginning when students enter school and continuing as they progress through the grades.

Effective school counseling programs are a collaborative effort between the counselor and other educators to create an environment which promotes school success. Staff and counselors value and respond to the diversity and individual differences in our society and communities. Comprehensive school counseling programs help ensure equal opportunities for all students to participate fully in the educational process.

This school counseling model is compatible with the *National Education Goals* and the *National Standards for School Counseling Programs*.

THE COUNSELOR'S ROLE

Within a comprehensive school counseling program, counselors will focus their skills, time, and energy on direct service to students, staff, and families. ASCA recommends a realistic counselor-student ratio to be 1:250. School counselors will spend 70% of their time in direct service to students. Indirect services will include counseling program planning, maintenance and evaluation, participation in school site planning and implementation, partnerships and alliances with postsecondary institutions, businesses, and community agencies, and other tasks which enhance the mission of the program.

The comprehensive school counseling program balances many components. It requires counselors to deliver individual and small group counseling and large group guidance; to teach skill development in academic, career, and personal/social areas; to provide consultation and case management; and to coordinate, manage, and evaluate the school counseling program.

As student advocates, school counselors participate as members of the educational team. They consult and collaborate with teachers, administrators, and families to assist students to be successful academically, vocationally, and personally. School counselors are indispensable partners with the instructional staff in the development of contributing members of society. They assure, on behalf of students and their families, that all school programs facilitate the educational process and offer the opportunity for school success.

SUMMARY

A written comprehensive, developmentally based preK–12 school counseling program should be implemented in every school district. It should include a systematic and planned program delivery that productively involves all students and promotes and enhances the learning process.

The comprehensive school counseling program facilitates student development in three areas:

- academic development which includes the acquisition of skills, attitudes, and knowledge which contributes to effective learning in school and throughout the life span;
- career development which includes the foundation for the acquisition of skills, attitudes, and knowledge which will enable students to make a successful transition from school to careers;
- personal/social development which includes the acquisition of skills, attitudes and knowledge to help students understand and respect self and others, acquire effective interpersonal skills, understand and practice safety and survival skills, and develop into contributing members of society.

The comprehensive school counseling program should be supported by appropriate resources and implemented and coordinated by a credentialed professional school counselor.

1. **Standards of Online Practice:** The site developers and professional counselors employed by this site have read and adhere to the American Counseling Association Code of Ethics and Standards for the Practice of Online Counseling. Specific issues and concerns in said codes and standards that are of critical importance include the following:

   Consumer protection issues are addressed such as fee schedules, site security, reporting of unethical behavior, and addressing complaints or concerns about the site itself. Appropriate orientation is provided to site visitors/clients and intake procedures are established as needed. Procedures for addressing the needs of potentially suicidal site visitors/clients are displayed on the home page of the site as needed. Links are provided to the professional counselor's state licensure board(s), the American Counseling Association and other relevant codes of ethics, (i.e., NCDA, NBCC), and the ACA and other relevant standards for the practice of online counseling.

2. **Professional Qualifications**—Professional counseling services provided and hosted on this site will only be given by qualified professional counselors unless a clear statement is made that the intervention or information offered is from a differently credentialed professional or organization (i.e., psychology or social work). The words "counselor" or "professional counselor" will only be used to identify service providers who are properly licensed or certified as such by appropriate state or professional counseling organizations.

Counselors employed by this site avail themselves of appropriate cyber training and continuing education opportunities.

3. **Online v. Onsite Presence**—The information provided on this site is designed to support, not replace, the relationship that exists between a client/site visitor and his/her existing professional counselor. Further, as counselors are an integral part of the system in which they function, i.e., their school system, their behavioral health organization, or their counselor education program, the range of information and services they provide cannot be replaced by online services. Because counselors have many roles in addition to that addressed by online counseling, their physical presence in the system is critical.

4. **Confidentiality**—Confidentiality of data and video transmissions relating to individual clients and visitors to a professional counseling Web site, including their identity, is respected by this Web site. The Web site owners undertake to honor or exceed the legal requirements of professional counseling information privacy that apply in the country and state where the Web site and mirror sites are located. Information acquired about clients/site visitors will not be sold or distributed to other vendors without the express written permission of the ACA Technology Committee or the ACA Executive Director.

5. **Attribution of Sources**—Where appropriate, information contained on this site will be supported by clear references to source data and, where possible, have specific HTML links to that data. The

date when a page was last modified will be clearly displayed (e.g., at the bottom of each page).

6. **Justification of Claims**—Any claims relating to the benefits/performance of a counseling intervention, commercial product or service will be supported by appropriate, balanced evidence.

7. **Visibility of and Access to Developers**—The developers of this Web site will seek to provide information online concerning their professional qualifications in the clearest possible manner and provide contact addresses, phone numbers, and e-mail addresses for visitors that seek further information or support. The Webmaster will display his/her E-mail address clearly throughout the Web site.

8. **Visibility of Site Backers**—Support for this Web site will be clearly identified, including the identities of commercial and non-commercial organizations that have contributed funding, services or material for the site.

9. **Advertising and Editorial Policy**—Sources of advertising funding are clearly stated. A brief description of the advertising policy adopted by the Web site owners will be displayed on the site. Advertising and other promotional material will be presented to viewers in a manner and context that facilitates differentiation between it and the original materials created by the institution operating the site.

10. **Research**—The site collaborates with the American Counseling Association research efforts to determine best online practice. Collaboration can include, but is not limited to, financially supporting ACA research efforts, providing legal and ethical access to clients and counselors and their records, and utilizing outcome research to modify practice.

Appendix N
The Practice of Internet Counseling

This document contains a statement of principles for guiding the evolving practice of Internet counseling. In order to provide a context for these principles, the following definition of Internet counseling, which is one element of technology-assisted distance counseling, is provided. The Internet counseling standards follow the definitions presented below.

A TAXONOMY FOR DEFINING FACE-TO-FACE AND TECHNOLOGY-ASSISTED DISTANCE COUNSELING

The delivery of technology-assisted distance counseling continues to grow and evolve. Technology assistance in the form of computer-assisted assessment, computer-assisted information systems, and telephone counseling has been available and widely used for some time. The rapid development and use of the Internet to deliver information and foster communication has resulted in the creation of new forms of counseling. Developments have occurred so rapidly that it is difficult to communicate a common understanding of these new forms of counseling practice.

The purpose of this document is to create standard definitions of technology-assisted distance counseling that can be easily updated in response to evolutions in technology and practice. A definition of traditional face-to-face counseling is also presented to show similarities and differences with respect to various applications of technology in counseling. A taxonomy of forms of counseling is also presented to further clarify how technology relates to counseling practice.

NATURE OF COUNSELING

Counseling is the application of mental health, psychological, or human development principles, through cognitive, affective, behavioral or systemic intervention strategies, that address wellness, personal growth, or career development, as well as pathology.

Depending on the needs of the client and the availability of services, counseling may range from a few brief interactions in a short period of time, to numerous interactions over an extended period of time. Brief interventions, such as classroom discussions, workshop presentations, or assistance in using assessment, information, or instructional resources, may be sufficient to meet individual needs. Or, these brief interventions may lead to longer-term counseling interventions for individuals with more substantial needs. Counseling may be delivered by a single counselor, two counselors working collaboratively, or a single counselor with brief assistance from another counselor who has specialized expertise that is needed by the client.

FORMS OF COUNSELING

Counseling can be delivered in a variety of forms that share the definition presented above. Forms of counseling differ with respect to participants, delivery location, communication medium, and interaction process. Counseling *participants* can be **individuals, couples, or groups**. The *location* for counseling delivery can be **face-to-face or at a distance** with the assistance of technology. The *communication medium* for

Source: From the National Board for Certified Counselors, Inc. (2001). *The Practice of Internet Counseling.* Copyright © 2001. National Board for Certified Counselors, Inc. Reprinted with the permission of the National Board for Certified Counselors and Affiliates, 3 Terrace Way, Suite D., Greensboro, NC 27403-3660.

counseling can be what is **read** from text, what is **heard** from audio, or what is **seen** and **heard** in person or from video. The *interaction process* for counseling can be **synchronous** or **asynchronous**. Synchronous interaction occurs with little or no gap in time between the responses of the counselor and the client. Asynchronous interaction occurs with a gap in time between the responses of the counselor and the client.

The selection of a specific form of counseling is based on the needs and preferences of the client within the range of services available. Distance counseling supplements face-to-face counseling by providing increased access to counseling on the basis of **necessity** or **convenience**. Barriers, such as being a long distance from counseling services, geographic separation of a couple, or limited physical mobility as a result of having a disability, can make it **necessary** to provide counseling at a distance. Options, such as scheduling counseling sessions outside of traditional service delivery hours or delivering counseling services at a place of residence or employment, can make it more **convenient** to provide counseling at a distance.

A Taxonomy of Forms of Counseling Practice. Table 1 presents a taxonomy of currently available forms of counseling practice. This schema is intended to show the relationships among counseling forms.

TABLE 1   A Taxonomy of Face-to-Face and Technology-Assisted Distance Counseling

Counseling

- Face-to-Face Counseling
  - Individual Counseling
  - Couple Counseling
  - Group Counseling
- Technology-Assisted Distance Counseling
  - Telecounseling
    - Telephone-Based Individual Counseling
    - Telephone-Based Couple Counseling
    - Telephone-Based Group Counseling
  - Internet Counseling
    - E-Mail-Based Individual Counseling
    - Chat-Based Individual Counseling
    - Chat-Based Couple Counseling
    - Chat-Based Group Counseling
    - Video-Based Individual Counseling
    - Video-Based Couple Counseling
    - Video-Based Group Counseling

DEFINITIONS

Counseling is the application of mental health, psychological, or human development principles, through cognitive, affective, behavioral or systemic intervention strategies, that address wellness, personal growth, or career development, as well as pathology.

Face-to-face counseling for individuals, couples, and groups involves synchronous interaction between and among counselors and clients using what is seen and heard in person to communicate.

Technology-assisted distance counseling for individuals, couples, and groups involves the use of the telephone or the computer to enable counselors and clients to communicate at a distance when circumstances make this approach necessary or convenient.

Telecounseling involves synchronous distance interaction among counselors and clients using one-to-one or conferencing features of the telephone to communicate.

Telephone-based individual counseling involves synchronous distance interaction between a counselor and a client using what is heard via audio to communicate.

Telephone-based couple counseling involves synchronous distance interaction among a counselor or counselors and a couple using what is heard via audio to communicate.

Telephone-based group counseling involves synchronous distance interaction among counselors and clients using what is heard via audio to communicate.

Internet counseling involves asynchronous and synchronous distance interaction among counselors and clients using e-mail, chat, and videoconferencing features of the Internet to communicate.

E-mail-based individual Internet counseling involves asynchronous distance interaction between counselor and client using what is read via text to communicate.

Chat-based individual Internet counseling involves synchronous distance interaction between counselor and client using what is read via text to communicate.

Chat-based couple Internet counseling involves synchronous distance interaction among a counselor or counselors and a couple using what is read via text to communicate.

Chat-based group Internet counseling involves synchronous distance interaction among counselors and clients using what is read via text to communicate.

Video-based individual Internet counseling involves synchronous distance interaction between counselor and client using what is seen and heard via video to communicate.

Video-based couple Internet counseling involves synchronous distance interaction among a counselor or counselors and a couple using what is seen and heard via video to communicate.

Video-based group Internet counseling involves synchronous distance interaction among counselors and clients using what is seen and heard via video to communicate.

STANDARDS FOR THE ETHICAL PRACTICE OF INTERNET COUNSELING

These standards govern the practice of Internet counseling and are intended for use by counselors, clients, the public, counselor educators, and organizations that examine and deliver Internet counseling. These standards are intended to address *practices* that are unique to Internet counseling and Internet counselors and do not duplicate principles found in traditional codes of ethics.

These Internet counseling standards of practice are based upon the principles of ethical practice embodied in the NBCC Code of Ethics. Therefore, these standards should be used in conjunction with the most recent version of the NBCC ethical code. Related content in the NBCC Code are indicated in parentheses after each standard.

Recognizing that significant new technology emerges continuously, these standards should be reviewed frequently. It is also recognized that Internet counseling ethics cases should be reviewed in light of delivery systems existing at the moment rather than at the time the standards were adopted.

In addition to following the NBCC® Code of Ethics pertaining to the practice of professional counseling, Internet counselors shall observe the following standards of practice:

Internet Counseling Relationship

1. In situations where it is difficult to verify the identity of the Internet client, steps are taken to address impostor concerns, such as by using code words or numbers. (Refer to B.8)
2. Internet counselors determine if a client is a minor and therefore in need of parental/guardian consent. When parent/guardian consent is required to provide Internet counseling to minors, the identity of the consenting person is verified. (Refer to B.8)
3. As part of the counseling orientation process, the Internet counselor explains to clients the procedures for contacting the Internet counselor when he or she is off-line and, in the case of asynchronous

counseling, how often e-mail messages will be checked by the Internet counselor. (Refer to B.8)
4. As part of the counseling orientation process, the Internet counselor explains to clients the possibility of technology failure and discusses alternative modes of communication, if that failure occurs. (Refer to B.8)
5. As part of the counseling orientation process, the Internet counselor explains to clients how to cope with potential misunderstandings when visual cues do not exist. (Refer to B.8)
6. As a part of the counseling orientation process, the Internet counselor collaborates with the Internet client to identify an appropriately trained professional who can provide local assistance, including crisis intervention, if needed. The Internet counselor and Internet client should also collaborate to determine the local crisis hotline telephone number and the local emergency telephone number. (Refer to B.4)
7. The Internet counselor has an obligation, when appropriate, to make clients aware of free public access points to the Internet within the community for accessing Internet counseling or Web-based assessment, information, and instructional resources. (Refer to B.1)
8. Within the limits of readily available technology, Internet counselors have an obligation to make their Web site a barrier-free environment to clients with disabilities. (Refer to B.1)
9. Internet counselors are aware that some clients may communicate in different languages, live in different time zones, and have unique cultural perspectives. Internet counselors are also aware that local conditions and events may impact the client. (Refer to A.12)

Confidentiality in Internet Counseling

10. The Internet counselor informs Internet clients of encryption methods being used to help insure the security of client/counselor/supervisor communications. (Refer to B.5).

Encryption methods should be used whenever possible. If encryption is not made available to clients, clients must be informed of the potential hazards of unsecured communication on the Internet. Hazards may include unauthorized monitoring of transmissions and/or records of Internet counseling sessions.
11. The Internet counselor informs Internet clients if, how, and how long session data are being preserved. (Refer to B.6)

Session data may include Internet counselor/ Internet client e-mail, test results, audio/video session recordings, session notes, and counselor/ supervisor communications. The likelihood of electronic sessions being preserved is greater because of the ease and decreased costs involved in recording. Thus, its potential use in supervision, research, and legal proceedings increases.

12. Internet counselors follow appropriate procedures regarding the release of information for sharing Internet client information with other electronic sources. (Refer to B.5)

Because of the relative ease with which e-mail messages can be forwarded to formal and casual referral sources, Internet counselors must work to insure the confidentiality of the Internet counseling relationship.

Legal Considerations, Licensure, and Certification

13. Internet counselors review pertinent legal and ethical codes for guidance on the practice of Internet counseling and supervision. (Refer to A.13)

Local, state, provincial, and national statutes as well as codes of professional membership organizations, professional certifying bodies, and state or provincial licensing boards need to be reviewed. Also, as varying state rules and opinions exist on questions pertaining to whether Internet counseling takes place in the Internet counselor's location or the Internet client's location, it is important to review codes in the counselor's home jurisdiction as well as the client's. Internet counselors also consider carefully local customs regarding age of consent and child abuse reporting, and liability insurance policies need to be reviewed to determine if the practice of Internet counseling is a covered activity.

14. The Internet counselor's Web site provides links to websites of all appropriate certification bodies and licensure boards to facilitate consumer protection. (Refer to B.1)

Adopted November 3, 2001

- Introduction to Career Counseling Competency Statements
- Minimum Competencies
- Professional Preparation
- Ethical Responsibilities
- Career Counseling Competencies and Performance Indicators
  - Career Development Theory
  - Individual and Group Counseling Skills
  - Individual/Group Assessment
  - Information/Resources
  - Program Promotion, Management, and Implementation
  - Coaching, Consultation, and Performance Improvement
  - Diverse Populations
  - Supervision
  - Ethical/Legal Issues
  - Research/Evaluation
  - Technology

INTRODUCTION TO CAREER COUNSELING COMPETENCY STATEMENTS

These competency statements are for those professionals interested and trained in the field of career counseling. For the purpose of these statements, career counseling is defined as the process of assisting individuals in the development of a life-career with focus on the definition of the worker role and how that role interacts with other life roles.

NCDA's Career Counseling Competencies are intended to represent minimum competencies for those professionals at or above the Master's degree level of education. These competencies are reviewed on an ongoing basis by the NCDA Professional Standards Committee, the NCDA Board, and other relevant associations.

Professional competency statements provide guidance for the minimum competencies necessary to perform effectively a particular occupation or job within a particular field. Professional career counselors (Master's degree or higher) or persons in career development positions must demonstrate the knowledge and skills for a specialty in career counseling that the generalist counselor might not possess. Skills and knowledge are represented by designated competency areas, which have been developed by professional career counselors and counselor educators. The Career Counseling Competency Statements can serve as a guide for career counseling training programs or as a checklist for persons wanting to acquire or to enhance their skills in career counseling.

MINIMUM COMPETENCIES

In order to work as a professional engaged in Career Counseling, the individual must demonstrate minimum competencies in 11 designated areas. These 11 areas are: Career Development Theory, Individual and Group Counseling Skills, Individual/Group Assessment, Information/Resources, Program Management and Implementation, Consultation, Diverse Populations, Supervision, Ethical/Legal Issues, Research/Evaluation, and Technology. These areas are briefly defined as follows:

- Career Development Theory: Theory base and knowledge considered essential for professionals engaging in career counseling and development.
- Individual and Group Counseling Skills: Individual and group counseling competencies considered essential for effective career counseling.
- Individual/Group Assessment: Individual/group assessment skills considered essential for professionals engaging in career counseling.
- Information/Resources: Information/resource base and knowledge essential for professionals engaging in career counseling.
- **Program Promotion, Management and Implementation:** Skills necessary to develop, plan, implement, and manage comprehensive career development programs in a variety of settings.
- **Coaching, Consultation, and Performance Improvement:** Knowledge and skills considered essential in enabling individuals and organizations to impact effectively upon the career counseling and development process.
- Diverse Populations: Knowledge and skills considered essential in providing career counseling and development processes to diverse populations.
- **Supervision:** Knowledge and skills considered essential in critically evaluating counselor performance, maintaining and improving professional skills, and seeking assistance for others when needed in career counseling.
- Ethical/Legal Issues: Information base and knowledge essential for the ethical and legal practice of career counseling.
- **Research/Evaluation:** Knowledge and skills considered essential in understanding and conducting research and evaluation in career counseling and development.
- **Technology:** Knowledge and skills considered essential in using technology to assist individuals with career planning.

PLEASE NOTE: *Highlighted competencies are those that must be met in order to obtain the Master Career Counselor Special Membership Category.*

PROFESSIONAL PREPARATION

The competency statements were developed to serve as guidelines for persons interested in career development occupations. They are intended for persons training at the Master's level or higher with a specialty in career counseling. However, this intention does not prevent other types of career development professionals from using the competencies as guidelines for their own training. The competency statements provide counselor educators, supervisors, and other interested groups with guidelines for the minimum training required for counselors interested in the career counseling specialty. The statements might also serve as guidelines for professional counselors who seek in-service training to qualify as career counselors.

ETHICAL RESPONSIBILITIES

Career development professionals must only perform activities for which they "possess or have access to the necessary skills and resources for giving the kind of help that is needed" (see NCDA and ACA Ethical Standards). If a professional does not have the appropriate training or resources for the type of career concern presented, an appropriate referral must be made. No person should attempt to use skills (within these competency statements) for which he/she has not been trained. For additional ethical guidelines, refer to the NCDA Ethical Standards for Career Counselors.

CAREER COUNSELING COMPETENCIES AND PERFORMANCE INDICATORS

Career Development Theory

Theory base and knowledge considered essential for professionals engaging in career counseling and development. Demonstration of knowledge of:

1. Counseling theories and associated techniques.
2. Theories and models of career development.
3. Individual differences related to gender, sexual orientation, race, ethnicity, and physical and mental capacities.
4. Theoretical models for career development and associated counseling and information-delivery techniques and resources.
5. Human growth and development throughout the life span.
6. Role relationships which facilitate life-work planning.
7. Information, techniques, and models related to career planning and placement

Individual and Group Counseling Skills

Individual and group counseling competencies considered essential to effective career counseling. Demonstration of ability to:

1. Establish and maintain productive personal relationships with individuals.
2. Establish and maintain a productive group climate.

3. Collaborate with clients in identifying personal goals.
4. Identify and select techniques appropriate to client or group goals and client needs, psychological states, and developmental tasks.
5. Identify and understand clients' personal characteristics related to career.
6. Identify and understand social contextual conditions affecting clients' careers.
7. Identify and understand familial, subcultural and cultural structures and functions as they are related to clients' careers.
8. Identify and understand clients' career decision-making processes.
9. Identify and understand clients' attitudes toward work and workers.
10. Identify and understand clients' biases toward work and workers based on gender, race, and cultural stereotypes.
11. Challenge and encourage clients to take action to prepare for and initiate role transitions by:
    • locating sources of relevant information and experience,
    • obtaining and interpreting information and experiences, and acquiring skills needed to make role transitions.
    • acquiring skills needed to make role transitions.
12. Assist the client to acquire a set of employability and job search skills.
13. Support and challenge clients to examine life-work roles, including the balance of work, leisure, family, and community in their careers.

Individual/Group Assessment

Individual/group assessment skills considered essential for professionals engaging in career counseling. Demonstration of ability to:

1. Assess personal characteristics such as aptitude, achievement, interests, values, and personality traits.
2. Assess leisure interests, learning style, life roles, self-concept, career maturity, vocational identity, career indecision, work environment preference (e.g., work satisfaction), and other related life style/development issues.
3. Assess conditions of the work environment (such as tasks, expectations, norms, and qualities of the physical and social settings).
4. Evaluate and select valid and reliable instruments appropriate to the client's gender, sexual orientation, race, ethnicity, and physical and mental capacities.
5. Use computer-delivered assessment measures effectively and appropriately.

6. Select assessment techniques appropriate for group administration and those appropriate for individual administration.
7. Administer, score, and report findings from career assessment instruments appropriately.
8. Interpret data from assessment instruments and present the results to clients and to others.
9. Assist the client and others designated by the client to interpret data from assessment instruments.
10. Write an accurate report of assessment results.

Information/Resources

Information/resource base and knowledge essential for professionals engaging in career counseling. Demonstration of knowledge of:

1. Education, training, and employment trends; labor market information and resources that provide information about job tasks, functions, salaries, requirements and future outlooks related to broad occupational fields and individual occupations.
2. Resources and skills that clients utilize in life-work planning and management.
3. Community/professional resources available to assist clients in career planning, including job search.
4. Changing roles of women and men and the implications that this has for education, family, and leisure.
5. Methods of good use of computer-based career information delivery systems (CIDS) and computer-assisted career guidance systems (CACGS) to assist with career planning.

Program Promotion, Management, and Implementation

Knowledge and skills necessary to develop, plan, implement, and manage comprehensive career development programs in a variety of settings. Demonstration of knowledge of:

1. Designs that can be used in the organization of career development programs.
2. Needs assessment and evaluation techniques and practices.
3. Organizational theories, including diagnosis, behavior, planning, organizational communication, and management useful in implementing and administering career development programs.
4. Methods of forecasting, budgeting, planning, costing, policy analysis, resource allocation, and quality control.
5. Leadership theories and approaches for evaluation and feedback, organizational change, decision-making, and conflict resolution.

6. Professional standards and criteria for career development programs.
7. Societal trends and state and federal legislation that influence the development and implementation of career development programs.

Demonstration of ability to:

8. Implement individual and group programs in career development for specified populations.
9. Train others about the appropriate use of computer-based systems for career information and planning.
10. Plan, organize, and manage a comprehensive career resource center.
11. Implement career development programs in collaboration with others.
12. Identify and evaluate staff competencies.
13. Mount a marketing and public relations campaign in behalf of career development activities and services.

Coaching, Consultation, and Performance Improvement

Knowledge and skills considered essential in relating to individuals and organizations that impact the career counseling and development process. Demonstration of ability to:

1. Use consultation theories, strategies, and models.
2. Establish and maintain a productive consultative relationship with people who can influence a client's career.
3. Help the general public and legislators to understand the importance of career counseling, career development, and life-work planning.
4. Impact public policy as it relates to career development and workforce planning.
5. Analyze future organizational needs and current level of employee skills and develop performance improvement training.
6. Mentor and coach employees.

Diverse Populations

Knowledge and skills considered essential in relating to diverse populations that impact career counseling and development processes. Demonstration of ability to:

1. Identify development models and multicultural counseling competencies.
2. Identify developmental needs unique to various diverse populations, including those of different gender, sexual orientation, ethnic group, race, and physical or mental capacity.

3. Define career development programs to accommodate needs unique to various diverse populations.
4. Find appropriate methods or resources to communicate with limited-English-proficient individuals.
5. Identify alternative approaches to meet career planning needs for individuals of various diverse populations.
6. Identify community resources and establish linkages to assist clients with specific needs.
7. Assist other staff members, professionals, and community members in understanding the unique needs/characteristics of diverse populations with regard to career exploration, employment expectations, and economic/social issues.
8. Advocate for the career development and employment of diverse populations.
9. Design and deliver career development programs and materials to hard-to-reach populations.

Supervision

Knowledge and skills considered essential in critically evaluating counselor or career development facilitator performance, maintaining and improving professional skills. Demonstration of:

1. Ability to recognize own limitations as a career counselor and to seek supervision or refer clients when appropriate.
2. Ability to utilize supervision on a regular basis to maintain and improve counselor skills.
3. Ability to consult with supervisors and colleagues regarding client and counseling issues and issues related to one's own professional development as a career counselor.
4. Knowledge of supervision models and theories.
5. Ability to provide effective supervision to career counselors and career development facilitators at different levels of experience.
6. Ability to provide effective supervision to career development facilitators at different levels of experience by:
   - knowledge of their roles, competencies, and ethical standards
   - determining their competence in each of the areas included in their certification
   - further training them in competencies, including interpretation of assessment instruments
   - monitoring and mentoring their activities in support of the professional career counselor; and scheduling regular consultations for the purpose of reviewing their activities

Ethical/Legal Issues

Information base and knowledge essential for the ethical and legal practice of career counseling. Demonstration of knowledge of:

1. Adherence to ethical codes and standards relevant to the profession of career counseling (e.g. NBCC, NCDA, and ACA).
2. Current ethical and legal issues which affect the practice of career counseling with all populations.
3. Current ethical/legal issues with regard to the use of computer-assisted career guidance systems.
4. Ethical standards relating to consultation issues.
5. State and federal statutes relating to client confidentiality.

Research/Evaluation

Knowledge and skills considered essential in understanding and conducting research and evaluation in career counseling and development. Demonstration of ability to:

1. Write a research proposal.
2. Use types of research and research designs appropriate to career counseling and development research.
3. Convey research findings related to the effectiveness of career counseling programs.
4. Design, conduct, and use the results of evaluation programs.

5. Design evaluation programs which take into account the need of various diverse populations, including persons of both genders, differing sexual orientations, different ethnic and racial backgrounds, and differing physical and mental capacities.
6. Apply appropriate statistical procedures to career development research.

Technology

Knowledge and skills considered essential in using technology to assist individuals with career planning. Demonstration of knowledge of:

1. Various computer-based guidance and information systems as well as services available on the Internet.
2. Standards by which such systems and services are evaluated (e.g. NCDA and ACSCI).
3. Ways in which to use computer-based systems and Internet services to assist individuals with career planning that are consistent with ethical standards.
4. Characteristics of clients which make them profit more or less from use of technology-driven systems.
5. Methods to evaluate and select a system to meet local needs.

REFERENCES

Abbe, A. E. (1961). Consultation to a school guidance program. *Elementary School Journal, 61*, 331–337.

ACES (Association for Counselor Education and Supervision) Technology Network. (2000). Technical competencies for counselor education students: recommended guidelines for program development. In J. W. Bloom & G. R. Walz (Eds.), *Cybercounseling and cyberlearning: Strategies and resources for the millennium.* (pp. 429–430). Alexandria, VA: American Counseling Association and Greensboro, NC: CAPS, Inc., with the ERIC Counseling and Student Services Clearinghouse.

Agar, M. (1994). *Language shock: Understanding the culture of conversation.* New York: Morrow.

Allsopp, A., & Prosen, S. (1988). Teacher reactions to a child sexual abuse training program. *Elementary School Guidance and Counseling, 22,* 299–305.

Altekruse, M. K. & Brew, L. (2000). Using the Web for distance learning. In J. W. Bloom & G. R. Walz (Eds.), *Cybercounseling and cyberlearning: Strategies and resources for the millennium* (pp. 129–141). Alexandria, VA: American Counseling Association and Greensboro, NC: CAPS, Inc. (ERIC Counseling and Student Services Clearinghouse)

American College Testing, Inc. (2001). DISCOVER. Iowa City, IA: Author.

American Psychiatric Association. (2000). *Diagnostic and statistical manual of mental disorders (DSM IV-TR).* (4th ed.). Washington, DC: Author.

American School Counselor Association (ASCA). (1964). *Statement of policy for secondary school counselors.* Washington, DC: Author.

American School Counselor Association. (1988). The school counselor and child abuse/neglect prevention. *Elementary School Guidance and Counseling, 22,* 261–263.

American School Counselor Association. (1999). *Position statement: Child abuse.* The professional school counselor and child abuse and neglect prevention. Alexandria, VA: Author.

American School Counselor Association. (1999). *The role of the professional school counselor.* Alexandria, VA: Author

Americans with Disabilities Act handbook. (1991). Washington, DC: U.S. Government Printing Office.

Anastasi, A. (1992). Tests and assessment: What counselors should know about the use and interpretations of psychological tests. *Journal of Counseling and Development, 70*(5), 610–615.

Anastasi, A., & Urbina, S. (1997). *Psychological testing* (7th ed.). Upper Saddle River, NJ: Prentice Hall.

Anderson, D. J., & Cranston-Gingras, A. (1991). Sensitizing counselors and educators to multicultural issues: An interactive approach. *Journal of Counseling and Development, 70,* 91–98.

Arredondo, P. M. (1986). Counseling Latinas. In C. C. Lee and B. L. Richardson (Eds.). *Multicultural issues in counseling: New Approaches to diversity*. Alexandria, VA: American Association of Counseling and Development.

Arredondo, P. M. (1986). Immigration as a historical moment leading to an identity crisis. *Journal of Counseling and Human Service Professionals, 1*(1), 79–87.

Arthur, G. L., Jr., & Swanson, C. D. (1993). Confidentiality and privileged communication. In T. P. Remley, Jr. (Ed.), *ACA Legal Series, 6*. Alexandria, VA: American Counseling Association.

Association for Specialists in Group Work. (2000). *Professional standards for the training of group workers*. (F. R. Wilson & L. S. Rapin, Co-Chairs, Standards Committee). Alexandria, VA: Author.

Baker, S. B. (1996). *School counseling for the twenty-first century*. Upper Saddle River, NJ: Merrill/Prentice Hall.

Baker, S. B., Sursher, P., Nadenichek, P., & Popowitz, C. (1984). Primaray effects of primary prevention strategies. *Personnel and Guidance Journal, 62*, 459–464.

Bandura, A. (1982). The psychology of chance encounters and life paths. *The American Psychologist, 37*(7), 747–755.

Bandura, A. (1997). *Social learning theory*. Upper Saddle River, NJ: Prentice Hall.

Basile, S. K. (1996). A guide to solution-focused brief therapy. *Counseling and Human Development, 29*(4), 1–10.

Beers, C. (1953). *A mind that found itself*. New York: Doubleday. (Original work published in 1908)

Belkin, G. S. (1975). *Practical counseling in the schools*. Dubuque, IA: Brown.

Bell, T. (1983). *A nation at risk: The imperative for educational reform*. Washington, DC: National Commission on Excellence in Education.

Bissell, L., & Royce, J. E. (1992). Ethics for addiction professionals. *Professional Counselor, 6*(4), 33–38.

Blanchard, K. H. (1982). *The one-minute manager*. New York: Morrow.

Blau, P. M., Gustad, J. W., Jessor, R., Parnes, H. S., & Wilcock, R. G. (1956). Occupational choice: A conception framework. *Industrial and Labor Relations Review, 9*, 531–543.

Blocher, D. H. (1987). *The professional counselor*. New York: Macmillan.

Blocher, D. H., & Biggs, D. A. (1983). *Counseling psychology in community settings*. New York: Springer.

Bloom, B. L. (1984). *Community mental health: A general introduction* (2nd ed.). Belmont, CA: Brooks/Cole.

Bloom, B. S. (1976). *Human characteristics and school learning*. New York: McGraw-Hill.

Bloom, J. W., and Walz, G. R. (Eds.). (2000). *Cybercounseling and cyberlearning: Strategies and resources for the millennium*. Alexandria, VA: American Counseling Association and Greensboro, NC: CAPS, Inc. (ERIC Counseling and Student Services Clearinghouse)

Blum, L. (1986). Building constructive counselor-teacher relationships. *Elementary School Guidance and Counseling, 20*, 236–239.

Borow, H. (1964). *Man in a world at work*. Ellicott City, MD: National Career Development Association.

Bowlsbey, J. H., Dikel, M. R., & Sampson, J. P., Jr. (1998). *A tool for career planning*. Columbus, OH: National Career Development Association.

Brammer, L. M., Shostrom, E. L., & Abrego, P. J. (1989). *Therapeutic psychology: Fundamentals of counseling and psychotherapy* (5th ed.). Upper Saddle River, NJ: Prentice Hall.

Brewer, J. M. (1932). *Education as guidance.* New York: Macmillan.

Brown, D. (1995). A values-based approach to facilitating career transitions. *Career Development Quarterly, 44,* 4–11.

Brown, D. (1996). Brown's value-based, holistic model of career and life-role choices and satisfaction. In D. Brown, L. Brooks, & Associates (Eds.), *Career choice and development* (3rd ed., pp. 337–338). San Francisco: Jossey-Bass.

Brown, D., Brooks, L., & Associates (Eds.). (1996). Career choice and development (3rd ed.). San Francisco: Jossey-Bass.

Brown, D., & Kurpius, D. J. (Eds.). (1985). Consultation. [Special issue]. *The Counseling Psychologist, 13*(3).

Brown, D., Kurpius, D. J., & Morris, J. R. (1988). *Handbook of consultation with individuals and small groups.* Alexandria, VA: Association for Counselor Education and Supervision.

Brown, J. H., & Christensen, D. N. (1986). *Family therapy: Theory and practice.* Monterey, CA: Brooks/Cole.

Brunner, B. (Ed. in chief). (2000). *Time Almanac 2001, with Information Please.* Boston: Information Please.

Bureau of Labor Statistics. (1996). *Occupational outlook handbook: 1996–1997.* Washington, D.C.: U.S. Department of Labor.

Burnham, J. J., & Jackson, C. M. (2000). School counselor roles: Discrepancies between actual practice and existing models. *Professional School Counseling, 4*(1), 45.

Campbell, C. A., & Dahir, C. A. (1997). *Sharing the vision: The national standards for school counseling programs.* Alexandria, VA: American School Counselor Association.

Capuzzi, D., & Gross, D. R. (1997). *Introduction to the counseling profession* (2nd ed.). Boston: Allyn & Bacon.

Centers for Disease Control and Prevention. (1995). *Morbidity and mortality weekly report: A compilation of 1995 MMWR articles on HIV infection and AIDS.* November 24, 1995, Vol. 44 (46), pp. 849–853.

Centers for Disease Control and Prevention. (1997a). *HIV/AIDS surveillance report.* U.S. HIV and AIDS cases reported through June 1997. Midyear edition, Vol. 9(1), pp. 16 and 25.

Centers for Disease Control and Prevention. (1997b). *Morbidity and mortality weekly report.* February 28, 1997, Vol. 46(8).

Chase, C. I. (1984). *Elementary statistical procedures* (3rd ed.). New York: McGraw-Hill.

Christensen, S. P. (1989). Cross-cultural awareness development: A conceptual model. *Counselor Education and Supervision, 28,* 270–287.

College Entrance Examination Board. (1986, October). *Keeping the options open: Recommendations.* Final report of the Commission on Precollege Guidance and Counseling. New York: Author

Conyne, R. K. (1987). *Primary preventative counseling.* Muncie, IN: Accelerated Development.

Corey, G. (2000). *Theory and practice of group counseling* (5th ed.). Belmont, CA: Brooks/Cole.

Corey, M. S., & Corey, G. (2002). *Groups: Process and practice* (6th ed.). Pacific Grove, CA: Brooks/Cole.

Cormier, S., & Hackney, H. (1999). *Counseling strategies and interventions* (5th ed.). Needham Heights, MA: Allyn & Bacon.

Corsini, R. J., & Wedding, D. (Eds.). (2000). *Current psychotherapies* (6th ed.). Itasca, IL: F. E. Peacock.

Crocker, E. C. (1964). Depth consultation with parents. *Young Children, 20,* 91–99.

Crow, L. D., & Crow, A. (1960). *An introduction to guidance* (2nd ed.). New York: American Book Company

Cubberly, E. P. (1934). *Public education in the United States.* Boston: Houghton Mifflin.

Cutshall, S. (2001, October). Help wanted. *Techniques,* 30–32.

Dahir, C. A., Sheldon, C. B., & Valiga, M. J. (1998). *Vision into action: Implementing the national standards for school counseling programs.* Alexandria, VA: American School Counselor Association.

Daly, M. (1979). How good is your child's school counselor? *Better Homes and Gardens, 57,* 15–22.

Donovan, C. E. (1959). A new era of guidance. *School and Society, 87,* 241.

Driver, H. (1958). *Counseling and learning through small group discussions.* Madison, WI: Monona.

Drummond, R. J. (1996). *Appraisal procedures for counselors and helping professionals* (3rd ed.). Upper Saddle River, NJ: Prentice Hall.

Dziekan, K. I., & Okocha, A. A. G. (1993, June). Accessibility of rehabilitation services: Comparison by racial-ethnic status. *Rehabilitation Counseling Bulletin, 36,* 183–189.

Eckerson, L., & Smith, H. (1962). *Elementary school guidance: The consultant.* (Reprint of three articles in *School Life*). Washington, DC: U.S. Department of Health, Education and Welfare, Office of Education.

Elias, M. (2001, May 22). Online therapy clicks. *USA Today,* p. 19.

Erchak, G. (1992). *The anthropology of self and mind.* New Brunswick, NJ: Rutgers University Press.

Erikson, E. H. (1994). *Identity and the life cycle.* New York: W. W. Norton.

Ewing, D. B. (1975). Direct from Minnesota—E. G. Williamson. *Personnel and Guidance Journal, 54,* 77–87.

Exum, H. A., & Moore, Q. L. (1993). Transcultural counseling from African-American perspectives. In J. McFadden (Ed.). *Transcultural counseling: Bilateral and international perspectives* (pp. 193–212). Alexandria, VA: American Counseling Association.

Faust, V. B. (1967). The counselor as a consultant to teachers. *Elementary School Guidance and Counseling, 1,* 112–117.

Feingold, G. A. (1947). A new approach to guidance. *School Review, 4,* 542–550.

Felner, R. D., Jason, L. A., Moritsugu, J. N., & Farber, S. S. (Eds.). (1983). *Preventive psychology: Theory, research, and practice.* New York: Pergamon.

Fischer, L., & Sorenson, G. P. (1996). *School law for counselors, psychologists and social workers.* New York: Longman.

Fisher, C. F., & King, R. M. (1995). *Authentic assessment: A guide to implementation.* Thousand Oaks, CA: Corwin.

Fiske, E. B. (1988). America's test mania. *New York Times*, Education Life, Section 12, pp. 16–20.

Flygare, T. (1975). *The legal rights of students*. Bloomington, IN: Phi Delta Kappa Educational Foundation.

Fretz, B. R. (Ed.). (1988). Third National Conference for Counseling Psychology: Planning the future. [Special issue]. *The Counseling Psychologist, 16*(3). Thousand Oaks, CA: Sage Publications, Inc.

Friedan, B. (1993). *The fountain of age*. New York: Simon and Schuster.

Froehlich, C. P. (1958). *Guidance services in schools* (2nd ed.). New York: McGraw-Hill.

Fuqua, D. R., & Kurpius, D. J. (1993). Conceptual models in organization consultation. *Journal of Counseling and Development, 71*(6), 607–18.

Gazda, G. M. (Ed.). (1982). *Basic approaches to group psychotherapy and group counseling* (3rd ed.). Springfield, IL: Charles C. Thomas.

Geertz, C. (1983). *Local knowledge*. New York: Basic Books.

George, R. L. , & Cristiani, T. S. (1995). *Counseling: Theory and practice* (4th ed). Upper Saddle River, NJ: Prentice Hall.

Gibson, R. L. (1973). The counselor as curriculum consultant. *American Vocational Journal, 48*, 50–51, 54.

Gibson, R. L. (1989). Prevention and the elementary school counselor. *Elementary School Guidance and Counseling, 24*(1), 30–36.

Gibson, R. L. (1990). Teachers' opinions of high school counseling and guidance programs: Then and now. *The School Counselor, 37*, 248–255.

Gibson, R. L., & Higgins, R. E. (1966). *Techniques of guidance: An approach to pupil analysis*. Chicago: Science Research Associates.

Gibson, R. L., Mitchell, M. H., & Basile, S. K. (1993). *Counseling in the elementary school: A comprehensive approach*. Boston: Allyn & Bacon.

Gibson, R. L., Mitchell, M. H., & Higgins, R. E. (1983). *Development and management of counseling programs and guidance services*. New York: Macmillan.

Gilliland, B. E., & James, R. K. (1998). *Theories and strategies in counseling and psychotherapy* (4th ed.). Needham Heights, MA: Allyn & Bacon.

Ginter, E. J. (Ed.). (2001). Archival Feature: 2000–2001. Accreditation and credentialing information. [Special Section]. *Journal of Counseling and Development, 79*(2), 231–249.

Ginzberg, E., Ginsburg, S. W., Axelrad, S., & Herma, J. L. (1951). *Occupational choice: An approach to a general theory*. New York: Columbia University Press.

Ginzberg, E. (1972). Restatement of the theory of occupational choice. *Vocational Guidance Quarterly, 20*(3), 169–176.

Glasser, W. (1965). *Reality therapy*. New York: Harper & Row.

Glasser, W. (1969). *Schools without failure*. New York: Harper Collins.

Glasser, W. (1981). *Stations of the mind*. New York: Harper & Row.

Glasser, W. (1984). Reality therapy. In R. J. Corsini (Ed.), *Current psychotherapies* (3rd ed., 320–353). Itasca, IL: Peacock.

Glasser, W. (1989). Control theory in the practice of reality therapy. In N. Glasser (Ed.), *Control theory in the practice of reality therapy: Case studies*. New York: Harper & Row.

Glosoff, H. L., Herlihy, B., & Spence, E. B. (2000). Privileged communication in the counseling/client relationship. *Journal of Counseling and Development, 78*(4), 454–462.

Goodenough, W. H. (1981). *Culture, language and society*. Reading, MA: Benjamin Cummings.

Goodyear, R. K., & Shaw, M. C. (Eds.). (1984). Primary prevention on campuses and in communities [Special issue]. *Personnel and Guidance Journal, 62*(9).

Goshen, C. E. (1967). *Documentary history of psychiatry: A sourcebook on history principles* New York: Philosophical Library.

Grohol, J. M. (2000/2001). *The insider's guide to mental health resources online*. New York: Guilford Press.

Gross, B., & Gross, R. (1974). *Will it grow in a classroom?* New York: Dell.

Gross, M. L. (1963). *The brain watchers*. New York: Signet Books.

Gysbers, N. C., & Henderson, P. (2000). *Developing and managing your school guidance program* (3rd ed.). Alexandria, VA: American Counseling Association.

Hackney, H. L., & Cormier, L. S. (1996). *The professional counselor: A process guide to helping* (3rd ed.). Boston: Allyn & Bacon.

Hadley, R. G., & Mitchell, L. K. (1995). *Counseling research and program evaluation*. Pacific Grove, CA: Brooks/Cole.

Hardesty, P. H., & Dillard, J. M. (1994). The role of elementary school counselors compared with their middle and secondary school counterparts. *Elementary School Guidance and Counseling, 29*(2), 83–91.

Hatch, R. N., & Costar, J. W. (1961). *Guidance services in the elementary school*. Dubuque, IA: Brown.

Havighurst, R. J. (1953). *Human development and education*. New York: Longmans, Green.

Havighurst, R. J. (1964). Youth in exploration and man emergent. In H. Borow (Ed.), *Man in a world at work* (pp. 215–236). Alexandria, VA: National Career Development Association.

Hawes, G. R. (1973). Criterion referenced testing — No more losers, no more norms, no more parents raising storms. *Nation's Schools, 91*(2), 35–41.

Heppner, P. P., Kivlighan, D. M., Jr., & Wampold, B. E. (1992). *Research design in counseling*. Pacific Grove, CA: Brooks/Cole.

Herndon, T. (1976). Standardized tests: Are they worth the cost? *Educational Digest, 42*, 13–16.

Herr, E. L. (1979). *Guidance and counseling in the schools: The past, present, and future*. Falls Church, VA: American Personnel and Guidance Association.

Herr, E. L., & Cramer, S. H. (1996). *Career guidance and counseling through the life span: Systematic approaches* (5th ed.). New York: HarperCollins.

Holland, J. L. (1966). *The psychology of vocational choice*. Lexington, MA: Blaisdell/Ginn.

Holland, J. L. (1973). *Making vocational choices: A theory of careers*. Upper Saddle River, NJ: Prentice Hall.

Holland, J. L. (1985a). *Making vocational choices: A theory of careers*. (2nd ed.). Upper Saddle River, NJ: Prentice Hall.

Holland, J. L. (1985b). *The self-directed search: Professional manual — 1985 edition*. Odessa, FL: Psychological Assessment Resources.

Hollis, J.W. with Dodson, T. A. (2000). *Counselor preparation 1999–2001: Programs, faculty trends* (10th ed.). Philadelphia: Taylor & Francis and Greensboro, NC: National Board for Certified Counselors. (also www.routledge-ny.com)

Hopkins, B. R., & Anderson, B. S. (1990). *The counselor and the law* (3rd ed.). Alexandria, VA: American Association for Counseling and Development.

Hoyt, K. (1993). Guidance is not a dirty word. *The School Counselor, 40*(4), 267–274.

Humes, C. W. (1987). *Contemporary counseling: Services, applications, issues.* Muncie, IN: Accelerated Development.

Humes, C. W., & Hohenshil, T. H. (1987). Elementary counselors, school psychologists, school social workers. Who does what? *Elementary School Guidance and Counseling, 22*(1), 37–45.

Hutson, P. W. (1958). *The guidance function in education.* New York: Appleton-Century-Crofts.

Iacocca, L., & Novack, W. (1984). *Iacocca: An autobiography.* New York: Bantam Books.

Inamori, K. (1995). *A passion for success.* New York: McGraw-Hill.

Isaacson, L. E., & Brown, D. (1993). *Career information, career counseling, and career development.* Boston: Allyn & Bacon.

Ishisaka, H. A., Nguyen, Q. T., & Okimoto, J. T. (1985). The role in the mental health treatment of Indochinese refugees. In T. C. Owan (Ed.), *Southeast Asian mental health treatment, prevention services, training and research.* Washington, DC: National Institute of Mental Health.

Ivey, A. E., M. D'Andrea, Ivey, M. B., & Simek-Morgan, L. (2002). *Theories of counseling and psychotherapy: A multicultural perspective.* (5th ed.). Boston: Allyn & Bacon.

Ivey, A. E., Ivey, M. B., & Simek-Morgan, L. (1997). *Counseling and psychotherapy: A multicultural perspective* (4th ed.). Boston: Allyn & Bacon.

Jacques, M. E. (1969). *Rehabilitation counseling: Scope and services.* Boston: Houghton Mifflin.

James, W. (1890). *The principles of psychology: Vol. 1.* New York: Holt.

Jeger, A. M., & Slotnick, R. S. (1982). *Community mental health and behavioral ecology: A handbook of theory, research and practice.* New York: Plenum.

Jenkins, W., Patterson, J. B., & Szymanski, E. M. (1992). Philosophical, historic, and legislative aspects of the rehabilitation counseling profession. In R. M. Parker & E. M. Szymanski (Eds.), *Rehabilitation counseling: Basics and beyond* (2nd ed., pp.1–41). Austin, TX: PRO-ED.

Job Outlook 2001. (2001, Summer). National Association of Colleges and Employers, Cam report. In *National Employment Counseling Association Newsletter*, p. 7.

Johansen, J. H., Collins, H. W., & Johnson, J. A. (1975). *American Education* (2nd ed.). Dubuque, IA: Brown.

Jones, A. J. (1963). *Principles of guidance* (5th ed.). New York: McGraw-Hill.

Kameen, M. C., Robinson, E. H., & Rotter, J. C. (1985). Coordination activities: A study of perception of elementary and middle school counselors. *Elementary School Guidance and Counseling, 20* 97–104.

Kennedy, E. M. (1990, November). Community-based care for the mentally ill: Simple justice. *American Psychologist, 45*(11), 1238–1240.

Keyes, R. (1976). *Is there life after high school?* Boston: Little, Brown.

Kiedler, T. (1993). *Old friends.* Boston: Houghton Mifflin.

Klopf, G. (1960). The expanding role of the high-school counselor. *School and Society, 88*, 417–419.

Krumboltz, J. D. (Ed.). (1966). *Revolution in counseling: Implications of behavioral science.* Boston: Houghton Mifflin.

Krumboltz, J. D. (1979). A social learning theory of career decision-making. In A. M. Mitchell, G. B. Jones, & J. D. Krumboltz (Eds.), *Social learning and career decision making* (pp.19–49). Cranston, RI: Carroll Press.

Krumboltz, J. D., Mitchell, A., & Gelatt, H. G. (1979). Applications of social learning theory of career selection. *Focus on Guidance*, *8*, 1–16.

Krumboltz, J. D., & Nichols, C. (1990). Integrating the social learning theory of career decision making. In W. B. Walsh & S. H. Osipow (Eds.), *Career counseling: Contemporary topics in vocational psychology* (pp. 159–192). Hillsdale, NJ: Erlbaum.

Kurpius, D. J. (1978). Consultation theory and process: An integrated model. *Personnel and Guidance Journal*, *56*(6), 335–338.

Kurpius, D. J., & Brown, D. (1988). *Handbook of consultation: An intervention for advocacy and outreach*. Alexandria, VA: Association for Counselor Education and Supervision.

Kurpius, D. J., & Fuqua, D. R. (Eds.). (1993a). Consultation: A paradigm for helping: Consultation I: Conceptual, structural and operational dimensions [Special issue]. *Journal of Counseling and Development*, *71*(6).

Kurpius, D. J., & Fuqua, D. R. (1993b). Fundamental issues in defining consultation. *Journal of Counseling and Development*, *71*(6), 598–600.

Kurpius, D. J., & Fuqua, D. R. (Eds.). (1993c). Consultation: A paradigm for helping: Consultation II: Prevention, preparation and key issues [Special issue]. *Journal of Counseling and Development*, *72*(2).

Kurpius, D. J., & Robinson, S. E. (Eds.). (1978a). Consultation I: Definition-models-programs [Special issue]. *Personnel and Guidance Journal*, *56*(6).

Kurpius, D. J., & Robinson, S. E. (Eds.). (1978b). Consultation II: Topical issues and features in consultation [Special issue]. *Personnel and Guidance Journal*, *56*(7).

La Fromboise, T. D. & Rowe, W. (1983). Skills training for bicultural competence: Rationale and application. *Journal of Counseling Psychology*, *30*, 589–595.

Lambert, R. G. & Lambert, M. J. (1984). The effects of role preparation for psychotherapy on immigrant clients seeking mental health services in Hawaii. *Journal of Community Psychology*, *12*, 263–275.

Lazarus, A. A. (2000). Multimodal therapy. In R. J. Corsini & D. Wedding (Eds.), *Current Psychotherapies* (6th ed., pp. 340–374). Itasca, IL: F. E. Peacock.

Leahy, M. J., & Szymanski, E. M. (1995, November/December). Rehabilitation counseling: Evolution and current status. *Journal of Counseling and Development*, *74*(2), 163–166.

Leahy, M. J., Szymanski, E. M., & Linkowski, D. C. (1993). Knowledge importance in rehabilitation counseling. *Rehabilitation Counseling Bulletin*, *37*, 130–145.

Leedy, P. D. (1997). *Practical research: Planning & design* (6th ed.). Upper Saddle River, NJ: Prentice Hall.

Lee, C. C. & Richardson, B. L. (eds.). (1991). *Multicultural issues in Counseling: New approaches to diversity*. Alexandria, VA: American Association of Counseling and Development

Lewin, K. (1936). *Principles of topological psychology*. New York: McGraw-Hill.

Lewis, J. A., Lewis, M. D., & Souflee, F., Jr. (1993). *Management of human service programs*. Pacific Grove, CA: Brooks/Cole.

Lewis, M. D., Hayes, R. L., & Lewis, J. A. (1986). *An introduction to the counseling profession*. Itasca, IL: Peacock.

Lewis, M. D., & Lewis, J. A. (1991). *Management of human service programs* (2nd ed.). Pacific Grove, CA: Brooks/Cole.

Lieberman, M., Yalom, I., & Miles, M. (1973). *Encounter groups: First facts.* New York: Basic Books.

Lorenzo, M. K., & Adler, D. A. (1984). Mental health services for Chinese in a community health center. *Social Casework, 65*, 600–610.

Lum, C. (March, 2001). *A guide to state laws and regulations on professional school counseling.* Alexandria, VA: American Counseling Association: Office of Public Policy and Legislation and the American School Counselor Association.

Mallart, M. (1955). *The history of the guidance movement: Western civilization — 1955.* Cleveland: Collins & World.

Marshall, J. (1983). Reducing the effects of work-oriented values on the lives of male American workers. *Vocational Guidance Quarterly, 32*, 109–115.

Maslow, A. H. (1970). *Motivation and personality* (2nd ed.). New York: Harper & Row.

May, R. & Yalom, I. (2000). Existential psychotherapy. In R. J. Corsini & D. Wedding (Eds.), *Current psychotherapies* (6th ed., pp. 273–302). Itasca, IL: F. E. Peacock.

McCandless, B. R., & Coop, R. H. (1979). *Adolescents: Behavior and development* (2nd ed.). New York: Holt, Rinehart & Winston.

McCully, C. H. (1962). The school counselor: Strategy for professionalization. *Personnel and Guidance Journal, 61*, 597–601.

McCully, C. H. (1965). The counselor: Instrument of change. *Teachers College Record, 66*, 405–412.

McCully, C. H. (1969). *Challenges for change in counselor education.* (L. L. Miller, Compiler). Minneapolis, MN: Burgess.

McFadden, J. (Ed.). (1993). *Transcultural counseling: Bilateral and international perspectives.* Alexandria, VA: American Counseling Association.

McKown, H. C. (1934). *Home room guidance.* New York: McGraw-Hill.

Mitchell, L. K., & Krumboltz, J. D. (1990). Social learning approach to career decision making: Krumboltz's theory. In D. Brown & L. Brooks (Eds.), *Career choice and development: Applying contemporary theories to practice* (2nd ed.), (pp. 145–196). San Francisco: Jossey-Bass.

Mitchell, L. K., & Krumboltz, J. D. (1996). Krumboltz's learning theory of career choice and counseling. In D. Brown, L. Brooks & Associates (Eds.), *Career choice and development* (3rd ed.), (pp. 233–276). San Francisco: Jossey-Bass.

Moreno, J. L. (Ed.). (1960). *The sociometry reader.* New York: Free Press.

Munson, H. L. (1971). *Foundation of developmental guidance.* Boston: Allyn & Bacon.

Murray, H., Barrett, W. G., & Honburger, E. (1938). *Exploration in personality: A clinical and experimental study of fifty men of college age.* New York: Oxford University Press.

Myers, J. E., Emmerling, D., & Leafgren, F. (Eds.) (1992). Wellness throughout the lifespan [Special issue]. *Journal of Counseling and Development, 71*(2).

National Board for Certified Counselors, Inc. (2000, Summer/Fall). The face of national certified counselors. *The National Certified Counselor, 17*(1), 1.

National Board for Certified Counselors, Inc. and Center for Credentialing and Education, Inc. (2001). *The practice of internet counseling.* Greensboro, NC: Author.

National Center for Education Statistics. (2000, October). The condition of education 2000. In *Techniques: Connecting education and careers*. Washington, DC: Association for Career and Technical Education, p.13.

National Commission on the Reform of Secondary Education. (1973). *The reform of secondary education*. New York: McGraw-Hill.

National Employment Counseling Association Newsletter. (Fall, 2000). *Copy editor*, 10. (A division of the American Counseling Association).

Nelson, R. C. (1992). Spa in counseling. *Journal of Counseling and Development*, *71*(2), 214–220.

New York State Teachers Association. (1935). *Guidance in the secondary school*. New York State Teachers Association Educational Monograph #3. New York: Author.

Nidorf, J. F. (1985). Mental health and refugee youths: A model for diagnostic training. In T. C. Owan (Ed.), *Southeast Asian mental health treatment, prevention services, training, and research*. Washington, DC: National Institute of Mental Health.

Nolte, M. C. (1975). Use and misuse of tests in education: Legal implications. *Evaluation Horizons*, *54*, 10–16.

Ohlsen, M. M. (1955). *Guidance: An introduction*. New York: Harcourt Brace Jovanovich.

Okun, B. F., Fried, J., & Okun, M. L. (1999). *Understanding diversity: A learning-as-practice primer*. Pacific Grove, CA: Brooks/Cole.

Omizo, M. M., Omizo, S. A., & D'Andrea, M. J. (1992). Promoting wellness among elementary school children. *Journal of Counseling and Development*, *71*(2), 194–198.

Ornstein, A. C. (1976). IQ tests and the culture issue. *Phi Delta Kappan*, *57*, 403–404.

Owan, T. C. (Ed.). (1985). *Southeast Asian mental health treatment, prevention services, training, and research*. Washington, DC: National Institute of Mental Health.

Parsons, F. (1909). *Choosing a vocation*. Boston: Houghton Mifflin.

Passons, W. R. (1975). *Gestalt approaches in counseling*. New York: Holt, Rinehart & Winston.

Pedersen, P. (1988). *A handbook for developing multicultural awareness*. Alexandria, VA: American Association for Counseling and Development.

Peregoy, J. J. (1993). Transcultural counseling with American Indians and Alaskan Natives: Contemporary issues for consideration. In J. McFaddden (Ed.), *Transcultural counseling: Bilateral and international perspectives* (pp. 163–191). Alexandria, VA: American Counseling Association.

Perls, F. (1948). Theory and technique of personality integration. *American Journal of Psychotherapy*, *2*(4), 565–586.

Peter, L. I., & Hull, R. (1959). *The Peter principle*. New York: Harper & Row.

Peters, T. J., & Waterman, R. H., Jr. (1982). *In search of excellence*. New York: Harper & Row.

Peterson, M. (2000). Electronic delivery of career development university courses. In J. W. Bloom and G. R. Walz (Eds.), *Cybercounseling and cyberlearning: Strategies and resources for the millennium* (pp. 143–159). Alexandria, VA: American Counseling Association and Greensboro, NC: CAPS, Inc. with the ERIC Counseling and Student Services Clearinghouse.

Plake, B. S., & Impara, J. C. (Eds.). (2001). *The fourteenth mental measurements yearbook*. Lincoln, NE: Buros Institute.

Ponzo, Z. (1992). Promoting successful aging: Problems, opportunities, and counseling guidelines. *Journal of Counseling and Development, 71*(2), 210–213.

Prediger, D., Swaney, K., & Vansickle, T. (1992, March). Beyond the "ASVAB Code": Using the Other ASVAB Aptitude Scores to Expand Career Exploration. Paper presented at the national convention of the American Counseling Association. Baltimore, MD.

Proctor, W. M., Benefield, W., & Wrenn, C. G. (1931). *Workbook in vocations*. Boston: Houghton Mifflin.

Pyszowski, I. S. (1986). Moral values and the school: Is there a way out of the maze? *Chronicle guidance, 107*(1), 87–92.

Remley, T. P., Jr. (1991, August). On being different. *Guidepost*, p. 2.

Remley, T. P., Jr. and Herlihy, B. (2001). *Ethical, legal and professional issues in counseling*. Upper Saddle River, NJ: Pearson Education.

Rencken, R. H. (1989). *Intervention strategies for sexual abuse*. Alexandria, VA: American Association for Counseling and Development.

Report of the Council for Accreditation of Counseling and Related Educational Programs, (CACREP), (2001, Spring). *Journal of Counseling and Development, 79*(2), 238–249.

Ridley, C. R. (1995). *Overcoming unintentional racism in counseling and therapy. A practitioner's guide to intentional intervention* (pp. 9, 82–83, 88–100). Thousand Oaks, CA: Sage.

Ridley, C. R., & Thompson, C. E. (1999). Managing resistance to diversity training: A social systems perspective. In M. S. Kiselica (Ed.), *Confronting prejudice and racism during multicultural training* (pp. 3–24). Alexandria, VA: American Counseling Association.

Robinson, S. E. (1983). Nader versus ETS: Who should we believe? *Personnel and Guidance Journal, 61*, 260–262.

Robinson, S. E., & Roth, S. L. (Eds.). (1992). Women and health [Special issue]. *Journal of Mental Health Counseling, 14*(1).

Rockwell, P. J., & Rothney, J. W. M. (1961). Some social ideas of pioneers in the guidance movement. *Personnel and Guidance Journal, 40*, 349–354.

Roe, A. (1956). *The psychology of occupations*. New York: Wiley.

Roe, A., & Klas, D. (1972). Classifications of occupations. In J. W. Whiteley & A. Resnikoff (Eds.), *Perspectives on vocational development* (pp. 199–221). Washington, DC: American Personnel and Guidance Association.

Rogers, C. R. (1942). *Counseling and psychotherapy*. Cambridge, MA: Riverside.

Rogers, C. R. (1951). *Client-centered therapy*. Boston: Houghton Mifflin.

Rogers, C. R. (1959a). A theory of therapy, personality and interpersonal relationships as developed in the client-centered framework. In S. Koch (Ed.), *Psychology: A study of science: Vol. 3* (pp. 184–256). New York: McGraw-Hill.

Rogers, C. R. (1959b). Significant learning: In theory and in education. *Educational Leadership, 16*, 232–242.

Rogers, C. R. (1967). The process of the basic encounter group. In J. F. T. Bugental (Ed.), *Challenges of humanistic psychology* (pp. 261–276). New York: McGraw-Hill.

Rude, S. S., Weissberg, M., & Gazda, G. M. (1988). Looking to the future: Themes from the third national conference for counseling psychology. *The Counseling Psychologist, 16*, 423–430.

Sampson, J. P., Jr., Kolodinsky, R. W., & Greeno, B. P. (1997). Counseling on the information highway: Future possibilities and potential problems. *Journal of Counseling and Development, 75*(3), 203–212.

Sampson, J. P., Jr., & Pyle, K. R. (1983). Ethical issues involved with the use of computer-assisted counseling, testing and guidance systems. *Personnel and Guidance Journal, 61,* 283–287.

Sapir, E. (1958). *Culture, language and personality.* Berkeley, CA: University of California Press.

Savickas, M. L., & Lent, R. W. (Eds.). (1994). *Convergence in career development theories.* Palo Alto, CA: Consulting Psychologists Press.

Schein, E. H. (1978). The role of the consultant: Content expert or process facilitator? *Personnel and Guidance Journal, 56,* 339–345.

Schein, E. H. (1991). Process consultation. *Consulting Psychology Bulletin, 43,* 16–18.

Schor, J. (1993). *The overworked American: The unexpected decline of leisure.* New York: Basic Books (Harper Collins).

Shaw, M. C., & Goodyear, R. K. (Eds.). (1984). Primary prevention in schools [Special issue]. *Personnel and Guidance Journal, 62*(8).

Shertzer, B., & Stone, S. C. (1981). *Fundamentals of guidance* (4th ed.). Boston: Houghton Mifflin.

Shifron, R., Dye, A., & Shifron, G. (1983). Implications for counseling the unemployed in a recessionary economy. *Personnel and Guidance Journal, 61,* 527–529.

Shuman, D. W., & Weiner, M. F. (1987). *The psychotherapist-patient privilege: A critical examination.* Springfield, IL: Charles C. Thomas.

Smead, R. (1995). *Skills and techniques for group work with children and adolescents.* Champaign, IL: Research Press.

Soska, M. (1997). How can we enable children to live a drug-free life? *Chronicle Guidance Publications,* CGP Professionals P97-2 Mental Hygiene 10.1 Drugs and Alcohol.

Sprinthall, N. A. (1990). Counseling psychology from Greyston to Atlanta: On the road to Armageddon? *The Counseling Psychologist, 18*(3), 454–462.

Stevens, P., & Smith, R. L. (2001). *Substance abuse counseling: Theory and practice.* (2nd ed.). Upper Saddle River, NJ: Merrill/Prentice Hall.

St. John, W. D., & Walden, J. (1976). Keeping student confidence. *Phi Delta Kappan, 57,* 682–684.

Stockton, R. (1980). The education of group leaders: A review of the literature with suggestions for the future. *Journal for Specialists in Group Work, 5,* 55–62.

Stockton, R., Barr, J. E., & Klein, R. (1981). Identifying the group dropout: A review of the literature. *Journal for Specialists in Group Work, 6,* 75–82.

Stockton, R., & Morran, D. K. (1982). Review and perspective of critical dimensions in therapeutic small group research. In G. M. Gazda (Ed.), *Basic approaches to group psychotherapy and group counseling* (3rd ed.). Springfield, IL: Charles C. Thomas.

Stockton, R., & Toth, P. (1993). Small group counseling in school settings. In J. Wittmer (Ed.), *Managing your school counseling program: K-12 developmental strategies.* Minneapolis: Educational Media Corporation.

Sturtevant, S. M. (1937). Some questions regarding the developing guidance movement. *School Review, 58,* 14–23.

Sue, D. W., & Sue, D. M. (1990). *Counseling the culturally different: Theory and practice* (2nd ed.). New York: John Wiley & Sons, Inc.

Super, D. E. (1990). A life-span, life-space approach to career development. In D. Brown, L. Brooks, & Associates (Eds.), *Career choice and development* (2nd ed.). San Francisco: Jossey-Bass.

Swenson, L. C. (1993). *Psychology and law for the helping professions.* Pacific Grove, CA: Brooks/Cole.

Taylor, S. E., Falke, R. L., Shapton, S. J., & Lichtmen, R. R. (1986). Social support, support groups and the cancer patient. *Journal of Consulting and Clinical Psychology, 54,* 608–615.

Tharp, R. G., & Wetzel, R. (1969). *Behavior modification in the natural environment.* New York: Academic Press.

Thorndike, R. M., & Hagen, E. P. (1977). *Measurement and evaluation in psychology and education* (4th ed.). New York: Macmillan.

Traxler, A. E. (1950). Emerging trends in guidance. *School Review, 58,* 14, 23.

Tung, T. M. (1985). Psychiatric care for southeast Asians: How different is different? In T. C. Owan (Ed.), *Southeast Asian mental health, treatment, prevention services, training, and research.* Washington, DC: National Institute of Mental Health.

Tyler, L. E. (1980). The next twenty years. *The Counseling Psychologist, 8*(4), 19–21.

U.S. Bureau of the Census. (1995). *Current population reports.* (Series P-20). Washington, DC: U. S. Government Printing Office.

Walz, G. R., & Reedy, L. S. (2000). The international career development library: The use of virtual libraries to promote counselor learning. In J. W. Bloom & G. R. Walz (Eds.), *Cybercounseling and cyberlearning: Strategies and resources for the millennium.* (pp. 162–164). Alexandria, VA: American Counseling Association and Greensboro, NC: CAPS, Inc., with the ERIC Counseling and Student Services Clearinghouse.

Watson, J. B. (1913). Psychology as the behaviorist views it. *Psychological Review, 20,* 159–170.

Weikel, W. J., & Hughes, P. R. (1993). The counselor as expert witness. In T. P. Remley, Jr. (Ed.), *ACA Legal Series, 5.* Alexandria, VA: American Counseling Association.

Werner, J. L. (1978). Community mental health consultation with agencies. *Personnel and Guidance Journal, 56*(6), 364–368.

Whiston, S. C. (2000). *Principles and applications of assessment in counseling.* Belmont, CA: Brooks/Cole.

Whiston, S. C., & Sexton, T. L. (1998). A review of school counseling outcome research: Implications for practice. *Journal of Counseling and Development, 76*(4), 412–426.

Whiteley, J. M. (1980). Counseling psychology in the year 2000 A.D. *The Counseling Psychologist, 8*(4), 2–8.

Wigmore, J. H. (1961). Evidence in trials at common law. In J. T. McNaughton (Ed.), *Rules of evidence* (Vol. 8, rev. ed.). Boston: Little, Brown.

Williamson, E. G. (1939). *How to counsel students: A manual of techniques for clinical counselors.* New York: McGraw-Hill.

Woody, R. H., Hansen, J. C., & Rossberg, R. H. (1989). *Counseling psychology: Strategies and services.* Pacific Grove, CA: Brooks/Cole.

Worthen, B. R., White, K. R., & Borg, W. R. (1993). *Measurement and evaluation in the schools.* New York: Longman.

Wrenn, C. G. (1962). *The counselor in a changing world*. Washington, DC: American Counseling Association.

Wrenn, C. G. (1973). *The world of the contemporary counselor*. Boston: Houghton Mifflin.

Yalom, I. D. (1995). *The theory and practice of group psychotherapy* (4th ed.pp. 6, 277, 279). New York: Basic Books.

Zirbes, L. (1949). Why guidance? *Childhood Education*, 25, 197–201.Zeran, F. R., & Riccio, A. C. (1962). *Organization and administration of guidance services*. Skokie, IL: Rand McNally.

Zytowski, D. G. (1972). Four hundred years before Parsons. *Personnel and Guidance Journal*, *50*, 443–450.

Author Index

Subject Index